Family Therapy
CONCEPTS AND METHODS
Third Edition

MICHAEL P. NICHOLS, Ph.D.
College of William and Mary

RICHARD C. SCHWARTZ, Ph.D.
Institute for Juvenile Research, Chicago
University of Illinois College of Medicine

Foreword by
SALVADOR MINUCHIN, M.D.
Family Studies, Inc.

ALLYN AND BACON
Boston London Toronto Sydney Tokyo Singapore

Vice President and Publisher: Susan Badger
Editorial Assistant: Laura Ellingson
Production Administrator: Susan McIntyre
Editorial-Production Service: Ruttle, Shaw & Wetherill, Inc.
Cover Administrator: Linda Dickinson
Composition Buyer: Linda Cox
Manufacturing Buyer: Megan Cochran
Marketing Manager: Joyce Nilsen

Copyright © 1995, 1991, 1984 by Allyn and Bacon
A Simon & Schuster Company
160 Gould Street
Needham Heights, MA 02194

 This book is printed on recycled,
acid-free paper.

Library of Congress Cataloging-in-Publication Data
Nichols, Michael P.
   Family therapy : concepts and methods / Michael P. Nichols,
Richard C. Schwartz; foreword by Salvador Minuchin. — 3rd ed.
    p. cm.
   Includes bibliographical references and indexes.
   ISBN 0-205-16395-5
   1. Family psychotherapy. I. Schwartz, Richard C. II. Title.
   [DNLM: 1. Family Therapy. WM 430.5.F2 N621f 1994]
RC488.5.N53 1994
616.89′156—dc20
DNLM/DLC
for Library of Congress   94-14096
                                       CIP

Printed in the United States of America
10 9 8 7 6 5 4 3 2 1   99 98 97 96 95 94

To our wives, Melody Nichols and Nancy Schwartz,
and our children, Sandy and Paul Nichols,
Jessie, Sarah, and Hali Schwartz

The publisher gratefully acknowledges permission from the following sources to reprint material in this book:

For material on pages 88, 89, and 90: Copyright © 1984 by M. Davidson. From the book *Uncommon Sense* and reprinted with permission from Jeremy P. Tarcher, Inc., Los Angeles, CA.

For material on pages 100 and 101: From *Family Therapy in Clinical Practice,* by Murray Bowen, M.D., copyright © 1985, 1983, 1978 by Jason Aronson Inc. Reprinted with permission of the publisher.

For material on pages 446, 447, and 449: From *In Search of Solutions, A New Direction in Psychotherapy,* by William Hudson O'Hanlon and Michele Weiner-Davis, by permission of W. W. Norton & Company, Inc. Copyright © 1989 by William Hudson O'Hanlon and Michele Weiner-Davis.

For materials on pages 305, 306, and 307: From Steve Andreas, *Virginia Satir: The Patterns of Her Magic* available through Science & Behavior Books, Inc., Palo Alto, California.

For material on pages 456, 457, 459, and 460: From *Schizophrenia and the Family,* by C. Anderson, D. Reiss, and B. Hogarty. Copyright © 1986. Reprinted by permission of The Guilford Press.

For material on pages 464, 465, 466, and 467: From *Selected Papers,* by Michael White, Copyright © 1989 by Michael White. Reprinted with permission of the author.

Contents

Foreword

In this volume Mike Nichols and Dick Schwartz tell the story of family therapy—and tell it very well. It's hard to imagine a more readable and informative guide to the field.

Born in the late 1950s, family therapy seemed to spring fully formed out of the heads of a group of seminal thinkers and practitioners. Nearly four decades later both theory and practice show the uncertainties and doubts that define maturity. But in the beginning—as the storytellers say—there was Gregory Bateson on the West Coast, a tall, clean-shaven, angular intellectual, who saw families as systems, carriers of ideas. On the East Coast was Nathan Ackerman, short, bearded, portly, the quintessential charismatic healer, who saw families as collections of individuals struggling to balance feelings, irrationalities, and desires. Bateson, the man of ideas, and Ackerman, the man of passion, complemented each other perfectly, the Don Quixote and Sancho Panza of the family systems revolution.

For all the diversity of the 1960s and 1970s that saw the new clinical practice called family therapy take a variety of names—systemic, strategic, structural, Bowenian, experiential—there was also a remarkable solidarity in the shared beliefs that defined the field. The pioneers were united in their rejection of psychoanalysis and their embrace of systems thinking, however much they might have differed in their therapeutic techniques.

From the mid 1970s on, as family therapy succeeded and expanded, it was extended to encompass different client populations, with specific interventions for various special groups; with drug addiction, hospitalized psychiatric patients, the welfare population, family violence. . . . All posed their own challenges. Practitioners responded to this expanded family therapy with an array of new approaches, some of which even challenged the fundamental allegiance to systems thinking.

The challenge to systems theory (the official science of the time) took two forms. One was purely theoretical: a challenge to the assumption that systemic thinking was a universal framework, applicable without modification to the organization and functioning of all human collectives. A major broadside came from feminists who questioned the absence of concepts of gender and power in systems thinking, and pointed to the distorting consequences of genderless theory when focusing on family violence. The other concerned the connection between theory and practice: a challenge to the imposition of systems theory as the basis for therapeutic practice. The very techniques that once defined the field were called into question. Inevitably, the field began to recover specificity and to reopen for examination its old taboos: the individual, intrapsychic life, emotions, biology, the past, and the particular place of the family in culture and society.

As is always the characteristic of an official science, the field tried to preserve established concepts while a pragmatic attention to specific cases was demanding new and specific responses. As a result, today we have an official family therapy that claims direct descendence from Bateson, and a multitude of excellent practitioners doing sensitive and effective work that is frequently quite different from what systems theory prescribes. The result has often produced conflict and controversy. One such controversy centers on the power of the therapist.

From the perspective of today, with its many challenges to the therapist's authority and responsibility, the early family therapists were all "conductors"—forceful advocates for change, with committed positions about how that change should occur. Therapy was always a joint endeavor, but the responsibility for leading the way was the therapist's.

A number of schools of family therapy now seek to protect the family from the intrusiveness of the therapist. They are concerned that a forceful therapist's interventions might dominate and disempower families. Starting with the Milan Associates' concern with neutrality, this stance has reappeared recently in the constructivists who propose that therapy can only be a dialogue between two coconstructors of a story that is not rooted in any testable reality. (Academic fashion being what it is, the story of family therapy is sometimes told in such a way that the contributions of Ackerman, Bowen, Boszormenyi-Nagy, Fleck, Haley, Lidz, Minuchin, Satir, Whitaker, and Wynne among others disappear in favor of a straight and narrow line from Bateson to the Milan group to the narrative constructivists.) The contemporary constructivist emphasis on language and meaning and their caution to restrain the power of the therapist was presented as radically new. But in some way this concern that therapists not intrude on patients is a throwback to the Freudian concept of the therapist as a tabula rasa onto whom patients projected transferential fantasies.

Lurking between the lines in many recent family therapy articles and books is a straw man, a power-hungry therapist who measures patients against the Procrustean bed of his or her own biases and then stretches or diminishes them to fit. It is to save families from the misguided intrusiveness of this kind of expertise that many of the new modalities of therapy have been constructed. But equating expertise with domination is false mathematics. Besides, control doesn't disappear from family therapy by changing the language from "intervene" to "cocreate." All that happens is that the influence of the therapist goes underground. Made invisible, it may remain unexamined.

Narrative constructivism is an interesting way of looking at human experience—emphasizing as it does one important aspect of the thinking, feeling, and acting beings we all are. But such a philosophical point of view imported unmodified into an interventionist enterprise like family therapy (which is, after all, about reducing suffering) constructs a fairy tale ogre: a therapist unaware of the effect of his interventions, operating from a power base invisible to him. The only way to avoid wielding such a sledgehammer, many now believe, is to intervene only as a coconstructor of stories—as though people were not only influenced by but were nothing but the stories they tell about themselves.

But there is another way of thinking about families and their problems, one held by a group who believes that therapy is a field of human transactions and that it is impossible for the therapist not to influence that field. Therapists in this group tend to be proximal, inventive, committed, interventive, and optimistic that their involvement with families will help family members solve their problems. Positioned in this group, I think that only a clear recognition of the idiosyncrasies of the individual therapist and the partialities of any therapeutic approach offers the possibility of true respect for each family's unique and individual character. I see the therapeutic process as an encounter between distinct interpersonal cultures. Real respect for clients and their integrity can allow therapists to be other than fearfully cautious, can encourage them to be direct and authentic—respectful and compassionate—but also at times honest and challenging. Such a therapist accepts that family members have their own experience and their own integrity, and also that they project their own wishes and fantasies into the therapeutic area, which then becomes a field of forces in which all the participants pull each other in different directions.

The advantage of this position is that the therapist, as a repository of multiple "transferences," experiences varying pulls of behavior. As the therapist, a discreet self, his or her own person, experiences those pulls, he or she responds by creating contexts in which family members encounter themselves in new positions that foster the exploration of novelty and alternative choices.

This conception of the therapist as an active knower—of himself or herself *and* of the different family members—is very different from the neutral therapist of the constructivists. But, of course, these two prototypes are entirely too simplified. Most practitioners fall somewhere between these two poles of neutrality and decisiveness.

The choice between action and interventionism, on the one hand, and meaning and conversation, on the other, is but one of the questions the field is grappling with today; there are many others. Are there useful models of human nature and of functional families, or must every situation be responded to de novo? Are the norms of human behavior and family function universal, or are they culturally constructed products of political and ideological constraint? How do we become experts? How do we know what we know? If we become experts, are we creating the fields that we then discover? Can we influence people? Can we not influence them? How do we know that we are not simply agents of social control? How do we know that we are accomplishing anything at all? What right do we have to constrain diversity, imposing ways of being on others? Are questions better than statements?

These questions and the rich history and contemporary practice of family therapy are explored magnificently in *Family Therapy: Concepts and Methods.* It is a thorough and thoughtful, fair and balanced guide to the ideas and techniques that make family therapy such an exciting enterprise. Nichols and Schwartz have managed to be comprehensive without becoming tedious. Perhaps the secret is the engaging style of their writing, or perhaps it is how they avoid getting lost in abstraction while keeping a clear focus on clinical practice. In any case, this superb book has long set the standard of excellence as the best introduction and guide to the practice of family therapy.

Much has changed in the field in the last few years, and this new edition brings readers right up to date. Considerably improved over the previous edition, this one describes the latest approaches and continues to offer insightful and balanced commentary. The inclusion of a separate chapter on research is also a welcome addition. Without a doubt the definitive textbook of family therapy, this volume offers a wealth of information presented with refreshing clarity and a total absence of cant. It all adds up to an exciting, highly readable book. It is a fascinating journey. Enjoy it.

Salvador Minuchin, M.D.
New York, New York, 1994

Preface

Amazingly, the sprawling field of family therapy changed more in the three years between the second and third editions of this book than it did in the seven years between the first and second. Looking back on the 1970s and 1980s—the time when most teachers formed their strongest impressions of the field—we see an era when various schools had defined and entrenched themselves. There were doctrinaire approaches to follow and charismatic leaders to look up to. Much has changed. Forceful ideologies that once competed are now being combined. Aggressive techniques are giving way to subtler, more collaborative methods, as a shift from action to meaning brings about a decreased urgency to control and manipulate families in the name of helping them. The call for more research is no longer a cry in the wilderness; now at last we are beginning to test our assumptions and put data ahead of enthusiasm as the measure of what works.

These changes as well as the rich history and contemporary practice of family therapy—no, therapies—are all described in this edition. We hope you like it.

So many people have contributed to my development as a family therapist and to the writing of this edition that it's impossible to thank them all. But I would like to single out a few. To the people who taught me family therapy— Rodney Shapiro, Lyman Wynne, Murray Bowen, Michael Kerr, and Salvador Minuchin—thank you. Gardner Spungin, of Gardner Press, believed in me when no one else did. He took a chance on an unknown young psychologist, and when the original manuscript of the first edition was finished, he took a pile of scribblings and turned it into a book. Since then he has always stood by me, and I will always be grateful.

Without Doug Sprenkle's and Richard Bischoff's encyclopedic knowledge and thoroughness, we wouldn't have been able to provide nearly as comprehensive a review of the vast and growing research literature. Thanks guys.

Once again I count myself lucky to have Dick Schwartz as coauthor. Collaborating with another writer is a little like a marriage: it's easiest in the courtship stage. Later on, when visions collide, there's a tremendous challenge to compromise without caving in. I think Dick and I have done a good job of that, and the result is a collaboration that expresses the best of both of us. Maybe it's the respect and affection we have for each other that makes that possible.

Some of the people who went out of their way to help us prepare this third edition were: Joe Eron, Tom Lund, Michael Rohrbaugh, Varda Shoham, Howard Liddle, Robert Jay Green, Edith Lawrence, Faith Bonecutter, Peter Steinglass, Jim Keim, Jay Haley, Cloe Madanes, Michele Weiner-Davis, Bill O'Hanlon, Don Efron, Vince Fish, and Salvador Minuchin. To paraphrase John, Paul, George, and Ringo, *we* get by with *a lot* of help from our friends— and we thank them one and all.

We are grateful to Bill Barke, Susan Badger, and Laura Ellingson at Allyn and Bacon for the encouragement and support that made a hard job a little easier.

Finally, I would like to thank my post-graduate instructors in family life: my wife Melody and my children Sandy and Paul. In the brief span of twenty-six years, Melody has seen me grow from a shy young man, totally ignorant of how to be a husband and father, to a shy middle-aged man, still bewildered and still trying. Like any marriage, ours has survived many inclemencies; like some, it continues to grow stronger. Each year Sandy and Paul teach me a little something new. This year Sandy taught me what it means to watch the best daughter any father could ever hope for move out of the house and off to college. Proud of her? You're darn right I am! And my son Paul, to whom (masculine reticence being what it is) maybe I haven't always shown the depth of my love, has grown to young manhood true to himself, true to his friends, and true to his mother and me. If in my wildest dreams I had described children to love and be proud of, I could never have imagined any as fine as Sandy and Paul.

Michael P. Nichols
Albany, New York, 1994

Even though I see my kids every day, occasionally I find myself stepping back and looking at them as if I hadn't seen them for years. I'm always shocked at how much they have changed right under my nose, and I always have mixed emotions. I feel proud of their growth but nostalgic for aspects of our earlier relationships; concerned about their future but excited about sharing it.

Working on this third edition was a similar experience. I have passionate and protective feelings for family therapy similar to those that I have for my children. Since I exist in the field, I hadn't noticed how much it had changed until this book forced Mike and me to step outside and look at it from a distance. Not surprisingly, I've experienced the same mixture of concern and excitement, pride and nostalgia. The last three years have produced so many challenges to and breaks from family therapy traditions that I sometimes feel like my parents must have felt in the 1960s when they kept telling me that not all of the established culture had to be rejected or rebelled against. Yet, no doubt also like my parents back then, I am intrigued by some of the new ideas and live vicariously through the adventures of those pursuing them.

I'll confess to still another parent-like emotion. I feel sorry for the beginning family therapy student. When I was smitten by the field in the early 1970s, things were much simpler and a student had far fewer choices. There were a handful of models and all you had to do was pick one and then idolize and impersonate its creator. The field was adequately covered in one semester and therapy was so straightforward that you could work right from a book.

Now there is so much more detail about different kinds of families, so many different, rapidly evolving approaches and perspectives, and so few charismatic leaders to impersonate or clear-cut techniques to employ. The novice facing all these choices and all this information is understandably daunted.

The task of those teaching courses in (or writing texts about) family therapy has become much more arduous. The field has become impossible to digest quickly—it must be savored over many years.

Yet, while all this diversity and change has increased the challenge we face, it also represents a welcome new approach to learning. There is less of the closed-minded fervor and chauvinism of those earlier, simpler days and more humility and openness both within the field and toward other disciplines. Family therapy became more complex once we recognized that having simple answers was not always useful. Perhaps it's good that we all have to work harder to grasp the complexity of the human condition.

I remain eternally grateful to Mike Nichols for inviting me to accompany him on this periodic perspective-taking. In addition to enjoying our collaboration, which is always highly stimulating and enriching, I have come to value our friendship a great deal. It's nice that every three years we have an excuse to strengthen it.

As with previous editions, Mike and I have tried to provide a fair representation of the concepts and methods of the approaches we cover and to openly discuss our opinions of them rather than pretending to be totally objective. This book then is a perspective on family therapy, not the truth about family therapy. I have my biases (and a model, described in Chapter 11, in which these biases are evident), and Mike has his. Our collaboration produces a binocular view that is richer than either of ours would be alone.

Once again I want to express my gratitude to the Institute for Juvenile Research for supporting this enterprise and the faculty of the Family Systems Program within the IJR for creating, over the past fourteen years, an intellectual incubator in which the best of my perspectives were born and nurtured. They have included Doug Breunlin, Rocco Cimmarusti, Betty Mac Kune Karrer, and Howard Liddle. Special thanks are also due to several other of my teachers, including Doug Sprenkle, Rich Simon, Debbie Gorman-Smith, and Ted and Gen Schwartz.

Finally, I thank my wife Nancy and our daughters Jessie, Sarah, and Hali for their sacrifice, support, and instruction. Each time I step back and look, my heart fills with joy.

Richard C. Schwartz
Chicago, Illinois, 1994

The Historical Context of Family Therapy

W_e are by now so used to hearing about "family therapy" that we may be beguiled into thinking of it as a monolithic enterprise, a programatic approach to treatment with a coherent set of concepts and methods. As family therapists are well aware, however, there is not one, but many family therapies, each with distinctly different ways of conceptualizing and treating families. Still the general impression persists that the history of family therapy is one continuous line of development with subsequent specialization. Yes, today we have a proliferation of competing approaches, but aren't they all variations on a common theme? And weren't the early family therapists pretty much in agreement about the general principles of treatment? In fact, such consensus never existed. Family therapy was developed by a heterogeneous group of investigators working in distinctly different contexts and with different purposes. These pioneers discovered family therapy before they discovered each other. While it is true that there are unifying principles that most family therapists share, variety, not unity, has always been a major theme of the story of family therapy.

Like the country family therapy grew up in, the field is a melting pot in which the ingredients never really melted. Family therapy's rich history of diversity complicates the task of the historian. The challenge is to describe the differences among various approaches without losing track of the common threads uniting them. Our response to this challenge is to divide the task among the first three chapters. In this chapter, focusing on the 1950s and 1960s, we describe the rivulets that fed into what was to become the mainstream of family therapy. In Chapter 2 we take a closer look at the ideas that shaped the field's identity, especially during the 1960s and 1970s. In Chapter 3, which covers the turbulent 1980s, we discuss the controversies and rude awakenings of that decade.

PSYCHOTHERAPEUTIC SANCTUARY

It is tempting to look back at the days before family therapy and see those who insisted on segregating individual mental patients from their families as naive and wrongheaded, exponents of a fossilized view of mental disorder according to which psychiatric maladies are firmly embedded in the heads of individuals. When we consider that clinicians didn't begin treating whole families together until the mid 1950s, we may be tempted to ask, what took them so long?

For one thing, there are very good reasons for conducting psychotherapy in private, in isolation from distressed and distressing relationships.

The two most influential approaches to psychotherapy in the middle of the twentieth century, Freud's psychoanalysis and Rogers's client-centered therapy, were both predicated on the assumption that psychological problems arose from unhealthy interactions with others and could best be alleviated in a private relationship between patient and therapist.

Freud's discoveries indicted the family, first as a breeding ground for childhood seduction, and later as the agent of cultural repression. Since the natural child is oriented toward pure pleasure, the family must stand for anti-pleasure. Ideally this dialectic tames the animal underside of our natures, making us fit to live in society and able to find healthy gratification without undue conflict with others. All too often, though, repression is excessive; instead of learning to express our needs in moderation, we bury them, settling for security instead of satisfaction. Unfortunately a life without pain is a life without passion. When we grow up a little bit neurotic—unconsciously afraid of our natural drives—whom else do we blame except our parents?

Given that neurotic conflicts were spawned in the family, it seemed only natural to assume that the best way to undo the family's influence was to isolate the family from treatment, to keep its contaminating influence out of the psychoanalytic operating room.

Freud also discovered that the less he revealed of his own personality and feelings, the more his patients reacted toward him as though he were a significant figure from their own families. At first these *transference* reactions seemed a hindrance, but Freud soon realized that they provided an invaluable glimpse into the past. Thereafter, fostering and analyzing transference became the cornerstone of psychoanalytic treatment, which meant that since the analyst was interested in the patient's memories and fantasies about the family, having the real family present in the treatment room would only obscure the subjective truth of the past. Freud was not interested in the living family; he was interested in the family-as-remembered, locked away in the unconscious.

By conducting treatment in private, Freud safeguarded the patient's trust in the sanctity of the therapeutic relationship and thus maximized the likelihood that the patient would repeat, in relation to the analyst, the understandings and misunderstandings of childhood.

Carl Rogers also believed that psychological problems stemmed from destructive early interactions with others. Each of us, Rogers said, is born with an innate tendency toward *self-actualization,* an idea that became the premise of all humanistic psychotherapies. Left to our own devices, we tend to follow our own best interests. Since we are curious and intelligent, we explore and learn; since we have strong bodies, we play and exercise; and since being with others brings us joy, we tend to be outgoing, loving, and affectionate.

Unhappily, said Rogers, our healthy instinct toward actualization gets warped and subverted. We crave the approval of others so badly that we learn to do what we think others want, even when it may not be what is best for us. Little boys act tough to please daddies who wish they were tougher themselves, and little girls subdue their competitive strivings to conform to what they think their parents expect.

Gradually this conflict between self-fulfillment and the need for approval leads to denial and distortion of our inner promptings and even of the feelings that signal them. Thus we learn to deny feelings of anger when we are unfairly criticized, lest we encounter disapproval. In fact, some people spend their whole lives in vocations that were selected as a means of getting approval, rather than as a means of fulfilling what is best in their own natures. It has been said that marriage is the most important and most neurotic choice that most people make. That may be, but choosing a career, too, is often influenced, directly or indirectly, more by the expectations of others than by following one's own inclinations and talents. Young men and women often fall into careers that their parents encourage, or choose the opposite of what their parents wish, confusing counter-conformity with independence. The consequences of this decision may be a life of vague unhappiness, with or without obvious psychological symptoms, but the real cause of unhappiness—the unfulfilled basic needs—may never be recognized.

The therapy that Rogers developed was designed to help patients rediscover their real feelings, urges, and basic self-actualizing tendencies. Given his faith that people will find their own best interests, Rogers's view of the proper role of the therapist was that of a midwife—passive, but supportive. The therapist does not do anything to the patient, but rather provides conditions to help the patient discover what needs to be done, primarily by providing *unconditional positive regard.* The therapist listens carefully and sympathetically, communicating understanding, warmth, and respect. In the presence of such an accepting listener, the patient is gradually able to get in touch with his or her own feelings and inclinations. Although this sounds simple, it is a unique relationship. If you doubt that, try telling a friend about a problem. Most likely you will find that the friend soon interrupts to tell you a similar story or to give you some advice—advice which may suit the friend more than it does you.

The client-centered therapist, like the psychoanalyst, maintains absolute privacy in the therapeutic relationship in order to avoid any situations in which patients' feelings and impulses might be denied or distorted to win the approval of others. Only a specially trained person can communicate the unconditional acceptance that helps patients rediscover their basic selves; therefore family members and other outsiders have no place in the work of client-centered therapy.

When one of the authors (MPN) finished giving a talk on family therapy to a group of psychiatrists, the question was asked: "But does this brief family intervention result in lasting change, or does the patient's personality reassert itself?" It was a good question. What is needed for real change: a brief intervention in the family or a long-term exploration of personality? Actually family therapy is not simply predicated on changing the individual patient in context. Family therapy can exert change on the entire family and therefore improvement can be lasting because each and every family member changes and continues to exert synchronous change on each other. Still there are some basic aspects of personality—say, a father's oversensitiveness, or a mother's insecurity—that may be best treated in individual psychotherapy.

Almost any sort of human difficulty can be treated by either individual or family therapy (the best therapy for a given problem is that provided by the best therapist in town). But certain problems are especially likely to benefit from a family approach, among them problems with children (who must, regardless of what happens in therapy, return home to the influence of their parents), complaints about a marriage or other intimate relationship, family feuds, and symptoms that develop in an individual around the time of a major family transition. A common example of the latter is depression in a young mother.

God made babies adorable and helpless so that everybody would want one. But their demands are so intense and unrelenting that the first months are a blur of fatigue and frustration. The little bundles of joy holler to be fed and wail when they're wet; they cry to be held, and sometimes they cry for no discernable reason. Without a great deal of emotional and physical support, young mothers have a reason to get depressed.

If problems that arise around the time of family transitions should make a therapist consider the role of the family, individual therapy may be useful when people identify something about themselves that they've tried in vain to change *and* their social environment seems to be stable. Thus, if a woman gets depressed during her first year at college, we might wonder if her sadness is related to leaving home, and leaving her parents alone with each other. But if the same woman were to get depressed in her forties, say, during a long period of stability in her life, we might rather wonder if there's something about the way she approaches life, something about the way she hasn't fulfilled herself that's responsible for her unhappiness.

It's tempting to describe the deliberate exclusion of relatives as naive and wrongheaded—part of a fossilized view of emotional disorder, namely, that problems are hardened remains of the past, firmly embedded inside the patient's head. Actually, this view is not entirely wrong. Our personalities *are* shaped by earliest experience. But this is only half the story. Both the memory of past experience and the current reality of family relationships affect our lives. There are, however, two very practical reasons for starting with the outer part of the equation, the contemporary family context.

For one thing, the present-day family has an immediate impact and a continuing influence. Unlike the family of the past, they can be included— and influenced to change—in therapy. Thus, the existing family offers more leverage for change than the remembered one.

As we have seen, then, there are and continue to be valid reasons for conducting psychotherapy in a private, safe, confidential relationship. But individual therapy also plays a political role, serving as another social institution that displaces the family's function as the primary agency for the support and guidance of its members.

Ordinarily the question of individual versus family therapy is posed as a technical one—which approach works best with a given problem? But the choice between individual and family therapy also reflects a philosophical understanding of human nature. Although most therapists are too busy trying to help people to contemplate philosophical questions about their work, they are, nevertheless, shaped by the context in which they work, an important aspect of which is the prevailing climate of opinion about the place of the individual and the role of the family.

The rise of individualism and the legitimization of selfhood led many people to place the needs of the individual over those of the group. "Authenticity" was once equated with radical individualism, just as it often is among adolescents struggling to define identities as individuals separate from their families. Perhaps family therapy has flourished at the close of the twentieth century, not only because of its proven clinical effectiveness, but also because American society is rediscovering the interconnectedness that characterizes our planet.

One of the cherished myths of psychotherapy is that it is value-free: Psychotherapists don't impose solutions; they help people discover their own. That sounds good, but psychotherapy is inevitably a moral enterprise. The type of treatment we choose to help people reflects our view of the proper balance between individualism and group membership. Most people value the claims of the individual *and* the group. Still, there is almost inevitably a greater emphasis on one or the other, and this emphasis is reflected in a greater or lesser tendency to turn to individual or family therapy to solve life's problems.

THE IMPACT OF THE FAMILY ON HOSPITALIZED PATIENTS

Except for purposes of footing the bill, hospital psychiatrists have generally kept families of patients at a distance. Although the family's role in the etiology of psychiatric problems has long been widely acknowledged, most clinicians believed that excluding the family was a necessary condition for undoing their destructive influence. Eventually, however, therapists were forced to acknowledge the family's continuing power to influence the course of treatment, especially for patients who go mad and require hospital care. Individual psychotherapy is predicated on the patient's having a stable, dependable, and relatively constant environment, so that the therapist can take a continuing family context for granted and concentrate on the individual's personality, unconscious, and past. This approach is less reasonable when the patient's environment is itself undergoing crisis, conflict, and change. All too often the hospitalized individual is an emotional prisoner of a chaotic environment.

Two consistent observations betrayed the reciprocal influence between psychiatric patients and their families. First, many therapists noticed that when the patient got better, someone else in the family got worse. It was almost as though the family *needed* a symptomatic member, and that any member would do. In the early 1950s Don Jackson documented the dramatic effect psychotherapy had on other members of the patient's family (Jackson, 1954). In one case Jackson was treating a woman for depression; when she began to improve, her husband called to complain that her emotional condition was getting worse. When she continued to improve, the husband lost his job. Eventually he killed himself. Apparently this man's stability was predicated on having a sick wife.

In another case, a husband urged his wife to seek psychotherapy for frigidity. When, after several months of treatment, she became less inhibited and more sexually responsive, he became impotent. Another example of dysfunctional balance is a marriage in which one spouse is an alcoholic and the other spouse subtly encourages the drinking. Some people seem better able to accept a needy, dependent partner than one who is competent and capable.

A similar pattern of shifting disturbance was discovered in families with an identified schizophrenic patient. When the patient improved, disruptions often occurred at home. The behavior of other family members changed in such a way as to push the patient back into psychosis; or if the patient recovered, others in the family began to show pathological distress (Bateson, 1959; Haley, 1959; Jackson, 1961; Jackson & Weakland, 1959). Otto Will (quoted in Stierlin, 1977, p. 12) noted, "Frequently it is at the first sign of progress with schizophrenics that their relatives want to take them out of treatment. "

The impact of a patient's improvement on the family is not always negative. Fisher and Mendell (1958) reported a spread of positive changes from patients to other family members. However, whether the effect that patient change has on the family is positive or negative is not the point. The fact is, change in one person changes the system.

The validity of these clinical observations was first corroborated in a study conducted at the Maudsley Hospital in England, in which a group of schizophrenic patients discharged either to their parents' homes or to live with their spouses was compared to a similar group of patients who lived alone. A significantly higher relapse rate was observed in the group who returned to their families (Brown, 1959). At least in this sample, the disrupting influence of living with families outweighed any positive effects of family support and nurturance. Furthermore the fact that family visits may disturb psychiatric patients is so well documented that to this day many hospitals do not allow patients to have family visitors, at least during the initial period of their hospital stay.

The shortsightedness of isolating mental patients from their families in psychiatric hospitals has recently been movingly documented in *Institutional-*

izing Madness by Joel Elizur and Salvador Minuchin (1989). Through the stories of four disturbed young people, the authors explore the consequences of labeling people as sick and then treating them as such—"a mode of therapy based on seclusion and forced contact with an insane world"—instead of supporting families in caring for their members. In one of the cases, a sixteen-year-old boy tragically drifts into the status of chronic mental patient, in part because of a progression of uncoordinated institutional vested interests. "Although he could act competently in many ways, the diagnosis of madness organized a rocklike reality that constrained possibilities, restricting his life so that the most morbid expectations were fulfilled" (p. 61).

As we head further into the 1990s, over forty years after the development of family therapy, most psychiatric hospitals still segregate patients from their families. True, there are some enlightened hospitals with enough trained staff to work with patients *and* their families; and there are some patients (battered women, for example, and severely abused children) whose families are pernicious and from whom the patient needs shelter. However, in the vast majority of hospitals, the pressure to stabilize patients on medication and return them as quickly as possible to the community (in order to free beds for the next round of admissions) means that patients are released into the same chaotic environments that helped precipitate hospitalization in the first place. Moreover even in those hospitals that make some attempt to recognize that patients have families, efforts at family therapy often mean no more than conducting family meetings with some attempt to help family members "communicate," when often as not the problem in these families is that family members communicate too much and need to develop more independence.

SMALL GROUP DYNAMICS

Those who wished to understand and treat families found a ready parallel between families and small groups. One reason that group dynamics are relevant to family therapy is that group life is a complex blend of individual personalities and superordinate properties of group structure. The bitter battle between Rousseau and Diderot throughout the middle of the eighteenth century about which had priority—society or the individual—is echoed among social scientists who debate whether groups and families are a product of *either* the individual *or* the larger system. In groups are met the provinces of the psychologist—individuals and what makes them tick—and the sociologist—the laws of group interaction.

During the 1920s social scientists began studying natural groups in society, hoping to solve political problems by coming to understand social interaction in organized groups. In 1920, the pioneering social psychologist William McDougall published *The Group Mind,* in which he described how a group's continuity depends in part on the group being an important idea in the minds of its members; the need for boundaries and structures in which differentiation and specialization of function could occur; and the importance of customs and habits, so that member-to-member relations could be fixed and defined. A more scientific and empirical approach to group dynamics was ushered in during the 1940s by Kurt Lewin, whose *field theory* (Lewin, 1951) guided a generation of researchers, industrial psychologists, group therapists, and agents of social change.

Lewin's field theory described the organic interactions between individuals and their environment. Drawing on ideas from the Gestalt school of perceptual psychology, Lewin developed the notion that the group as a whole is different from, and more than, the sum of its parts. This transcendent property of groups has obvious relevance to family therapists who must work not only with idividuals but also with family systems—and their famous resistance to change.

Another of Lewin's important discoveries was that group discussions are superior to individual instruction or lecturing for changing ideas and behavior. This finding suggests that family meetings are often more effective than separate meetings with individuals. Trying to coach a wife to behave more assertively, for example, is far less likely to succeed than working with her and her husband together. By meeting with both partners, the therapist can help the wife deal better with her spouse's counterreactions, and at the same time can make the husband more aware of the indignity—to both of them—of failing to treat his partner as an equal.

Analyzing what he called *quasi-stationary social equilibrium,* Lewin pointed out that change in group behavior requires "unfreezing" and "refreezing." First something must shake up and unsettle the group's accustomed beliefs and behavior; only then will group members be prepared to accept change. In individual therapy the unfreezing process is initiated by the disquieting experiences that lead a person to become a patient. Once he or she accepts the status of patient and meets individually with a therapist, the person has already begun to unfreeze old habits. When families come for treatment, it's quite a different matter. Many of them haven't been sufficiently unsettled by the symptomatic member's behavior to be prepared to change their own behavior. Furthermore, family members bring their primary reference group with them, with all its traditions, mores, and habits. Consequently, much more effort is required to unfreeze, or shake up, a family than an individual before therapeutic change can take place. Examples of unfreezing maneuvers include Minuchin's promotion of crises in family lunch sessions, Norman Paul's use of cross-confrontations, and Peggy Papp's family choreography. The idea of unfreezing foreshadows early family therapists' great concern with disrupting family *homeostasis*—a notion that dominated family therapy for decades.

Wilfred Bion is another major figure in the study of group dynamics who emphasized the group as a whole, with its own dynamics and hidden structure. He is best known for his description of three basic assumptions of groups (Bion, 1948). According to Bion, most groups become diverted from their primary tasks by engaging in patterns of *fight-flight, dependency,* or *pairing.* In *fight-flight* groups, members become so preoccupied with interpersonal conflict that battling or avoiding it, rather than problem-solving, becomes the real purpose of meeting. In *dependency* groups, maintaining a dependent relationship with the leader is more important to members than the group's avowed purpose. This kind of dependency is operating when students select courses in order to be entertained by witty instructors or to be enthralled by attractive ones. Finally, in *pairing* groups, members are more interested in being with each other than they are in working toward the group's goals. Even in therapy groups, members may be more concerned with socializing than with personal exploration and change.

Bion's basic assumptions are easily extrapolated to family therapy. Some families are so afraid to face conflict that they skirt around hot issues, like a cat circling a snake. Others use therapy sessions just to vent their spleen, preferring to fight endlessly rather than to contemplate compromise, much less change.

Lewin's and Bion's influences continue to be felt through their students, their wonderful writings, and two major centers for analysis and change of small group behavior, which bear the mark of their inspiration—The National Training Laboratory (NTL) in the United States and the Tavistock Institute of Human Relations in Britain.

Warren Bennis, a student of Lewin's, described group development as going through two main phases, each with three subphases (Bennis, 1964): Phase I *Dependence* (1) dependence-flight, (2) counterdependence-flight, and (3) resolution-catharsis; Phase II *Interdependence* (4) enchantment-flight, (5) disenchantment-flight, and (6) consensual validation. Understanding that groups go through standard phases of development has been put to use by family therapists who plan therapy in stages, and later into notions about predictable changes as families go through the life cycle. Bennis's conception of dependence and interdependence as the central problems in group life antedates similar notions among family therapists, among them Minuchin's description of enmeshment and disengagement and Bowen's concepts of fusion and differentiation.

The *process/content* distinction in group dynamics has likewise had a major impact on family treatment. Many family therapists have learned to attend more to *how* families talk than to the content of their discussions. For example, a mother might tell her young daughter that she shouldn't play with Barbie dolls because she shouldn't aspire to an image of bubble-headed beauty. The *content* of the mother's message is: respect yourself as a person, not as an ornament. But if the mother expressed her point of view by attacking or negating the daughter's feelings, then the *process* of her message would be: your feelings don't count. Strategic therapists even go so far as to say that the process by which family members try to solve their difficulties often becomes a way of inadvertently maintaining problems.

Students of small group dynamics have also explored the factors involved in developing a productive atmosphere in groups (group cohesiveness); the effectiveness of high- and low-structured groups; implications of authoritarian and democratic groups; scapegoating; the sociometric assessment of how friendship choices dictate channels of communication more than does formal structure; leadership and power, formal and informal, autocratic, democratic, or laissez faire; and how effective leadership contributes to the emotional needs as well as tasks of the group (Luft, 1970; Lakin, 1985).

Role theory, explored in the literatures of psychoanalysis and group dynamics, has had particularly important applications to the study of families. The expectations that roles provide bring regularity to complex social situations. A narrowing of roles shrinks the possibilities of family life; too many roles may lead to conflicting loyalties.

According to role analysis, multiple roles and multiple group affiliations are keys to understanding individual motives. We often think of family members in terms of a single role (wife or husband), but we need to remember that a wife may also be a mother, a friend, a daughter, and an employee. (Husbands should remember this too.) Furthermore, even those roles that aren't currently being performed are potential and therefore important. A mother who is a single parent is also potentially a wife or lover. Her neglect of these potential roles may impoverish her life and cause her to smother her children. When members of unhappy families get bogged down in few and rigid roles, they develop interpersonal arthritis, a disease that leads to family rigidity and the atrophy of unused life.

Sherif (1948) and others have shown that multiple roles, required to belong to various groups, can create problems. Dutifully doing what you're told and patiently waiting for recognition may work when you're in the role of son or daughter, but these attitudes probably won't work for a lover or an employee, where more outgoing and assertive action is called for.

Roles tend to be stereotyped in most groups and so there are characteristic behavior patterns of group members. Bales (1950) described twelve broad categories of group behavior, including: "shows solidarity" (raises others' status, gives help); "shows tension-release" (jokes, laughs); "agrees" (passive-accepting compliance); "gives suggestions"; and "asks for suggestions." Similar role patterns also characterize family members, most of whom learn roles in the family that become more or less fixed. Sometimes these roles are transferred to extrafamilial relationships where they may be less appropriate. Virginia Satir (1972) described family roles, such as the placator or the disagreeable one, in her book *Peoplemaking*. If you think about it, you may be able to recognize that you played a fairly predictable role growing up in your family. Perhaps you were "the good boy," "mother's helper," "the quiet one," "the family joker," "the counselor," "the thinker," or "the successful one." The trouble is that roles, once learned, are hard to put aside.

The encounter group movement, which had enormous clinical and social consequences, was a direct offshoot of studies of group dynamics. T-groups, forerunners of encounter groups, were begun in 1964 by Kurt Lewin and his colleagues Leland Bradford, Kenneth Benne, and Ronald Lippit (Benne, 1964). These groups were begun as a means of using participant observation to study small group dynamics. The aim gradually shifted from simply understanding group behavior to helping members clarify their goals and learn methods by which to realize these goals in group interactions. These modest aims proved very successful in increasing effectiveness and satisfaction; as a result, T-groups evolved into encounter groups, the main purposes of which are personal growth and enrichment. Influential as the encounter group movement has been (Nichols & Zax, 1977), it came too late to have any impact on the early history of family therapy. However, the experiential school of family therapy has been influenced by the encounter group movement, as we shall explain in Chapter 7.

Group therapy, which had a formative influence on family therapy, was originally developed in the early part of this century as an inspirational, persuasive, and supportive technique until the psychoanalytic conceptual framework was applied by Trigant Burrow, Louis Wender, and Paul Schilder (Nichols &

Zax, 1977). The analytic approach, which incorporated the dynamics of small groups with the dynamics of personality structure, was consolidated into a coherent theory and technique by Samuel Slavson (1943), who was a founder of the American Group Psychotherapy Association in 1948. Analytic group leaders regarded the group as a recreation of the family, with the therapist as an object of transference and other group members as sibling figures. Thus, ironically, analytic group therapy, which later became one of the prototypes for family treatment, began by treating the group as an ersatz family.

Analytic groups were designed to be frustratingly unstructured, in order to arouse latent unconscious conflicts and revive problems from the original family group. Group members' basic motives were considered to be conflicting combinations of love and hate, pain and pleasure, and strictures of the superego versus demands of primitive impulses. The developing ego was seen as the basic coping mechanism, and the growth and dissolution of psychological defenses the battleground on which these forces met. Notice that the emphasis was on the individual, rather than the group as a whole.

In the group dynamics approach, developed by Foulkes, Bion, Ezriel, and Anthony in Great Britain, the focus shifted from individuals to the group itself, seen as a transcendent entity with its own inherent laws. These therapists studied group interaction not only for what it revealed about individual personalities, but also to discover overall themes or dynamics common to all patients. This *group process* was considered a fundamental characteristic of social interaction and a major vehicle for change.

Another clear departure from psychoanalytic group therapy was the existential or experiential model. Experiential group therapy, stimulated by existential psychiatrists Ludwig Binswanger, Medard Boss, and Rollo May in Europe and by Carl Rogers, Carl Whitaker, and Thomas Malone in the United States, emphasized deep personal involvement with patients as opposed to dissection of people as objects. Phenomenology took the place of analysis, and immediate experience, especially emotional experience, was seen as the royal road to personal growth. Instead of transference, experiential therapists emphasized the profoundly real aspects of the therapeutic relationship, conceived as an authentic "I-thou" encounter.

Moreno's psychodrama, in which patients act out their conflicts instead of discussing them, was one of the earliest approaches to group treatment (Moreno, 1945). Psychodramas are dramatic enactments from the lives of participants, using a number of techniques to stimulate emotional expression and clarify conflicts. Because the focus is on interpersonal action, psychodrama is a direct and powerful means of exploring family relationships and resolving family problems. Although psychodrama has remained tangential to the mainstream of group therapy, Moreno's role-playing techniques have been widely adopted by group leaders and family therapists.

Fritz Perls's Gestalt therapy aims to enhance patients' awareness in order to increase spontaneity, creativity, and personal responsibility. Even though it is frequently used in groups, Gestalt therapy discourages group members from interacting while one person at a time works with the therapist. Although more widely used in individual than in group or family treatment, Gestalt techniques have been borrowed by encounter group leaders and some family therapists to stimulate emotional interaction (Kempler, 1974).

Given the extensive and diverse procedures for exploring interpersonal relationships developed by group therapists, it was natural that some family therapists would apply group treatment models to working with families. "Family group therapy" was an application of small group theory and group therapy technique to the natural group of the family. After all, what are families but collective groups with various subgroups?

Before examining the question of how suitable the group treatment model is for family therapy, I must mention one more historical fact. Even before John Elderkin Bell and Rudolph Dreikurs began to apply group psychotherapy to families in the early 1950s, a number of workers had used the group format to enlist cooperation from family members in planning treatment for individual patients. L. Cody Marsh, for instance, lectured to groups of relatives at Worcester State Hospital (Marsh, 1935); and A. A. Low also used this technique in his work (Low, 1943). Other therapists concentrated on group meetings with mothers whose children were in treatment (Amster, 1944; Burkin, Glatzer, & Hirsch, 1944; Lowrey, 1944). Some, including Ross at McGill, held weekly discussion groups for families of adult patients (Ross, 1948). In all these group meetings, relatives were treated like helpers who were not themselves in need of therapy. The "real" patients were not even included in the meetings. This work was similar to the long tradition of group counseling with parents, especially in child welfare agencies (Grunwald & Casell, 1958), and is still the way most adolescent inpatient units try to "involve" families.

One step closer to family therapy is "family group counseling" (Freeman, Klein, Riehman, Lukoff, & Heisey, 1963), a sociological, problem-solving approach. Counselors facilitate communication but de-emphasize individual goals and change. Intrapsychic conflicts are avoided. Family counselors foster understanding at the social level of external reality by helping family members recognize and modify social role conflicts. They aim for change in the social functioning of the family unit, rather than in its individual members. Although changes in the social functioning of whole families can effect profound changes in individuals, Freeman and his colleagues did not try or claim to achieve anything more than superficial support. Refreshing modesty!

By the 1970s, when family therapy had become thoroughly sophisticated and thoroughly systemic, these early group counseling approaches seemed naive, treating as they did individuals as the real patients and families as playing only a supporting role in patients' recovery. However, in the 1980s there was a growing recognition that some problems may, in fact, be primarily problems of individuals—or at least best treated that way. Carol Anderson and her colleagues at the University of Pittsburgh, as well as Michael Goldstein and his associates at UCLA, developed programs of *psychoeducation* for families with schizophrenics (Anderson, Reiss, & Hogarty, 1986; Goldstein, Rodnick, Evans, May, & Steinberg, 1978). Consistent with mainstream psychiatry, this approach treats schizophrenia as a disease that can best be dealt with using medication, and counseling for families faced with the terrible ordeal of coping with a schizophrenic member. Alcohol and drug abuse is another area where many believe that treatment must be directed primarily at individuals and only secondarily at families (Kaufman & Kaufmann, 1979; Steinglass,

1987). Where once family group counseling, which preserved the primacy of the individual patient, seemed naive, today treating schizophrenia or alcohol and drug abuse exclusively as byproducts of family stress now seems equally naive.

The psychoeducation approach was prefigured by the work of Kirby and Priestman (1957), who described a group that went on for fourteen months with six young schizophrenic women and their mothers at Brooklyn State Hospital. When the group began, the patients were quiet and withdrawn, while the mothers talked on and on about all they tried to do for their children. Gradually, however, the young patients overcame their submissiveness and began to speak up to their mothers, using words instead of symptoms. Encouraged by the support of the therapists and other patients, the daughters eventually found their own distinct voices. Eventually another significant shift took place—the mothers gave up their defensive preoccupation with their children's problems and began to discuss their own needs. This shift from the usual scapegoating pattern greatly benefited the daughters. Even though this group closely approximated conjoint family therapy, its focus still remained on individual expression. The daughters were encouraged to speak up, but the therapists neither sought nor sustained interaction; and though the mothers finally started talking about their own problems, no attempt was made to resolve their marital conflicts, nor were their husbands ever invited to attend.

All these approaches to group treatment were available to be applied in family therapy. Some of the techniques were useful, some not. It was a short step, for instance, from observing a patient's reactions to others in a group—some of whom might be similar to siblings, parents, or other children—to observing interactions with real, rather than transference, families.

Furthermore, from a technical point of view, group and family therapies are similar. Both involve several people. Both are more complex and amorphous, more like everyday social reality, than individual therapy. In groups and families each patient must react to a number of people, not just the therapist, and therapeutic use of this interaction is a definitive mechanism of change in both settings. Consequently, many group and family therapists endeavor to remain relatively inactive and decentralized so that patients in the room will relate to each other.

In individual treatment the therapist is a safe but artificial confidant. Patients expect their therapists to be understanding and accepting, an audience of one friendly person. Not so with groups and families. In both, the situation is more naturalistic, more threatening perhaps, but also more like everyday experience. Transfer to life outside the consulting room is therefore more direct.

On closer examination, however, we can see that the differences between families and groups of strangers are so many and so significant that group therapy has only limited application for family treatment. Families are different from therapy groups: Family members have a long history, and—more important—a future together. Groups are comprised of strangers, families of intimates. Revealing yourself to strangers is easier and safer than exposing yourself to members of your own family. In fact great harm can be done to patients by therapists who are so naive as to push family members to always be "completely honest and open" with each other. Once blurted out, there's no taking back thoughts that perhaps better remain private—the affair, long since over, or the admission that a woman *does* care more about her career than her children. Continuity, commitment, and shared distortions all mean that treatment for families has to differ from therapy for groups.

In one of the few small group studies using families, Strodtbeck (1954) tested a variety of propositions derived from groups of strangers and found major differences, which he ascribed to the enduring relationship of family members. Strodtbeck (1958) later substantiated the opinion that family interactions, unlike those in ad hoc groups, can only be understood in terms of the history of the family group.

Group therapy is predicated on a few basic conditions inherent in the structure of the group (Yalom, 1985). Some of the differences between family structure and that of groups are trivial, others are significant enough to make group therapy techniques inappropriate for families. Therapy groups are designed to provide an atmosphere of warmth and support. By being with others, patients feel less alone. They may have felt isolated before, but now they see the group as a place where they can be helped and where they can help others. This feeling of safety among sympathetic strangers cannot be part of family therapy, for instead of separating treatment from a stressful environment, the stressful environment, itself, is brought into treatment. Furthermore, in group therapy, all patients can have equal power and status, but this is not appropriate in families. Someone has to be (or should be) in charge. What's more, the official patient in the family is likely to remain isolated and to feel stigmatized. After all, he or she is "the problem." The sense of protection felt in being part of a therapeutic group made up of strangers, who will not have to be faced at home, cannot be part of family therapy, where it isn't always safe to speak openly because no therapist will be there to protect you from retaliation on the ride home.

Another basic therapeutic mechanism of groups is that they stimulate typical patterns of social interaction which then can be analyzed and changed. This function of groups has been likened to a "laboratory for social change" or a "social microcosm" (Nichols & Zax, 1977). Families, however, are less flexible and less open to experimentation. They have a complex shared mythology that dictates certain roles and ways of behaving. These highly developed and patterned communications make families far less able to experiment with new responses.

Family therapy is a less productive context for testing social reality than group therapy. Groups are specifically designed to provide opportunities for reality testing in a relatively nonthreatening atmosphere (Handlon & Parloff, 1962) so that distorted perceptions may be corrected and new ways of behaving tried out. But families share distortions of reality which must be maintained for the sake of family equilibrium. Individual members are thus less able to reexamine their perceptions than they are when they receive feedback from observers who have different points of view.

Therapy groups also provide opportunities for members to resolve transference distortions, played out with a variety of group members (Handlon & Parloff, 1962). The family therapy situation is different; the real figures are actually present. Transference still occurs, but is less amenable to exploration and correction. Parents may see their adolescent children in ways that fit the past better than the present. Children may see their parents accurately but transfer these perceptions on to the therapists. Therapists are generally hamstrung by powerful countertransference reactions when dealing with families. Furthermore, transference distortions are often supported by family mythology. "Daddy is a monster" is a myth that pervades the thinking of some mother-child coalitions—that he isn't is a myth in others. Such distortions and misperceptions are certainly available as grist for the therapeutic mill, but they are more difficult to deal with in families.

Although group therapy was used as a model for family therapy by some early practitioners, only the process/content distinction and role theory had any lasting impact on the mainstream of family therapy. One application of group methods that has persisted in family therapy are couples groups, and we shall examine this form of treatment in later chapters.

THE CHILD GUIDANCE MOVEMENT

Early in this century major social reforms and changes in the legal status of children led to universal compulsory education, attempts to control juvenile delinquency, restrictions on child labor, and a greater respect for children's rights. This new concern for children also extended to emotionally disturbed children and thus led to the child guidance movement.

The child guidance movement was founded on the belief that since emotional disorders begin in childhood, treating problems of children is the best way to prevent mental illness in adults. It was Freud who introduced the idea that psychological disorders of adulthood were the consequence of unsolved problems of childhood. Among his followers, Alfred Adler was the principal one to pursue the implication that treating the growing child might be the most effective way to prevent adult neuroses from developing. To this end Adler organized child guidance clinics in Vienna, where not only children but also families and teachers were counseled. Adler's approach was to offer encouragement and support in an atmosphere of optimism and confidence. His technique helped to alleviate the child's feeling of *inferiority* so that he or she could work out a healthy *life-style,* directed toward achieving competence and success through *social usefulness.* Adler's methods are still practiced in child guidance clinics in Europe and America.

By 1909 the psychiatrist William Healy had founded the Juvenile Psychopathic Institute in Chicago, a forerunner among child guidance clinics (now known as the Institute of Juvenile Research). By 1917 Healy had moved to Boston and established the Judge Baker Guidance Center, devoted to diagnostic evaluation and treatment of delinquent children.

When the child guidance movement in the United States expanded in the 1920s, under a grant from the Commonwealth Fund (Ginsburg, 1955), Rudolph Dreikurs, one of Adler's students, was one of its most effective proponents. In 1924 the American Orthopsychiatric Association was organized to work toward the prevention of emotional disorders in children. Although they remained few in number until after World War II, child guidance clinics now exist in every city in the United States. American child guidance clinics provided a setting for the study and treatment of childhood psychological problems and of the complex social and family forces contributing to these problems. Treatment was carried out by psychiatrist-psychologist-social worker teams, who focused much of their attention on the child's family environment.

Gradually child guidance workers concluded that the real problem was not the obvious one brought to the clinic, the child's symptoms, but the tensions in the family that were their source. At first there was a tendency to blame the parents, especially the mother, for the child's problems. Mothers were viewed as enemies to be vanquished and fathers were generally ignored (Burgum, 1942). The usual arrangement was for a psychiatrist to treat the child and a social worker to see the mother. Treatment of the mother was secondary to the primary goal of treating the child. The major purpose of seeing the mother was to reduce emotional pressure and anxiety, redirect hostility away from the child, and modify childrearing attitudes. In this model the family was viewed as an extension of the child, rather than the other way around.

Although the importance of the family's influence was recognized, mothers and children were treated as separate individuals. They were not seen together, and discussion between therapists was discouraged on the grounds that it might impair the privacy of the separate therapeutic relationships. Under the reigning influence of psychoanalysis, there was a tremendous emphasis on the individual psyche, with its unconscious conflicts and irrational motivations. Attempts to apply a social approach to disturbances in family life were dismissed as "superficial"—the ultimate indictment from psychoanalytic clinicians.

In this climate much was learned about individual childhood development, but clinicians often lost sight of the interpersonal context. It was assumed that resolution of the child's problems would also clear up family problems. Occasionally this happened, but more often it did not. Neurotic problems in individuals are only one problem in relationships, the others are interactional. Unfortunately, individual therapy may cause patients to increase their preoccupation with themselves, exclusive of others in the family. After analysis the patient may be wiser but sadder—and lonelier.

Researchers in child guidance clinics tended to focus on parental psychopathology throughout the 1940s and 1950s. David Levy (1943) was among the first to establish a relationship between pathogenic traits in parents and psychiatric disturbance in their offspring. The chief cause of childhood psychological problems, according to Levy, was *maternal overprotectiveness*. Mothers who themselves had been deprived of love while growing up became overprotective of their children. Some did so in a domineering manner, others were overly indulgent. Children with domineeringly overprotective mothers were submissive at home but had difficulty making friends; children with indulgent mothers were disobedient at home but well-behaved at school.

During this period Frieda Fromm-Reichmann (1948) introduced her famous concept of the *schizophrenogenic mother*, domineering, aggressive, rejecting, and insecure. Such women, especially when they were married to inadequate, passive, and indifferent men, were thought to provide the pathological parenting that produces schizophrenia. Adelaide Johnson's description of the transmission of *superego lacunae* was another example of how parents were blamed for causing their children's problems (Johnson

& Szurek, 1954). According to Johnson, antisocial behavior in delinquents and psychopaths was due to defects in their superegos, passed on by their parents.

Eventually the emphasis in the child guidance movement shifted from seeing parents as noxious agents to the view that pathology was inherent in the relationships that developed among patients, parents, and significant others. This shift had profound consequences. No longer was psychopathology located within the individual; no longer were parents seen as villains, and patients as victims. Now the nature of the interaction was seen to be the problem, which resulted in a more optimistic prognosis and changed the very nature of treatment. The goal shifted from weaning patients from their families to clarifying the relationships between parents and patients in hopes of improving them. Instead of trying—in vain—to separate children from their families, child guidance workers began to help families support their children.

John Bowlby's work at the Tavistock Clinic exemplified the transition from an individual to a family approach. Bowlby (1949) was treating a child psychoanalytically and making very little progress. Feeling frustrated, he decided to see the child and his parents together for one session. During the first half of this two-hour session, child and parents took turns complaining, each blaming the other. During the second half of the session, Bowlby interpreted to each of them what he thought their contributions to the problem were. Eventually, all three members of the family developed some sympathy for the others' points of view.

Although he was intrigued by the possibilities of these conjoint interviews, Bowlby was still wedded to the one-to-one format, which he believed should precede and follow joint sessions. For Bowlby, family meetings were a useful catalyst but only as an adjunct to the *real* treatment—individual psychoanalytic therapy. Nevertheless by eliminating the strict separation of the child's treatment from the mother's treatment, and pioneering the use of conjoint family interviews, Bowlby began the transition from what had been individual therapy to what would become family therapy.

What Bowlby began as an experiment, Nathan Ackerman carried through—family therapy as the major form of treatment in child guidance clinics. As early as 1938, Ackerman went on record as suggesting the clinical utility of viewing the family as a single, whole entity when dealing with disturbance manifest in any of its members (Ackerman, 1938). Subsequently he (Ackerman & Sobel, 1950) recommended studying the family as a means of understanding the child—instead of the other way around. Once he saw the need to understand the family in order to diagnose problems, Ackerman soon took the next step—family treatment. Before we get to that, however, let us examine parallel developments in social work and research on schizophrenia that led to the beginning of family therapy.

THE INFLUENCE OF SOCIAL WORK

No history of family therapy would be complete without mention of the enormous contribution of social workers and their tradition of community service.

(We are indebted to Donald Bardhill & Benjamin Saunders [1988] for point-ing out earlier omissions of this important contribution.) Since the beginning of the profession, social workers have been concerned with the family, both as the critical social unit and the focus of intervention (Ackerman, Beatman, & Sherman, 1961).

The profession of social work grew out of the charity movements in Great Britain and the United States in the late nineteenth century. Then, as now, social workers were dedicated to improving the condition of society's poor and underprivileged. In addition to ministering to basic needs for food, clothing, and shelter, social workers have also tried to relieve emotional dis-tress in their client families and to address the social forces responsible for extremes of poverty and privilege.

The *friendly visitor* was a social worker who visited clients in their homes in order to assess their needs and offer help. By bringing helpers out of their offices and into the homes of the helped, these visits served to break down the artificiality of the doctor-patient model that prevailed for so long. Friendly visitors were directly involved in treating problems of troubled marriages and difficulties of childrearing. Workers at *settlement houses* offered social services, not only to individuals, but to family groups as well.

Family casework was probably the most important focus of early social work training. In fact the first course taught by the first school of social work in the United States was entitled "The Treatment of Needy Families in Their Own Homes" (Siporin, 1980). Friendly visitors were taught the importance of interviewing both parents at the same time to get a complete and accurate picture of a family's problems, this at a time when mothers were considered responsible for family life, and long before traditional mental health workers began experimenting with conjoint family sessions.

These turn-of-the-century family caseworkers were well aware of some-thing it took psychiatry fifty more years to discover—that families must be considered as whole units. Thus, for example, Mary Richmond (1917) in her classic text *Social Diagnosis* prescribed treatment of "the whole family" and warned against isolating family members from their natural context. Rich-mond's concept of *family cohesion* had a strikingly modern ring, anticipating, as it did, later work by role theories, group dynamics research, and, of course, structural family therapy. According to Richmond, the degree of emotional bonding between family members was a critical determinant of their ability to survive and flourish.

Richmond also anticipated developments that family therapy became concerned with in the 1980s by viewing families as systems within systems. As Bardhill and Saunders (1988) pointed out,

> She recognized that families are not isolated wholes (closed systems), but exist in a particular social context, which interactively influences and is influenced by their functioning (i.e. they are open). She graphi-cally depicted this situation using a set of concentric circles to represent various systemic levels from the individual to the cultural. Her approach to practice was to consider the potential effect of all interventions on every systemic level, and to understand and to use the reciprocal inter-

action of the systemic hierarchy for therapeutic purposes. She truly took a systemic view of human distress. (p. 319)

Ironically, social workers, who pioneered in seeing the family as the unit of intervention, retreated to a more traditional individual-as-patient approach as they came under the sway of psychiatry in the 1920s. Social workers in the mental healthwing of the profession were strongly influenced by the prevailing psychoanalytic model, which emphasized individuals, not families.

When the family therapy movement was launched, social workers were among the most numerous and most important contributors. Among the leaders of family therapy who are social workers have been: Virginia Satir, Ray Bardhill, Peggy Papp, Lynn Hoffman, Froma Walsh, Insoo Berg, Jay Lappin, Richard Stuart, Harry Aponte, Michael White, Doug Breunlin, Olga Silverstein, Lois Braverman, Steve de Shazer, Peggy Penn, Betty Carter, Braulio Montalvo, and Monica McGoldrick. Incidentally, even starting such a list is difficult because unless it went on for pages it would have to omit a host of important names.

RESEARCH ON FAMILY DYNAMICS AND THE ETIOLOGY OF SCHIZOPHRENIA

Families with schizophrenic members proved to be an especially fertile area for research because their strange patterns of interaction were so dramatic and striking. Human nature is exaggerated under stress. However, as we shall see, the fact that family therapy emerged from research on schizophrenia led to an overly optimistic hope that family therapy might be the way to cure this baffling form of madness. Moreover, because abnormal families are so resistant to change, the early family therapists probably exaggerated the homeostatic properties of family life.

Family therapists did not discover the role of the family in schizophrenia, but, by actually observing families interacting, they witnessed patterns that their predecessors had only speculated about. Recognition of family influences on schizophrenia has existed at least since Freud's famous account (1911) of Dr. Schreber. In this first psychoanalytic formulation of psychosis, Freud discussed psychological factors in paranoia and schizophrenia, and also suggested how the patient's bizarre relationship with his father played a role in his fantastic delusions.

Harry Stack Sullivan focused on interpersonal relations in his brilliant work with schizophrenics. Beginning in 1927, he emphasized the importance of the "hospital family"—physicians, nurses, and aides—as a benevolent substitute for the patient's real family. Sullivan did not, however, take his ideas one step further and directly involve families in treatment. Frieda Fromm-Reichmann also believed that the family played a part in the dynamics of schizophrenia and considered the hospital family important to the resolution of schizophrenic episodes; however, she also failed to recommend family treatment. Although these interpersonal psychiatrists recognized the importance of family life in schizophrenia, they continued to treat the family as a pathogenic environment from which patients must be rescued.

In the 1940s and 1950s research on the link between family life and schizophrenia led to the pioneering work of the first family therapists.

Gregory Bateson—Palo Alto

One of the groups with the strongest claim to originating family therapy was Gregory Bateson's schizophrenia project in Palo Alto, California. There were actually two Palo Alto groups. The first was the "Project for the Study of Schizophrenia," under the direction of Gregory Bateson. Project members— Jay Haley and John Weakland, with Don Jackson and William Fry as principal consultants—were primarily interested in the study of communication, secondarily interested in families, and only tangentially interested in treatment. The other group was the Mental Research Institute, directed by Don Jackson, who was primarily interested in treating families. Bateson's project was thus mainly devoted to scientific study, and Jackson's group to the problems of treating families.

A scientist in the classic mold, Gregory Bateson did research on animal behavior, learning theory, evolution, and ecology, as well as psychiatry. He worked with Margaret Mead in Bali and New Guinea; then, becoming interested in cybernetics, he wrote *Naven,* and worked on synthesizing cybernetic ideas with anthropological data. He entered the psychiatric field when he worked with Jurgen Ruesch at the Langley Porter Clinic. Together they wrote *Communication: The Social Matrix of Psychiatry.* In 1962 Bateson shifted to studying communication among animals, and after 1963 worked at the Oceanographic Institute in Hawaii until his death in 1980.

The Palo Alto project began in the fall of 1952 when Bateson received a grant from the Rockefeller Foundation to study the general nature of communication in terms of its levels. All communications, Bateson had written (Bateson, 1951), have two different levels or functions—*report* and *command.* Each message has a stated content, as, for instance, "Wash your hands, it's time for dinner"; but, in addition, the message carries how it is to be taken. In this case the second message is that the speaker is in charge. This second message—*metacommunication*—is at a higher level and often goes unnoticed. Bateson's idea about levels of communication was derived from Bertrand Russell's *Theory of Logical Types* (Whitehead & Russell, 1910), which dealt with hierarchies in levels of abstraction, or logical types. Russell pointed out that a class cannot be a member of itself, nor can a member of the class be the class. That is, classes and members are of different logical types. For example, the class of chairs is not a chair, but neither is it some *thing* other than a chair; the class of chairs is a different level of abstraction. Another illustration is that the noun *university* is a higher-level, more abstract, or collective, noun than the separate buildings subsumed as members of the class "university." Bateson wanted to analyze a variety of phenomena using this insight.

In early 1953 Bateson was joined by Jay Haley and John Weakland. Haley was primarily interested in social and psychological analysis of fantasy; Weakland was a chemical engineer who had become interested in cultural anthropology. Later that same year, a psychiatrist, William Fry, joined them; his major interest was the study of humor. This group of eclectic talents and catholic interests began a number of different studies: otters at play, the training of guide dogs, the meaning and uses of humor, the social and psychological significance of popular movies, and the utterances of schizophrenic patients. Jay Haley (1976) has explained that Bateson gave the project members free rein, but although they investigated many kinds of complex human and animal behavior, all their studies had to do with possible conflicts between messages and qualifying messages.

In 1954 Bateson received a two-year grant from the Macy Foundation to study schizophrenic communication. Shortly thereafter they were joined by Don Jackson, who served as a clinical consultant and supervisor of psychotherapy with schizophrenics.

The group's interests turned to developing a communication theory that might explain the origin and nature of schizophrenic behavior, particularly in the context of families. Worth noting, however, is that in the early days of the project none of them thought of actually observing schizophrenics and their families.

Bateson and his colleagues hypothesized that family stability is achieved by feedback that monitors the behavior of the family and its members. Whenever the family system is threatened—that is, disturbed—it moves toward balance or *homeostasis*. Thus, apparently puzzling behavior might become understandable if it were perceived as a homeostatic mechanism. For example, if whenever two parents argue one of the children exhibits symptomatic behavior, the symptoms may be a way to interrupt the fighting by uniting the parents in concern for the child. In this manner the symptomatic behavior serves the cybernetic function of preserving the family's equilibrium by keeping the parents from fighting. Unhappily, in the process, one of the family members may have to assume the role of "identified patient."

In addition to applying systems ideas to explain the overall nature and purpose of family interactions, the group used communication theory to analyze specific sequences of family interaction. Even animals, Bateson had observed (1951), metacommunicate. Notice, for example, how two dogs or cats or monkeys play-fight. One leaps at the other, they tussle, they nip each other, but neither fights seriously and inflicts damage. How do they know they're playing? Clearly they must have some way of metacommunicating, of indicating that the attack is only playful. Humans achieve considerable complexity in framing and labeling messages and meaningful actions. Typically the qualifying metamessages are conveyed through nonverbal signals, including gesture, tone, posture, facial expression, and intonation. "I hate you," may be said with a grin, with tears, or with a fixed stare and clenched teeth. In each case the metacommunication alters the message.

Hypothesizing that schizophrenia might be a result of family interaction, Bateson's group wanted to identify sequences of experience that would induce such symptomatology. They were not interested in traumatic childhoods, but in characteristic family patterns of communication. Their basic premise was, at this time, simply conjecture; only later was it supported by observation (Bateson, Jackson, Haley, & Weakland, 1963). Once they agreed that schizophrenic communication had to be a product of what was learned inside the family, the group looked for the kind of circumstances that could

lead to such confused and confusing patterns of speech. In 1956 they published a preliminary report on their findings, "Toward a Theory of Schizophrenia," in which Bateson, Jackson, Haley, and Weakland (Fry was off doing military service) introduced the concept of the *double bind.*

They assumed that psychotic behavior might not be the result of a collapse ("breakdown") of one's ability to deal with reality, but may stem from
having to learn how to cope with a reality of disturbed communication. Consider someone who has an important relationship where escape is not feasible
and response is important; when he or she receives two related but contradictory messages on different levels, but finds it difficult to detect or comment
on the inconsistency or leave the relationship (Bateson, Jackson, Haley, &
Weakland, 1956); that person is in a double bind.

Because this difficult concept is often misused as a synonym for paradox or simply contradictory messages, it is worthwhile to review each feature
of the double bind as the authors listed them. The double bind has six characteristics:

1. Two or more persons are involved in an important relationship;
2. The relationship is ongoing;
3. A primary negative injunction is given, such as "Do not do X or I will
   punish you," or "If you don't do X, I will punish you";
4. A second injunction is given that conflicts with the first, but at a more
   abstract level; this injunction is also enforced by punishment or perceived threat. The second injunction is often nonverbal and frequently involves one parent negating the injunction of the other;
5. A tertiary negative injunction prohibits escape from the field, and
   demands a response. Without this crucial factor the "victim" will not
   feel bound and therefore there will be no bind;
6. Finally, once the victim is conditioned to perceive the world in terms
   of a double bind, the necessity for every injunction to be present
   disappears, and almost any part is enough to precipitate panic or
   rage.

Most of the examples of double binds in the literature are inadequate
because they don't include all the critical features of the definition. Skynner,
for instance, cites (1976): "Boys must stand up for themselves and not be
sissies"; but "Don't be rough . . . don't be rude to your mother." These two
messages are confusing and may cause conflict, but they hardly constitute a
double bind; they are merely a contradiction. Faced with those two statements, a child is free to obey either one, to alternate, or even to complain that
there is a contradiction. This and many similar examples neglect the specification that the two messages exist on different levels of communication. A
better example is the one given in the original article by Bateson, Jackson,
Haley, and Weakland (1956). A young man, recovering in the hospital from a
schizophrenic episode, was visited by his mother. When he put his arm around
her, she stiffened. But when he withdrew, she asked, "Don't you love me anymore?" He blushed, and she said, "Dear, you must not be so easily embarrassed and afraid of your feelings." Following this exchange, the patient became upset; after the visit with his mother was over he assaulted an aide and

had to be put into seclusion. Notice that all the features of the double bind were present in this conversation, and also that the young man was obviously caught. There is no bind if the subject is not bound. The concept is interactional.

Furthermore we may say that this mother was made anxious by intimacy with her son, but couldn't accept her feelings; consequently she behaved overtly as a loving mother who always does the right thing. Typically in such a family, there is no one else, such as a strong and insightful father, who can intervene and support the child. The mother tries to control her anxiety by controlling the closeness between herself and her child. But because she can't admit her anxiety, even to herself, she has to hide important aspects of her communication, that is, her own anxiety or hostility. In addition she forbids comments about her messages. Hence the child grows up unskilled in the ability to communicate about communication, unskilled in determining what people really mean, and unskilled in the ability to relate. Although it sounds esoteric, people need to metacommunicate in order to get along. It is often necessary to ask such questions as "What do you mean?" or "Are you serious?" In the double-binding family, however, such questions are not possible; comment and questioning are threatening to the parents, and the contradictory injunctions are obscure, occurring on different levels of communication.

We're all caught in occasional double binds, but the schizophrenic has to deal with them continually—and the effect is maddening. Unable to comment on the dilemma, the schizophrenic must respond defensively, perhaps by being concrete and literal, perhaps by speaking in disguised answers or in metaphors. Eventually the schizophrenic, like the paranoid, may come to assume that behind every statement is a concealed meaning; alternatively, he or she may gradually withdraw from the external world and grow progressively detached.

This 1956 double bind paper has proved to be one of the most influential and controversial in the history of family therapy.

Members of the Bateson group continued to clarify the concept of double bind and tried to document its occurrence in schizophrenic families. Other researchers created laboratory analogues of the double bind so they might test its effects under controlled conditions. Among the laboratory situations designed to imitate the double bind have been studies on: inconsistent reward and censure (Ciotola, 1961); nonzero sum games, such as the prisoner's dilemma (Potash, 1965); the shifts and evasions that occurred when mothers of schizophrenics were asked about their feelings (Beavers, Blumberg, Timken, & Weiner, 1965); schizophrenics rating the frequency with which their mothers had used a list of double-binding verbal-nonverbal contradictions (Berger, 1965); double binds in written communications (Ringuette & Kennedy, 1966); incongruent instructions for a task (Sojit, 1969); impossible tasks with helpers who wouldn't help (Kingsley, 1969); tasks in which anxiety was generated but denied (Schrieber, 1970); written tests of parent-to-child messages (Phillips, 1970); channel-discrepant messages and paradoxical injunctions (Guindon, 1971); training schizophrenics and neurotics to recognize double binds (Schaeffer, 1972); punishment and contradictory material (Smith, 1972); and paradoxical alternatives in a testing situation (Ables, 1975). All of these efforts were confident attempts to bring laboratory precision to the evaluation of a highly complex construct, but most of these researchers failed to document the destructive effects of the double bind.

The problem with these double bind studies was that they all failed to include one or more of the essential ingredients. A genuinely crucial relationship such as child/parent or patient/therapist must be involved; otherwise the victim can simply ignore the situation and walk away from the relationship. Laboratory experiments rarely involve anything like a critical relationship. In fact, the atmosphere tends to be one of gamesmanship and skepticism. And even if all the essential conditions seem to be met, what is being studied is merely a potential bind, because a bind is not a bind unless it binds. Some studies present contradictions between verbal and nonverbal messages, paradigms of the double bind, but this situation, too, is an inadequate substitute, since the levels in a true double bind are, by definition, different *logical* levels, not simply different ways to communicate. In the final analysis it appears that the essential features of the double bind have eluded operationalism.

Those who studied the double bind tended to look for evidence that it does or does not cause schizophrenia. But this approach is based on linear causality—A's response causes B's response. A more appropriate approach is to use the systems idea of *circular causality* and ask what's going on in schizophrenic families—A's response, then B's response, then A's response. It's more useful to think of the double bind as a pattern of relationship than as a discrete event, and we concur with those reviewers (Ables, 1976) who have suggested that a natural-history approach (observing without attempting to control) may be the most fruitful means of understanding the phenomenon.

The double bind theory undeniably offered us an enormously productive way to look at schizophrenia. Since its introduction the concept has been extended to humor, creativity, poetry, fiction, delinquency, hypnosis, religion, art, and psychotherapy—that is, to both creative and productive behavior as well as to pathological—on the basis of the response of the person who is the victim. There are four possible ways to respond to double binds or, indeed, to disqualifying messages of any kind: comment; withdrawal from the relationship; acceptance; or counterdisqualification (Sluzki, Beavin, Tarnopolsky, & Veron, 1967). The first two avoid or offset the double bind, and if these responses are able to circumvent the bind, they may lead to creativity (Bateson, 1978). The reason for this is that an adaptive solution to a double bind involves stepping out of the frame, recognizing the different logical types. The ability to step back like this is a creative act, based on the rare capacity to take an objective view of one's own context. Although the double bind was originally described as dependent on the motivation of one person (the mother's need to mask her anxiety or hostility), a comprehensive description would involve interaction with the other person's motivation. To describe interchanges between two people, one must postulate functions (motives, intentions, behavior) that involve both of them.

Bateson's original paper focused on a two-person interaction, essentially between mother and child. Father was described only in a negative way, as being unable to help the child resist being caught in the bind. Family analyses limited to two persons, although frequent (notably among child behavior therapists and couples therapists), are inadequate. A mother's relationship with her child is shaped by her relationship with her husband and, in turn, reshapes that relationship. So, too, a therapist's relationship with a patient is mutually defined by and defines the therapist's relationship with supervisors and administrators. In 1960 Weakland attempted to extend the double bind from two- to three-person interactions (Weakland, 1960) and discussed the fact that three people are involved in the double bind, even though one may not be immediately apparent. However, in general, the Bateson group was more concerned with broad applications than with the intricacies of three-person systems. Thus they suggested that the double bind concept may be useful for analyzing three-person systems in the family, clinic, business world, government, and organized religion, but they dealt with the father's effect on the mother-child dyad in a fairly superficial fashion. Indeed, the Bateson group, as well as their communications therapy and strategic therapy off-shoots, have persistently failed to deal effectively with three-person systems. In a similar way, although they espoused open systems concepts, their analyses have always tended to be limited to closed systems.

The Bateson group did not stop with their work on double binds. In 1956 members of the project began seeing parents jointly with their schizo-phrenic offspring. These meetings were held to observe and explore rather than to treat, but they were nonetheless an attempt to study actual behavior rather than speculate about it. Live observation of families was so revealing that it could be considered the beginning of the family therapy movement.

After 1956 the project went in several directions at once. The group continued to observe and try to understand double binds and, at the same time, to compile descriptions of communication and families. Haley began making regular visits to Phoenix to consult with Milton Erickson about the nature of hypnosis (Haley, 1976). Haley was fascinated by issues of power and control, and he considered the struggle for control between people as the relationship context—that is, the motive—for double-binding. His ideas on this subject will be developed below.

In 1959 the group received one grant from the National Institute of Mental Health for a family therapy project and another from the Foundations Fund for Research in Psychiatry for a series of experimental studies on family dynamics. A good deal of this work was done by Haley who, as a result, became skeptical about the possibility of doing meaningful controlled research with families.

In 1959 Don Jackson also founded the Mental Research Institute (MRI) and invited Virginia Satir to join him. Although the Bateson group and MRI staff shared the same building in downtown Palo Alto for a while, there was never any formal connection between them (Haley, 1976). Bateson, always more interested in theory than treatment, wrote: "As regards psychotherapy, all I would claim as a contribution from double bind theory is greater insight; and I do not mean insight for the patient which some practitioners think useless or harmful. I mean that the theory gives the therapist who works with schizophrenics or with families more insight into his patients and perhaps more insight into his own actions—if that be desirable" (Bateson, 1978, p. 42). Although clinical work was never a major goal for the project, Haley, and Weakland did do psychotherapy with families; so, naturally, did the psy-chiatrists of the group, Jackson and Fry.

All the diverse efforts of the Bateson group were united on one point, the importance of communication on the organization of families; but within this point of view there was also considerable disagreement. Bateson, for example, was most interested in pursuing the double bind, while others were more interested in the varying patterns of communication in different types of families. Therapists have also been attracted to the appealing notion that different kinds of symptoms might be linked to different kinds of families. Thus, in the 1950s, there was great interest in the characteristics of psychotic families; in the 1960s, families of delinquent boys; in the 1970s, psychosomatic families. The hunt for family types is linked to the linear idea that families *cause* symptomatic behavior in their members, rather than the systemic idea that family patterns and symptoms are circular, each one affecting the other.

Members of the project also disagreed about what constitutes the central motivating forces of families. Haley thought it was control; Bateson and Weakland thought it was concealment of unacceptable feelings. They all agreed that to understand families they had to use systems theory to identify the patterns of rules and stability; they also agreed that to understand interaction, they had to identify levels of messages, rules, and governing processes. All believed that schizophrenic behavior was, in some way, adaptive to the family context and that family members respond in error-activated ways to each other and so govern each other's behavior. However, given the diversity of talents and interests, it was not surprising that the output of this group was more a collection of ideas than a homogeneous theoretical presentation. Some of their ideas are summarized in *Pragmatics of Human Communication* (Watzlawick, Beavin, & Jackson, 1967), but to get any clear idea of the full scope of their work it is necessary to examine their papers individually. In 1962 the group disbanded.

Theodore Lidz—Yale

Theodore Lidz's investigations of the family dynamics of schizophrenia were grounded in psychoanalytic theory, and he sought the roots of schizophrenia in family object relationships. Much of his work focused on two traditional psychoanalytic concerns: rigid roles of family members and the effects of faulty parental models on identification and incorporation.

When Lidz began his studies of the families of schizophrenics in 1941, while he was completing his residency at Johns Hopkins, he and his colleagues surveyed the gross features of the family environment in which schizophrenics were reared. This original study, published in 1949 (Lidz & Lidz, 1949), surveyed fifty case histories. They exhibited a prevalence of broken homes and seriously disturbed family relationships. Forty percent of the young schizophrenic patients in the sample had been deprived of at least one parent by death, divorce, or separation; 61 percent of the families exhibited serious marital strife; 48 percent of the families contained at least one extremely unstable parent (psychotic, seriously neurotic, or psychopathic); and 41 percent of the families exhibited bizarre or unusual patterns of childrearing. In all, only five of fifty randomly selected schizophrenic patients appeared to have come from stable homes, raised by two well-adjusted and compatible parents.

Lidz challenged the then current belief that maternal rejection is a major distinguishing feature of schizophrenic families, and in one of his most notable findings, observed that the father's influence was frequently more destructive than the mother's.

Lidz followed up this initial exploration with an extensive longitudinal study of sixteen families containing a schizophrenic member. These intensive studies on a relatively small number of cases over the course of several years yielded an intimate glimpse of the environment in which young schizophrenics grew up. The primary method of study was to interview repeatedly all available family members over periods ranging from six months to several years. Additional information was gleaned from observing the interaction between families and hospital staff. Finally, projective testing was done with all members of the families. Since each of the patients in the sample had been hospitalized at the Yale Psychiatric Institute, a private hospital, they were all from middle- and upper-class families. Thus there was a bias in the sample toward a relatively high socioeconomic status, which meant there was a greater likelihood that the families were intact and better integrated than typical schizophrenic families. In the face of this bias toward better functioning, the consistent observation of severe family disruption and psychopathology is all the more striking.

Findings were categorized by parent-child relationships, marital interaction and its influence on the child, the dynamics of the family as a small group, the manner in which the family fosters ego integration, and the nature of family communication. And although Lidz was firmly rooted in the traditional psychoanalytic way of thinking about families, and many of his concepts focused on individuals and their roles, some of his observations went beyond one- and two-person systems and ideas about identification and incorporation to include consideration of three-person systems and the whole family as a unit. Thus Lidz bridged older theories about the impact of individual parents' personalities on their children and the more modern interest in families as systems.

Lidz believed that the major psychodynamic explanations of schizophrenia were too narrow. He rejected Freud's idea that schizophrenia was due to fixation at an early oral level and subsequent regression in the face of stress during young adulthood. Lidz did not find overt rejection of their children by any of the mothers he studied; consequently he also rejected the idea propounded by Frieda Fromm-Reichmann and John Rosen that severe and unqualified rejection by mothers was a major cause of schizophrenia. Furthermore Lidz considered the entire period of maturation, not just infancy, and tried to correct the tradition of ignoring the role of fathers.

Early in his studies Lidz's attention was drawn to the fathers, who were as frequently and severely disturbed as the mothers (Lidz, Parker, & Cornelison, 1956). In a landmark paper entitled "Intrafamilial Environment of the Schizophrenic Patient II: The Father" (Lidz, Cornelison, Fleck, & Terry, 1957a), Lidz and his colleagues described five patterns of pathological fathering in families of schizophrenics.

The first group was domineering and rigidly authoritarian, constantly in severe conflict with their wives. Having failed to establish intimate relationships with their wives, they sought to win over their daughters, who thus abandoned their mothers as objects of identification and tried to follow their fathers' inconsistent and unrealistic demands.

The second group of fathers were hostile toward their children rather than toward their wives. These men rivaled their sons for the mother's attention and affection, and behaved like jealous siblings rather than parents. They strutted and bragged, belittling their sons' achievements and sabotaging their self-confidence.

The third group of fathers exhibited frankly paranoid grandiosity. They were aloof and physically distant. The sons of these men were too weak to be like their fathers, but they continued desperately to emulate the parent's bizarre characteristics.

The fourth group of fathers were failures in life and nonentities in their homes. Children in these families grew up as though fatherless. They could hardly look up to the pathetic figures who were treated with such disdain by their wives.

The fifth group of fathers were passive and submissive men who acted more like children than parents. They were pleasant, almost motherly, but offered weak models of identification. These submissive fathers failed to counterbalance the strong domineering influence of their wives. Lidz concluded that it may be better to grow up without a father than with one who is too aloof or too weak to serve as a healthy model for identification.

After elucidating some of the characteristics of the fathers in schizophrenic families, Lidz turned his attention to defects in the marital relationship. The theme underlying his findings was an absence of *role reciprocity*. The partners in these marriages did not function cooperatively as a unit. In a successful marriage it's necessary first to fill one's own role and then to support the role of the spouse. In these families the spouses were inadequate to fulfill their own roles and disinclined to support their mate's. Lidz followed Parsons and Bales in saying that the father's role is primarily *adaptive-instrumental* while the mother's is primarily *integrative-expressive*. If each parent fulfills a version of one of these roles, then they can fit together harmoniously. However, if fathers are unsuccessful at their instrumental tasks, or mothers reject expressive nurturing, difficulties will arise in their relationship.

(Notice how wedded to traditional sex roles the investigators' assumptions were: Fathers should be "masculine," not "motherly," and a good marriage is rigidly complementary—fathers were forceful and made their way in the world; women were soft and selfless; they stayed home, serving children, and the men.)

Lidz found highly disturbed parental relationships in all cases that he studied (Lidz, Cornelison, Fleck, & Terry, 1957b). In focusing on the failure to arrive at reciprocal, interrelating roles, Lidz identified two general types of marital discord. In the first, *marital schism*, there is a chronic failure of the spouses to accommodate to each other or to achieve role reciprocity. These husbands and wives chronically undercut each other's worth and compete aggressively and blatantly for their children's loyalty and affection. Their marriages are combat zones in which every member of the family is wounded and scarred. The second pattern, *marital skew*, involves serious psychopathology in one marital partner who dominates the other. Thus one parent becomes extremely dependent while the other appears to be a strong parent figure, but is, in fact, a pathological bully. The weaker spouse, in Lidz's cases usually the father, goes along or even supports the pathological tendencies and distortions of the dominant one. In all these families, unhappy children are torn by conflicting loyalties and weighted down with the pressure to balance their parents' precarious marriages.

Lyman Wynne—NIMH

None of the leaders of family therapy has had as long and distinguished a career in family studies as Lyman Wynne. His impeccable scholarship and passionate concern for the unfortunate have been guiding inspirations for forty years of hard-nosed and enormously productive empirical research. Like others before him, Wynne examined the effects of communication and family roles, but what distinguished his work was his focus on how pathological thinking is transmitted in families of schizophrenics.

After completing his medical training at Harvard in 1948, Wynne went on to earn a Ph.D. in the Department of Social Relations. There he encountered the work of leading figures in sociology, social psychology, and social systems, including Talcott Parsons, from whom he came to see personality as a subsystem within a larger family system. For Wynne, the notion that we are part of something larger than ourselves has been the hallmark of his professional approach to troubled individuals and to his personal commitment to the problems of society. In these twin concerns, Lyman Wynne stands as a model for the entire field.

Wynne saw his first families in 1947 when he was working with Erich Lindemann at Massachusetts General as part of the treatment of patients with severe mental and physical disorders. Lindemann's understanding of the importance of working with the whole family in dealing with crisis and grief was the perfect practical complement to what Wynne was learning academically.

In 1952, Wynne took a position as psychiatrist in John Clauson's Laboratory of Socioenvironmental Studies at the National Institute of Mental Health (NIMH), where he first began working intensively with the families of mental patients (Broderick & Schrader, 1991). In 1954, when Murray Bowen came to NIMH as head of a research project on schizophrenics and their families, Wynne found a colleague who shared his belief that the family should be the unit of treatment, even if the two didn't quite agree about the nature of that treatment. When Bowen left NIMH in 1959, Wynne took over as chief of the family research section, where he remained until the early 1970s.

During his tenure at NIMH, Wynne also received training at the Washington Psychoanalytic Institute and was on the faculty of the Washington School of Psychiatry. From the 1950s through the 1970s Wynne published many research reports; he also trained several talented researcher-clinicians, including Shapiro, Beels, and Reiss. In 1972 Wynne left NIMH to become Professor and Chairman of the Department of Psychiatry in Rochester. He is still actively pursuing his research at Rochester, although he stepped down from the chair in 1978.

Wynne's study of families of schizophrenics began in 1954 when he started seeing the parents of his hospitalized patients in twice-weekly psychotherapy. He was fascinated by the chaos he observed in these families, and sought to make sense out of it by extending psychoanalytic concepts and role theory to the systems level. What struck Wynne most forcefully about disturbed families were the strangely unreal qualities of both positive and negative emotions within them, which he labeled *pseudomutuality* and *pseudohostility,* and the nature of the boundaries around them—*rubber fences*—apparently yielding, but actually impervious to outside influence (especially from therapists).

Pseudomutuality (Wynne, Ryckoff, Day, & Hirsch, 1958) is a facade of togetherness that masks conflict and blocks intimacy. Such families have an unnatural dread of separateness. They are preoccupied with fitting together so closely that there is no room for differentiation of separate identities, and no room for recognition and appreciation of any divergence of self-interest. The family cannot tolerate deeper, more honest relationships, or independence. This surface togetherness submerges deep affectionate and sexual feelings, and keeps both conflict and greater intimacy from emerging.

Pseudohostility is a different guise for a similar collusion to obscure *alignments* and *splits* (Wynne, 1961). Sequences of splits and alignments may be observed during family sessions; they are used to maintain a kind of dynamic equilibrium in which change in any part of the system, either an alignment or a split, reverberates to produce change in other parts of the system. A typical situation is an alignment between one parent and the patient, with a split between the parents. But the truth of these coalitions is threatening and, therefore, often covered up.

Pseudohostility is a self-rescuing operation. Although noisy and intense, it signals only a superficial split. Like pseudomutuality, it blurs intimacy and affection as well as deeper hostility; and, like pseudomutuality, pseudohostility distorts communication and impairs realistic perception and rational thinking about relationships.

In disturbed families, various mechanisms are employed to quell any sign of separateness, either inside or outside the family. The *rubber fence* is an invisible barrier that stretches to permit essential extrafamilial involvement, such as going to school, but springs back tightly if the involvement goes too far. The family's rigid role structure persists, protected by the family's isolation. The most damaging feature of the rubber fence is that precisely those who most need outside contact to correct family distortions of reality are the ones allowed it least. Instead of being a subsystem of society (Parsons & Bales, 1955), the schizophrenic family becomes a complete society, with a rigid boundary and no openings.

In a context where togetherness is everything and significant outside relationships aren't tolerated, recognition of personal differences may be impossible, short of the blatantly bizarre behavior seen in schizophrenic reactions. The person may thus finally achieve the status of separateness but is then labeled schizophrenic and extruded from the family; and like mud oozing back over where a rock has been removed from a swamp, the family's pseudomutuality is restored. In these terms, acute schizophrenia may be considered a desperate attempt at individuation which not only fails but also costs the person membership in the family. If acute schizophrenia becomes chronic, the now defeated patient may later be reaccepted into the family.

Wynne also linked the new concept of *communication deviance* with the older notion of *thought disorder.* He saw communication as the vehicle for transmitting thought disorder, the defining characteristic of schizophrenia. Communication deviance is a more interactional concept than thought disorder and more readily observable than double binds. By 1978 Wynne and his colleagues had studied over six-hundred families, and had gathered incontrovertible evidence that disordered styles of communication are a distinguishing feature of families with young adult schizophrenics. Similar disorders also appear in families of borderlines, neurotics, and normals, but they are progressively less severe (Singer, Wynne, & Toohey, 1978). This observation—that communication deviance is not confined solely to schizophrenic families, but exists on a continuum (greater deviance with more severe pathology)—is consistent with other studies that describe a "spectrum of schizophrenic disorders."

Role Theorists

Other researchers and clinicians used role theory to explain the deviant patterns in schizophrenic families. In 1934 Kasanin, Knight, and Sage described the parent-child relationships of schizophrenics and suggested that family relationships were an important and specific etiological factor in schizophrenia. In forty-five cases of schizophrenia, they found *maternal overprotection* in twenty-five and *maternal rejection* in two. Kasanin described a pair of identical twins discordant for schizophrenia and suggested that the differences in their relationships with family members were responsible for the differences in their fates (Kasanin, Knight, & Sage, 1934). David Levy (1943) found that *maternal overprotection* was much more frequently associated with schizophrenia than was *rejection.* While the mother's overprotection was generally more obvious, Levy also found many cases of paternal overprotection. Moreover, he observed that overprotection was not simply imposed by parents on their children; children in these families met their overprotecting parents more than halfway. Thus Levy introduced an interactional dimension to what had previously been regarded as another way that parents victimize their children.

In 1951 the Group for the Advancement of Psychiatry (GAP) decided that families had been neglected in the field of psychiatry. They therefore appointed a committee, chaired by John Spiegel, to review the field and report their findings. The committee not only went beyond the individual patient, but also beyond the influence of individual persons on individual patients to consider the total family. When they began to think at this level, they were impressed by the degree to which families are embedded in and shaped by culture and society. This illustrates the point that individual behavior can be seen as reflecting progressively wider social influences, depending upon the focus of observation. Nevertheless Spiegel's committee decided that limiting their observations to the level of the family would be optimally comprehensive and pragmatic.

The GAP committee's report (Kluckhohn & Spiegel, 1954) emphasized roles as the primary structural component of families. They concluded that healthy families contained relatively few and stable roles, and that this pattern was essential to teach children a sense of status and identity. There were norms for every role, and children learned these norms by imitation and identification. Family roles do not exist independently from each other; each role is circumscribed by other, reciprocal roles. Role behavior on the part of two or more people involved in a reciprocal transaction defines and regulates their interchange. The committee explained roles as a function, not only of external social influences, but also of inner needs and drives. Thus role theory served as a link between *intra*personal and *inter*personal structures.

Spiegel went on to Harvard Medical School in 1953 where he followed up his interests in role theory and family pathology. He observed that symptomatic children tend to be involved in their parents' conflicts; nonsymptomatic children may also have parents in conflict, but these children do not get directly involved. Spiegel (1957) described his observations in psychoanalytic terms: The child identifies with the unconscious wishes of the parents and acts out their emotional conflict. The child's acting out serves as a defense for the parents, who are thereby able to avoid facing their own problems, and each other.

R. D. Laing's analysis of family dynamics was often more polemical than scholarly, but his observations helped popularize the family's role in psychopathology. Laing (1965) borrowed Marx's concept of *mystification* (class exploitation) and applied it to the "politics of families." Mystification refers to the process of distorting children's experience by denying or relabeling it. One example of this is a parent telling a child who is feeling sad, "You must be tired" (*Go to bed and leave me alone*). Similarly, the idea that "good" children are always quiet breeds compliant, but lifeless, children.

According to Laing, labeling behavior as pathology, even "family pathology," tends to mystify it. The prime function of mystification is to maintain the status quo. Mystification contradicts perceptions and feelings—and, more ominously, reality. When parents continually distort a child's experience, the child's existence becomes inauthentic. Because their feelings are not accepted, these children project a *false self*, while keeping the *real self* private. In mild instances this produces unassertiveness, but if the real self/false self split is carried to an extreme, the result is madness (Laing, 1960).

Murray Bowen at NIMH and Ivan Boszormenyi-Nagy at the Eastern Pennsylvania Psychiatric Institute also studied family dynamics and schizophrenia, but since they are better known for their clinical contributions, their work will be considered below.

MARRIAGE COUNSELING

The history of professional marriage counseling is a less well known contributory to family therapy because much of it took place outside of the mainstream of psychiatry. For many years there was no apparent need for a separate profession of marriage counselors. People with marital problems are likely to discuss them with their doctors, clergy, lawyers, and teachers before they seek out professional mental health workers. Some students in courses on marriage and the family stay after class to talk to their instructors about personal as well as academic problems, and many women discuss sexual problems in marriage with their gynecologists.

The first professional centers for marriage counseling were established in about 1930. Paul Popenoe opened the American Institute of Family Relations in Los Angeles and Abraham and Hannah Stone opened a similar clinic in New York City. A third center for marriage counseling was the Marriage Council of Philadelphia, begun in 1932 by Emily Hartshorne Mudd (Broderick & Schrader, 1981). Members of this new profession started meeting annually in 1942 and formed the American Association of Marriage Counselors in 1945 in order to share ideas, establish professional standards, and foster research.

In the 1940s the movement spread from the initial three centers to fifteen, located throughout the country. Between then and now the profession has evolved from an informal service-oriented group to an organized profession, with a code of ethics and several training centers (Nichols, 1979).

At the same time these developments were taking place, there was a parallel trend among some psychoanalysts leading to conjoint marital therapy. Although the majority of psychoanalysts have always followed Freud's prohibition against contact with the patient's family, a few have broken the rules and experimented with concomitant and conjoint therapy for married partners.

The first report on the psychoanalysis of married couples was made by Clarence Oberndorf at the American Psychiatric Association's 1931 convention (Oberndorf, 1938). Oberndorf advanced the theory that married couples have interlocking neuroses and that they are best treated in concert. This view was to be the underlying point of agreement among those in the analytic community who became interested in couples. "Because of the continuous and intimate nature of marriage, every neurosis in a married person is strongly anchored in the marital relationship. It is a useful and at times indispensable therapeutic measure to concentrate the analytic discussions on the complementary patterns and, if necessary, to have both mates treated" (Mittleman, 1944, p. 491).

In 1948, Bela Mittleman of the New York Psychoanalytic Institute became the first to publish an account of concurrent marital therapy in the United States. Previously Rene LaForgue had reported in 1937 on his experience analyzing several members of the same family concurrently. Mittleman suggested that husbands and wives could be treated by the same analyst and that by seeing both it was possible to disentangle their irrational perceptions of each other from rational ones (Mittleman, 1948). This was truly a revolutionary point of view from an analyst: that the reality of relationships may be at least as important as their intrapsychic representations. Nathan Ackerman (1954) agreed that the concomitant treatment of married partners was a good idea and also suggested that mothers and children could profitably be treated together.

Meanwhile in Great Britain, where object relations were the central concern of psychoanalysts, Henry Dicks and his associates at the Tavistock Clinic established a Family Psychiatric Unit. Here couples referred by the divorce courts were helped to reconcile their differences (Dicks, 1964). Subsequently the Balints affiliated their Family Discussion Bureau with the Tavistock, adding the prestige of that clinic to their marital casework agency and, indirectly, to the entire field of marriage counseling.

In 1956, Victor Eisenstein, Director of the New Jersey Neuropsychiatric Institute, published an edited volume entitled *Neurotic Interaction in Marriage.* In it were several articles describing the state of the art in marital therapy. Frances Beatman, Associate Executive Director of Jewish Family Services in New York, described a casework treatment approach to marital problems (Beatman, 1956); Lawrence Kubie wrote a psychoanalytic analysis of the dynamics of marriage (Kubie, 1956); Margaret Mahler described the effects of marital conflict on child development (Mahler, 1956); and Ashley Montague added a cultural perspective to the dynamic influences on marriage (Montague, 1956). In the same volume Mittleman (1956) wrote a more extensive description of his views on marital disorders and their treatment. He described a number of complementary marital patterns, including aggressive/submissive and detached/demanding. These odd matches are made, according to Mittleman, because courting couples distort each other's personalities through the eyes of their illusions; she sees his independence as strength, he sees her dependency as sexy and giving. Mittleman also pointed out that the couple's reactions to each other may be shaped by their relationships to their parents. Without insight, unconscious motivation may dominate marital behavior, leading to patterns of reactive neurotic circles. For treatment, Mittleman believed that 20 percent of the time one therapist could handle all members of the family but, in other cases, separate therapists may be better.

At about this time Jackson and Haley were also writing about marital therapy within the framework of communications analysis. As their ideas gained prominence among marital therapists, the field of marital therapy was absorbed into the larger family therapy movement.

FROM RESEARCH TO TREATMENT: THE PIONEERS OF FAMILY THERAPY

We have seen how family therapy was preceded by clinical and research developments in several areas, including hospital psychiatry, group dynamics, interpersonal psychiatry, the child guidance movement, research on schizophrenia, and marriage counseling. But who actually started family therapy? Although there are rival claims to this honor, the distinction should probably be shared by John Elderkin Bell, Don Jackson, Nathan Ackerman, and Murray Bowen. In addition to these originators of family therapy, Jay Haley, Virginia Satir, Carl Whitaker, Lyman Wynne, Ivan Boszormenyi-Nagy, James Framo, Gerald Zuk, Christian Midelfort, and Salvador Minuchin were also significant pioneers of family treatment. Of these, Don Jackson, Jay Haley, and Virginia Satir in Palo Alto, Murray Bowen in Washington, DC, and Nathan Ackerman in New York probably had the greatest influence on the first decade of the family therapy movement. Among the others, those with the most lasting influence on the field are Carl Whitaker (Chapter 7), Salvador Minuchin (Chapter 5), and John Bell (Chapter 4).

John Bell

John Elderkin Bell, a psychologist at Clark University in Worcester, Massachusetts, who began treating families in 1951, occupies a unique position in the history of family therapy. Although he may have been the first family therapist, he is mentioned only tangentially in two of the most important historical accounts of the movement (Guerin, 1976; Kaslow, 1980). The reason for this is that although he began seeing families in the 1950s, he did not publish his ideas until a decade later. Moreover, unlike the other parents of family therapy, he had few offspring. He did not establish an important clinical center, develop a training program, or train well-known students. Therefore, although he was a significant early figure, his influence on the first decade of family therapy was not great.

Bell's approach (Bell 1961, 1962) to treating families was based on group therapy. In "family group therapy," Bell relied primarily on stimulating an open discussion in order to help families solve their problems. Like a group therapists, he intervened to encourage silent participants to speak up, and he interpreted the reasons for their defensiveness.

Bell believed that family group therapy goes through certain phases just as do groups of strangers. In his early work (Bell, 1961), he carefully structured treatment in a series of stages, each of which concentrated on a particular segment of the family. Later he became less directive and allowed families to evolve through a naturally unfolding sequence of stages. As they did so, he would tailor his interventions to the needs of the moment. For a more complete description of Bell's family group therapy, see Chapter 4.

Palo Alto

While conducting their landmark studies of family dynamics and schizophrenia, the Bateson group stumbled onto family therapy. Once the group began to meet with schizophrenic families in 1954, hoping to better understand their patterns of communication through unobtrusive, naturalistic observation, project members found themselves drawn into helping roles by the pain of these families (Jackson & Weakland, 1961). While Bateson was the undisputed scientific leader of the group, Don Jackson and Jay Haley were most influential in developing family therapy.

Jackson's work offers a rare example of the development of psychotherapy following the development of a theory—and secondary to theory. As a therapist, Jackson rejected the intrapsychic role theory and psychoanalytic concepts he learned in training and focused instead on the dynamics of interchange between persons. Analysis of communication was always his tool for understanding and treatment. Like Bateson, Don Jackson believed that behavior and communication were synonymous.

Jackson's thinking about family therapy was first stimulated by encounters with patients' relatives in his private practice and by occasional visits to the homes of individual schizophrenic patients (Jackson & Weakland, 1961). Observing the impact of families on patients—and vice versa—was not new, but Jackson's conclusions were. Since Freud, the family was understood to be the critical force in shaping personality, for better or worse. But the family was dealt with by segregation, physical and emotional, like removing a sick person from a germ-ridden environment. Jackson began to see the possibility of treating patients in the family as an alternative to trying to eliminate the family's influence.

By 1954 Jackson had developed a rudimentary family interactional therapy, which he reported in a paper, "The Question of Family Homeostasis," delivered to the American Psychiatric Association convention in St. Louis. His main emphasis was still on the effect of patients' therapy on their families, rather than on the prospect of family treatment (Jackson, 1954). Borrowing ideas from biology and systems theory, Jackson described families as homeostatic units that maintain relative constancy of internal functioning.

Jackson's concept of *family homeostasis*—families as units that resist change—was to become the defining metaphor of family therapy's first three decades. This view underestimates how families evolve and change shape as they move through the life cycle, and how families undergo sudden change at times of disequilibrium. Looking back, we can see that Jackson's emphasis on homeostasis was partly a function of the families he studied and partly a function of his efforts to change them. Abnormal families highlight homeostasis because they are the ones most likely to resist change. And therapists who see families as pathological and who try to rescue "family scapegoats" by challenging the way the family operates are certainly likely to provoke resistance.

Although Jackson and his colleagues probably overemphasized the homeostatic nature of families, their theoretical papers became increasingly sophisticated. Consistency, they realized, does not necessarily mean rigidity. Instead, family homeostasis is a nonstatic, dynamic state, an equilibrium within which the family may be at point A on Monday and point B on Tuesday. Families seek to maintain or restore the status quo; family members function as governors, and the family is said to act in error-activated ways (Haley, 1963). The result is not invariance, but stability in variance of behavior. A clinical illustration of homeostasis is to be found in families in which the symptomatic behavior of children serves to restore the status quo. Frequently, parental argument is followed by disturbed behavior from one of the children, after which the parents stop arguing and become concerned about the now "identified patient's" symptoms. (We'll take a closer look at some of the problems with the concept of homeostasis in Chapters 2 and 3.)

In "Schizophrenic Symptoms and Family Interaction" (Jackson & Weakland, 1959) Jackson illustrated how patients' symptoms preserve stability in their families. In one case a young woman diagnosed as a catatonic schizophrenic had as her most pronounced symptom a profound indecisiveness. However, when she did behave decisively her parents fell apart. Mother became helpless and dependent; father became, literally, impotent. In one family meeting the parents failed to hear the patient when she made a simple decision. Only after listening to a taped replay of the session *three times* did the parents finally hear their daughter's statement. The patient's indecision was neither crazy nor senseless but protected her parents from facing their own difficulties. This case is one of the earliest published examples of how schizophrenic symptoms are meaningful in the family context. The paper also contains the shrewd observation that this patient's symptoms were often an exaggerated version of her parents' problems. The parents simply had established better social covers. In addition, the case demonstrates how parents obscure and mystify feelings and conflicts. Jackson noted that often when the parents were asked to discuss their own thoughts and feelings, they quickly returned the focus to the patient, lest disagreements emerge.

In moving away from inference to observation of communication among family members, Jackson found that he needed a new language of interaction. His basic assumption was that all people in continuing relationships develop patterns of interaction. This patterning he called "behavioral (or communicational) redundancy" (Jackson, 1965). The term *redundancy* not only captures an important feature of family behavior, but also reflects Jackson's phenomenological stance. Traditional psychiatric terms like *projection, defense,* and *regression* imply far more about inner states of motivation than the simple descriptive language of early family therapists. Even when using concepts that imply prescription, Jackson remained committed to description. Thus his *rules hypothesis* was simply a means of summarizing the observation that within any committed unit (dyad, triad, or larger group) there were redundant behavior patterns. Rules (as any student of philosophy learns when studying determinism) can describe regularity, rather than regulation. A second part of the *rules hypothesis* was that family members use only some of the full range of behavior available to them. This seemingly innocent fact is precisely what makes family therapy possible. Families who come to therapy can be seen as stuck within a narrow range of options—unnecessarily rigid rules. Since the rules in most families are not spelled out, no one ratifies them and they are hard to change. The therapist, however, as an outsider can help families see—and re-examine—the rules they live by.

By 1963 Jackson had delineated three types of family rules: (1) norms, which are covert; (2) values, which are consciously held and openly acknowledged; and (3) homeostatic mechanisms, which are rules about how norms and values are enforced (*metarules*). Many of these rules are inculcated by families of origin, but Jackson generally did not look beyond the nuclear family.

Since families operate by rules, and rules about rules, Jackson concluded that family dysfunction was due to lack of rules for change. Therefore he sought to make explicit and to change the rules by which family transactions are governed. This is, in fact, a fancy way of describing interpretation, a technique that characterizes the treatment of communications therapists far more than their writings suggest. Although he denied that pointing out family patterns of interactions is useful (Jackson & Weakland, 1961), this technique was, in fact, part of his style and part of his influence.

Jackson's therapeutic strategies were based on the premise that psychiatric problems resulted from the way people behave with each other in a given context. He saw human problems as interactional *and* situational. Problem resolution involves shifting the context in which problems occur. Although Jackson had more to say about understanding families than treating them, many of his explanatory concepts (*homeostatic mechanisms, quid pro quo, double bind, symmetry,* and *complementarity*) informed his strategies and tactics of therapy, and became the early language of systems-oriented family therapists. He sought first to distinguish interactions ("redundant behavior patterns") that were functional from those that were dysfunctional or *problem-maintaining*. To do this, he observed routine behavior patterns and noted when problems occurred and in what context, who was present, and what the people did about the problems. Given the belief that symptoms are homeostatic mechanisms, Jackson also considered how the family might get *worse* if the problem got better. The individual might want to get better, but the family may need someone to play the sick role. Sometimes progress is a threat to the defensive order of things.

Jackson's model of the family as a homeostatic system emphasized the equilibrium-maintaining qualities of symptomatic behavior. This led directly to the idea that deviation or deviance, including symptomatic and irrational behavior, was not necessarily negative—at least if you abandon the point of view of those who want to correct it. A child's symptoms, for example, might distract the parents from conflict between them, and unite them in concern for the child. Unfortunately, following Jackson, some family therapists jumped from the observation that symptoms *may* serve a purpose to the assumption that some families *need* a sick member—which often led, in turn, to a view of parents victimizing *scapegoated* children. Unfortunately when early family therapists thought of themselves as avenging knights out to rescue innocent victims by slaying family dragons, they often took up an adversarial stance, which only exaggerated family resistance.

Among Jackson's most popular and trenchant papers was "Family Rules: Marital Quid Pro Quo" (Jackson, 1965). In a marriage, husband and wife play a variety of different roles. Jackson denied that these roles were the result of sexual differences; instead he considered that they resulted from a series of *quid pro quos*, worked out in a long-term collaborative relationship. The traditional view is that marital roles stem from sex role differences; it thus ascribed behavior to individual personalities instead of recognizing that relationships depend in large measure upon the interactions and rules for interaction worked out between people. Jackson's view is not that sexual differences don't exist, but that they are relatively unimportant. The major differences in marriages were worked out, not given. (In their enthusiasm for newly discovered interactional forces, early family therapists may have underestimated the importance of gender and the effect of gender bias on families.) *Quid pro quo* refers to the bargains struck between husband and wife, analogous to a legal contract. The rights and duties of each are established in mutual exchange. Jackson cites as one of the major quid pro quos among middle-class families the arrangement where the husband plays an instrumental role, dealing with things in a logical and practical manner, and the wife plays an emotional role, dealing more with people than with things. This division of labor is highly practical because the dyad then contains two specialists who combine their talents. The fact that such quid pro quos are not overt or conscious is significant for family therapists who must ferret out these agreements in order to help couples modify those that are not serviceable.

Another construct important to Jackson's thinking was the dichotomy between relationships that are *complementary* and those that are *symmetrical*. (Like so many of the seminal ideas of family therapy, this one was first articulated by Bateson.) *Complementary* relationships are those in which people are different in ways that fit together. If one is dominant, for instance, the other is submissive; if one is logical, the other is emotional; if one is weak, the other is strong. *Symmetrical* relationships are based on equality and similarity. Marriages between two people who both have careers and share housekeeping chores are symmetrical. (Once, the complementary marriage was the norm in this country, giving families stability if not equality. Perhaps the most profound change in family life in the second half of the twentieth century has been the advent of the symmetrical pattern in two-paycheck families. Unfortunately, in the process of transition from complementarity toward a more egalitarian, symmetrical norm, the American family has undergone a great deal of instability and conflict on the road to equality.)

Most of Jackson's descriptive concepts (*complementary/symmetrical, quid pro quo, double bind*) describe relationships between only two people. Although his intent was to develop a descriptive language of whole family interactions, Jackson's major success was in describing relationships between husband and wife. This limited focus on the marital dyad is one of the shortcomings of the Palo Alto group. Their sophisticated interest in communication led to an adult-centered bias, and they tended to neglect children as well as various triads that made up families. As a consequence many of their students tend to reduce family problems, even where small children are presented as the patients, to marital problems.

Like the other members of the Palo Alto group, Jay Haley's major focus was on the marital pair. Symptoms in a marriage partner, Haley argued, represent an incongruence between levels of communication. The symptomatic spouse does something, such as touching a doorknob six times before turning it, while at the same time indicating that he is not doing it, because he can't help it. Haley goes on to argue that the patient's symptoms are perpetuated both by the way the patient behaves and how others respond. From this follows Haley's basic tactic of psychotherapy: to persuade family members to change their behavior in relation to the patient.

Control in relationships is the theme underlying all of Haley's work. He describes everyday relationships as significantly determined by people struggling to achieve control over each other, and the therapeutic relationship as one in which patients attempt to control therapists (Haley, 1961). Therapists, therefore, need to outwit and manipulate patients, to defeat their resistance and subtle uncooperativeness. Haley, who borrowed many of his maneuvers from Milton Erickson, the renowned hypnotherapist, treated symptoms just as he treated resistance. Since symptoms are seen as ways of dealing with people, therapy must provide other ways of dealing with people. Thus Haley analyzed patients' manipulative and rebellious ways of dealing with family members. For example, a wife's handwashing compulsion may be seen as a means of rebelling against a tyrannical husband. A psychoanalyst would describe this as "secondary gain"; Haley sees this interpersonal payoff as the primary gain. As he put it, "From the point of view offered here, the crucial aspect of the symptom is the advantage it gives the patient in gaining control of what is to happen in a relationship with someone else" (Haley, 1961, p. 151).

Haley pointed out that the initial contact with the patient often involves subtle and not so subtle maneuvering for position. Thus when the patient says, "I work days and can only meet with you in the evenings," the therapist will respond either by accepting the control or resisting it. While such struggles indeed take place—as most therapists realize—it may be simplistic to see them as the major feature of the psychotherapeutic relationship. True, if the patient gains control of what happens in therapy, he or she may lose by winning—perpetuating difficulties by continued reliance on a destructive pattern. But it doesn't follow that therapists can succeed merely by achieving control themselves.

Haley (1963) defined his therapy as a directive form of treatment, and acknowledged that many of his methods were developed by Milton Erickson. Indeed it is sometimes difficult in Haley's early writings to determine where Erickson leaves off and Haley begins. In what he called "brief therapy," Haley zeroed in on the patient's context and the possible function of the patient's symptoms. His first moves were often designed to gain control of his own relationship with the patient. Thus Haley cites Erickson's device of advising the patient that since this is only the first interview there will be things that the patient may be willing to say and other things that the patient will want to withhold, and that these, of course, should be withheld. Here Erickson is directing patients to do precisely what they do anyway, and thus, subtly, gaining the upper hand.

Even while gaining initial information, the brief therapist begins to establish a context for therapeutic change. Accordingly a history may be taken in such a way as to suggest that progressive improvement has and will continue to occur. Alternatively, with a pessimistic patient, the therapist accepts the pessimism and says that since things have become so terribly bad it is time for a change. In either case the therapist gathers information while at the same time encouraging a commitment to change.

The decisive technique in brief therapy (then and now) is the use of directives. As Haley put it, it isn't enough to explain problems to patients; what counts is getting them to *do* something about them. However, as he points out, "One of the difficulties involved in telling patients to do something is the fact that psychiatric patients are noted for their hesitation about doing what they are told" (Haley, 1963, p. 45). Haley's solution was to use directives so cleverly that patients couldn't help but do what's wanted. Typical of this procedure is to prescribe symptomatic behavior, but add something in the instructions so that the symptoms come under therapeutic direction, and may slowly be modified. In one instance Haley was asked to treat a freelance photographer who compulsively made silly blunders which ruined every picture. Naturally this person became so preoccupied with avoiding mistakes that he was too tense to take satisfactory pictures. Haley instructed him to go out and take three pictures, making one deliberate error in each. While seeming to perpetuate the patient's problem, Haley was, in fact, paradoxically directing symptomatic behavior in such a way that the patient gained control over it. In another case Haley prescribed that an insomniac spend his wakeful late night hours performing arduous, unpleasant tasks, like going for long walks or polishing floors. The patient reported that he dared not suffer from insomnia once he knew that if he failed to fall asleep immediately he had to spend the night polishing floors.

Central to Haley's thinking is the idea that people develop problems when they are bound by paradoxical directives from their parents; yet they can be helped to overcome these problems by a therapist's benign use of paradox. Haley cites John Rosen as a therapist who used therapeutic paradoxes in an authoritarian manner, and Frieda Fromm-Reichmann as one who used paradoxes in a warm, gentle manner. In one famous instance Rosen dealt with a young schizophrenic patient who claimed to be God by having the ward attendants force the patient to his knees before Rosen, thus demonstrating vividly that he, Rosen, was in charge. The patient was, therefore, in a paradoxical dilemma. Once on his knees, he had to acknowledge either that God was subservient to the therapist, or that he was not indeed God.

Frieda Fromm-Reichmann's more gentle approach is described in her book *Principles of Intensive Psychotherapy* (Fromm-Reichmann, 1950). She once treated a patient who said that everything she did occurred in relation to her own private and powerful God, rather than in relation to other people. This, of course, provided a convenient excuse for her refusing to relate to Dr. Fromm-Reichmann. Here's what Fromm-Reichmann said to the patient: "Tell him that I am a doctor and you have lived with him in his kingdom now from 7 to 16—that's nine years—and he has not helped you. So now he must permit me to try and see whether you and I can do that job." This patient, too, was caught in a position where she had to respond to the therapist whatever she did. She could either go to her God and repeat what she was told, thereby conceding that the doctor was in charge; or she could rebel against the doctor, which meant she was relating to her, an action which also renders questionable the existence of her God. Hence, in order to acknowledge her God, she must deny him; similarly if she defies Fromm-Reichmann, she must acknowledge her. What Haley salutes in these examples is the use of *therapeutic paradox*—a benign version of damned if you do, damned if you don't.

In describing marriage therapy, Haley devoted most of his attention to analyzing the dynamics of marital relationships, leaving little room for discussion of the actual techniques of therapy. As we shall see, Haley has written several extremely informative books on doing therapy; his early writing, however, left the reader intrigued and fascinated, but uninformed as to how to proceed technically. One may infer from Haley's description of marital dynamics, and from those few techniques he did describe, that he pointed out to couples some of the dynamics of their interaction and encouraged them to communicate openly about how they are dealing with each other. In one place he said, "One of the functions of a marriage therapist might be to provoke a couple to fight and say what is on their minds so they do not continue to punish each other indirectly for crimes which have never been brought up as accusations. When a couple cannot fight, all issues which require defining an area of the relationship are avoided" (Haley, 1963, p. 125).

Haley based his recommendations for therapy with whole families on an amalgam of concepts from the Bateson group. As in traditional individual psychotherapy, conflict was a major focus; but conflict was seen as occurring *between,* rather than within, people. The model was cybernetic: One person's behavior was seen as provoking a response in other family members; family members set limits on one another's behavior in a self-corrective process by responding in error-activated ways when any individual goes beyond the acceptable limits. This process of mutually responsive behavior defines rules in the family system. Haley relied on the metaphor of a power struggle when describing who sets the rules. The therapeutic task was to help families resolve power struggles.

Virginia Satir was another member of the Palo Alto group who played a major role in the development of family therapy. Satir saw troubled family members as trapped in narrow family roles like *victim, placator, defiant one,* and *rescuer.* Her concern with identifying such life-constricting roles and freeing family members from their grip was consistent with her major focus, which was always on the individual. Thus Satir was a humanizing force, even in the early days of family therapy, when many were so enamored of the new systems metaphor that they sometimes neglected the emotional life of families—their disappointments, pain, and hopes.

In her work with families Satir concentrated on clarifying communication, expressing feelings, and fostering a climate of mutual acceptance and warmth. The 1964 publication of Satir's book *Conjoint Family Therapy* did much to popularize the family therapy movement. This book, along with *Pragmatics of Human Communication* (Watzlawick, Beavin, & Jackson, 1967), helped spread the influence of the Palo Alto group's brand of systemic thinking. Eventually Satir went on from family therapy to become a major force in the human potential movement, and we will consider her work more fully in Chapter 7, Experiential Family Therapy.

Murray Bowen

Like many of the founders of family therapy, Murray Bowen was a psychiatrist who specialized in schizophrenia. Unlike others, however, he emphasized theory in his work, and to this day Bowenian theory is the most thoughtful and thorough system of ideas family therapy has produced.

Bowen began his clinical work at the Menninger Clinic from 1946 to 1954, where he studied mothers and their schizophrenic children who lived together in small cottages. His major interest at the time was mother-child symbiosis, which led to the formation of his concept of *differentiation* (autonomy from others and independence of thought from feeling). From Menningers, Bowen moved to NIMH, where he developed a project to hospitalize whole families with a schizophrenic member. It was this project that expanded the concept of mother-child symbiosis to include the role of fathers, and led to the concept of *triangulation* (diverting conflict between two people by involving a third). In 1959, Bowen left NIMH for Georgetown Medical School, where he was a professor of psychiatry and director of his own training program until his death in the fall of 1990.

In the first year of the NIMH project (1954), Bowen provided separate therapists for individual family members. What he discovered, however, was that these efforts tended to fractionate families. Instead of working out their mutual problems, family members had a tendency to think, "I'll take up my problems with *my* therapist" (Bowen, 1976). (Of course, this never happens when nice people like you and me go to *our* individual therapists.) After a year, concluding that the family was the unit of disorder, Bowen began treating the families together. Thus, in 1955, Bowen became one of the first to invent family therapy.

Beginning in 1955, Bowen also held large group therapy sessions for the entire project staff and all of the families. In this early form of network therapy, Bowen assumed that togetherness and open communication would be therapeutic for problems within families and between family members and the staff.

The history of Bowen's methods of therapy marks the evolution of his thinking. At first he used four therapists to manage the large multifamily meetings, but he became dissatisfied when he noticed that the therapists tended to pull in different directions. So he put one therapist in charge, with the others consigned to supporting roles. However, just as the therapists tended to pull in different directions, so did the families. As soon as a crucial point was being developed within one family, someone from another family would become anxious and change the subject. Finally, Bowen decided that families would have to take turns—one family was the focus for each session, with the others as silent auditors.

At first, Bowen's approach to single families was the same one he employed with the large meetings. He did what many people new to family therapy do; he brought family members together and just tried to get them talking. He reasoned that simply by being together and discussing mutual concerns families would improve. Although Bowen soon rejected this idea, many people continue to approach family treatment this way. Nondirective participant observation has little utility beyond getting family members started talking together and perhaps resolving relatively transient problems. Bowen soon learned this, and he developed a structured and directive approach which paralleled the evolution of his theory.

When he brought family members together to define problems and discuss solutions, Bowen was most struck by their intense *emotional reactivity.* Feelings overwhelmed thinking and tended to involve the whole group in chaos and conflict. Bowen felt the family's tendency to pull him into the center of this *undifferentiated ego mass,* and he had to make a concerted effort to remain objective (Bowen, 1961). He believed that if they were forced to solve their own problems, families would become more responsible and competent. So Bowen sat with them, remaining neutral and detached, while he observed the process of family interactions. His major active effort was to discourage scapegoating by pointing out when family members used the patient as an excuse for avoiding other problems. At the end of each session he summed up what he observed, emphasizing the process by which the family went about trying to solve their problems.

Bowen found that observing whole families was invaluable as a source of information, but he was disappointed with the results of therapy. Beginning in 1960 he began meeting with just the parents of symptomatic children. His purpose was to block scapegoating and help parents focus on problems in their own relationship, without being distracted by their children. He was much happier with the results of seeing parents alone, and has continued to do so, only rarely including children. When he first began interviewing couples, Bowen analyzed one spouse at a time, focusing heavily on dreams for his interpretations. He soon abandoned this intrapsychic focus and shifted to explore the relationship system between partners. Bowen experimented with different methods of working with couples until about 1964, when he developed his final method which has four basic elements:

1. *Defining and Clarifying Relationships between Partners.* Bowen encouraged each spouse to talk directly to the therapist, not to his or her mate. In this way the therapist, not the couple, controls the affect in the interchange. The Bowenian therapist tries to keep things calm, low-keyed, and objective. A spouse who is neither speaking nor being spoken to is less emotionally reactive and, therefore, better able to listen. The therapist focuses on cognition—thoughts and ideas, rather than feelings. Only after a couple makes a great deal of progress toward understanding each other rationally, does the therapist invite them to talk about their emotional reactions and feelings. When feelings are stirred up, the therapist encourages couples to discuss the issues about which they have feelings, not the feelings themselves. Emotions that do emerge from these issue-oriented discussions are probably more spontaneous than those elicited when couples are encouraged to express feelings.

2. *Keeping Self Detriangled.* Bowen believed that a prerequisite to avoiding emotional entanglement with client families was a mature resolution of emotional conflicts within one's own family and emotional system at work. In the absence of such personal maturity, therapists are liable to react emotionally to family members who restimulate conflicts and blind spots. To avoid emotional entanglement, therapists should focus on process, not content, and avoid taking sides, being charmed, or getting angry. The Bowenian therapist remains calm at all times.

3. *Teaching Partners about the Functioning of Emotional Systems.* This should only be attempted when anxiety is reduced. Otherwise whatever the therapist says is liable to be interpreted as siding with one or the other partner. When anxiety in a couple was moderately low, Bowen might discuss progress made in other cases, to illustrate certain points. When anxiety between spouses was very low, he taught them directly about functioning of emotional systems. If they were motivated, he also encouraged them to work on differentiating themselves in relation to their families of origin.

4. *Taking "I-Position" Stands.* The more a therapist can define him- or herself in relationship to a family, the more family members can follow suit and define themselves in relation to the rest of the family. Defining oneself means to become clear about and express convictions, beliefs, and actions in relation to other people. By knowing what one believes, and saying so in a calm, straightforward manner, one can avoid *fusion*, or *undifferentiation*.

The goal of Bowen's work with parents was to help them achieve a reasonable level of differentiation of self, from each other and from their families of origin, to learn enough about family systems to handle future crises, and to develop the motivation to continue working toward further differentiation after therapy is terminated.

Besides treating couples Bowen also used two other methods of treatment: couples groups and individual sessions.

When he found himself covering similar issues with different couples, session after session, Bowen decided that he might save time by working with several families at once. This seemed particularly appropriate for Bowen's therapy because it is relatively didactic. So, beginning in about 1965 (Bowen, 1976), he began treating couples in groups. Bowen's use of Multiple Family Therapy was paradoxical because his major emphasis had been to avoid the fusion inherent in social and emotional togetherness. When he worked with groups, though, Bowen minimized emotional interaction between families and forbade contact outside group sessions. Although he found it no easier to teach families about emotional systems and much harder to remain neutral, the couples in these groups made rapid progress. Apparently families learned a great deal about the process of emotional systems, with less anxiety, as they listened to discussions of other people's problems. For several years, the Multiple Family Therapy method was the bulk of Bowen's practice.

In addition to couples and couples groups, Bowen also worked frequently with single family members. This is a unique approach, and it challenges facile assumptions about family therapy. Family therapy is both a method and an orientation. As an orientation, it means understanding people in context of significant emotional systems; as a method, it usually means working with whole families. But some might argue that Bowen's work with individual family members is more exclusively focused on family issues, systems concepts, and emotional process than is almost any other family therapy approach.

In 1966 there was an emotional crisis in Bowen's family, and his personal experience in resolving that crisis was a formative event in teaching him about changing families.

Murray Bowen was the oldest of five children from a tightly knit family that for several generations resided in the same small town in Pennsylvania. After growing up, he kept his distance from his parents and maintained relations on a comfortable but superficial basis. Like many of us, Bowen mistook avoidance for emancipation. But as he later realized, emotional tension in the family remains with us, making us vulnerable to repeat similar patterns in new relationships, until our family conflicts are finally resolved.

Bowen's personal resolution of emotional reactivity in his family was as significant for his work as Freud's self-analysis had been for psychoanalysis. In neither case was it easy. Bowen spent twelve years trying to understand his family, using the framework of his theory, and seven or eight years of active effort to modify himself in relation to the family before the major breakthrough occurred. The going is usually slower for explorers of unknown territory than for those who come later with maps to guide them.

In his attempt to understand and improve relationships with his own family, Bowen turned first to his nuclear family and only later to his family of origin. Although this seems a natural sequence, Bowen's experience convinced him that the most productive course is to begin with the original family. Only then is it possible to make genuine progress in reducing tension in the more significant, but more reactive, nuclear family. *Differentiation of self* in the family of origin is begun by developing an individual, person-to-person relationship with each parent and with as many members of the family as possible. If visiting is difficult, letters and phone calls can help re-establish relationships, particularly if they are personal and intimate. Differentiating one's self from the family is completed when these relationships are maintained without fusion or triangulation. Differentiated people can talk about the full range of personal issues between them without getting anxious and detouring the conversation to a third person or impersonal subject.

Bowen's most important achievement was detriangling himself from his own parents. His parents had been accustomed to complaining to him about unresolved conflicts between them. Most of us are flattered to receive these confidences and consider them a form of intimacy born of respect for our judgment. Bowen recognized this triangulation for what it was, and when his mother complained about his father, he told his father: "Your wife told me a story about you; I wonder why she told me instead of you?" Naturally father discussed this with mother and, naturally, she was annoyed. Moves to differentiate oneself violate family norms and cause emotional upheaval. If there is no upheaval, then the differentiation effort is probably insignificant. Although his mother fussed about it, Bowen's maneuver was effective in keeping his parents from trying to get him to take sides—and made it harder for them to avoid discussing things between themselves. Telling the third person what a second person says to you about him or her is one of the most effective detriangling moves.

Bowen also discovered that it's important to define self around significant issues. Since emotionally significant issues are usually dormant, the most productive visits home are during a crisis or stressful occasion, such as a death, serious illness, wedding, or birth. At these times, the family's emotional reactivity is at high tide. It was at such a point that Bowen returned home for a carefully orchestrated effort to differentiate himself from a series of interlocking family triangles. The details of that venture are complex but make rewarding reading for the serious student (Anonymous, 1972).

Bowen's trip came on the heels of a family squabble over problems with the family business. He prepared the way by writing a series of intimate and provocative letters to the major players in the family drama. These letters were designed to open hidden conflicts and promote a lively confrontation. Thus, he wrote to his brother, a family scapegoat, and told him all the stories and gossip about him. That did the trick.

When Bowen arrived home, the whole family was present—and hopping mad. Every segment of the family tried to engage him in an emotional tug of war. But differentiation requires thinking, instead of hasty reaction, and remaining objectively neutral about conflicts between others. Although his letters had provoked the showdown, the issues were among the family members who lived together in Pennsylvania. Bowen saw his task as stirring things up, but not taking sides. Armed with his understanding of family systems theory and knowing what to expect from the family, Bowen was able to remain absolutely neutral. This forced the feuding parties, all of whom were present, to work things out among themselves.

The trip was a great success. Bowen was able to remain in personal contact with each member of his family at a time of crisis, but without becoming triangled or emotionally reactive.

After he told them about his experience with his own family, many of Bowen's trainees began to return to their own families and work on differentiating themselves. They did so even though Bowen had not directly encouraged them. When he noted how productive these trainees became as therapists, as compared with those who had not returned to their own families, Bowen decided that the best way to become a family therapist was to resolve emotional problems in the family of origin. Thus, beginning in 1971, studying one's own family became the core of Bowen's approach to training. The major emphasis is on returning to the family of origin, making contact, and developing an honest personal relationship with every possible member of the family, while remaining detriangled.

Nathan Ackerman

Nathan Ackerman came to family therapy from psychoanalysis, and his thinking about families continued to reflect that background. He emphasized psychodynamic conflict more than the communication and interaction that systems-oriented family therapists stressed, but he had a keen sense of the overall organization of families. Families, Ackerman said, give an appearance of unity, but underneath they are emotionally divided into competing factions. This you may recognize as similar to the psychoanalytic model of individuals who, despite apparent unity of personality, are actually minds in conflict, driven by the interplay of drives and defenses and competing structural forces. Just as an individual expresses the dynamic conflicts of id, ego, and superego, so too are families dynamic coalitions, sometimes of mother and daughter against father and son, sometimes of one generation against the next.

Ackerman was a psychoanalytically trained child psychiatrist. After completing his residency training during the Depression, he joined the psychiatric staff at Southard School, a facility for disturbed children at the Menninger Clinic in Topeka, Kansas. In 1937 he became chief psychiatrist of the Child Guidance Clinic. At first he followed the child guidance model of having a psychiatrist treat the child and a social worker see the mother. But by the mid 1940s he began to experiment with having the same therapist see both. Unlike Bowlby, however, Ackerman did more than use this as a temporary expedient to resolve treatment impasses. Instead he reevaluated his whole conception of psychopathology and began to see the family as the basic unit for diagnosis and treatment.

In 1955, Ackerman organized and led the first session on family diagnosis at a meeting of the American Orthopsychiatric Association. Two years later, in 1957, he opened the Family Mental Health Clinic of the Jewish Family Services in New York City and taught at Columbia University. From there he founded the Family Institute, in 1960, which was renamed the Ackerman Institute following his death in 1971.

In addition to his clinical innovations, Ackerman also published several important articles and books. As early as 1938 he wrote "The Unity of the

Family," and some consider his article, "Family Diagnosis: An Approach to the Preschool Child" (Ackerman & Sobel, 1950), as the beginning of the family therapy movement (Kaslow, 1980). In 1962, Ackerman, with Don Jackson, cofounded the field's first journal, *Family Process*. Under the editorial leadership of Jay Haley (1962–1969), Donald Bloch (1969–1982), Carlos Sluzki (1983–1990), and Peter Steinglass (1990–present), *Family Process* has for many years been the major scholarly and scientific vehicle through which family therapists communicate their ideas.

While other family therapists de-emphasized the psychology of individuals, Ackerman was always concerned with what goes on inside people, as well as between them. He never lost sight of individuals' feelings, hopes, and desires. In fact, Ackerman's model of the family was like the psychoanalytic model of an individual writ large; instead of conscious and unconscious issues, Ackerman talked about how families confront some issues while they avoid and deny others, particularly conflictual ones involving sex and aggression. He described his role as therapist as one of stirring things up and bringing the family's secrets into the open.

Ackerman recommended that everyone living under the same roof be present in all family interviews. As he put it, "It is very important at the outset to establish a meaningful emotional contact with all members of the family, to create a climate in which one really touches them and they feel they touch back" (Ackerman, 1961, p. 242). Once contact was made, Ackerman encouraged an open and honest expression of feeling. As a therapist he was an *agent provocateur*, stirring up revelations and confrontations with his legendary wit, ebullience, and willingness to stick his nose into personal family issues.

Ackerman pointed out that identity has various aspects: one has identity as an individual, a member of various family subsystems, and as a member of the family as a whole. In order to pinpoint these various components of identity, he was alert to the coalitions revealed in family interviews. One clue to such coalitions is found in the seating arrangement; that is, as family members enter the room they tend to pair off in ways that reveal alignments. But to see these various alignments and conflicts clearly, Ackerman recommended mobilizing spontaneous interaction among family members. Once family members are interacting among themselves and with the therapist, it's possible to see how the family is emotionally divided, as well as what problems and prohibitions are present. He also paid close attention to nonverbal cues, because he believed that disguised feelings were conveyed in body language far more eloquently than in words.

In order to promote more honest emotional interchange, Ackerman "tickled the defenses" of family members—his phrase for teasing, provoking, and stimulating people to open up and say what's really on their minds. The phrase nicely reflects Ackerman's charismatic and provocative style.

What are thought to be family secrets, Ackerman said, generally turn out to be known by all family members but simply not spoken of. Children know a good deal more than parents think. They also know what they're not supposed to talk about. However as long as the therapist is in control, the family is reassured and, therefore, feel free to speak more plainly about matters that they usually avoid.

Ackerman himself was spontaneous, lively, and outspoken, which put him in the center of things. He didn't hesitate to confront, provoke, challenge, or even argue with family members. According to him, it's more therapeutic for the therapist to become a target for anger and hostility than other family members.

In order to encourage families to give up their emotional restraint, Ackerman himself was unrestrained. He willingly sided first with one part of the family and later with another. He didn't think it was necessary—or possible—to be neutral and objective; instead, he believed that an impartial balance was achieved in the long run by moving about and giving support now to one, and now to another family member. He was also unabashedly blunt with family members. If he thought someone was lying, he said so. To critics who suggested this bluntness might produce too much anxiety in patients, Ackerman replied that people derive more reassurance from honesty than from bland support.

Ackerman also made use of psychoanalytic processes like transference, resistance, and interpretation. He used the feelings aroused in countertransference because he thought therapy was lifeless unless the therapist was fully and feelingly engaged.

Ackerman explained many family events as the product of conflict. He said that conflicts within individuals, among family members, and between families and the larger community must be identified and resolved if psychological hurts are to be mended. Conflicts between family members and within the mind of an individual family member are related in a circular feedback system—that is, interpersonal conflict affects intrapsychic conflict and vice versa (Ackerman, 1961). Conflicts of identity, values, and strivings may produce rifts among family members or subsystems, mobilizing one segment against the other. Likewise, conflicts between segments of the family may produce subsequent disturbance within family members. Ackerman considered symptoms to be products of the internalization of persistent pathological family conflict. To reverse symptomatic disturbances, the therapist must bring conflicts into the open, into the field of family interaction, where new solutions can be found. As long as conflicts remain locked within individuals, Ackerman believed, psychopathology remains fixed.

Ackerman's treatment procedure was problem-oriented rather than technique-oriented (Ackerman, 1970a). Rather than approach families with a preordained plan, he preferred to use procedures determined by the needs of the family group and its individual members. He was not wedded to seeing any particular family unit; he might begin by seeing the nuclear family, but then subsequently meet with parents and grandparents, parents alone, or parents with their children. This creative flexibility makes it very difficult to describe or to teach Ackerman's approach. He was a clinical artist, not a systematizer.

While it may be impossible to neatly characterize Ackerman's method, there were clear themes. One was the necessity for depth of commitment and involvement with families. He himself became quickly and deeply emotionally involved with the families he treated, in contrast, say, to Murray Bowen, who consistently cautioned therapists to remain somewhat distant in order to avoid being triangulated. Depth also characterized the type of material on which Ackerman focused—family analogues of the kinds of conflicts, feelings, and fantasies that lie buried in the individual unconscious. He believed that there are similar currents of highly significant conflict, feeling, and fantasy excluded from the family's awareness—a kind of interpersonal unconscious of the family group. Ackerman's psychoanalytic orientation sensitized him to these hidden themes, and his provocative style enabled him to help families vividly enact them.

In one very interesting paper, "The Art of Family Therapy" (Ackerman, 1970), he reflected on the fact that in previous descriptions of his approach he had never really said much about his personal style. He had never mentioned his use of first names, his humor, and how he tried to make family encounters interesting and pleasant for himself and for the family, apparently because his long training as a psychoanalyst had inculcated certain taboos against informality and intimacy with patients. He concluded that if teachable principles did underlie his work, they were probably inextricably bound up with his personal performance as a therapist. Thus Ackerman came to see family therapy as a unique and spontaneous expression of the therapist's personality.

Ackerman's contributions to the field of family psychotherapy were extensive and important: He was one of the first to envision whole family treatment, and he had the personal inventiveness and energy to initiate it. As far back as the late 1940s, he was pointing out that treating family members in individual therapy without considering the configuration of the family was often futile. Very early, Ackerman (1954) recommended that family groups be evaluated as wholes, and that these evaluations be followed by therapy of the family group and individual therapy for selected family members.

Ackerman's second major impact was as a brilliant artist of family therapy technique. He was one of the great geniuses of the movement. Those who studied with him and observed his treatment of families all attest to his clinical wizardry. He was a dynamic catalyst, active, open, and forthright, never rigid or shy. He interacted with families in a highly emotional and effective manner. Nor was he content to remain always in the office, for he recommended and made frequent home visits (Ackerman, 1966).

Despite his brilliance as a therapist, however, Ackerman's theoretical papers don't go much beyond pointing out that individuals are inextricably embedded in families. Moreover, his clinical writings offer little in the way of systematic strategy for working with families. He is often colorful, but rarely concrete or explicit. Some of his recommendations are vague; for instance, that the therapist must evaluate the outer and inner reality of the family and then stir family members to open up (Ackerman, 1966).

Finally there are Ackerman's contributions as a teacher, which may be his most important legacy. On the East Coast his name was synonymous with family therapy throughout the late 1950s and 1960s. Among those fortunate enough to study with him was Salvador Minuchin, who openly acknowledges his debt to Ackerman's genius.

Ackerman consistently urged therapists to become emotionally engaged with families and to use confrontation to transform dormant conflicts into open discussions. How does a therapist provoke candid disclosures? Ackerman did it by calling attention to avoidance and emotional dishonesty ("tickling the defenses"), challenging clichés, and interrupting fruitless bickering over unimportant matters. Ackerman's techniques suggest that he was somewhat more concerned with the content of family conflicts than with the process by which family members dealt with them, and more interested in secrets conflicts (particularly those involving sex and aggression) than in emotional distance and proximity among family members or their patterns of communication. Perhaps his major enduring contribution was his consistent stress on individual persons and whole families; he never lost sight of the fact that people are both individuals and members of a family.

Carl Whitaker

Even among the strong-willed and colorful founders of family therapy, Carl Whitaker stands out as the most irreverent. His approach to psychotherapy has always been radical and provocative, and he brought this same style to his innovative work with families. Whitaker's view of psychologically troubled people is that they are alienated from their emotions and frozen into devitalized routine (Whitaker & Malone, 1953). Whitaker turns up the emotional temperature. His "Psychotherapy of the Absurd" (Whitaker, 1975) is a blend of warm support and unpredictable emotional goading, designed to loosen people up and help them get in touch with their immediate experience.

Given his bold and inventive approach to treatment, it is not surprising that Whitaker was one of the first to break with psychiatric tradition in order to experiment with family treatment. In 1943 he and John Warkentin, working as cotherapists in Oakridge, Tennessee, began including spouses and, eventually, children in their patients' treatment. Whitaker also pioneered the use of cotherapy for treatment, and he continues to feel that a supportive cotherapist is essential to enable family therapists to react spontaneously without fear of unchecked countertransference.

In 1946 Whitaker accepted the chair of psychiatry at Emory University in Atlanta, where he was joined by Warkentin and Thomas Malone. Together they continued to experiment with family treatment and shifted their interest to working with schizophrenics and their families. During this period Whitaker initiated a series of conferences that eventually led to the first major meeting of the family therapist movement. Beginning in 1946 Whitaker, Warkentin, and Malone began twice-yearly conferences during which they observed and discussed each other's work with families. The group found these sessions to be enormously helpful, and mutual observation, using one-way vision screens, has since then been one of the hallmarks of family therapy.

In 1953 Whitaker invited John Rosen, Albert Scheflen, Gregory Bateson, and Don Jackson to participate in the semiannual conference on families, which was held that year in Sea Island, Georgia. Each took turns demonstrating his own approach with the same family, while the others observed and, afterwards, joined in for a group discussion and analysis. The cross-fertilization of ideas that occurred has continued to characterize the family therapy movement; family clinicians openly display their work, both for teaching and for mutual enrichment.

Whitaker resigned from Emory's Department of Psychiatry in 1955 and entered private practice with Warkentin, Malone, and Richard Felder. He and his partners at the Atlanta Psychiatric Clinic developed an "experiential" form of psychotherapy, utilizing a number of highly provocative techniques, as well as the force of their own personalities, in the treatment of families, individuals, groups, and couples (Whitaker, 1958).

In 1965 Whitaker left Atlanta to become a professor of psychiatry at the University of Wisconsin, and became professor emeritus in 1982. Since he has been in Madison he has worked exclusively with families and is now one of the elder statesmen of the family therapy movement. He travels widely, giving workshops and presentations at conventions, and he has been on the editorial board of *Family Process* since its inception.

When the family therapy movement first began, Whitaker was less well known to students than were many of the other first generation family therapists. Perhaps this was due to his atheoretical position. Whereas Jackson, Haley, and Bowen developed concepts that were intriguing and easy to grasp, Whitaker always eschewed theory in favor of creative spontaneity. His work has, therefore, been less accessible to students than that of his colleagues. Nevertheless he has always had the respect of his peers, and people who have had the chance to observe his work can see that there is method to his madness.

To begin with, Whitaker deliberately creates tension by teasing and confronting families, in the belief that stress is necessary for change. In the process he does not have an obvious strategy, nor does he use structured techniques, preferring, as he says, to let his unconscious run the therapy (Whitaker, 1976). Although his work seems totally spontaneous, even outrageous at times, there is a consistent theme. All of his interventions have the effect of promoting flexibility and change. He views the core problem in families as emotional sterility, and his treatment is to open individuals up to their own feelings and help them share these feelings within the family.

Ivan Boszormenyi-Nagy

Ivan Boszormenyi-Nagy came to family therapy from psychoanalysis, and he has been one of the seminal thinkers in the family therapy movement since its earliest days. In 1957 he founded the Eastern Pennsylvania Psychiatric Institute (EPPI), in Philadelphia, as a center for research and training in families and schizophrenia. Because he was a respected scholar-clinician and an able administrator, Nagy was able to attract a number of highly talented colleagues and students. Among these were James Framo, one of the few psychologists in the early family therapy movement; David Rubenstein, a psychiatrist who later conducted a separate family therapy training program; and Geraldine Spark, a social worker who worked with Nagy as a cotherapist, codirector of the unit, and coauthor of *Invisible Loyalties* (Boszormenyi-Nagy & Spark, 1973). This group was joined by Gerald Zuk, a psychologist who became interested in families while working with mentally retarded persons. Zuk later developed a "triadic-based" approach to family therapy (1971) in which he conceptualized the therapist as a member of the system in treatment. In triadic-based family therapy, the therapist begins as a mediator but then takes sides in order to shift power alignments in the family. According to Zuk (1971, p. 73), "By judicious siding, the therapist can tip the balance in favor of more productive relating, or at least disrupt a chronic pattern of pathogenic relating."

In 1960 Albert Scheflen moved from Temple University to EPPI and joined with Ray Birdwhistell to study body language in the process of psychotherapy. Ross Speck, who did his psychiatric residency in the early 1960s, developed, along with Carolyn Attneave, "network therapy," which broadened the context of treatment far beyond the nuclear family. In this approach as many people as possible who are connected to the patient are invited to attend therapy sessions. Frequently as many as fifty people, including the extended family, friends, neighbors, and teachers, are brought together for approximately three 4-hour sessions and helped by a minimum of three therapists to discuss ways to support and help the patient change (Speck & Attneave, 1973).

Aside from his sponsorship of these students and colleagues, Nagy himself has made major contributions to the study of schizophrenia (Boszormenyi-Nagy, 1962) and family therapy (Boszormenyi-Nagy, 1966, 1972; Boszormenyi-Nagy & Spark, 1973). Nagy described himself as a therapist who went from being an analyst, prizing secrecy and confidentiality, to a family therapist, fighting the forces of pathology on an open battlefield. One of his most important contributions was to introduce the criterion of morality to therapeutic goals and techniques. According to Nagy, neither the pleasure-pain principle nor transactional expediency are sufficient guides to human behavior. Instead, he believes that family members have to base their relationships on trust and loyalty, and that they must balance the ledger of entitlement and indebtedness.

In 1980, after thousands of professionals had been trained at the Eastern Pennsylvania Psychiatric Institute, the Commonwealth of Pennsylvania abruptly closed it down. Nagy and some of his colleagues continue to be associated with nearby Hahnemann University Medical School, but the critical mass was lost. Since then Nagy has continued to refine his own approach, contextual therapy, which many believe is among the most thoughtful and underappreciated approaches to family therapy.

Salvador Minuchin

Although he was not one of the very first family therapists, Minuchin was an early entry into the field, and his accomplishments rank him as one of the most influential of all family therapists. Salvador Minuchin is a psychiatrist, trained in his native Argentina, who developed a family approach to treating delinquents at the Wiltwyck School for Boys in New York. The use of family therapy with urban slum families was a new development, and publication of his ideas (Minuchin, Montalvo, Guerney, Rosman, & Schumer, 1967) led to his being invited to become the director of the Philadelphia Child Guidance Clinic in 1965. Minuchin brought Braulio Montalvo and Bernice Rosman with him, and they were joined in 1967 by Jay Haley; together they set about transforming a traditional child guidance clinic into one of the great centers of the family therapy movement.

Minuchin's first notable achievement at the Philadelphia Child Guidance Clinic was a unique program for training indigenous members of the local black community as paraprofessional family therapists. The reason for this special effort is that cultural differences often make it very difficult for white middle-class therapists to understand and relate successfully to urban blacks and Latinos.

In 1969 Minuchin received a grant to support his training program. This helped launch an intensive two-year program in which Minuchin, Haley, Montalvo, and Rosman developed a highly successful approach to training as well as one of the most important systems of family therapy. According to Haley, one of the advantages to training people with no previous experience as clinicians to become family therapists is that they have less to unlearn, and are, therefore, less resistant to thinking in terms of systems. Minuchin and Haley sought to capitalize on this by developing an approach with the least possible number of theoretical concepts. Conceptual elegance became one of the hallmarks of "structural family therapy."

The major features of the training were hands-on experience, on-line supervision, and extensive use of videotapes. Minuchin himself is a practical, technique-oriented clinician, and he believes that therapists are best taught by experience. Once they have seen a few families, therapists, he believes, are ready to appreciate and utilize systems theory. Traditional psychotherapy supervision is done after the session and takes the form of telling students what they should have done. In contrast Minuchin and Haley supervised by actually observing sessions and interrupting to provide redirection when necessary. Instead of learning afterward what they did wrong, therapists learned, on the spot, how to do it right. Later the group studied videotapes for a more in-depth analysis of what works and what doesn't.

The structural family therapy that Minuchin and his colleagues developed (Minuchin, 1974) begins with the observation that family transactions, when they are repeated, develop a patterned regularity, or *structure*. For example, when new parents bring home their first baby from the hospital, they must work out a system for parenting. Since they have no previous experience, their initial interactions are unprogrammed and somewhat unpredictable. When the baby cries in the middle of the night, will the mother get up and nurse him in his room, or will the father get up and bring him to her; who will change the baby's diapers when both parents are present; and how early and often will the new parents leave the baby with a babysitter in order to resume their relationship as husband and wife? These questions are soon answered, and the results shape the family's structure.

The nature of the family's structure is determined by emotional *boundaries* which keep family members close or distant. Either pattern, closeness leading to *enmeshment,* or distance leading to *disengagement,* may be more or less functional for any particular family. This is a point frequently missed by beginning family therapists, who often assume that any family pattern that differs from their own should be changed. Problems begin, according to Minuchin, when a family fails to modify its structure to fit changing circumstances. When this happens, the family needs help.

The techniques of structural family therapy fall into two general strategies. First the therapist must accommodate to the family in order to join them. To begin by confronting and challenging the family's preferred mode of relating is to ensure that they will resist. If, instead, the therapist begins by trying to understand and accept the family, they will be more likely to accept treatment. Once this initial *joining* is accomplished, the structural family therapist begins to use *restructuring* techniques. These are active and directive maneuvers designed to disrupt dysfunctional structures by strengthening diffuse boundaries and softening rigid ones (Minuchin & Fishman, 1981).

In the 1970s, under Minuchin's leadership, the Philadelphia Child Guidance Clinic became the world's leading center for family therapy and training. The clinic itself is a large and marvelously equipped building with excellent facilities for videotaping, live supervision, workshops, and conferences; and it even has small apartments for hospitalizing whole families. When Minuchin stepped down as director in 1975, he was succeeded first by Harry Aponte, then by Ron Liebman. Today, Alberto Serrano is the medical director, Bernice Rosman is director of education, and Marion Linblad-Goldberg directs the family therapy training center. Resigning the directorship left Minuchin free to pursue his special interest in treating psychosomatic families, especially those with anorexia nervosa (Minuchin, Rosman, & Baker, 1978).

Since 1981 Minuchin has moved to New York where he runs the Family Studies Institute and pursues his dedication to teaching family therapists from all over the world and his burning commitment to social justice by working with the foster care system, as well as continuing to turn out a steady stream of the most influential books in the field. His 1974 *Families and Family Therapy* is deservedly the most popular book ever written in family therapy, and his 1993 *Family Healing* has the most thorough and moving descriptions of actual therapy sessions ever written by a family therapist.

Other Early Centers of Family Therapy

In New York, Israel Zwerling, who had been analyzed by Nathan Ackerman, and Marilyn Mendelsohn, who was analyzed by Don Jackson, organized the Family Studies Section at Albert Einstein College of Medicine and Bronx State Hospital. Andrew Ferber was named Director in 1964, and later Philip Guerin, a protégé of Murray Bowen's, joined the section. Nathan Ackerman served as a consultant to the group, and they assembled an impressive array of family therapists with diverse orientations. These included Chris Beels, Betty Carter, Monica Orfanidis (now McGoldrick), Peggy Papp, and Thomas Fogarty (Guerin, 1976).

Philip Guerin became Director of Training of the Family Studies Section in 1970 and in 1972 established an extramural training program in Westchester. Shortly afterward, in 1973, he founded the Center for Family Learning in New Rochelle, New York. Here Guerin developed one of the strongest family therapy training programs in the nation.

In Galveston, Texas, Robert MacGregor and his colleagues developed "multiple impact therapy" (MacGregor, 1967). It was a case of necessity being the mother of invention. The clinic where MacGregor was located served a large population scattered widely over southeastern Texas, and many of his clients had to come from hundreds of miles away. Because they had to travel such distances, most of these people were unable to return for weekly therapy sessions. Therefore, in order to make the maximum possible impact in a short time, MacGregor assembled a large team of professionals who worked intensively with the families for two full days. The treatment team consisted of psychologists, social workers, psychiatric residents, and trainees. They met with the family together and in various subgroups in a series of sessions; between sessions the treatment team discussed their findings and refined their strategies of intervention. Although few family therapists have used such marathon sessions, the team approach to treating families has continued to be one of the hallmarks of the field.

In conservative and proper Boston the two most significant early contributions to family therapy were both in the existential-experimental wing of the movement. Norman Paul developed an "operational mourning" approach to family therapy, designed to uncover and express unresolved grief. According to him, this cathartic approach is useful in almost all families, not only those who have suffered an obvious recent loss.

Also in Boston, Fred and Bunny Duhl set up the Boston Family Institute, where they developed "integrative family therapy." The Duhls, along with David Kantor and Sandy Watanabe, combined ideas from several family theories and added a number of expressive techniques, including *family sculpting*.

In Chicago, the Family Institute of Chicago and the Institute for Juvenile Research were important parts of the early scene in family therapy (Guerin, 1976). At the Family Institute, Charles and Jan Kramer developed a clinical training program, which was later affiliated with the Northwestern University Medical School. The Institute for Juvenile Research also mounted a training program under the leadership of Irv Borstein, with the consultation of Carl Whitaker.

The work of Nathan Epstein and his colleagues, first formulated in the department of psychiatry at McMaster University in Hamilton, Ontario, is a problem-centered approach (Epstein et al., 1981). The "McMaster Model of Family Functioning" goes step by step from elucidating the problem to gathering data, through considering alternatives for resolution, to assessing the procedures involved in learning to cope more effectively, in order to help families understand their own interaction and build mechanisms for evaluating their own functioning and newly acquired coping skills. Epstein later relocated to Brown University in Providence, Rhode Island.

Some of the important developments in family therapy outside the United States included: Robin Skynner's (1976) use of psychodynamic family therapy at the Institute of Family Therapy in London; British psychiatrist John Howells's (1975) system of family diagnosis as a necessary step for planning therapeutic intervention; West German Helm Stierlin's (1972) integrative efforts bringing together psychodynamic and systemic ideas to bear on understanding and treating troubled adolescents; in Rome, Maurizio Andolfi started working with families early in the 1970s, and in 1974 founded the Italian Society for Family Therapy; and Mara Selvini Palazolli and her colleagues who founded the Institute for Family Studies in Milan in 1967.

We conclude this section by mentioning the contributions of Christian Midelfort. Even more than was the case with John Bell, Midelfort's pioneering work in family therapy was slow to gain recognition. He began treating families of hospitalized patients in the early 1950s; delivered what was probably the first paper on family therapy at a professional meeting in 1952, at the American Psychiatric Association Convention; and published one of the first complete books on family therapy in 1957. Nevertheless he remained isolated from the rest of the family therapy movement while he continued to practice as a staff psychiatrist at a clinic in LaCrosse, Wisconsin. Only recently are his pioneering efforts being recognized (Broderick & Schrader, 1991). Midelfort's method of treating families was based on the group therapy model and its combined psychoanalytic insights with techniques of support and encouragement. At first his concern was to counsel family members on the best ways to help the identified patient, but gradually he evolved a systems viewpoint and conceived of the family as the patient. His technique, which is described in Chapter 4, was to encourage family members to give each other the love and support that was initially provided by the therapist.

THE CURRENT SCENE

Family therapy was born in the 1950s, grew up in the 1960s, and came of age in the 1970s. The initial wave of enthusiasm for seeing the whole family as a unit was followed by an increasing split between schools, each vying for a corner of the truth, and of the market for services.

The most widely read and talked about approach in the 1960s was the Palo Alto group's communications therapy. Gregory Bateson, Don Jackson, and Jay Haley were the dominating figures, and *Pragmatics of Human Communication* was the most popular book. The 1970s belonged to structural family therapy. Salvador Minuchin was the most admired and influential family therapist of the time, and his *Families and Family Therapy* was the book of the decade. In the 1980s, strategic and systemic family therapies dominated the scene, including the approaches of Jay Haley and Cloe Madanes; the brief therapy group at MRI, including Paul Watzlawick, John Weakland, and Richard Fisch; and the Milan associates, Mara Selvini Palazzoli, Gianfranco Cecchin, Luigi Boscolo, and Guiliana Prata. The book that excited the most interest was *Paradox and Counterparadox,* and its authors, the Milan associates, were the intellectual darlings of the period. But it was probably Milton Erickson who exercised the most influence in the decade of strategic therapy, albeit from beyond the grave.

Some day we may look back on the years from 1975 to 1985 as family therapy's golden age. That was the time of the full flowering of the most imaginative and vital approaches to treatment, and it was, too, a time of enthusiasm and confidence. Family therapists might have had their differences about technique, but they shared a sense of optimism and common purpose. Since then, in the late 1980s and into the 1990s, several developments have shaken the field out of its zealousness and overconfidence. The pioneering models were challenged (on both clinical and sociocultural grounds) and their boundaries blurred to the point where today far fewer family therapists identify themselves exclusively with any one particular school. Even the distinction between individual and family therapists is less clear-cut, as more and more therapists are practicing both forms of treatment.

While it's comforting to see change—especially if one is a part of it—as progress, it may not be that all the changes we've seen in family therapy are progressive.

Thus far, the dominating trends of the 1990s are social constructionism (the idea that our experience is a function of the way we think about it), integrative approaches, and a growing concern with social and political issues. We will explore these and other developments in the chapters that follow, but here we simply want to suggest that as you read about these developments you consider the possibility that, like all new developments, these have pluses and minuses.

If the animating idea of family therapy is that human behavior is interactive and that problems can best be addressed by helping people change the way they interact, to what extent are the innovations of the 1990s useful corrections and extensions of family therapy's original focus, and to what extent do some of the new developments take us beyond our expertise or back toward linear thinking?

To what extent does the constructivist notion that we invent rather than discover reality correct a myopic and authoritarian bias of family therapists, and to what extent does it take us back from action to insight? When an integrative approach to therapy means that well-schooled and experienced therapists with coherent strategies of treatment borrow some useful ideas from people of other approaches, then it is enriching. But when is more less? When therapists are so skeptical of dogmatism that they mix too many elements from various approaches, they end up with a hodgepodge that robs the muscle of a consistent way of approaching problems.

Family therapy's contemporary emphasis on social issues, especially sexism, family violence, and multiculturalism, is consistent with its history of concern for social justice and human rights. But it would be unfortunate if in the process of getting away from parochial factionalism between different schools of treatment, family therapy accepted or encouraged a new factionalism—between men and women, between gays and straights, or between ethnic and cultural groups.

SUMMARY

As we have seen, family therapy has a short history but a long past. For many years therapists resisted the idea of seeing members of a patient's family, in order to safeguard the privacy of the patient-therapist relationship. (That this arrangement also preserved the shame associated with psychological disorder as well as the myth of the individual as hero was not noticed, or at least not mentioned.) Freudians excluded the real family in order to uncover the unconscious, introjected family; Rogerians kept the family away in order to provide unconditional positive regard; and hospital psychiatrists discouraged family visits which might disrupt the benign milieu of the ersatz hospital family.

Several converging developments in the 1950s led to a new view, namely that the family is a living system, an organic whole. Hospital psychiatrists noticed that often when a patient improved someone else in the family got worse. Moreover, despite good reasons for keeping family members isolated from an individual's therapy, there were also distinct disadvantages to this approach. To begin with, individual treatment is predicated on relative stability in the patient's environment—otherwise, trying to change the individual but then returning him or her to a destructive environment wouldn't make sense. When families were undergoing crisis and conflict, the patient's improvement sometimes made the family worse. Thus it became clear that change in any one person changes the whole family system. Eventually it also became apparent that changing the family might be the most effective way to change the individual.

Although practicing clinicians in hospitals and child guidance clinics prepared the way for family therapy, the most important breakthroughs were achieved in the 1950s by workers who were scientists first, healers second.

In Palo Alto, Gregory Bateson, Jay Haley, Don Jackson, and John Weakland, studying communication, discovered that schizophrenia made sense in the context of pathological family communication. Schizophrenics weren't crazy in some meaningless way; their apparently bizarre behavior could be understood as an extension of their crazy families. At Yale, Theodore Lidz found a striking pattern of instability and conflict in the families of schizophrenics. *Marital schism* (open conflict) and *marital skew* (pathological balance) had profound effects on the pathological development of children. Murray Bowen's observation of how mothers and their schizophrenic offspring go through cycles of closeness and distance was the forerunner of the *pursuer-distancer* dynamic. Behind these cycles, Bowen believed were cycles of anxiety: separation anxiety and incorporation anxiety. By hospitalizing whole families for observation and treatment, Bowen implicitly located the problem of schizophrenia in an *undifferentiated family ego mass* and even extended it beyond the nuclear family to three generations. Lyman Wynne, at NIMH and later Rochester, linked schizophrenia to the family by demonstrating how communication deviance contributes to thought disorder. *Pseudomutuality* described the maddening unreality of some families, and the *rubber fence* described the psychological membrane that surrounds them, like a thick skin surrounding a living organism.

These observations launched the family therapy movement, but the excitement they generated blurred the distinction between what the researchers observed and what they concluded. What they observed was that the behavior of schizophrenics *fit* with their families; what they concluded was far more momentous. First it was implied that since schizophrenia fit (made sense) in the context of the family, then the family must be *the cause* of schizophrenia. A second conclusion was even more influential. Family dynamics—double binds, pseudomutuality, undifferentiated family ego mass—began to be seen as products of a "system," rather than features of persons who share certain qualities because they live together. Thus was born a new creature, "the family system."

Once the family became the patient, there was a need for new ways to think about and treat human problems. The systems metaphor was the pivotal concept in this endeavor. And, though neither could be considered the founder of family therapy, no one had greater influence on how we think about families than Gregory Bateson and Milton Erickson—the anthropologist and the alienist.

Erickson's legacy to family therapy was the pragmatic, problem-solving approach. He helped us learn to figure out what keeps families stuck, how to get them unstuck—using creative, sometimes counterintuitive ideas—and then get out, letting families get on about their business, rather than incorporating a therapist into the family as an expensive crutch. But Erickson's mesmerizing artistry also promoted a tradition of the quick fix, done *to* rather than done *with* families.

Inspired by Bateson's scientific commitment to observation and study, early family therapists spent a good deal of time watching and listening. They were willing to observe and learn because they knew they were in unknown territory. Unfortunately, many family therapists have gotten away from this receptive openness. So much has been written about family dynamics and technique that therapists too often approach families with a set of precooked techniques and generic preconceptions that they impose on the family's reality.

Bateson is also the patron saint of the intellectual wing of family therapy. His ideas were so profound that they are still being mined by the most sophisticated thinkers in the field. On the other hand, Bateson also set an example of overly abstract theorizing and importing ideas from other—"more scientific"—disciplines. In the early days of family therapy, perhaps we needed models from fields like cybernetics to help us get started. But when so many family therapists continue to lean so heavily on the intellectual underpinnings of physics and biology, one wonders, why this physics envy? Perhaps, after all this time, we're still insecure about the legitimacy of psychology and about our ability to observe human behavior in human terms without losing our objectivity.

Another reason family therapists gravitated to abstract theories from mechanics and the natural sciences is that they totally rejected the major body of literature about human psychology: psychoanalysis. The psychoanalytic establishment was none too enthusiastic about this new challenge to their way of thinking, and in many quarters family therapists had to fight to win a place for their beliefs. Perhaps it was this resistance that pushed family therapists into a reactive position. The extreme hostility between family therapists and psychodynamic therapists cooled off in the 1970s after family therapy established itself as part of the mental health establishment. One reason family therapy gained acceptance was that it carved out its domain in areas traditionally neglected by the psychiatric power structure—services to children and the poor. An unfortunate legacy of this early antagonism, however, was a prolonged period of ignorance and neglect. Now, in the 1990s, the pendulum is beginning to shift. Family therapists are beginning to discover that at the same time we are trying to understand hidden forces in the family, it may also be useful to pay attention to the hidden forces in the individuals who make up the family (see Chapters 6 and 11). Perhaps the fullest appreciation of human nature lies in the fullest understanding of self *and* system.

Obvious parallels between small groups and families led some family therapists to treat families as though they were just another form of group.

They were well served in this endeavor by a large volume of literature on group dynamics and group therapy. Some even saw therapy groups as models of family functioning, with the therapist as father, group members as siblings, and the group collectively as mother (Schindler, 1951). While group therapists experimented with married couples in groups, some family therapists began to conduct group therapy with individual families. Among these John Bell was the most significant and his family group therapy was one of the most widely imitated of the early models (see Chapter 4).

As therapists gained more experience with families, they discovered that the group therapy model was not entirely appropriate for families. Therapy groups are made up of separate individuals, strangers with no past or future outside the group. Families, on the other hand, consist of intimates who share the same myths, defenses, and points of view. Moreover, family members are not peers who can relate democratically as equals; generational differences create hierarchical structures that cannot be ignored. For these reasons family therapists eventually abandoned the group therapy model, replacing it with a variety of systems models.

The child guidance movement contributed the team approach to family therapy. At first members of interdisciplinary teams were assigned to different family members but, gradually, as they came to appreciate the interlocking behavior patterns of their separate clients, they started integrating and later combining their efforts. The child guidance movement began in this country in 1909 as a creation of the juvenile courts in order to treat delinquent children who were considered disturbed. Soon these clinics broadened their scope to include a wide range of disorders, and at the same time they broadened the unit of treatment from the child to include the family. At first family therapy was seen as a better means of helping the patient; later it was conceived as a way to serve the needs of the entire family.

Who was the first to practice family therapy? This turns out to be a difficult and controversial question. As in every field there were some visionaries who anticipated the recognized development of family therapy. Freud, for example, occasionally saw "Little Hans" together with his father in 1909. However, such experiments were not sufficient to challenge the hegemony of individual therapy until the climate of the times was receptive. In the early 1950s family therapy was begun independently in four different places: John Bell began family group therapy at Clark University (Chapter 4), Murray Bowen started treating families of schizophrenics at the Menninger Clinic and later at NIMH (Chapter 9), Nathan Ackerman began his psychoanalytic family therapy in New York (Chapter 6), and Don Jackson and Jay Haley started communications family therapy in Palo Alto (Chapters 4 and 10).

All of these pioneers had distinctly different backgrounds and clinical orientations. Not surprisingly, therefore, the approaches they developed to family therapy were also quite different. This diversity still characterizes the field today. Had family therapy been started by a single person, as was psychoanalysis, it is unlikely that there would have been so much creative competition so soon.

In addition to those people just mentioned, others who made significant contributions to the beginning of family therapy include Wynne, Lidz, Satir,

Whitaker, Nagy, Midelfort, MacGregor, and Minuchin. Even this list leaves out a number of important figures for what began after a long period of incubation quickly grew and spread. By the 1960s there were literally hundreds of family therapists. Today the field is so large and complex that it will take an entire chapter (Chapter 3) just to provide a descriptive overview.

All the complexity of the family field should not, however, obscure its basic premise: The family is the context of human problems; and, like all human groups, the family has emergent properties—the whole is greater than the sum of its parts. Moreover, no matter how many and varied the explanations of these emergent properties, they all fall into two categories: structure and process. The structure of families includes triangles, subsystems, and boundaries. Among the processes that describe family interaction—emotional reactivity, dysfunctional communication, and so on—the central concept is *circularity*. Rather than worrying about who started what, family therapists understand and treat human problems as a series of moves and countermoves, in repeating cycles.

REFERENCES

Ables, G. 1975. The double-bind: Paradox in relationships. Ph.D. diss., Boston University.

Ables, G. 1976. Researching the unresearchable: Experimentation on the double-bind. In *Double-bind: The foundation of the communication approach to the family*, C. E. Sluzki and D. C. Ransom, eds. New York: Grune & Stratton.

Ackerman, N. W. 1938. The unity of the family. *Archives of Pediatrics*. 55:51–62.

Ackerman, N. W. 1954. Interpersonal disturbances in the family: Some unsolved problems in psychotherapy. *Psychiatry*. 17:359–368.

Ackerman, N. W. 1961. A dynamic frame for the clinical approach to family conflict. In *Exploring the base for family therapy*, N. W. Ackerman, F. L. Beatman and S. N. Sherman, eds. New York: Family Services Association of America.

Ackerman, N. W. 1966. Family psychotherapy—theory and practice. *American Journal of Psychotherapy*. 20:405–414.

Ackerman, N. W. 1970. The art of family therapy. In *Family therapy in transition*, N. W. Ackerman, ed. Boston: Little, Brown.

Ackerman, N. W., Beatman, F., and Sherman, S. N., eds. 1961. *Exploring the base for family therapy*. New York: Family Service Assn. of America.

Ackerman, N. W., and Sobel, R. 1950. Family diagnosis: An approach to the preschool child. *American Journal of Orthopsychiatry*. 20:744–753.

Amster, F. 1944. Collective psychotherapy of mothers of emotionally disturbed children. *American Journal of Orthopsychiatry*. 14:44–52.

Anderson, C. M., Reiss, D. J., and Hogarty, G. E. 1986. *Schizophrenia and the family*. New York: Guilford Press.

Andres, F. D. 1971. An introduction to family systems theory. Paper presented at Georgetown Family Symposium, Washington, DC.

Anonymous. 1972. Differentiation of self in one's family. In *Family interaction*, J. L. Framo, ed. New York: Springer.

Bales, R. F. 1950. *Interaction process analysis*. Cambridge, MA: Addison-Wesley.

Bardhill, D. R., and Saunders, B. E. 1988. In *Handbook of family therapy training and supervision*, H. A. Liddle, D. C. Breunlin, and R. C. Schwartz, eds. New York: Guilford Press.

Bateson, G. 1951. Information and codification: A philosophical approach. In *Communication: The social matrix of psychiatry*, J. Ruesch and G. Bateson, eds. New York: Norton.

Bateson, G. 1959. Cultural problems posed by a study of schizophrenic processes. In *Schizophrenia: An integrated approach*, A. Auerbach, ed. New York: Ronald Press.

Bateson, G. 1978. The birth of a matrix or double-bind and epistemology. In *Beyond the double-bind*, M. M. Berger, ed. New York: Brunner/Mazel.

Bateson, G., Jackson, D. D., Haley, J., and Weakland, J. 1956. Toward a theory of schizophrenia. *Behavioral Science. 1*:251–264.

Bateson, G., Jackson, D. D., and Weakland, J. H. 1963. A note on the double bind— 1962. *Family Process. 2*:154–161.

Beatman, F. L. 1956. In *Neurotic interaction in marriage*, V. W. Eisenstein, ed. New York: Basic Books.

Beavers, W. R., Blumberg, S., Timken, K. R., and Weiner, M. F. 1965. Communication patterns of mothers of schizophrenics. *Family Process. 4*:95–104.

Bell, J. E. 1961. *Family group therapy*. Public Health Monograph #64. Washington, DC: U.S. Government Printing Office.

Bell, J. E. 1962. Recent advances in family group therapy. *Journal of Child Psychology and Psychiatry. 3*:1–15.

Benne, K. D. 1964. History of the T-group in the laboratory setting. In *T-group theory and laboratory method*, L. P. Bradford, J. R. Gibb, and K. D. Benne, eds. New York: Wiley.

Bennis, W. G. 1964. Patterns and vicissitudes in T-group development. In *T-group theory and laboratory method*, L. P. Bradford, J. R. Gibb, and K. D. Benne, eds. New York: Wiley.

Berger, A. 1965. A test of the double-bind hypothesis of schizophrenia. *Family Process. 4*:198–205.

Bion, W. R. 1948. Experience in groups. *Human Relations. 1*:314–329.

Boszormenyi-Nagy, I. 1962. The concept of schizophrenia from the point of view of family treatment. *Family Process. 1*:103–113.

Boszormenyi-Nagy, I. 1966. From family therapy to a psychology of relationships; fictions of the individual and fictions of the family. *Comprehensive Psychiatry. 7*:408–423.

Boszormenyi-Nagy, I. 1972. Loyalty implications of the transference model in psychotherapy. *Archives of General Psychiatry. 27*:374–380.

Boszormenyi-Nagy, I., and Spark, G. L. 1973. *Invisible loyalties: Reciprocity in intergenerational family therapy*. New York: Harper & Row.

Bowen, M. 1960. A family concept of schizophrenia. In *The etiology of schizophrenia*, D. D. Jackson, ed. New York: Basic Books.

Bowen, M. 1961. Family psychotherapy. *American Journal of Orthopsychiatry. 31*:40–60.

Bowen, M. 1965. Family psychotherapy with schizophrenia in the hospital and in private practice. In *Intensive family therapy*, I. Boszormenyi-Nagy and J. L. Framo, eds. New York: Harper & Row.

Bowen, M. 1976. Principles and techniques of multiple family therapy. In *Family therapy: Theory and practice*, P. J. Guerin, ed. New York: Gardner Press.

Bowen, M., Dysinger, R. H., and Basamania, B. 1959. The role of the father in families with a schizophrenia patient. *American Journal of Psychiatry. 115*:1017–1020.

Bowlby, J. P. 1949. The study and reduction of group tensions in the family. *Human Relations. 2*:123–138.

Broderick, C. B., and Schrader, S. S. 1981. The history of professional marriage and family therapy. In *Handbook of family therapy*, A. S. Gurman and D. P. Kniskern, eds. New York: Brunner/Mazel.

Broderick, C. B., and Schrader, S. S. 1991. The history of professional marriage and family therapy. In *Handbook of family therapy* Vol. II, A. S. Gurman and D. P. Knishern, eds. New York: Bruner/Mazel.

Brown, G. W. 1959. Experiences of discharged chronic schizophrenia patients in various types of living groups. *Milbank Memorial Fund Quarterly.* 37:105–131.

Burgum, M. 1942. The father gets worse: A child guidance problem. *American Journal of Orthopsychiatry.* 12:474–485.

Burkin, H. E., Glatzer, H., and Hirsch, J. S. 1944. Therapy of mothers in groups. *American Journal of Orthopsychiatry.* 14:68–75.

Ciotola, P. V. 1961. The effect of two contradictory levels of reward censure on schizophrenics. Ph.D. diss., University of Missouri.

Cooley, C. H. 1902. *Human nature and the social order.* New York: Scribners.

Dicks, H. V. 1964. Concepts of marital diagnosis and therapy as developed at the Tavistock Family Psychiatric Clinic, London, England. In *Marriage counseling in medical practice,* E. M. Nash, L. Jessner, and D. W. Abse, eds. Chapel Hill, NC: University of North Carolina Press.

Elizur, J., and Minuchin, S. 1989. *Institutionalizing madness: Families, therapy, and society.* New York: Basic Books.

Epstein, N. B., Bishop, D. S., and Baldarin, L. M. 1981. McMaster Model of Family Functioning. In *Normal family problems,* F. Walsh, ed. New York: Guilford Press.

Fisher, S., and Mendell, D. 1958. The spread of psychotherapeutic effects from the patient to his family group. *Psychiatry.* 21:133–140.

Freeman, V. J., Klein, A. F., Riehman, L., Lukoff, I. F., and Heisey, V. 1963. Family group counseling as differentiated from other family therapies. *International Journal of Group Psychotherapy.* 13:167–175.

Fromm-Reichmann, F. 1948. Notes on the development of treatment of schizophrenics by psychoanalytic psychotherapy. *Psychiatry.* 11:263–274.

Fromm-Reichmann, F. 1950. *Principles of intensive psychotherapy.* Chicago: University of Chicago Press.

Ginsburg, S. W. 1955. The mental health movement and its theoretical assumptions. In *Community programs for mental health,* R. Kotinsky and H. Witmer, eds. Cambridge: Harvard University Press.

Goldstein, M. J., Roderick, E. H., Evans, J. R., May, P. R., and Steinberg, M. 1978. Drug and family therapy in the aftercare treatment of schizophrenia. *Archives of General Psychiatry.* 35:1169–1177.

Greenberg, G. S. 1977. The family interactional perspective: A study and examination of the work of Don D. Jackson. *Family Process.* 16:385–412.

Grunwald, H., and Casell, B. 1958. Group counseling with parents. *Child Welfare.* 1:1–6.

Guerin, P. J. 1976. Family therapy: The first twenty-five years. In *Family therapy: Theory and practice,* P. J. Guerin, ed. New York: Gardner Press.

Guindon, J. E. 1971. Paradox, schizophrenia and the double bind hypothesis: An exploratory study. Ph.D. diss., University of Washington.

Haley, J. 1959. The family of the schizophrenic. *American Journal of Nervous and Mental Diseases.* 129:357–374.

Haley, J. 1961. Control in brief psychotherapy. *Archives of General Psychiatry.* 4:139–153.

Haley, J. 1963. *Strategies of psychotherapy.* New York: Grune & Stratton.

Haley, J. 1973. *Uncommon therapy.* New York: Norton.

Haley, J. 1976. Development of a theory: A history of a research project. In *Double-bind: The foundation of the communication approach to the family,* C. E. Sluzki and D. C. Ransom, eds. New York: Grune & Stratton.

Haley, J., and Hoffman, L., eds. 1968. *Techniques of family therapy.* New York: Basic Books

Handlon, J. H. and Parloff, M. B. 1962. Treatment of patient and family as a group: Is it group therapy? *International Journal of Group Psychotherapy.* *12:*132–141.

Hare-Mustin, R. T., and Marecek, J. 1988. The meaning of difference: Gender theory, postmodernism, and psychology. *American Psychologist.* *43:*455–464.

Hirsch, S. R., and Leff, J. P. 1975. *Abnormalities in parents of schizophrenics: A review of the literature and an investigation of communication defects and deviances.* London: Oxford University Press.

Howells, J. G. 1971. *Theory and practice of family psychiatry.* New York: Brunner/Mazel.

Jackson, D. D. 1954. Suicide. *Scientific American.* *191:*88–96.

Jackson, D. D. 1957. The question of family homeostasis. *The Psychiatric Quarterly Supplement.* *31:*79–90.

Jackson, D. D. 1961. Family therapy in the family of the schizophrenic. In *Contemporary psychotherapies*, M. Stein, ed. Glencoe, IL: The Free Press.

Jackson, D. D. 1965. Family rules: Marital quid pro quo. *Archives of General Psychiatry.* *12:*589–594.

Jackson, D. D., and Weakland, J. H. 1959. Schizophrenic symptoms and family interaction. *Archives of General Psychiatry.* *1:*618–621.

Jackson, D. D., and Weakland, J. H. 1961. Conjoint family therapy, some considerations on theory, technique, and results. *Psychiatry.* *24:*30–45.

Johnson, A. M., and Szurek, S. A. 1954. Etiology of anti-social behavior in delinquents and psychopaths. *Journal of the American Medical Association.* *154:*814–817.

Kaplan, H. and Sadock, B. 1983. *Comprehensive group psychotherapy.* Baltimore: Williams & Wilkins.

Kasanin, J., Knight, E., and Sage, P. 1934. The parent-child relationships in schizophrenia. *Journal of Nervous and Mental Diseases.* *79:*249–263.

Kaslow, F. W. 1980. History of family therapy in the United States: A kaleidoscopic overview. *Marriage and Family Review.* *3:*77–111.

Kaufman, E., and Kaufmann, P., eds. 1979. *Family therapy of drug and alcohol abuse.* New York: Gardner Press.

Kempler, W. 1974. *Principles of Gestalt family therapy.* Salt Lake City: Desert Press.

Kingsley, V. C. 1969. The effects of the double-bind conflict and sex of the experimenter on the conceptual functioning and visual discrimination of male good and poor premorbid schizophrenics. Ph.D. diss., New York University.

Kirby, K., and Priestman, S. 1957. Values of a daughter (schizophrenic) and mother therapy group. *International Journal of Group Psychotherapy.* *7:*281–288.

Kluckhohn, F. R., and Spiegel, J. P. 1954. *Integration and conflict in family behavior.* Group for the Advancement of Psychiatry, Report No. 27. Topeka, Kansas.

Knoblochova, J., and Knobloch, F. 1970. Family therapy in Czechoslovakia: An aspect of group-centered psychotherapy. In *Family therapy in transition*, N. W. Ackerman, ed. Boston: Little, Brown.

Kubie, L. S. 1956. Psychoanalysis and marriage. In *Neurotic interaction in marriage*, V. W. Eisenstein, ed. New York: Basic Books.

Laing, R. D. 1960. *The divided self.* London: Tavistock Publications.

Laing, R. D. 1965. Mystification, confusion and conflict. In *Intensive family therapy*, I. Boszormenyi-Nagy and J. L. Framo, eds. New York: Harper & Row.

Lakin, M. 1985. *The helping group: Therapeutic principles and issues.* Reading, MA: Addison-Wesley.

Levy, D. 1943. *Maternal Overprotection.* New York: Columbia Unversity Press.

Lewin, K. 1951. *Field theory in social science.* New York: Harper.

Lidz, R. W., and Lidz, T. 1949. The family environment of schizophrenic patients. *American Journal of Psychiatry.* *106:*332–345.

Lidz, T., Cornelison, A., Fleck, S., and Terry, D. 1957a. Intrafamilial environment of the schizophrenic patient. I: The father. *Psychiatry,* *20:*329–342.

Lidz, T., Cornelison, A., Fleck, S., and Terry, D. 1957b. Intrafamilial environment of schizophrenic patients. II: Marital schism and marital skew. *American Journal of Psychiatry.* 114:241–248.

Lidz, T., and Fleck, S. 1960. Schizophrenia, human integration, and the role of the family. In *The etiology of schizophrenia,* D. D. Jackson, ed. New York: Basic Books.

Lidz, T., Parker, B., and Cornelison, A. R. 1956. The role of the father in the family environment of the schizophrenic patient. *American Journal of Psychiatry. 113:*126–132.

Low, A. A. 1943. *The technique of self-help in psychiatry after-care.* Vol. 3, *Lectures to relatives of former patients.* Chicago: Recovery, Inc.

Lowrey, L. G. 1944. Group treatment for mothers. *American Journal of Orthopsychiatry. 14:*589–592.

Luft, J. 1970. *Group processes.* Palo Alto, CA: National Press Books.

MacGregor, R. 1967. Progress in multiple impact theory. In *Expanding theory and practice in family therapy,* N. W. Ackerman, F. L. Beatman, and S. N. Sherman, eds. New York: Family Services Association.

Mahler, M. S. & Rabinovitch, R. 1956. The effects of marital conflict on child development. In *Neurotic interaction in marriage,* V. W. Eisenstein, ed. New York: Basic Books.

Marsh, L. C. 1935. Group therapy and the psychiatric clinic. *American Journal of Nervous and Mental Diseases. 82:*381–393.

Midelfort, C. F. 1957. *The family in psychotherapy.* New York: McGraw-Hill.

Minuchin, S. 1974. *Families and family therapy.* Cambridge, MA: Harvard University Press.

Minuchin, S., and Fishman, H. C. 1981. *Family therapy techniques.* Cambridge, MA: Harvard University Press.

Minuchin, S., Montalvo, B., Guerney, B. G., Rosman, B. L., and Schumer, F. 1967. *Families of the slums.* New York: Basic Books.

Minuchin, S., Rosman, B. L., and Baker, L. 1978. *Psychosomatic families: Anorexia nervosa in context.* Cambridge, MA: Harvard University Press.

Mittleman, B. 1944. Complementary neurotic reactions in intimate relationships. *Psychoanalytic Quarterly. 13:*474–491.

Mittleman, B. 1948. The concurrent analysis of married couples. *Psychoanalytic Quarterly. 17:*182–197.

Mittleman, B. 1956. Analysis of reciprocal neurotic patterns in family relationships. In *Neurotic interactions in marriage.* V. W. Eisenstein, ed. New York: Basic Books.

Montague, A. 1956. Marriage—A cultural perspective. In *Neurotic interaction in marriage,* V. W. Eisenstein, ed. New York: Basic Books.

Moreno, J. L. 1945. *Psychodrama.* New York: Beacon House.

Nichols, M. P., and Zax, M. 1977. *Catharsis in psychotherapy.* New York: Gardner Press.

Nichols, W. 1979. Doctoral programs in marital and family therapy. *Journal of Marital and Family Therapy.* 5:23–28.

Oberndorf, C. P. 1938. Psychoanalysis of married couples. *Psychoanalytic Review.* 25:453–475.

Parsons, T., and Bales, R. F. 1955. *Family socialization and interaction.* Glencoe, IL: Free Press.

Phillips, M. 1970. Response to "double-bind" messages in relation to four dimensions of personality and two maternal child rearing attitudes: A study of interpretational and feeling preferences of late adolescents. Ph.D. diss., New York University.

Potash, H. M. 1965. Schizophrenic interaction and the concept of the double-bind. Doctoral diss., Michigan State University.

Richmond, M. E. 1917. *Social diagnosis.* New York: Russell Sage.

Ringuette, E. L., and Kennedy, T. 1966. An experimental study of the double-bind hypothesis. *Journal of Abnormal Psychology.* *71*:136–141.

Ross, W. D. 1948. Group psychotherapy with patient's relatives. *American Journal of Psychiatry.* *104*:623–626.

Satir, V. 1964. *Conjoint family therapy.* Palo Alto, CA: Science and Behavior Books.

Satir, V. 1972. *Peoplemaking.* Palo Alto, CA: Science and Behavior Books.

Schaeffer, R. L. 1972. Training schizophrenics and neurotics to recognize double-binds: A comparison. Ph.D. diss., Adelphi University.

Schindler, W. 1951. Counter-transference in family-pattern group psychotherapy. *International Journal of Group Psychotherapy.* *1*:100–105.

Schrieber, A. W. 1970. An experimental double-bind and communicativeness. Ph.D. diss., City University of New York.

Sherif, M. 1948. *An outline of social psychology.* New York: Harper and Brothers.

Singer, M. T., Wynne, L. C., and Toohey, M. L. 1978. Communication disorders and the families of schizophrenics. In *The nature of schizophrenia,* L. C. Wynne, R. L. Cromwell, and S. Matthysse, eds. New York: Wiley.

Siporin, M. 1980. Marriage and family therapy in social work. *Social Casework.* *61*:11–21.

Skynner, R. 1976. *Systems of family and marital psychotherapy.* New York: Brunner/Mazel.

Slavson, S. R. 1943. *An introduction to group therapy.* New York: The Commonwealth Fund.

Sluzki, C. E., Beavin, J., Tarnopolsky, A., and Veron, E. 1967. Transactional disqualification. *Archives of General Psychiatry.* *16*:494–504.

Smith, E. K. 1972. *The effect of double bind communications upon the state of anxiety of normals.* Ph.D. diss., University of New Mexico.

Sojit, C. M. 1969. Dyadic interaction in a double bind situation. *Family Process.* *8*:235–259.

Speck, R., and Attneave, C. 1973. *Family networks: Rehabilitation and healing.* New York: Pantheon.

Spiegel, J. P. 1957. The resolution of role conflict within the family. *Psychiatry.* *20*:1–16.

Steinglass, P. 1987. *The alcoholic family.* New York: Basic Books.

Stierlin, H. 1972. *Separating parents and adolescents.* New York: Quadrangle/New York Times Books.

Stierlin, H. 1977. *Psychoanalysis and family therapy.* New York: Jason Aronson.

Strodtbeck, F. L. 1954. The family as a three-person group. *American Sociological Review.* *19*:23–29.

Strodtbeck, F. L. 1958. Family interaction, values, and achievement. In *Talent and society,* D. C. McClelland, A. L. Baldwin, A. Bronfenbrenner, and F. L. Strodtbeck, eds. Princeton, NJ: Van Nostrand.

Uzoka, A. F. 1979. The myth of the nuclear family. *American Psychologist.* *34*:1095–1106.

Watzlawick, P. A., Beavin, J. H., and Jackson, D. D. 1967. *Pragmatics of human communication.* New York: Norton.

Weakland, J. H. 1960. The 'double bind' hypothesis of schizophrenia and three-party interaction. In *The etiology of schizophrenia,* D. D. Jackson, ed. New York: Basic Books.

Whitaker, C. A. 1958. Psychotherapy with couples. *American Journal of Psychotherapy.* *12*:18–23.

Whitaker, C. A. 1975. Psychotherapy of the absurd: With a special emphasis on the psychotherapy of aggression. *Family Process.* *14*:1–16.

Whitaker, C. A. 1976. A family is a four-dimensional relationship. In *Family therapy: Theory and practice,* P. J. Guerin, ed. New York: Gardner Press.

Whitaker, C. A., and Malone, T. P. 1953. *The roots of psychotherapy.* New York: Balkiston.

Whitehead, A. N., and Russell, B. 1910. *Principia mathematica.* Cambridge, MA: Cambridge University Press.

Wynne, L. C. 1961. The study of intrafamilial alignments and splits in exploratory family therapy. In *Exploring the base for family therapy,* N. W. Ackerman, F. L. Beatman, and S. N. Sherman, eds. New York: Family Services Association.

Wynne, L. C. 1978. Knotted relationships, communication deviances, and metabinding. In *Beyond the double bind,* M. M. Berger, ed. New York: Brunner/Mazel.

Wynne, L. C., Ryckoff, I., Day, J., and Hirsch, S. I. 1958. Pseudomutuality in the family relationships of schizophrenics. *Psychiatry. 21:*205–220.

Yalom, I. D. 1985. *The theory and practice of group psychotherapy.* 3rd ed. New York: Basic Books.

Zuk, G. H. 1971. *Family therapy: A triadic-based approach.* New York: Behavioral Publications.

The Conceptual Context of Family Therapy

One of family therapy's greatest contributions to the mental health field is to stress the importance of understanding people's behavior in context. As Bateson (1979) wrote, "It is the context that fixes the meaning." Prior to this recognition, the symptoms of a psychiatric patient were examined in isolation, apart from his or her network of family relationships. So the only available explanation was that the person was defective. Once therapists began to view people in the context of the family, their behavior not only seemed less strange, but it could be understood as an inevitable and necessary aspect of the way the family had evolved.

Similarly, when viewed apart from *its* context in the evolution of our scientific culture, family therapy seems a strange and radical departure from psychotherapy. The purpose of this chapter is to do more than simply introduce the reader to family therapy's concepts and methods, but also to provide perspective on the evolution of these ideas and techniques. Once viewed in this context, family therapy also can be seen as an inevitable development in the evolution of psychotherapy.

THE EVOLUTION OF IDEAS

Before exploring the specific case of family therapy, we would like to discuss the way science in general evolves, so we can have a larger perspective on the emergence of family therapy, and, perhaps, have some idea of where the field is headed.

69

Science historian Thomas Kuhn (1977) traced the evolution of scientific disciplines. He found that most disciplines begin in what he called a preparadigmatic period, during which practitioners are split into many competing schools, each of which approach the same subject differently, while claiming that theirs is the best way. This stage lasts until a major scientific breakthrough makes most of the rival schools obsolete, after which, in the postparadigmatic period, the discipline is dominated by one school.

Kuhn cites many examples from the physical sciences of this evolutionary process. One of these relates to our understanding of the nature of light. Before Newton's work, there was no scientific consensus regarding the nature of light.

> From remote antiquity . . . many men advanced a large number of different views about the nature of light. Some of these views found few adherents, but a number of them gave rise to continuing schools of optical thought. Although the historian can note the emergence of new points of view as well as changes in the relative popularity of older ones, there never was anything resembling consensus. As a result, a new man entering the field was inevitably exposed to a variety of conflicting viewpoints; he was forced to examine the evidence for each, and there always was good evidence. (p. 231)

Eventually, Newton's idea that light consisted of material corpuscles won out and became the agreed-upon view, until that paradigm was replaced in the early nineteenth century by the view of light as wave motion, which, in turn, was replaced early this century by the quantum-mechanical view of light as photons, which have some characteristics of waves and some of particles.

Kuhn proposes that this pattern of evolution of science, from a period during which there are many competing schools to the dominance of one school which is subsequently overthrown by a new one, is characteristic of all fields. Different disciplines reach their first consensus during different centuries and, Kuhn suggests, "This century appears to be characterized by the emergence of a first consensus in parts of a few of the social sciences" (p. 232).

Psychotherapy is not one of those social sciences to have reached consensus. Instead, the current state of psychotherapy is a classic example of the preparadigmatic or preconsensual phase, in which a number of competing schools each claim validity. This state of the art can be accounted for, in part, by the relative youth of the field, but also by the complexity of the phenomena that theories of psychotherapy try to deal with. Unlike the physical sciences, the social sciences are faced with more diverse and changing variables, and have few and imprecise instruments with which to measure them.

To illustrate the difference between the physical and biological sciences, Gregory Bateson (1979) used the example of kicking a stone versus kicking a dog. The effect of kicking a stone can be predicted precisely by measuring the force and angle of the kick, and the weight of the stone. If a man kicks a dog, on the other hand, the effect is far less predictable. The dog may respond to a kick in any number of ways, from cringing to running away to turning and biting the man, depending on the temperament of the dog and how it interprets the kick. In response to the dog's reaction, the man may modify his behavior in any number of ways, and so on, so that the number of possible outcomes is immense.

Given this complexity, it's difficult for a field like psychotherapy to test the validity of its theories. Kuhn's (1977) description of astrology hits uncomfortably close to home: "The occurrence of failures [of prediction] could be explained, but particular failures did not give rise to research puzzles, for no man, however skilled, could make use of them in a constructive attempt to revise the astrological tradition. There were too many possible sources of difficulty, most of them beyond the astrologer's knowledge, control, or responsibility" (p. 276).

In the absence of ironclad validity tests and solid conclusions, how are schools within a preparadigmatic field born or retired? Richard Schwartz (1985) proposed a framework for understanding the differentiation of psychotherapy and family therapy, as well as the various schools of family therapy. We elaborate on this framework below to help the reader understand how family therapy arrived at its present state.

The marketplace of models in psychotherapy can be compared to the evolution of biological systems. Stephan Jay Gould (1985), a leading scholar of evolution, summarizes the process this way: "When systems first arise, they probe all the limits of possibility. Many variations don't work; the best solutions emerge, and variation diminishes" (p. 220). For example, mollusks now exist as snails, clams, octopuses, and a few other groups, but early in their history there were ten to fifteen fundamental variations.

The same process applies to theories in a field like psychotherapy. When this new approach to human problems was first developed—the idea that people could be helped through some form of contact with a "therapist"—all the limits of possibility were probed. Many models were generated. Eventually such trial innovations should either merge or die from lack of success and, ideally, we would be left with a few models that represent the most effective ways to do psychotherapy.

In this early stage of the evolution of psychotherapy, there is not only great variation but also a high degree of polarization. One model is countered by a rival, based on opposite assumptions. This pendulum-swinging process seems to be useful in that the extremes are quickly explored, allowing for a gradually increasing drift toward a middle ground. For example, Freud's extreme focus on the power of the psyche was countered by the behaviorist movement that discounted the mind and emphasized environmental reinforcers. Next, the reductionistic focus on the individual of both the Freudian and behaviorist schools was countered by family therapy's extreme emphasis on the power of the family. It's only lately that common ground among these three extreme approaches is being explored.

Stages within a Model

Essentialistic. This pendulum-swinging process seems a natural artifact of the way people react to new ideas. The proponents of an advance usually consider it the long-sought understanding that captures the *essence* of the phenomenon being investigated. This begins an *essentialistic stage* in the model's development, which is often characterized by tunnel vision, zeal, and chauvinism—enthusiasms that are understandable and even useful, if they don't persist indefinitely. Tunnel vision is expedient temporarily in order to fully explore the complex possibilities of the new approach without the distraction of old or alternative points of view. Zeal and chauvinism arise from the belief that the essence has finally been found, but also provide a defense against attacks from the establishment.

An essentialistic stage is often a period of high productivity and creativity, fueled by the excitement and commitment that accompanies the belief that one is on the brink of something big. This stage can have a down side, however, because essentialistism breeds either-or thinking: our model is right and all others are wrong. Any failure of the model is explained away by essentialists as a misapplication of its principles or as faulty documentation of outcome.

The duration and extremism of the essentialistic stage is likely to depend on (1) how long it takes to explore the model to the point where its limitations begin to emerge, and (2) the degree to which the established orthodoxy accepts or accommodates to the new model. The more the essentialists must defend their model, the more they feel like enlightened crusaders, and the less able they are to examine their discoveries critically. The less critically they examine their efforts, the longer it takes to discover that the model is limited or flawed.

Transitional. The *transitional stage* begins when some essentialists begin to recognize that their model is limited or flawed. This can be a tumultuous period, depending on how extreme the essentialistic period was. If hopes of having found the essence were raised high, they have a long way to fall when prophecies fail. When this happens, the transitional period is marked by intramodel polarization, with some adherents defending the model while others desert in disillusionment.

Thus we can see how the zealousness and over-optimism of an essentialistic stage generates the pendulum-swinging process, as disillusioned former adherents of the model and outsiders polarized by the essentialists' chauvinism and zeal, spin off new, opposite but equally extreme models.

Some of those who remain loyal to the original model through this transitional stage will be inclined to retrench in the face of the chaos and polarization and become even more rigidly dogmatic about the model's assumptions and methods. Others, however, gradually accept the model's limitations—that it may not have full essentialistic power or universality—and begin to see it in context. They are able to broaden the tunnel vision that was necessary earlier and see commonalities as well as the differences with other models. Their zeal is replaced with a new openness and modesty, as they become comfortable with a shift from finding the truth to contributing a piece to a larger puzzle.

Ecological. This opening of the boundaries of a model is often accompanied by the fear that its unique qualities will dissipate, or will be co-opted by the establishment. This can be a real danger and adherents walk a tightrope in trying to maintain the model's integrity while considering other possibilities.

Ideally, the tension of this process forces theorists to a "meta" position—a perspective from which they can look down on the larger field and see their model as one among an ecology of models. From this meta and modest state of mind they are better able to see the "pattern that connects" (Bateson, 1979) their model with other models, which they once believed to be incompatible. This period is characterized by increased communication and cooperation among models. In this way, the *ecological period* may produce a new meta-theory that is able to account for and deal with a much wider range of phenomena than any of the individual models within the ecology.

CONTEXTUAL INFLUENCES ON THE EVOLUTION OF FAMILY THERAPY

The field of family therapy emerged as part of this pendulum-swinging, stage-wise process within the larger mental health field, and the various schools of family therapy emerged as a subpart of that process. This explains why family therapy, and many of its schools, have often been characterized by tunnel vision, zeal, and chauvinism. In the 1980s, family therapy emerged from its essentialistic stage, survived the disillusionment, retrenchment, and challenge of the early transitional stage, and is now showing some of the modesty and openness characteristic of the transitional period. This characterization also applies to some schools of family therapy, while, as we shall see, others remain relatively essentialistic and isolated.

Let us now take a more careful look at how family therapy has arrived at this stage. Accounts that summarize the emergence and evolution of the field fit well with our pendulum-swinging, stages framework. Consider Lynn Hoffman's (1981) observations:

> The family movement in therapy resembles the Protestant movement in religion. It follows on the heels of a highly organized body of ideas and practice which has a well-recognized founding father, Sigmund Freud. Despite multiple heresies and schisms, psychoanalysis has formed the basis for a mental health establishment. Some pioneers in the family therapy field have mounted a revisionistic assault, almost amounting to revolution, against the ideas of this Freudian establishment. . . . (p. 219)

Many family therapy pioneers were disillusioned psychoanalysts frustrated by the limits of psychoanalytic orthodoxy and its focus on the individual out of context, its overemphasis on intrapsychic and historical factors, its pessimistic and pathological assumptions about people, its esoteric theorizing, its impracticality for the majority of Americans and for many syndromes, and its rigid dogmatism. In fairness to psychoanalysis, many of these criticisms apply more to its essentialistic stage than to its current practice. Nevertheless, the extreme essentialism of psychoanalysis helped generate the reactive essentialism of early family therapy, with its overemphasis on the power of the family context, its rejection of intrapsychic and historical considerations, its overly optimistic assumptions, its overemphasis on being pragmatic, simple, and short, and its own dogmatism. When the pendulum swings, it swings all the way.

During this early period, family therapy's rhetoric reflected the need to differentiate from mainstream thought and to recruit converts. There existed an us-versus-them mentality characteristic of revolutionary groups: We are systemic/they are linear; we can cure all problems/they can cure none; we are the therapy of the people/they are for the wealthy; we are good/they are bad. In a chapter entitled "Family Therapy: A Radical Change," Jay Haley (1971), probably the most radical and polemic of the pioneers, wrote "the ideas of the past are not building blocks but become stumbling blocks in grasping a new way of thinking" (p. 272).

As family therapy became more widely accepted as a valid orientation to human problems, much of the extreme dogma and essentialistic thinking abated. It's less necessary to attack the establishment now because there are fewer attacks from the establishment and more converts. As the field moves through its transitional phase and communicates with the establishment, the fear of co-option grows. As Salvador Minuchin lamented,

> The psychiatric field has incorporated family therapy as a modality of treatment—without, of course, changing the diagnostic categories of individual patients . . . This is the way society works. It co-opted a movement that was challenging basic ways of thinking about human problems by making it official. (Simon, 1984, p. 30)

Indeed, versions of family therapy, such as the psychoeducation movement, have emerged and become increasingly popular seeming more closely tied to the assumptions of the medical model than to the systemic paradigm that Minuchin and others want to preserve. Other models, like the psychoanalytic and behavioral schools of family therapy (see Chapters 6 and 8), which have always been considered outgrowths of the individual therapy establishment rather than part of the systems revolution, have also been gaining in popularity.

Whether these trends represent a fatal dilution of the essence of family therapy or steps toward an ecological stage in the field that will result in a valuable synthesis or meta-theory is yet to be determined.

DIFFERENTIATION WITHIN FAMILY THERAPY

The process by which family therapy differentiated into competing models parallels the pendulum-swinging, stages framework by which family therapy as a whole differentiated from the psychiatric establishment. In the 1950s family therapy was a radical new experiment, practiced in relative isolation by a small number of clinician-researchers around the country. These theorists shared a sense of awe at the magnitude of the task they faced in making sense of phenomena that no one before had studied, and a sense of solidarity against the establishment that all revolutionary groups start out with. Carlos Sluzki (1983) likened these early family therapists to pioneers of the old west:

> During its first 10 or 15 years, the situation in the family therapy field was akin to that of the western frontier of the U.S. during the mid-1800s.

There was a lot of territory to occupy and explore, an undeclared war with the previous inhabitants (in family therapy's case, psychodynamically-oriented and classical psychiatrists) and a prevailing spirit of adventure and expansionism. Back then, family therapists were, for the most part, not too preoccupied with staking out their personal domains since like-minded neighbors were few and far between and they were concerned with developing common defenses against the unfriendly elements in the mental health establishment. (p. 24)

Gradually and, from the perspective of our pendulum-swinging, stages framework, naturally, the field began to differentiate and polarize. Systems theory was abstract and had a number of different versions so that it could be, and was, translated in a number of ways, depending on the inclination of the theorist. As with the proverbial blind men exploring different parts of an elephant, many of the family therapy pioneers stressed the importance of different aspects of family systems, each believing that their aspect was the essence of what caused problems in families. These early essences, which will be described later in this chapter, were encapsulated in terms like *incongruent communication,* lack of *differentiation,* poorly defined *boundaries, function of the symptom,* and *positive feedback loops.* Differences in theory translated into even larger differences in technique, and in this way a series of idiosyncratic models of family therapy entered their essentialistic stage.

Economic Influences

Since family therapy was an antiestablishment movement, it was not born, nor could it take root, within the established institutions like medical schools or universities. Students who wanted training in family therapy couldn't get it through established academic avenues and, instead, looked to the training institutes that sprang up around the country and to private workshops put on by the peripatetic pioneers. This privatization of family therapy training released it from the economic constraints of academia and made it a lucrative enterprise. During family therapy's boom period of the late 1970s and early 1980s a big-name presenter could make $10,000 in a weekend.

Sluzki (1983) colorfully described the effect this profit motive has had on the differentiation of the field.

Over the last 10 years . . . there has been a population explosion within the field as well as a dramatic increase in the commercial advantages of having control of part of its territory. As a result, people have been known to surreptitiously move fences, erect huge stockages, dispute certain areas and even claim as their own territories that were previously defined as common grounds. During the past 10 years, we have witnessed a Balkanization of the field into sectors based on political rather than scientific boundaries. We have also seen the rise of a "star" system, based on maintaining those artificial boundaries for politico-economic reasons. The consequence of all this has been the development of more and more "brand-name" models and increased bickering about whose technique washes whiter. (p. 24)

Minuchin also recognized that the motives of the various schools to maintain their essentialistic differences were not pure. In describing the pioneers (in part autobiographically) he stated that,

> . . . lo and behold, their institutions grew and they needed large buildings to accommodate all their students. Slowly, before anyone realized it, the buildings became castles with turrets and drawbridges, and even watchmen in the towers. The castles were very expensive and they had to justify their existence. Therefore, they demanded ownership of the total truth. (Simon, 1984, p. 88)

Today, there are still many different castles. Some inhabitants guard them as ferociously as ever and rarely venture out. One harbinger of the transitional stage, however, is the increasing number of family therapists who have traveled widely enough to see their own castles in perspective and can move back and forth between conceptual realms. This is a generation of therapists with less direct allegiance to the charismatic rulers of the castles and, therefore, less constrained by personal loyalties.

The Influence of Free Market Research

Another effect of the field's development outside academia is that the pioneering theorists were relatively immune to traditional academic publication standards. They could (and sometimes did) make dramatic outcome claims without the scrutiny that traditional institutions and review processes afford. Alan Gurman, former editor of the *Journal of Marital and Family Therapy*, complained that,

> The prominent purveyors of family therapy often seemed to be making across-the-board assertions about what their methods could accomplish —as if they were saying they had the cleanest wash no matter what the dirt was. Mostly this has been communicated indirectly by rarely reporting failures and not providing clear research data. (Quoted in Schwartz & Perrotta, 1985)

On the other hand, subjecting the field to standard professional constraints might have stifled creativity and innovation. Seminal ideas and practices might have been watered down if the goal had been to reduce family therapy to the kind of easily controlled or operationalized studies that academic journals demand—where the findings are sometimes rigorous but trivial. Perhaps a few questionable notions and inflated claims is part of the price for creative freedom.

Don Ransom, associate editor of *Family Systems Medicine*, provides another rationale for exaggerated claims during the essentialistic stage:

> Creating a climate of enthusiasm is a stage in the sociology of any new profession. The early claims made by family therapy—the idea that it might be the panacea—were important in turning many of us on, getting us involved in the field. (quoted in Schwartz & Perrotta, 1985)

The flaw in these ends-justify-the-means arguments lies in the damage done to those clients whose problems were oversimplified and whose hopes were raised and dashed, as clinicians around the country rushed to try out the latest exciting techniques.

The danger of naive enthusiasm is exemplified by the actions of a fledgling therapist who, in 1974, discovered *Change: Principles of Problem Formation and Problem Resolution* (Watzlawick, Weakland, & Fisch, 1974), a classic text for strategic family therapy. This eager convert embraced this book as the solution to all his therapeutic muddles.

> This attitude was not discouraged by the authors who made statements like " . . . second order change through paradox—is undoubtedly the most powerful and elegant form of problem resolution known to us," and "We see our basic views on problem formation and resolution, persistence and change, as usefully and appropriately applicable to human problems generally."
>
> He seized on what amounted to a small footnote in the book that said a wide range of psychiatric problems were at least significantly improved in 73 percent of nearly 100 cases, and in an average of less than 10 sessions. Taking this as compelling proof of the validity of the paradoxical approach, he brazenly prescribed that all kinds of psychiatric morasses he encountered in his crisis work remain the same.
>
> On one occasion he made a home visit to a chronically depressed older man who had an established pattern of becoming bedridden for weeks, being hospitalized, getting better, returning to work, then getting depressed and returning to bed for weeks . . . with barely hidden sarcasm, [the therapist] told the now bedridden man that he should continue in his current helpless state because his wife was a retired nurse and needed to have a patient to care for. Enraged, the man bounded out of bed, grabbed a broomstick, and chased the well-meaning young therapist out of his house.
>
> Did this incident point towards a positive outcome? After all, the man was activated to get out of bed and express his anger directly. But the couple never wanted to see the therapist again and quickly fell back into their old pattern. (Schwartz & Perrotta, 1985, p. 21)

The point of this story isn't that paradoxical techniques are without value (see Chapter 10 for a discussion of paradox), but that in the excitement of discovery, these authors oversold them.

This has been the case with the debut of other models. Therapists around the world were inspired to try the methods of the Milan Associates based on their book *Paradox and Counterparadox* (Selvini Palazzoli, Cecchin, Boscolo, & Prata, 1978), which contains few warnings or guidelines, while promoting paradoxical technique with impressive anecdotal outcome claims. A decade later, Selvini Palazzoli had totally abandoned this paradoxical approach which had seemed so miraculous, stating that "I had too many failures using paradoxical methods with psychotic and anorectic families" (Simon, 1987, p. 26).

She then adopted a new method, the *invariant prescription,* for which she claimed equally miraculous results. Based on ten cases in which she claimed there was a complete alleviation of symptoms in anorexic and schizophrenic patients, she concluded that "the therapeutic power of the invariable prescription, when obeyed, had now been confirmed beyond all doubt" (Simon, 1987, p. 20). More recently she has renounced that approach as well.

The same criticism applies to Haley's (1980) "Leaving Home Model," a difficult and risky approach, based on a handful of anecdotal outcome reports and accompanied by few guidelines or warnings. It was packaged, instead, as an instrument that "causes positive change and has a low risk of doing harm" and with the suggestion that it could be applied to most troubled young adults regardless of diagnosis or symptoms. Years later, after hearing how therapists had been misapplying this model, Haley confessed that "Sometimes what you write for therapists spills into the community in unfortunate ways and then you're sorry you ever wrote it" (Simon, 1984).

A model that rises rapidly on the wings of great promise is more likely to crash and burn when it doesn't fulfill that promises. This rapid rise and fall characterized the field's pendulum-swinging essentialistic stage. Family therapists have become more skeptical over the years, however, and the frequency of exaggerated claims seems to have decreased correspondingly. In addition, the number and scale of rigorous outcome studies has increased (see Chapter 13).

Gender and Class Bias

The various pioneering models of family therapy differed in large part because of the idiosyncrasies of personality and background of the various theorists. They viewed the families they studied through entirely different lenses. If, for example, Nathan Ackerman and Virginia Satir were observing the same family, their observations, assessments, and interventions would have been very different. That's because the assumptions and beliefs we hold about the world color the way we see it.

Family therapy has struggled to give up the Lockean notion that there is a reality out there that we can objectively perceive and, with the help of both the feminists and constructivists (two groups otherwise often in conflict), now realizes the importance of understanding the belief systems of the observers, and the contextual influences on those belief systems.

Let us briefly examine the personalities, backgrounds, and cultural contexts of the family therapy pioneers and speculate as to how these factors might have affected what they saw. With few exceptions, these pioneers were white, male psychiatrists, exploring and writing during a very conservative period of American history, the late 1950s. As might be expected, they shared many of the biases of their time. Beginning in the early 1980s, feminist family therapists reexamined many of the premises and techniques that two generations of family therapists held sacred (see Chapter 3). Their critique stunned a field that prided itself on its liberalism. It was as if the feminists switched on a light in a dark room; once the bias in the original theories was pointed out, it's hard to understand how we could have been so blind. Perhaps the length of family therapy's essentialistic stage accounts for some of this blindness. It took a while for the insecurity and excitement of exploring unknown territory and making new discoveries to wear off to the point that we could take another look at our theories.

At any rate, it seems clear now that sexism had an impact on the field. Deborah Luepnitz, in *The Family Interpreted* (1988), presented a scathing yet scholarly feminist critique of the thinking of the pioneers. The patriarchal belief system of someone like Nathan Ackerman (1958) (see Chapter 6), who has been called "the father of family therapy," is easy to identify. Luepnitz cites the following passage where Ackerman wrote:

> In certain families, there is a reversal of sexual roles. The woman dominates and makes the decisions; she "wears the pants." The father is passive and submits to avoid argument. The mother pushes the father towards many of the maternal duties . . . Such trends as these have had an immeasurable effect in distorting the functions of mothering and in confusing the sexual and emotional development of the child. (pp. 172–73) . . . He [the father] has been stripped of all semblance of arbitrary authority in the family. His power to discipline and punish family offenders, whether wife or child, has been sharply undercut. (p. 79)

Patriarchal assumptions in other models are less blatant but still evident. For example, Luepnitz (1988) criticized Bowen's (1978) implication of the mother in the development of pathology in her child. Additionally, she and others (Hare-Mustin, 1978; Lerner, 1986) criticize Bowen's emphasis on male-oriented traits like "autonomous," "goal-directed," and "intellectual" in describing the "differentiated" way people should strive to be, while he uses qualities that women have traditionally been socialized for, such as "seeking approval," "relatedness," and "being-for-others," to describe the poorly differentiated person. Finally, Bowen's thesis that to differentiate one should separate the emotional from the intellect and put the intellect in control can also be seen as a reflection of a male value system that reveres reason and fears feelings.

Salvador Minuchin, the founder of structural family therapy (see Chapter 5), one of the field's most popular models, has not escaped the feminist critique. In watching tapes of Minuchin work, feminists noticed the frequency with which he tried to disengage what he considered to be an enmeshed and overwhelmed mother from her children by getting the father to take over, rather than encouraging and supporting the mother to become more effective (Luepnitz, 1988). Many of these pioneers saw mothers as incompetent or enmeshing people partly because mothers were the most central figures. They were given the most burdens in the family, and so were the easiest targets. But, as we'll discuss in the next chapter, these pioneers also were viewing families in isolation—out of their social-political context. They didn't see how our culture makes families dangerous to the health of mothers.

Strategic family therapists as a whole (including the MRI group, Haley and Madanes, and the Milan associates; see Chapter 10) are indicted by Luepnitz (1988) for acts of omission. While there is little overt sexism in their writing and technique, they show inadequate concern over how their techniques might be used in the service of, rather than in opposition to, patriarchy. In striving to be pragmatic, using any means to solve the presenting problem, strategic therapists have shown little interest in examining the larger implications of their solutions. As Luepnitz (1988) asserts, . . . "there is nothing in strategic therapy that would rule out making a wife more submissive to her husband if such a change would remove a symptom" (p. 77).

The attempt on the part of strategic therapists to be value-free is directly related to Gregory Bateson's distaste for the metaphor of power, which led him to imply that all parts of a system are equally influential. This idea is rejected by feminists and those who work with victims of sexual or physical abuse because it can be used to excuse the abuser. In addition, Bateson led the group that constructed the famous double bind theory of schizophrenia (Bateson, Jackson, Haley, & Weakland, 1956; see previous chapter), which seemed to blame mothers for the schizophrenia in their children. Despite the fact that this group later refuted this theory as too linear, it has had an impact on the field.

It's interesting to note that Bateson's caveats about the use of power metaphors haven't prevented many family therapy theorists (most notably Haley) from emphasizing the importance of power relations between the generations, otherwise known as family hierarchy. Yet these same theorists ignore the power differential between the sexes in families, except to the extent that it interferes with parenting (Goldner, 1988).

By presenting elements of the feminist critique of some pioneers, we don't mean to diminish their contributions but to highlight the power of a theorist's cultural and intellectual context and background on his or her observations. We're all subject to the blind spots of our time.

Our culture not only affected the way the pioneers saw (or didn't see) gender relations within families, but also had an impact on what these theorists considered to be a normal family structure. Family therapy received another jolt in the early 1980s, this time from clinicians who had worked with families from other cultures and recognized that many characteristics of these ethnic families would be considered dysfunctional by conventional family therapy standards (McGoldrick, Pearce, & Giordano, 1982). Practitioners were awakened to their ethnocentric and absolutist ideas of what's normal by the recognition that families from other cultures have different values, and that these differences don't necessarily represent dysfunction. Now when we work with a family from southern Italy, for example, we are aware of the importance of family loyalty; we don't assume that they're sick just because they seem more inclined than middle-class American families to sacrifice their own desires for the interests of the family.

The map of the healthy family that has been the most influential for the family therapy is presented by the structural school. The picture of a normative family they paint is one that fits well in the American middle-class culture. It has clear boundaries between the generations, it emphasizes hierarchy in terms of the primacy and smooth functioning of the *executive subsystem* (usually the parents), it advocates an "age-appropriate" parenting style designed to create autonomous, independent children, and it values an open boundary around the family; all useful qualities for surviving in our highly mobile and competitive society. Therapists routinely measure the families they treat against this structural ideal. While many family therapists use this map flexibly and with respect for the variety in family forms, some will see pathology in families from different cultures or classes that don't fit this ideal.

Celia Falicov (1983) draws on the work of anthropologist Francis Hsu (1971) to point out that in many cultures the dominant or governing dyad in a family isn't the husband/wife, but instead is intergenerational, for example, husband/son in some cultures, wife/son in others, or even brother/brother in still others. Thus, the very *cross-generational coalitions* we seize on as the root of some families' problems may be normative in their culture. As the feminists remind us, however, just because a family's structure is normative does not mean that it's balanced or fair.

Returning to family therapy's normative map, it can be seen as promoting a streamlined, nuclearized family structure and values that fit well with our highly mobile, materialistic society but might create problems for families in nonmobile societies. We will present briefly some elements of middle-class American culture that make this structural model fit so well with it.

Ours is an economy based on a white-collar work force, willing to put the corporation, and advancement within it, ahead of the interests of the family. The economy also needs voracious consumers who, likewise, are willing to put their families in debt or work long hours, depriving family members of their energy, to buy luxuries. To maintain these values, the media bombards us with materialistic messages that create an insatiable hunger for things and for success. These strivings can easily override concern for family relationships, which in turn are increasingly ungratifying and impoverished because of these strivings.

In addition, the decline in the standard of living over the last few decades has meant that family leaders must work harder and longer just to help the family survive, much less to live in luxury. With all this pressure and worry, parents often want to spend what little time they have away from work trying to decompress with soothing, passive distractions rather than engaging in meaningful conversations or meting out discipline.

The restless mobility of American families also takes its toll. In their climb up the corporate ladder, families routinely moved, and still move, every two or three years. As Robert Bellah and his colleagues (1985) reported in *Habits of the Heart,* their study of American values, "Being tied to one particular job, in one particular location, is tantamount to being stuck, trapped, denied the opportunity for personal fulfillment" (p. 186). The not so funny joke among IBM employees is that the initials stand for "I've Been Moved." The roots of relational networks have barely taken hold before they have to be dug up and transplanted. With higher unemployment, more working-class families have become urban nomads, following job opportunities across the country as tribes once followed animal herds.

The isolation resulting from this repeated uprooting tends to reinforce a materialistic orientation to life because, as the family is perpetually having to present an image to strangers and getting fewer rewards from emotional connections, issues of status and appearance come to dominate. In turn, the materialistic, rather than relational, striving reinforces mobility, which again reinforces materialism, and we get caught in an American vicious circle.

Young and Willmott (1957) saw this same phenomenon in their classic study of the effects on families who moved from a highly stable, homogeneous working-class borough in East London to a housing development outside London.

> One might even suggest, to generalize, that the less the personal respect received in small group relationships, the greater is the striving for the kind of impersonal respect embodied in a status judgment. The lonely man, fearing he is looked down on, becomes the acquisitive man; possession the balm of anxiety; anxiety the spur to unfriendliness. (p. 164)

The lonely husband, wife, and children also are more likely to make television the centerpiece of family life which, in turn, diminishes the quality of relationships and increases materialistic striving.

In our highly mobile middle-class society, we're expected to leave our parents at an early age and, likewise, our children expect to leave us. The only constant relationship amid all these transitional ones is marriage. Thus, in lieu of a network of emotionally satisfying relationships, we put most of our emotional eggs in one basket. Spouses are expected to be far more than just partners in parenthood or in the struggle for economic survival or a bridge connecting two extended families, as is the case in many other cultures. The ideal middle-class marriage is a union of soulmates who selected each other and who enjoy a consistently high level of intellectual, emotional, and sexual intimacy throughout their long lives together.

We stay with our marriage partners because they satisfy us, turn us on, more than any other, and if that were to change, we want to be free to change partners. Thus, not only does modern middle-class marriage carry unprecedented emotional expectations, it also has an unprecendred lack of traditional obligation. All this is in keeping with the need in a capitalistic society for a professional and managerial workforce, willing to put materialistic and achievement values ahead of family commitments or considerations. Bellah and his colleagues (1985) interviewed "Brian" who exemplifies this ethic.

> Still rising toward the peak of a career that has defined his identity by its progress, Brian looks back on his twenties and thirties, devoted to advancing his career at the expense of tending his marriage and family life, and concedes, "I got totally swept up in my own progress, in promotions and financial success." Yet even now, Brian's definition of success revolves around an open-ended career on the upswing. . . . "Where I come as close as I can to performing at the absolute limits of my capacity. That's success." (p. 68)

With a multitude of Brians and a culture that reinforces them, love and marriage must accommodate accordingly.

American childrearing values, too, have conformed to the needs of our corporate culture. More than in any other culture, American children are encouraged to bargain with parents for what they want, to compete with peers in all arenas, to desire and expect material possessions, and to think for themselves rather than rely on tradition or authority. Middle-class children are expected to leave home at eighteen, to enter and succeed in a harsh survival economy. In many ways, childhood is a long proving ground for a reality that is very different from life in cultures where children are socialized for obedience, loyalty, conformity, and to put the interests of the family before personal advancement.

American models of therapy have evolved that reinforce many of the same values responsible for creating problems in the first place. Psychoanalysis is an obvious target of this critique in its view of anyone who can't cope with the world of competitive striving as maladjusted; its measure of growth being the degree to which people separate from their families.

Because family therapy does attempt to view people's problems in context, it's a less obvious culprit in supporting competitive individualism. But the goal of differentiating individuals from their families so they can rely on themselves, so they don't have to live up to their family's expectations, so they can leave home and pursue individual interests, are no less products of and contributions to the American middle-class value system. To varying degrees, the models of many family therapy pioneers seem designed to reduce the sense of social or family obligation or guilt that constrains clients from achieving their personal ambitions. Perhaps we have been helping people shed baggage and streamline so they are better able to compete, without considering whether these extremely competitive, individualistic values, themselves, are healthy for our clients or for the global ecology.

Ivan Boszormenyi-Nagy was an exception in that he emphasized the loyalty and obligation that family members owe one another, both within and across generations (Boszormenyi-Nagy & Spark, 1973). In light of this critique, it isn't surprising that his ideas never generated a large school of family therapy.

This isn't to suggest that normative family maps haven't been useful. We need a template of the family-of-best-fit for our society so that we can help families decide if they want to fit into it. What has been largely missing in family therapy, with the exception of the feminist critique, however, is a critical evaluation of the society we are helping people fit into that could enable us to help clients make educated decisions about their value systems.

Another bias in many family therapy models, which also stems from our individualistic heritage, is the belief that families are inherently able to find their own best solutions, and that when they fail to do so, it's because of the interference of social control agents or because they've tripped over a bump in the life cycle. In reexamining this assumption, Virginia Goldner (1988) wrote: "Were it not for developmental snags and external meddlers, families would 'naturally' grow and develop, and in the process emerge as more complex forms of life" (p. 26). The implication is that if we just get the control agents and other "helpers" off the family's back and jump-start its natural problem-solving mechanisms, the family will heal itself.

This view of the family is consistent with the image that grew out of the industrial revolution when home and workplace became separated. Since then middle-class Americans have viewed their families as "havens in a heartless world," private retreats where one can find respite from the competitive jungle of the business world (Hareven, 1982; Lasch, 1977).

The instinct to idealize and protect these havens from meddlers is deeply rooted in conservative American politics, and is reflected most directly in the brief, strategic, and systemic schools of family therapy (see Chapter 9). Running throughout the literature of these schools are the themes that (1) therapy should not be political, therapists should not be agents of social control; (2) families should be left alone as quickly as possible; and (3) after minimal intervention, families can be trusted to find their own best solutions. As Boscolo and Cecchin (Boscolo et al. 1987) assert, "If you let them alone, they improve" (p. 115, cited in Luepnitz, 1988).

This trust in the healing resources of people and respect for their strengths was a refreshing counterpoint to the pessimistic orientation of the psychiatric establishment that turned therapists into psychopathologists, and led to "parentectomies" (long-term hospitalization of children) or other disrespectful intrusions into families. Carried too far, however, the minimalist attitude blinds therapists to the political and ecological impact of their interventions (Goldner, 1987; Luepnitz, 1988; Keeney & Sprenkle, 1982), and encourages the tendency of some families to deny the existence of shameful problems (as, for example, violence, sex abuse, and addictions).

Finally, we cannot ignore the impact of the pioneers' personal characteristics on their theories and techniques. It has often been suggested that therapists find out what they like to do in therapy and then construct elaborate theories to rationalize these preferences. Anyone who saw Salvador Minuchin present, particularly in the 1970s or early 1980s, would not be surprised to learn that structural family therapists were taught to be directive, dramatic, and provocative. Likewise, those who have experienced Murray Bowen first-hand are not surprised that therapists using his model are to be rational, low-key, and controlled.

Along these lines, it's interesting to contrast the language and concepts used by the late Virginia Satir, the only woman among the pioneers. Satir was no less exposed to the exciting new ideas of systems theory and was closely associated with the men who infused the field with those concepts, yet she spoke of the importance of self-esteem, compassion, and the expression of feelings, while her colleagues were speaking of feedback loops, homeostasis, and hierarchy. She touched and nurtured her clients while her colleagues strategized to trick them into changing or used their authority to command change. As a result, Satir was viewed as a fuzzy thinker, too naive for the real systems thinkers. Ironically, some of these same systems thinkers are currently reevaluating the authoritarian relationships of their prior models, and moving toward Satir-like collaborative, supportive positions.

Not only did each blind man and woman have personal perspectives that made the elephant seem different to them, they were also seeing different elephants. The families struggling with schizophrenia, that formed the basis of the concepts introduced by Bowen, the Bateson group, Wynne, Lidz, and Whitaker, were very different from the families of the slums studied by Minuchin and his colleagues, or even from the families of Italian schizophrenics upon which the Milan group based their model. What works with a family organized around one kind of syndrome in one cultural context may be totally ineffective with another kind of syndrome or culture, yet, for the most part, these early models became generalized and applied universally.

Furthermore, these models of family functioning were developed from observations of families in crisis. A family organized around their child's recent schizophrenic break may look entirely different from the same family one or two years before or later. Crises tend to exaggerate conflict and rigidity, and it is probably unfair to base generalized models of "psychosomatic families" or "schizophrenic families" on observations made when these families were at their worst.

In sum, we consider the influence of the personalities and cultural contexts and backgrounds of the field's founding parents, not to denigrate their approaches or assumptions, but to remind the reader that their theories don't describe some objective reality of family process. Each theorist has made valuable contributions, but it's important to see their ideas in context. Thus, instead of trying to compare the models in this book based on which best describes "real" family process, we recommend using such standards as how effective, ethical, ecologically, and politically sensitive an approach is. In other words, consider how well it fits your values, personal style, and intuition rather than how much truth it contains.

CONCEPTUAL INFLUENCES ON THE EVOLUTION OF FAMILY THERAPY

If we were to poll family therapists as to the most important conceptual influence on the development of the field, the winner by a landslide would be something called "systems theory." If we followed up that survey and asked those therapists to describe this systems theory, most would mumble phrases like "the whole is greater than the sum of its parts," or words like *equifinality* or *homeostasis,* while feeling uneasy about their inability to articulate a theory they believe they should know by heart.

This inarticulateness of family therapists isn't entirely their fault. Systems theory isn't really a coherent, standardized doctrine, but is more like a way of thinking, and there are many variations on the systemic theme. This incoherence has been reflected in much of the writing regarding the application of systemic thinking to family therapy. Systemic ideas are abstract enough to provide a wide variety of interpretations. What we describe below is no less an interpretation, but we hope it's one that provides some coherence and clarity.

Many family therapists don't fully realize that most of the concepts the pioneers used to try to understand families weren't developed by them, but were imported from other fields of study, all of which were changing in a similar direction at the time family therapy emerged. Jay Haley (1971) summarized some of those changes:

> The idea of trying to change a family appeared in the 1950s at the same time as other happenings in the social sciences in America. At midcentury the social sciences became more social: the study of small groups flourished, animals were observed in their natural environments instead of in the zoo or laboratory, psychological experiments were seen as social situations in experimenter-bias studies, businesses began to be thought of as complex systems, mental hospitals were studied as total institutions, and ecology developed as a special field, with man and

other creatures looked upon as inseparable from their environments. (p. 1)

Functionalism

Of these fields, the changes within anthropology most closely paralleled the changes brought to psychotherapy by family therapy. This isn't surprising when we consider that the person most responsible for bringing systems ideas into psychotherapy was Gregory Bateson, an anthropologist.

Until the turn of the century, anthropology was dominated by the cultural evolutionists who applied Darwinian theory to cultures, and theorized about the various stages through which humankind evolved from primitive savagery to modern civilization. Their theories were based on artifacts brought back by archaeologists, and on tales of travelers or merchants, so they were more like philosophers than scientists.

Beginning around the turn of the century, but not dominating the anthropological scene until the 1930s, an approach known as *functionalism* emerged as a reaction against the evolutionist tendency to tear cultural traits out of their context and to disregard cultures as meaningful wholes. British anthropologists Bronislaw Malinowski and A. R. Radcliffe-Brown took the position that historical studies were futile because the data are scant and unverifiable. They were interested in studying cultures as social systems in the present and had little concern for their history. Thus, they studied cultures ethnographically, as "participant observers," and tried to understand cultural ceremonies or customs—in context—looking for the function that a cultural practice served for the larger social network.

These functionalists were as affected by Darwin's theory as the historical evolutionists against whom they reacted, only in a different way. They speculated about the function of social behavior for the larger group in much the same way that Darwinians speculated about the survival value of animal traits. Thus, functionalists believe that the adaptive function of any activity can be found if the behavior is viewed in the context of its environment.

The parallels between this shift in anthropology and a later shift in psychotherapy are striking. Psychoanalysts tried to reconstruct a person's history by searching for and studying, out of context, events in the person's past. Like the evolutionary anthropologists, psychoanalysts developed theories based on historical speculation. Indeed, Freud was fascinated by archaeology and compared his psychological explorations to archaeological excavations.

Family therapy's reaction against the historical and out-of-context theorizing of psychoanalysis was similar to the reaction of anthropological functionalists against the same historical and out-of-context qualities of evolutionism. Like the functionalists, systems-oriented family therapists weren't interested in history, and instead tried to become participant observers of families in the present. They were interested in understanding the function that the behavior of family members served for the family system.

One of the hazards of family therapy's functionalist inclination is to view *any* behavior as potentially adaptive. As Luepnitz (1988) asserts, "Functionalist explanations can justify almost anything in terms of some putative social need. Functionalist historians have even argued that lynchings and witch hunts serve a social need, i.e., a cathartic or 'therapeutic' need. Therapeutic for whom? one might well ask" (p. 65).

An example relevant to family therapy is the assumption by Talcott Parsons (Parsons & Bales, 1955), probably the most influential functionalist sociologist, that the mother's proper role in a family is *expressive*, and the father's *instrumental*. The *expressive role* involves emotional support, management of tensions, and care and support of the children. The *instrumental role* involves managerial decisions, solution of group tasks, and discipline of the children. In this case, Parsons took an observation of the sex-role polarity that existed in many families in the 1950s and used functionalism to imply that this division was adaptive, serving the needs of the family and society.

This functionalist bent entered sociology through the work of Emile Durkheim. Durkheim studied modern society and speculated that many kinds of behavior that society considers deviant or pathological may perform a socially useful role in bringing the larger group together. Later, sociologists who studied social deviance, like Erving Goffman, took Durkheim's ideas even further and suggested that social groups may *need* deviants for their stability or survival.

Before moving on, another sociological study bears mentioning because its findings closely paralleled and corroborated the function-of-the-symptom ideas of family therapists. Alfred Stanton and Morris Schwartz (1954) studied the interaction among patients and staff in a mental hospital. They noticed that patients were often caught in triangles in which one staff member tried to uphold the rules of the institution and didn't want patients to have any special treatment, while another staff member resented this rigidity and thought that rules should be flexible enough to accommodate individual needs. A patient who stumbled into this polarization became the battlefield over which this staff conflict was played out, and immediately had a permissive ally pitted against a restrictive antagonist. The more the one staff member protected the patient, the more the other would punish him or her, and the whole hospital unit might be pulled into the escalating polarization, forced to take sides. As the tension mounted, the patient became increasingly disruptive on the unit. Stanton and Schwartz's description of this triangular process is remarkably similar to the process of *triangulation* or *cross-generational coalition* that family therapists were reporting.

Functionalist Influence in Family Therapy

Family therapists took the functionalist notion that deviant behavior may serve a protective function for a social group and applied it to the symptoms of family members. Initially their view of a family's "identified patient" was similar to Stanton and Schwartz's view of the patient in the hospital. The family's "identified patient" was a scapegoat, a victim on whom the other family members focused, or over whom they fought, to avoid having to deal with each other. Later, family therapists suspected that many of these scapegoats were active volunteers for the position. It was thought that these "symptom-bearers" were willingly sacrificing their own welfare for the greater good. This idea that a symptom served a function for the family became a cornerstone of family therapy theory that, more recently, has been challenged and will be discussed in more detail in the next chapter.

To summarize functionalism's influence on family therapy, families were viewed as living organisms that needed to survive or thrive, but also had to adapt to their environment. The behavior and traits of the family organism were examined in this context to see how they helped the family adapt or better meet its needs. Symptoms were viewed as signs that the family wasn't adapting well to its environment or was, for some reason, unable to meet its needs. Descriptions and techniques based on these assumptions can be found throughout the family therapy literature. Functionalism has proven useful in understanding how families try to adapt but, like Darwin, functionalists saw the environment as a given that the organism must fit into, and, consequently, turned the field's attention away from questioning whether the environment that the family was trying to adapt to was healthy. Thus, functionalism could be used to support a conservative political agenda.

General Systems Theory

Ludwig von Bertalanffy was a prominent biologist who began to wonder if the laws that applied to biological organisms might also apply to other areas, from the human mind to the global ecosphere. He developed a model that was mistranslated from the German as General Systems Theory (GST), the last word of which he intended to have been "teaching," because it is not so much a theory as an approach, a way of thinking or a set of assumptions that can be applied to all kinds of systems (Davidson, 1983).

Bertalanffy published widely and had some influence on all the social sciences, but, unlike Bateson, had no extended direct contact with the pioneers of family therapy (although Dick Auerswald [1969] was excited by Bertalanffy's ideas and, in turn, strongly influenced Minuchin's thinking). In addition, as will be discussed later, Bertalanffy had a lifelong disdain for mechanism and was highly critical of cybernetics, the mechanistic systems approach that, through Bateson, came to dominate family therapy. Consequently, while many of the concepts of GST seem to have seeped into the family therapy literature, Bertalanffy's work is rarely cited, and where it is noted, it is often described as being basically the same as cybernetics (Bateson, 1971; Becvar & Becvar, 1988).

Part of Bertalanffy's obscurity may be because he was a generalist, spreading his ideas over the fields of medicine, psychiatry, psychology, sociology, history, education, philosophy, and biology, and also because GST is not a clear-cut theory with a list of testable hypotheses. Until Mark Davidson's thoughtful biography of Bertalanffy, *Uncommon Sense,* in 1983, there was no overview or summary of his voluminous work that could help us recognize the immensity of his contribution. In explaining Bertalanffy, we will draw heavily on Davidson's book, and recommend it to the reader. Davidson (1983) summarized Bertalanffy's definition of a system as:

> . . . any entity maintained by the mutual interaction of its parts, from atom to cosmos, and including such mundane examples as telephone, postal, and rapid transit systems. A Bertalanffian system can be physical

like a television set, biological like a cocker spaniel, psychological like a personality, sociological like a labor union, or symbolic like a set of laws . . . A system can be composed of smaller systems and can also be part of a larger system, just as a state or province is composed of smaller jurisdictions and also is part of a nation. Consequently, the same organized entity can be regarded as either a system or a subsystem, depending on the observer's focus of interest. (p. 26)

Bertalanffy pioneered the idea that a system was more than the sum of its parts, in the sense that a watch is more than a pile of machine parts or a piece of music is more than a cluster of notes. There is nothing mysterious or mystical about this assertion, just the idea that when things are organized into a pattern, something emerges out of the pattern and the relationship of the parts within it that is more or different, the way water emerges from the interaction of hydrogen and oxygen. Thus, Bertalanffy conveyed the importance of focusing on the pattern of relationships within a system or among systems rather than on the substance of their parts.

For these reasons, Bertalanffy believed that science had become far too *reductionistic* in its tendency to analyze phenomena by breaking whole systems up and studying their parts in isolation. While he believed that such analysis had a place in science and had led to certain advances, the study of whole systems had been grossly neglected and he urged scientists to learn to "think interaction" rather than striving to find and study the basic elements of a system.

Applied to family therapy, these ideas—that a family system should be seen as more than just a collection of people, and that therapists should focus on interaction among family members rather than individual qualities—became central tenets of the field.

Like the functionalists, Bertalanffy used the metaphor of an organism for social groups, but an organism that was an *open system*, continuously interacting with its environment. Open systems, in contrast to closed systems (which are nonliving), sustain themselves by continuously exchanging substances—for example, taking in food and oxygen and expelling carbon dioxide and nitrogenous waste—with their environment.

One difference in Bertalanffy's view of organisms from the functionalist perspective, implied in this open systems concept, is his emphasis on the importance of the relationship between an organism and its environment which, of course, includes other organisms, rather than seeing organisms as simply reactors to their environment. The mechanists didn't recognize that organisms don't just react to stimuli, they actively initiate creative efforts to enhance themselves.

Indeed, Bertalanffy was a life-long crusader against the mechanistic view of living systems, particularly of those living systems called people. He believed that, unlike machines, living organisms demonstrate *equifinality*,

. . . the ability of organisms to reach a given final goal from different initial conditions and in different ways. (In nonliving systems, the final state and the means to that state are fixed by the initial conditions.) He and other biologists used that term to identify the organism's inner-directed ability to protect or restore its wholeness, as in the human body's mobilization of antibodies and its ability to repair skin and bone. (Davidson, 1983, p. 77)

Thus, living organisms are creatively, spontaneously active, and can use many methods to maintain their organization, but are not solely motivated to maintain the status quo. As we will discuss later, family therapy picked up on the concept of *homeostasis*, that is the tendency of a system to regulate itself so as to maintain a constant internal environment in response to changes in external environment. This term, coined by French physiologist Claude Bernard in the nineteenth century to describe the regulation of such conditions as body temperature or blood sugar level, does describe some of the behavior of organisms, but Bertalanffy believed that an overemphasis on this reactive, homeostatic aspect of an organism reduced it to the level of a machine. Bertalanffy wrote that "If [this] principle of homeostatic maintenance is taken as a rule of behavior, the so-called well-adjusted individual will be [defined as] a well-oiled robot" (quoted in Davidson, p. 104). "In the sense of homeostasis, Michelangelo should have followed his father's advice and gone into the stone-cutting business. He would have had a much happier life than the one he led painting the Sistine Chapel in a very uncomfortable position" (quoted in Davidson, p. 127).

As we shall discuss later, homeostasis is a more central concept in cybernetics, which is the study of self-regulating systems like thermostats, endocrine systems, or guided missiles, than it is in GST. Homeostasis was introduced into family therapy by Don Jackson (1957), as a way to explain the tendency of families to resist change. While it remains a central concept in family therapy, its limited ability to account for the wide variety of human behavior has been repeatedly acknowledged by family therapists in ways that echo Bertalanffy's concerns (Hoffman, 1981; Speer, 1970; Dell, 1982). The cyberneticians had to propose new concepts like "morphogenesis" (Speer, 1970) to account for what Bertalanffy believed was simply a property of organisms—to seek, in addition to resist, change.

One of Bertalanffy's chief quarrels with the mechanistic view of people was that it led to valuelessness, a concern that foreshadowed the feminist critique of family therapy. If families are like machines, then we simply study how they work, determine how they become "dysfunctional," and repair the dysfunction. None of this requires that we evaluate the family's functional state or, for that matter, the culture in which it exists, in terms of inequity or violence.

For example, when a family mechanic encounters a rebellious adolescent daughter embedded in a striving American family, where father is never home because of his job and mother fights bitterly with the girl about her friends and her appearance, the mechanic might try to break the covert alliance between the father and daughter against mother and encourage father to support mother's attempts to discipline the girl. This structural repair might, at least temporarily, calm the situation and decrease the girl's defiance so that the family could become more "functional." But the therapist wouldn't have helped the family examine or question the effect of the father's job and the values associated with it on the health of the family members. A Bertalanffian therapist might encourage the family to weigh the economic benefits of father's job next to the effects of his lack of involvement with the family and high level of stress.

If you think ecologically, you can't avoid values because it becomes clear that certain values are ecological and others aren't, whether they're held by an individual, a family, a community, or a nation. A balance must exist among the parts of a system, and whenever one part strives for unrestrained growth or power, the system and those systems above and below it, will lose this healthy balance. Family therapists, by and large, have tried to remain value-free mechanics.

Bertalanffy sought to raise ecological and ethical questions at all levels of human endeavor because he saw that there are systems of belief that have as much or more power than systems of living beings. Thus, like the Bertalanffian therapist's questions to a family, the Bertalanffian politician would ask us to weigh the economic benefit of an industrial plant next to the long-term damage of its pollution. Thus, by underscoring our interconnectedness and the ecological impact of our decisions, Bertalanffy sought to broaden our loyalties beyond ourselves or our families or our nations to our planet, and in that sense he predated and influenced the environmental movement that emerged in the 1960s.

Bertalanffy's insistence on the importance of human belief systems also predated the recent shift in family therapy's focus from behavior to belief, a shift that will be discussed in Chapter 3. Bertalanffy's emphasis on values and beliefs, like family therapy's, is the result in part of his understanding of the inadequacies of *logical positivism,* the philosophy that has dominated western science since the nineteenth century.

Logical positivism holds that the only valid data are those derived from observations that can be empirically verified. This paradigm divorced science from philosophy or ethics with the assumption that only through empirical science can we truly know reality. Logical positivism and its assumptions about our ability to know reality was wounded by the discovery in physics earlier this century that subatomic particles didn't really exist, in the sense that we are used to thinking about things existing. Fritzjov Capra (1982), whose book *The Turning Point* provides a good overview of systems thinking among the sciences, describes the discovery this way: "At the subatomic level, matter does not exist with certainty at definite places, but rather shows 'tendencies to exist' . . . subatomic particles have no meaning as isolated entities but can be understood only as interconnections, or correlations, between various processes of observation and measurement" (p. 80). Thus, it seems that there are no elementary particles to be found and analyzed. This discovery, captured by the famous Heisenberg uncertainty principle, led theorists in many fields to question the absolutist position on reality.

To counter logical positivism, Bertalanffy (1968) used the term "perspectivism" to characterize his belief that while reality exists, the reality we *know* can never be fully objective because our view of it is filtered through our particular perspective. To a man with a hammer, everything looks like a nail. To a physicist, a table is a collection of electrons. A chemist sees the same table as organic compounds, the biologist sees a set of wood cells, and the art historian sees a baroque object. To Bertalanffy, all those views have some validity, but each is incomplete and none should be seen as more authentic than the others.

Bertalanffian perspectivism is quite similar to a philosophy, derived from Kant, known as *constructivism,* that recently had a major impact on family therapy and will be discussed further in Chapter 3. In fact the following Bertalanffian quote might just as well have come from Paul Watzlawick or any of the other constructivist writers that have influenced, in particular, the strategic or brief family therapies.

> There are no facts flying around in nature as if they are butterflies that you put into a nice orderly collection. Our cognition is not a mirroring of ultimate reality but rather is an active process, in which we create models of the world. These models direct what we actually see, what we consider as fact. (quoted in Davidson, p. 214)

Bertalanffy also recognized that the act of observation has an effect on the phenomena being observed. This awareness strengthened his perspectivist conviction that one should be humble about one's observations and theories, rather than believing that they are the absolute truth, so as to keep one's mind open to valuable new ideas.

Some family therapists have interpreted constructivism to mean that since no one has the corner on absolute reality, any interpretation is as valid as any other and, therefore, the therapist is free to "reframe" reality in any way he or she wants as long as the family seems to buy the reframe and it produces a change (Duncan & Solovey, 1989). In all likelihood, Bertalanffy would have objected to this relativistic position. Instead, he believed the opposite: that our inability to know absolute reality implies that we should be increasingly concerned with values and assumptions because some perspectives are far more ecologically destructive than others. This implies that therapists should carefully scrutinize their own values and those of their theories, and should not become too attached to the truth or objectivity of their observations. Bertalanffy had this to say to the theorists and philosophers of the world: "It is we who, in the last resort, manufacture the glasses through which people look at the world and at themselves—little as they may know it . . . I dare say we are the great spectacle makers in history" (quoted in Davidson, p. 69).

To summarize, Bertalanffy anticipated many of the concepts and issues that have shaped and are still shaping family therapy:

- concept of a system as more than the sum of its parts;
- emphasis on interaction within and among systems versus reductionism;
- human systems as ecological organisms versus mechanism;
- concept of equifinality;
- homeostatic reactivity versus spontaneous activity;
- importance of ecological beliefs and values versus valuelessness;
- perspectivism or constructivism versus logical positivism.

Many of these issues will reappear in the ensuing discussion of cybernetics and throughout the book.

Cybernetics of Families

Cybernetics was developed and named (from the Greek word for helmsman) by Norbert Weiner, a mathematician at MIT. During World War II, Weiner was asked to work on the problem of how to get guns to hit moving targets. From that work he expanded his ideas about cybernetic systems—that is, systems that are self-correcting—to the way people or animals operate.

At the core of cybernetics is the concept of the *feedback loop,* the process by which a system gets information necessary to self-correct in its effort to maintain a steady state or move toward a preprogrammed goal. This feedback may be information regarding the system's performance relative to its external environment or regarding the relationship among the system's parts. Feedback loops can be *negative* or *positive*. This distinction refers to the effect they have on deviations from a steady, homeostatic state within the system, not to whether they are beneficial or not. *Negative feedback* reduces deviation or change; *positive feedback* amplifies it.

Because cybernetics developed out of the study of machines, where positive feedback loops led to destructive "runaways" in which the machinery would break down, the emphasis was on negative feedback and the maintenance of homeostasis in the face of change. The system's environment would change— the temperature outside a house would go up or down exceeding a certain temperature range—and this change would trigger the negative feedback mechanisms to bring the system back to homeostasis—the air-conditioning or heat would go on.

As applied to families, cybernetics focused attention on several phenomena: (1) *family rules*, which govern the range of behaviors that the family system can tolerate (i.e., the family's homeostatic range); (2) *negative feedback* processes that families use to enforce those rules (e.g., guilt, double messages, symptoms); (3) *sequences of family interaction* around a problem that characterize the system's reaction to it (i.e., the feedback loops around a deviation); and (4) what happens when the system's traditional negative feedback is ineffective, triggering *positive feedback loops*.

For example, in a family with a low threshhold for the overt expression of anger, Johnny, the adolescent son, blows up at his parents over their insistence that he not stay out past curfew. Mother is shocked and begins to cry. Father is outraged and responds by grounding Johnny for a month. Rather than reducing Johnny's deviation—bringing his anger back within homeostatic limits—this negative feedback from the parents produces the opposite effect. Johnny explodes and challenges their authority. They respond with more of the same crying and punishing, which further escalates Johnny's anger, and so on. In this way the parents' original negative feedback (crying and punishing) becomes positive feedback in the sense that it begins to amplify rather than diminish his deviation. The family is caught in a positive feedback "runaway," otherwise known as a vicious cycle, that threatens to break up the family, much as positive feedback loops, if unabated, cause cybernetic machines to break down.

Later, cyberneticians like Walter Buckley and Ross Ashby recognized that positive feedback loops aren't all bad and can help systems adjust to changed circumstances if they don't get out of hand. Thus, Johnny's family needed to recalibrate their rules for anger to accommodate an adolescent's increased assertiveness. The crisis that this positive feedback loop produced could lead to a reexamination of the family's rules, if the family could step out of the loop long enough to get some perspective. In so doing they would be *metacommunicating,* that is communicating about their ways of communicating, a process that can lead to a change in communication rules (Satir, 1972). This recognition that positive feedback loops can lead to change paved the conceptual foundation for some of the crisis-inducing forms of family therapy like the Milan (Chapter 10) or structural (Chapter 5) models. As Haley (1971) suggested, "If a treatment program subdues and stabilizes the family, change is more difficult.... To change a stabilized, miserable situation and create space for individual growth of family members, the therapists often must induce a crisis which creates instability" (p. 8).

Such a change in family rules is what cybernetically-oriented family therapists strive for and call *second-order change,* to distinguish it from *first-order change,* in which the family changes some behaviors but those behaviors are still governed by the same rules (Watzlawick, Weakland, & Fisch, 1974). For example, Johnny's family may shift the focus of their disagreements from his curfew to his sister's boyfriend (first-order change), yet their patterns around the issues would not change drastically because their stifling rules regarding anger (second-order) remain unchanged. Faulty or unclear communication results in inaccurate or incomplete feedback so the system cannot self-correct (change its rules) and, consequently, overreacts or underreacts to change.

Cybernetics was introduced to family therapy by Gregory Bateson. Bateson encountered Weiner and cybernetics shortly after World War II during the Macy Conferences, a series of gatherings of high-level thinkers from diverse disciplines who tried to apply their theories to problems in a variety of fields. Bateson became interested in the feedback processes of systems and pioneered a conceptual shift that has become central to family systems thinking, the shift from linear to *circular causality.*

Before the advent of family therapy, explanations of psychopathology were based on linear models—medical, psychodynamic, and behavioral. In all of these, etiology was conceived in terms of prior events—disease, emotional conflict, or learning history—which caused symptoms in the present. Using the concept of circularity, Bateson helped us change the way we think about psychopathology, from something caused by events in the past to something that's a part of ongoing, circular feedback loops.

The concept of linear causality is based on a Newtonian model, in which the universe is like a billiard table where the balls act unidirectionally on each other. Bateson believed that while linear causality was useful for describing the nonliving world of forces and objects, it was a poor model for the world of living things, because it neglects to account for communication and relationships as well as force, as illustrated by the example of the man kicking a dog.

In addition to observable circular feedback loops, Bateson was also interested in how messages are interpreted by those receiving them. The mechanistic cyberneticians believed one could understand systems simply by studying their behavioral inputs and outputs and, in that sense, as Bertalanffy asserted, they were basically behaviorists but with the addition of the feedback loop. Bateson, however, didn't limit his interest to behavioral sequences, but studied the meaning that people derived from communication and its context.

When they began to study families directly the Bateson group split into two camps (Haley, 1981; Simon, 1982). On one side was Bateson, continuing to focus on the way the receiver of communication processes it, and interested in the way individuals learn and perceive. On the other side, Haley and Weakland were taken by the cybernetic metaphor and wanted to focus exclusively on the observable interaction patterns among family members.

The Bateson project ended in 1962 and Bateson shifted his interests away from psychiatric phenomena. The legacy of the project to psychotherapy was left to the other Bateson project and MRI members who (with the exception of Satir) advanced the mechanistic notions of homeostasis and feedback loops, keeping a logical positivistic focus on observable behavior sequences, and ignoring for the most part Bateson's concerns about the individual's perception and learning (Breunlin, Schwartz, & Mac Kune-Karrer, 1992). These theorists borrowed the "black box" metaphor to justify their mechanistic position:

> The impossibility of seeing the mind "at work" has in recent years led to the adoption of the Black Box concept from the field of telecommunication. . . . The concept is more generally applied to the fact that electronic hardware is by now so complex that it is sometimes more expedient to disregard the internal structure of a device and concentrate on the study of its specific input-output relations. . . . This concept, if applied to psychological and psychiatric problems, has the heuristic advantage that no ultimately unverifiable intrapsychic hypotheses need to be invoked, and that one can limit oneself to observable input-output relations, that is, to communication. (Watzlawick, Beavin, & Jackson, 1967, pp. 43–44)

Viewing people as black boxes seems the ultimate expression of the mechanistic tendencies that Bertalanffy lamented. But this metaphor had the behavioristic advantage of simplifying one's field of study by eliminating concerns about the mind and emotions of the individual as well as the history of the family. In addition, one could judge the outcome of therapy equally simply—if the problem was solved, the system returned to a functional state, the outcome was positive, and therapy could end. Hence the evolution of brief, strategic therapy.

Power and Control

Another important rift developed in this group that by the early 1960s was theorizing from the Mental Research Institute (MRI) in Palo Alto. Haley believed that these black boxes were wired to move in a certain direction; that is, that people's communication was motivated by the desire to control each other. His first law of relationships states that "when one person indicates a change in relation to another, the other will act upon the first so as to diminish and modify that change" (Haley, 1963, p. 189). Bateson strongly objected to the use of power and control metaphors, and the other family cyberneticians at the MRI strove to avoid imputing any motivation to people's behavior and instead to simply observe feedback loops (Haley, 1981).

Haley's view of social behavior as attempts to control others led him, more than any other family therapy pioneer, to maintain the functionalist legacy from anthropology and sociology described earlier. It should be noted that Haley's position regarding control has shifted over the years. He now believes that the underlying motive for attempts to control others is love rather than power. He has also become less attached to the reality of his functionalist assumptions and now sees them as useful clinical hypotheses rather than as explanations of actual family processes. Nonetheless, therapists who use the brand of strategic therapy developed by Haley and his later collaborator, Cloe Madanes, search for the function that a symptom serves, not only for the symptom-bearer, but also for the family.

Considering Haley's interest in interpersonal control, it's not surprising that he was also drawn to hypnosis. During the years of the Bateson project, as the emphasis shifted from research to therapy, Haley, along with John Weakland, began visiting Phoenix to study with the well-known hypnotherapist, Milton Erickson. Haley (1985) reports, "As we sought consultation and supervision, Dr. Erickson was the only person who could advise us on interview technique with couples and families" (p. 32).

Bateson had strong reservations about psychotherapy and was wary of changing systems in general. Haley remembers that:

> Bateson was an anthropologist to his soul and an anthropologist doesn't believe you should tamper with the data or change it in any way. . . . After I met Erickson and began to go into a very directive style of therapy in which you produce a change, Bateson got more and more uncomfortable, particularly when I began describing the therapy relationship as a struggle for control or power. (Simon, 1982, p. 22)

Thus, with the exception of Bateson himself, the interests of Bateson Project members were shifting from studying people's behavior in context to using people's interpersonal context to influence their behavior, and Erickson was a master at manipulating interpersonal contexts.

Haley (1985) again explains, "At that time we were studying communication, focusing on how messages are classified and the paradoxes that occur when levels of messages conflict. Erickson's work was replete with deliberate use of paradox" (p. 32; see Chapter 10 for more on using paradox and Erickson's influence on technique). Thus, through Erickson these researchers-cum-therapists were introduced to a wide array of powerful and unorthodox techniques, including such famous maneuvers as paradoxical directives, reframing, and using the client's language, that they applied to families. Paul Watzlawick has suggested that the MRI model (see Chapter 10) of brief therapy is essentially an elaboration of Erickson's techniques (Bogdan, 1983).

Erickson's beliefs about people had a strong impact on family therapy, countering some of the pessimistic assumptions from cybernetics. Haley

(1985) relates that "As we applied the notion [of homeostasis] to families in therapy, it took the form of resistance to change. When we offered these ideas to Dr. Erickson, he responded with polite irritation. He thought, correctly I believe, that a theory that encouraged the notion that people resist change was a noxious theory for a therapist, since expecting resistance encourages it" (p. 32). Erickson's optimistic view of people—that they wanted to change and possessed the resources to do so—was, perhaps, his most important contribution to the family therapy movement. At a time when the psychotherapy establishment was extremely pessimistic about change and was long term, interpretive, nondirective, and highly suspicious of symptom removal, Erickson's approach was optimistic, brief, directive, problem-focused, and, at times, included the client's family or others in treatment (Bogdan, 1983). Erickson offered Haley, Weakland, and their colleagues in Palo Alto, an antidote to all the things they didn't like about psychoanalysis, and to the pessimism of the homeostatic model.

From Cybernetics to Structure

Haley's interest in power led him to focus on the hierarchy, or generational power structure, of families. He pioneered the understanding of child problems as being the result of coalitions that cross the boundary between children and parents, much like the stressful coalitions that crossed the line of authority between patients and staff in Stanton and Schwartz's mental hospital. With these concepts of hierarchy and boundary, Haley's interest was moving toward the structure of families rather than just their communication circuits. In 1967 he left the MRI and joined the founders of structural family therapy, Salvador Minuchin and Braulio Montalvo at the Philadelphia Child Guidance Clinic.

In contrast to the focus of the family cyberneticians at MRI, structural family theory owes a debt to the organismic (Bertalanffy and cellular biology) and structural-functional (Malinowski, Radcliffe-Brown, Levi-Strauss, and Parsons) trends in the social sciences mentioned earlier. The family is viewed as an organism, an open system, made up of subsystems each of which is surrounded by a semipermeable *boundary,* which is really a set of rules governing who is included within that subsystem and how they interact with those outside it.

To appreciate structural family therapy's functionalist heritage, consider this passage by Talcott Parsons (Parsons & Bales, 1955):

That the [nuclear family] is itself a subsystem of a larger system is of course a sociological commonplace. But to break it in turn down into subsystems is a less familiar way of looking at it. Yet we will treat the family in this way and say that, in certain crucially important respects, the very young child does not participate in, is not fully a "member," of his whole family, but only of a subsystem of it, the mother-child subsystem. The marriage pair constitute another subsystem as may, for certain purposes, also the child with all his siblings, all the males in the family, all the females, etc. In fact, any combination of two or more members as differentiated from one or more other members may be treated as a social system which is a subsystem of the family as a whole. (p. 37)

Thus, as early as 1955, families were viewed in this structural way—as having subsystems with boundaries separating them.

According to structural theory, a healthy structure for the family organism requires clear boundaries, particularly generational boundaries. Unclear boundaries (overly rigid or overly diffuse) create a dysfunctional family structure, one manifestation of which is the symptomatic family member. If the structural flaw is corrected, the family organism will return to health (Bertalanffian equifinality).

Thus where the family cyberneticians saw circular interactions maintaining problems, structural family therapists saw boundary violations resulting in inappropriate alliances and coalitions. Where family cyberneticians were interested in the temporal (tracking sequences over time), structural family therapists were interested in the spatial (the proximity of family members to one another).

Concerns with generational boundaries and the importance of the proper functioning of the parental subsystem predate Minuchin's creative application of these ideas to family treatment. Theodore Lidz (1963), who frequently cited his debt to functionalist sociologist Talcott Parsons, said in a lecture in 1961, "Failure to achieve a parental coalition will often lead to infractions of the generation boundaries within the family" (p. 62). Lidz elaborated that violations of this boundary lead to the entanglement of the child in the parent's struggle. "Often, the child becomes a scapegoat. His difficulties are magnified into the major source of dissent between the parents, and he comes to feel responsible for it. At times, the child falls in with the assignment and obliges by creating further unhappiness that masks the friction between the parents" (p. 57).

The structural perspective can be best characterized by this premise: that the key to changing an individual is to change his or her context—the network of relationships in which the individual is embedded. A related assumption within this philosophy is that, no matter how incompetent or pathological a family member appears, an improvement in family structure will elicit a more competent "partial self" of that family member which, in turn, will reinforce the family change. Thus, the structural view of people is essentially optimistic.

To summarize our speculations on the development of structural family therapy, it seems that in his struggle to find a model effective with a disadvantaged population, Minuchin borrowed the Bertalanffian view of systems as open and organismic and the Parsonian concepts of structure and emphasis on generational boundaries, concepts that were in the social science air at that time and had been adopted to varying degrees by more psychoanalytically oriented family theorists such as Lidz and Ackerman. Minuchin, however, deleted the psychoanalytic aspects of their theories and techniques, and, in the process of experimenting with action-oriented techniques, discovered the power of an individual's external context as well as ways to harness that power.

In so doing, Minuchin provided the first clear map to understanding and reorganizing families, a map that was received as a godsend by the legions of bewildered therapists who were lost amid a confusing jungle of family entanglements. As a therapist and a speaker, Minuchin was charismatic, dramatic, and authoritative at a time when the field was hungry for dynamic leadership. He was the street fighter who would stand up to the psychiatric establishment, eventually armed with outcome data that could not be dismissed. For all these reasons, structural family therapy became the most popular and influential brand of family therapy in the 1970s.

Satir's Humanizing Effect

Family therapy is often associated with the concept of hierarchy because of its emphasis on motivating parents to become effective disciplinarians. Through the work of Minuchin and Haley, that disciplinary power, or authority aspect of hierarchy has been the primary focus of systems-based family therapists, including the MRI family cyberneticians. Virginia Satir was the only family therapy pioneer to promote and focus on the other side of family leadership. She was devoted to getting parents to be more affectionate and loving to each other and to their children, in addition to being more firm.

As an early member of MRI, Satir was exposed to the same functionalist and cybernetic influences that produced Watzlawick and Weakland and Haley's version of strategic therapy. Thus, her theorizing included the idea that children's symptoms can serve the function of distracting from an unhappy marriage and that communication is the key to family process. Satir's philosophy of therapy, however, was very different. She brought some yin into what was becoming an overly yang field through her involvement with the human potential movement pioneered by Abraham Maslow and Carl Rogers.

In contrast to the MRI model's view of people as cybernetic black boxes, Haley's view of people as power-game players, and Minuchin's view of people as context reactors, Satir saw people as motivated by the need for self-esteem, that is to feel good about themselves and to get close to others. "The critical factor in what happens both inside and between people is the picture of individual worth that each person carries around with him" (Satir, 1972, p. 21). Her interest in promoting the self-esteem of each family member led her to maintain a focus on the humanity of individuals at a time when her contemporaries were actively ignoring individual feelings in their struggle to understand families.

Her humanistic orientation led Satir to try to change families into incubators for the positive, loving qualities that she believed to be at the core of every family member. Thus, her interest in family communication was not so much to track and break the dysfunctional interaction sequences that surrounded a problem, but instead to encourage family members to drop their protective masks and to discover and express their real feelings.

To illustrate the differences between Satir and the other models, suppose a father says angrily to his teenaged daughter, "You can't go out tonight!" The MRI cyberneticians might see this as the beginning of an escalating positive feedback loop; Haley might hear the command message of "I am in control of you; I am still one-up in relation to you" beneath the father's outburst; and Minuchin might hear the father's anger as a reaction to a mother-daughter coalition that renders him powerless. Satir, on the other hand, might hear the father as wanting but afraid to say, "I want you to stay home tonight because I miss you and feel you slipping away from me."

The father doesn't speak openly about his love because he's afraid of being rejected, which would be a blow to his self-esteem. If the father could be honest, however, his daughter would have a chance to express her mixed feelings about growing up and away from him, and they'd both feel better about themselves for having leveled with each other. Thus, Satir believed that the relationship between self-esteem and communication was circular. Low self-esteem begets protective, incongruent communication, which elicits similarly protective communication from others, which, in turn, engenders low self-esteem, and so on. Fortunately, however, the cycle can be virtuous as well as vicious: honest communication engenders high self-esteem, which encourages more honesty and so on (Satir, 1972, 1988).

The key to increasing self-worth is direct, straight-from-the-heart communication. To achieve this, therapists must be able to create an atmosphere within sessions that allows family members to feel safe and accepted so they will risk this kind of openness. The therapist must be able to challenge people without threatening their self-esteem, and so must be a model of honesty and acceptance.

To summarize, Satir deviated from the norms established by the systems theorists in Palo Alto. She focused on nurturance where they were interested in control and feedback loops. She was concerned with the experience of individual family members where the others believed that such a focus distracted from seeing interactional patterns. She worked to improve communication and self-esteem where her male colleagues remained problem-focused. She generated and advocated a close, collaborative relationship with clients where the others maintained an air of distant authority. While Satir was seen by many of these theorists as touchy-feely and naive, it may be that she was ahead of her time.

Bowen and Differentiation of Self

Up to this point all of the seminal family therapy theorists described—the MRI group, Haley, Minuchin, and Satir—had at least indirect contact with Bateson and his cybernetic/functionalist perspective. Despite the differences among them, they all had in common an interest in changing ongoing interaction patterns of the primary family system, which they generally viewed as the nuclear family, rather than the family-of-origin. Murray Bowen, the last family therapy pioneer we will consider here, evolved a version of systems theory apart from this cybernetic/functional influence, so his ideas are quite different from these other models. To bolster the originality of his ideas, Bowen (1978) wrote,

> There are those who believe family systems theory [the name he originally gave to what is now known as Bowen theory] was developed from general systems theory. Back in the 1940s, I attended one lecture by Bertalanffy, which I did not understand, and another by Norbert Weiner, which was perhaps a little more understandable. . . . The degree to which I

heard something in those lectures that influenced my later thinking is debatable. (p. 359)

What did influence Bowen's ideas was the biological sciences, hence the compatibility with GST. In describing his reasons for looking to biology, Bowen (1978) said:

> On the premise that psychiatry might eventually become a recognized science, perhaps a generation or two in the future, and being aware of the past conceptual problems of psychoanalysis [that used metaphors from literature and hydraulics] . . . I therefore chose to use only concepts that would be consistent with biology and the natural sciences. It was easy to think in terms of the familiar concepts of chemistry, physics, and mathematics, but I carefully excluded all concepts that dealt with inanimate things. . . . The concept of differentiation was chosen because it has specific meaning in the biological sciences. When we speak of "differentiation of self," we mean a process similar to the differentiation of cells from each other. The same applies to the term fusion. (p. 354)

Initially, Bowen was struck by the amount of *fusion* between schizophrenic patients and their mothers; that is, that they were highly emotionally reactive to each other. He later noticed that this was the case with the whole family and coined the phrase *undifferentiated family ego mass* to suggest that, because of their emotional reactivity, the whole family was like one undifferentiated cell. Similarly, he found that each family member had a low level of *differentiation of self;* that is, their emotions overwhelmed their intellect to the point that they reacted automatically and impulsively. Thus, the goal of Bowen therapy became the differentiation of self of key family members such that they could help differentiate the whole family.

This emphasis on differentiation, meaning control of reason over emotion, betrays Bowen's psychoanalytic roots. Freud's famous dictum "Where id is, there ego shall be," fits differentiation quite well. Indeed, Bowen (1978) saw the emotional system as "an intimate part of man's phylogenetic past which he shares with all lower forms of life," while the intellectual system was "a function of the cerebral cortex which appeared last in man's evolutionary development and is the main difference between man and the lower forms of life" (p. 356).

In contrast to the optimistic position taken by many of the other family therapy pioneers, Bowen saw a person's level of differentiation as a relatively fixed trait that took a long time to change. He also believed that about 90 percent of the population is not well differentiated. In this judgment, too, we hear Freud's echo.

The theory of evolution reappears in Bowen's speculations about how people arrive at a level of differentiation. He called this the *multigenerational transmission process* and believed that most children emerge from their families with the same level of differentiation that their parents had, while some emerge with lower and some with higher levels. Thus the transmission of differentiation follows a "genetic-like pattern" (Bowen, 1978, p. 410) across generations.

With these beliefs about people, it's understandable that Bowen was less interested in family communication patterns than were the other theorists. He saw the quality of communication in a family as the product of each family member's level of differentiation. Consequently, communication is unlikely to change lastingly until differentiation levels change. Along these lines, Bowen (1978) asserted that while approaches that work with the whole family to improve their communication "can produce dramatic shifts in the feeling system, and even a period of exhilaration . . . [but] I have not been able to use this as a long-term method for resolving underlying problems" (p. 151).

Like the other family therapy pioneers, Bowen believed that child problems were related to the parents' marriage and, in his theory, the concept of triangles is central. He saw the forming of triangles as a natural human tendency in the face of anxiety. That is, when a two-person relationship, particularly where those two people are not highly differentiated, experiences stress, a third person will become involved. "The twosome might 'reach out' and pull in the other person, the emotions might 'overflow' to the third person, or the third person might be emotionally programmed to initiate the involvement. With the involvement of the third person, the anxiety level decreases" (Bowen, 1978, p. 400). From this we can see that Bowen made many of the same function-of-the-symptom observations that became the centerpiece of other models, but, like the psychoanalysts, he saw these patterns as manifestations of an underlying process that had to be changed, rather than as direct targets of change.

Instead he believed that if people became educated to the existence of the emotional triangling process within their nuclear and extended families, and learned to avoid being pulled into it, they would gradually differentiate. Bowen's interest in the evolution of levels of differentiation made him one of the few pioneers who paid much attention to a family's history. This was one area where he differed from Freud, because Bowen's focus was not on a client's childhood trauma or early relationships, instead it was on the multigenerational history of the extended family. In this interest in family history, Bowen also differentiated from the other pioneers, most of whom viewed history as an explanatory background for problems in a family's current structure or feedback loops.

Family Life Cycle

The concept of the *family life cycle* was borrowed from sociology to become this explanatory background to the structural and strategic approaches. Sociologists Evelyn Duvall and Reuben Hill began applying a developmental framework to families in the 1940s that is characterized by dividing a family's development into discrete stages with different tasks to be performed at each stage (Duvall, 1957, 1977; Hill & Rodgers, 1964). Duvall's eight stages of family development set the tone, although later theorists have come up with different frameworks by adding or subtracting stages (Solomon, 1973; Barnhill & Longo, 1978).

Family therapists Betty Carter and Monica McGoldrick (1980) enriched this framework by adding a multigenerational point of view and by considering stages of divorce and remarriage. Their book, *The Family Life Cycle,* with

TABLE 2.1 Duvall's Stages of the Family Life Cycle

Stage	Developmental tasks
1. Married couples without children.	Establishing a mutually satisfying marriage. Adjusting to pregnancy and the promise of parenthood. Fitting into the kin network.
2. Childbearing families (oldest child birth–30 months).	Having, adjusting to, and encouraging the development of infants. Establishing a satisfying home for both parents and infants.
3. Families with preschool children (oldest child 2½–6 years).	Adapting to the critical needs and interests of preschool children in stimulating, growth-promoting ways. Coping with energy depletion and lack of privacy.
4. Families with children (oldest child 6–13 years).	Fitting into the community of school-age families. Encouraging children's educational achievement.
5. Families with teenagers (oldest child 13–20 years).	Balancing freedom with responsibility. Establishing postparental interests and careers.
6. Families launching young adults (first child gone to last child's leaving home).	Releasing young adults with appropriate rituals and assistance. Maintaining a supportive home base.
7. Middle-aged parents (empty nest to retirement).	Rebuilding the marriage relationship. Maintaining kin ties with older and younger generations.
8. Aging family members (retirement to death of both spouses).	Coping with bereavement and living alone. Closing the family home or adapting it to aging. Adjustment to retirement.

chapters on the various stages, greatly popularized the family life cycle concept within family therapy. Their second edition (Carter & McGoldrick, 1989) updates the developments in this area over the decade. Other family therapists injected systems ideas into the family life cycle framework so that the transitions between stages are not so discrete and the family as a whole can be characterized. Lee Combrinck-Graham (1983, 1985, 1988) views the three-generational family as alternating between centrifugal and centripetal states as events in their life cycle alternately call for more interdependence or individuation among family members. Douglas Breunlin's (1983, 1988; Breunlin,

Schwartz, & Mac Kune-Karrer, 1992) oscillation theory provides a sophisticated understanding of the transitions among family or individual life cycle stages. Breunlin demonstrates how such transitions are never discontinuous shifts but instead occur as gradual oscillations between stages or levels of functioning.

Like so many other new ideas, the concept of the family life cycle was first introduced to family therapy by Jay Haley (1973) who, in his book *Uncommon Therapy,* also presented Milton Erickson to the field. Haley saw symptoms as the result of a family becoming stuck at a transition between life cycle stages because the family was unable or afraid to make the transition. Later Haley (1980) focused on one particular life cycle stuck-point in his book *Leaving Home,* which provided strategies for working with families having difficulty launching their young adults.

The formulations of Minuchin (1974; Minuchin & Fishman, 1981) were also influenced by the life cycle concept. The structural model contained many of the ideas from sociology regarding stages and tasks, but couched in terms of the development of various subsystems within the family system and changes in hierarchy and parenting style as children mature. Problems develop when a family with a dysfunctional structure encounters a transition point to another stage and, because of their structural problems, cannot make the transition adequately.

The MRI group (Watzlawick et al., 1974) also used the life cycle in their theory of problem formation. Life cycle transitions present a family with predictable difficulties which become problems because of the family's ill-fated attempted solutions. They used this life cycle understanding as a way to reframe the family's problem as normal rather than pathological.

As we will discuss in the next chapter, this use of historical, life cycle material as a reframe for current family problems was expanded by the Milan Associates, who would explore a family's history in some detail to find information with which to build a "positive connotation" of each family member's behavior. In addition, the Milan Associates pioneered the use of *family rituals* for facilitating the transitions between life cycle stages. The use of ritual in family therapy was later elaborated on and has become a prominent interest of many family therapists (Imber-Black, Roberts, & Whiting, 1989).

For reasons discussed above, Bowen was less interested in the life cycle of a nuclear family than the longer-term development of the parents' extended family. Other psychodynamically-oriented family therapists, however, proposed family life cycle models that were influenced by psychoanalytic models of individual development. According to these theorists the development of families can become fixated or arrested at earlier stages, just as it can with individuals (Wachtel & Wachtel, 1986; Skynner, 1981; Paul, 1969; Barnhill & Longo, 1978). The goal becomes to help families recognize and work through these developmental arrests by, for example, mourning unresolved loss.

In summary, most of the schools of family therapy have at least paid lip service to the concept of the family life cycle in their theorizing, if not in their therapy. Structural and strategic therapists, with their primary interest in changing current family processes, did not see much value in accompanying the family in historical investigations, other than to find life cycle information with which to "normalize" the problems. Thus, the major schools have not taken the concept far beyond the original sociological frameworks. Others have refined and improved the thinking about the family life cycle and, while there remains little consensus as to the best way to use the concept, it has received renewed interest and more sophisticated treatment recently (Falicov, 1988; Pittman, 1987; Carter & McGoldrick, 1989).

SUMMARY OF CONCEPTUAL INFLUENCES

To summarize the conceptual influences on the field, each of these pioneers was faced with the same set of questions for which there were no previous answers:

- How do families operate?
- How do families develop?
- What is the difference between healthy and pathological families?
- What is the relationship between a family member's symptom and the family's operation?
- How can families change the way they operate?
- Why do families sometimes resist taking obvious steps toward improvement?

As we have seen, despite the similarity of many of their initial observations, the pioneers' answers to these questions varied enormously, and the therapeutic techniques derived from their answers varied even more. This variation is due in part to differences among the metaphors or conceptual traditions to which each pioneer turned for help. We have seen the influence of a panoply of disparate ideas on the development of the field: functionalism and structuralism, General Systems Theory, Ericksonian hypnotherapy, cybernetics and Bateson's interpretation of it, communication theory, the humanistic movement, cell biology and evolutionary theory, family life cycle theory from sociology, and psychoanalysis.

Each of these traditions conveys a different view of the nature of people and how they can change. We agree with Bertalanffy's assertion that a theory's basic assumptions regarding the human personality will dictate, to a large degree, the practices of its adherents. Those who view people as mechanistic black boxes will try anything to alter the communications among those boxes, and do so from a position of distance, like the expert repairman. Those who understand people through a lens of power and see symptoms as control operations, also work from a strategic distance and develop strategies to diffuse the power of the symptom or the power arrangements in the family that made it necessary.

Those who see people as chameleon-like in the degree to which they change when family relationships change, use their own relationship with the family to change its structure and, consequently, work from a position of proximity. Those who believe people basically want intimacy and love, will get close to family members in order to help them feel and share tender feelings. Those who see people as dominated by irrational emotionality will create a reflective atmosphere in which clients learn to stay rational in the face of family upset.

In family therapy's attempt to focus on the system rather than the individuals who comprise it, these fundamental assumptions about people, at times, have not been clearly articulated. Given the degree to which the methods of each model of family therapy are driven by its basic view of people, we recommend that those assumptions be carefully examined when evaluating a model.

ENDURING CONCEPTS AND TECHNIQUES

In this chapter, we have explored the contextual factors that influenced the early development of family therapy, including the general nature of change within a field; free market influence relative to money and research; the personalities, cultural biases, and target populations of the pioneers; and the conceptual traditions from which they drew.

Given the complexity of these ideas, we will summarize what we believe to be the concepts and methods that endured from this early period and continue to shape the field.

The Importance of Family Context

For a long time, individual therapists recognized the importance of family influences in shaping the personality, but assumed that the internal representations of childhood events exerted a more powerful influence than ongoing family interactions. Consistent with this viewpoint, psychotherapists isolated patients from their natural environment in order to manipulate aspects of their internally organized behavior. Family therapists, on the contrary, believe that the dominant forces in personality development are located externally in current interactions in the family system. This is the fundamental premise of family therapy as an orientation: that people are products of their social context, and that any attempt to understand them must include an appreciation of their families.

A corollary of the family orientation is that the most effective way to treat people is to alter their family interactions. As a method, family therapy usually, but not always, involves bringing the whole family together for treatment. But even those therapists—for example, Bowen and strategic therapists—who don't necessarily meet with an entire family, design their interventions to affect family interactions.

In summary, context is central to family therapy in two ways. The first is related to understanding people and their problems—that they can best be understood when their family context is considered. The second is related to treatment—that changes in family context create powerful changes in people and their problems.

Dyads to Triads

In attempting to organize observations of family context, family therapy passed through a series of conceptual stages, from regarding individuals as the units of pathology, to dyadic and triadic models, and finally to models that tried to include the whole family's structure. Locating pathology in the individual personality didn't begin with psychoanalysis; it was always a natural way to think about psychological problems. If someone has a problem, something inside must be bothering them, right? This point of view has been maintained in Freudian theory, as well as in most other theories of psychotherapy. The *monadic* model was later extended by social psychiatrists and object relations theorists to include the dyadic concept of interlocking pathology or *object relations*. Behavior therapists also extended their view to include two people and how they reinforced each other.

Family therapists demonstrated that the dyad's relationship also reflects the influence of third parties. A boy's behavior depends on his relationship with his father and that, in turn, depends on father's relationship with his wife. As family therapy's view expanded to include more family members, the need increased for metaphors for understanding how groups of people interact.

Family Structure

The field borrowed metaphors of *subsystems* and *boundaries* from cell biology and functionalism in sociology. The idea that families can be understood best by assessing the boundaries around the various subsystems within them, with particular importance given to the boundaries between generations, has become a cornerstone of the field. There is an ideal level of permeability to the boundaries around a subsystem. When boundaries are too open, relationships are described as *enmeshed* or *fused,* and when boundaries are too closed, relationships are *disengaged* or *cut-off.* Therapists informed by these ideas are interested in who is close to or distant from whom in families and how to reorganize those alliances or coalitions.

Boundaries around the "executive subsystem," that is, the leadership in the family, are of particular import because the *hierarchy* of the family is seen as crucial to its well-being. Therapists concerned with family hierarchy assess how well those who are supposed to be leading the family, commonly the parents, are able to work together and how much children are being thrust into that position inappropriately, creating *incongruent hierarchies.*

Psychopathology as Serving a Function in Families

Severely disturbed families provide a magnified focus on processes that operate in all families, but are not always as easy to observe. Studies of the etiology of schizophrenia led to the conclusion that deviance wasn't necessarily negative, but that, on the contrary, symptoms made sense when seen in the light of their family contexts, and served a function in those families.

Another important finding was that often when the patient got better, someone else in the family got worse. This, and the tenacity with which some families seemed to resist change, led Jackson to coin the term *family homeostasis.* The concept of homeostasis emphasized the sanctions that family members imposed on each other, referred to as *negative feedback,* to keep the system from changing.

Eventually, most schools of family therapy subscribed in one way or another to the idea that a family member's problems may somehow be functional for the larger system. The idea was that when a family dyad is stressed they will "triangulate" a third person to diffuse the stress. That person may become the object of concern or criticism, and may actively seek the distractive role or have it imposed on him or her. Following this logic, symptoms become *homeostatic mechanisms*, or ways to help the system avoid threatening changes. As we discuss in the next chapter, these concepts of homeostasis and the need of families for symptoms have been reexamined and challenged as the field develops, but they still exert a powerful influence.

Circular Sequences of Interaction

Our language trains us to think *linearly*, that is, to think that there is a specific cause for a specific effect or problem. If Johnny is withdrawn and shy, something inside must be bothering him—he probably has low self-esteem. Before family therapy, explanations of psychopathology were based on linear models—medical, psychodynamic, and behavioral. In all of these, etiology was conceived of in terms of prior events—disease, emotional conflict, or learning history—which caused symptoms in the present. The patient was the locus of malfunction. Linear thinking isn't limited to a focus on one person. It's also linear to assume that one person caused another to behave or think in a problematic way. Johnny is withdrawn and shy because father overprotects him.

Using the concept of *circularity*, family therapists changed the way we think of psychopathology, from something caused by events in the past or inside the person, to something that is a part of ongoing, circular causal sequences of behavior. Johnny is withdrawn and shy because father overprotects; father overprotects because Johnny is so withdrawn and shy.

A family therapist may be able to expand this circular sequence, involving other family members or people outside the family that fit into this vicious circle (*positive feedback loop*). No matter how many people or levels of system are involved in a family therapist's understanding of a problem, however, the formulation will be circular rather than linear. For many family therapists, then, assessment involves tracking or observing the circular sequences of interaction that surround a problem or illustrate the family's structure.

In taking the concept of circularity seriously, family therapists had to include themselves in their assessments of problems. No longer could we see the therapist as an active subject and the client as a passive object. Therapist and family react to each other in circular ways too and, consequently, family therapists began to consider themselves as elements in the fields they were trying to change.

Family Life Cycle

The idea that families evolve over time as they enter and leave different stages of the life cycle added depth to these systemic formulations. A family's inability to successfully navigate one of these predictable stages could initiate the kinds of circular sequences that eventually lead to problems. Shy and withdrawn Johnny reaches the age where he starts to think about living on his own; but he's been overprotected by his parents and caught up in their marital differences. He fears for himself and for his parents if he were to leave home, and his parents are also ambivalent. The family is stuck at the launching stage of their life cycle. Johnny gets and loses several jobs, makes a few aborted attempts to live on his own and, with each failure, feels increasingly incompetent and dependent. His parents are increasingly concerned about and embarrassed by his failures, and the stage is set for some sort of chronic symptom that might excuse Johnny's failures and diffuse the growing pressure. Rather than seeing this family as defective—symbiotic, enmeshed, dependent—the life cycle perspective allows us to see them as stuck. They merely need help navigating the difficult transition from a unit of three to a restabilized couple and launched son.

Multigenerational Patterns

Bowen's idea that a family's problems are not simply due to current interactions or to bumps along the family's life cycle, but instead evolve over many generations, wasn't of interest to many of the other pioneers who were enamoured by the power of current circular family interactions. Gradually, however, the field began to conclude that the evolution of a family system over generations can explain many of their present circular knots.

Today, even many structural or strategic therapists routinely take a family's genogram to detect multigenerational patterns and to help the family understand their problems in a longitudinal perspective that reduces the blame and guilt they feel. As family and therapist examine together this encapsulated history of the family's evolution, their current predicament often seems to make sense given the pattern of syndromes, traumas, and crises over the decades.

Views of the Individual

Family therapy has presented a wide array of portraits of personality, some original and some borrowed. Each school of family therapy carries different fundamental assumptions about the nature of people and, earlier, we reviewed several conceptions of personality: the black box, the power motivated, the self-esteem motivated, the context reactor, the undifferentiated (between reason and emotion), and the psychodynamic (impelled by basic drives). All of these views continue to have an impact on the field, just as each of the schools on which they are based continue to have a following, and none has emerged as the prevailing view.

These fundamental assumptions about people will determine many of the concepts and methods of a family therapy model. For example, the first four of those views, all of which are optimistic about the possibility of rapid internal change, informed models that tend to be brief and active, and have more in common than the last two, which are pessimistic about rapid change and, consequently, are long-term and less directive. Once again, we can't overemphasize the importance of clarifying and evaluating a model's basic assumptions about people when deciding whether to adopt it.

FUNDAMENTALS OF TREATMENT _____

The first people to actually treat families began with few established concepts and methods. They borrowed and invented as they went along, gradually evolving distinctive techniques that came to define the various schools of family therapy. Although each school developed its own way of doing things, some procedures became fundamentals—methods most family therapists use regardless of school.

Contextualizing the Problem

Families come for help not only because they face difficult problems, but also because they are looking at their problems in ways that are keeping them stuck. Principal among these is viewing problems as located exclusively in one person and ignoring that person's interpersonal context. "It's Lonnie; he doesn't do his homework—he just won't do it." "It's Mom; she's depressed." Family therapists try to help family members explore the patterns of relationship that surround the problem; that is, to see the problem in context. What does Dad or Mom do when Lonnie blows off his homework? What's going on in the family that might contribute to Mom's depression? Does she have her hands full, without sufficient support, appreciation, and affection?

Let's say a therapist asks Lonnie's parents to discuss their concerns about homework with him. Maybe the father begins by trying to convince Lonnie that school is important, and Lonnie argues back, saying he doesn't care about school because he's not interested in getting a job that requires schooling. If Lonnie is seven and his father accepts such a debate, as though it were necessary for parents to convince a small child of the importance of doing what they think best, we might conclude that Lonnie doesn't do his homework because his parents fail to take a position of leadership with him. If, on the other hand, Lonnie is sixteen and his father doesn't acknowledge his point of view, but says instead, "You have to do homework because I say so," it may be that the family hasn't accommodated to an adolescent's need to have his perspective considered. If we also notice that Lonnie's father and mother are polarized around how to handle him, we would try to include that relationship in our exploring of the problem's context.

In addition to simply asking questions of family members about the patterns surrounding problems, early family therapists tried to contextualize problems more actively by giving families interpretations called variously *reframing*, *relabeling*, or *creating a workable reality*. The therapist restated the family's problems, or presented a family member, in such a way that allowed for more possibilities. For example, if the family considers Lonnie a rebellious teenager, they will feel powerless to help him other than to escalate their coercion or take him to doctors. If, on the other hand, the therapist reframes Lonnie's rebellious behaviors as his way of saying he doesn't feel a part of the family, then the family can reorganize to include him.

The goal in broadening the family's understanding of the problem is to expand the family's options for producing change. If, however, family members feel blamed and defensive by being implicated in the problem, this will narrow their options. It took some time before family therapists learned how to explore with a family their problem's context with sensitivity and respect, in the spirit of collaboration, rather than just concocting a reframe they thought the family would buy and aggressively selling it.

Dealing with Resistance

One of the things that most impressed early family therapists was the tenacity with which families resisted change. Therapists first saw families as powerful adversaries, who victimized the scapegoated "identified patient." They believed families were organized to automatically resist change in order to maintain a putative conservative force they called homeostasis.

But, of course, family therapists didn't observe families resisting change, they observed families resisting *their* efforts to change them. The resistance that therapists encountered was, at least in part, a product of the way they interacted with families. One reason therapists encountered so much resistance was that they were too eager to change people and too slow to understand them.

Families *do* resist change. We all do. Anyone who's ever tried to lose weight or stick to an exercise program knows that. It's easy to interpret a family's natural sense of caution or fear as the desire to remain stuck. In general, families will gladly change once they believe it's safe to do so and they understand and believe in the direction of the change. The job of the therapist is to respectfully help find direction, explore fears, and convey a sense of safety. The process by which therapists convey respect came to be known as *joining*, which means making each family member feel accepted and heard. To be effective, joining must flow from the heart, rather than be considered a technique for gaining leverage.

You will have trouble joining in a sincere way, however, if you feel insecure about your ability to have an impact. Out of anxiety about their own abilities, early family therapists sometimes resorted to leaning on their authority in an aggressively directive way, or to manipulative indirection. One reason for the fascination with hypnotic techniques from Milton Erickson—techniques like *restraining* (urging families to move slowly, or even to consider not changing, in hopes they will do the opposite) and other *paradoxical directives*— is that families were too often considered objects of intervention or opponents to be outwitted, instead of as partners in a collaborative effort.

Changing Interaction

Family therapists often encourage family members to speak directly to each other and then try to change the way they are interacting. These *enactments* allow the therapist to observe the family's process directly, rather than having to rely on their report, and to intervene directly into that process and see the results of their interventions.

One common type of enactment, pioneered by Satir, is to direct family members to communicate the more vulnerable feelings or desires that often lie behind their hostility, and to listen with empathy to each other. Thus, family therapists often strive to *change the style of communication* of the family. Along these lines, some therapists will send clients on *family-of-origin voyages*, in which they are to meet with extended family members outside of sessions and try to communicate in a new, more differentiated, way with them.

As we mentioned above, the structural concept of boundaries around subsystems has become widely used, and so the technique of *boundary-making* is also widespread. This phrase encompasses a variety of interventions designed to separate family members who are too close or bring together those who are too distant. For example, when two disengaged family members start to speak to each other, the therapist will strengthen the boundary around them by preventing others from interrupting.

Similarly, family therapists may *prescribe the symptom;* that is, ask the family to act out the sequences around their problem, with the hope that they will not be able to comply, or will change their pattern or, at least, will become more aware of these sequences. All of these action-changing techniques require skill in *giving directives* clearly and with some authority, while remaining joined with the family. This directive stance is another quality that differentiates many forms of family therapy from many forms of individual therapy, and it often takes students time before they are comfortable with this directiveness.

The use of directives has become one of the most widespread techniques of family therapy. Experientialists use directives to promote emotional experiencing in therapy sessions; behaviorists use directives to teach parents better ways to discipline their children; structural family therapists use directives to realign boundaries; Bowenian therapists use directives to advise patients how to be different with their parents; and strategic therapists give directives in the form of between-session tasks and also use directives to outwit resistance. This directiveness of early family therapy reflects the belief of many of the pioneers that they were primarily responsible for getting families to change. As we will see later, this belief, and the directiveness it fosters, has also been challenged.

MISCELLANEOUS CONTRIBUTIONS

In this chapter we have tried to summarize the major contextual and conceptual influences on family therapy during its formative years. In focusing this summary on only a few of the most influential theorists, we haven't done justice to the contribution of several other theorists whose work had an impact but didn't develop into a distinct school of family therapy. John E. Bell treated families as groups, helped parents learn to negotiate with their children, and introduced the idea that therapy can be conducted in planned stages. Christian Midelfort worked with families in order to help them mobilize latent forces of love and support. Norman Paul's technique of *operational mourning* was another attempt to stimulate healing emotional experiences in families.

Ivan Boszormenyi-Nagy's work initially drew little attention outside the scholarly wing of family therapy. Recently, however, his combination of psychoanalytic, systems, and ethical principles has become more influential, as increasing numbers of family therapists are becoming interested in integrating psychoanalytic theory and family therapy.

Carl Whitaker is one of the major figures in the field, but his impact has been more personal than conceptual, in part because he argues against therapists having a preconceived theory that might interfere with their intuitions. His contributions include emphasizing the value of cotherapy, and teaching—by example—that family therapy can be a spontaneous and provocative experience. Theodore Lidz and Lyman Wynne also made early conceptual contributions derived from their work with schizophrenic families, which are described in Chapter 1.

Finally, no summary of influences would be complete if it didn't include the impact of the *one-way mirror* and *videotaping*. The one-way mirror opened a window to the world of family process and therapy that had never existed before. It and the videotaping of sessions offered the ability to directly observe families in action, an ability that accounts in part for the rapid conceptual and technical strides that family therapy has made.

In addition, these technologies allowed students to directly observe and emulate the technique of master therapists, and allowed supervisors to give direct and immediate feedback to students struggling with families. So-called "live" and video supervision have become standard training practices in institutes around the country. These technologies have also promoted the more recent "teamwork" approaches to family therapy, in which a team of therapists watch a session from behind the mirror and work with the therapist in treating the family (see Liddle, Breunlin, & Schwartz, 1988, for more on how training influenced family therapy).

REFERENCES

Ackerman, N. 1958. *The psychodynamics of family life.* New York: Basic Books.

Auerswald, E. H. 1969. Interdisciplinary versus ecological approach. In *General systems theory and psychiatry,* W. Gray, F. J. Duhl, and N. D. Rizzo, eds. Boston: Little, Brown.

Barnhill, L., and Longo, D. 1978. Fixation and regression in the family life cycle. *Family Process. 17:*469–478.

Bateson, G. 1956. *Naven.* Stanford, CA: Stanford University Press.

Bateson, G. 1971. *Steps to an ecology of mind.* New York: Ballatine.

Bateson, G. 1979. *Mind and nature.* New York: E. P. Dutton.

Bateson, G., Jackson, D. D., Haley, J., and Weakland, J. H. 1956. Towards a theory of schizophrenia. In *Steps toward an ecology of mind,* G. Bateson, ed. New York: Ballantine.

Bateson, G., Jackson, D. D., Haley, J., and Weakland, J. 1963. A note on the double bind. *Family Process. 2*(1): 154–161.

Bateson, M. C. 1984. *With a daughter's eye.* New York: William Morrow.

Becvar, D. S., and Becvar, R. J. 1988. *Family therapy: A systemic integration.* Boston: Allyn and Bacon.

Bellah, R. N., Madsen, R., Sullivan, W. M., Swidler, A., and Tipton, S. M. 1985. *Habits of the heart: Individualism and commitment in American life.* New York: Harper & Row.

Bertalanffy, L. von 1968. *General system theory.* New York: George Braziller.

Bogdan, J. 1983. The Ericksonian Rorshach. *Family Therapy Networker. 7*(5):36–38.

Bogdan, J. 1987. "Epistemology" as a semantic pollutant. *Journal of Marital and Family Therapy. 13*(1): 27–36.

Boscolo, L., Cecchin, G., Hoffman, L., and Penn, P. 1987. *Milan systemic family therapy.* New York: Basic Books.

Boszormenyi-Nagy, I., and Spark, G. 1973. *Invisible loyalties: Reciprocity in intergenerational family therapy.* New York: Harper & Row.

Bowen, M. 1978. *Family therapy in clinical practice.* New York: Jason Aronson.

Breunlin, D. 1983. Therapy in stages: a life cycle view. In *Clinical implications of the family life cycle,* H. Liddle, ed. Rockville, MD: Aspen Systems Corporation.

Breunlin, D. 1988. Oscillation theory and family development. In *Family transitions,* C. Falicov, ed. New York: Guilford Press.

Breunlin, D. C., Cornwell, M., and Cade, B. 1983. International trade in family therapy: Parallels between societal and therapeutic values. In *Cultural perspectives in family therapy,* C. J. Falicov, ed. Rockville, MD: Aspen.

Breunlin, D. C., and Schwartz, R. C. 1986. Sequences: Toward a common denominator for family therapy. *Family Process, 25:*67–87.

Breunlin, D. C., Schwartz, R. C., and Mac Kune-Karrer, B. M. 1992. Metaframeworks: Transcending the models of family therapy. San Francisco: Jossey-Bass.

Capra, F. 1982. *The turning point.* New York: Simon & Shuster.

Carter, E., and McGoldrick, M., eds. 1980. *The family life cycle: A framework for family therapy.* New York: Gardner Press.

Carter, E., and McGoldrick, M., eds. 1989. *The changing family life cycle: A framework for family therapy,* 2nd ed. Boston: Allyn and Bacon.

Combrinck-Graham, L. 1983. The family life cycle and families with young children. In *Clinical implications of the family life cycle.* H. Liddle, ed. Rockville, MD: Aspen Systems.

Combrinck-Graham, L. 1985. A model for family development. *Family Process. 24:* 139–150.

Combrinck-Graham, L. 1988. Adolescent sexuality in the family life cycle. In *Family transitions,* C. Falicov, ed. New York: Guilford Press.

Davidson, M. 1983. *Uncommon sense.* Los Angeles: J. P. Tarcher.

Dell, P. F. 1982. Beyond homeostasis: Toward a concept of coherence. *Family Process. 21*(1): 21–42.

Duncan, B. L., and Parks, M. B. 1988. Integrating individual and systems approaches: Strategic-behavior therapy. *Journal of Marital and Family Therapy. 14*(2): 151–162.

Duvall, E. 1957. *Family development.* Philadelphia: Lippincott.

Duncan, B. L., and Solevey, D. 1989. Strategic-brief therapy: An insight-oriented approach. *Journal of Marital and Family Therapy. 15*(1):1–10.

Falicov, C. J., ed. 1983. *Cultural perspectives in family therapy.* Rockville, MD: Aspen.

Falicov, C. J., ed. 1988. *Family transitions.* New York: Guilford Press.

Goldner, V. 1987. Instrumentalism, feminism and the limits of family therapy. *Journal of Family Psychology. 1*(1):109–116.

Goldner, V. 1988. Generation and gender: Normative and covert hierarchies. *Family Process. 27*(1):17–33.

Gould, S. J. 1985. *The flamingo's smile: Reflections in natural history.* New York: Norton.

Haley, J. 1963. *Strategies of psychotherapy.* New York: Grune & Stratton.

Haley, J. 1971. Family therapy: A radical change. In *Changing families: A family therapy reader,* J. Haley, ed. New York: Grune & Stratton.

Haley, J., ed. 1971. *Changing families: A family therapy reader.* New York: Grune & Stratton.

Haley, J. 1973. *Uncommon therapy: The psychiatric techniques of Milton H. Erickson.* New York: Norton.

Haley, J. 1976. *Problem-solving therapy.* San Francisco: Jossey-Bass.

Haley, J. 1980. *Leaving home.* New York: McGraw-Hill.

Haley, J. 1981. *Reflections on therapy and other essays.* Chevy Chase, MD: The Family Therapy Institute of Washington, DC.

Haley, J. 1985. Conversations with Erickson. *Family Therapy Networker. 9*(2):30–43.

Hare-Mustin, R. C. 1978. A feminist approach to family therapy. *Family Process.* *17*:181–194.

Hareven, T. 1982. American families in transition: Historical perspectives on change. In *Normal family processes,* F. Walsh, ed. New York: Guilford Press.

Hill, R., and Rodgers, R. 1964. The developmental approach. In *Handbook of marriage and the family,* H. T. Christiansen, ed. Chicago: Rand McNally.

Hoffman, L. 1971. Deviation-amplifying processes in natural groups. In *Changing families: A family therapy reader,* J. Haley, ed. New York: Grune & Stratton.

Hoffman, L. 1981. *Foundations of family therapy.* New York: Basic Books.

Hsu, F. K., ed. 1971. *Kinship and culture.* Chicago: Aldine.

Imber-Black, E., Roberts, J., and Whiting, R. 1989. *Rituals in families and family therapy.* New York: Norton.

Jackson, D. 1957. The question of family homeostasis. *Psychiatric Quarterly Supplement.* *31*:79–90.

Keeney, B. P., and Sprenkle, D. H. 1982. Ecosystemic epistemology: Critical implications for the aesthetics and pragmatics of family therapy. *Family Process.* *21*(1): 1–20.

Kuhn, T. S. 1977. *The Essential tension: Selected studies in scientific tradition and change.* Chicago: The University of Chicago Press.

Lasch, C. 1977. *Haven in a heartless world.* New York: Basic Books.

Liddle, N., Breunlin, D., and Schwartz, R. eds. 1988. *The boundbook of family therapy and supervision.* New York: Guilford Press.

Lidz, T. 1963. *The family and human adaptation.* New York: International Universities Press.

Lerner, H. G. 1986. Dianna and Lillie: Can a feminist still like Murray Bowen? *Family Therapy Networker.* *9*:36–39.

Luepnitz, D. A. 1988. *The family interpreted: Feminst theory in clinical practice.* New York: Basic Books.

McGoldrick, M., Pearce, J. K., and Giordano, J. 1982. *Ethnicity and family therapy.* New York: Guilford Press.

Minuchin, S. 1974. *Families and family therapy.* Cambridge: Harvard University Press.

Minuchin, S., and Fischman, H. C. 1981. *Family therapy techniques.* Cambridge: Harvard University Press.

Parsons, T., and Bales, R. F. 1955. *Family, socialization and interaction process.* New York: Free Press.

Paul, N. 1969. The role of mourning and empathy in conjoint marital therapy. In *Family therapy and disturbed families,* G. Zuk, and I. Boszormenyi-Nagy, eds. Palo Alto: Science and Behavior Books.

Pittman, F. 1987. *Turning points: Treating families in transition and crisis.* New York: Norton.

Satir, V. 1972. *Peoplemaking.* Palo Alto, CA: Science and Behavior Books.

Satir, V. 1988. *The new peoplemaking.* Palo Alto, CA: Science and Behavior Books.

Schwartz, R. C. 1985. Has family therapy reached the stage where it can appreciate the concept of stages? In *Stages: Patterns of change over time,* D. C. Breunlin, ed. Rockville, MD: Aspen.

Schwartz, R. C., and Perrotta, P. 1985. Let us sell no intervention before its time. *Family Therapy Networker.* *9*(4):18–25.

Selvini-Palazzoli, M., Boscolo, L., Cecchin, G., and Prata, G. 1978. *Paradox and counterparadox.* New York: Jason Aronson.

Simon, R. 1982. Reflections on family therapy: An interview with Jay Haley. *Family Therapy Networker.* *6*(5):18–26.

Simon, R. 1984. Stranger in a strange land: An interview with Salvador Minuchin. *Family Therapy Networker.* *8*(6):51.

Simon, R. 1987. Good-bye paradox, hello invariant prescription: An interview with Mara Selvini Palazzoli. *Family Therapy Networker.* *11*(5):16–33.

Skynner, R. 1981. An open systems, group analytic approach to family therapy. In *Handbook of family therapy,* A. Gurman, and D. Kniskern, eds. New York: Brunner/Mazel.

Sluzki, C. 1983. Interview on the state of the art. *Family Therapy Networker.* 7(1):24.

Solomon, M. 1973. A developmental, conceptual premise for family therapy. *Family Process.* *12:*179–188.

Speer, D. C. 1970. Family systems: Morphostasis and morphogenesis, or "Is homeostasis enough?" *Family Process.* *9*(3):259–278.

Stanton, A., and Schwartz, M. 1964. *The mental hospital.* New York: Basic Books.

Wachtel, E. F., and Wachtel, P. L. 1986. *Family dynamics in individual psychotherapy.* New York: Guilford Press.

Watzlawick, P., Beavin, J. H., and Jackson, D. D. 1967. *Pragmatics of human communication.* New York: Norton.

Watzlawick, P., Weakland, J., and Fisch, R. 1974. *Change: Principles of problem formation and problem resolution.* New York: Norton.

Young, M., and Willmott, P. 1957. *Family and kinship in East London.* London: Routledge and Kegan Paul.

The Contemporary Context
of Family Therapy

During the 1960s and 1970s family therapy grew from a radical new experiment to an established force, complete with its own journals, conferences, and thousands of adherents. Unlike other fields that were relatively homogeneous because they were organized around one theory or approach (behavior therapy, psychoanalysis, hypnotherapy), or by professional degree (psychology, psychiatry, social work), family therapy had a wide variety of leaders and theories and drew followers from many backgrounds.

If differences in professional degree or in orientation to therapy were apparent in the way clinicians looked, then family therapy conferences might resemble the bar scene in *Star Wars*. Family therapy gatherings attracted refugees and renegades from all over the psychotherapy universe, with precious little in common beyond a dissatisfaction with their former haunts and a hope that involving families might be the answer. They tried out one or another of the handful of pioneering models but, unless they received training directly from one of these pioneers, their loyalty to any one model, while intense, was subject to change.

As we discussed in Chapter 2, these were the decades of family therapy's essentialistic stage. The systems-oriented family therapy models had differentiated from each other in large pendulum swings and were equally polarized from the psychoanalytic or behavioral establishments (though both behaviorism and analysis had their own representative models of family therapy). Boundaries around each model were rigid. If, for example, you were a structuralist and met someone at a conference who identified himself or herself as interested in Bowen or Satir, the conversation was not likely to last long.

In the early 1970s family therapy was like the American auto industry in its heyday. Just as the "big three" automakers competed among themselves but, otherwise, dominated the booming market, the big four or five models of family therapy competed with each other, also in a booming market. As a result, both automakers and schools of family therapy felt the chauvinism and complacency that typify organizations on the rise—organizations that because of their prosperity, have little incentive to question their own beliefs or practices.

"The family" that each of these models was trying to understand was not well differentiated. Most descriptions related to two-parent nuclear family systems, with scant attention paid to the importance of ethnic or class differences, or to family variations (single parent or step-families), and even less attention given the power differences between men and women within families. The pioneers rarely considered the possibility that their observations might not be objective and unbiased. They explored a family as if they were dissecting a specimen—as if that specimen was unaffected by their behavior or assumptions, by the strange context in which they observed it, or, possibly, by the crisis state it was in.

In these early days family therapists saw themselves as experts who would overcome the family's homeostatic tendencies and reorganize their structure or convert them to a better way to view their problems. In their enthusiasm for patterns of interaction, family therapists often lost sight of the personal experience of individual family members, and viewed their feelings as distractions from the real—systemic—issues. In addition, just as individual therapists had ignored the family system, our fascination with the family blinded us to the impact of larger systems like schools, social agencies and institutions, peer groups, and work settings.

POSTMODERNISM

The 1980s ushered in a new stage in the field's development during which family therapy's biases and blind spots were challenged. The resulting changes in family therapy that will be described in this chapter parallel changes occurring in many other fields during this period in which established truths were challenged everywhere. This era of skepticism and reexamination has been called postmodernism. To understand what happened to family therapy, we must first try to understand postmodernism.

To get a feel for postmodernism, you might remember the time when you first realized your parents didn't know everything. Indeed, it suddenly seemed that they often presented opinion as fact and sometimes just made things up. In all likelihood, that realization was both disturbing and liberating. You left the security of a world where there is a truth and your parents know what it is, for the exhilaration of a world where there is no absolute truth—where your truth may be as good as theirs.

This questioning of authority is what has been happening in our culture for the past one and one-half decades. Not only are we losing faith in the absolute validity of scientific, political, and religious truths, we are also coming to doubt whether absolute truth can be known. This is a big shift from the modern era, during which we assumed that truth existed and we fought fiercely over who possessed it. As Walter Truett Anderson (1990) writes in his thoughtful book *Reality Isn't What It Used To Be,* "Most of the conflicts that tore the now-ending modern era were between different belief systems, each of which professed to have the truth: this faith against that one, capitalism against communism, science against religion. On all sides the assumption was that somebody possessed the real item, a truth fixed and beyond mere human conjecture" (p. 2). In family therapy it was structural truth versus psychodynamic; Bowen versus Satir.

Modernists not only believed that truth could be known, but that universal principles could be discovered to explain all human behavior. In this, modernists are what we have been calling essentialists—they look inside a phenomenon for its essence. The effort to identify these universal factors, these essences, governed most fields of science from medicine and genetics to physics and mathematics. This search for the essence of things contributed to the reductionism of the times, where history and context were ignored, because it was assumed that the essence resided in the structure of a thing itself (Doherty, 1991).

Even during the modern period, many people wrote of the difficulty of knowing reality objectively (e.g., Bertalanffy's perspectivism discussed in Chapter 2). As Minuchin (1991) points out, ". . . the idea that all truth is relative, that there is no way of escaping the closed perceptual limitations of the individual mind, has haunted thinkers throughout recorded history" (p. 48). Thus, the conviction that all belief systems are social constructions is not entirely new. What is new is how pervasive this skepticism has become and how willing people are to challenge accepted truths in every human endeavor.

Skepticism has been building in our culture this century. Einstein's relativity undermined our faith in the solid certainties of Newtonian physics. Marx challenged the right of one class to dominate another. In the 1960s we lost trust in the establishment and, from drug experiences and Eastern religion, gained a sense that there were other realities besides those of ordinary consciousness. The feminist movement challenged patriarchal assumptions about gender, which had been considered laws of nature. As the world shrank and we were increasingly exposed to people of different cultures, we had to reexamine our assumptions regarding their "primitive" or "exotic" beliefs. Instead, we had to look at our reality as only one of many ways people see the world.

This accumulating skepticism became a major force in the 1980s and the pillars of many fields were shaken. In literature, law, education, architecture, religion, political science, art, and psychology, accepted practices and knowledges were "deconstructed." That is, they were shown to be social conventions developed by people with their own biased perspectives and motives. French philosopher Michel Foucault interpreted the accepted knowledges in many fields, presented as objective reality, as stories perpetuated to maintain power structures and marginalize alternative stories.

With this postmodern assumption—that there are no realities, only points of view—comes an interest in how the narratives that organize people's lives are generated. Postmodern psychologies concern themselves with how people make meaning in their lives; how they construct reality. One of these psychologies, called *constructivism,* took hold of family therapy in the early 1980s and has exerted a powerful impact on the field.

The various constructivist theorists (Paul Watzlawick, Humberto Maturana, Heinz von Foerster, & Ernst von Glaserfeld) take the Kantian position that the image of the world we carry in our mind isn't a direct replica of the "world out there." We can no longer judge theories by how well they match objective reality. We can only assess how well theories help us fit with our environment; that is, how useful, ethical, and ecologically sensitive the theory is. There may be many useful theories.

These ideas inject humility into the clinical discourse. Rather than believing our favorite therapy approach accurately reflects reality, we now see it as only one of many potentially useful stories about people. We also lose some of our status as experts. Our client families are no longer "homeostatic systems of enmeshed relationships," the individuals in them are no longer "borderline personalities" or "adult children of alcoholics." Instead, we now see these labels as part of the stories we bring to the therapy room. Our clients also bring their own stories, which may be more or less useful than ours, but no more or less true.

Constructivism tends to focus on how individuals create their own realities, but family therapy has always emphasized the power of interaction. As a result, a variant of constructivism called *social constructionism* has recently been embraced by many family therapists. Its main proponent, social psychologist Kenneth Gergen (1985, 1991a, 1991b), emphasizes the power of social interaction in generating meaning for people. Thus, not only are we unable to perceive an objective reality, the realities we do construct are anchored in the language systems in which we exist. Gergen challenges the notion that we are autonomous individuals holding independent beliefs, and implies instead that our beliefs are highly plastic, changing drastically with changes in our social context. Gergen (1991b) asks, "Are not all the fragments of identity the residues of relationships, and aren't we undergoing continuous transformation as we move from one relationship to another? Indeed, in postmodern times, the reality of the single individual, possessing his/her own values, emotions, reasoning capacities, intentions and the like, becomes implausible. . . . The sense of what is real and what is good emerges from relationships" (pp. 28, 32).

Social constructionism was welcomed with open arms by those family therapists who were trying to shift the field's focus toward meaning rather than action. It fortified their position with an academic theory that suggested the therapist's job was to cocreate new realities with families, not to direct or advise them.

To consolidate this discussion, we will summarize the changes in family therapy over the past fifteen years, which parallel in many ways the changes in our culture that accompanied the postmodernist movement.

First was the loss of faith in truth and objectivity. This spelled the demise of orthodox adherence to the various schools of family therapy. Battles among the schools over who had the most objective picture of family dynamics were reduced to battles over who had the most convincing—or least objectionable—story about families. The sense that there wasn't just one correct way to work with families, but many useful ways, also diminished the territorial wars. As a result, family therapy, like the culture in general, became more pluralistic. Therapists were free to sample among the various schools, extracting the concepts and methods they liked best and creating new, more comprehensive perspectives (see, for example, Breunlin, Schwartz, & Mac Kune-Karrer, 1992).

Second was the movement to deconstruct established knowledge. In family therapy the reevaluation took form in the feminist critique, discussed later in this chapter, which pointed out the patriarchal bias behind many of family therapy's basic assumptions and practices.

Third was disillusion with experts. Postmodern family therapy has become a more collaborative endeavor. Contemporary family therapists are far less apt to impose their frameworks or solutions on families and try instead to respect the untapped wisdom of clients themselves. In addition, as family therapists became less attached to their role as experts, they became more respectful of various self-help movements. A cross-fertilization has begun, with many self-help leaders popularizing family therapy concepts and some family therapists incorporating 12-step ideology in their work.

Fourth, postmodern psychology has been interested in the generation of meaning—in the stories that organize people's lives and the language process that produces those stories. In the 1990s, many leading family therapists have rejected the mechanistic aspects of systems thinking that informed the field's development in favor of the narrative metaphor. Their focus is on the stories that govern a family's life rather than on its structure or interactional sequences of behavior.

Fifth, postmodernists gave up the search for essential, universal patterns and instead became interested in diversity and pluralism. Likewise, in the 1990s there is very little writing in family therapy journals about the generic family and its properties and a great deal of ink devoted to the variety of family forms created by ethnicity, race, social class, and sexual preference. Writing about techniques of family therapy has also diversified. There are fewer articles devoted to generic techniques and more to the application of family therapy to specific populations and problems.

The postmodernization of family therapy is far from complete. In the past decade the field, like the culture, entered a whirlwind and has yet to land. The next sections of this chapter attempt to cover these changes in more detail, to make some guesses as to where it may stop, and to provide perspective on what we may have gained and lost in the process.

RUDE AWAKENINGS

Postmodernization begins with disillusionment with established truths. During the 1980s, with far fewer attacks from the mental health establishment to unite and distract the field, family therapy took a good look at itself and found the image not entirely pleasing. As we described in Chapter 2, some family therapists began to question whether their model really captured the essence—

whether there might be more limitations in effectiveness or application than they had thought. Braulio Montalvo, one of the principal architects of structural family therapy, summarized these sentiments when he said, "We have to learn how to lower our sights and realize what we can accomplish. I think our effort now has to be highlighting the various areas in which we have some honest knowledge and away from clinical myth-making" (Schwartz & Perrotta, 1985).

The Milan Revolution

While second thoughts were growing regarding our American models, a new, radically different model was gaining adherents in Europe. Promoted as a cure for the most difficult cases (chronic schizophrenics and anorexics) and as being a purer translation of Bateson's thinking into practice, the Milan model took the field by storm following the publication of the book *Paradox and Counterparadox* (Selvini Palazzoli, Boscolo, Cecchin, & Prata, 1978). It emerged at a time when structural family therapy and Haley's version of strategic therapy were the dominant influences in the field. Because the emphasis of these models was on assessing and changing a family's current structure, therapists paid scant attention to history or internal conflicts within families. Therapists were encouraged to size up a family's dysfunctional structure (or problem-maintaining interchanges) very quickly, often in the first session, and then use the power of their personalities (or paradoxical techniques) to attack these patterns.

Structural and strategic therapists, then, focused basically on assessing and changing interactional behavior and were less interested in the beliefs family members held that might govern their behavior. Therapists were highly directive and active, telling family members what to do in and out of sessions, and deliberately siding, at least temporarily, with one member against another. The therapist was responsible for getting families to change, and to change in a certain way. This was a uniquely American form of therapy—highly pragmatic and impatient for change. The therapist-as-expert should quickly understand, take command of, and solve any family's problem.

Apparently there were many therapists who, while trying to be structural or strategic, weren't entirely comfortable with what they were doing. To these therapists the Milan model, with its emphasis on thoroughly and systemically understanding the family's evolution over time and how it came to need the problem; its focus on meaning, not just behavior; its view of therapist as distant and neutral asker of "circular questions," rather than as opinionated, pushy giver of directives; therapist as perturber of the system which will change as it sees fit, rather than as forger of new family structures or interactions, was a welcome change. Peggy Papp, a prominent strategic therapist, described her excitement when she tried the Milan model: "Instead of trying too hard to persuade people to change, I was sitting back, throwing out messages, and watching families react in remarkable ways. . . . In some way, I was leaving the decision to change up to the family. I thought to myself, 'Oh what a relief. . . .' " (Simon, 1987, p. 23).

It was such a relief to so many therapists, that the Milan model spread with amazing speed across Europe and then North America, promoted and interpreted here by other former strategic therapists Carl Tomm and Lynn Hoffman. The field woke up to several new ideas. Therapists didn't have to push so hard. They could take time to explore and ask questions before acting. They didn't have to be powerful or clever to be effective. Families could figure out and change some things on their own, if asked the right questions. Questions were powerful.

It also didn't hurt the popularity of the Milan model that it had an exotic and mysterious shape. Therapists worked in nonhierarchical teams and strove for a sort of "group mind" in which the therapist was simply the extension of that mind in the room. The therapist asked strange, sometimes convoluted, questions and, through most of any session, did little else. During sessions the therapist would leave the family and go behind the one-way mirror for long stretches to brainstorm with the team. Sessions were scheduled with long intervals (a month or more) between them and the team would have no contact with the family between sessions. Once the team had an hypothesis they felt good about, the therapist would deliver it to the family in a dramatic speech, often read from a letter for the family to take home and reread regularly. Every family member's intentions were *positively connoted* in this dramatic message.

Thus, not only was the Milan model a relief from the aggressive American approaches, it also appealed to the more cerebral therapists who liked to work from a comfortable distance, liked to discuss and solve puzzles, and liked to enjoy the camaraderie and shared responsibility of being part of a team. In addition, because it claimed to be more systemic—truer to Bateson's ideas— than the American models, Milan adherents could look down on their structural and strategic colleagues, in much the same way that those therapists used to look down on individual therapists. What Liddle and Saba (1981) called "systemic chic" was all the rage.

While many of the Milan ideas and practices were revolutionary, the original version of the model shared some elements with American approaches that would later seem undesirable. First, while the team tried to be relatively leaderless and democratic, their relationship to families was distinctly hierarchical. The therapist remained distant and authoritarian; families weren't privy to the mysterious discussions the experts were having behind the mirror. Instead, the therapist imposed the team's verdict on the family, and declined to discuss it with them.

Second, these pronouncements usually attributed a sacrificial function to the identified patient. The rationales Milan therapists gave for the family's need to have a symptomatic member were usually far more elaborate, often involving a whole network of people or events in the family's history, than the simple distracting-from-parents'-marriage function assumed in American models. In addition, the team was careful to positively connote every family member's motives for their role in the network of relationships that led to the need for the symptom. In this way the team reduced resistance to the message, implying that it was the system that needed the symptom, not its members. In searching for the putative function of the symptom, Milan therapist remained modernist in that they were looking for the pattern of truth that, once revealed, would powerfully change a family. It was only later that they adopted the postmodern view that they were cocreating useful realities.

The Milan model's view of people was strongly influenced by the belief that people manipulate each other. Despite positively connoting the motives of family members in sessions, the Milan Associates portrayed family members as power-game players, whose objective was to win at the expense of others. For example, when a family member expressed an emotion, Milan therapists were trained to say, "He is *showing* sadness" rather than "He *is* sad," to highlight the interpersonally manipulative aspect (the function) of showing emotions.

Third, the Milan model's emphasis on remaining neutral and letting the family find its own solutions runs counter to feminist thinking (discussed later in this chapter) because, in the words of Laurie MacKinnon and Dusty Miller (1987), it

> assumes that families are voluntary organizations functioning for the ultimate good of all members. This does not take into consideration the fact that families have "found their own solutions" for centuries and that these solutions have been primarily at the expense of women and children. (p. 150)

That is, the attempt to simply perturb family systems without a view to how they should change ignores the sociopolitical context that *will* influence the direction of families' solutions if the therapist doesn't. The Milan Associates represented a combination of modernism (expert stance and objectivist view of families) and postmodernism (relativistism about goals), and in that sense is a transitional model. This early controversy over the Milan Associates' neutral, relativistic stance regarding goals and outcome foreshadows attacks on the relativistic nature of much postmodern thought.

Finally, the Milan model shared the American fascination (particularly in strategic models) with technology. Questioning was a prelude to the powerful part of the therapy—the "positive connotations" delivered at the end of sessions to stop families in their tracks.

From Rambo to Columbo.   In fairness, the Milan fascination with big-bang interventions shifted in the early 1980s and they began giving the questioning process more credit for producing change. As Matteo Selvini (1988), Selvini Palazzoli's son, described the period after the Milan group's "interventionist" phase,

> The focus of attention was now shifted to what happens *during* the session, to the interviewing techniques and to the strategies and tactics of conducting the session. The therapeutic effectiveness of the entire course of the therapy, during and between the sessions, was being taken into account, when the earlier view had been that all the team's work was a mere preliminary to the elaboration of the final intervention, of the resolving counterparadox. With this transformation, the therapeutic atmosphere, too, became changed: it was now less "athletic" and competitive. (p. 413)

The Milan Associates' shift away from imposing forceful interventions and toward simply helping families explore their predicaments marks the advent of the postmodern era in family therapy. The original group split at that point, and the two male members (Gianfranco Cecchin and Luigi Boscolo) pursued their interest in the questioning process and in constructivism. They traveled extensively, giving workshops around the world, which spread interest in the questioning process. The two women (Mara Selvini Palazzoli & Guiliana Prata) remained modernist, searching for the basic dysfunctional patterns of schizophrenic families.

When all is said and done, the most important impact of the Milan movement may be the permission it gave a generation of therapists to break away from the narrow rules and aggressiveness of models developed in the United States. It provided the opening through which postmodern ideas could enter the field. More specifically, the lasting contributions of the Milan movement are: (1) recognizing the importance of the historical evolution of problems within family systems; (2) increasing therapists' trust in families to come up with their own solutions and, consequently, decreasing their need to force families to change in preconceived ways; (3) increasing the field's appreciation of the beliefs that lie behind family behaviors; and (4) elevating the art of interviewing, in particular, of asking questions.

This fourth contribution merits some elaboration. The Milan Associates introduced a type of interviewing called *circular questioning,* developed further by Karl Tomm (1985, 1987, 1988), which generates the kind of systemic information that enables families to see their problems differently. The basic method involves asking questions that highlight differences among family members or define relationships, rather than asking for the beliefs or feelings of any one family member without reference to another. For example, a mother might be asked to describe the relationship between her son and husband, or the whole family might be asked which of them would suffer the most if the son were to leave home, or the son might be asked who would worry the most if he left.

When asked questions that force them to define positions relative to each other, family members have to think in new ways, and the network of relationships surrounding problems becomes clearer to all. Because the therapist is eliciting this information through sincerely curious (rather than rhetorical) questioning, and because family members are describing each other rather than themselves, these discussions are often less inhibited or defensive.

DECONSTRUCTING FAMILY THERAPY'S
PHILOSOPHICAL ROOTS

It's no accident that the spread of the Milan movement coincided with a period during which the field's basic philosophical premises were being questioned and, in many cases, rejected by some of its more thoughtful practitioners. Until the late 1970s, family therapy concentrated on developing pragmatic techniques. The pioneers were struggling to find ways to understand and tame this strange new animal, the family system, and to convert a skeptical psychotherapy field. Having succeeded to varying degrees in both arenas by the end of the 1970s, family therapy had a chance to catch its breath and take a look at the foundations upon which it rested. Finally, family therapists could afford the luxury of self-criticism, and it came in two forms: the feminist critique and the new epistemologies.

This reappraisal began with a series of attacks on the narrow pragmatism of family therapy models, calling into question such basic concepts as *homeostasis, resistance,* and *paradox* (Keeney & Sprenkle, 1982; Keeney, 1983; Dell, 1982, 1985). The general thrust of these brash critiques was that the field had gone astray, become too results- and technique-oriented and, in the process, lost touch with broader considerations about families. Pragmatists took strong exception to this criticism and countered with ridicule, calling these papers "epistobabble" (Coyne, 1982).

This antimechanist critique can be seen as a reaction against cybernetics and functionalism, with which there was little need to consider the effect on the family of the act of observing, or of the influence of the observer's preconceptions. That is, therapists were too often making the modernist mistake of believing that their map was the territory; believing that the "structural flaws," "positive feedback loops," "undifferentiated family ego masses" somehow existed in reality, rather than as useful metaphors.

Constructivism

This critique functioned as a crowbar to pry family therapy away from its belief in objectivity—the belief that what one *sees* in families is what *is* in families. Emerging from the smoke of all this debate and exotic theorizing were some new assumptions that have led groups of clinicians to adventure in new directions. These new assumptions fall loosely under the rubric constructivism, a philosophy that arises from some ideas from neurobiology—for example, Maturana and Varela's (1980) belief that living systems are self-contained neural units that can have no direct experience of their environments; von Foerster's (1981) reminder that observers have an effect on the systems they interpret; and von Glaserfeld's (1984) "radical constructivism" which says that we can never know the real world, only our internal images of it. These ideas were imported into family therapy by Paul Dell (1985), Paul Watzlawick (1984), and Lynn Hoffman (1985, 1988).

Constructivism asserts that reality doesn't exist "out there," but instead is a mental construction of the observer. The implications for therapy of the constructivist position are that therapists should not consider what they're seeing in families as existing in the family. Instead, they should understand that what they are seeing is the product of their assumptions—about people, families, and problems—and of their interactions with the family.

This concern about the influence of therapists' preconceptions was expanded to an interest in belief systems in general. Through Bateson's influence, family therapy adopted the term *epistemology* as a synonym for belief system, perspective, or world view (even though the term properly refers to the branch of philosophy concerned with the development of knowledge). Family therapy has always shown some interest in changing meanings, as evidenced by the early popularity of reframing techniques or the value put on "creating a workable reality." But these meaning changes were generally in the service of behavioral changes, which remained the primary target.

Instead of focusing on patterns of family interaction, constructivists shifted focus to exploring and reevaluating people's assumptions about their problems. Meaning itself became the primary target. Extending this thinking, some writers have proposed that we jettison our arbitrary focus on family systems and, instead, examine the total meaning systems in which problems are embedded, which might include family members but also include all the other helpers, including the therapist (Anderson, Goolishian, & Winderman, 1986).

The idea that our belief systems influence what we see may not come as a great revelation to students of philosophy, and it had been a cliche within family therapy from the beginning—Bateson frequently cited Alfred Korzybski's (1942) saying, "The map is not the territory." But until this philosophical mid-life crisis, many structural and strategic family therapists were acting as if their maps *were* the territory.

One clinical consequence of constructivism has been to make therapists humbler in their dealings with families. For example, many structural family therapy maneuvers, such as unbalancing or creating intensity, require a high level of confidence in the correctness of one's assessment. If the therapist wavers, intensity will be lost and, theoretically, the family's homeostasis will not be perturbed. But if therapists believe that their assessment is just one of many stories about the family, it is hard to avoid wavering. Lynn Hoffman (1988) describes her initial reaction to constructivism this way: "One suddenly doesn't know how to 'teach' therapy, much less how to 'do' it. One loses one's status, one loses one's expert position" (p. 124).

Thus, many constructivist therapists have gravitated toward a kinder, gentler therapy in which they are more like collaborators with the family than like experts or directors. Many of the groups in North America and Europe that have moved in this direction began as Milan-style teams, fertilized by visits from Cecchin and Boscolo. As the constructivist bug spread, the resulting collaborative, meaning-focused family therapy became known as the post-Milan movement or "second-order" family therapy, to differentiate it from the strategic, hierarchical aspects of the earlier brands of family therapy.

The second-order teams have invented several techniques for engaging with families in "conversations" about their problems, during which the constructions of each member of the system, including therapist and team members, are examined and critiqued collectively and nonjudgmentally. Rather than presupposing that family members' views are incorrect and in need of change, second-order therapists try to promote an understanding of everyone's private reality and create an atmosphere of respect in which various viewpoints can be discussed nondefensively (Anderson & Goolishian, 1988; Hoffman, 1985, 1988). Toward these ends, team members have openly conveyed their views to the family in various formats, including having the family come behind the one-way mirror and watch the team conference (Andersen, 1987).

These second-order groups are, in some ways, circling family therapy back toward a Rogerian, nondirective position, although Carl Rogers gets little citation in their literature. The therapy teams strive to create an atmosphere of acceptance and empathy, in which the defensiveness or aggressiveness of family members can recede, allowing the whole group to brainstorm creatively and flexibly about problems. Lynn Hoffman (1988) summarized this brand of therapy this way:

> It avoids the implication of fixing something that has been broken down or is not functioning and comes closer to being some kind of hopeful discourse. It is, as far as possible, nonjudgmental, and nonperjorative. It is not control-oriented. It is lateral rather than hierarchical in structure. It is wary of an instructive stance. It shrinks away from an influence that is primarily intentional. It is pluralistic in nature, focusing on many views rather than one. There is no assumption of objectivity or truth. (p. 126)

As Hoffman's quote illustrates, at this point the second-order movement, like many new approaches that emerge as reactions to an establishment, seems clearer about what it isn't than what it is.

This movement seems to be more of an attitude than a model. Harlene Anderson, who, with the late Harry Goolishian, led the development of one second-order variant, said in an interview (Winderman, 1989):

> I try to learn about [the family's] views and create through learning an "in there together" process that leads to new meaning, narrative, and agency. . . . In the therapy room I am a learner. I adopt a "puzzling" position. This flips the position of the client and the therapist. The client is now the knower and the therapist is the not-knower. . . . It is not just the therapist trying to understand the client, collecting information and data and placing it on some kind of cognitive map in a unilateral way. Rather, it is a mutual search in which client and therapist puzzle together in search for understanding, to develop a story that has not been told before. (p. 12)

With Anderson's last phrase about developing a story, we segue into another emphasis of postmodernist approaches. The Anderson/Goolishian (1988) approach is the one most heavily influenced by Gergen's *social constructionism*. As a result, they have "conversations" with a family out of which emerge new, more optimistic or empowering stories about the problem or the family.

There are other postmodern approaches that also emphasize the importance of new stories or narratives about the family, the problem, or the patient, but have less faith in a democratic conversational process to achieve this re-storying and, therefore, actively lead families to new stories.

Australian Michael White leads families to participate in what he calls "externalizing conversations" about their problems; that is, view the problem as a separate entity, external to the person who has it. For example, an encopretic child is asked how his "poo" is affecting his life, and when he had been able to resist "sneaky poo." Similar questions are put to other family members regarding the influence of poo in their lives and when they were able to not let it have these consequences. After a round of these questions, White (1989) reports that ". . . Nick could recall a number of occasions during which he had not allowed Sneaky Poo to outsmart him. These were occasions during which he could have cooperated by 'smearing,' 'streaking,' or 'plastering,' but when he declined to do so. He had not allowed himself to be tricked into this" (p. 10).

This externalizing allows families new options for escaping the oppression of problems because they can work together to defeat the problem rather than blame each other for it. White (1989) describes the way families usually view problems this way:

> Although the problem was usually defined as internal to the child, all family members were affected by it, and often felt overwhelmed, dispirited and defeated. In various ways, they took the ongoing existence of the problem, and their failed attempts to solve it, as a reflection on themselves, each other and/or on their relationships. (p. 5)

In this sense, families with problems present a story about themselves that is, in White's words, "problem-saturated"; it focuses on their impotence and frustration. By externalizing the problem and asking family members to focus on "unique outcomes," that is, times when the problem did not defeat them, White helps people identify how they were able to triumph. In the process, people are able to separate from the problem-saturated story that had been shaping their lives and, thereby, see alternative aspects of themselves that lead them to "re-author" themselves in a new, empowered story.

In the 1990s, White has become increasingly postmodern in the political sense due to his interest in the late philosopher Michel Foucault (1980, 1984). White's externalizing technique has become one of many ways to help people deconstruct realities they are socialized to take for granted but that are subjugating them. For example, White (1991) encouraged a parent who believed she was a failure as a mother to explore how she had been "recruited" into this belief. "What experiences had been most instrumental in this recruitment? Did she think that women [or men] were more vulnerable to being recruited into the view that they had failed their children?" (p. 1). In response to these questions, she discussed being abused by her former husband and the prevalence of mother-blaming in our culture. During this discussion she began to experience herself differently and to identify areas in her life that were not dominated by this failure story. Ultimately, through this questioning process, alternative versions of who she was emerged, versions that she much preferred.

The contrast between White's style of interviewing (asking pointed questions designed to separate people from the oppressive stories given them by our culture) and the Anderson/Goolishian style (unstructured, empathic conversations about problems) highlights the clinical applications of two different strains of postmodern thought. White was influenced by what philosopher Pauline Rosenau (1992) calls the *affirmative postmodernists* who use the message that no one can know the truth to show how privileged groups create stories that keep others marginalized. Thus, White is highly political. He aims to liberate alternative stories that have been oppressed by the dominant culture.

The other postmodern strain, what Rosenau calls the *skeptical postmodernists*, takes the same message—that no one can know the truth—to a relativistic conclusion. For the skeptics, no value system, narrative, or perspective can be assumed superior to any other. Logically, then, there's nothing wrong with any story a family comes up with, except if it's not working for them. Any new story the family accepts and makes the problem disappear will do. This relativistic position has a long tradition in family therapy, dating back to Bateson's disdain for issues of power and his implication that everyone in a system is equally responsible for its problems, as well as the reframing techniques of the MRI group. Not surprisingly, Paul Watzlawick (1984), a prime mover within the MRI group, is a leading advocate of relativistic constructivism. It is also not surprising that Kenneth Gergen's brother is David Gergen, the consummate spin doctor who created realities for Presidents Nixon and Reagan and is now doing so for Bill Clinton. Where formerly the therapist created realities (reframes) and tried to sell them to the family (à la David Gergen), in the postmodern update of this relativistic position, the therapist does not guide clients away from or toward certain stories but instead tries to create a conversational atmosphere in which new stories emerge spontaneously (à la Kenneth Gergen).

It seems ironic that out of constructivism should emerge two such contradictory strains of thought—skeptical and affirmative. One leads to value-free conversations in which everyone's position is respected and heard. The other leads to a political therapy of liberation, with therapist as deconstructor. This important distinction is often obscured because both strains fall under the rubric of postmodern constructivism.

Steve de Shazer (1985, 1988, 1991, 1992) and his colleagues, notably Bill O'Hanlon and Michele Weiner-Davis (1989), have developed another popular constructivist approach that contains elements of both strains of thought. The "solution-focused" approach is similar to White's in that it uses leading questions to separate clients from their problem-focused stories. In this sense, the therapist is affirmative because he or she is deconstructing the problem story by having clients focus on "exceptions"—times when their problems did not occur. The therapist then helps them find ways to expand those exceptions.

Solution-focused therapists are ultimately skeptical relativistists, however. de Shazer's roots are in the MRI tradition and he retains their minimalist, intervene-as-little-as-possible philosophy. That is, while he deconstructs the problem story by allowing clients to only discuss their solutions and exceptions, he makes no judgment regarding the solutions they come up with, as long as they seem to be satisfactory to the family. This is because, as Berg and de Shazer (1993, p. 7) assert "language is reality." So, change the language and you change the only reality you need to change.

The solution-focused model is of interest in this chapter for one more reason. Its popularity grew rapidly in the 1980s when mental health budgets were slashed and managed care began to limit the number of sessions for which practitioners could be reimbursed. This produced a tremendous demand for a brief, prescriptive, commonsensical approach, and solution-focused is all of those.

Where will constructivism ultimately take the field? It's hard to tell. Much as was the case when the pioneers shifted their focus from individuals to families, this recent shift from action to narrative—from challenging to collaborating—opened a whole new world of possibilities for doing therapy. It's likely that the pendulum will continue to swing until these possibilities have been explored.

We believe, however, that this shift has already led to some valuable changes that will last whether the specific models do or not. These changes include (1) the elevation of meaning to a position at least equal in importance to behavioral interaction patterns; (2) increased humility about our theoretical models; (3) increased attention to the values behind our assumptions (including political values); and (4) decreased urgency to change or control people, and increased trust in their own resources.

On the other hand, we have questions and concerns regarding constructivism's influence on family therapy. For example, all of these postmodern therapies tend to discount much of what came before, implying that it was all the product of that bad modernist, essentialist thinking. Do we really have to continue erasing our heritage with each swing of the pendulum? As Walter Truett Anderson (1990) reminds us: "A social construction of reality does not have to be discarded the moment one has recognized that that is what it is. The Wizard of Oz, upon being exposed as human, may still be a very good man; and the belief, tradition, value, religion, norm or Constitution that stands revealed as nothing more than a social construct may still be a very useful item" (p. 259). Can we accept, for example, that Minuchin did not have a God's eye view when he described common family alliances and coalitions, and still keep open the possibility that aspects of his understanding of families may have utility? The point is to remain humble and critical about our maps, and open to maps of others, not necessarily to throw them out because the mapmaker had some biases.

Relatedly, while Bateson spent his life searching for the "pattern that connects," postmodernists eschew attempts to find larger patterns or to create universal theories. White (1992), for example, takes the position that, "all essentialist notions about human nature are actually ruses that disguise what is really taking place" (p. 8). He implies that what is really taking place are power grabs by those making essentialist or universal claims. In taking this position, White has ruled out any attempts to describe families generically or to speculate about human nature. Yet his descriptions of therapy are rife with assumptions about people and the way they change—for example, people are dominated by subjugating stories but have access to alternatives once separated from the oppressing ones.

It is difficult to have no essential assumptions—to have no world view or psychology of human nature. As philosopher Harvey Cox notes (Smith, 1989), all these "critics will have to face the contention that no one ever really escapes metaphysics, that its derogators end up hiding it, obscuring it, or doing it badly" (p. 42). The trick is to remain humble about one's assumptions, to critically examine their roots and implications, while remaining curious about and appreciative of human diversity.

Leadership in therapy is another concern. As a reaction against the hierarchical, authoritative therapist of earlier models, some interpretations of constructivism may lead therapists to abdicate leadership in their efforts to be collaborative and not impose their viewpoint on families (Atkinson, 1992;

Nichols, 1993). Leadership doesn't mean pushing, confronting, or controlling, but it does mean creating an atmosphere of safety and a context in which difficult issues are addressed. Being a collaborative partner for families doesn't mean being passive and going along with whatever clients say, or allowing their conflicts to escalate or remain underground.

Another concern about relativistic family therapies has to do with denial. There is the tendency in many troubled families to want to deny their problems or their pain. If, for example, one has a nondirective "conversation" with many alcoholic or abusive families, it's possible to cocreate with them a reality that their problems aren't as bad as they think and everyone will walk away, at least temporarily, feeling better. This is not to imply that constructivist therapists routinely cocreate problem-denying realities with families, but instead to suggest that there is nothing in the theory that precludes such a possibility.

Others are beginning to voice serious concerns regarding the way family therapy has interpreted postmodern thinking. In a recent scholarly and scathing critique, Vincent Fish (1993) attacks relativistic approaches because they

> reinforce tendencies, already present in Batesonian and constructivist-based therapies, to conceptually isolate the therapist-family system from any social, historical, economic, or institutional context, and to deny the existence or relevance of differences in power at an interpersonal level. Splitting off a separate world of language, divorced from any notion of a relevant social and material realm, they enforce a conceptual blackout which begins at the edges of the family's story, or conversation. There is nothing for the therapist who operates solely within these models to mentally see, hear or touch but the content and arrangement of words the family uses while in the therapist's office. (p. 228)

Fish claims that the relativistic assumption that every family member's story is equally valid maintains a politically conservative tendency to ignore or gloss over the plight of those who are oppressed in families. This is because "perpetrators of abuse almost always attempt to control information—to dictate the family story" (p. 229). Might not the stories of abused children and women, when they feel safe to relate them, more accurately reflect the conditions in the home than that of the abuser? These are some of the concerns that the field must address in the coming years so that the opportunities postmodernism offers are not "squandered on dressing up old Batesonian and constructivist assumptions in the latest academic fashions" (p. 230).

Indeed, it was family therapy's denial of the gender inequities, violence, and sexual abuse within families that led to the field's other rude awakening, the feminist critique.

THE FEMINIST CRITIQUE OF FAMILY THERAPY

Feminist family therapists not only deconstructed existing models, as described in Chapter 2, they also advocated a style of therapy that, like the second-order movement, is collaborative and interested in meaning. Feminism and skeptical postmodernism are not, however, entirely compatible (Rosenau, 1992). Feminist family therapists don't advocate relativistic neutrality, and have trouble with the idea of trusting the family, steeped as it is in patriarchal values, to find its own solutions. For feminists, all realities are not created equal.

The feminist critique was family therapy's rudest awakening. The field's increasing popularity through the 1970s left us feeling a little smug. We were the progressive avant-garde whose theories and techniques were going to revolutionize psychotherapy. It was inconceivable that we could have been blind to sexism along the way. As Lois Braverman (1988) confessed,

> As long as we thought systemically and did not buy into a traditional linear long-term psychotherapy approach to treatment, we considered ourselves to be far ahead of other helping professionals. So while other therapeutic frameworks and treatment modalities of the 1970s were marked by feminist critiques . . . which questioned traditional psychodynamic theory and practice, we, as family therapists, had our heads buried in the sand. (p. 6)

The Apolitical Machine

Heads came out of the sand in the early 1980s and began to look around at our model of the functional family and at our precious systems theory. It became increasingly and painfully clear that cybernetics and functionalism had led us astray. Cybernetics encouraged us to view a family system as a flawed machine. Judith Meyers Avis's complaints about cybernetics are remarkably similar to Fish's (1993) words that critique the new relativistic constructivism. Meyers Avis (1988) described this family machine as one that

> . . . functions according to special systemic rules and is divorced from its historical, social, economic, and political contexts. By viewing the family out of context, family therapists locate family dysfunction entirely within interpersonal relationships in the family, ignore broader patterns of dysfunction occurring across families, and fail to notice the relationship between social context and family dysfunction. (p. 17)

Thus the mechanistic philosophy of cybernetics narrowed our vision and made us oblivious to the parallels between disharmonies in our culture and in our families.

Additionally, the Batesonian version of cybernetics was strongly opposed to the use of power metaphors. He claimed that unilateral control in systems was impossible because all elements are continually and circularly influencing one another in repetitive feedback loops. If all parts of a system are equally involved in its problems, no one is to blame. This idea had great appeal for family therapists because family members often enter therapy pointing fingers at each other, and failing to see their own steps in their circular dances.

To feminists, however, this idea of equal responsibility for problems looked "suspiciously like a hypersophisticated version of blaming the victim and rationalizing the status quo" (Goldner, 1985, p. 33). This critique was particularly evident in crimes against women like battering, incest, and rape, for which psychological theories have long been used to imply that the woman either provoked or consented to the crime (James & MacKinnon, 1990).

But those crimes are only the most obvious instances in which the systemic doctrine of equal responsibility is troublesome. The larger issue is that if one accepts the feminist premise that in our patriarchal society, marriage and family life inherently subjugates women, then to suggest that husbands and wives have contributed equally to and have equal responsibility for changing their problems is to collude with the rules of these patriarchal microcosms of society.

Mother Blaming

The dysfunctional family constellation most commonly cited by family therapists is the peripheral father, overinvolved mother, and symptomatic child caught up in the parents' relationship. For years, psychodynamic therapists blamed mother's attachment to the child for the symptoms. Family therapy's apparent advance was to show how father's lack of involvement contributed to mother's overinvolvement, and so therapists tried to pry mother loose by inserting father in her place. This, however, was not the advance for women that it might seem because, in too many cases, mothers were viewed no less negatively. Mothers were still enmeshed and incompetent, but now we had a new solution—to bring competent, rational fathers to the children's rescue.

What the feminists contend we failed to see, and to help our client families see, is that "the archetypal 'family case' of the overinvolved mother and peripheral father is best understood not as a clinical problem, but as the product of an historical process two hundred years in the making" (Goldner, 1985, p. 31). Women are overinvolved, insecure, controlling, ineffectual, overemotional—not because of psychopathology, but because they are put in, and encouraged by society to desire, emotionally isolated, economically dependent, overresponsible positions in families, positions that are crazy-making.

Feminist family therapists help families reorganize so that no one, male or female, remains stuck in such positions. Thus, instead of further diminishing an insecure mother's self-esteem by replacing her with a peripheral father (who is likely to have been critical of her parenting all along), a feminist family therapist might help the family examine and change the rules and roles that kept mother down and father out. During this process, fathers may be encouraged to become more involved with parenting—but not because mothers are incompetent. Rather they become involved because it is a father's responsibility as a parent and because it will allow the mother to begin to move out of that crazy-making position (Ault-Riche, 1986; Goodrich, Rampage, Ellman, & Halstead, 1988; Walters, Carter, Papp, & Silverstein, 1988; McGoldrick, Anderson, & Walsh, 1989).

Looking through the Lens of Gender

Feminist family therapists, then, are not simply asking us to be more sensitive to gender issues in working with families. Instead they assert that issues of gender or, more specifically, patriarchy, permeate all of our work as therapists, even though we have been conditioned not to notice them. They believe, therefore, that gender should be a primary organizing concept for family therapists, on a par with the concept of generation (Goldner, 1988, 1993).

Only when we look through this lens of gender can we effectively stop blaming mothers, or stop looking to them to do most of the changing simply because they are the most invested in change or the most cooperative. Only then will we be able to fully counter our unconscious biases toward seeing women as primarily responsible for childrearing or housekeeping; as needing to support their husbands' careers by neglecting their own; as needing to be married, or at least, to have a man in their lives. Only then can we stop relying on traditional male traits like rationality, independence, and competitiveness as our standards of health and stop denigrating or ignoring traits traditionally encouraged in women like emotionality, nurturance, and relationship focus.

In essence, the feminist revolution in family therapy differs from the Milan or constructivist revolutions because it isn't just asking that we try on some new concepts or techniques. It's not theoretical—it's personal. It forces us, as therapists, to look in the mirror at our own attitudes and our lives outside of the professional safety of our offices.

As one might anticipate, the feminist critique wasn't immediately welcomed or accepted by the established models in the field. The early to mid 1980s was a period of polarization and tension between male and female therapists at conferences, as feminists tried to exceed the establishment's "threshold of deafness." By the 1990s, that threshold has been exceeded, in the sense that many of the major feminist points are no longer debated and the field is evolving toward a more collaborative, but socially enlightened, form of therapy.

Family Violence

In the early 1990s family therapy took its first real look at the dark side of family life. Perhaps it wasn't until the other aspects of the feminist critique had been accepted that the field was ready to take this step, because other fields had been exploring the problems of wife battering and sex abuse for years. In the late 1980s and early 1990s books and articles on these topics began appearing in the mainstream family therapy literature (e.g., Controneo, 1987; Trepper & Barrett, 1989; Dell, 1989; Goldner, Penn, Sheinberg, & Walker, 1990; Friedrich, 1990; Markowitz, 1992; Schwartz, 1992, 1993; Barrett & Trepper 1992; Sheinberg, 1992; Canavan, Higgs, & Meyer 1992; Serra, 1993; Calof, 1993; Gorman-Smith & Tolan, 1993). But it wasn't until 1991 that the field of family therapy was shaken out of its collective denial regarding the horrifying extent of male to female abuse in families by a slap in the face. This slap took the form of three plenary addresses at the annual meeting of the American Family Therapy Academy (AFTA), which were later published in the *Journal of Marital and Family Therapy* (Meyers Avis, 1992; Kaufman, 1992; Bograd, 1992).

Judith Meyers Avis (1992) delivered a barrage of staggering statistics regarding such things as the proportion of women who have experienced sexual abuse before the age of 18 (37%), percent of abusers who are male (95%), number of women abused each year by the man they live with (1 in 6), and percent of male college students who had coerced sex from an unwilling partner (25%) and who said they would commit rape if guaranteed immunity from detection or punishment (20%). After reiterating the indictment of family therapy theories that strive for therapist neutrality and see the abused as partially responsible for abuse, she concluded that:

> As long as we train therapists in systemic theories without balancing that training with an understanding of the non-neutrality of power dynamics, we will continue producing family therapists who collude in the maintenance of male power and are dangerous to the women and children with whom they work. Taking a feminist position in relation to male power means taking a non-neutral position, challenging male control and domination, naming the abuse, and naming the abuser. (p. 231)

Gus Kaufman (1992) increased the rhetorical intensity with statements like:

> Constructivists and systems theorists . . . should know this: violence follows the old Newtonian physics of mass, velocity, momentum and inertia—as in a fist hitting a face and breaking bones. . . . We don't hear [about violence in the families we treat] because we never ask the right questions in the right context of the right people. We are like Red Cross workers visiting the P.O.W. camp asking "How are they treating you?" as the guards stand by. She is a prisoner; he is a guard; and we—the well-meaning helper—won't be there to insure her safety after the visit. (pp. 236-237)

Michele Bograd (1992) concluded with a series of questions that we believe summarize some of the central predicaments for family therapy in this decade.

> In working with family violence, how do we balance a relativistic world view with values about human safety and the rights of men and women to self-determination and protection? When is the clinical utility of neutrality limited or counterproductive? When is conviction essential to the change process? How do we confront the batterer about the destructive nature of his behavior without condemning him? How strongly and passionately do we employ our values to therapeutic advantage while maintaining a caring and respectful connection with family members struggling with the trauma of violence? (pp. 248-249)

Part of what made these presentations so controversial was their rejection of the family therapy's traditional point of view, according to which family violence, like many other problems that occur in families, involves the interacting influence of all members of the family. The traditional, systemic view, now under attack, was that such violence was the outcome of cycles of mutual provocation, an escalation, albeit unacceptable, of the emotionally destructive behavior that characterizes many marriages. Moreover, the audience of therapists was told that they themselves might be part of the problem by excusing or minimizing wife beating. Violent men, from this perspective, don't lose control, they *take* control, and will only stop once they are accountable.

While these presentations generated complaints that they were unnecessarily inflammatory and unfairly stereotyping men (Meth, 1992; Erickson, 1992; Combrinck-Graham, 1991), they also provided a wake-up call. Domestic violence—let's call it what it is, wife battering and child beating—is a major public health problem, right up there with alcoholism and depression.

As family therapists become more sensitive to family violence, they will encounter it more often; more client families will reveal these dirty secrets, ongoing or former abuses that had formerly passed unnoted through therapist caseloads. As they listen to stories of beating and molestation they will become more aware of the devastating effects of trauma and terror on people. They will be less satisfied with approaches that solve all problems in ten sessions and claim that historic traumas or abuses are irrelevant to present problems or solutions. They will become more aware of the social and political climate of violence in our culture. The field will be rudely awakened yet again.

THE DIFFERENTIATION OF THE FAMILY

The postmodern movement was triggered, in part, by recent developments in the United States. First came the gradual recognition, beginning in the 1960s with a growing awareness of mounting problems in our culture, that our own world view may not be all that healthy. This eroded our ethnocentrism and made us more open to other points of view. Second, due to increased immigration and contact with the global media, we were exposed to cultures with entirely different perspectives and lifestyles. This has led to a shift in the goal for our country from a melting pot, where ethnic differences were assimilated, to a stew pot, where different groups coexist but all lend flavor to the whole dish. We now strive to be a pluralistic society that values diversity.

This postmodern pluralism launched another assault on our comfortable image of how families should look. It turned out that the map of the "healthy family" that we inherited from family therapy's pioneers contained not only patriarchal but also ethnocentric biases. What American middle-class therapists had been seeing as pathological family structures may simply have been different. Those differences aren't necessarily problematic just because they do not match the American middle-class norm.

Ethnicity

Monica McGoldrick and her colleagues (McGoldrick, Pearce, & Giordano, 1982) dealt one of the first blows to our ethnocentricity with an edited book, each chapter of which described the characteristic values and structure of a different ethnic group. Following this and a spate of related books (e.g., Falicov, 1983, and in press; Boyd-Franklin, 1989; Szapocznik & Kurtines, 1989; Saba, Karrer, & Hardy, 1990; Mirkin, 1990; Breunlin, Schwartz, & Mac Kune-Karrer, 1992), we are now more sensitive to the importance of knowing some of the characteristics of the ethnic group from which a family descends, so we don't assume they're sick just because they're different. For example, many non-American, middle-class families have a strong rule that each family member is to think of the good of the family before what might be good for himself or herself. While navigating by the early maps, family therapists were likely to view this selfless loyalty to the family as pathological—demonstrating a lack of differentiation, evidence of enmeshment or overprotectiveness—and would challenge it. Now, when encountering such a family value, therapists are more likely to consider, or even explore with the family, the ethnic heritage of the family's belief while evaluating its functionality.

In trying to overcome our ethnocentrism, we had to look again at many of the things we previously considered pathology. For example, Celia Falicov (Falicov & Brudner-White, 1983) drew from the work of anthropologist Francis Hsu to point out that in many cultures the dominant or governing dyad in a family is not the husband and wife. Instead, the primary dyad is often intergenerational—husband-son in some cultures, and wife-son in others. Thus, the very cross-generational coalitions we had been trained to seize upon as the root of a family's problem, may well be normative in that family's culture. This same kind of critique can apply also to many of our other ideas about family life, such as the importance of democratic versus autocratic parenting styles, of open, expressive communication, and of encouraging autonomy versus loyalty in children.

As Monica McGoldrick (1993) writes,

> Ethnicity patterns our thinking, feeling, and behavior in both obvious and subtle ways, although generally operating outside our awareness. It plays a major role in determining what we eat, how we work, how we relate, how we celebrate holidays and rituals, and how we feel about life, death, and illness. (p. 335)

In other words, ethnicity is a powerful meaning generator. Given family therapy's current obsession with belief systems, this interest in ethnicity also makes sense, although the major constructivist schools, with their exclusive focus on the family's language in the session and their reluctance to generalize, have had little to say about ethnicity (McGoldrick, 1993).

It's one thing for therapists to be respectful of the ethnic legacy on a client family's beliefs and structure, but it's also important to help families assess how well that legacy fits with their current context (Breunlin, Schwartz, & Mac Kune Karrer, 1992; Schwartz, 1994). For example, if a family that's structured to fit best within a stable, homogeneous ethnic network finds itself isolated in a middle-class American suburb, they are in for trouble. Simply helping families understand their problems in terms of lack of fit can help them find new solutions.

The multiculturalism of the 1990s has become a dominant theme in family therapy, and this is reflected in the agenda of the major organizations in the field. For example, the 1993 annual AFTA meeting was titled "Social, Cultural and Economic Diversity," and the preconference workshop, "Culture, Power and the Family," gathered as presenters forty of the field's top experts on diversity. The popularity of these issues represents a welcome sensitizing to issues of ethnicity. Yet there are some problems with this focus that remain to be resolved in the coming years.

First, ethnicity is just one of many factors that influence a family's belief system. Other factors such as race, economic class, and education can be obscured by an overemphasis on ethnicity (Breunlin, Schwartz, & Mac Kune-Karrer 1992). For example, a poor family in Guatemala may have more in common with a poor family in Chicago than with a wealthy Guatemalan family. Second, an overemphasis on ethnicity can focus therapists on the differences between themselves and their clients, which can constrain the therapeutic connection. Despite the vast diversity of our backgrounds, we are all more human than otherwise. While we should honor our differences, there are commonalities among us that transcend our backgrounds and can provide crucial empathy and rapport. These commonalities can be obscured when any source of difference becomes foreground.

Multiculturalism is certainly an advance over American ethnocentrism. Yet in highlighting differences, the danger exists of creating a new ethnocentrism around the highlighted group. Segregation, even in the name of ethnic pride, still isolates people within their own group which can foster prejudice. Perhaps pluralism is a better term than multiculturalism because it implies more balance between ethnic identity and connection to the larger group.

Third, the conflict between relativism and political or ethical values, which has reared its head throughout this chapter, is no less an issue here. For example, just because a belief or behavior pattern is normative in another culture, does that mean that it's healthy and shouldn't be challenged? Many cultures are at least as patriarchal as our own. Should we respect a husband's domination over his wife simply because it's customary in their native country? If a family's culture condones using a belt to discipline the children, should we not intervene? In other words, can we become so afraid of imposing our cultural values that we condone inequity and violence? McGoldrick (1993) takes a decidedly nonrelativistic position on this issue.

> Even as we learn to appreciate cultural differences and the limitations of any one perspective, it makes no sense to say that just because a culture proclaims a certain value or belief that it is sacrosanct. We must not move away from responsibility for the complex ethical stance required of us in our clinical work. All cultural practices are not equally ethical. Every intervention we make is political. We must not use notions of

neutrality or deconstruction to shy away from committing ourselves to the values we believe in. (p. 357)

These issues are complex and difficult. While we cannot dictate where therapists should draw the line of tolerance, we can encourage them to draw the line somewhere. The key is to find respectful ways to convey alternative perspectives to clients or help them find those perspectives within themselves.

Race and Class

Where awareness of ethnicity shattered family therapy's homogenized image of families in the early 1980s, the issues of racism and poverty are just beginning to break through. In the early days of family therapy poor African-American families received some attention (e.g., Minuchin et al., 1967), but for many years it seemed that the field, like the rest of the country, tried to forget about this group and the racism they endure. Recently, African-American family therapists such as Nancy Boyd-Franklin (1993) and Ken Hardy (1993), through lectures and writing, have brought these issues out of the shadows and forced them on our consciousness.

One thrust of this work is to help therapists understand African-American families and break through stereotypes, fears, and pessimism. As Boyd-Franklin (1993) laments,

> . . . for poor, inner-city, African-American families, the day-to-day realities of racism, discrimination, classism, poverty, homelessness, violence, crime, and drugs create forces that continually threaten the family's survival. Many clinicians who have no framework with which to view these complicated interrelationships become overwhelmed. (p. 361)

To help overwhelmed clinicians refocus away from family deficits and cultural obstacles, Boyd-Franklin (1989) describes the strengths of African-American families including: a large and strongly bonded kinship network, an adaptability of family roles, a strong religiosity and connection to the church, and an ability to adapt to economic hardship.

Boyd-Franklin (1993) also describes the predicaments that face African-American families. For example, what messages do parents give their children regarding the racism they will encounter? "Parents must walk a fine line between giving children the tools with which to understand racism so they do not internalize the process and instilling in their children a belief that they can achieve despite the odds and overcome racism without becoming consumed with rage and bitterness" (p. 363). African-American families not only have to overcome barriers to opportunity and achievement but also the anxiety and despair that such obstacles create. In addition, it is impossible to survive the war zone in which many inner-city families dwell without some symptoms of post-traumatic stress syndrome, symptoms which are often misunderstood by clinicians, and in this context are anything but abnormal.

Thus, the task of therapists working with poor, African-American families is to avoid being overwhelmed by the obstacles they face, and to understand their symptoms, reluctance to engage in treatment, and distance or

hostility (particularly if the therapist is white) in the context of their environment and their history of negative or unhelpful interaction with white people,
including the many agents of social control they encounter. In addition, the
therapist must focus on the family's many strengths, draw from their networks, or, if the family is isolated, help create networks.

Finally, the therapist must look inside and face his or her attitudes about
race, class, and poverty. Toward this end, several authors recommend curric-
ula which go beyond didactic lectures to personal, experiential encounters—
that is, confronting our own demons of racism (Pinderhughes, 1989; Boyd-
Franklin, 1989).

Ignoring our racial attitudes can harm clients. As an example, Laura
Markowitz (1993) quotes an African-American woman's therapy experience.

> I remember being in therapy years ago with a nice white woman who
> kept focusing me on why I was such an angry person and on my parents
> as inadequate individuals. . . . We never looked at my father as a poor
> black man, my mother as a poor black woman and the context in which
> they survived and raised us. . . . Years later, I saw a therapist of color and
> the first thing out of her mouth was, "Let's look at what was going on for
> your parents." It was a joyous moment to be able to see my dad not as a
> terrible person who hated us but as a survivor living under amazingly
> difficult conditions. I could embrace him, and I could understand my
> anger instead of blaming myself for feeling that way. (p. 29)

Racism has also become an issue within the field of family therapy. As
Markowitz (1993) points out,

> the largest of the professional associations, the AAMFT, has never had
> a person of color as board president, executive director, nor included
> more than one or two as board members in its 51-year history, despite
> having a reported 10 percent of members identified as minorities.
> (p. 29)

In contrast NASW, the national organization for social workers, which has the
same percentage of minorities, is structured such that at least every third term
a minority person is elected president.

In a recent issue of the *Family Therapy Networker,* African-American family
therapists spoke out about their experience in a predominantly white field.
Ken Hardy (1993), for example, described the masquerade that many African-American professionals live and the bonds they feel,

> To avoid being seen by whites as troublemakers, we suppress the part of
> ourselves that feels hurt and outraged by the racism around us, instead
> developing an "institutional self"—an accommodating facade of calm
> professionalism calculated to be nonthreatening to whites. . . . Familiar
> only with our institutional selves, white people don't appreciate the
> sense of immediate connection and unspoken loyalty that binds black
> people together. . . . We are united by being raised with the same mes-
> sages most black families pass on to their children: "You were born into

one of the most despised groups in the world. You can't trust white people. You are somebody. Be proud, and never for one minute think that white people are better than you." (pp. 52-53)

These voices mark the beginning of an important discussion that we hope will make family therapy a more hospitable place for African-American therapists and clients alike.

Gay and Lesbian Issues

Family therapy's consciousness was raised about gay and lesbian issues in the same way it was for race. After a long period of neglect or denial (we could find only one article: Krestan & Bepko, 1980) in the late 1980s, family therapy began to face these issues with which a sizable percentage of the population struggle (Crawford, 1988; Goodrich et al., 1988; Krestan, 1988; Roth & Murphy, 1986; Roth, 1989; Carl, 1990; Markowitz, 1991; Hersch, 1991; Dahlheimer & Feigal, 1991; Laird, 1993; Sanders, 1993).

As for African Americans, the signs of sensitization in family therapy to gay and lesbian issues have included a special issue of the *Family Therapy Networker* (January, 1991) and a powerful AFTA conference plenary (1992) titled "The Love That Dares to Speak Its Name." Perhaps the biggest sign of change in the field's attitude, however, is that the second edition of *Normal Family Processes*, an influential text, includes a chapter on gay and lesbian families, whereas the first edition, ten years earlier, did not. That gay and lesbian families are now considered one of many normal family types is quite a change for our field and our culture.

Yet many straight family therapists ignore this literature and receive little if any exposure to gay and lesbian issues in graduate school, despite the fact that even if they don't work with many openly gay or lesbian clients, many of their client families struggle with polarizations from having a gay or lesbian child. To avoid doing harm to these families or to other gay and lesbian clients, therapists must examine their attitudes about sexuality and must understand what such clients face in a homophobic world.

Harmonious relationships are more difficult to achieve for gay and lesbian couples, not because they are inherently more pathological than straight couples, but because our society presents them with far more obstacles. After a childhood full of confusion, shame, secrecy, and fear of discovery, many gays and lesbians are disowned by their families once they come out. Where heterosexual couples are often supported and encouraged to remain together by their families, gay and lesbian couples often have the opposite experience. Despite gains in tolerance in some segments of our society, they continue to face humiliation, discrimination, and even violence because of their sexuality. Due to the lack of social support, the bonds in gay and lesbian relationships can be tenuous, generating jealousy and intense involvement.

Rather than explore the impact of these constraints on their lives or relationships, many therapists (even those who consider themselves tolerant) continue to push gay and lesbian clients to look into their pasts to find the cause of their homosexuality, or to try to resolve their "sexual confusion."

Relatedly, many therapists carry unexamined prejudices regarding these couples having children through adoption or alternative insemination.

We hope the day will arrive soon when gay and lesbian families, as well as those of African Americans and other marginalized groups, are studied by family therapists to learn not only about the problems they face but also about how they survive and thrive against such great odds. As Laird (1993) suggests, these families have much to teach us, "about gender relationships, about parenting, about adaptation to tensions in this society, and especially about strength and resilience" (p. 284). The question is whether we are ready to learn.

Specialization

Another trend, begun in the 1980s and related to the recognition of ethnicity as an important consideration, was the increased specialization of treatment models. Books emerged that focused on how to do family therapy with a host of specific types of problems and family constellations. In fact, this trend predated the 1980s (for example, Minuchin and his colleagues had written books on "families of the slums" and on "psychosomatic families"), but the number of recent specialized texts and articles reflects a maturing of the field.

There are books on working with families of people who abuse drugs (Stanton, Todd, & Associates, 1982; Kaufman, 1985); abuse alcohol (Steinglass, Bennett, Wolin, & Reiss, 1987; Bepko & Krestan, 1985; Treadway, 1989; Elkin, 1990; Berg & Miller, 1992); abuse food (Root, Fallon, & Friedrich, 1986; Schwartz, 1994); and abuse each other (Trepper & Barrett, 1989; Friedrich, 1990; Madanes, 1990).

In addition there are books for treating: single-parent families (Morawetz & Walker, 1984); step-parent families (Visher & Visher, 1979, 1988); divorcing families (Issacs, Montalvo, & Abelsohn, 1986; Sprenkle, 1985; Wallerstein & Kelley, 1980; Ahrons & Rogers, 1989); blended families (Hansen, 1982; Sager et al., 1983); families in transition among these states (Pittman, 1987; Falicov, 1988); and for all combinations of relationships within families (Walters, Carter, Papp, & Silverstein, 1988).

There are also books for families with young children (Zilbach, 1986; Combrinck-Graham, 1989); with troubled adolescents (Mirkin & Koman, 1985) and young adults (Haley, 1980); with problems among siblings (Bank & Kahn, 1982; Kahn & Lewis, 1988); as well as a book about "normal families" (Walsh, 1982, 1993) and another about "successful families" (Beavers & Hampson, 1990).

There are books for working with schizophrenic families (Anderson, Reiss, & Hogarty, 1986); families with AIDS (Walker, 1991); families who have suffered trauma (Figley, 1989); families with chronic illness or disability (Rolland, 1994; McDaniel, Hepworth, & Doherty, 1992); and those who are grieving a death (Walsh & McGoldrick, 1991).

Extending the ethnicity theme, there is a book for working with African-American families (Boyd-Franklin, 1989), Latino families (Falicov, in press), and with minority families in general (Saba, Karrer, & Hardy, 1989).

In addition to these specialized books, the field has broadened its scope and extended systems thinking beyond the family to include the impact on families and their problems of larger systems like other helping agents or social agencies and schools (Schwartzman, 1985; Berger, Jurkovic & Associates, 1984; Imber-Black, 1988; Minuchin, 1984; Elizur & Minuchin, 1989); and the impact of the absence of family rituals and their use in therapy (Imber-Black, Roberts, & Whiting, 1988), and the sociopolitical context in which families exist (Mirkin, 1990).

One point to be made about this trend is that many of these books transcend individual models of family therapy. The author may have a particular orientation but that orientation takes enough of a backseat to the specific content that the book can be read by therapists from other orientations without engendering rivalry. Thus, as opposed to the 1960s and 1970s, during which the followers of a particular model read little but what came out of that school and eagerly awaited the next offering from the school's leadership, this recent trend toward specialization by content area rather than by model has decreased factionalism and increased communication among the models. The field itself has become more pluralistic in this postmodern age.

WHAT HAPPENED TO FUNCTIONALISM?

Functionalism, the philosophy discussed in Chapter 2 that influenced therapists to search for the function that a problem serves for the family, is another cornerstone of family therapy that has been challenged by postmodernists. Michael White (1989), for example, believes that problems oppress families rather than are created by them. This turns functionalism on its ear. Rather than examine the effect the family has on the symptom, White focuses on the effect the symptom has on the family, and tries to get family members to unite in an effort to wrestle control of their lives from the oppressive symptom.

Functionalism has also been challenged by those who work with severe disorders like schizophrenia. Rather than seeing families as causing or needing the schizophrenia in their offspring, psychoeducational family therapists see schizophrenics as having a disease that impedes their ability to process information and makes them hypersensitive to environmental stimulation. Family stress, according to this way of thinking, may cause problems for schizophrenic members, but families don't cause schizophrenia. Families don't need symptoms or a scapegoat for distraction; they are themselves victims of the disease. Psychoeducational therapists join forces with families to help them understand the nature of schizophrenia, to alleviate their guilt, and to help them work together to help the patient (Anderson, Reiss, & Hogarty, 1986).

This represents a significant shift in thinking for family therapy from looking at the impact of families on symptoms to the reverse: the impact of symptoms on families. It is a shift that, in threatening its functionalist base, has profound implications for family therapy that extend well beyond the example of schizophrenia (see Chapter 11).

As might be expected, this shift away from functionalism has generated protest. Jay Haley (1988), for example, spoke out against the psychoeducational movement. Others, like Salvador Minuchin (Elizur & Minuchin, 1989) were more circumspect:

When Jay Haley made it clear that he had not deviated from a position he has held for decades—that schizophrenia is a sociopsychological entity and that hospitalization and drug treatment produce iatrogenic results—Carol Anderson and Michael Goldstein . . . responded with a broadside: Haley was blind not to see the importance of joining with a family's pain at having a schizophrenic member. Immediately the lines were drawn, and family therapists of different persuasions chose up sides, joining one of the parties and becoming deaf to what the other was saying. (p. 65)

Part of this debate centers around the disease metaphor for syndromes. Traditionally family therapy has opposed the medical model, preferring more interactional explanations. This field had a similarly difficult time seeing alcoholism as a disease, a metaphor with a powerful and growing grip on the consciousness of the American public. Through the popularity of the 12-step, Alcoholics Anonymous (AA) model, the idea that an alcoholic has an incurable illness, from which he or she can recover but never be cured, has become so pervasive that all mental health professions have been forced to take it seriously. Indeed, the disease metaphor has been expanded to apply to all the people intimately related to the alcoholic. An alcoholic's spouse is "codependent" and goes to Codependency Anonymous groups; an alcoholic's child becomes an Adult Child of an Alcoholic and goes to 12-step groups for ACoAs.

In the case of alcoholism, the disease metaphor has different implications for treatment than it does for schizophrenia (AA versus medication), implications that perhaps are more palatable for family therapists. Many of the principles advocated in 12-step programs complement or echo principles outlined in this book: helping family members differentiate from each other and break out of dysfunctional patterns. A growing number of books written by family therapists about alcoholism advocate AA support and language (Bepko & Kresten, 1985; Elkin, 1990; Treadway, 1989). In addition, Sharon Wegscheider-Cruse (1985) borrowed Virginia Satir's (1972) typology of family roles (blamer, placater, distracter, and computer) and applied it to children in alcoholic families (hero, scapegoat, lost child, and mascot). Far from ignoring this amazingly popular movement, family therapy, despite its ambivalence about the disease metaphor, is keeping pace with and contributing to the AA, ACoA movement.

Those who subscribe to the disease model believe that family therapy's search for the hidden function a patient's behavior serves for the family has done both patients and their families a terrible disservice, implying as it does that the patient's behavior is voluntary and that family members either want or need it. As a result, these critics say, family members have been made to feel unnecessarily guilty and inept, and patients to feel unnecessarily angry with themselves and their families.

The idea that symptoms serve protective functions in families is by no means dead in the field, however. In a survey of family therapists, over three quarters of the sample responded with "often" or "almost always" to the question: "Do you believe that symptoms arise to serve an interpersonal function in families?" (Raitt, 1988). While there continues to be a growing disenchantment with the idea that families somehow need their problems to preserve their equilibrium, it is difficult to imagine that the family therapy field will ever totally divorce itself from this seminal belief.

Antifunctionalist sentiment, while useful and warranted, may also represent a pendulum swing in reaction to the many unfortunate consequences of the way that family therapy has incorporated functionalism. There is no question that family therapists have done damage by presupposing and conveying to families, overtly or covertly, that they are so selfish as to be willing to have their children suffer rather than face scary issues. Too often functionalism has turned therapists into pathology detectives, hunting for clues to the underlying function and suspicious that the family's reports about their problems are attempts to mislead or obfuscate. Such detectives don't trust improvements in the problem until the putative function or structural flaw that underlies it has been rooted out and corrected.

These negative consequences, rather than being inherent in the notion that symptoms sometimes play a protective role in families, are the result of the way that observation has been interpreted. Recognition of the protectively functional nature of symptoms was such a revelation to many therapists that they came to certain essentialist conclusions: *all* symptoms serve protective functions in families, the function a symptom serves in the family is the primary factor maintaining it, patients behave as they do to distract or protect other family members, and the family's need for a distraction was the primary precipitant of the symptom.

Such extreme beliefs tended to make the function-of-the-symptom element of assessment and treatment overshadow all others, and cast therapists into the pathology detective role. It's possible to believe, instead, that in some cases families are so distressed that they will seize on distractions from painful and hard to face issues and that, sometimes, they will use a child's symptoms as one (Schwartz, 1990).

Thus, the idea that families may need a distraction is different from the idea that they need or want symptoms. Unhappy couples will often need or want to be diverted from their most painful concerns and will seize anything available for that purpose. Since their child's symptoms are there and are available, they may use those symptoms, along with any number of other distractions. They may not make the connection between their use of the symptom and its maintenance or exacerbation, and, instead, strongly wish it were not there; but since it is, they use it.

But this distractive process is involved only in *some* cases—many, if not most, problems are attempts to protect other family members. Where evidence suggests that such a protective process is involved, many other processes are also at work on which it may be better to focus. In other words, even where a therapist believes such distractive or protective sequences are involved, this doesn't have to be pointed out to or admitted by a family for the symptom to be resolved. If people can lift themselves out of their fear and desperation in other ways, the need for symptomatic distractions will vanish, if it ever existed.

We don't need to make functionalist investigations the centerpiece of our therapy. Nor, on the other hand, do we have to deny or ignore the protective operation of symptoms when this information emerges and where the family may benefit from discussing it. We also don't have to minimize the oppressive impact that symptoms have on family life, while insinuating that they want things that way. Instead, we can genuinely empathize with our client families' predicaments.

TRENDS COUNTER TO POSTMODERNISM

While there are many trends in family therapy that seem consistent with postmodernist relativism, there are a few that go against that grain and imply that all is not relative.

Research Groups

Groups of clinician-researchers have been struggling for years to develop family therapy approaches that work with multi-problem families and violent, antisocial behavior. Funded by large federal grants, they strive to carefully test the results of their interventions and use this knowledge to refine their approach. In doing rigorous, quantitative research they are swimming against the postmodern current of research skepticism.

Since they believe there is no such thing as objectivity, skeptical postmodernists contend that research is used to bolster established knowledges and marginalize alternatives. They believe that since each theory or model is just another story about families or therapy, none better than any other, there's no point in trying to compare or test them. In addition, the approaches these researchers are testing generally involve aspects of behavioral and/or structural family therapies—approaches which have been deemed modernist and passe by the new wave in the field.

As a result, many of these projects operate in relative obscurity as far as most family therapists are concerned. This is unfortunate because, despite what the skeptical postmodernists say, this research movement is vital to the future of the field. We have an ethical obligation to evaluate the effectiveness of our approaches and to address our society's most difficult problems. In addition, our economic future depends on our ability to demonstrate to third-party payers that family therapy is effective. We hope and trust that the obscurity of these projects is temporary; that once their results are completed and fully published, they will have the influence they deserve.

The best known of these research projects is led by Gerald Patterson who has been refining his behavioral methods for two decades at the Oregon Social Learning Center in Eugene. Other prominent leaders in this movement include Jose Szapocznik at the University of Miami, Jim Alexander at the University of Utah, Scott Henggeler at the Medical College of South Carolina in Charleston, Pat Tolan at the University of Illinois at Chicago, and Howard Liddle at Temple University in Philadelphia. Their research is described in Chapter 13.

Ironically, these groups are well-known and highly regarded outside family therapy. Because of the desperate need for ways to work with the problems these projects target, national policy makers are well aware of them and look to them for direction. These researchers provide credibility for family therapy within the larger mental health field, credibility that has been strained by the eccentric practices and unsubstantiated outcome claims of some of the other models described in this book.

The Self Reenters the System

The final trend we want to highlight reverses the postmodern swing away from intrapsychic speculation and grand theories. The pendulum that swung family therapy away from intrapsychic, individual models of psychotherapy began to swing back in the 1980s, despite the postmodern disdain for the idea that we have a separate self that can be explored and mapped. The reasons for this new appreciation for the individual are many.

The first of these reasons is developmental. Family therapy has become sufficiently accepted as a valid discipline that it no longer has to maintain the us-versus-them attitude of its early days. Like an adolescent taking a second look at parents she once rejected, the field has grown strong and confident enough to admit that it may not have all the answers after all and that psychological considerations may also be important.

A second factor has to do with the immigration of increasing numbers of psychodynamically trained clinicians into the family therapy field as family therapy became more popular and less polarized from the psychotherapy establishment. This influx has created an increasing demand for models that can bridge the gap between the self and the system.

Finally, several offshoots of psychoanalysis have evolved to the point that they seem more compatible with family therapy. Classic Freudian drive theory gives people's environment little credit for their problems and, consequently, gives little justification for working with their families. Freud taught us that human nature is propelled by unconscious forces buried deep within the psyche. Both object relations theory and self psychology put more emphasis on a person's interactions with family.

The essence of object relations theory is quite simple: We relate to people in the present partly on the basis of expectations formed by early experience. For the more interpersonally oriented object relations theorists like Ronald Fairbairn and Donald Winnicott, interpersonal relatedness replaces drives, aggression, and the pleasure principle as the driving force in human personality.

Object relations theory says that the past is alive—in memory—and it runs people's lives more than they know. From our early relationships with caretakers, we formed mental images, called *internal objects,* that structure the way we experience the world. As adults, we react to other people based in large part on how much those people resemble these internal objects, rather than on the real characteristics of the people.

As applied to family therapy then, the idea is that the dysfunctional patterns that family therapists have identified are often maintained by the internal object relations of key family members. Through a process called *projective identification,* the images of certain internal objects are projected onto other family members, who are then induced to act out these projections. Object relations family therapists interpret these projections to families so that their members can be more aware of the unseen forces behind their unhappy interactions and more able to change them.

In the 1980s a number of books were written on object relations and family therapy (Nichols, 1987; Leupnitz, 1988; Wachtel & Wachtel, 1986; Kirschner & Kirschner, 1986; Slipp, 1984; Scharff & Scharff, 1987). In addition the self psychology of Heinz Kohut (1971, 1977) has had a revolutionizing impact on the psychoanalytic world and, indirectly, on family therapy. Kohut replaced Freud's raging id with an insecure self at the core of human nature and taught us that our lives are organized around a striving for fulfillment and longing for acceptance, more than around sex and aggression.

These ideas have strong implications for the nature of the relationship between therapist and patient. Therapists are to be more nurturant and empathic—to provide a safe, warm envelope known as a *holding environment*—rather than remaining distant, passive, and neutral. This is a large and controversial step for psychoanalysis, and also for family therapy.

The attempted marriage of even these more interpersonally oriented psychoanalytic theories with family therapy is a delicate matter. These models still contain concepts and assumptions that do not blend well with systems thinking, and various writers have handled this problem in different ways. Some advocate giving up on systems theory and replacing it with object relations as a basis for family therapy. Others try to use both, but keep them separated and use them sequentially or to complement each other. Still others have tried to integrate the concepts and methods of the two paradigms, a process very much like trying to mate animals across species.

One model has taken a different tack. Instead of trying to work with the incompatibilities between object relations and systems thinking, Schwartz (1987, 1994) extended systems principles and techniques to intrapsychic process, applying them to the interaction of internal subpersonalities. In the process, he stumbled onto a new method of working intrapsychically and a useful language for therapy, as well as a way to move fluidly from family to internal considerations (see Chapter 11).

Many family therapists continue to maintain the systemic position of the pioneers and view this return to the individual as regressive. For them, the discovery of systemic concepts and techniques was as clarifying as turning on a light in a dark room. Where once there was only chaos and confusion, they could now see triangles, boundary violations, and circular interaction sequences. The idea of going back into the murky, speculative, and emotional intrapsychic arena, from which they were rescued by family therapy, is quite unsavory.

We agree that there are dangers in this swingback. It's easy to get lost in the fascinating inner life of individuals and, once again, to minimize the importance of their external context. It's easy to become daunted by stories of pathological interactions in a person's early life and underestimate their ability to change in the present. It's easy to become overwhelmed by the complexity of trying to understand the many psyches that comprise a family system. We mustn't forget, however, that even though families act like systems, it is still individuals who do the acting—and they, as you may have noticed, can sometimes be pretty courageous.

If the field proceeds carefully toward a systemic appreciation of individuals, then these dangers can be addressed. When this is achieved, our models will be enriched and blind spots will be filled as we will be able to appreciate both internal and external levels of the system and shift between them as needed. We will respect the power of family systems without losing sight of the abilities of individuals to control their own lives. We will be able to identify problematic interaction patterns in the family while also knowing each family member as a flesh and blood person rather than as a cog in the machine. That is an exciting prospect.

THE FAMILY THERAPY ESTABLISHMENT

Having now described the evolution of family therapy's concepts and methods, we will, in this section, present something of a consumer's guide to the field as it appears in the spring of 1994. In the four decades since its inception, family therapy has had a tremendous influence on the psychotherapeutic community and has grown so large that it is impossible to cover adequately in a few pages. Nonetheless, we will attempt to orient readers to some of what is available.

Professional Organizations

The *American Association for Marriage and Family Therapy* (AAMFT), located in Washington, D.C., was organized in 1942 by Lester Dearborn and Ernest Graves as a professional organization to set standards for marriage counselors. In 1970 it was expanded to include family therapists, and has become the major credentialing body for the field. Through its requirements for membership, standards have been set for becoming a family therapist that are used by the various states that regulate the profession. AAMFT also lobbies state and federal governments for the interests of family therapists, interests such as state licensing.

AAMFT's membership has grown enormously, reflecting the growth of the field. In the decade since the first edition of this book, membership has more than doubled, from 9,000 in 1983 to nearly 20,000 in 1990. This kind of membership and the money generated from it has made AAMFT a powerful player in mental health politics, and has aided in public and governmental recognition of family therapy as a distinct field.

The *American Family Therapy Academy* (AFTA) was organized in 1977 to serve the needs of the field's senior researchers, clinicians, and trainers who wanted a smaller, more intimate context for sharing ideas and developing common interests. Despite high standards for membership regarding years of teaching and clinical experience, and an interest in remaining small, AFTA's membership has also doubled since 1983, going from 500 to over 1,000. AFTA is a high-level think tank focused around its annual conference, described below, and its newsletter.

Conferences

Besides the multitude of workshops and conferences privately sponsored or put on by local chapters of AAMFT, there are four main national meetings. By far the largest is AAMFT's annual conference each October which has grown to the point (between three and four thousand) that only a few cities have the facilities to accommodate it. With over 200 presentations on various family therapy topics to select from, there is something for everyone. In addition, the conference features the Masters Series, in which well-known therapists interview families while an audience watches, as well as a series of plenary addresses by leaders in the field.

The second largest (over 2,000) is the Family Therapy Network Symposium each March in Washington, D.C. Sponsored by the *Family Therapy Networker* magazine (described below), all presenters are invited so that quality throughout the 80 workshops is ensured. Each year the symposium has a theme and invited plenary speakers are often famous for work done from outside the field of family therapy; one of these is often a writer such as, in recent years, Tom Wolfe, Maya Angelou, and John Updike.

AFTA's annual meeting deliberately has a different flavor than these other conferences. Because of its small size (usually around 300—it is not open to nonmembers), it's the one place where many of the leaders of the field can gather in a relatively informal setting to discuss ideas. Rather than workshops, the meeting is organized around interest groups and brief presentations designed to promote interaction.

The other conference where many family therapists can be found is not devoted exclusively to family therapy. The American Orthopsychiatric Association is a multidisciplinary organization whose annual conference usually contains a sizable percentage of presentations devoted to family therapy or to issues that would interest systems-oriented clinicians.

Publications

The first book devoted entirely to the diagnosis and treatment of families was Nathan Ackerman's, *The Psychodynamics of Family Life*, published in 1958. The field's first journal, *Family Process*, was founded in 1961. Since these early publications, the family therapy literature has proliferated to the point where it is virtually impossible to stay on top of it. We count over 20 journals or newsletters devoted to some aspect of family therapy published in the United States, with many other countries publishing their own journals. The number of books is equally overwhelming, so we refer the reader to the *Recommended Readings* section in the back of this volume for a selective guide to some of the most useful books and articles in the field. Below we will describe some of the major periodicals.

Family Process continues to exert a powerful influence on the field. Many of the debates and developments described in the first three chapters of this book appeared first in its pages. Founded in 1961 by Don Jackson and Nathan Ackerman, its editors have included Jay Haley, Don Bloch, Carlos Sluzki, and, starting in 1990, Peter Steinglass. The *Journal of Marital and Family Therapy* is a close second in prestige and, as the official journal of AAMFT, has a large readership. Under the editorship of Alan Gurman during the 1980s and now Douglas Sprenkle in the 1990s, *JMFT* increased its focus on research and improved its standards.

The *Family Therapy Networker,* a magazine devoted to issues related to family therapy or psychotherapy in general, also has a strong influence. Its huge readership (upwards of 70,000) has been won through tackling provocative issues with high-quality writing. Rich Simon has turned what began as a small newsletter (*The Family Schtick*) into the most widely read publication on psychotherapy and, in so doing, has introduced many of family therapy's ideas to therapists throughout the country. In 1993, the *Family Therapy Networker* won the American Magazine Award for feature writing, the highest honor possible for a magazine.

There are a number of other well-established journals that, like *Family Process* and *JMFT,* are devoted to general issues in the field. These include the *American Journal of Family Therapy, Journal of Family Psychotherapy, The International Journal of Family Therapy, Contemporary Family Therapy,* and *Family Therapy Collections.* In addition, a number of specialized journals have emerged. For example, the *Journal of Systemic Therapies* (formerly the *Journal of Strategic and Systemic Therapies*) is widely read by therapists who use those adjectives to describe themselves, while Bowenian therapists will soon be reading *Family Systems* and those interested in Michael White's work subscribe to the *Dulwich Centre Review* and *Family Therapy Case Studies.*

The cross-fertilization of family therapy with other fields is represented by *Family Systems Medicine,* a journal devoted to the collaboration between medicine and family therapy, by the *Journal of Family Psychology,* published by a division of the American Psychological Association, and by *Feminism and Family Therapy,* which reflects the growing influence of feminist thought on the field.

News within the field and digests of important developments are conveyed through AAMFT's newsletter, *Family Therapy News,* and through the *Marriage and Family Review* and the *Brown University Family Therapy Newsletter.* Those interested in the branch of sociology called family studies have much in common with family therapists and read *Family Relations* and the *Journal of Marriage and the Family.*

TRAINING CENTERS

As we have already discussed, family therapy developed primarily outside academia. There are, however, a handful of doctoral programs and a larger number of masters programs specializing in marital and family therapy in universities around the country. The American Association for Marriage and Family Therapy (1100 Seventeenth St., NW, 10th Floor, Washington, DC 20036-4601) accredits 29 masters programs and ten doctoral programs and can provide a list of them. Because we are aware of no comparable list of the major nonacademic training centers, we will offer below a description of some of the best known centers in the United States. There are other major centers throughout the world, but our space is limited. The reader may notice that the large majority of these are clustered in the northeast where family therapy is most strongly rooted. We will begin there and move west.

The *Family Institute of Cambridge* in Massachusetts was founded in 1976. Now located in Watertown, it is a nonprofit center of training and research in applied systems theory. Faculty members include such notable therapists as Evan Imber-Black, Michele Bograd, Laura Chasin, Richard Chasin, Thelma Jean Goodrich, Natalie Schwartzberg, and Sallyann Roth. The institute offers four training sequences: (1) fundamentals of family systems, (2) intensive clinical, (3) couples therapy, and (4) narrative approaches to therapy. The institute also offers a wide variety of long- and short-term courses, group supervision, and conferences and has some training scholarships for supervision at inner-city clinics and research stipends for its students. While the faculty is strongly interested in family therapy, they also do systems-oriented work with individuals, couples, organizations, and communities. The institute's Public Conversation Project is exploring the use of family therapy skills and techniques to foster dialogue as an alternative to debate on divisive public issues such as the abortion controversy. For more information, contact the Administrator, 51 Kondazian St., Watertown, MA 02172.

The *Kantor Family Institute*, in Somerville, Massachusetts, was founded by David Kantor after he left the Family Institute of Cambridge in 1980, and is informed by his structural/analytic model of therapy, as well as psychodynamic and other family therapy influences. The institute offers a sequence of three one-year training programs that build upon each other but can be taken independently. They also offer a specialized program in couples treatment, and in organizational consultation, as well as a variety of apprenticeships, internships, and courses. For more information contact: Ulrike Dettling, Kantor Family Institute, 7 Shepard Street, Cambridge, MA 02138.

Family Studies, Inc., is a small private training institution in New York City, founded in 1981 by Salvador Minuchin. The faculty also includes Jorge Colapinto, Ema Genijovich, Daniel Minuchin, Patricia Minuchin, and George Simon. Special programs are designed for on-site training and consultation with agencies that work with poor families, foster care, substance abuse, the homeless, or children in psychiatric facilities. The year-long extern training program is at three levels: beginning family therapists, more experienced therapists, and administrators and supervisors. The orientation emphasizes structural family therapy and the connection between families and larger systems. Inquiries may be directed to Salvador Minuchin, P.O. Box 1035, Cooper Station, New York, NY 10276.

The *Ackerman Institute for Family Therapy* in New York City was founded as the Family Institute by Nathan Ackerman in 1965. Following Ackerman's death in 1971, the center was renamed in his honor and the directorship was assumed by Donald Bloch, who has recently passed the baton to Peter Steinglass, current editor of *Family Process*. In addition to Bloch and Steinglass, the institute also has such noted family therapists and theorists as Peggy Penn, Peggy Papp, Olga Silverstein, Marcia Sheinberg, Virginia Goldner, and Gillian Walker. The institute offers training in systemic family therapy. It offers a one-year introductory training program and a two-year clinical externship program for more experienced family therapists. In addition, the institute offers weekend workshops throughout the year. For further information contact: Marcia Sheinberg, Director of Training, 149 East 78th St., New York, NY 10021.

The *Family Institute of Westchester* is located in Mount Vernon, New York, and is directed by Betty Carter. FIW teaches the multicontextual approach, which includes aspects of structural and strategic techniques, and is based on the Bowen model. The institute has been in operation since 1977 and is primarily known for its training program, which usually takes three years to complete. There is also a two-year externship which meets weekly. Specialized training programs are offered in multicultural family therapy, and therapy with gay and lesbian couples and families. Additional information is available from Lillian Fine, Director of Administration, Family Institute of Westchester, 147 Archer Ave., Mount Vernon, NY 10550.

The *Center for Family Learning* in Rye Brook, New York, was founded in 1973 by Philip Guerin, who was trained by Murray Bowen. The center provides a three-year training program in family systems therapy which includes a clinical externship year for experienced clinicians, followed by a fellowship year with center faculty working on the Child and Adolescents Project. The third year is another fellowship studying marital conflict. The center also offers a wide variety of seminars and workshops, as well as a Community Education Program which is taped for cable television. For additional information contact: Eileen Guerin Pendagast, Director of Post Graduate and Community Education, 28 Rye Ridge Plaza, Rye Brook, NY 10573.

The *Family Therapy Training Program at the University of Rochester* was established in 1983 by Judith Landau-Stanton and M. Duncan Stanton. The current director is Susan McDaniel. The FTTP teaches the Rochester Model, an integration of structural, strategic, transgenerational, and experiential approaches in a series of externships and seminars. Special areas of interest are cultural transition and medical family therapy. Cases are provided for trainees. The faculty includes such notable family therapists as Lyman C. Wynne. For more information contact: Judith Mincher, Family Therapy Training Program, Department of Psychiatry, University of Rochester, 300 Crittenden Boulevard, Rochester, NY 14642.

The *Family Institute of New Jersey* was founded in 1992 by its director, Monica McGoldrick. It is committed to training, research, and service in support of cultural diversity and the empowerment of those voices our society silences. In addition to a three-year certificate program, the institute offers a variety of workshops, free lectures to the community, and consultation to schools and other organizations. Minority scholarships are available. Faculty includes notable therapists such as Nydia Garcia Preto and Paulette Moore Hines. For further information contact: Monica McGoldrick, 312 Amboy Ave., Metuchen, NJ 08840.

The *Family Therapy Institute of Washington, D.C.* is the training center and clinic codirected by Jay Haley and Cloe Madanes. Haley and Madanes teach, supervise, and conduct therapy emphasizing their strategic, problem-focused approach. A variety of training programs are offered in which Haley and Madanes present seminars, videotaped examples of therapy, and live supervision. The institute's clinic offers treatment provided by a multidisciplinary staff, all of whom have previously trained with Haley and Madanes. Haley and Madanes offer workshops and seminars to professionals throughout the United States and Europe. Inquiries may be made to: Executive Director, Family Therapy Institute of Washington, D.C., 5850 Hubbard Dr., Rockville, MD 20852.

The *Georgetown Family Center,* located in Washington, D.C., exists to refine, test, extend, and define Bowen theory. Murray Bowen founded and directed this center until his death in 1990. The current director is Michael Kerr. Training programs include a weekly, postgraduate program, and a special program for out-of-towners that meets for three consecutive days, four times a year. Other learning opportunities include the monthly Clinical Conference Series and the annual Main Symposium. A description of these programs is available from: Daniel Papero, Director of Training, Georgetown Family Center, 4380 MacArthur Blvd. N.W., Washington, DC 20007.

The *Family Therapy Practice Center of Washington, D.C.* was founded in 1980 by Marianne Walters, after she left the Philadelphia Child Guidance Clinic. The center has a strong structural family therapy base and offers a postgraduate externship. In addition, the center develops programs for dealing with at-risk populations and changing family structures such as their adolescent foster care project, family violence assistance project, and runaway youth/multiple family group project. For more information contact: Director of Training, 2153 Newport Place N.W., Washington, DC 20037.

The *Philadelphia Child Guidance Center* became one of the leading centers of family therapy in the world during the 1970s. It was here that Salvador Minuchin and his colleagues defined and promulgated the concepts of structural family therapy. It provides the full range of children's services: outpatient, home-based, day hospital, and inpatient. The outpatient specialty services include: early childhood intervention, sexual abuse (victims and offenders), divorce and remarriage, and pain control. Three home-based programs serve children and adolescents at risk for placement and provide specialized foster care. The inpatient service includes family apartments so that families are maximally involved in the treatment process.

Unlike most of the other centers of family therapy training, which are located in small clinics and old houses, PCGC is a large, modern, well-equipped facility that is physically part of the Children's Hospital of Philadelphia. The center is affiliated with the Departments of Psychiatry and Pediatrics of the University of Pennsylvania School of Medicine. PCGC probably has trained more family therapists than any other center in the world. The training programs include internships and externships for psychology, social work, child psychiatry, or postgraduate students. Additional information can be obtained by writing to: Marion Lindblad-Goldberg, Director, Family Therapy Training Center, Philadelphia Child Guidance Center, 34th Street and Civic Center Blvd., Philadelphia, PA 19104.

The *Atlanta Institute for Family Studies* was founded in 1977 by Carrell Dammann (who left to found The Open Hand). The current director, Michael Berger and faculty teach an integration of structural, strategic, and Bowen approaches as well as hypnosis in externships and internships. The institute also is doing research on developing support networks for families struggling with AIDS or with handicapped children. For more information contact: Michael Berger, Glenridge 400 Office Park, Bldg. 1, Suite 133, 5825 Glenridge Dr., Atlanta, GA 30328.

The *Brief Family Therapy Center* (BFTC) of Milwaukee is known for its specialization in the research, training, and clinical practice of brief, solution-focused therapy. BFTC provides short- and long-term training in solution-focused therapy that attracts practitioners from North America, Europe, and Asia. The staff includes Steve de Shazer, Insoo Kim Berg, Scott Miller, and Larry Hopwood, who have presented workshops and seminars in more than 30 countries and written extensively on solution-focused therapy. For further information contact: Brief Family Therapy Center, 6815 West Capitol Drive, Suite 300, Milwaukee, WI 53216.

The *Family Institute* (formerly of Chicago) was founded in 1968 by Charles Kramer to provide training, research, and clinical services. William Pinsof, the president of the institute, and the large faculty, including notable family therapists Douglas Breunlin and Cheryl Rampage, offer a variety of training programs grounded in a multilevel, integrative approach. Elements of the approach include Integrative Problem Centered Therapy, the Metaframeworks perspective, feminism, and multiculturalism. They offer a two-year certificate program that is accredited by AAMFT and a masters in family therapy in affiliation with Northwestern University, as well as a one-year clinical training practicum, a psychology internship, and a postdoctoral fellowship. Students in these programs see clients through their clinic. In 1994 the institute will move to a new facility in Evanston. For more information contact: Marina Eovaldi, The Family Institute, 680 N. Lake Shore Drive, Suite 1306, Chicago, IL 60611.

The *Family Systems Program* (FSP) at the Institute for Juvenile Research in Chicago was founded in 1974. It is a part of the Department of Psychiatry of the University of Illinois at Chicago. The current faculty includes Director Betty Mac Kune Karrer and Richard Schwartz, who, with Doug Breunlin, developed the metaframeworks approach which integrates and transcends the various models of family therapy. FSP offers a variety of postgraduate training experiences including six-week courses, one-year introductory and clinical externships, advanced training in supervision or in Schwartz's Internal Family Systems model, and (in collaboration with the *Family Therapy Networker*) an international visitors program which trains practitioners from around the world. In addition, FSP provides training for internships, in psychology, social work, and child psychiatry. For more information contact: Betty Karrer, Institute for Juvenile Research, 907 South Wolcott, Chicago, IL 60612.

The *Chicago Center for Family Health* (CCFH) was begun in 1991 by codirectors John Rolland and Froma Walsh. Affiliated with the University of Chicago, the center's orientation integrates systems theory with a multigenerational family life cycle framework. In addition to general training in family therapy, CCFH offers specialized training in couples therapy, divorce mediation, and medical family therapy. Training programs include a two-year certificate program, workshops and courses, and consultation groups. Faculty also includes notable family therapists such as Mary Jo Barrett, Gene Combs, Jill Freedman, Jay Lebow, John Schwartzman, and Tom Todd. For more information contact: John Rolland, CCFH, North Pier, Suite 651, 445 E. Illinois St., Chicago, IL 60611.

The *Houston Galveston Institute* is a private, nonprofit organization that was founded in 1977. The current theoretical orientation of the institute is a "collaborative language systems approach" which informs the educational program to emphasize openness and sharing of clinical experiences. This is exemplified by group learning, teamwork, live consultation, and observation of faculty work. Programs include: (1) residential (fellowships, internships, and apprenticeships), (2) external programs (externships, seminars, supervision, and workshops), and (3) international visitor study programs. For more information contact: Harlene Anderson, Director, 3316 Mount Vernon, Houston, TX 77006.

The *Mental Research Institute* (MRI) in Palo Alto, California, was founded in 1969 by the late Don Jackson and is considered one of the birthplaces of family therapy. The MRI is best known for it's brief therapy approach to families. Its faculty includes such notable names as Paul Watzlawick, John Weakland, Richard Fisch, and Arthur Bodin. The MRI offers a wide variety of training programs, including workshops, continuing seminars, four- or six-week residency programs, and intensive programs in brief therapy or in Michael White's approach. A program for on-site training has also begun recently. For further information contact: Karin Schlanger, Director of Training, 555 Middlefield Rd., Palo Alto, CA 94301.

REFERENCES

Ahrons, C., and Rogers, R. 1989. *Divorced families: Meeting the challenges of divorce and remarriage.* New York: Norton.

Alexander, J. F., Barton, C., Schiavo, R. S., and Parsons, B. V. 1977. Systems-behavioral intervention with families of delinquents: Therapist characteristics, family behavior and outcome. *Journal of Consulting and Clinical Psychology. 44*:656–664.

Andersen, T. 1987. The reflecting team: Dialogue and meta-dialogue in clinical work. *Family Process. 26*:415–428.

Anderson, C. M. 1986. The all-too-short trip from positive to negative connation. *Journal of Marital and Family Therapy. 12*(4):351–354.

Anderson, C. M. 1988. Psychoeducational model different than paradigm. *Family Therapy News. 19*(3).

Anderson, C. M., Reiss, D., and Hogarty, G. E. 1986. *Schizophrenia and the family: A practitioner's guide to psychoeducation and management.* New York: Guilford Press.

Anderson, H., Goolishian, H., and Winderman, L. 1986. Problem determined systems: Toward transformation in family therapy. *Journal of Strategic and Systemic Therapies. 5*:14–19.

Anderson, H., and Goolishian, H. 1988. Human systems as linguistic systems: Preliminary and evolving ideas about the implications for clinical theory. *Family Process. 27*:371–394.

Anderson, W. T. 1990. *Reality isn't what it used to be.* San Francisco: Harper & Row.

Arnold, J., Levine, A., and Patterson, G. R. 1975. Changes in sibling behavior following family intervention. *Journal of Consulting and Clinical Psychology. 43*:683–688.

Atkinson, B. 1992. Aesthetics and pragmatics of therapy revisited. *Journal of Marital and Family Therapy. 18*:389–393.

Ault-Riche, M., ed. 1986. *Women and family therapy.* Rockville, MD: Aspen Systems.

Avis, J. M. 1988. Deepening awareness: A private study guide to feminism and family therapy. In *Women, feminism, and family therapy*, L. Braverman, ed. New York: Haworth Press.

Avis, J. M. 1992. Where are all the family therapists? Abuse and violence within families and family therapy's response. *Journal of Marital and Family Therapy*. *18*:223–230.

Bank, S., and Kahn, M. 1982. *The sibling bond*. New York: Basic Books.

Barrett, M. J., and Trepper, T. 1992. Unmasking the incestuous family. *Family Therapy Networker*. *16*:39–46.

Baucom, D. H. 1982. A comparison of behavioral contracting and problem-solving/communications training in behavioral marital therapy. *Behavior Therapy*. *13*:162–174.

Baucom, D. H., and Hoffman, J. A. 1985. The effectiveness of marital therapy: Current status and application to the clinical setting. In *Clinical handbook of marital therapy*, N. Jacobson and A. Gurman, eds. New York: Guilford Press.

Beach, S. R., and O'Leary, K. D. 1985. The current status of outcome research in marital therapy. In *Handbook of family psychology and psychotherapy*, L. L'Abate, ed. Pacific Grove, CA: Wadsworth.

Beavers, W., and Hampson, R. 1990. *Successful families: Assessment and intervention*. New York: Norton.

Bednar, R. L., Burlingame, G. M., and Masters, K. S. 1988. Systems of family treatment: Substance or semantics? *Annual Review of Psychology*. *39*:401–434.

Bepko, C., and Krestan, J. 1985. *The responsibility trap*. New York: The Free Press.

Berg, I. K., and Miller, S. 1992. *Working with the problem drinker*. New York: Norton.

Berg, I. K., and de Shazer, S. 1993. Making numbers talk: Language in therapy. In *The new language of change*, S. Friedman, ed. New York: Guilford Press.

Berger, M., Jurkovic, G., and Associates, eds. 1984. *Practicing family therapy in diverse settings*. San Francisco: Jossey-Bass.

Berkowitz, R., Kuipers, L., Eberlain-Frief, R., and Leff, J. 1981. Lowering expressed emotion in relatives. In *New developments in interventions with families of schizophrenics*, M. J. Goldstein, ed. San Francisco: Jossey-Bass.

Bograd, M. 1992. Values in conflict: Challenges to family therapists' thinking. *Journal of Marital and Family Therapy*. *18*:243–253.

Borlens, W., Emmelkamp, P., MacGillarry, D., and Markvoort, M. 1980. A clinical evaluation of marital treatment: Reciprocity counseling versus system-theoretic counseling. *Behavioral Analysis and Modification*. *4*:85–96.

Boyd-Franklin, N. 1989. *Black families in therapy. A multisystems approach*. New York: Guilford Press.

Boyd-Franklin, N. 1993. Race, class, and poverty. In *Normal family processes*, F. Walsh, ed. New York: Guilford Press.

Braverman, L., ed. 1988. *Women, feminism, and family therapy*. New York: Haworth Press.

Breunlin, D., Schwartz, R., and Mac Kune-Karrer, B. 1992. *Metaframeworks: Transcending the models of family therapy*. San Francisco: Jossey-Bass.

Calof, D. 1992. Adult children of incest and child abuse: Holograms of the trance generational family. *AFTA Newsletter*. Winter, 35–40.

Canavan, M., Higgs, D., and Meyer, W. 1992. The female experience of sibling incest. *Journal of Marital and Family Therapy*. *18*:129–142.

Carl, D. 1990. *Counseling same-sex couples*. New York: Norton.

Chamberlain, P., Patterson, G., Reid, J., Kavanaugh, K., and Forgatch, M. 1984. Observation of client resistance. *Behavior Therapy*. *15*:144–155.

Coleman, S. 1987. Milan in Bucks Country. *Family Therapy Networker*. *11*(5):42–47.

Combrinck-Graham, L. 1989. *Children in family contexts*. New York: Guilford Press.

Combrinck-Graham, L. 1991. Review of the plenary, "Violence: The dark side of the family." *AFTA Newsletter. 45*:12–14.

Controneo, M. 1987. Women and abuse in the context of the family. *Journal of Psychotherapy and the Family. 3*:81–96.

Coyne, J. 1982. A brief introduction to epistobabble. *Family Therapy Networker. 6*(4):27–28.

Crawford, S. 1988. Cultural context as a factor in the expansion of therapeutic conversation with lesbian families. *Journal of Strategic and Systemic Therapies. 7*:2–10.

Dahlheimer, D., and Feigal, J. 1991. Bridging the gap. *Family Therapy Networker. 15*:44–53.

Dell, P. 1982. Beyond homeostasis: Toward a concept of coherence. *Family Process. 21*(1):21–41.

Dell, P. 1985. Understanding Bateson and Maturana. *Journal of Marital and Family Therapy. 11*:1–20.

Dell, P. 1989. Violence and the systemic view: The problem of power. *Family Process. 23*:1–14.

de Shazer, S. 1984. The death of resistance. *Family Process. 23*(1):11–16.

de Shazer, S. 1985. *Keys to solutions in brief therapy*. New York: Norton.

de Shazer, S. 1988. *Clues: Investigating solutions in brief therapy*. New York: Norton.

de Shazer, S. 1991. *Putting difference to work*. New York: Norton.

DeWitt, K. N. 1978. The effectiveness of family therapy: A review of outcome research. *Archives of General Psychiatry. 35*:549–561.

Doherty, W. 1991. Family therapy goes postmodern. *Family Therapy Networker. 15*:36–42.

Duncan, B. L. and Solevey, D. 1989. Strategic-brief therapy: An insight-oriented approach. *Journal of Marital and Family Therapy. 15*(1):1–10.

Elizur J., and Minuchin, S. 1989. *Institutionalizing madness: Families, therapy and society*. New York: Basic Books.

Elkin, M. 1990. *Families under the influence*. New York: Norton.

Emmelkamp, P., vander Hulm, M., MacGillarry, D., and van Zanten, B. 1984. Marital therapy with clinically distressed couples: A comparative evaluation of system-theoretic, contingency contracting and communication skills approaches. In *Marital therapy and interaction*, K. Hahlweg, & N. Jacobson, eds. New York: Guilford Press.

Erickson, B. 1992. Feminist fundamentalism: Reactions to Avis, Kaufman and Bograd. *Journal of Marital and Family Therapy. 18*:263–267.

Everett, C. A. 1987. *The divorce process: A handbook for clinicians*. New York: Haworth Press.

Falicov, C. 1983. *Cultural perspectives in family therapy*. Rockville, MD: Aspen Systems.

Falicov, C. 1988. *Family transitions: Continuity and change over the life cycle*. New York: Guilford Press.

Falicov, C. *Latino families in therapy*. New York: Guilford Press.

Falicov, C., and Brudner-White, L. 1983. The shifting family triangle: The issue of cultural and contextual relativity. In *Cultural perspectives in family therapy*, C. Falicov, ed. Rockville, MD: Aspen Systems.

Falloon, I. R. H., Boyd, J. L., McGill, C. W., Razani, J., Moss, H. B., and Gilderman, A. M. 1982. Family management in the prevention of exacerbations of schizophrenia. *New England Journal of Medicine. 306*:1437–1440.

Falloon, I., Boyd, J. L., and McGill, C. W. 1985. *Family care of schizophrenia*. New York: Guilford Press.

Figley, C. 1989. *Helping traumatized families*. New York: Plenum.

Fish, V. 1993. Poststructuralism in family therapy: Interrogating the narrative/conversational mode. *Journal of Marital and Family Therapy. 19*:223–232.

Fleishmann, M. J. 1981. A replication of Patterson's "Intervention for boys with conduct problems." *Journal of Consulting and Clinical Psychology. 49*:343–351.

Fleischman, M. J., and Szykula, S. A. 1981. A community setting replication of a social learning treatment for aggressive children. *Behavior Therapy. 12*:115–122.

Foucault, M. 1980. *Power/knowledge: Selected interviews and other writings.* New York: Pantheon Books.

Foucault, M. 1984. *The history of sexuality.* Great Britain: Peregrine Books.

Friedrich, W. 1990. *Psychotherapy of sexually abused children and their families.* New York: Norton.

Gergen, K. 1985. The social constructionist movement in modern psychologist. *American psychologist. 40*:266–275.

Gergen, K. 1991a. *The saturated self.* New York: Basic Books.

Gergen, K. 1991b. The saturated family. *Family Therapy Networker. 15*:26–35.

Goldner, V. 1985. Feminism and family therapy. *Family Process. 24*:31–47.

Goldner, V. 1988. Generation and gender: Normative and covert hierarchies. *Family Process. 27*:17–33.

Goldner, V., Penn, P., Sheinberg, M., and Walker, G. 1990. Love and violence: Gender paradoxes in volatile attachments. *Family Process. 29*:343–364.

Goldstein, M. 1988. Correction on views offered by awardee. *Family Therapy News. 19*(3):7–9.

Goodrich, T. J., Rampage, C., Ellman, B., and Halstead, K. 1988. *Feminist family therapy: A casebook.* New York: Norton.

Gorman-Smith, D., and Tolan, P. 1992. Ethics and empirical basis of treatment of adult survivors of childhood sexual abuse. *AFTA Newsletter.* Winter, 41–44.

Grunberg, L., and Pinsof, W., eds. 1985. *The psychotherapeutic process: A research handbook.* New York: Guilford Press.

Gurman, A. S., and Kniskern, D. P. 1978. Research on marital and family therapy: Progress, perspective, and prospect. In *Handbook of psychotherapy and behavior change,* 3rd ed., S. L. Garfield and A. E. Bergin, eds. New York: Wiley.

Gurman, A. S., Kniskern, D. P., and Pinsof, W. M. 1986. Research on marital and family therapies. In *Handbook of psychotherapy and behavior change,* 3rd ed., S. L. Garfield and A. E. Bergin, eds. New York: Wiley.

Hahlweg, K., Schindler, L., Revenstorf, D., and Brengelmann, J. C. 1984. The Munich marital therapy study. In *Marital interaction: Analysis and modification,* K. Hahlweg and N. Jacobson, eds. New York: Guilford Press.

Haley, J. 1980. *Leaving home.* New York: McGraw-Hill.

Haley, J. 1988. Schizophrenics deserve family therapy, not dangerous drugs and management. *Family Therapy News. 19*(2).

Hansen, J. C. 1982. *Therapy with remarriage families.* Rockville, MD: Aspen Systems.

Hardy, K. 1993. War of the worlds. *Family Therapy Networker. 17*:50–57.

Hare-Mustin, R. T. 1986. The problem of gender in family therapy theory. *Family Process. 26*:15–27.

Held, B., and Pols, E. 1987. Dell on Maturana: A real foundation for family therapy. *Psychotherapy. 24*(3):455–461.

Held, B. S. 1990. What's in a name? Some confusions and concerns about constructivism. *Journal of Marital and Family Therapy. 16*:179–186.

Hersch, P. 1991. Secret lives. *Family Therapy Networker. 15*:36–43.

Hoffman, L. 1985. Beyond power and control: Toward a second-order family systems therapy. *Family Systems Medicine. 3*:381–396.

Hoffman, L. 1988. A constructivist position for family therapy. *The Irish Journal of Psychology. 9*(1):110–129.

Imber-Black, E. 1988. *Families and larger systems: A family therapist's guide through the labyrinth.* New York: Guilford Press.

Jacobson, N. S. 1977. Problem-solving and contingency contracting in the treatment of marital discord. *Journal of Consulting and Clinical Psychology. 45:*92–100.

Jacobson, N. S., and Bussod, N. 1983. Marital and family therapy. In *The clinical psychology handbook,* M. Hersen, A. E. Kazdin, and A. S. Bellack, eds. New York: Pergamon.

Jacobson, N. S., Follette, W. C., and Elwood, R. W. 1984. Outcome research on behavioral marital therapy: A methodological and conceptual reappraisal. In *Marital interaction: Analysis and modification,* K. Hahlweg and N. Jacobson, eds. New York: Guilford Press.

James, K., and MacKinnon, L. 1990. The "incestuous family" revisited: A critical analysis of family therapy myths. *Journal of Marital and Family Therapy. 16:*71–88.

Kahn, M., and Lewis, K. G. 1988. *Siblings in therapy.* New York: Norton.

Kaufman, E. 1985. *The power to change.* New York: Gardner Press.

Kaufman, G. 1992. The mysterious disappearance of battered women from family therapists' offices. *Journal of Marital and Family Therapy. 18:*231–241.

Kazdin, A. E. 1984. Treatment of conduct disorders. In *Psychotherapy research: Where are we and where should we go?* J. Williams and R. Spitzer, eds. New York: Guilford Press.

Keeney, B. P., 1983. *Aesthetics of change.* New York: Guilford Press.

Keeney, B. P., and Sprenkle, D. H. 1982. Ecosystemic epistemology: Critical implications for the aesthetics and pragmatics of family therapy. *Family Process. 21*(1):1–20.

Kiesler, D. J. 1971. Experimental designs in psychotherapy research. In *Handbook of psychotherapy and behavior change: An empirical analysis,* A. Bergin and S. Garfield, eds. New York: Guilford Press.

Kirschner, D. A., and Kirschner, S. 1986. *Comprehensive family therapy: An integration of systemic and psychodynamic models.* New York: Brunner/Mazel.

Kohut, H. 1971. *The analysis of the self.* New York: International University Press.

Kohut, H. 1977. *The restoration of the self.* New York: International University Press.

Korzybski, A. 1942. *Science and sanity: An introduction to non-Aristotelian systems and general semantics,* 2nd ed. Lancaster PA: Science Books.

Krestan, J. 1988. Lesbian daughters and lesbian mothers: The crisis of disclosure from a family systems perspective. *Journal of Psychotherapy and the Family. 3:*113–130.

Krestan, J., and Bepko, C. 1980. The problem of fusion in the lesbian relationship. *Family Process. 19:*277–289.

Laird, J. 1993. Lesbian and gay families. In *Normal family processes,* 2nd ed., F. Walsh, ed. New York: Guilford Press.

Langsley, D., Flomenhaft, K., and Machotka, P. 1969. Follow-up evaluation of family crisis therapy. *American Journal of Orthopsychiatry. 39:*753–759.

Langsley, C., Pittman, F., Machotka, P., and Flomehaft, K. 1968. Family crisis therapy—results and implications. *Family Process. 7:*145–158.

Leff, J., Kuipers, L., Berkowitz, R., Eberlein-Vries, R., and Sturgeon, D. 1982. A controlled trial of social intervention in the families of schizophrenic patients. *British Journal of Psychiatry. 141:*121–134.

Leupnitz, D. 1988. *The family interpreted: Feminist theory in clinical practice.* New York: Basic Books.

Liddle, H. A., and Saba, G. W. 1981. Systemic chic: Family therapy's new wave. *Journal of Strategic and Systemic Therapies. 1*(2):36–39.

MacKinnon, L. K., and Miller, D. 1987. The new epistemology and the Milan approach: Feminist and sociopolitical considerations. *Journal of Marital and Family Therapy. 13*(2):139–156.

Madanes, C. 1990. *Sex, love and violence.* New York: Norton.

Markowitz, L. 1992. Reclaiming the light. *Family Therapy Networker. 16:*17–24.

Markowitz, L. 1993. Walking the walk. *Family Therapy Networker. 17:*18–24, 27–31.

Mashal, M., Feldman, R., and Sigal, J. 1989. The unraveling of a treatment paradigm: A followup study of the Milan approach to family therapy. *Family Process. 28:*457–470.

Maturana, H., and Varela, F. 1980. *Autopoiesis and cognition: The realization of living.* Boston: D. Reidel.

McDaniel, S., Hepworth, J., and Doherty, W. 1992. *Medical family therapy.* New York: Basic Books.

McGoldrick, M. 1993. Ethnicity, cultural diversity, and normality. In *Normal family process,* F. Walsh, ed. New York: Guilford Press.

McGoldrick, M., Anderson, C., and Walsh, F., eds. 1989. *Women in families: A framework for family therapy.* New York: Norton.

Meth, R. 1992. Marriage and family therapists working with violence: Strained bedfellows or compatible partners? A commentary on Avis, Kaufman, and Bograd. *Journal of Marital and Family Therapy, 18:*257–261.

Meyers Avis, J. 1992. Where are all the family therapists? Abuse and violence within families and family therapy's response. *Journal of Marital and Family Therapy. 18:*225–232.

Minuchin, S. 1984. *Family kaleidoscope.* Cambridge, MA: Harvard University Press.

Minuchin, S. 1991. The seductions of constructivism. *Family Therapy Networker, 15:*47–50.

Minuchin, S., Baker, L., Rosman, B., Liebman, R., Milman, L., and Todd, T. 1975. A conceptual model of psychosomatic illness in children. *Archives of General Psychiatry. 32:*1031–1038.

Minuchin, S., and Fishman, H. C. 1981. *Techniques of family therapy.* Cambridge, MA: Harvard University Press.

Minuchin, S., Montalvo, B., Guernery, B., Rosman, B., and Schumer, F. 1967. *Families of the slums.* New York: Basic Books.

Minuchin, S., Rosman, B., and Baker, L. 1978. *Psychosomatic families.* Cambridge, MA: Harvard University Press.

Mirkin, M. P. 1990. *The social and political contexts of family therapy.* Boston: Allyn and Bacon.

Mirkin, M. P., and Koman, S. L., eds. 1985. *Handbook of adolescents and family therapy.* Gardner Press.

Morawetz, A., and Walker, G. 1984. *Brief therapy with single-parent families.* New York: Bruner/Mazel.

Nichols, M. P. 1987. *Self in the system.* New York: Brunner/Mazel.

Nichols, M. P. 1993. The therapist as authority figure. *Family Process. 32:*163–165.

O'Hanlon, W., and Wilk, J. 1987. *Shifting contexts: The generation of effective psychotherapy.* New York: Guilford Press.

O'Hanlon W., and Weiner-Davis, M. 1989. *In search of solutions.* New York: Norton.

Patterson, G. R. 1974. Interventions for boys with conduct problems: Multiple settings, treatment and criteria. *Journal of Consulting and Clinical Psychology. 42:*471–481.

Patterson, G. R., Chamberlain, P., and Reid, J. B. 1982. A comparative evaluation of a parent-training program. *Behavior Therapy. 13:*638–650.

Patterson, G. R., and Fleishmann, M. J. 1979. Maintenance of treatment effects: Some considerations concerning family systems and follow-up data. *Behavior Therapy. 10:*168–185.

Piercy, F. P., and Sprenkle, D. H. Marriage and family therapy: A decade review. *Journal of Marriage and the Family.*

Pinderhughes, E. 1989. *Understanding race, ethnicity and power: The key to efficacy in clinical practice.* New York: The Free Press.

Pinsof, W. M. 1981. Family therapy process research. In *The handbook of family therapy,* A. S. Gurman and D. Kniskern, eds. New York: Brunner/Mazel.

Pinsof, W. M. 1982. Integrative problem-centered therapy: Toward the synthesis of family and individual psychotherapies. *Journal of Marital and Family Therapy.* 9(1):19–36.

Pittman, F. 1987. *Turning points: Treating families in transition and crisis.* New York: Norton.

Raitt, D. 1988. The family therapy survey. *Family Therapy Networker. 12:*52–57.

Rolland, J. 1994. *Helping families with chronic and life-threatening disorders.* New York: Basic.

Root, M., Fallon, P., and Friedrich, W. 1986. *Bulimia: A systems approach to treatment.* New York: Norton.

Rosenau, P. M. 1992. *Post-modernism and the social sciences.* Princeton, NJ: Princeton University Press.

Roth, S. 1989. Psychotherapy with lesbian couples: Individual issues, female socialization, and the social context. In *Women in families,* M. McGolrick, C. Anderson, and F. Walsh, eds. New York: Norton.

Roth, S., and Murphy, B. 1986. Therapeutic work with lesbian clients: A systemic therapy view. In *Women and family therapy,* M. Ault-Riche and J. Hansen, eds. Rockville, MD: Aspen Systems.

Saba, G., Karrer, B., and Hardy, K. 1989. *Minorities and family therapy.* New York: Haworth.

Sager, C., Brown, H. S., Crohn, H., Engel, T., Rodstein, E., and Walker, L. 1983. *Treating the remarried family.* New York: Brunner/Mazel.

Sanders, G. 1993. The love that dares not speak its name: From secrecy to openness in gay and lesbian affiliations. In *Secrets in families and family therapy,* E. Imber-Black, ed. New York: Norton.

Satir, V. 1972. *Peoplemaking.* Palo Alto, CA: Science and Behavior Books.

Scarff, D., and Scarff J. 1987. *Object relations family therapy.* New York: Jason Aronson.

Schwartz, R. C. 1987. Our multiple selves. *Family Therapy Networker. 11:*23–31, 80–83.

Schwartz, R. C. 1990. The concept of the function of the symptom in family therapy. Unpublished manuscript.

Schwartz, R. C. 1992. Rescuing the exiles. *Family Therapy Networker. 16:*33–37,75.

Schwartz, R. C. 1993. Constructionism, sex abuse, and the self. *American Family Therapy Academy Newsletter. Winter,* 6–10.

Schwartz, R. C., 1994 *Internal family systems therapy.* New York: Guilford Press.

Schwartz, R. C., Barrett, M. J., and Saba, G. 1985. Family therapy for bulimia. In *Handbook for the psychotherapy of anorexia nervosa and bulimia,* D. Garner and P. Garfinkel, eds. New York: Guilford Press.

Schwartz, R. C., and Breunlin, D. C. 1983. Research: Why clinicians should bother with it. *Family Therapy Networker. 7*(4):22–27, 57–59.

Schwartz, R. C., and Perrotta, P. 1985. Let us sell no intervention before its time. *Family Therapy Networker.* July–August, 18–25.

Schwartzman, J. 1985. *Families and other systems: The macrosystemic context of family therapy.* New York: Guilford Press.

Selvini, M., ed. 1988. *The work of Mara Selvini Palazzoli.* Northvale, NJ: Jason Aronson, Inc.

Selvini Palazzoli, M. 1986. Towards a general model of psychotic family games. *Journal of Marital and Family Therapy. 12*(4):339–349.

Selvini Palazzoli, M., Boscolo, L., Cecchin, G., and Prata, G. 1978. *Paradox and counterparadox.* New York: Jason Aronson.

Serra, P. 1993. Physical violence in the couple relationship: A contribution toward the analysis of the context. *Family Process. 32:*21–34.

Sheinberg, M. 1992. Navigating treatment impasses at the disclosure of incest: Combining ideas from feminism and social constructionism. *Family Process. 31:* 201–216.

Simon, R. 1986. An interview with Cloe Madanes. *The Family Therapy Networker. 10*(5):64–65.

Simon, R. 1987. Good-bye paradox, hello invariant prescription: An interview with Mara Selvini Palazzoli. *Family Therapy Networker. 11*(5):16–33.

Slipp, S. 1984. *Object relations: A dynamic bridge between individual and family treatment.* New York: Jason Aronson.

Smith, H. 1989. *Beyond the post-modern mind.* Wheaton, IL: Theosophical Publishing House.

Sprenkle, D. 1985. *Divorce therapy.* New York: Haworth Press.

Stanton, M. D. 1981. Strategic approaches to family therapy. In *Handbook of Family Therapy,* A. Gurman and D. Kniskern, eds. New York: Brunner/Mazel.

Stanton, M. D., Todd, T., and Associates 1982. *The family therapy of drug abuse and addiction.* New York: Guilford Press.

Steinglass, P., Bennett, L., Wolin, S. J., and Reiss, D. 1987. *The alcoholic family.* New York: Basic Books.

Szapocznik, J., and Kurtines, W. M. 1989. *Breakthroughs in family therapy with drug abusing and problem youth.* New York: Springer.

Taggert, M. 1989. Epistemological equality as the fulfillment of family therapy. In *Women in families: A framework for family therapy,* M. McGoldrick, C. Anderson, and F. Walsh, eds. New York: Norton.

Tolan, P. H., Cromwell, R. E., and Brasswell, M. 1986. Family therapy with delinquents: A critical review of the literature. *Family Process. 25:*619–649.

Tomm, K. 1985. Circular interviewing: A multifaceted clinical tool. In *Applications of systemic therapy: The Milan approach,* D. Campbell and R. Draper, eds. London: Grune & Stratton.

Tomm, K. 1987. Interventive interviewing: Part II. Reflexive questioning as a means to enable self-healing. *Family Process. 26:*167–183.

Tomm, K. 1988. Interventive interviewing: Part III. Intending to ask linear, circular, strategic or reflexive questions? *Family Process. 27:*1–15.

Treadway, D. 1989. *Before its too late: Working with substance abuse in the family.* New York: Norton.

Trepper, T. S., and Barrett, M. J. 1989. *Systemic treatment of incest: A therapeutic handbook.* New York: Brunner/Mazel.

Ulrici, D. 1983. The effects of behavioral and family interventions on juvenile recidivism. *Family Therapy. 10:*25–36.

Vaughn, C., and Leff, J. 1976. The measurement of expressed emotion in the families of psychiatric patients. *British Journal of Psychology. 15:*157–165.

Visher, E., and Visher, J. 1979. *Stepfamilies: A guide to working with stepparents and stepchildren.* New York: Brunner/Mazel.

Visher, C., and Visher, J. 1988. *Old loyalties, new ties: Therapeutic strategies with stepfamilies.* New York: Brunner/Mazel.

von Foerster, H. 1981. *Observing systems.* Seaside, CA: Intersystems Publications.

von Glasserfeld, H. 1984. An introduction to radical constructivism. In *The invented reality,* P. Watzlawick, ed. New York: Norton.

Wachtel, E. F., and Wachtel, P. L. 1986. *Family dynamics in individual psychotherapy: A guide to clinical strategies.* New York: Guilford Press.

Walker, G. 1991. *In the midst of winter: Systemic therapy with families, couples, and individuals with AIDS infection.* New York: Norton.

Wallerstein, J., and Kelly, J. 1980. *Surviving the breakup: How children and parents cope with divorce.* New York: Basic Books.

Walsh, F. 1982. *Normal family processes.* New York: Guilford Press.

Walsh, F. 1993. *Normal family processes,* 2nd ed. New York: Guilford Press.

Walters, M., Carter, B., Papp, P., and Silverstein, O. 1988. *The invisible web: Gender patterns in family relationships.* New York: Guilford Press.

Watzlawick, P., ed. 1984. *The invented reality.* New York: Norton.

Wegscheider-Cruse, S. 1985. *Choicemaking: For co-dependents, adult children and spirituality seekers.* Pompano Beach, FL: Health Communications.

White, M. 1986. Negative explanation, restraint, and double description: A template for family therapy. *Family Process.* 25:169–184.

White, M. 1989. *Selected papers.* Adelaide Australia: Dulwich Centre Publications.

White, M., and Epston, D. 1990. *Narrative means to therapeutic ends.* New York: Norton.

White, M. 1991. Deconstruction and therapy. *Dulwich Centre Newsletter.* 3:21–40.

White, M. 1992. Men's culture, the men's movement, and the constitution of men's lives. *Dulwich Center Newsletter.* 3 & 4:1–21.

Winderman, L. 1989. Generation of human meaning key to Galveston Paradigm: An interview with Harlene Anderson & Harold Goolishian. *Family Therapy News.* 20(6):11–12.

Zilbach, J. 1986. *Young children in family therapy.* New York: Brunner/Mazel.

Early Models and Basic Techniques: Group Processes and Communications Analysis

Most people who practiced family therapy in the early years used some combination of a group therapy approach and the communications model that came out of Bateson's schizophrenia project. In this chapter, we will explore those two models and see how they had to be modified to fit the unique challenges of treating troubled families. We will conclude with a section on the basic techniques of family therapy, as they are applied from the first telephone contact through the various stages of treatment to termination.

Those of us who practiced family therapy in the 1960s could often be seen engaged in a strange ritual. When a family filed in for their first session, all anxious and uncertain, the therapist, all smiles, would go over and kneel in front of one of the small children. "Hi! And what's your name?" Then, often as not, "Do you know why you're here?" meanwhile ignoring the parents. The most common answers to this question were: "Mommy said we were going to the doctor's," in a frightened voice; or, confused, "Daddy said we were going for a ride." Then the therapist, trying not to be scornful, would turn to the parents and say, "Perhaps you could explain to Johnny why you *are* here."

The reason for this little charade was that before they understood how families were structured, many therapists treated the family as a group, in which the youngest members were presumed to be the most vulnerable and, therefore, in need of "expert" help to express themselves—as though the parents weren't in charge, as though everybody's opinion was equal.

Another common scene was therapists making solemn comments about patterns of communication: "I notice that when I ask Suzie a question, she first turns to Mom to see if it's okay to answer . . ." Very clever. Not only did we expect families to be impressed by such bright remarks, we imagined that they'd somehow instantly reform and start communicating according to some ideal model in *our* heads—"I statements" and all the rest. *And* we thought that such clear communication would somehow resolve their problems.

Are we being a little condescending here? Absolutely. The first family therapists turned somewhat naively to models from group therapy and communications analysis because there were no other models available.

Early family therapists availed themselves of the techniques of group therapy because, after all, families are groups, aren't they? It was certainly convenient to have a ready-made set of principles to rely on, and for a long time the group therapy model was one of the most widely used approaches to families. Even today, when therapists with little understanding of systems dynamics or family structure see families, they often treat the family as though it were a group of equals.

The communications model that emerged from Palo Alto in the 1950s had an enormous impact on the entire field. Communications family therapy was no mere application of individual psychotherapy to families; it was a radically new conceptualization that altered the very nature of imagination. What was new was the focus on the *process,* the form of communication, rather than its *content.* The communications family therapists developed techniques of treatment, but their lasting contribution was a whole new way of thinking about families.

Bateson's observations led to the conclusion that the interchange of messages between people defined their relationships and that these relationships were stabilized by homeostatic processes in families. His interest was scientific, not therapeutic, and his goal was to develop a general model of human behavior. When Jay Haley and Don Jackson began interviewing families, they were more interested in studying them than in treating them. Gradually, however, they began to intervene in order to help these families overcome their problems. At first they used interpretations because they still believed that awareness would bring about change. But, finding that this didn't work, they developed new techniques to fit their new ways of thinking. Directives replaced interpretations as the major technique to change family systems by changing the way that family members communicate with one another.

The paradigms of communications theory were so well received that they were adopted by other schools of family therapy. Virtually every approach now treats communication as synonymous with behavior, and concepts like the *double bind* and *family homeostasis* have been absorbed in the literature. In fact it might be said that communications family therapy died of success.

SKETCHES OF LEADING FIGURES

Group therapy influenced the beginnings of family therapy in two ways. First, many of the early family therapists turned to the group therapy literature to guide their efforts at treating families. Second, many of the pioneers of family therapy were themselves products of group therapy training. By far the most influential of these was John Elderkin Bell.

Bell (1975) credits his start as a family therapist to a fortunate misunderstanding. When he was in London in 1951, Bell heard that Dr. John Bowlby of the Tavistock Clinic was experimenting with group therapy for families. This remark caught Bell's interest and stimulated him to try this approach as a means of dealing with behavior problems of children. It turned out that Bowlby had only interviewed one family as an adjunct to treating a troubled child; but Bell didn't learn this until years after. As Bell later put it, if so eminent an authority as John Bowlby was using family therapy, it must be a good idea.

While none of the early pioneers of family group therapy are as well known as John E. Bell, their work had a direct impact on many of those who took up family therapy in the late 1950s and early 1960s, among them: Rudolph Dreikurs, Christian Midelfort, S. H. Foulkes, and Robin Skynner.

Rudolph Dreikurs was a student of Alfred Adler's who put Adler's ideas into practice in child guidance clinics in Chicago. Dreikurs translated Adler's ideas about the need to overcome *feelings of inferiority* by developing *social interest* in a variety of formats, including children's groups, community groups, parents' groups, and family therapy groups. His techniques with families combined emotional support and encouragement with interpretations and suggestions about modifying unhappy interactions. He encouraged families to discuss their mutual problems in an open, democratic spirit; and he urged them to institute regular "family councils," in order to carry the model of family group therapy into the family's daily life.

Christian Midelfort is another early figure in family therapy whose influence was largely restricted to his own place and time. He practiced at the Lutheran Hospital in LaCrosse, Wisconsin. Charged with responsibility for treating fairly seriously disturbed patients, Midelfort decided that the only way to achieve lasting results was to include the patients' families in treatment. Although he still considered the patient as the focus of treatment, Midelfort (1957) developed an array of family therapy techniques that anticipated many later developments.

S. H. Foulkes was an English psychoanalyst and one of the organizers of the group therapy movement in Great Britain. Although he began conducting conjoint family therapy interviews early in the 1940s, his work is little known to family therapists because his major interest and publications were in analytic group therapy. Among Foulkes's students was Robin Skynner, whose work overlaps the psychoanalytic (Chapter 6) and group approaches to families. More of a synthesizer than an innovator, Skynner has written a useful guide to analytic and group-oriented family therapy (Skynner, 1976). Skynner's (1976) orientation to families is revealed in the following remark: "The family, like the small group of strangers, is seen as possessing inherent potentials for constructive understanding and for facilitating growth and positive change, as well as for creating confusion and blocking development" (p. 192).

Communications therapy was one of the earliest approaches to family therapy, and the history of this approach is inextricably intertwined with the history of the first decade of the family therapy movement (see Chapter 1). The leading characters in this history were the members of Bateson's schizophrenia project and the Mental Research Institute (MRI) in Palo Alto. Don Jackson and Jay Haley were the leaders who created and popularized the communications approach to treating families. Nothing in Jackson's traditional psychiatric background portends his radical departure from conventional psychotherapy. He graduated in 1943 from Stanford University School of Medicine where the major influences were Freudian and Sullivanian. He completed his residency training at Chestnut Lodge in Rockville, Maryland, in 1949 and remained there as a member of the staff until 1951. During this period he was also a candidate at the Washington-Baltimore Psychoanalytic Institute. In 1951 Jackson moved to Palo Alto, California, where he maintained a private practice and worked as Chief of the Psychiatric Department of the Palo Alto Medical Clinic. He also was a candidate at the San Francisco Psychoanalytic Institute until 1954, and was associated with the Department of Psychology at Stanford University from 1951 until 1960. He became a consultant to the Palo Alto Veterans Administration Hospital in 1951, which led to his association with the Bateson project.

Jackson established the Mental Research Institute in November 1958, and received his first grant in March 1959. The original staff consisted of Jackson, Jules Riskin, and Virginia Satir. They were joined later by Jay Haley, John Weakland, and Paul Watzlawick. Gregory Bateson served as a research associate and teacher.

When he died tragically in 1968 at the age of 48, Don Jackson left behind a legacy of seminal papers, the leading journal in the field, *Family Process,* which he cofounded with Nathan Ackerman, and a great sadness at the passing of such a vibrant and creative talent.

Jay Haley has always been somewhat of an outsider. He entered the field without clinical credentials, and first established his reputation as a commentator and critic. His initial impact came from his writing, in which he infused irony and sarcasm with incisive analysis of psychotherapy. In "The Art of Psychoanalysis" (reproduced in Haley, 1963), Haley redefined psychoanalysis, not as a search for insight, but as a game of "oneupmanship":

> By placing the patient on a couch, the analyst gives the patient the feeling of having his feet up in the air and the knowledge that the analyst has both feet on the ground. Not only is the patient disconcerted by having to lie down while talking, but he finds himself literally below the analyst and so his one-down position is geographically emphasized. In addition, the analyst seats himself behind the couch where he can watch the patient but the patient cannot watch him. This gives the patient the kind of disconcerted feeling a person has when sparring with an oppo-

nent while blindfolded. Unable to see what response his ploys provoke, he is unsure when he is one-up and when one-down. Some patients try to solve this problem by saying something like, "I slept with my sister last night," and then whirling around to see how the analyst is responding. These "shocker" ploys usually fail in their effect. The analyst may twitch, but he has time to recover before the patient can whirl fully around and see him. Most analysts have developed ways of handling the whirling patient. As the patient turns, they are gazing off into space, or doodling with a pencil, or braiding belts, or staring at tropical fish. It is essential that the rare patient who gets an opportunity to observe the analyst see only an impassive demeanor. (pp. 193–194)

In this same paper Haley (1963) also tossed a few barbs at other popular forms of psychotherapy.

There is, for example, the Rogerian system of ploys where the therapist merely repeats back what the patient says. This is an inevitably winning system. When the patient accuses the therapist of being no use to him, the therapist replies, "You feel I'm no use to you." The patient says, "That's right, you're not worth a damn." The therapist says, "You feel I'm not worth a damn." This ploy, even more than the orthodox silence ploy, eliminates any triumphant feeling in the patient and makes him feel a little silly after a while (a one-down feeling). Most orthodox analysts look upon the Rogerian ploys as not only weak but not quite respectable. They do not give the patient a fair chance. (p. 198)

Haley saw patients and families during the years he worked on the Bateson project, but retired from clinical practice in 1962 when the project disbanded. Since that time he's concentrated on studying families and teaching and supervising family therapy. His writing continues to be witty and critical, and his relationship to the rest of the field continues to be adversarial and iconoclastic. Recently, for example, writing about what he called "the plague of drugs in psychiatry," Haley said that today psychotic people are "routinely medicated into a state of zombydom" (Haley, 1986, p. 98).

Haley was studying for a master's degree in communication at Stanford University when he met Gregory Bateson, who hired him to work on the communications project. Haley began to interview schizophrenic patients in order to analyze the strange style of their communication. As a therapist Haley was greatly influenced by Milton Erickson, with whom he began studying hypnosis in 1953. Then, after the Bateson project broke up in 1962, Haley worked in research at MRI until 1967 when he joined Minuchin at the Philadelphia Child Guidance Clinic. It was here that Haley became especially interested in training and supervision, areas in which he may have made his greatest contribution to the field of family therapy. At present Haley codirects the Family Therapy Institute of Washington, D.C., with Cloe Madanes.

Bateson himself had a superbly analytic mind, nurtured from an early age in a variety of scientific disciplines, and his scientific background shaped the character of the group's approach to families. Under Bateson's influence, the orientation of the project was anthropological. The group didn't set out to develop a clinical approach: their goal was to observe, not change, families. In fact they stumbled onto family therapy more or less by accident. When Bateson developed the double bind hypothesis in 1954 he had never seen a family. It wasn't until 1956 or 1957 that the group began seeing families. At first the group merely wanted to observe patterns of communication; onlylater were they moved to try to help the unhappy people they had been studying.

Virginia Satir was another prominent member of the MRI group, but because her emphasis shifted to emotional experiencing, we will consider her in Chapter 7.

THEORETICAL FORMULATIONS

Although he's better known for studying the psychology of individuals, Freud was also interested in interpersonal relationships, and many would consider his *Group Psychology and the Analysis of the Ego* (Freud, 1921) the first major text on the dynamic psychology of the group. According to Freud, the major requirement for transforming a collection of individuals into a group is the emergence of a leader. In addition to manifest tasks of organization and direction, the leader also serves as a parent figure on whom the members become more or less dependent. Members *identify* with the leader as a parent surrogate, and with other group members as siblings. *Transference* occurs in groups when members repeat unconscious attitudes formed in the process of growing up. Freud's concept of *resistance* in individual therapy also applies to groups, because group members, seeking to ward off anxiety, may oppose the progress of treatment with silence, hostility, refusing to attend sessions, or avoiding painful topics. Family groups resist treatment by scapegoating, superficial chatting, prolonged dependency on the therapist, refusal to follow therapeutic suggestions, and allowing difficult family members not to show up.

Like Freud, Wilfred Bion (1961) also attempted to develop a group psychology of the unconscious, and he described groups as functioning on *manifest* and *latent* levels. The group's official task is on the manifest level, but people also join groups to fulfill powerful, but unconscious, primal needs. At the latent level groups seek a leader who will permit them to gratify their needs for *dependence, pairing,* and *fight-flight.*

Freudian concepts, extrapolated from the individual to the group, remain part of group dynamics theory, but most of the working concepts focus less on individuals than on the interactions among them. Whole groups, including families, are usually defined by structure; subgroups, by function. Most of the time groups, including families, operate as subgroups. The Family doesn't clean the house—Mom and the kids do. The Family doesn't plan a move, Dad and Mom do.

According to Kurt Lewin's (1951) *field theory,* conflict is an inevitable feature of group life, as members vie with one another for adequate *life space.* Just as animals need their own territory, people seem to need their own "space" (or turf), and for this reason there is an inherent tension between the needs of the individual and those of the group. The amount of conflict generated by this tension depends upon the amount of restriction imposed by the group, compared with the amount of mutual support it gives in exchange. (People who give up a lot for their families expect to get a lot in return.)

What distinguished Lewin's model of group tensions from earlier theories is that it was *ahistorical*. Instead of worrying about who did what to whom in the past, Lewin concentrated on what was going on in the *here-and-now*. This focus on *process* (how people talk), rather than *content* (what they talk about), is one of the keys to understanding the way a group (or family) functions.

Role theory, which influenced so many branches of psychology, also played a prominent place in theories of group functioning. Every position in a group structure has an associated role, which consists of expected and prohibited behavior for the occupant of that position. In family groups some roles are biologically determined, while others depend on the specific dynamics of the group. Sex roles; kinship roles of mother, father, son, and daughter; and age roles of infant, child, teenager, and adult, are obvious, but not necessarily more significant than such assigned roles as "the strong one," "the scapegoat," or "the baby."

In families, role conflicts can occur within or between roles. *Intra-role* conflict exists when a single role calls for contradictory performances, such as when a child is expected to be both independent and obedient. *Inter-role* conflict exists when two or more roles are incompatible, as, for example, when a woman is expected to be strong as a mother but helpless as a wife. Notice that the notion of role conflict makes no reference to personalities. The problem isn't in the person but in the design of the system.

There can also be problems in how well roles and personalities fit each other. An introverted, narcissistic man may have trouble filling the role of a warm and loving father. Thus personality and role are mutually determinative. Talcott Parsons (1950), speaking as an analytically oriented sociologist, emphasized the internalization of family roles as a determining influence on the formation of character. Over time, roles tend to become stereotyped, and thus limit flexibility in individuals and in the group (Bales, 1970). Clinicians like Spiegel (1971) and Bell (1975) developed the therapeutic implications of role theory and applied them to the diagnosis and treatment of families.

Communications therapists adopted the *black box* concept from telecommunications and applied it to the individuals within the family. This model disregards the internal structure of individuals in order to concentrate on their input and output—that is, communication. It isn't that these clinicians denied the phenomena of mind—thinking and feeling—they just found it useful to ignore them. By limiting their focus to what goes on between, rather than within, family members, communications theorists qualify as "systems purists" (Beels & Ferber, 1969).

Communications theorists also disregarded the past, leaving that to psychoanalysts, while they searched for patterns with which to understand behavior in the present. They considered it unimportant to figure out what's cause and what's effect, preferring to use a model of circular causality in which chains of behavior are seen as effect-effect-effect.

Families were treated as error-controlled, goal-directed systems, and their interactions were analyzed using cybernetic theory, general systems theory, and games theory. For example, interactions can be described using a games analogy. Someone who doesn't know how to play chess could discover the rules by watching the game being played and noting the pattern of moves. This is precisely the strategy used by communications theorists in their analyses of family communications. Beginning with schizophrenic families and branching out to a wide variety of families, these workers observed the patterns of communication to discover regularities, which acted as "rules" of family interaction (Jackson, 1965).

Human communication can be analyzed according to *syntax, semantics,* and *pragmatics* (Carnap, 1942; Morris, 1938). *Syntax* refers to the way words are put together to form phrases and sentences; it is the manner in which information is transmitted. Errors of *syntax* are particularly likely in persons learning a new language. This is the domain of the information theorist, who is concerned with who speaks to whom, the percentage of speaking time for each member, the parsimony of speech, and the ratio of information to noise. Thus *syntax* is concerned with the stylistic properties of language, not with its meaning. Meaning is the realm of *semantics.* In families, *semantics* refers to the clarity of language, the existence of private or shared communicational systems, and concordance versus confusion of communication. Finally there is the *pragmatics,* or behavioral effect, of communication. In order to evaluate the effects of communication, it's necessary to take into account nonverbal behavior and the context of communication, as well as the words used. The *pragmatics* of communication is the primary concern of communications therapists, and is their basis for understanding behavior in any family system.

In *Pragmatics of Human Communication,* Watzlawick, Beavin, and Jackson (1967) sought to develop a "calculus" of human communication, which they stated in a series of axioms about the interpersonal implications of communication. These axioms are an aspect of *metacommunication,* which means communicating about communication. The first of these axioms is that people are always communicating. Since all behavior is communicative, and one cannot *not* behave, then it follows that one cannot *not* communicate. Consider the following example.

> Mrs. Snead began the first family therapy session by saying, "I just don't know what to do with Roger anymore. He's not doing well in school, he doesn't help out around the house; all he wants to do is hang around with those awful friends of his. But the worst thing is that he refuses to communicate with us."
>
> At this point, the therapist turned to Roger and said, "Well, what do you have to say about all of this?" But Roger said nothing. Instead he continued to sit slouched in a chair at the far corner of the room, with an angry, sullen look on his face.

Roger isn't "not communicating." He's communicating that he's angry, and that he refuses to negotiate. Communication also takes place when it isn't intentional, conscious, or successful—that is, in the absence of mutual understanding.

A second major proposition is that all messages have a *report* and a *command* function (Ruesch & Bateson, 1961). The report (or content) of a message conveys information, while the command is a statement about the definition of the relationship. For example, the message, "Mommy, Sandy hit me," conveys information but also suggests a command—"Do something about it." Notice, however, that the implicit command is ambiguous. The reason for this is that the printed word omits nonverbal and contextual clues. This statement shrieked by a child in tears would have a different command value than if it were spoken by a giggling child.

The relationship between speakers is another factor that significantly affects how the command aspects of communication are responded to. For example, a therapist whose aim is to help patients express their feelings would be likely to respond to a husband who is crying by listening sympathetically and encouraging him to continue. The man's wife, on the other hand, might be upset by his display of "weakness," and try to "cheer him up" by telling him that the problem doesn't really exist or by suggesting ways for him to solve it. In this instance, the therapist can listen to the man's feelings without hearing (or responding to) a command to "do something about them." The wife feels threatened and obligated by the inferred command, and so cannot simply listen.

The command aspect of communications functions to define relationships. "Mommy, Sandy hit me" suggests that the speaker accepts a one-down relationship with Sandy, and insists that mother will intercede to settle any problems. This defining is often obscured because it's usually not deliberate or done with full awareness, and, as we have seen, it depends upon how it's received. In healthy relationships this aspect recedes into the background. Conversely, problematic relationships are characterized by frequent struggles about the nature of the relationship: "Don't tell me what to do!"

In families, command messages are patterned as *rules* (Jackson, 1965). The regular patterning of interactions stabilizes relationships. These patterns, or rules, can be deduced from observed redundancies in interaction. Jackson used the term *family rules* as a description of regularity, not as a causal or determining concept. Nobody "lays down the rules." In fact, families are generally unaware of them.

The rules, or regularities, of family interaction operate to preserve family *homeostasis* (Jackson, 1965, 1967), an acceptable behavioral balance within the family. Homeostatic mechanisms bring families back to a previous balance in the face of any disruption, and thus serve to resist change. Jackson's notion of family homeostasis describes the conservative aspect of family systems and is similar to the general systems theory concept of *negative feedback*. Thus, according to a communications analysis, families operate as goal-directed, rule-governed systems.

Communications theorists found in *general systems theory* (von Bertalanffy, 1950) a number of ideas useful in explaining how families work. But while they (Watzlawick, Beavin, & Jackson, 1967) described families as *open systems* in their theoretical statements, they tended to treat them as *closed systems* in their clinical work. Thus they concentrated their therapeutic efforts on the nuclear family, with little or no consideration of inputs from the community or extended family,

Relationships between communicants are also described as being either *complementary* or *symmetrical. Complementary* relationships are ones based on differences that fit together. A common complementary pattern is where one person is assertive and the other submissive, with each mutually reinforcing and sustaining each other's position. It's important to understand that these are descriptive terms, not evaluative. Moreover, it's a mistake to assume that one person's position *causes* the other's, or that one is weaker than the other. As Sartre (1964) pointed out, it is the masochist as well as the sadist who creates the possibility of a sado-masochistic relationship.

Symmetrical relationships are based on equality; the behavior of one person mirrors that of the other. Symmetrical relationships between husbands and wives, where both are free to pursue careers and share housekeeping and childrearing responsibilities, are often thought of as ideal by today's standards. However, from a communications analysis, there's no reason to assume that such a relationship would be any more stable or functional for the system than a traditional, complementary one.

Another aspect of communication is that it can be *punctuated* in various ways (Bateson & Jackson, 1964). An outside observer may hear a dialogue as an uninterrupted flow of communication, but each of the participants may believe that what he or she says is caused by what the other says. Thus punctuation organizes behavioral events and reflects the bias of the observer. Couples therapists are familiar with the impasse created by each spouse saying, "I only do X, because he (or she) does Y." A common example is the wife who says she only nags because her husband withdraws; while he says he only withdraws because she nags. Another example is the wife who says she'd be more in the mood for sex if her husband was more affectionate; to which he counters that he'd be more affectionate if she'd have sex more often.

As long as couples punctuate their interactions in this fashion, there is little likelihood of change. Each insists that the other causes the impasse and each waits for the other to change. The impasse is created by the universal tendency for people to punctuate a sequence of interactions so that it appears the other one has initiative, dominance, or dependency—in other words, power. Children illustrate this when they have a fight and run to a parent, both crying, "He started it!" Their mutual illusion is based on the mistaken notion that such sequences have a discrete beginning, and that one person's behavior is caused by another's in linear fashion.

Communications theory doesn't accept linear causality or look for underlying motives for behavior; instead, this model assumes circular causality and analyzes specific behaviors occurring at the present time. Considerations of underlying causality are treated as conceptual noise, with no practical therapeutic value. The behaviors that the communications theorist observes are patterns of communications linked together in additive chains of stimulus *and* response. This model of sequential causality enables therapists to treat behavioral chains as *feedback loops*. When the response to one family member's problematic behavior exacerbates the problem, that chain is seen to be a *positive feedback loop*. The advantage of this formulation is that it focuses on interactions that perpetuate problems, which can be changed, instead of inferring underlying causes, which aren't observable and often not subject to change.

NORMAL FAMILY DEVELOPMENT

Now that we have rich literatures on child development and the family life cycle, it doesn't seem particularly fruitful to turn to the group dynamics literature to help us understand normal family development. Nevertheless, in the early days of family therapy, many therapists borrowed concepts of group development and applied them to families. Among the most notorious of these was Talcott Parsons' idea (1950) that groups needed an *instrumental* leader and an *expressive* leader to look after the *social-emotional* needs of the group. Guess who was elected to which roles—and consider how that helped to legitimize an artificial and unfair division of labor.

William Schutz's (1958) discussion of three phases of group development—*inclusion, control,* and *affection*—was more useful. Other studies in the group dynamics literature called attention to the critical need for *cohesiveness*. One factor that helps determine cohesiveness is *need compatibility* (Shaw, 1981). If members of a group have compatible needs, they tend to function well together; if not, not. Likewise, compatible needs—compatible, not identical—make good marriages. This assumption has been supported by studies demonstrating that need compatibility predicts marital choice (Winch, 1955) and marital adjustment (Meyer & Pepper, 1977).

As "systems purists," communications family therapists treat behavior as ahistorical. Whether they're describing or treating family interactions, their attention is on the here-and-now, with very little interest in development. Normal families are described as functional systems, which like all living systems, depend upon two important processes (Maruyama, 1968). First, they must maintain constant integrity in the face of environmental vagaries. This is accomplished through *negative feedback*, which is often illustrated by the example of the thermostat on a home heating unit. When the heat drops below a set point, the thermostat activates the furnace until the heat returns to the desired temperature.

No living system can survive without a regular pattern or structure. On the other hand, too rigid a structure leaves the system ill-equipped to adapt to changing circumstances. This is why normal families must also have mechanisms of *positive feedback*. Negative feedback minimizes change to maintain a steady state; positive feedback alters the system to accommodate to novel inputs. As children grow older, they change the nature of their input to the family system. The most obvious instance of this is adolescence, at which time children seek more involvement with peers and demand more freedom and independence. A family system limited to negative feedback can only resist such changes. Normal families, on the other hand, also have positive feedback mechanisms and can respond to new information by modifying their structure.

Normal families become periodically unbalanced (Hoffman, 1971) during transition points in the family life cycle. No family passes through these changes in a totally harmonious fashion; all experience stress, resist change, and develop vicious cycles. But normal families aren't trapped in these cycles; they're able to engage in positive feedback to modify themselves. Symptomatic families remain stuck, using a symptomatic member to avoid change.

Concepts from general systems theory, such as positive feedback, have the virtues of wide applicability and theoretical elegance, but often seem esoteric and abstract. When we recognize that the channel for positive feedback is communication, it's possible to state the case more plainly. Healthy families are able to change because they communicate clearly and are flexible. When their children say they want to grow up, healthy parents listen.

DEVELOPMENT OF BEHAVIOR DISORDERS

From a group theory perspective, symptoms were considered products of disturbed and disturbing group processes. But groups weren't thought to *cause* disturbance in their members; rather, the behavior of the members was part of the disturbance of the group. Thus group researchers and therapists rejected linear causality in favor of a form of circular causality that they called "group dynamics." Family group therapists were less concerned with the origins of psychopathology than with the conditions that support and maintain it. These include stereotyped roles, breakdowns in communication, and blocked channels for giving and receiving support.

Rigidity of roles forces group interactions to occur in a narrow, stereotyped range. When the number of options are reduced for individuals, their flexibility as a group is constrained. Groups stuck with inflexible roles and unvarying structures tend to malfunction when called upon to handle changed circumstances. Moreover, if flexibility is threatening, such groups don't risk communicating about unmet needs; the result is often frustration and sometimes symptomatic disturbance in one of the group's members. If the needs that generate acute disturbance continue to go unmet, the symptoms themselves may be perpetuated as a role, and the group organizes itself around a "sick" member.

According to communications family therapists, the essential function of symptoms is to maintain the homeostatic equilibrium of family systems. (As we have seen, the notion that symptoms are functional—implying that families *need* their problems—was to become controversial.) Pathological families were considered to be trapped in dysfunctional, but very strong, homeostatic patterns of communication (Jackson & Weakland, 1961). Their interactions may seem odd, and they may be unsatisfying, yet they are powerfully self-reinforcing. These families cling to their rigid and inflexible structures and respond to signs of change as negative feedback. That is, change is treated not as an opportunity for growth but as a threat and a signal to change back. Changes that threaten stability are labeled as "sick," as the following example illustrates.

Tommy was a quiet, solitary boy, the only child of East European immigrant parents. The parents left their small farming community and came to the United States, where they both found factory work in a large city in the Northeast. Although they were now safe from religious persecution and their standard of living improved, the couple felt alien and out of sympathy with their new neighbors. They kept to themselves and took pleasure in raising Tommy.

Tommy was a frail child with a number of peculiar mannerisms, but to his parents he was perfect. Then he started school. He began to make friends with other children, and, eager to be accepted, he picked up a number of American habits. He chewed bubble gum, watched television cartoons, and rode his bicycle whenever he had the chance. His parents were annoyed by the gum chewing and by Tommy's fondness for television, but they were genuinely distressed by his eagerness to play with his friends. They began to feel that he was rejecting their values, and that "something must be wrong with him." By the time they called the child guidance clinic, they were convinced that Tommy was disturbed, and they asked for help to "make Tommy normal again."

In their theoretical papers, communications theorists maintained the position that pathology inheres in the system as a whole (Hoffman, 1971; Jackson, 1967; Watzlawick, Beavin, & Jackson, 1967). The *identified patient* was considered a role with complementary counterroles all of which contributed to the maintenance of the system. The identified patient may be the victim, but in this framework "victim" and "victimizer" are seen as mutually determined roles—neither is good or bad, and neither causes the other. However, although this circular causality was a consistent feature of their theorizing, communications therapists often lapsed into demonizing parents.

The foundations for a family theory of the etiology of schizophrenia, focusing on disturbed patterns of communication, were laid down by Gregory Bateson (Bateson, Jackson, Haley, & Weakland, 1956), Theodore Lidz (Lidz, Cornelison, Terry, & Fleck, 1958), and Lyman Wynne (Wynne, Ryckoff, Day, & Hirsch, 1958). All of these researchers emphasized the pathological effect of parents' irrationality on their offspring, suggesting that the disordered thinking observed in the schizophrenic children was caused by their parents.

Despite the enthusiastic response to the idea that schizophrenia might be caused by disordered communication in the family, the fact is, that it isn't. Communication deviance isn't found in all schizophrenic families, nor is it limited to families so diagnosed. Wynne's view (1968, 1970) is that communications patterns can be regarded as building upon attention-response deficits which probably have an innate, genetically determined component.

It's difficult to judge a single communication as normal or pathological. Instead the judgment must be made on a series or sequence of communications. One can look at syntax and semantics, that is the content of speech, for clarity or confusion. This approach is exemplified by Lyman Wynne's studies in which he found that schizophrenics' speech could be differentiated from that of normals or delinquents (Wynne & Singer, 1963). Alternatively one can look at the pragmatics of communication, as did the members of the Palo Alto group. Here the emphasis wasn't on clarity or content, but on the *metacommunication* or command aspects of language.

Symptoms were seen as messages in response to persistent communicational quandaries. The nonverbal message of a symptom is: "It is not I who does not (or does) want to do this, it is something outside my control—my nerves, my illness, my anxiety, my bad eyes, alcohol, my upbringing, the Communists, or my wife" (Watzlawick, Beavin, & Jackson, 1967, p. 80). As the group became more sophisticated, they tried to get past blaming parents for victimizing their children. Symptoms were no longer considered to be *caused* by communication problems in the family; they were seen as embedded in a pathological context, within which they may be the only possible reaction. Among the forms of pathological communication identified by the Palo Alto group were: denying that one is communicating, disqualifying the other person's message, confusing levels of communication, discrepant punctuation of communication sequences, symmetrical escalation to competitiveness, rigid complementarity, and paradoxical communication.

The most pervasive feature of pathological family communications is the use of *paradox*. A paradox is a contradiction that follows correct deduction from logical premises. In family communications, paradoxes usually take the form of *paradoxical injunctions*. A frequent example of paradoxical injunction is to demand some behavior which by its very nature can only be done spontaneously—"Be spontaneous!" "You should have more self-confidence." "Tell me you love me." A person exposed to such paradoxical injunctions is caught in an untenable position. To comply—to act spontaneous or self-confident— means to be self-consciously deliberate or eager to please. The only way to escape the dilemma is to step outside the context and comment on it, but such metacommunication rarely occurs in families. (It's difficult to communicate about communication.)

Paradoxical communications are a frequent feature of everyday life. They are relatively harmless in small doses, but when they take the form of double binds the consequences are malignant. In a double bind the two contradictory messages are on different levels of abstraction, and there is an implicit injunction against commenting on the discrepancy. A common example of a double bind is the wife who denounces her husband for not showing feelings, but then attacks him when he does.

Continual exposure to paradoxical communication is like the dilemma of a dreamer caught in a nightmare. Nothing the dreamer tries to do in the dream works. The only solution is to step outside the context by waking up. Unfortunately, for people who live in a nightmare, it isn't easy to wake up.

GOALS OF THERAPY

The goal of treating family groups was the same as treating stranger groups: promoting individuation of group members and improving their relationships. Individual growth is promoted when unmet needs are verbalized and understood, and when overly confining roles are explored and expanded. When family members are released from their inhibitions, it was assumed that they would develop greater family cohesiveness. Notice the difference in emphasis between this—considering families as groups of individuals, each of whom must be helped to develop—and the systemic view of the family as a unit.

Treating families as though they were like any other group failed to appreciate the need for hierarchy and structure.

Improved communication was seen as the primary way to meet the goal of improved group functioning. The aims of this approach reflect the fairly simple view of families and their problems that was prevalent among clinical practitioners before they learned to think systemically. While Bateson and his colleagues were laboring with their complex systems analyses, the average therapist still thought that the way to help troubled families was simply to have them sit down and talk to one another. In fact, as most families begin to converse, they have enough communication problems to keep therapists busy for a long time correcting their "mistakes," without getting to the individual and systems dynamics that generate them.

The goal of communications family therapy was to take "deliberate action to alter poorly functioning patterns of interaction . . ." (Watzlawick, Beavin, & Jackson, 1967, p. 145). Because "patterns of interaction" are synonymous with communication, this meant changing patterns of communication. In the early days of communications family therapy, especially in Virginia Satir's work, this translated into a general goal of improving communication in the family. Later the goal was narrowed to altering those specific patterns of communication that maintained problems. By 1974 Weakland wrote that the goal of therapy was resolving symptoms, not reorganizing families: "We see the resolution of problems as primarily requiring a substitution of behavior patterns so as to interrupt the vicious, positive feedback circles" (Weakland, Fisch, Watzlawick, & Bodin, 1974, p. 149).

The goal of the communications therapist is, like that of the behavior therapist, to interdict behavior that stimulated and reinforced symptoms. These two models also share the assumption that once pathological behavior is blocked, it will be replaced by constructive alternatives, instead of other symptoms. The limitation of the behavioral model is that it treats the symptomatic person as the problem, and conceives of the symptom as a response rather than as both a response and a stimulus in a chain of interaction. The limitation of the communications model is that it isolates the sequence of behavior that maintains the symptoms, and focuses on two-person interactions without considering triangles or other structural problems. If, for example, a child is fearful because her overinvolved father yells at her, and her father yells at her because his wife isn't emotionally involved, then changing the father's behavior might result in a different form of a symptomatic behavior in the child, unless the relationship with the wife is addressed.

CONDITIONS FOR BEHAVIOR CHANGE

As we've already indicated, group family therapists thought the way to bring about change was to help family members open up and talk to each other. The therapist encourages them to talk openly, supports those who seem reticent, and then critiques the process of their interaction. It is the power of the therapist's support that helps family members open up where they once held back, and this, in turn, often shows them in a new light, which enables others in the family to relate to them in new ways. For example, children who aren't accustomed to being listened to by grown-ups, tend to make themselves "heard" by disruptive behavior. But if the therapist demonstrates a willingness to listen, the children may learn to express their feelings in words rather than in actions. As they begin to interact with someone who takes them seriously, they may suddenly "grow up."

Group-oriented therapists promote communication by concentrating on *process* rather than *content* (Bion, 1961; Yalom, 1985; Bell, 1975). This is an important point, and one easy to lose sight of. The minute a therapist gets caught up in the details of a family's problems or thinks about solving them, he or she may lose the opportunity to discover the process of what family members are doing that prevents them from working out their own solutions.

One of the ways therapists influence the process of family dialogue is to model listening. As the family members talk, the therapist listens intently, demonstrating to the speaker what it feels like to be heard and understood, and to other family members how not to interrupt, argue, or blame. After expression comes analysis. Once members of the family have a chance to express their feelings—and to be listened to—the family group therapist begins to explore why those feelings are present, and why they were held back. The assumption is that what families can understand they can change.

If behavior is communication, then the way to change behavior is to change communication. According to the communications theorists, all events and actions have communicative properties: Symptoms can be considered as covert messages, commenting upon relationships (Jackson, 1961). Even a headache that develops from prolonged tension in the occipital muscles is a message, since it is a report on how the person feels and also a command to be responded to. If a symptom is seen as a covert message, then by implication making the message overt eliminates the need for the symptom. Therefore one of the important ways to change behavior is to bring hidden messages out into the open.

As we pointed out above, an essential ingredient of the double bind is that it is impossible to escape or look at the binding situation from the outside. But no change can be generated from within; it can only come from outside the pattern. So, according to communications theorists (Watzlawick, Beavin, & Jackson, 1967), the paradigm for psychotherapy is an intervention from the outside to resolve relational dilemmas. The therapist is an outsider who supplies what the relationship cannot, a change in the rules.

From the outside position the therapist can either point out problematic sequences or simply manipulate them to effect therapeutic change. The first strategy relies on the power of insight and depends upon a willingness to change, but the second does not; it's an attempt to beat families at their own games, with or without their cooperation. Included in the second strategy are many of the most clever and interesting tactics of communications therapy, and much more is written about these than about simple interpretation. Nevertheless, in the early days of family therapy, therapists relied more on the pointing out of communicational problems than on any other technique.

The first strategy, simply pointing out communicational problems, was represented in Virginia Satir's work and was widely practiced by those who were new to family therapy. The second, less direct, approach was characteristic of Haley and Jackson and eventually it became the predominant strategy. By the time they wrote *Pragmatics of Human Communication*, Watzlawick, Beavin, and Jackson (1967) believed that:

> Therapeutic communication, then, must necessarily transcend such counsel as is customarily but ineffectually given by the protagonists themselves, as well as their friends and relatives, [because] bona fide patients—by which we simply mean persons who are not deliberately simulating—usually have tried and failed in all kinds of self-discipline and exercises in will power long before they revealed their distress to others and were told to "pull themselves together." It is in the essence of a symptom that it is something unwilled and therefore autonomous. (pp. 236–237)

Therefore they recommended interventions to *make* people behave in ways that would produce change. These manipulative strategies formed the basis of strategic family therapy (Chapter 9), which is an offshoot of communications theory.

Jackson and Haley's early work with families was influenced by the hypnotherapy they learned from Milton Erickson. The hypnotherapist works by giving explicit instructions whose purpose is often obscure. However, before patients will follow directions the therapist must gain control of the relationship. Jackson sometimes began by giving patients advice about their symptoms. He did so to point up the problem area, just as interpretation would do; but at the same time his comments made the patient focus on the relationship with the therapist—regardless of whether the patient accepted or rejected the advice. Haley (1961) recommended asking certain kinds of patients to do something in order to provoke a rebellious response, which served to make them concede that they were relating to the therapist. He mentions, as an example, directing a schizophrenic patient to hear voices. If the patient hears voices, then he is complying with the therapist's request; if he doesn't hear voices, then he can no longer claim to be crazy.

Haley's (1961) direction to hear voices illustrates the technique of *prescribing the symptom*. By instructing the patient to enact a symptomatic behavior the therapist is demanding that something "involuntary" be done voluntarily. This is a paradoxical injunction which forces one of two changes. Either the patient performs the symptom and thus admits that it isn't involuntary, or the patient gives up the symptom. Prescribing the symptom is a form of what the communications theorists called *therapeutic double binds* (Jackson, 1961). The same technique that drives people crazy is used to drive them sane.

Actually "therapeutic double bind" is somewhat loose usage because it doesn't necessarily involve two levels of message, one of which denies the other. To illustrate what he meant by a therapeutic double bind, Jackson (1961) cited the following case report.

> The patient was a young wife with a martyr complex, who felt that despite her best efforts to please her husband he just would not be satis-

fied. Jackson sensed that she was probably just "acting nice" in order to cover her intense, but unacceptable, rage at her husband. But the patient bridled when he even suggested that she might be "dissatisfied." In the face of this resistance, Jackson suggested that since her marriage was so important and since her husband's mood had such a profound effect on her, that she should learn to be really pleasing.

By accepting the therapist's suggestion, the patient was admitting that she wasn't really pleasing. Moreover, she was forced to change.

In the above example, the patient was directed to change by doing more of the same. The object was to force the patient to step outside the frame set by her dilemma, with or without her awareness. In order to succeed, therapeutic double binds, or paradoxical injunctions, must be so cleverly designed as to leave no loopholes through which a patient can escape.

According to Jackson's notion of family homeostasis, family systems regulate themselves by using symptoms as negative feedback to maintain their equilibrium. In this way, symptomatic families become caught in an increasingly inflexible set of patterns. The task of therapy is to loosen them up by introducing positive feedback to break up stability and equilibrium. The goal is to change the family system so that deviance is no longer necessary to preserve homeostasis. Timing is considered to be an important factor in how the family will respond to attempts to change them. At a period of steady-state equilibrium, families will resist change; at times of crisis, they are more likely to accept change.

The tactics of change employed by the communication therapists focused on altering discrete sequences of interaction that perpetuate symptomatic behavior. Despite their claims to include triadic sequences in their analyses (Sluzki, 1978), most of their interventions were limited to dyadic interactions.

TECHNIQUES

The techniques of family group therapy were similar to those of analytic and supportive group therapy. The role of the therapist was that of a *process leader.* The model of the family was a democratic group, and the therapist related to the family members democratically, just as the members are expected to do with each other. The therapist saw all of them as people with something to say, often in need of help saying it, and encouraged everyone in the family to open up and express their points of view. There was little concern with structure and few attempts to reinforce the parents' hierarchical position. If anything, there was a tendency to give extra support for children and encourage them to assume a more equal role in family interactions.

John Bell's original approach (1961) was orchestrated in a series of stages. First was a *child-centered phase,* in which children were helped to speak up and express their wishes and concerns. Bell was so anxious to help children participate that he held preliminary meetings with parents to encourage them not only to listen but also to go along with some of the children's requests as a means of gaining their cooperation.

After the children spoke up and were rewarded with some additional privileges, then it was the parents' turn. In the *parent-centered stage,* parents usually began by complaining about their children's behavior. During this phase, Bell was careful to soften the harshest of parental criticisms and to focus on problem-solving. In the final, or *family-centered,* stage, the group family therapist equalized support for the entire family while they continued to improve their communication and work out solutions to their problems. The following vignette illustrates Bell's (1975) directive style of intervening.

> After remaining silent for a few sessions, one father came in with a great tirade against his son, daughter, and wife. I noticed how each individual in his own way, within a few minutes, was withdrawing from the conference. Then I said, "Now I think we should hear what Jim has to say about this, and Nancy should have her say, and perhaps we should also hear what your wife feels about it." This restored family participation without closing out the father. (p. 136)

It also kept the therapist in charge, preventing him from seeing how the family handled their own confrontations, and from possibly being in a position to point out problems in their way of handling things.

Anything that interfered with balanced self-expression was considered resistance and dealt with accordingly. Often this meant confronting nonverbal signs of unexpressed feeling. "Mr. Brown, you've been silent, but I wonder if your drumming your fingers is trying to tell us something."

Three specialized applications of group methods to family treatment were *multiple family group therapy, multiple impact therapy,* and *network therapy.*

Peter Laqueur began *multiple family group therapy,* in 1950, at Creedmore State Hospital in New York, and he refined this approach as Director of Family Therapy at Vermont State Hospital (Laqueur, 1966, 1972a, 1972b, 1976). Multiple family group therapy involved the treatment of four to six families together for weekly sessions of ninety minutes. Laqueur and his cotherapists conducted multiple family groups like traditional therapy groups with the addition of encounter group and psychodrama techniques. Structured exercises were used to increase the level of interaction and intensity of feeling; families were used as "cotherapists" to help confront members of other families from a more personal position than therapists could take.

Although multiple family therapy lost its most creative force with Peter Laqueur's untimely death, it is still occasionally used, especially in hospital settings, both inpatient (McFarlane, 1982) and outpatient (Gritzer & Okum, 1983).

Robert MacGregor and his colleagues at the University of Texas Medical Branch in Galveston developed *multiple impact therapy* as a way to have maximum impact on families with a disturbed adolescent in crisis (MacGregor, Richie, Serrano, Schuster, McDonald, & Goolishian, 1964; MacGregor, 1967, 1972). These families came from all over Texas to Galveston to spend several days in intense therapy with a large team of professionals. Team members met with several combinations of family members and then assembled in a large group to review findings and make recommendations. Although multiple impact therapy is no longer practiced, its intense but infrequent meetings were a powerful stimulus for change and prefigured later developments in experiential therapy (Chapter 7) and the Milan model (Chapter 10).

Network therapy was an approach developed by Ross Speck and Carolyn Attneave for assisting families in crisis by assembling their entire social network—family, friends, neighbors—in gatherings of as many as fifty people. Teams of therapists were used to work with these large groups, and their emphasis was on breaking up destructive patterns of relationship and mobilizing support for new options (Speck & Attneave, 1973; Ruevini, 1975).

Therapeutic teams meet with networks in meetings lasting from two to four hours; groups typically meet three to six times. Encounter group techniques are used to alleviate defensiveness and foster a climate of warm involvement. After five or ten minutes of shaking hands, jumping up and down, shouting, huddling together, and swaying back and forth, the group experiences a release of tension and a sense of cohesiveness.

The polarization phase begins when the leader identifies and activates conflicting points of view in the network. These may be dramatized by arranging people into concentric circles and inviting them to confront their differences. Under the guidance of the leaders, confrontation is moved toward compromise and synthesis. During the mobilization phase, tasks are presented, and subgroups of involved and active members are asked to develop plans for solving concrete problems. If the identified patient needs a job, a committee might be formed to help; if young parents are stuck at home fighting over who's going to take care of the baby, a group might be asked to develop babysitting resources and allow the couple to get out together.

After the initial enthusiasm wears off, network groups often fall into exhaustion and despair as members begin to realize just how entrenched certain problems are and how difficult it is to resolve them. Uri Ruevini (1975) described one case in which a period of depression set in, and the problem family felt isolated and abandoned by the network. Ruevini broke through this impasse by prescribing a cathartic encounter group exercise, "the death ceremony." Family members were asked to close their eyes and imagine themselves dead. The rest of the network members were asked to share their own feelings about the members of the family: their strengths, their weaknesses, and what each of them meant to their family and friends. This dramatic device produced an outpouring of feeling and support which roused the network out of depression.

Speck and Attneave (1973) described breaking the network into problem solving subgroups, using action instead of affect to move beyond despair. In one case they assigned a group of friends to watch over an adolescent patient who was abusing drugs and another group to arrange for him to move out of his parents' house. Breakthrough is achieved when the network's energies are unleashed and directed toward active resolution of problems. Network sessions often produce what Speck and Attneave called the "network effect"—a feeling of euphoric connectedness and the satisfaction of solving problems once thought to be overwhelming. Once a network has been activated, there's always someone to call when the need arises.

In communications family therapy, technique followed theory more so than in almost any other treatment approach. These therapists wrote a great deal about the theory of human communications before they began applying their ideas to treatment, and even after they began to describe their work with families, most of their publications had a distinctly theoretical flavor. As a result, communications family therapists appear to have had an intellectual stance and more emotional distance from the families they worked with than other early family therapists. Communications therapy seems to have been done *to* families, more than *with* them.

Formal assessment was typically not used by communications therapists, although Watzlawick (1966) did introduce a *structured family interview*. In this procedure, families were given five tasks to complete, including:

1. Deciding their main problem
2. Planning a family outing
3. The parents discussing how they met
4. Discussing the meaning of a proverb
5. Identifying faults and placing the blame on the correct person

While the family worked on these tasks, the therapist, watching behind a one-way mirror, observed the family's patterns of communication, methods of decision making, and scapegoating. Although it was useful for research, the structured family interview never gained wide acceptance as a clinical tool.

Most of the actual techniques of communications family therapy consisted of teaching rules of clear communication, analyzing and interpreting communicational patterns, and manipulating interactions through a variety of strategic maneuvers. The progression of these three strategies from more straightforward to more strategic reflected the growing awareness of how families resist change.

In their early work (Jackson & Weakland, 1961), communications therapists opened by indicating their belief that the whole family was involved in the presenting problem. Then they explained that all families develop habitual patterns of communication, including some that are problematical. This attempt to convert families from seeing the identified patient as the problem to accepting mutual responsibility underestimated the family's resistance to change. Later these therapists were more likely to begin by asking for and accepting a family's own definition of their problems (Haley, 1976).

After the therapists made their opening remarks, they asked the family members, usually one at a time, to discuss their problems. While they did so the therapist listened, but concentrated on the process of communication, rather than the content. When someone in the family spoke in a confused or confusing way, the therapist would point this out and insist on certain rules of clear communication. Satir (1964) was the most straightforward teacher. When someone said something that was unclear, she would question and clarify the message, and as she did so she impressed on the family some basic guidelines for clear speaking.

One rule is that people should always speak in the first person singular when saying what they think or feel. For example:

HUSBAND: We always liked Donna's boyfriends.

THERAPIST: I'd like you to speak for yourself; later your wife can say what she thinks.

HUSBAND: Yes, but we've always agreed on these things.

THERAPIST: Perhaps, but you are the expert on how you think and feel. Speak for yourself, and let her speak for herself.

A similar rule is that people should make personal statements ("I statements") about personal matters. Opinions and value judgments must be understood as that, not passed off as facts or general principles. Owning opinions, as such, is a necessary step to discussing them in a way that permits legitimate differences of opinion, much less the possibility of changing opinions.

WIFE: People shouldn't want to do things without their children.

THERAPIST: So you like to bring the kids along when you and your husband go out.

WIFE: Well yes, doesn't everybody?

HUSBAND: I don't. I'd like to go out, just the two of us, once in a while.

Another rule is that people should speak directly to, not about, each other. This avoids ignoring or disqualifying family members and prevents the establishment of destructive coalitions. For example:

TEENAGER: (To therapist) My mother always has to be right. Isn't that so, Dad?

THERAPIST: Would you say that to her?

TEENAGER: I have, but she doesn't listen.

THERAPIST: Tell her again.

TEENAGER: (To therapist) Oh, okay. (To mother) Sometimes I get the feeling . . . (Shifts back to therapist) Oh, what's the use!

THERAPIST: I can see how hard it is, and I guess you've kind of decided that it's no use trying to talk to your mom if she isn't going to listen. But in here, I hope we can all learn to speak more directly to each other, so that no one will give up on having their say.

As this exchange illustrates, it's difficult to teach people to communicate clearly just by telling them how. It seemed like a good idea, but it didn't work very well. The reason a directive approach to family therapy persists at all is that, with enough insisting, most people will follow therapeutic directions, at least as long as the therapist is there to insist.

In the early days of communications family therapy, Virginia Satir was probably the most transparent and directive therapist, and Jay Haley was the least; Don Jackson occupied a position somewhere in between.

When he began treating families of schizophrenics, Jackson thought he needed to protect patients from their families (Jackson & Weakland, 1961) but came to realize that parents and children were all bound together in mutually destructive ways. Even now those who are new to family therapy, especially if they themselves haven't yet become parents, tend to identify with the children and see the parents as the bad guys. Not only is this wrong, as Jackson himself later realized, it alienates parents and drives them out of treatment. Young therapists often begin "knowing" that parents are responsible for most of their children's problems. Only later, when they become parents themselves, do they achieve a more balanced perspective—namely, that family problems are all the children's fault.

Jackson emphasized the need for structure and control in family therapy sessions. He began first sessions by saying, "We are here to work together on better understanding one another so that you all can get more out of your family life" (Jackson & Weakland, 1961, p. 37). Not only does this remark structure the meeting, it also conveys the idea that all members of the family are to become the focus of discussion. Furthermore it reveals the therapist's intentions and may, therefore, precipitate a struggle with parents who have come only to help the patient, and may resent the implication that they are part of the problem. Thus we see that Jackson was an active therapist who set the rules right at the outset and explained openly what he was doing in order to anticipate and disarm resistance. Today most family therapists find it more effective to be subtler, meeting the families' resistance not with psychological karate but with jujitsu—using their own momentum for leverage, instead of opposing them head on.

Jackson may have found it so difficult to deal with schizophrenic families that he became active and intrusive to avoid being caught up in their craziness. In any case, there is a suggestion of combativeness in his writings, as though he saw himself battling families, beating them at their own game (Jackson & Weakland, 1961), using dual or multiple messages, provoking them to do something in defiance of therapeutic directives whose real purpose may be concealed (therapeutic double binds).

Jackson may have been subtly combative with families; Jay Haley wasn't subtle about it. He was clear and explicit in defining therapy as a battle for control between therapist and patients.[1] Haley believed that therapists need to maneuver into a position of power over their patients in order to manipulate them into changing. Although the notion of manipulation may have unpleasant connotations, moral criticism should be reserved for those who use patients covertly for their own ends, rather than used against those who seek the most effective means of helping patients achieve their goals.

In *Strategies of Psychotherapy*, Haley (1963) described the marital relationship in terms of conflicting levels of communication. Conflicts occur not only over what rules the couple will follow in dealing with each other, but also over who sets the rules. Complexity is introduced because couples may be complementary in some spheres and symmetrical in others. But the complexity goes still further; although it may appear that a wife dominates a dependent husband, the husband may, in fact, provoke the wife to be dominating, thus him-

---

[1]Haley has continued to develop and revise his thinking and, today, he is far from this blunt and provocative. See Chapter 9 on strategic family therapy for a description of Haley's contemporary work.

self controlling the type of relationship they have. Sometimes it takes a coward to make a bully.

Although Haley's analysis of human relations was highly intellectual and rational, he believed that family members can't be rational about their problems. In fact he still tends to exaggerate people's inability to understand their own behavior. His therapy therefore tends to be done *to* patients rather than done *with* them. Although Haley criticizes to the point of ridicule the idea that insight is curative, he used to put a lot of faith in simple openness of communication as a way of dealing with problems in couples and marriages.

According to Haley the mere presence of a third person, the therapist, helps couples solve their problems. By dealing fairly with each spouse and not taking sides, the therapist disarms the usual blaming maneuvers; in other words, the therapist serves as a referee. In addition to being a referee, the communications therapist relabeled or redefined the activity of family members with each other. One strategy is to redefine what family members say, stressing the positive aspects of their relationship. "For example," Haley (1963) says, "if a husband is protesting his wife's constant nagging, the therapist might comment that the wife seems trying to reach her husband and achieve more closeness with him. If the wife protests that her husband constantly withdraws from her, the husband might be defined as one who wants to avoid discord and seeks an amiable relationship" (p. 139). This technique was later to be called *reframing* and to become a central feature of strategic therapy.

One of Haley's major strategies was to make explicit the implicit or covert rules that govern family relationships. Dysfunctional rules made explicit become more difficult to follow. For example, some wives berate their husbands for not expressing themselves, but the wives talk so much and criticize so loudly that the husbands hardly have a chance. If the therapist points this out, it becomes more difficult to follow the implicit rule that the husband should not talk. Haley believed that disagreements about which rules to follow are relatively easily solved through discussion and compromise. Conflicts about who is to set rules are stickier and require that the therapist be less straightforward. Because the issue of control is too explosive to be dealt with openly, Haley recommends subtle directives.

Haley's directives are of two sorts: suggestions to behave differently and suggestions to continue to behave the same. Straightforward advice, he says, rarely works. When it does, it's likely that the conflict is minor or that the couple is moving in that direction anyway. Some of Haley's directives are for changes that seem so small that the full ramifications aren't immediately apparent. In a couple, for example, where the wife seems to have her own way most of the time, the husband is asked to say "no" on some minor issue once during the week. This seems trivial, but it accomplishes two things: It makes the husband practice speaking up for himself, and it makes the wife aware that she's been domineering. (Unfortunately, it also seems to blame the wife for problems in the relationship.) This small beginning gives both spouses a chance to work on changing their part of the interaction. The fact that they're doing so under therapeutic direction often, though not always, makes them more likely to follow the advice.

Haley's suggestion that family members continue to behave in the same way was, in fact, a therapeutic paradox. When a teenager who is rebellious against his parents is instructed to "continue to rebel," he or she is caught in a paradoxical position. Continuing to rebel means following the direction of an authority figure (and admitting that what you're doing is "rebellious"). Only by giving up this behavior can the teenager maintain the illusion of freedom. Meanwhile the problematic behavior ceases. Sometimes it's more effective to have one spouse suggest that the other continue symptomatic behavior. This may produce a major shift because it alters who defines the nature of the relationship.

LESSONS FROM THE EARLY MODELS

The most important contribution from group studies to family therapy was the idea that all groups, including families, have emergent properties. Group functioning transcends individual personalities, and groups cannot be understood merely by adding up the characteristics of their members. When people join together to form a group, relational processes emerge which reflect not only the individuals involved, but also their collective patterns of interaction known as *group dynamics.*

Family therapists applied notions of group dynamics to families and used systems theory to elaborate the nature of these interpersonal forces. Among the group processes that family therapists deal with are triangulation, scapegoating, alignments, coalitions, and splits.

Group theorists also taught us the importance of *roles,* official and unofficial, and how they organize behavior in groups. Family therapists draw on role theory when they support and enhance parents in their role as leaders, or point out how covert roles can detract from group functioning, such as how a father who constantly plays the role of jokester undermines his wife and distracts the family group from discussing and solving problems. Family therapists also help family members realize how certain rigid roles trap them in narrow and inflexible performances, such as when teenagers play counterconformist and are so busy *not* being their parents that they never figure out how to be themselves.

The process/content distinction was also profoundly important to family therapists. When families seek help, they expect expert information about their problems and help solving them. They might want to know how to encourage a shy youngster to make friends or how to get a recalcitrant teenager to show more respect to his parents. But what the family therapist tries to figure out is: Why hasn't the family been able to solve their own problems? What about the way they've been going about it isn't working? Therefore, when the family discusses their problems, the therapist listens as much to the process of the discussion—who speaks to whom and in what way—as to the content of what they're saying.

The shift from attending to what people say to how they say it—openly or defensively, cooperatively or competitively—is one of the important strategies of all forms of therapy. Another way of saying this is that most family therapists focus on the here-and-now, bringing problems into the consulting room in the form of the way family members relate to one another.

The primary group therapy technique—promoting free and open discussion—helped family therapists encourage dialogue and mutual understanding in families. But although helping families talk over their problems may enable them to resolve a minor crisis, mere conversation is rarely sufficient to solve more difficult problems. Moreover, the model of a democratic group on which this technique is predicated overlooked the unique structural properties of families. Unlike therapy groups, families are *not* made up of equals. Every member of a family may have an equal right to his or her feelings and point of view, but someone has to be in charge. Therapists who speak first to children, or invite everyone in the family to have an equal say, fail to respect the family's need for leadership and hierarchy.

The other major technique used by group therapists is the process interpretation, of which Bell (1961) delineated four varieties: *Reflective interpretations* describe what's going on at the moment—"I notice that when your wife says something critical, you just hang your head, as if to say 'Poor me.' " *Connective interpretations* point out unrecognized links between different actions among family members—"Have you noticed that Jenny starts to misbehave the minute you two start to argue?" *Reconstructive interpretations* explain how events in the family's history provide the context for current experience. *Normative interpretations* are remarks designed to support or challenge a family member by comparing that person to what most people do—"Big deal, most teenagers are sassy with their parents. It's part of growing up."

The most obvious comment we can make about process interpretations is that simply pointing out what family members are doing may not help them to see that their behavior isn't productive, or to change it. Therapists make interpretations to be helpful, but the people at whom they are directed often feel such comments as hurtful, as if the therapist were saying, "Look what you're doing; it's wrong—you're wrong."

The real reason people don't usually change when something is pointed out to them isn't that they are mindless puppets of a family system, but that even constructive criticism often feels more critical than constructive. Family therapists, already inimical to the analytic approach, came to doubt the usefulness of interpretation, even to mock insight in favor of action. They did so because they believed that individuals were often powerless over the systemic forces of their families. In hindsight it seems that, while individual change is often complicated by the actions of others, it isn't true that family members lack the capacity to reflect on the consequences of their behavior—depending on how it is pointed out to them. Perhaps the same respect for people's capacity to understand and change their behavior also leads therapists to phrase interpretative comments that sound more like permission to be honest than like an attack. Maybe people *can* learn hard truths, when they're told with respect.

Group family therapists were directive to the extent of encouraging people to speak up when they appeared to have something to say. Otherwise they were relatively passive and confined themselves to describing the processes they saw in families. In therapy groups of strangers with contrasting defenses and personality styles, this approach is effective; moreover therapists in these groups can act as catalysts who stir members to confront and challenge each other. Families, however, share defenses and pathological attitudes, and therapists cannot rely on other group members to challenge family norms. That's why contemporary family therapists, who treat families more actively, confront family patterns of interaction (rather than individual reticence) and look for ways to circumvent defenses that are more powerful in families than in groups of strangers.

The three specialized applications of group methods with families considered in this chapter—multiple family group therapy, multiple impact therapy, and network therapy—were experiments of the 1960s and early 1970s. Treating more than one family at the same time allows members of one family to see how others deal with similar problems. However when there are other families present to serve as distractions, it makes it hard to focus for any length of time or depth on entrenched or anxiety-arousing problems. What works in group therapy may not work with families.

Both multiple impact therapy and network therapy brought tremendous resources to bear on families stuck in crisis. Although family therapists in clinics often work in teams, today we usually rely on one therapist to treat a family. Perhaps there are times when it makes sense to launch the all-out effort that multiple impact therapy represented. The additional advantage of network therapy was that the resources it mobilized were the natural resources of a family's community. Perhaps this model, too, is still useful: It uses community resources that are still available after treatment is over, and it's a useful antidote to the isolation of many families.

Communications family therapy was one of the first and most influential forms of family treatment. Its theoretical development was closely tied to general systems theory and the therapy that emerged was a systems approach *par excellence*. Therapy was a by-product of Gregory Bateson's schizophrenia project. The main product was a set of ideas about human communication and family systems. The fact that their studies had a profound impact on the entire field of psychotherapy was largely an artifact of the psychiatric context that was the source of their funding. Many of these ideas—homeostasis, double bind, feedback—were absorbed by the entire field of family therapy, so that there is no longer a separate school of communications family therapy.

Bateson assembled a unique group with diverse talents, and he gave them free rein to develop their interests. Among the many subjects that interested them, communication was the common denominator. Communication was the detectable input and output they used to analyze the black box of interpersonal systems. Communication was described as feedback, as a tactic in interpersonal power struggles, and as symptoms. In fact, all behavior was considered communication. The trouble is, when "communication" is used so broadly, the concept loses precision. If all events and actions are treated as communication, then communications analysis may be taken to mean everything, and therefore nothing. Human relations are not all a matter of communication; communication may be the matrix in which interactions are embedded, but human interactions have other attributes as well—love, hate, fear, conflict.

The Bateson group may be best remembered for the concept of the double bind, but their enduring contribution was applying communications analysis to a wide range of behavior, including family dynamics. In fact, the idea of metacommunication is a much more useful concept than that of the double bind, and it has been incorporated not only by family therapists but also by the general public. Whether or not they are familiar with the term *metacommunication*, most people understand that all messages have both report and command functions.

Another of the most significant ideas of communications therapy is that families are rule-governed systems, maintained by homeostatic, negative feedback mechanisms. This accounts for the stability of normal families and the inflexibility of dysfunctional families. Because such families don't have adequate positive feedback mechanisms, they're unable to adjust to changing circumstances.

Communications theorists borrowed the open systems model from general systems theory, but their clinical analyses and interventions were based on the closed systems paradigm of cybernetics. This is another example of how this approach was more useful theoretically, than pragmatically. In their clinical descriptions, relationships were portrayed as struggles for power and control. Haley emphasized the power struggle between spouses, and Watzlawick said that the major problem of control in families is cognitive. The therapy that they developed from these ideas was conceived as a power struggle in which the therapist takes control to outwit the forces of symptom maintenance.

When communication takes place in a closed system—an individual's fantasies, or a family's conversations—there's little opportunity for adjusting the system. Only when someone outside the system provides communicational input can correction occur. This is the premise on which communications family theory was based. The rules of family functioning are largely unknown to the family, and the best way to examine and correct them is to consult an expert in communications.

While there were major differences among the intervention strategies of Haley, Jackson, Satir, and Watzlawick, they were all committed to altering self-reinforcing and mutually destructive patterns of communication. They pursued this goal by direct and indirect means. The direct approach, favored by Satir, sought change by making family rules explicit and by teaching principles of clear communication. This approach could be described as establishing ground rules, or metacommunicational principles, and included such tactics as telling people to speak for themselves and pointing out nonverbal and multileveled channels of communication.

The trouble is, as Haley noted, "One of the difficulties involved in telling patients to do something is the fact that psychiatric patients are noted for their hesitation about doing what they are told." For this reason, communications therapists began to rely on more indirect strategies, designed to provoke change, not to foster awareness. Telling family members to speak for themselves, for instance, may challenge a family rule and therefore meet with strong resistance. With this realization, communications therapy began a treatment of resistance.

Resistance and symptoms were treated with a variety of paradoxical directives, known loosely as therapeutic double binds. Milton Erickson's technique of prescribing resistance was used as a lever to gain control—for example, when a therapist tells family members not to reveal everything in the first session. The same ploy was used to prescribe symptoms, an action which made unrecognized rules explicit, implied that such behavior was voluntary and placed the therapist in control.

Eventually communications therapy became symptom-focused, brief, and directive. The focus on symptoms is consistent with the general systems concept of *equifinality* which means that no matter where systems change begins the final result is the same. Moreover, even when they convened whole families, the communications therapists focused on the marital pair, and they were always more adept with dyadic than triadic thinking.

Today the theories of communications therapy have been absorbed into the mainstream of family therapy and the symptom-focused interventions are the basis of the strategic school of family therapy. Unfortunately, when group and communications therapists were confounded by the obdurate inflexibility of families, they may have exaggerated the irrational power of the family system.

SYSTEMS ANXIETY[2]

Therapists first encountered the family as a powerful adversary. Freud's discoveries indicted families as seducers of innocent children, and later as agents of cultural repression, source of all guilt and anxiety. Hospital psychiatrists also saw patients as victims of their families and, except for purposes of footing the bill, kept them at arms length. Child guidance workers approached domestic life with a built-in prejudice. Their vision that flawed relations in the family held the key to psychopathology was blurred by their loyalty to their child patients, with whom they identified. Bent on saving the child, they saw mothers as enemies to be overcome and fathers as peripheral figures to be ignored.

Communications family therapists rescued schizophrenics from psychiatric invalidation by demonstrating that their crazy conversation made sense as a desperate solution to desperate family situations. It wasn't the patient but the family system that was deranged. Family therapy aimed to humanize mental illness, but it created a nonhuman, mechanistic entity—the system—to do so.

In their efforts to make individual family members unrepressed agents in their own right, practicing therapists ran smack into powerful family opposition to personal autonomy. The individual may want to get better, but the family may need someone to play the sick role. Some families apparently re-

[2]The ideas in this section were adapted from *The Self in the System* (Nichols, 1987).

quire a "scapegoat" to maintain their equilibrium; the patient's sickness becomes necessary for the family's precarious health. This led Don Jackson to characterize families as "rule-governed homeostatic systems." Little noticed at the time was how this description portrayed patients as helpless and passive victims, and attention (as well as blame) was shifted to the family.

The Bateson group's observations were meant to be scientific, yet their language for describing family systems was combative and bellicose, often suggesting not just resistance, but willful opposition to change. The idea that families were oppositional put family therapists in an adversarial stance. Because families were seen as mindless systems, at once rigid (holding fast to their own ways) and slippery (hard to pin down), interviewing them became a struggle for strategic advantage.

Even when family therapists got past the naive idea that patients were innocent victims of malevolent kinfolk, they felt themselves in opposition to families who stubbornly resisted their well-meaning efforts to change them.

The shift from working with individuals to working with families was discontinuous and required new ways of thinking. Therapists, unused to seeing whole families interacting, eagerly imported nonclinical models to help them conceptualize patterned interactions.

Cybernetics and general systems theory provided useful metaphors to help clinicians organize some of the patterned interactions of family life. Describing the family as a system helped them see that a group of interacting personalities can function like a composite entity, a unit. Families were said to be like systems in that the behavior of every member of the system is related to and dependent on the behavior of all the others.

The great advance of systemic thinking was the recognition that people's lives are linked together such that behavior in families becomes a product of mutual influence. The danger of forgetting that systems metaphors are just that is the danger of overestimating their influence—and of dehumanizing individual family members. One myth of the system is that it is determinative rather than influential. Thus, for example, an overinvolved mother who steps back makes room for her husband to become more involved, but this shift in the system doesn't *make* him become involved. By the same token, while it may be difficult for a disengaged parent to spend more time with the children as long as they are enmeshed with the other parent, it isn't impossible.

The systems metaphor was thought to have the advantage of shifting blame away from individuals who were seen as caught up in the systemic structure of their families. Avoiding blame and fault-finding is all to the good, but avoiding the possibility of self-determination is an invidious myth. The danger here is the danger of mechanism.

Systems thinking deals with action—really behavior—but often with little distinction between human action and physical movement. An act is seen as the causal outcome of a mechanistic interaction of elemental "systemic forces." Therapy, therefore, can and should be arational. The truth is that action is also rational, mediated by individuals and their creation of meaning—and responsibility. Much of what we do is automatic and channeled by patterns of interaction. But although we do not always reflect and act rationally, we sometimes do. We are not just links in a circular chain of events; we are people with names who experience ourselves as centers of initiative. Certainly we are linked to others. Much of what we do is with other people in mind, some of what we do is with others, and once in a while for others. But the "we" who are the authors of the doing are single organisms, with hearts and minds and bodies all encased within our skin.

Family therapists taught us that our behavior is controlled in unseen but profound ways by the actions of those around us. Family rules and roles operate as invisible constraints influencing all that we do. The idea that people behave as they do because they are induced to live out defined roles can have a liberating effect; if one is playing a role, it is possible to play a new one. For example, modifying roles of manhood and womanhood that were based on sexual stereotypes permits a broader and more authentic definition of the self. If overextended, however, this kind of thinking implies that the role is everything.

Systems thinking in the extreme dismisses selfhood as an illusion. The problem is when roles become reified and rigidified as prescribed determinants of behavior *and* as independent of personal agency. Systems thinkers unfortunately implied that the role plays the person, rather than the other way around. But whether they act in concert or separately, it is finally the selves in the system who must act to bring about change.

Early family therapists treated the family as a *cybernetic system* that governs itself through feedback. Perhaps they overemphasized negative feedback, which enables families to resist change and maintain homeostasis, in part because they were studying schizophrenic families, who tend to be particularly rigid, and in part because they were reacting against the prevailing psychodynamic focus on the mental life of the individual. Nevertheless, as we came to realize, although systems thinking alerts us to our interconnections, the metaphor of an inanimate system is not an adequate model for human systems. When we think systemically, we realize that individuals are systems within systems, and that although they respond to forces outside themselves, they are also initiators, with imagination, abstract reasoning, creativity, memory, and desire.

THE STAGES OF FAMILY THERAPY[3]

The Initial Telephone Call

The goal of the initial contact is to get a minimal amount of information and arrange for the entire family to come for a consultation. Listen briefly to the caller's description of the presenting problem and then identify all members of the household and others who might be involved (including the referral source and other agencies). Then arrange for the first interview, specifying who will attend (usually everyone in the household), and the date, time, and place.

[3]The following description of how family therapists typically conduct treatment at times reflects the senior author's (M.P.N.) background in structural family therapy.

The reason for speaking only briefly to the caller is to avoid becoming caught up in one person's point of view about the problem (which is usually linear and blaming). The only uncomplicated calls to handle are those explicitly requesting family therapy—a husband or wife asking for couples therapy, or worried parents who expect to participate in the treatment of their child. In most cases, however, people calling for help think of one person as "the problem" and expect treatment to be focused on that person.

While there are things you can learn to say to convert requests for individual therapy into family cases, the most important consideration is attitudinal. First, understand and respect that the parent who wants you to treat his or her child individually, or the partner who wants to talk to you alone, has a perfectly legitimate point of view—even if it doesn't happen to agree with yours. Second, if you expect to meet with the whole family, your intention to do so and calm insistence that that is necessary, at least for the initial session, will get most families to agree to a consultation. It's not so much not knowing what to say as being anxious and uncertain about the need to meet with the entire group that makes beginning therapists have a hard time convincing families to come in together. (One way to decrease the no-show rate is to help novice therapists avoid feeling relief when the family doesn't show up.)

When the caller presents the problem as limited to one person, a useful way to broaden the complaint is to ask how it affects other members of the family. If the caller balks at the idea of bringing in the whole family, or says that a particular family member won't attend, say that you'll need to hear from everyone, at least initially, in order to get as much information as possible. Most people accept the need to give their point of view; what they resist is any implication that they're to blame for the problem—or in some cases, even that they are involved.

When a child is the identified patient, parents may be willing to come but reluctant to bring siblings whom they consider well-adjusted. Like the "uninvolved husband" who's "too busy" to attend, nonsymptomatic brothers and sisters may be important to help broaden the focus from the identified patient's failings to relationship issues in the entire family.

Broadening the focus does not, however, mean broadening the blame. Family members can often acknowledge a role in problematic family patterns if they sense that the therapist genuinely respects them and isn't looking to pin all the responsibility on one person. And it certainly isn't necessary or useful to get family members to openly admit their involvement in the problem; what's important is getting everyone to work together toward a solution.

Although the goal of the first telephone contact is primarily to arrange for a face-to-face meeting with the family, the clinician needs to find out if there are any circumstances that might preclude his or her ability to work with the family. Although many young therapists are equally expert on every imaginable problem, experienced therapists learn that there are some problems they aren't equipped to deal with—severe eating disorders, for example, or active alcohol or drug abuse.

Not all family therapists routinely meet with the entire family. Some find they have more room to maneuver by meeting with individuals or subgroups in the initial meeting and then gradually involving others. Others attempt to work with what the late Harry Goolishian called the "problem-determined system," not necessarily the family but everyone intimately affected by the problem. Still others try to determine who the "customers" are—namely, those people who seem most concerned. If the therapist suspects violence or abuse, confidential individual sessions may enable family members to reveal what they might not dare to discuss in front of the whole family. The point to remember is that family therapy is more a way of looking at things than a treatment technique based on seeing families.

Finally, because *most* families are reluctant to sit down together and face their conflicts, a reminder call before the first session helps cut down on the no-show rate.

The First Interview

The goal of the first interview is to build an alliance with the family and develop a hypothesis about what's maintaining the presenting problem. It is a good idea to come up with a tentative hypothesis (in technical terms, a "hunch") after the initial phone call, and then to test it in the first interview. (In order to avoid imposing pet theories on patient families, recreating them in the image of one's own bias, it's important to remain open to refuting, not just confirming, one's initial hypothesis.) The point isn't to jump to conclusions, but to start actively thinking.

The first objective of a consultation is to establish rapport. Unlike people who request individual psychotherapy, family members often don't think that they are part of the problem, and many don't want to be there. The key to building an alliance is to accept people where they are—listen respectfully to their points of view and appreciate their attitudes. Few people will put up with anyone's attempt to change them before they feel understood and accepted as they are.

Introduce yourself to the contact person and then to other adults in the household. Ask parents to introduce their children. Shake hands and greet everyone present. Orient the family to the room (e.g., observation mirrors, videotaping, toys for children) and to the format of the session (length and purpose). Repeat *briefly* (a sentence or two) what the caller told you over the phone (so as not to leave others wondering), and then ask for elaboration. Once you've heard and acknowledged that person's point of view ("So what you're saying is . . . ?"), ask each succeeding member of the family for their viewpoint.

At this stage, the objective is to hear from each person one at a time, and therefore arguments or interruptions should be politely but firmly blocked ("Excuse me, but I need to hear from each of you one at a time"). By listening to each person's perspective on the presenting problem, the therapist gathers information and establishes rapport.

While most of the session should be taken up with a discussion of the major problem, this negative focus can have a disheartening effect, and therefore spending some time exploring family members' interests, accomplishments, and strengths is never wasted and sometimes changes the emotional energy of sessions dramatically.

Strive for a balance between warmth and professionalism. Being friendly and accepting doesn't, however, mean spending a great deal of time making small talk, as though this were a social visit. Respectful interest in the family's problems and individual members' points of view is the best way to build trust.

In gathering information, some therapists find it useful to take a family history and many use *genograms* to diagram the extended family network. Others believe that whatever facts are essential will emerge in the natural course of events and prefer to concentrate on the family's presenting concerns and the circumstances surrounding them. (Why search history for an answer that only the living expression of it can give?)

Family therapists develop hypotheses about how family members might be involved in the presenting problem by asking them how they've attempted to solve it, and by watching how they interact as they discuss it among themselves.

Two kinds of information (*content*) that are particularly important are solutions that don't work and transitions in the life cycle to which the family hasn't yet adjusted. If whatever the family has been doing to solve their problems hasn't worked, then it may be that those attempts are part of the problem. A typical example would be overinvolved parents trying to help a shy child make friends by spending a lot of time coaxing and criticizing and controlling her. Sometimes family members will say they've "tried everything" to solve their problems and then list the full gamut of possible responses. In this case, the problem may be inconsistency. They try everything but give up too quickly in the face of opposition.

Despite the natural tendency to focus on problems and what causes them, it is a family's strengths not their weaknesses that will be most important in successful therapy. Therefore the therapist should search for resilience, accentuating the positive, and hope. What have these people been doing well? How have they successfully handled difficulties in the past? What would a hopeful future look like? Even the most discouraged families have had times where they were successful, even though those positive episodes are obscured by the frustration they feel over their current difficulties. By simply asking about family successes and what was different about those occasions, therapists may find that clients have more resources than they give themselves credit for. Successful therapy isn't so much about finding out what's wrong, as it is discovering and releasing unused human potential.

Although it isn't always immediately apparent (especially to them), most families seek treatment having failed to adjust to changing circumstances. If a husband or a wife develops problems within the first few months after a baby's birth, it may be because the couple hasn't shifted effectively from being a unit of two to being a unit of three. A young mother may be depressed because she doesn't have enough support (from her husband or extended family or friends) for meeting the consuming demands of caring for a new baby. A young father may feel neglected, jealous of all the time and attention his wife now lavishes on the baby, and hurt that she seems too tired to do anything with him when they do have time.

Although the strain on a couple of having a new baby seems obvious, you'd be amazed at how often depressed young mothers are treated by therapists as though there were something wrong with them—"unresolved dependency needs," perhaps, or maybe a Prozac deficiency. The same is true when families develop problems around the time a child enters school or reaches adolescence, or any other developmental shift: The transitional demands on the family are obvious, *if* you think about them.

Novice family therapists may be in their twenties or thirties and have no personal experience with some of the life transitions their clients are struggling with. Where this is the case, it underscores the need for the therapist to remain curious and respectful of a family's predicament rather than jump to uninformed conclusions. For example, as a young single man one of the authors (R. C. S.) couldn't understand why so many client couples with young children rarely went out on dates together anymore. He assumed that they were overly focused on their children and afraid of being alone together. Subsequent events in his own life taught him differently. With small children of his own, he now wonders how those couples got out so often!

Family therapists explore the *process* of family interaction by asking questions to get at how family members relate to each other and by inviting them to discuss their problems with one another in the session. The first strategy, asking "process" or "circular" questions, is favored by Bowenians and systemic therapists; the second, by structural therapists. In either case, the key question for the therapist is: What's keeping the family stuck? What is the force keeping them from adapting to the pressures of development and change?

Once they have met the family, learned about the problem that brings them to treatment, and developed a conjecture about what needs to be done to resolve the problem, therapists should make a recommendation to the family. This may include consulting another professional (a therapist who specializes in the problem the family presents with, a learning disability expert, a medical doctor, a lawyer), or even that the family doesn't need—or doesn't seem ready to profit from—treatment. Most often, however, the recommendation will be for a course of family therapy. Although most therapists try to make their recommendation at the end of the first interview, this may be hasty. If it takes two sessions to form a bond with the family, understand their situation, and find out if you can work with them, then take two sessions.

If you think you can help the family solve their problem, then offer them a treatment contract. Acknowledge why they came in, say that it was a good idea, and say that you can help. Then specify a regular meeting time, the length of sessions, who will attend, the presence of observers or use of videotape, the fee, and how insurance is handled. Remember that family resistance doesn't magically disappear after the first (or fourteenth) session. So stress the importance of regular meetings and the need for everyone to attend. Finally, don't forget to emphasize the family's goals and the strengths you have observed in people that can help meet the goals.

First Session Checklist:

1. Make contact with each member of the family and acknowledge his or her point of view about the problem and feelings about coming to therapy.

2. Establish leadership by controlling the structure and pace of the interview.
3. Develop a working alliance with the family by balancing warmth and professionalism.
4. Compliment family members on specific positive actions and family strengths.
5. Maintain empathy with individuals and respect for the family's way of doing things.
6. Focus on specific problems and attempted solutions.
7. Develop hypotheses about unhelpful interactions around the presenting problem.
8. Consider the possible involvement of family members, friends, or helpers who aren't present.
9. Negotiate a treatment contract that acknowledges the family's goals and specifies the therapist's framework for structuring treatment.
10. Ask if family members have any questions.

The Early Phase of Treatment

The early phase of treatment is devoted to refining the therapist's hypothesis into a formulation about what's maintaining the problem and beginning to work on resolving it. Now the strategy shifts from an emphasis on alliance-building and accommodating the family to challenging them to produce change. Most therapists are able to figure out what needs to change. Once you have the whole family present, their inadvertent mistakes are often glaringly obvious. What sets good therapists apart is their ability to push for change forcefully. Some therapists prefer to avoid confrontation and find it more effective to work indirectly. However, regardless of whether they work directly [and at times use confrontation] or indirectly [and avoid it], good therapists are finishers.

Effective family therapy addresses interpersonal conflict, and the first step (especially in structural family therapy) is to bring it into the consulting room and put it between family members. Often this is not a problem. Couples in conflict or parents feuding with their children will usually speak right up about their disagreements. If the family is in therapy not because they want to be but because someone sent them (the court, the school, the Department of Protective Services), the therapist begins by addressing the family's problem dealing with these outside agencies. How must the family change so as to resolve their conflict with these agencies? How must the family change so that its members won't be in trouble?

When one person is presented as the problem, the therapist challenges linearity by asking others how they are involved (or affected). What was their role in creating (or managing) the problem? How have they responded to it?

For example: "The problem is Tommy. He's disobedient." "Who taught him to be disobedient?"

Less confrontive therapists might ask: "When do you notice this?" "What does he do that seems disobedient?" "How does this disobedience affect you?"

Or: "It's me, I'm depressed." "Who in the family is contributing to your depression?" "No one." "Then who's helping you get over being depressed?"

These challenges can be blunt or gentle, depending on the therapist's preferred style and assessment of the family. The point, incidentally, is not to switch from blaming one person (the disobedient child, say) to another (a parent who lacks authority and doesn't discipline effectively), but to broaden the problem as a triangular, interactional one. Maybe the mother is too lenient with Tommy because she finds father too strict, and moreover she may be overinvested in the boy because of emotional distance in the marriage.

The best way to challenge inappropriate interactions is to point out the patterns that are keeping people stuck. A useful formula for this is: "The more you do X, the more he does Y—and the more you do Y, the more she does X." For X and Y, try substituting nag and withdraw, or punish and indulge. Incidentally, when therapists point out what people are doing that isn't working, it's a tactical error to then tell them what they *should* be doing. Once a therapist shifts from pointing something out to giving advice, the family's attention shifts from themselves and their behavior to the therapist and his or her advice.

"When you criticize your son for feeling upset, he feels misunderstood and hurt. What you're saying may be true, but he doesn't feel supported." "What should I do?" "I don't know; ask your son."

Even though family therapists challenge assumptions, they continue to listen to family members' feelings and points of view. Listening is a silent activity, rare at times, even among therapists. Family members often don't listen to each other for long without become defensive and reactive. Therapists don't listen when they're too anxious to jump in to disagree or give advice. But remember that people aren't likely to change or even reconsider their assumptions until they feel they've been heard and understood.

Homework assignments can be used to test flexibility (simply seeing if they are carried out measures willingness to change), to make family members more aware of their role in problems (telling people just to notice something, without necessarily trying to change it, is very instructive), and to suggest new ways of relating. Typical homework assignments include: suggesting that overinvolved parents hire a babysitter and go out together, having argumentative partners take turns talking about their feelings while the other just listens without saying anything (but noticing tendencies to become reactive that make it hard to listen), and having dependent family members practice spending more time alone (or with someone outside the family) and doing more things for themselves. Homework assignments likely to generate conflict—such as negotiating house rules with teenagers—should be avoided, and such difficult discussions should be saved for when the therapist can act as referee.

Early Phase Checklist:

1. Identify major conflicts and bring them into the consulting room.
2. Develop a hypothesis and refine it into a formulation about what the family is doing to perpetuate or fail to solve their presenting problem. Formulations should consider: process and structure, family rules, triangles, and boundaries.

3. Keep the focus of treatment on primary problems and the interpersonal conditions supporting them.
4. Create homework assignments that address both problems and the underlying conditions supporting them.
5. Challenge family members to see their own role in the problems that plague them.
6. Push for change, in the session and between sessions at home.
7. Seek and make effective use of supervision and consultation to test validity of formulations and effectiveness of interventions.

The Middle Phase of Treatment

When therapy is anything other than brief and problem-focused, much of the middle phase is devoted to helping family members express themselves and achieve mutual understanding. If the therapist plays too active and central a role in this process—filtering all conversation between family members and himself or herself—family members won't learn how to deal with each other, and will continue to manage only as long as they keep coming in for therapy sessions. For this reason, in the middle phase of therapy, the therapist takes a less active role and encourages family members to talk and interact with each other. As they do so, the therapist steps back and observes the process. When dialogue bogs down, the therapist either points out what went wrong, or simply encourages them to keep talking—but with less interruption and criticism.

When family members address their conflicts directly they tend to become anxious and reactive. Anxiety is the enemy of listening. Some therapists (Bowenians, for example) make every effort to control and minimize anxiety by having family members talk mostly to the therapist. Others prefer to let family members deal with their own anxiety by helping them learn to talk with each other less defensively (by saying how they feel, and listening to and acknowledging what the other one says). However, even therapists who work primarily with family dialogue need to interrupt when anxiety starts to escalate and conversations become defensive and destructive.

Thus, in the middle phase of treatment the therapist takes a less directive role and encourages the family to begin to rely on their own resources. The level of conflict and anxiety is balanced by alternating between having family members talk among themselves or with the therapist. In either case, the therapist encourages family members to get beyond criticism and blaming to talking directly about what they feel and what they want—and to learn to see their own part in unproductive patterns of interaction.

Middle Phase Checklist:

1. Use intensity to challenge family members. (Or ingenuity to get around resistance; or empathy to get underneath defensiveness.)
2. Avoid being so directive and controlling that the family doesn't learn to rely on and improve their own ways of relating to each other.
3. Foster individual responsibility and mutual understanding.

4. Make certain that efforts to improve relationships are having a positive effect on the presenting complaint.

5. Even if you meet with subgroups, don't lose sight of the whole family picture, and don't neglect any individuals or relationships—*especially* not those "difficult" ones that are so tempting to avoid.

6. Is therapy stuck on a plateau? Have sessions taken on a sameness and predictability? Does the therapist assume too active a role in choosing what to talk about? Have therapist and family developed a friendly relationship that has become more important than addressing conflicts? Has the therapist assumed a regular role in the family (an empathic listener to the spouses, or a firm parent figure to the children), substituting for a missing function in the family (the spouses aren't listening to each other, the parents aren't nurturing and controlling their own children)?

Termination

Termination comes for brief therapists as soon as the presenting problem is resolved. For psychoanalytic therapists, therapy is a long-term learning process and may continue for a year or two, or more. For most therapists, termination comes somewhere between these two extremes and has to do both with the family feeling that they've gotten what they've come for and the therapist's sense that treatment has reached the point of diminishing returns. One clue that it may be time to terminate is when the family comes in with nothing to say but small talk (assuming, of course, that they aren't avoiding conflict).

In individual psychotherapy, where the relationship to the therapist is often the primary vehicle of change, termination focuses on reviewing the relationship and saying goodbye. In family therapy, the focus is more on what the family has been doing that doesn't work. Termination is, therefore, a good time to review and consolidate what they've learned. Although some strategic therapists are content to manipulate change without necessarily being concerned that the family understands it, most family therapy has some kind of teaching function, and termination is the time to make sure the family has learned something about how to get along.

It can be helpful at this point to ask the family to anticipate upcoming changes or challenges that might cause setbacks and discuss with them how they will handle those challenges. The question "How will you know when things are heading backwards and what will you do?" is useful in this regard. Families can also be reminded that their present harmony can't be maintained indefinitely and that people have a tendency to overreact to the first sign of relapse, which can trigger a self-fulfilling vicious cycle. To paraphrase Zorba the Greek, Life *is* trouble. To be alive is to encounter difficulties. The real test is how you handle them.

Although there are cases in which it seems likely that a family will run into additional problems and perhaps need additional treatment, at termination it may be best to recognize that the current relationship has come to an end—and to expressly support the family's strengths and coping skills.

Finally, although in the business of therapy, no news is usually good news, it might be a good idea to check in with the family to see how they're doing some months after termination. This can be done with a letter, a phone call, or a brief follow-up session. The family will appreciate the therapist's continued interest and concern, and the therapist will feel a greater sense of closure. The therapeutic relationship is, of necessity, somewhat artificial or at least constrained. But there's no reason to make it less than human—or to forget about families once you terminate with them.

Termination Checklist:

1. Is the presenting problem resolved or greatly improved?
2. Is the family satisfied that they got what they came for, or are they interested in continuing to learn about themselves and improve their relationships?
3. Does the family have an understanding of what they were doing that wasn't working, and how to avoid the recurrence of similar problems?
4. Do minor recurrences of problems reflect lack of resolution of some underlying dynamic or merely that the family has to readjust to function without the therapist?
5. Have family members developed and improved relationships outside the immediate family context as well as within it?

REFERENCES

Adler, A. 1931. *Guiding the child.* New York: Greenberg.

Bales, R. F. 1950. *Interaction process analysis: A method for the study of small groups.* Cambridge, MA: Addison-Wesley.

Bales, R. F. 1970. *Personality and interpersonal behavior.* New York: Holt, Rinehart and Winston.

Bateson, G., and Jackson, D. D. 1964. Some varieties of pathogenic organization. *Disorders of Communication.* 42:270–283.

Bateson, G., Jackson, D. D., Haley, J., and Weakland, J. H. 1956. Toward a theory of schizophrenia. *Behavioral Science.* 1:251–264.

Bateson, G., Jackson, D. D., Haley, J., and Weakland, J. H. 1963. A note on the double-bind–1962. *Family Process.* 2:154–161.

Beels, C. C., and Ferber, A. 1969. Family therapy: A view. *Family Process.* 8:280–318.

Bell, J. E. 1961. *Family group therapy.* Public Health Monograph No. 64. Washington, DC: U.S. Government Printing Office.

Bell, J. E. 1975. *Family group therapy.* New York: Jason Aronson.

Bell, J. E. 1976. A theoretical framework for family group therapy. In *Family therapy: Theory and practice,* P. J. Guerin, ed. New York: Gardner Press.

Bennis, W. G., and Shepard, H. A. 1956. A theory of group development. *Human Relations.* 9:415–437.

Bion, W. R. 1961. *Experiences in groups.* New York: Tavistock Publications.

Birdwhistell, R. L. 1952. *Introduction to kinesics.* Louisville, KY: University of Louisville Press.

Bleuler, E. 1950. *Dementia praecox or the group of schizophrenias.* New York: International Universities Press.

Brown, R. 1965. *Social psychology.* New York: The Free Press.

Carnap, R. 1942. *Introduction to semantics.* Cambridge, MA: Harvard University Press.

Cartwright, D., and Zander, A., eds. 1968. *Group dynamics: Research and theory.* New York: Harper & Row.

Cooley, C. H. 1902. *Human nature and the social order.* New York: Scribner.

Dreikurs, R. 1951. Family group therapy in the Chicago community child guidance centers. *Mental Hygiene. 35*:291–301.

Foulkes, S. H. 1965. *Therapeutic group analysis.* New York: International Universities Press.

Foulkes, S. H. 1975. *Group analytic psychotherapy: Method and principles.* London: Gordon & Breach.

Freud, S. 1921. *Group psychology and the analysis of the ego.* Standard Edition. Vol. 18. London: Hogarth Press, 1955.

Gleitman, H. 1981. *Psychology.* New York: Norton.

Gritzer, P. H., and Okum, H. S. 1983. Multiple family group therapy: A model for all families. In *Handbook of family and marital therapy,* B. B. Wolman and G. Stricker, eds. New York: Plenum Press.

Haley, J. 1961. Control in psychotherapy with schizophrenics. *Archives of General Psychiatry. 5*:340–353.

Haley, J. 1963. *Strategies of psychotherapy.* New York: Grune and Stratton.

Haley, J. 1968. Testing parental instructions to schizophrenic and normal children: A pilot study. *Journal of Abnormal Psychology. 73*:559–565.

Haley, J. 1976. *Problem-solving therapy.* San Francisco: Jossey-Bass.

Haley, J. 1986. *The power tactics of Jesus Christ,* 2nd ed. Rockville, MD: The Triangle Press.

Hearn, G. 1957. The process of group development. *Autonomous Groups Bulletin. 13*:1–7.

Hoffman, L. 1971. Deviation-amplifying processes in natural groups. In *Changing families,* J. Haley, ed. New York: Grune & Stratton.

Jackson, D. D. 1961. Interactional psychotherapy. In *Contemporary psychotherapies,* M. T. Stein, ed. New York: Free Press of Glencoe.

Jackson, D. D. 1965. Family rules: The marital quid pro quo. *Archives of General Psychiatry. 12*:589–594.

Jackson, D. D. 1967. Aspects of conjoint family therapy. In *Family therapy and disturbed families,* G. H. Zuk and I. Boszormenyi-Nagy, eds. Palo Alto: Science and Behavior Books.

Jackson, D. D., and Weakland, J. H. 1961. Conjoint family therapy: Some consideration on theory, technique, and results. *Psychiatry. 24*:30–45.

Laqueur, H. P. 1966. General systems theory and multiple family therapy. In *Handbook of psychiatric therapies,* J. Masserman, ed. New York: Grune & Stratton.

Laqueur, H. P. 1972a. Mechanisms of change in multiple family therapy. In *Progress in group and family therapy,* C. J. Sager and H. S. Kaplan, eds. New York: Brunner/Mazel.

Laqueur, H. P. 1972b. Multiple family therapy. In *The book of family therapy,* A. Ferber, M. Mendelsohn, and A. Napier, eds. Boston: Houghton Mifflin.

Laqueur, H. P. 1976. Multiple family therapy. In *Family therapy: Theory and practice,* P. J. Guerin, ed. New York: Gardner Press.

Lederer, W., and Jackson, D. D. 1968. *Mirages of marriage.* New York: Norton.

Lewin, K. 1951. *Field theory in social science.* New York: McGraw-Hill.

Lidz, T., Cornelison, A., Terry, D., and Fleck, S. 1958. Intra-familial environment of the schizophrenic patient: IV. The transmission of irrationality. *Archives of Neurology and Psychiatry. 79*:305–316.

Liem, J. H. 1974. Effects of verbal communications of parents and children: A comparison of normal and schizophrenic families. *Journal of Consulting and Clinical Psychology. 42*:438–450.

MacGregor, R. 1967. Progress in multiple impact theory. In *Expanding theory and practice in family therapy,* N. W. Ackerman, F. L. Beatman, and S. N. Sherman, eds. New York: Family Service Association.

MacGregor, R. 1972. Multiple impact psychotherapy with families. In *Family therapy: An introduction to theory and technique*, G. D. Erickson, and T. P. Hogan, eds. Monterey, CA: Brooks/Cole.

MacGregor, R., Richie, A. M., Serrano, A. C., Schuster, F. P., McDonald, E. C., and Goolishian, H. A. 1964. *Multiple impact therapy with families*. New York: McGraw-Hill.

Marayuma, M. 1968. The second cybernetics: Deviation-amplifying mutual causal processes. In *Modern systems research for the behavioral scientist*, W. Buckley, ed. Chicago: Aldine.

McFarlane, W. R. 1982. Multiple-family therapy in the psychiatric hospital. In *The psychiatric hospital and the family*, H. T. Harbin, ed. New York: Spectrum.

Meyer, J. P., and Pepper, S. 1977. Need compatibility and marital adjustment among young married couples. *Journal of Personality and Social Psychology*. *35*:331–342.

Midelfort, C. F. 1957. *The family in psychotherapy*. New York: McGraw-Hill.

Morris, C. W. 1938. Foundations on the theory of signs. In *International encyclopedia of united science*, O. Neurath, R. Carnap, and C. O. Morris, eds. Chicago: University of Chicago Press.

Nichols, M. P. 1987. *The self in the system*. New York: Brunner/Mazel.

Parsons, T. 1950. Psychoanalysis and the social structure. *Psychoanalytic Quarterly*. *19*:371–380.

Ruesch, J., and Bateson, G. 1951. *Communication: The social matrix of psychiatry*. New York: Norton.

Ruevini, U. 1975. Network intervention with a family in crisis. *Family Process*. *14*:193–203.

Ruevini, U. 1979. *Networking families in crisis*. New York: Human Sciences Press.

Sartre, J. P. 1964. *Being and nothingness*. New York: Citadel Press.

Satir, V. 1964. *Conjoint family therapy*. Palo Alto, CA: Science and Behavior Books.

Satir, V. 1971. The family as a treatment unit. In *Changing families*, J. Haley, ed. New York: Grune & Stratton.

Scheflen, A. E. 1966. Natural history method in psychotherapy: Communicational research. In *Methods of research in psychotherapy*, L. A. Gottschalk, and E. H. Auerbach, eds. New York: Appleton-Century-Crofts.

Scheflen, A. E. 1968. Human communication: Behavioral programs and their integration in interaction. *Behavioral Science*. *13*:86–102.

Schutz, W. C. 1958. *FIRO: A three-dimensional theory of interpersonal behavior*. New York: Holt, Rinehart and Winston.

Shaw, M. E. 1981. *Group dynamics: The psychology of small group behavior*. New York: McGraw-Hill.

Skynner, A. R. C. 1976. *Systems of family and marital psychotherapy*. New York: Brunner/Mazel.

Sluzki, C. E. 1978. Marital therapy from a systems theory perspective. In *Marriage and marital therapy*, T. J. Paolino and B. S. McCrady, eds. New York: Brunner/Mazel.

Speck, R. V., and Attneave, C. A. 1971. Social network intervention. In *Changing families*, J. Haley, ed. New York: Grune & Stratton.

Speck, R. V., and Attneave, C. A. 1973. *Family networks*. New York: Pantheon.

Spiegel, J. 1971. *Transactions*. New York: Science House.

Sullivan, H. S. 1944. The language of schizophrenia. In *Language and thought in schizophrenia*, J. S. Kasanin, ed. New York: Norton.

Von Bertalanffy, L. 1950. An outline of general system theory. *British Journal of the Philosophy of Science*. *1*:134–165.

Watzlawick, P. A. 1966. A structured family interview. *Family Process*. *5*:256–271.

Watzlawick, P., Beavin, J. H., and Jackson, D. D. 1967. *Pragmatics of human communication*. New York: Norton.

Waxler, N. E. 1974. Parent and child effects on cognitive performance: An experimental approach to the etiological and responsive theories of schizophrenia. *Family Process. 13:*1–22.

Weakland, J., Fisch, R., Watzlawick, P., and Bodin, A. M. 1974, Brief therapy focused problem resolution. *Family Process. 13:*141–168.

Winch, R. F. 1955. The theory of complementary needs in mate selection: A test of one kind of complementariness. *American Sociological Review. 20:*52–56.

Wynne, L. C. 1968. Methodologic and conceptual issues in the study of schizophrenics and their families. *Journal of Psychiatric Research. 6:*185–199.

Wynne, L. C. 1970. Communication disorders and the quest for relatedness in families of schizophrenics. *American Journal of Psychoanalysis. 30:*100–114.

Wynne, L. C., Jones, J. E., and Al-Khayyal, M. 1982. Healthy family communication patterns: Observations in families "at risk" for psychopathology. In *Normal family processes,* F. Walsh, ed. New York: Guilford Press.

Wynne, L. C., Ryckoff, I. M., Day, J., and Hirsch, S. 1958. Pseudomutuality in the family relations of schizophrenics. *Psychiatry. 21:*205–220.

Wynne, L., and Singer, M. 1963. Thought disorder and family relationships of schizophrenics: I. Research strategy. *Archives of General Psychiatry. 9:*191–198.

Wynne, L. C., Singer, M. T., Bartko, J. J., and Toohey, M. L. 1977. Schizophrenics and their families: Recent research on parental communication. In *Developments in psychiatric research,* J. M. Tanner, ed. London: Hodder and Stoughton.

Yalom, I. D. 1985. *The theory and practices of group psychotherapy,* 3rd ed. New York: Basic Books.

Structural Family Therapy

In the 1970s structural family therapy emerged as perhaps the most influential approach in the field. This predominance came about, not only because of the effectiveness of the approach, but also because of the stunning virtuosity of its primary exponent, Salvador Minuchin. Known initially as a clinician rather than a theoretician, Minuchin first established his reputation in dramatic and compelling teaching demonstrations; but he also described families as having an underlying organization in terms that provide clear guidelines for diagnosis and treatment.

One of the reasons family therapy is so difficult is that families often appear as collections of individuals who affect each other in powerful but unpredictable ways. Beginning therapists are usually puzzled by the complex transactions that make up family life. Structural family therapy offers a clear framework that brings order and meaning to those transactions. The consistent, repetitive, organized, and predictable patterns of family behavior are what allow us to consider that they have a structure, although, of course, only in a functional sense. The emotional boundaries and coalitions that make up family structure are abstractions; nevertheless, using the concept of family structure enables therapists to intervene in a systematic and organized fashion.

Salvador Minuchin began seeing families of institutionalized children in the late 1950s. Unlike other family therapists, he didn't have to make the transition from sitting in an office listening and talking to doing family therapy; as a child psychiatrist working with delinquents, he always had to use action and pressure. And he had to understand people in context, because even the hard-core toughs he worked with were always pushed and pulled by pressures of the gang and of the family. Moreover, given where he chose to start his career, it should come as no surprise that Minuchin has always been passionately concerned with social issues.

When he first burst onto the scene, Minuchin's immediate galvanizing impact was as an incomparable master of technique. But perhaps his most lasting impact will prove to be the development of a theory of family structure and a set of guidelines to organize therapeutic techniques: Families who come for treatment are seen as stuck for lack of alternatives; therapy is designed to unfreeze them from rigid habits, creating the opportunity for new structures to emerge. This approach was so successful that it captivated the field in the 1970s, and Minuchin helped build the Philadelphia Child Guidance Clinic into a world famous complex, where thousands of family therapists have been trained in structural family therapy.

SKETCHES OF LEADING FIGURES

Minuchin was born and raised in Argentina. He served as a physician in the Israeli army, then came to the United States, where he trained in child psychiatry with Nathan Ackerman at the Jewish Board of Guardians in New York City. After completing his studies, Minuchin returned to Israel in 1952 to work with displaced children—and to become absolutely committed to the importance of families. He moved back to the United States in 1954 to begin psychoanalytic training at the William Alanson White Institute, where he was imbued with the interpersonal psychiatry of Harry Stack Sullivan. After leaving the White Institute, Minuchin took a job at the Wiltwyck School for delinquent boys, where he suggested to his colleagues that they start seeing families. Other family therapists during this period, such as Nathan Ackerman and Don Jackson, were working with middle-class families; their approaches hardly seemed suitable to multiproblem, poor families with children at Wiltwyck. Therefore Minuchin had to develop new concepts and techniques applicable to these families, one of which was of the idea of *enactment*—that is, bringing problematic sequences into the treatment room by having families act them out so that the therapist can observe and change them. Most of Minuchin's techniques were concrete and action-oriented, qualities that have continued to characterize structural family therapy ever since.

At Wiltwyck, Minuchin and his colleagues—Dick Auerswald, Charlie King, Braulio Montalvo, and Clara Rabinowitz—taught themselves to do family therapy, inventing it as they went along. To do so, they built a one-way mirror and took turns observing each other work. In 1962 Minuchin made a hajj to what was then the Mecca of family therapy, Palo Alto. Here he met Jay Haley and began a friendship that was to bear fruit in an extraordinarily fertile collaboration. A couple of years later Minuchin renewed his contact with Nathan Ackerman, who from 1950 to 1952 had guided his early development as a child psychiatrist. Minuchin credits Ackerman with demonstrating the personal power of a therapist passionately engaged with the families he treats. While most family therapists are observers, Minuchin, like Ackerman, joins the families he treats, becoming for a time an active participant in their drama.

The clinical and conceptual success of Minuchin's work with the families at Wiltwyck led to a book, *Families of the Slums,* written with Montalvo, Guerney, Rosman, and Schumer. Minuchin's reputation as a practitioner of family therapy grew, and he became the Director of the Philadelphia Child Guidance Clinic in 1965. The Clinic, located in the heart of Philadelphia's black ghetto, then consisted of less than a dozen staff members. From this modest beginning Minuchin created one of the largest and most prestigious child guidance clinics in the world. When he stepped down ten years later, there were three hundred people on the staff and the clinic had become part of an elaborate modern complex along with the Children's Hospital of Philadelphia adjacent to the University of Pennsylvania campus.

Among Minuchin's colleagues in Philadelphia were Braulio Montalvo, Jay Haley, Bernice Rosman, Harry Aponte, Carter Umbarger, Marianne Walters, Charles Fishman, Cloe Madanes, and Stephen Greenstein, all of whom had an important role in shaping structural family therapy. Many other therapists associated with the Philadelphia Child Guidance Clinic as students and staff members have also influenced structural family therapy with their own ideas and styles; these second-generation structuralists are now dispersed throughout the country. By the late 1970s, structural family therapy had become the most influential and widely practiced of all systems of family therapy.

When he was working with poor people at Wiltwyck, Minuchin says he got no flack for doing family therapy. The flack came when he turned the Philadelphia Child Guidance Clinic into a family therapy center. Both the APA and AMA raised serious questions: Was family therapy proper for the training of child psychiatrists? Could Minuchin's unorthodox notion that family therapy and child psychiatry should be synonymous be right? Accused of heresy and summoned to constant meetings to defend his point of view, Minuchin responded strategically: He didn't show up at the meetings. But even more important than his refusal to take the defensive was the fact that the influential institution he created gave him a power base from which he was able to fight and win a place for family therapy in the medical establishment.

In 1976 Minuchin stepped down as Director of the Philadelphia Child Guidance Clinic, but stayed on as head of training until 1981. He now directs his own center, Family Studies, Inc., and travels around the world teaching and demonstrating his uniquely charismatic brand of family therapy. Less widely known, but also perhaps closer to his heart, is Minuchin's dedication to reforming the social welfare system in New York City, especially the foster care program that continues to separate children from their parents.

Like good players on the same team with a superstar, some of Minuchin's colleagues are not as well known as they might be. Chief among these is Braulio Montalvo, one of the great and underrated geniuses of family therapy. Born and raised in Puerto Rico, Montalvo, like Minuchin, has always been committed to treating minority families. He is also like Minuchin in being a brilliant therapist, though he favors a gentler, more supportive approach. Montalvo was instrumental in building the Philadelphia Child Guidance

Clinic, but his contributions are less well known because he is a quiet man who usually works behind the scenes.

THEORETICAL FORMULATIONS

The prominence of structural family therapy is due in part to Minuchin's renown as a clinician, and to the excellent training programs offered at the Philadelphia Child Guidance Clinic, but also to the fact that Minuchin's theory is both simple and practical.

Most therapists are impatient with theories: They see them as abstractions, which they are eager to bypass in order to learn techniques. But all the clever techniques and impressive interventions that one can pick up from books and supervisors are nothing but tactical maneuvers. Without a map you're lost—caught up in the detailed content of family discussions with no overall plan. This often occurs in individual psychotherapy, where therapists become experts at passivity: You can sit back and listen impassively, week after week, as Mr. Jones complains about his wife. As long as he gets some relief from just complaining, there's no need to do much but listen and nod sympathetically. In family work it's harder to be passive. Family members aren't confirmed into the status of patienthood and they won't put up with a passive therapist. They want action! They want solutions! They want a therapist to solve their problems. Families present problem after problem, crisis after crisis, and demand that therapists *Do Something!*

Beginners tend to get bogged down in the content of family problems because they don't have a theory to help them see the process of family dynamics. Structural family therapy is a blueprint for analyzing the process of family interactions. As such, it provides a basis for consistent strategies of treatment, which obviates the need to have a specific technique—usually someone else's—for every occasion.

Three constructs are the essential components of structural family theory: *structure, subsystems,* and *boundaries.*

Family structure, the organized pattern in which family members interact, is a deterministic concept, but it doesn't prescribe or legislate behavior; it *describes* sequences that are predictable. When they are repeated, family transactions establish enduring patterns. These repeated patterns determine how, when, and to whom family members relate. When a mother tells her daughter to pick up her toys and the daughter refuses until her father shouts at her, an interactional pattern is initiated. If it's repeated, it creates a structure in which father is competent as a disciplinarian, mother is incompetent. In addition, mother is likely to be more affectionate to her daughter, while father, the disciplinarian, remains on the outside.

Family structure involves a set of covert rules that govern transactions in the family. For example, a rule such as "family members must always protect one another" will be manifested in various ways depending on context and which family members are involved. If an adolescent son has to be up early for school, mother wakes him; father does all the shopping if driving makes the mother nervous; the kids intervene to diffuse conflict between the parents; and the parents' preoccupation with the kids' problems keeps the couple from spending time together. All of these sequences are isomorphic; they are structured. Changing any of them may or may not affect the underlying structure, but altering the basic structure will have ripple effects on all family transactions.

Family structure is shaped partly by universal and partly by idiosyncratic constraints. For example, all families have some kind of hierarchical structure, with parents and children having different amounts of authority. Family members also tend to have reciprocal and complementary functions. If one parent is supercompetent and responsible, the other will be less so; if the supercompetent one gets "sick" or less competent in some other way, the other will take over.

Transactional patterns foster expectations that determine future patterns. Often these become so ingrained that their origin is forgotten, and they are presumed necessary rather than optional. If a young mother, burdened by the demands of her infant, gets upset and complains to her husband, he may respond in various ways. Perhaps he'll move closer and share the heavy demands of childrearing. This creates a united parental team. On the other hand, if he decides, and his wife concurs, that she is "depressed," she may be sent into psychotherapy to get the emotional support she needs. This creates a structure where the mother remains distant from her husband, and learns to turn outside the family for emotional support. Whatever the chosen pattern, it tends to be self-perpetuating and resistant to change. Although alternatives are available, families are unlikely to consider them until changing circumstances produce stress and dysfunction in the system.

Family structure is not easily discerned. Two things are necessary: a theoretical system that explains structure, and seeing the family in action. The facts are not enough. Knowing that a family is a single-parent family with three children, or that two parents are having trouble with a middle child doesn't tell you what the family structure is. Structure only becomes evident when you observe the actual interactions among family members over time. Single interactions are affected by specific circumstances; repeated sequences reveal structural patterns.

Consider the following example. A mother calls the clinic to complain of misbehavior in her 17-year-old son. She is asked to bring her husband, son, and their three other children to the first session. When they arrive, the mother begins to describe a series of minor ways in which the son is disobedient around the house. He responds angrily, saying nobody understands him and he never gets any sympathy from his mother. This spontaneous dialogue between mother and son reveals an intense involvement between them—an involvement no less real or intense simply because it is conflictual. This dyadic sequence doesn't tell the whole story, however, because it doesn't include the father or the other three children. They must be engaged in interaction to observe their role in the family structure. If the father sides with his wife but seems unconcerned, then it may be that the mother's preoccupation with her son is related to her husband's lack of involvement. Further, if the three younger children tend to agree with the mother and describe their brother as bad, then it becomes clear that all the children are close to the mother—close and obedient up to a point, then close and disobedient.

Families are differentiated into *subsystems* of members who join together to perform various functions. Every individual is a subsystem, and dyads or larger groups make up other subsystems, determined by generation, gender, or common interests. Obvious groupings such as the parents or the teenagers are sometimes less significant than covert coalitions. A mother and her youngest child may form such a tightly bonded subsystem that others are excluded. Another family may be split into two camps, with Mom and the boys on one side, and Dad and the girls on the other. Though certain patterns are common, the possibilities for subgrouping are endless.

Every family member plays many roles in several subgroups. Mary may be a wife, a mother, a daughter, and a niece. In each of these roles she will be required to behave differently and exercise a variety of interpersonal options. If she's mature and flexible, she will be able to vary her behavior to fit the different subgroups in which she functions. Scolding may be okay from a mother, but it causes problems from a wife or a daughter.

Individuals, subsystems, and whole families are demarcated by interpersonal *boundaries*, invisible barriers that surround individuals and subsystems, regulating the amount of contact with others. Boundaries serve to protect the autonomy of the family and its subsystems, by managing *proximity* and *hierarchy*. A rule forbidding phone calls at dinner time establishes a boundary which protects the family from outside intrusion. When small children are permitted to freely interrupt their parents' conversation at dinner, the boundary separating the parents from the children is minimal. Subsystems that aren't adequately protected by boundaries limit the development of interpersonal skills achievable in these subsystems. If parents always step in to settle arguments between their children, the children won't learn to fight their own battles and will be impaired in their dealings with peers.

Interpersonal boundaries vary from being rigid to diffuse (Figure 5.1). Rigid boundaries are overly restrictive and permit little contact with outside subsystems, resulting in *disengagement*. Disengaged individuals or subsystems are relatively isolated and autonomous. On the positive side, this permits independence, growth, and mastery. If parents don't hover over their children, telling them what to do and fighting their battles, then the children will be forced to develop their own resources. On the other hand, disengagement limits warmth, affection, and nurturance; and disengaged families must be under extreme stress before they mobilize mutual support. If parents keep their children at a distance, affection is minimized, and the parents will be slow to notice when the children need support and guidance.

Enmeshed subsystems offer a heightened sense of mutual support, but at the expense of independence and autonomy. Enmeshed parents are loving

Rigid Boundary	Clear Boundary	Diffuse Boundary
————————	- - - - - - - - - - -	• • • • • •
Disengagement	Normal Range	Enmeshment

FIGURE 5.1 Interpersonal Boundaries

and considerate; they spend a lot of time with their kids and do a lot for them. However, children enmeshed with their parents learn to rely on the parents and tend to be dependent. They're less comfortable by themselves, and may have trouble relating to people outside the family.

Minuchin described some of the features of family subsystems in his most accessible work, *Families and Family Therapy* (Minuchin, 1974). Families begin when two people join together to form a spouse subsystem. Two people in love agree to share their lives and futures and expectations, but a period of often difficult adjustment is required before they can complete the transition from courtship to a functional spouse subsystem. They must learn to *accommodate* to each other's needs and preferred styles of interaction. In a normal couple, each gives and gets. He learns to accommodate to her wish to be kissed hello and goodbye. She learns to leave him alone with his paper and morning coffee. These little arrangements, multiplied a thousand times, may be accomplished easily or only after intense struggle. Whatever the case, this process of accommodation cements the couple into a unit.

The couple must also develop complementary patterns of mutual support. Some patterns are transitory and may later be reversed—perhaps, for instance, one works while the other completes school. Other patterns are more stable and lasting. Traditional sex-role stereotypes may allow couples to achieve complementarity, but at the expense of fully rounded functioning for each spouse. A traditional woman may not have to open doors, earn a living, or mow the lawn; on the other hand, she may have to deny her own intelligence, submerge her independence, and live in the shadow of her husband. A traditional husband may get to make all the decisions, not have to change dirty diapers, and be waited on hand and foot around the house; however, the price for these "masculine" prerogatives may be that he's not allowed to cry, never learns the pleasure of cooking a special meal, and doesn't share the joy of caring for his children.

Exaggerated complementary roles can detract from individual growth; moderate complementarity enables spouses to divide functions, to support and enrich each other. When one has the flu and feels lousy, the other takes over. One's permissiveness with children may be balanced by the other's strictness. One's fiery disposition may help to melt the other's icy reserve. Complementary patterns, such as pursuer-distancer, active-passive, dominant-submissive, exist in most couples. They become pathological when they are so exaggerated that they create a dysfunctional subsystem. Therapists must learn to accept those structural patterns that work, and challenge only those that do not.

The spouse subsystem must also have a boundary which separates it from parents, from children, and from the outside world. All too often, husband and wife give up the space they need for supporting each other when children are born. A rigid boundary around the couple deprives the children of the support they need; but in our child-centered culture, the boundary separating parents and children is often extremely diffuse.

The birth of a child instantly transforms the family structure; the pattern of interaction between the parental and child subsystems must be worked out and then modified to fit changing circumstances. A clear boundary enables the children to interact with their parents, but excludes them from the spouse subsystem. Parents and children eat together, play together, and share much of each others' lives. But there are some spouse functions which need not be shared. Husband and wife are sustained as a loving couple, and enhanced as parents, if they have time to be alone together—alone to talk, alone to go out to dinner occasionally, alone to fight, and alone to make love. Unhappily, the demands of small children often make parents lose sight of their need to maintain a boundary around their relationship.

In addition to maintaining some privacy for the couple, a clear boundary establishes a hierarchical structure in which parents exercise a position of leadership. All too often this hierarchy is disrupted by a child-centered ethos, which influences family therapists as well as parents. Parents enmeshed with their children tend to argue with them about who's in charge, and misguidedly share—or shirk—the responsibility for making parental decisions. Offering a child the choice in picking out clothes or choosing friends is respectful and flexible. Asking children whether they want to go to school, or trying to convince a toddler to agree that it's dangerous to play in the street simply blurs the line of authority.

In a recent book, *Institutionalizing Madness* (Elizur & Minuchin, 1989), Minuchin makes a compelling case for a systems view of family problems that extends beyond the family itself to encompass the entire community. As long as they confine their attention to the nuclear family, family therapists themselves suffer from a myopia that may produce solutions that don't work. Minuchin points out, forcefully, that unless family therapists learn to look beyond the limited slice of ecology where they work to the larger social structures within which their work is embedded, their efforts may amount to little more than spinning wheels.

NORMAL FAMILY DEVELOPMENT

A common presumption is that normal family life is happy and harmonious. This is an idealized myth. Normal families are constantly struggling with problems in living. What distinguishes a normal family isn't the absence of problems, but a functional family structure. Normal husbands and wives must learn to adjust to each other, rear their children, deal with their parents, cope with their jobs, and fit into their communities. The nature of these struggles changes with developmental stages and situational crises. Normal family life is neither static nor problem free. Nevertheless, as Minuchin (1974) put it, "the myth of placid normality endures, supported by hours of two-dimensional television characters" (p. 50).

When two people marry, the structural requirements for the new union are *accommodation* and *boundary making*. The first priority is mutual accommodation to manage the myriad details of everyday living. Each spouse tries to organize the relationship along familiar lines, and pressures the other to accommodate. Each must adjust to the other's expectations and wants. They must agree on major issues, such as where to live and if and when to have children; less obvious, but equally important, they must coordinate daily rituals, like what to watch on television, what to eat for supper, when to go to bed, and what to do there. Often the little things are the most irksome and problematic, and the couple may argue heatedly about who will take out the garbage, or wash the clothes.

In accommodating to each other, the couple must also negotiate the nature of the boundary between them, as well as the boundary separating them from the outside. A vague, diffuse boundary exists between the couple if they call each other at work frequently; if neither has separate friends or outside independent activities; and if they come to view themselves only as a pair rather than also as two separate personalities. On the other hand, they've established a rigid boundary between them if they spend little time doing things together, have separate bedrooms, take separate vacations, have different checking accounts, and each is considerably more invested in careers or outside relationships than in the marriage. While none of these markers by itself defines enmeshment or disengagement, each of them suggests the pattern that will develop.

Typically spouses come from families with differing degrees of enmeshment or disengagement. Each spouse tends to be more comfortable with the sort of proximity that existed in the family of origin. Since these expectations differ, a struggle ensues that may be the most difficult aspect of a new marriage. He wants to go play poker with the boys; she feels deserted. She wants to hold hands and whisper in the movies; he wants to concentrate on the picture. His major attention is on his career; her major attention is on the marriage. Each thinks the other wrong, unreasonable, and terribly hurtful.

Couples must also define a boundary separating them from their original families. Rather suddenly the families that each grew up in must take second place to the new marriage. This, too, is a difficult adjustment, both for newlyweds and their parents. Families of origin vary in the ease with which they accept and support the new union.

The addition of children transforms the structure of the new family into a *parental subsystem* and a *sibling subsystem*. It's typical for spouses to have different patterns of commitment to the babies. A woman's commitment to a unit of three is likely to begin with pregnancy, since the child inside her belly is an unavoidable reality. Her husband, on the other hand, may only begin to feel like a father when the child is born. Many men don't accept the role of father until the infants are old enough to begin to respond to them. Thus, even in normal families, children bring with them great potential for stress and conflict. The woman's life is usually more radically transformed than the man's. She sacrifices a great deal and typically needs more support from her husband. The husband, meanwhile, continues his job, and the new baby is far less of a disruption. Though he may try to support his wife, he's likely to resent some of her demands as inordinate and unreasonable.

The family takes care of the psychosocial needs of the children and transmits the culture to them. Children develop a dual identity within the family; a sense of belongingness and a sense of being separate. John Smith is both a Smith and also John; part of the family, yet a unique person.

Children require different styles of parenting at different ages. Infants primarily need nurturance and support. Older children need guidance and control; and adolescents need independence and responsibility. Good parenting for a two-year-old may be totally inadequate for a five-year-old or a four-teen-year-old. Normal parents adjust to these developmental challenges. The family modifies its structure to adapt to new additions, to the children's growth and development, and to changes in the external environment.

Minuchin (1974) warns family therapists not to mistake family growing pains for pathology. The normal family experiences anxiety and disruption as its members adapt to growth and change. Many families seek help at transitional stages, and therapists must keep in mind that they may simply be in the process of modifying their structure to accommodate to new circumstances.

All families face situations that stress the system. Although no clear dividing line exists between normal and abnormal families, we can say that normal families modify their structure to accommodate to changed circumstances; pathological families increase the rigidity of structures that are no longer functional.

DEVELOPMENT OF BEHAVIOR DISORDERS

Family systems must be stable enough to ensure continuity, but flexible enough to accommodate to changing circumstances. Behavior disorders arise when inflexible family structures cannot adjust adequately to maturational or situational challenges. Adaptive changes in structure are required when the family or one of its members faces external stress and when transitional points of growth are reached.

Family dysfunction results from a combination of stress and failure to realign themselves to cope with it (Colapinto, 1991). Stressors may be environmental (a parent is laid off, the family moves) or developmental (a child reaches adolescence, parents retire). The family's failure to handle adversity may be due to inherent flaws in their structure or merely to their inability to adjust to changed circumstances.

In disengaged families, boundaries are rigid, emotional distance is excessive, and the family fails to mobilize support when it's needed. Disengaged parents may be unaware that a child is depressed or experiencing difficulties at school until the problem is far advanced. In enmeshed families, on the other hand, boundaries are diffuse and family members overreact and become intrusively involved with one another. Enmeshed parents create difficulties by hindering the development of more mature forms of behavior in their children and by interfering with their ability to solve their own problems.

In their book of case studies, *Family Healing,* Minuchin and Nichols (1993) describe a common example of enmeshment as a father jumps in to settle minor arguments between his two boys—"as though the siblings were Cain and Abel, and fraternal jealousy might lead to murder" (p. 149). The problem, of course, is that if parents always interrupt their children's quarrels, the children won't learn to fight their own battles.

Although we may speak of enmeshed and disengaged families, it is more accurate (and useful) to speak of particular subsystems as being enmeshed or disengaged. In fact, enmeshment and disengagement tend to be reciprocal, so that, for example, a father who is overly involved with his work is likely to be less involved with his family. A frequently encountered pattern is the enmeshed mother/disengaged father syndrome—"the signature arrangement of the troubled middle-class family: a mother's closeness to her children substituting for closeness in the marriage" (Minuchin & Nichols, 1993, p. 121).

Feminists have criticized the notion of an enmeshed mother/disengaged father syndrome because they reject the stereotypical division of labor (instrumental role for the father, expressive role for the mother) that they think Minuchin's belief in hierarchy implies, and because they worry about blaming mothers for an arrangement that is culturally sanctioned. Both concerns are valid. But prejudice and blaming are due to insensitive application of these ideas, and are not inherent in the ideas themselves. Skewed relationships, whatever the reason for them, can be problematic, though naturally no single family member should be blamed or expected to unilaterally redress imbalances. Likewise, the need for hierarchy doesn't imply any particular division of roles in the family; it only implies that families need *some* kind of structure, *some* parental teamwork, and *some* degree of differentiation between subsystems.

Hierarchies can be excessively weak and ineffective, or excessively rigid and arbitrary. In the first case, younger members of the family may find themselves unprotected because of a lack of guidance; in the second, their growth as autonomous individuals may be impaired, or power struggles may ensue (Colapinto, 1991). Just as a functional hierarchy is necessary for a healthy family's stability, flexibility is necessary for them to adapt to change.

The most common expression of fear of change is *conflict-avoidance,* by which family members shy away from directly addressing their disagreements to protect themselves and each other from the pain of facing each other and telling hard truths. Disengaged families avoid conflict by avoiding contact; enmeshed families avoid conflict by denying differences or by constant bickering, which allows them to vent feelings without pressing each other for change or resolution of the conflict. A common expression of conflict-avoidance between partners involves diverting conflict to the children, in which case "conflicts between the spouses are played out in the parenting battlefield—and that as they pull in different directions, the confused children become casualties" (Minuchin & Nichols, 1993, p. 149).

Structural family therapists use a few simple symbols to diagram structural problems, and these diagrams usually make it clear what changes are required. Figure 5.2 on page 220 shows some of the symbols used to diagram family structure.

One problem often seen by family therapists arises when parents who are unable to resolve the conflicts between them divert the focus of concern onto a child. Instead of worrying about each other, they worry about the child (see Figure 5.3 on page 220). Although this reduces the strain on father (F) and mother (M), it victimizes the child (C) and is therefore dysfunctional.

An alternate but equally common pattern is for the parents to continue to argue through the children. Father says mother is too permissive; she says he's too strict. He may withdraw, causing her to criticize his handling of the child, which in turn causes further withdrawal. The enmeshed mother responds to the child's needs with excessive concern and devotion. The disen-

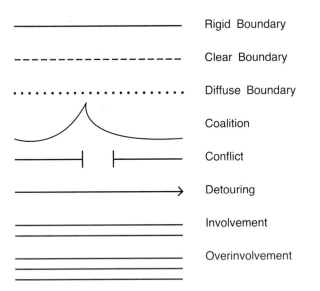

────────────────	Rigid Boundary
─ ─ ─ ─ ─ ─ ─ ─ ─	Clear Boundary
· · · · · · · · · · · · · · ·	Diffuse Boundary
	Coalition
	Conflict
────────────→	Detouring
════════════════	Involvement
════════════════	Overinvolvement

FIGURE 5.2   Symbols of Family Structure

gaged father tends not to respond even when a response is necessary. Both may be critical of the other's way, but both perpetuate the other's behavior with their own. The result is a *cross-generational coalition* between mother and child, which excludes the father (Figure 5.4).

Some families function quite well when the children are small, but are unable to adjust to a growing child's need for discipline and control. Parents may be particularly solicitous of children if they've had reason to worry about the children's health, if they had to wait a long time before they had them, or if they have few interests outside the family to give meaning to their lives. Parents who are unable to have children of their own, and finally decide to adopt, may find it difficult to set appropriate limits. They're too invested and enmeshed with their children to be able to exercise appropriate control (Figure 5.5).

Infants in enmeshed families receive wonderful care: their parents hug them, love them, and give them lots of stimulation. Although such parents

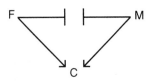

FIGURE 5.3   Scapegoating as a Means of Detouring Conflict

FIGURE 5.4 Mother-Child Coalition

may be too tired from caring for the children to have much time for each other or for outside interests, the system may be moderately successful. However, if these doting parents don't teach the children to obey rules and respect adult authority, the children may be unprepared to successfully negotiate their entrance into school. Used to getting their own way, they may be unruly and disruptive. Several possible consequences of this situation may bring the family into treatment. The children may be afraid to go to school, for instance, and their fears may be covertly reinforced by "understanding" parents who permit them to remain at home (Figure 5.6 on p. 222). Such a case may be labeled as school phobia, and may become entrenched if the parents permit the children to remain at home for more than a few days.

The children of such a family may go to school; but since they haven't learned to accommodate to others they may be rejected by their schoolmates. These children may become depressed and withdrawn. In other cases, children enmeshed with their parents become discipline problems at school, and the school authorities may initiate counseling.

A major change in family composition that requires structural adjustment occurs when divorced or widowed spouses remarry. Such "blended families" either readjust their boundaries or soon experience transitional conflicts. When a woman divorces, she and the children must first learn to readjust to a structure that establishes a clear boundary separating the divorced spouses, but still permits contact between father and children; then if she remarries, the family must readjust to functioning with a new husband and stepfather (Figure 5.7 on p. 222). Sometimes it is hard for a mother and children to allow a stepfather to participate as an equal partner in the new parental subsystem. Mother and children have long since established transactional rules and learned to accommodate to each other. The new parent may be treated as an outsider who's supposed to learn the "right" (accustomed) way of doing things, rather than as a new partner who will give as well as receive ideas about childrearing (Figure 5.8 on p. 223). The more mother and children insist on maintaining their familiar patterns without modifications required to absorb the stepfather, the more frustrated and angry he'll be-

F   M
• • • • • •
FIGURE 5.5 Parents Enmeshed with Children   Children

FIGURE 5.6   School Phobia

come. The result may lead to child abuse or chronic arguing between the parents. The sooner such families enter treatment, the easier it is to help them adjust to the transition. The longer they wait, the more entrenched structural problems become.

An important aspect of structural family problems is that symptoms in one member reflect not only that person's relationships with others, but also the fact that those relationships are a function of still other relationships in the family. If Johnny, aged sixteen, is depressed it's helpful to know that he's enmeshed with his mother. Discovering that she demands absolute obedience from him and refuses to let him develop his own thinking or outside relationships helps to explain his depression (Figure 5.9). But that is only a partial view of the family system, and therefore an incomplete guide to treatment.

Why is the mother enmeshed with her son? Perhaps she's disengaged from her husband; perhaps she's a widow who hasn't found new friends, a career, or any other outside interests. Helping Johnny resolve his depression may best be accomplished by helping his mother satisfy her needs for closeness with her husband or friends.

Because problems are a function of the entire family structure, it's important to include the whole group for assessment. For example, if a father complains of a child's misbehavior, seeing the child alone won't help the father to state rules clearly and enforce them effectively. Nor will seeing the father and child together do anything to stop the mother from undercutting

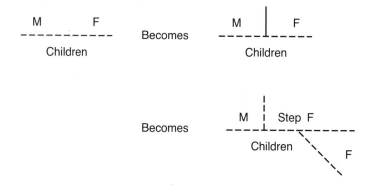

FIGURE 5.7   Divorce and Remarriage

FIGURE 5.8   Failure to Accept a Stepparent

the father's authority. Only by seeing the whole family interacting is it possible to get a complete picture of their structure.

Sometimes even seeing the whole family isn't enough. Structural family therapy is based on recognition of the importance of the context of the social system. The family may not be the complete or most relevant context. If one of the parents is having an affair, that relationship is a crucial part of the family's context. It may not be advisable to invite the lover to family sessions, but it is crucial to recognize the structural implications of the extramarital relationship.

In some cases, the family may not be the context most relevant to the presenting problem. A mother's depression may be due more to her relationships at work than at home. A son's problems at school may be due more to the structural context at school than to the one in the family. In such instances, structural family therapists work with the more relevant context to alleviate the presenting problems.

Finally, some problems may be treated as problems of the individual. As Minuchin (1974) has written, "Pathology may be inside the patient, in his social context, or in the feedback between them" (p. 9). Elsewhere Minuchin (Minuchin, Rosman, & Baker, 1978) referred to the danger of "denying the individual while enthroning the system" (p. 91). Family therapists should not overlook the possibility that some problems may be most appropriately dealt with on an individual basis. The therapist must not neglect the experience of individuals, although this is easy to do, especially with young children. While interviewing a family to see how the parents deal with their children, a careful clinician may notice that one child has a neurological problem or a learning disability. These problems need to be identified and appropriate referrals made. Usually when a child has trouble in school, there's a problem in the family or school context. Usually, but not always.

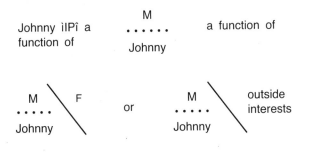

FIGURE 5.9

GOALS OF THERAPY

Structural family therapists believe that problems are maintained by dysfunctional family structures. Therefore therapy is directed at altering family structure so that the family can solve its problems. The goal of therapy is structural change; problem-solving is a by-product of this systemic goal.

The structural family therapist joins the family system in order to help its members change their structure. By altering boundaries and realigning subsystems, the therapist changes the behavior and experience of each of the family members. The therapist doesn't solve problems; that's the family's job. The therapist helps modify the family's functioning so that family members can solve their own problems. In this way, structural family therapy is like dynamic psychotherapy—symptom-resolution is sought not as an end in itself, but as a result of lasting structural change. The analyst modifies the structure of the patient's mind; the structural family therapist modifies the structure of the patient's family.

Symptomatic change and enhanced family functioning are seen as inextricably interrelated goals. The most effective way to change symptoms is to change the family patterns that maintain them. An effectively functioning family is a system that supports its members. The goal of structural family therapy is to facilitate the growth of the system in order to resolve symptoms and encourage growth in individuals, while also preserving the mutual support of the family.

Short-range goals may be to alleviate symptoms, especially life-threatening symptoms such as anorexia nervosa (Minuchin, Rosman, & Baker, 1978). At times, behavioral techniques, suggestion, or manipulation may be used to provide temporary surcease. However, unless structural change in the family system is achieved, short-term symptom-resolution may collapse.

The goals for each family are dictated by the problems they present and by the nature of their structural dysfunction. Although every family is unique, there are common problems and typical structural goals. Most important of the general goals for families is the creation of an effective hierarchical structure. Parents are expected to be in charge, not to relate as equals to their children. A frequent goal is to help parents function together as a cohesive executive subsystem. When only one parent is present, or when there are several children, one or more of the oldest children may be encouraged to be a parental assistant. But this child's needs must not be neglected, either.

With enmeshed families the goal is to differentiate individuals and subsystems by strengthening the boundaries around them. With disengaged families the goal is to increase interaction by making boundaries more permeable.

CONDITIONS FOR BEHAVIOR CHANGE

Structural family therapy changes behavior by opening alternative patterns of family interaction which can modify family structure. It's not a matter of creating new structures, but of activating dormant ones. If, once activated, the dormant sequences are functional, they will be reinforcing; and family structure will be transformed. When new transactional patterns become regularly repeated and predictably effective, they will stabilize the new and more functional structure.

The therapist produces change by joining the family, probing for areas of flexibility, and then activating dormant structural alternatives. *Joining* gets the therapist into the family; *accommodating* to their accustomed style gives him or her leverage; and *restructuring* interventions transform the family structure. If the therapist remains an outsider or uses interventions that are too dystonic, the family will reject him or her. If the therapist becomes too much a part of the family or uses interventions that are too syntonic, the family will assimilate the interventions into previous transactional patterns. In either case there will be no structural change.

For change to occur, the family must first accept the therapist, and then respond to his or her interventions as though to a novel situation. This increases stress, which in turn unbalances family homeostasis, and thus opens the way for structural transformation.

Joining and accommodating are considered prerequisite to restructuring. To join the family the therapist must convey acceptance of family members and respect for their way of doing things. Minuchin (1974) likened the family therapist to an anthropologist who must first join a culture before being able to study it.

To join the family's culture the therapist makes accommodating overtures—the sort of thing we usually do unthinkingly, although often unsuccessfully. If parents come for help with a child's problems, the therapist shouldn't begin by asking for the child's views. This conveys a lack of respect for the parents and may lead them to reject the therapist. Only after the therapist has successfully joined with a family is it fruitful to attempt restructuring—the often dramatic confrontations that challenge families and force them to change.

Structural family therapy changes behavior by reframing the family's presentation of their problems into a systemic model. Families define problems as a function of individuals or outside forces; structural family therapists redefine these problems as a function of the family structure. The first task is to understand the family's view of their problems. The therapist does this by tracking their formulation in the content they use to explain it and in the sequences with which they demonstrate it. Then the family therapist *reframes* their formulation into one based on an understanding of family structure.

In fact, all psychotherapies use reframing. Patients, whether individuals or families, come with their own views as to the cause of their problems—views that usually haven't helped them solve the problems—and the therapist offers them a new and potentially more constructive view of these same problems. What makes structural family therapy unique is that it uses *enactments* within therapy sessions to make the reframing happen. This is the *sine qua non* of structural family therapy: observing and modifying the structure of family transactions in the immediate context of the session. Although this sounds simple, it has important implications for treatment. Structural family therapists work with what they see going on in the session, not what family members describe about what happens outside, nor with the content of family discussions. Action in the session, family dynamics in process, is what structural family therapists deal with.

There are two types of live, in-session material on which structural family therapy focuses—*enactments* and *spontaneous behavior sequences.* An enactment occurs when the therapist stimulates the family to demonstrate how they handle a particular type of problem. Enactments commonly begin when the therapist suggests that specific subgroups begin to discuss a particular problem. As they do so, the therapist observes the family process. Working with enactments requires three operations. First, the therapist defines or recognizes a sequence. For example, the therapist observes that when mother talks to her daughter they talk as peers, and little brother gets left out. Second, the therapist directs an enactment. For example, the therapist might say to the mother, "Talk this over with your kids." Third, and most important, the therapist must guide the family to modify the enactment. If mother talks to her children in such a way that she doesn't take appropriate responsibility for major decisions, the therapist must guide her to do so as the family continues the enactment. All the therapist's moves should create new options for the family, options for new behavior sequences. A common mistake made by many family therapists is to simply criticize what they see by labeling it, without offering options for change.

Once an enactment breaks down, the therapist intervenes in one of two ways: commenting on what went wrong, or simply pushing them to keep going. For example, if a father responds to the suggestion to talk with his twelve-year-old daughter about how she's feeling by berating her, the therapist could say to the father: "Congratulations." Father: "What do you mean?" Therapist: "Congratulations; you win, she loses." Or the therapist could simply nudge the transaction by saying to the father: "Good, keep talking, but help her express her feelings more. She's still a little girl; she needs your help."

In addition to working with enacted sequences, structural family therapists are alert to spontaneous sequences that are the illustrative processes of family structure. Creating enactments is like directing a play; working with spontaneous sequences is like focusing a spotlight on action that occurs without direction. In fact, by observing and modifying such sequences very early in therapy the therapist avoids getting bogged down in the family's usual nonproductive ways of doing business. Dealing with problematic behavior as soon as it occurs in the first session enables the therapist to organize the session, to underscore the process, and to modify it.

An experienced therapist develops hunches about family structure even before the first interview. For example, if a family is coming to the clinic because of a "hyperactive" child, it's possible to guess something about the family structure and something about sequences that may occur as the session begins, since "hyperactive" behavior is often a function of the child's enmeshment with the mother. Mother's relationship with the child may be a product of a lack of hierarchical differentiation within the family; that is, parents and children relate to each other as peers, not as members of different generations. Furthermore, mother's overinvolvement with the "hyperactive" child is likely to be both a result of and a cause of emotional distance from her husband. Knowing that this is a common pattern, the therapist can anticipate that early in the first session the "hyperactive" child will begin to misbehave, and that the mother will be inadequate to deal with this misbehavior. Armed with this informed guess the therapist can spotlight (rather than enact) such a sequence as soon as it occurs, and modify it. If the "hyperactive" child begins to run around the room, and the mother protests but does nothing effective, the therapist might say, "I see that your child feels free to ignore you." This challenge may push the mother to behave in a more competent manner. The therapist may have to push further, saying, "Come on now, do something about it." Once such a theme is focused on, the therapist needs to pursue it relentlessly.

TECHNIQUES

In *Families and Family Therapy*, Minuchin (1974) taught family therapists to see what they are looking at. Through the lens of structural family theory, previously puzzling family interactions suddenly swam into focus. Where others saw only chaos and confusion, Minuchin saw structure: families organized into subsystems with boundaries. This enormously successful book (over 200,000 copies in print) not only taught us to see *enmeshment* and *disengagement*, but also let us hope that changing them was just a matter of *joining, enactment,* and *unbalancing*. Minuchin made changing families look simple. It isn't.

Anyone who watched Minuchin at work ten or fifteen years after the publication of *Families and Family Therapy* would see a creative therapist still evolving, not someone frozen in time back in 1974. There would still be the patented confrontations ("Who's the sheriff in this family?") but there would be fewer enactments, less stage-directed dialogue. We would also hear bits and pieces borrowed from Carl Whitaker ("When did you divorce your wife and marry your job?") and Maurizio Andolfi ("Why don't you piss on the rug, too?"), and others. Minuchin combines many things in his work. To those familiar with his earlier work, all of this raises the question: Is Minuchin still a structural family therapist? The question is, of course, absurd; we raise it to make one point: Structural family therapy is not a set of techniques; it's a way of looking at families.

In the remainder of this section, we will present the classic outlines of structural family technique, with the caveat that once therapists master the basics of structural theory, they must learn to translate the approach in a way that suits their own personal styles. Implementing specific techniques is an art, and therapists must discover and create techniques that fit each family's transactional style and therapist's personality. Since every therapeutic session has idiosyncratic features, there can be no interpersonal immediacy if the specific context is ignored. Imitating someone else's technique is stifling and ineffective—stifling because it doesn't fit the therapist, ineffective because it doesn't fit the family.

In *Families and Family Therapy*, Minuchin (1974) listed three overlapping phases in the process of structural family therapy. The therapist (1) joins the family in a position of leadership; (2) maps their underlying structure; and (3) intervenes to transform this structure. This program is simple, in the sense that it follows a clear and specifiable plan, but immensely complicated because it is difficult to accomplish these tasks, and furthermore because there is an endless variety of family patterns.

Observed in practice, structural family therapy is an organic whole, created out of the very real human interaction of therapist and family. If they are to be genuine and effective, the therapist's moves cannot be preplanned or rehearsed. Good therapists are more than technicians. The strategy of therapy, on the other hand, must be thoughtfully planned. In general, the strategy of structural family therapy follows these steps:

1. Joining and accommodating
2. Working with interaction
3. Diagnosing
4. Highlighting and modifying interactions
5. Boundary making
6. Unbalancing
7. Challenging the family's assumptions

The first three strategies constitute the opening phase of treatment. Without carefully planning and skillfully accomplishing the critical opening moves, therapy usually fails. When we begin, we're often too anxious or eager to consider opening wisely. Only after we get started and the jitters calm down, do we look around, assess the situation, and then act accordingly. Unfortunately this sort of catch-up strategy results in the loss of much valuable ground. The therapist who neglects the opening moves of treatment may lose all chance of having a significant impact.

Genuine preparation and an effective opening must be distinguished from obsessional rituals which do nothing but bind anxiety and use up energy. Habitually arriving ten minutes early for sessions, arranging and rearranging the furniture, and endlessly reading charts or books on technique—as many of us do—should not be confused with careful planning.

Joining and Accommodating

Because families have firmly established homeostatic patterns, effective family therapy requires strong challenge and confrontation. But assaults on a family's habitual style will be dismissed unless they are made from a position of acceptance and understanding. Families, like you and me, resist efforts to change them by people they feel don't understand and accept them.

The need for leverage is even more important in family treatment than in individual therapy. Individual patients generally enter treatment already predisposed to accept the therapist's authority. By seeking therapy, the individual tacitly acknowledges suffering, need for help, and willingness to trust the therapist. Not so with families.

The family outnumbers the therapist, and they have mutually agreed-upon and long-practiced ways of doing things. The family therapist is an unwelcome outsider. After all, why did the therapist insist on seeing the whole family rather than just the official patient? They expect to be told that they're doing things all wrong, and they're prepared to defend themselves. The family is thus a group of nonpatients who feel guilty and anxious; their set is to resist, not to cooperate.

First the family therapist must disarm defenses and ease anxiety. This is done by generously conveying understanding and acceptance to every single member of the family. The therapist greets each person by name and makes some kind of friendly contact.

These initial greetings convey respect, not only for the individuals in the family, but also for their hierarchical structure and organization. The therapist shows respect for parents by taking their authority for granted. They, not their children, are asked first to describe the problems. If a family elects the mother as their speaker, the therapist notes this but does not initially challenge it.

Children also have special concerns and capacities. They should be greeted gently and asked simple, concrete questions, "Hi, I'm so-and-so; what's your name? Oh, Shelly, that's a nice name. Where do you go to school, Shelly?" Those who wish to remain silent should be "allowed" to do so. They will anyway, but the therapist who accepts their reticence will have made a valuable step toward keeping them involved. "And what's your view of the problem?" (Grim silence.) "I see, you don't feel like saying anything right now? That's fine; perhaps you'll have something to say later."

Failure to join and accommodate produces tense resistance, which is often blamed on the family. It may be comforting to blame others when things don't go well, but it doesn't improve matters. Family members can be called "negative," "rebellious," "resistant," or "defiant," and seen as unmotivated"; but it is more useful to make an extra effort to connect with them.

It's particularly important to join powerful family members, as well as angry ones. Special pains must be taken to accept the point of view of the father who thinks therapy is hooey or of the angry teenager who feels like a hunted criminal. It's also important to reconnect with such people at frequent intervals, particularly as things begin to heat up.

A useful beginning is to greet the family and then ask for each person's view of the problems. Listen carefully, and acknowledge each person's position by reflecting what you hear. "I see, Mrs. Jones, you think Sally must be depressed about something that happened at school." "So Mr. Jones, you see some of the same things your wife sees, but you're not convinced it's a serious problem. Is that right?"

Working with Interaction

Family structure is manifest in the way family members interact. It cannot be inferred from their descriptions, nor from reconstructing previous discussions. Therefore, asking questions such as "Who's in charge?" "Do you two agree?" or "Can you show me what happened in yesterday's argument?" tend to be unproductive. Families generally describe themselves more as they think they should be than as they are.

Family dynamics are what happens when the family is in action, not what they *say* happens, or what the therapist *imagines* must happen. They have to talk among themselves for the dynamics to emerge. When they do, the therapist observes: Who talks to whom? when? in what way?

Getting family members to talk among themselves runs counter to their expectations, and they resist doing it. They expect to present their case to an expert, and then be told what to do. If asked to discuss something in the session, they'll say: "We've talked about this many times"; or "It won't do any good, he (or she) doesn't listen"; or "But *you're* supposed to be the expert."

If the therapist begins by giving each person a chance to speak, usually one will say something about another which can be a springboard for an enactment. When, for example, one parent says that the other is too strict, the therapist can develop an enactment by saying: "She says you're too strict; can you answer her?" Picking a specific point for response is more likely to stimulate a dialogue than a vague request, such as "Why don't you two talk things over?"

Once an enactment is begun, the therapist can discover many things about the family's structure. How long can two people talk without being interrupted—that is, how clear is the boundary? Does one attack, the other defend? Who is central, who peripheral? Do parents bring children into their discussions—that is, are they enmeshed?

Families may demonstrate enmeshment by frequently interrupting each other, speaking for other family members, doing things for children that they can do for themselves, or by constantly arguing. In disengaged families one may see a husband sitting impassively while his wife cries; a total absence of conflict; a surprising ignorance of important information about the children; a lack of concern for each other's interests.

If, as soon as the first session starts, the kids begin running wildly around the room while the parents protest ineffectually, the therapist doesn't need to hear descriptions of what goes on at home to see the executive incompetence. If a mother and daughter rant and rave at each other while the father sits silently in the corner, it isn't necessary to ask how involved he is at home. In fact, asking may yield a less accurate picture than the one revealed spontaneously.

Diagnosing

It's necessary to have a formulation to organize strategies of change. Clinicians must steer a course between the Scylla of unorganized experience and the Charybdis of rigid characterizations which don't capture the reality of the family's experience. Structural diagnostic categories organize what otherwise may be a confusing welter of impressions, without arbitrarily distorting the dynamic aspects of family interaction.

Families usually conceive of problems as located in the identified patient and as determined by events from the past. They hope the therapist will change the identified patient—with as little disruption as possible to the family homeostasis. Family therapists regard the identified patient's symptoms as an expression of dysfunctional transactional patterns affecting the whole family. A structural diagnosis broadens the problem beyond individuals to family systems, and moves the focus from discrete events in the past to ongoing transactions in the present. A family diagnosis is predicated on the goal of transforming the family in a way that benefits all of its members.

Even many family therapists categorize families with constructs that apply more to individuals than to systems. "The problem in this family is that the mother is smothering the kids," or "These kids are defiant," or "He's a placater." Structural family therapists diagnose in such a way as to describe the systemic interrelationships of all family members. Using the concepts of boundaries and subsystems, the structure of the whole system is described in a way that points to desired changes.

Diagnoses are based on observed interactions that take place in the first session. In later sessions the formulations are refined and revised. Although there is some danger of bending families to fit categories when they're applied early, the greater danger is waiting too long.

We see people with the greatest clarity and freshness during the initial contact. Later, as we come to know them better, we get used to their idiosyncrasies and soon no longer notice them. Families quickly *induct* therapists into their culture. A family that initially appears to be chaotic and enmeshed soon comes to be just the familiar Jones family. For this reason, it is critical to make structural formulations as quickly as possible.

In fact, it's helpful to make some guesses about family structure even before the first session. This starts a process of active thinking which sets the stage for observing the family. For example, suppose you're about to see a family consisting of a mother, a sixteen-year-old daughter, and a stepfather. The mother called to complain of her daughter's misbehavior. What do you imagine the structure might be, and how would you test your hypothesis? A good guess might be that mother and daughter are enmeshed, excluding the stepfather. This can be tested by seeing if mother and daughter tend to talk mostly about each other in the session—whether positively or negatively. The stepfather's disengagement would be confirmed if he and his wife are unable to converse without the daughter's intrusion.

The structural diagnosis takes into account both the problem that the family presents and the structural dynamics that they display. And it includes all family members. In this instance, knowing that the mother and daughter are enmeshed is not enough; you also have to know what role the stepfather plays. If he's reasonably close with his wife but distant from the daughter, finding mutually enjoyable activities for stepfather and stepdaughter will help increase the girl's independence from her mother. On the other hand, if the mother's proximity to her daughter appears to be a function of her distance from her husband, then the marital pair may be the most productive focus.

Without a diagnostic formulation and a plan, the therapist is defensive and passive. Instead of knowing where to go and moving forcefully, the therapist lays back and tries to cope with the family, put out brush fires, and help them through a succession of incidents. Consistent awareness of the family's structure and focus on one or two structural changes helps the therapist see behind the various content issues that family members bring up.

Highlighting and Modifying Interactions

Once families begin to interact, problematic transactions emerge. Noticing them demands focus on process, not content. Nothing about structure is revealed by hearing who is in favor of punishment or who says nice things about others. Family structure is revealed by who says what to whom, and in what way.

Perhaps a husband complains, "We have a communication problem. My wife just won't talk to me; she never expresses her feelings." The therapist then stimulates an interaction to see what actually does happen. "Your husband says it's a communication problem; can you respond to that? Talk with him." If, when they talk, the husband becomes domineering and critical while the wife grows increasingly silent and withdrawn, then the therapist sees what's wrong: The problem isn't that she doesn't talk, which is a linear explanation. Nor is the problem that he nags, also a linear explanation. The problem is that the more he nags, the more she withdraws, and the more she withdraws, the more he nags.

The trick is to highlight and modify this pattern of interaction. This requires forceful intervening. It's usually necessary to use therapeutic dynamite to break families loose from their patterns of equilibrium. Structural therapists use *intensity* to make these interventions.

Minuchin himself frequently speaks to families with dramatic and forceful impact. He regulates the intensity of his messages to exceed the threshold that family members have for not hearing challenges to the way they perceive reality. When Minuchin speaks, families listen.

Minuchin is forceful, but his intensity is not merely a function of his personality; it reflects his clarity of purpose. Knowledge of family structure and a serious commitment to help families change make powerful interventions possible. Families will usually respond to messages delivered with the kind of intensity that comes from being clear about the goal.

Structural therapists achieve intensity by selective regulation of affect, repetition, and duration. Tone, volume, pacing, and choice of words can be used to raise the affective intensity of statements. It helps if you know what you want to say. Here's an example of a limp statement: "People are always concerned with themselves, kind of seeing themselves as the center of attention and just looking for whatever they can get. Wouldn't it be nice for a change if everybody started thinking about what they could do for others? I mean, thinking about other people and the country before themselves." Compare that with, "Ask not what your country can do for you—ask what you can do for your country." John Kennedy's words had impact because they were carefully chosen and clearly put. Family therapists don't need to make speeches or be clever phrasemakers, but they do occasionally have to speak forcefully to get the point across.

Affective intensity is not simply a matter of crisp phrasing. You have to know how and when to be provocative. For example, one of us (M. P. N.) was recently working with a family in which a twenty-nine-year-old woman with anorexia nervosa was the identified patient. Although the family maintained a facade of togetherness, it was rigidly structured; the mother and her anorexic daughter were enmeshed, while the father was excluded. In this family, the father was the only one to express anger openly, and this was part of the official rationale for why he was excluded. His daughter was afraid of his anger, which she freely admitted. What was less clear, however, was that the mother had covertly taught the daughter to avoid him, because she, the mother, couldn't deal with his anger. Consequently, the daughter grew up afraid of her father, and men in general.

At one point the father described how isolated he felt from his daughter; he said he thought it was because she feared his anger. The daughter agreed, "It's his fault all right." The therapist asked the mother what she thought, and she replied, "It isn't his fault." The therapist said, "You're right." She went on, denying her real feelings to avoid conflict, "It's no one's fault." The therapist answered in a way that got her attention, "Like hell it isn't!" Startled, she asked what he meant. "It's your fault!" the therapist said.

This level of intensity was necessary to interrupt a rigid pattern of conflict-avoidance that sustained a pathogenic alliance between mother and daughter. The content—who really is afraid of anger—is less important than the structural goal: freeing the daughter from her position of overinvolvement with her mother.

Therapists too often dilute their interventions by overqualifying, apologizing, or rambling. This is less of a problem in individual therapy, where it's often best to elicit interpretations from the patient. Families are more like the farmer's proverbial mule—you sometimes have to hit them over the head to get their attention.

Intensity can also be achieved by extending the duration of a sequence beyond the point where the dysfunctional homeostasis is reinstated. A common example is the management of severe temper tantrums. Temper tantrums are maintained by parents who give in. Most parents *try* not to give in; they just don't try long enough. Recently a four-year-old girl began to scream bloody murder when her sister left the room. She wanted to go with her sister. Her screaming was almost unbearable, and the parents soon were ready to back down. However, the therapist urged that they not allow themselves to be defeated, and suggested that they hold her to "show her who's in charge" until she calmed down. She screamed for one solid hour! Everyone in the room was frazzled. But the little girl finally realized that this time she was not going to get her way, and so she calmed down. Subsequently, the parents were able to use the same intensity of duration to break her of this highly destructive habit.

Sometimes intensity requires frequent repetition of one theme in a variety of contexts. Infantilizing parents may have to be told not to hang up their child's coat, not to speak for her, not to take her to the bathroom, and not to do many other things that she is able to do for herself.

Shaping competence is another method of modifying interactions, and it is a hallmark of structural family therapy. Intensity is generally used to block the stream of interactions. Shaping competence is like altering the direction of the flow. By highlighting and shaping the positive, structural therapists help family members use functional alternatives that are already in their repertoire.

A common mistake made by beginning family therapists is to attempt to foster competent performance by pointing out mistakes. This is an example of focusing on content without due regard to process. Telling parents that they're doing something wrong, or suggesting they do something different has the effect of criticizing their competence. However well-intentioned, it is still a put-down. While this kind of intervention cannot be completely avoided, a more effective approach is to point out what they're doing right.

Even when people do most things ineffectively, it's usually possible to pick out something that they're doing successfully. A sense of timing helps the therapist punctuate sequences while they're going well. For example, in a large chaotic family the parents were extremely ineffective at controlling the children. At one point the therapist turned to the mother and said, "It's too noisy in here; would you quiet the kids?" Knowing how much difficulty the woman had controlling her children, the therapist was poised to comment immediately on any step in the direction of effective management. The mother had to yell "Quiet!" a couple of times before the children momentarily stopped what they were doing. Quickly—before the children resumed their misbehavior—the therapist complimented the mother for "loving her kids enough to be firm with them." Thus the message delivered was "You're a competent person, you know how to be firm." If the therapist had waited until the chaos resumed before telling the mother she should be firm, the message would be "You're incompetent."

Wherever possible, structural therapists avoid doing things for family members that they're capable of doing themselves. Here, too, the message is "You are competent, you can do it." Some therapists justify taking over the family's functions by calling it "modeling." Whatever it's called it has the impact of telling family members that they are inadequate. Recently a young mother confessed that she hadn't known how to tell her children that they were coming to see a family therapist and so had simply said she was taking them for a ride. Thinking to be helpful, the therapist then explained to the children that "Mommy told me there were some problems in the family, so we're all here to talk things over to see if we can improve things." This lovely explanation tells the kids why they came, but confirms the mother as incompetent to do so. If instead the therapist had suggested to the mother, "Why don't you tell them now?" Then the mother, not the therapist, would have had to perform as an effective parent.

Boundary Making

Dysfunctional family dynamics are developed from and sustained by overly rigid or diffuse boundaries separating subsystems in the family. Structural therapists intervene to realign boundaries, increasing either proximity or distance between family subsystems.

In highly enmeshed families the therapist's interventions are designed to strengthen boundaries between subsystems and to increase the independence of individuals. Family members are urged to speak for themselves, interruptions are blocked, and dyads are helped to finish conversations without intrusion from others. A therapist who wishes to support the sibling system and protect it from unnecessary parental intervention may say, "Susie and Sean, talk this over, and everyone else will listen carefully." If children frequently interrupt their parents, a therapist might challenge the parents to strengthen the hierarchical boundary by saying, "Why don't you get them to butt out so that you two grownups can settle this."

Although structural family therapy is begun with the total family group, subsequent sessions may be held with individuals or subgroups to strengthen the boundaries surrounding them. A teenager who is overprotected by her mother is supported as a separate person with individual needs by participating in some separate sessions. Parents so enmeshed with their children that they never have private conversations may begin to learn how if they meet separately with a therapist.

When a forty-year-old woman called the clinic for help with depression, she was asked to come in with the rest of the family. It soon became apparent that this woman was overburdened by her four children, and received little support from her husband, either as a husband or a father. The therapist's strategy was to strengthen the boundary between the mother and the children, and help the parents move closer toward each other. This was done in stages. First the therapist joined the oldest child, a sixteen-year-old girl, and supported her competence as a potential helper for her mother. Once this was done, the girl was able to assume a good deal of responsibility for her younger siblings, both in the sessions and at home.

Freed from some of the preoccupation with the children, the parents now had the opportunity to talk more with each other. They had very little to say to each other, however. This was not the result of hidden conflict or anger, but instead it reflected the marriage of a relatively nonverbal husband and wife, with different interests. After several sessions of trying to get the pair to enjoy talking with each other, the therapist realized that while talking may be fun for some people, it may not be for others. So to support the bond between the couple the therapist asked them to plan a special trip together. They chose a boat ride on a nearby lake. When they returned for the next session, the spouses were beaming. They reported having had a wonderful time, being apart from the kids and enjoying each other's company. Subsequently they decided to spend a little time out together each week.

Disengaged families tend to avoid or detour conflict, and thus minimize interaction. The structural therapist intervenes to challenge conflict avoidance, and to block detouring in order to help disengaged members increase contact with each other. The therapist creates boundaries in the session that permit family members to discuss their conflicts without being interrupted. In addition, the therapist prevents escape or avoidance, so that the disagreements can be resolved.

Without acting as judge or referee, the structural therapist creates conditions in which family members can face each other squarely and struggle with the difficulties between them. When beginners see disengagement, they tend to think first of ways to increase positive interaction. In fact, disengagement is usually a way of avoiding arguments. Therefore, spouses isolated from each other typically need to fight before they can become more loving.

Most people underestimate the degree to which their own behavior influences and regulates the behavior of those around them. This is particularly true in disengaged families. Problems are usually seen as the result of what someone else is doing, and solutions are thought to require that the others change. The following complaints are typical: "We have a communication problem; he won't tell me what he's feeling." "He just doesn't care about us.

All he cares about is that damn job of his." "Our sex life is lousy—my wife's frigid." "Who can talk to her? All she does is complain about the kids." Each of these statements suggest that the power to change rests solely with the other person. This is the almost universally perceived view of linear causality.

Whereas most people see things this way, family therapists see the inherent circularity in systems interaction. He doesn't tell his wife what he's feeling, because she nags and criticizes; *and* she nags and criticizes because he doesn't tell her what he's feeling.

Structural therapists move family discussions from linear to circular causality by stressing the complementarity of family relations. The mother who complains that her son is naughty is taught to consider what she's doing to stimulate or maintain his behavior. The one who asks for change must learn to change his or her way of trying to get it. The wife who nags her husband to spend more time with her must learn to make increased involvement more attractive. The husband who complains that his wife never listens to him may have to listen to *her* more, before she's willing to reciprocate.

Minuchin emphasizes complementarity by asking family members to help each other change. When positive changes are reported, he's liable to congratulate others, underscoring family interrelatedness.

Unbalancing

In boundary making the therapist aims to realign relationships between subsystems. In unbalancing, the goal is to change the relationship of members within a subsystem. What often keeps families stuck in stalemate is that members in conflict check and balance each other, and as a result remain frozen in inaction. In unbalancing, the therapist joins and supports one individual or subsystem at the expense of others.

Taking sides—let's call it what it is—seems like a violation of therapy's sacred cannon of neutrality. However, the therapist takes sides to unbalance and realign the system not because he or she is the judge of who's right and wrong, but in order to unfreeze and realign the system. Ultimately, balance and fairness is achieved because the therapist sides in turn with various members of the family.

For example, when Bob and Shirley came for help with marital problems, her complaint was that he never shared his feelings; his was that she always criticized him. This, of course, is a classic trading of complaints. Dr. Minuchin, the therapist in this case, chose to challenge Bob's side of this two-part disharmony. (Balanced challenges that mention both of their contributions sound elegant, and fair, but often allow both partners to think, "That's right. I hope he [or she] hears what the therapist is saying.")

To Bob, Minuchin said, "If you were a frog, what would you be like if Shirley changed you into a prince?" When Bob countered by saying that one reason he doesn't talk more with her is that she's so critical, it seemed to the couple like the old argument. But the therapist saw this as the beginning of change—Bob speaking up more. One way to create change in rigid families is to support the blamed person and help bring him back into the fray.

When Shirley criticized Bob for complaining, he tried to retreat, but Minuchin said, "No. Continue. You are still a frog."

Bob tried to shift responsibility back to Shirley. "Doesn't she have to kiss me first?" But Minuchin said, "No, in real life that comes afterwards. You have to earn it."

In another case of Dr. Minuchin's, a strange case of Oedipus revisited, twenty-three-year-old Kenny spent a year in Bellevue because he scratched his eyes so severely that doctors feared he would blind himself. In the hospital he functioned normally, but when he returned home he returned to self-destruction. Normal in the hospital; crazy at home. One solution would be to keep him in the hospital, normal in a crazy world, forever. Perhaps, like Oedipus Rex, the boy was blinding himself so as not to see his obsession with his mother and his hatred of his father.

But this family was neither ancient nor Greek, and Minuchin is more pragmatist than poet. So he challenged the father to protect his son by dealing directly with his wife—and then he challenged the father's demeaning, destructive attitude toward her, which made her feel hopeless, helpless, and all the more in need of her son's proximity and protection. Minuchin said to him: "As a father of children in danger, what you're doing isn't enough." When he tried to put the responsibility on the therapist by saying, "What should I do?" Dr. Minuchin said, "I don't know. Ask your son."

The familiar image of the therapist—kindly, benevolent, and relatively silent—is based on the analytic model of discovering meaning in a thoughtful, leisurely process.

Unbalancing is part of a struggle for change that sometimes takes on the appearance of combat. When a therapist says to a father that he's not doing enough or to a mother that she's unwittingly excluding her husband, it may seem that the combat is between the therapist and the family, that he or she is attacking them. But the real combat is between the therapist and fear—fear of change.

Challenging the Family's Assumptions

Although structural family therapy is not primarily a cognitive treatment, its practitioners sometimes challenge the way family members perceive reality. Changing the way family members relate to each other offers alternative views of reality. The converse is also true: Changing the way family members view reality enables them to change the way they relate to each other.

People have a habit of becoming the stories they tell about themselves. When memory speaks it tells a "narrative truth," which comes to have more influence than "historical truth." The "facts" presented to a therapist are partly historical truth and partly a construction. The constructions that are the shared reality of a family represent mutual understandings and shared prejudices, some of which are hopeful and helpful, some of which are not.

When six-year-old Cassie's parents complained about her behavior, they said she's "hyper," "sensitive," a "nervous child." Such labels convey how parents respond to their children and have a tremendous controlling power. Is a child's behavior "misbehavior" or is it a symptom of "nervousness?" Is it "naughty" or is it a "cry for help?" Is the child mad or bad, and who is in charge? What's in a name? Plenty.

Sometimes the structural family therapist acts as a teacher, offering information and advice based on training and experience. Information may be imparted to reassure anxious family members, to help them behave more competently, or to restructure their interactions. When family members feel embarrassed because they fight over little things, it may be helpful to tell them that most people do. Sometimes young parents will profit from a simple suggestion that they hire a baby-sitter and get out once in a while.

Minuchin occasionally teaches families about structure. Doing so is likely to be a restructuring maneuver and must be done in a way that minimizes resistance. He does this by delivering first a "stroke," then a "kick." If Minuchin were dealing with a family in which the mother speaks for her children, he might say to her, "You are very helpful" (stroke). But to the child, "Mommy takes away your voice. You can speak for yourself" (kick). Thus mother is defined as helpful, but intrusive (one stroke and one kick).

Structural therapists also use constructions, which are pragmatic fictions, to provide family members with a different frame for experiencing. This aim is not to educate or to deceive, but to offer a pronouncement which will help the family to change. For instance, telling children that they are behaving in a way that is consistent with being younger than they are is a very effective means of getting them to change. "How old are you?" "Seven." "Oh, I thought you were younger, because when you really get to be seven, you won't need Mommy to take you to school anymore."

Paradoxes are cognitive constructions which frustrate or confuse family members into a search for alternatives. Minuchin himself makes little use of paradox, but it can be an effective means of stimulating new transactional patterns (see Chapter 9).

EVALUATING THERAPY THEORY AND RESULTS

While he was Director of the Philadelphia Child Guidance Clinic, Minuchin developed a highly pragmatic commitment to research. As an administrator he learned that research demonstrating effective outcomes is the best argument for the legitimacy of family therapy. Both his studies of psychosomatic children and Stanton's studies of drug addicts show very clearly how effective structural family therapy can be.

In *Families of the Slums*, Minuchin and his colleagues (1967) at Wiltwyck described the structural characteristics of low socioeconomic families, and demonstrated the effectiveness of family therapy with this population. Prior to treatment mothers in patient families were found to be either over or under controlling; either way their children were more disruptive than those in control families. These observations were the basis of Minuchin's classification of families as either *enmeshed* or *disengaged*. After treatment mothers used less coercive control, yet were clearer and more firm. In this study, seven of eleven families were judged to be improved after six months to a year of family therapy. Although no control group was used, the authors compared their results favorably to the usual 50 percent rate of successful treatment at Wiltwyck. The authors also noted that none of the families rated as disengaged improved.

By far the strongest empirical support for structural family therapy comes from a series of studies with psychosomatic children and adult drug addicts. Studies demonstrating the effectiveness of therapy with severely ill psychosomatic children are convincing because of the physiological measures employed, and dramatic because of the life-threatening nature of the problems. Minuchin, Rosman, and Baker (1978) reported one study which clearly demonstrated how family conflict can precipitate ketoacidosis crises in psychosomatic-type diabetic children. The investigators compared three groups of families—psychosomatic, behavior disorder, and normal—in terms of their response to a sequence of stress interviews. In the baseline interview parents discussed family problems with their children absent. Normal spouses showed the highest levels of confrontation, while psychosomatic spouses exhibited a wide range of conflict-avoidance maneuvers. Next, a therapist pressed the parents to increase the level of their conflict, while their children observed behind a one-way mirror. As the parents argued, only the psychosomatic children seemed to be really upset. Moreover, these children's manifest distress was accompanied by dramatic increases in free fatty acid levels of the blood, a measure which is related to ketoacidosis. In the third stage of these interviews, the patients joined their parents. Normal and behavior-disorder parents continued as before, but the psychosomatic parents detoured their conflict, either by drawing their children into their discussions or by switching the subject from themselves to the children. When this happened, the free fatty acid levels of the parents fell, while the children's levels continued to rise. The study provided strong confirmation of the clinical observations that psychosomatic children are used (and let themselves be used) to regulate the stress between their parents.

Minuchin, Rosman, and Baker (1978) summarized the results of treating fifty-three cases of anorexia nervosa with structural family therapy. After a course of treatment which included hospitalization followed by family therapy on an outpatient basis, forty-three of these anorexic children were "greatly improved," two were "improved," three showed "no change," two were "worse," and three had dropped out. Although ethical considerations precluded using a control treatment with these seriously ill children, the 90 percent improvement rate is extremely impressive, especially compared with the usual 30 percent mortality rate for this disorder. Moreover, the positive results at termination were maintained at follow-up intervals of up to several years. Structural family therapy has also been shown to be extremely effective in treating psychosomatic asthmatics and psychosomatically complicated cases of diabetes (Minuchin, Baker, Rosman, Liebman, Milman, & Todd, 1975).

Finally, Duke Stanton has shown that structural family therapy can be an effective form of treatment for drug addicts and their families. In a well-controlled study, Stanton and Todd (1979) compared family therapy with a family placebo condition and individual therapy. Symptom reduction was significant with structural family therapy; the level of positive change was more than double that achieved in the other conditions, and these positive effects persisted at follow-up of six and twelve months.

SUMMARY

Minuchin may be best known for the artistry of his clinical technique, yet his structural family theory has become one of the most widely used conceptual models in the field. The reason that his theory is popular is that it is simple, inclusive, and practical. The basic structural concepts—boundaries, subsystems, alignments, and complementarity—are easily grasped and applied. They take into account the individual, family, and social context, and provide a clear organizing framework for understanding and treating families.

Minuchin first created his technique while working with disorganized families from inner-city slums. In order to gain entrance to these families he developed techniques of joining, and in order to change them he developed concrete and powerful restructuring techniques. It is therapy of action, directed at the here and now interactions of families, but designed to alter the basic structure underlying those interactions.

The single most important tenet of this approach is that every family has a structure, and that this structure is revealed only when the family is in action. According to this view, therapists who fail to consider the entire family's structure, and intervene in only one subsystem, are unlikely to effect lasting change. If a mother's overinvolvement with her son is part of a structure that includes distance from her husband, no amount of therapy for the mother and son is likely to change the family.

Subsystems are units of the family based on function. If the leadership of a family is taken over by a father and daughter, then they are the executive subsystem, not the husband and wife. Subsystems are circumscribed and regulated by interpersonal boundaries. In healthy families boundaries are clear enough to protect the separateness and autonomy of individuals and subsystems, and permeable enough to ensure mutual support and affection. Enmeshed families are characterized by diffuse boundaries; disengaged families by rigid boundaries.

Structural family therapy is designed to resolve the presenting problem by reorganizing the family structure. Assessment, therefore, requires the presence of the whole family, so that the therapist can observe the structure underlying the family's interactions. In the process, therapists should distinguish between dysfunctional and functional structures. Families with growing pains should not be treated as pathological. Where structural problems do exist, the goal is to create an effective hierarchical structure. This means activating dormant structures, not creating new ones.

Structural family therapists work quickly to avoid being *inducted* as members of the families they work with. They begin by making concerted efforts to accommodate to the family's accustomed ways of behaving, in order to circumvent resistance. Once they have gained a family's trust, structural therapists promote family interaction, while they assume a decentralized role. From this position they can watch what goes on in the family and make a diagnosis, which includes the problem and the structure that supports it. These diagnoses are framed in terms of boundaries and subsystems, which are easily conceptualized as two-dimensional maps that can be used to suggest avenues for change.

Once they have successfully joined and diagnosed a family, structural therapists proceed to activate dormant structures using techniques that alter alignments, and shift the power within and between subsystems. These restructuring techniques are concrete, forceful, and often highly dramatic. However, their success depends as much on the joining and assessment as on the power of the techniques themselves.

Structural family therapy's popularity is based on its theory and techniques of treatment; its central position in the field has been augmented by its research and training programs. There is now a substantial body of research which lends considerable empirical support to this school's approach. Moreover, the training programs at the Philadelphia Child Guidance Clinic have influenced an enormous number of family therapy practitioners throughout the world.

Although structural family therapy is so closely identified with Salvador Minuchin that they once were synonymous, it may be a good idea to differentiate the man from the method. When we think of structural family therapy, we tend to remember the approach as described in *Families and Family Therapy* published in 1974. That book adequately represents structural theory, but emphasizes only the techniques Minuchin favored at that time. Minuchin, the thinker, has always thought of families in organizational terms. He read Talcott Parsons and Robert Bales and George Herbert Mead; and in Israel he saw how children from unstructured Moroccan families often became delinquents, while those from organized Yemenite families did not. Minuchin the therapist has always been an opportunist, using whatever works. In the 1990s, you can see Carl Whitaker and constructivism in Minuchin's work. From Whitaker, he took the idea of challenging families' myths and engaging with them from a position of passionate involvement. The young Minuchin followed families and watched them in action; that's why he made such use of enactments. The older Minuchin, who has seen thousands of families, now sees things faster; he uses enactment less, and is likely to confront one family on the basis of what he has seen in hundreds of similar cases. Should we follow him in this? Yes, as soon as we have the same experience.

Minuchin has always been a constructivist, though he comes by it intuitively, not from reading books. He challenges families, telling them, essentially, that they are wrong; their stories are too narrow. And he helps them rewrite stories that work. Minuchin has always been interested in literature and story telling; perhaps he likes the doctrine of constructivism simply because it legitimizes his story telling. But, he cautions, when constructivism is not grounded in structural understanding or when it neglects the emotional side of human beings, it can become an arid intellectualism. Minuchin has moved toward eclecticism in technique, but not in theory. Although Minuchin the therapist has changed since 1974, his basic perspective on families, described in structural family theory, still stands, and continues to be the most widely used way of understanding what goes on in the nuclear family.

REFERENCES

Colapinto, J. 1991. Structural family therapy. In *Handbook of family therapy*, vol. II, A. S. Gurman and D. P. Kniskern, eds., New York: Brunner/Mazel.

Elizur, J., and Minuchin, S. 1989. *Institutionalizing madness: Families, therapy, and society.* New York: Basic Books.

Minuchin, S. 1974. *Families and family therapy.* Cambridge, MA: Harvard University Press.

Minuchin, S., Montalvo, B., Guerney, B., Rosman, B., and Schumer, F. 1967. *Families of the slums.* New York: Basic Books.

Minuchin, S., Baker, L., Rosman, B., Liebman, R., Milman, L., and Todd, T. C. 1975. A conceptual model of psychosomatic illness in children. *Archives of General Psychiatry.* *32*:1031–1038.

Minuchin, S., Rosman, B., and Baker, L. 1978. *Psychosomatic families: Anorexia nervosa in context.* Cambridge, MA: Harvard University Press.

Minuchin, S., and Fishman, H. C. 1981. *Family therapy techniques.* Cambridge, MA: Harvard University Press.

Minuchin, S., and Nichols, M. P. 1993. *Family healing: Tales of hope and renewal from family therapy.* New York: The Free Press.

Stanton, M. D., and Todd, T. C. 1979. Structural family therapy with drug addicts. In *The family therapy of drug and alcohol abuse*, E. Kaufman and P. Kaufmann, eds., New York: Gardner Press.

Psychoanalytic Family Therapy

Among the pioneers of family therapy many were psychoanalytically trained, including Nathan Ackerman, Ian Alger, Murray Bowen, Lyman Wynne, Theodore Lidz, Israel Zwerling, Ivan Boszormenyi-Nagy, Carl Whitaker, Don Jackson, and Salvador Minuchin. But with the eager enthusiasm so essential to innovation they turned away from the old—psychodynamics—and toward the new—systems dynamics. Some, including Jackson and Minuchin, went far indeed from their psychoanalytic roots. Others, including Bowen, Lidz, and Wynne, retained a distinctly analytic influence in their work.

In the 1960s and 1970s the burgeoning field of family therapy followed the lead of Jackson and Minuchin, not only ignoring, but at times denouncing, psychoanalytic thinking. Jackson went so far as to declare the death of the individual (Jackson, 1967). As Minuchin was to recall, "We understood that the decontexted individual was a mythical monster, an illusion created by our psychodynamic blinders" (Minuchin, 1989). Family therapists saw themselves as forward-looking modern progressives, liberating the field from a fossilized view of mental disorder, namely, that problems are firmly embedded inside people's heads. If at times they sounded a little self-righteous, perhaps that was due to the vehemence of the resistance they encountered from the entrenched powers of the psychiatric establishment. Understandable or not, the result was a prolonged and polarized alienation between family therapists and psychoanalysts.

Then in the 1980s a surprising shift occurred; family therapists took a renewed interest in the psychology of the individual. While the current reemergence of psychodynamics in family therapy may not be as significant as the crumbling of the Berlin wall, to those who remember the old antagonisms it was equally unexpected.

One reason for the revival of interest in psychodynamics is that there have been a number of recent innovations: within family therapy, a host of voices calling for a reintroduction of psychodynamic ideas; and, within psychoanalysis, the growth of object relations theory and the tremendous popularity of self psychology. Among the books and articles offering an integration of psychoanalytic ideas and family therapy are: *Individual and Family Therapy: Toward an Integration* (Sander, 1979); "Integrating Psychoanalytic Object Relations Understanding with Family Systems Intervention in Couples Therapy" (Friedman, 1980); "Integrative Marital Therapy" (Gurman, 1981); *Object Relations: A Dynamic Bridge Between Individual and Family Treatment* (Slipp, 1984); *The Self in the System* (Nichols, 1987); *Object Relations Family Therapy* (Scharff & Scharff, 1987); and *The Foundations of Object Relations Family Therapy* (Scharff, 1989).

The reason these psychodynamic approaches have found a receptive audience is that many clinicians believe that while family therapists discovered profound truths about systemic interactions, they were wrong to turn their backs on the lessons of depth psychology. There seems to be a paradox here: Psychoanalysis is a theory and therapy of individuals; family therapy is a theory of social systems and a therapy of families. How, then, can there be a psychoanalytic family therapy?

One way of answering this question, illustrated by the object relations family therapy of David and Jill Scharff, is to do psychoanalytic therapy with families. Another solution, suggested by Nichols in *The Self in the System,* is to selectively introduce psychoanalytic insights and interventions in systemic family therapy. In either case, the question—Can there be a psychoanalytic family therapy?—remains a good one.

SKETCHES OF LEADING FIGURES

We can distinguish four distinct groups of contributors to psychoanalytic family therapy: psychoanalytic forerunners; psychoanalytically trained pioneers who helped develop family therapy; the few who pursued psychoanalytic investigations even when mainstream family therapy was vociferously antipsychoanalytic; and those in the forefront of the contemporary resurgence of psychoanalytic family therapy.

It is appropriate to begin by acknowledging Freud's contribution to the psychoanalytic study of family life. Freud was interested in the family, but viewed it as old business—the context where people learned neurotic fears, rather than the contemporary context where such fears are maintained. Presented with a phobic Little Hans, Freud (1909) was more interested in analyzing the child's Oedipus complex than treating the family.

Flugel (1921) also put forth a psychoanalytic view of the family; but, like Freud's, his thinking was limited to intrapsychic processes and his therapy to individuals.

Major advances were achieved in the psychoanalytic understanding of family dynamics by child psychiatrists who began to analyze mothers and children concurrently (Burlingham, 1951). An example of the fruits of these studies is Adelaide Johnson's (Johnson & Szurek, 1952) explanation of the transmission of *superego lacunae*, gaps in personal morality passed on by parents who do things like telling their children to lie about their ages in order to save a couple of dollars at the movies.

Subsequently, the concurrent analysis of married couples revealed the family as a group of interlocking, intrapsychic systems (Oberndorf, 1938; Mittlemann, 1948; Martin & Bird, 1953). The notion of interlinked psyches remains an important feature of the psychoanalytic view of families (Sander, 1989). Most contemporary family therapists view the family as functioning in terms of a single organic unity, but psychoanalytic therapists are concerned with complex interactions among and within individual family members.

From the 1930s to the 1950s more and more psychoanalytic researchers became interested in the family. Erik Erikson explored the sociological dimensions of ego psychology. Erich Fromm's observations about cultural forces and the struggle for individuality foreshadowed later work by Bowen on the process of differentiation within the family. Harry Stack Sullivan's interpersonal theory emphasized the mother's role in transmitting anxiety to her children. Moreover, although he did not treat families, Sullivan transformed the treatment milieu at Sheppard and Enoch Pratt Hospital into a kind of surrogate family for young schizophrenic patients.

The psychoanalysts who helped create family therapy were moving away from psychodynamics, and the analytic influence retained in their work was deliberately muted. Murray Bowen, Lyman Wynne, Theodore Lidz, and Nathan Ackerman have been discussed elsewhere. Among this group, Nathan Ackerman retained the strongest tie to psychoanalytic theory in his approach to families.

In the first two decades of family therapy, Nathan Ackerman was the leading family therapist on the East Coast. Students, among them Salvador Minuchin, flocked to the Family Institute (now Ackerman Institute) in New York to observe this master therapist at work. His book, *The Psychodynamics of Family Life*, published in 1958, was the first one devoted to diagnosis and treatment of families. Classical Freudians assumed that the individuals they treated lived in stable environments. Dreams and fantasies were the royal roads to the unconscious and consequently they didn't think it necessary to know anything about the real family. Ackerman realized, though, that families are rarely stable, dependable, or predictable; rather than quarantine them, however, he believed they could be changed for the better (Ackerman, 1966). Moreover, he wrote (Ackerman, 1958) that accurate understanding of an individual's unconscious requires an understanding of its context in the reality of family interactions. Since people don't live in isolation, Ackerman believed they shouldn't be treated in isolation.

Ivan Boszormenyi-Nagy, also a psychoanalyst, developed another important center of family therapy at the Eastern Pennsylvania Psychiatric Institute (EPPI) in 1957. Among his colleagues and students at EPPI were David Rubenstein, James Framo, Geraldine Spark, and Ross Speck. Nagy's writings

(Boszormenyi-Nagy & Framo, 1965; Boszormenyi-Nagy & Spark, 1973; Boszor-menyi-Nagy & Ulrich, 1981; Boszormenyi-Nagy, 1987) merit careful study by serious students of family therapy.

Even when family therapy was most inhospitable to psychoanalytic think-ing, important, though not well-known, psychoanalytic investigations of the family were being carried out at Tavistock and NIMH.

In the 1940s Henry Dicks (1963) established the Family Psychiatric Unit at the prestigious Tavistock Clinic in England, where teams of psychiatric so-cial workers attempted to reconcile couples referred by the divorce courts. By the 1960s Dicks (1967) was applying object relations theory to the under-standing and treatment of marital conflict. Also at the Tavistock, John Bowlby (1949) described conjoint family interviews as an adjunct to individual psy-chotherapy; he saw the parents of one of his adolescent patients in an effort to resolve a treatment impasse. His report of this case is, like many others, an isolated example of a clinician experimenting with family sessions, but with-out much notice or lasting influence.

In the 1950s and 1960s American psychoanalysis was dominated by ego psychology (which focuses on intrapsychic structures), while object relations theory (which lends itself to interpersonal analysis) flourished an ocean away in Britain. Edith Jacobson (1954) and Harry Stack Sullivan (1953) were the most influential thinkers who helped bring American psychiatry to an inter-personal point of view. Less well known, but more important to the develop-ment of family therapy, was the work carried out at NIMH. When NIMH opened in 1953, Irving Ryckoff jumped at the chance to move from Chestnut Lodge, where he'd been working with chronic schizophrenics isolated from their fami-lies, to develop a research project on families of schizophrenics under the leadership of Robert Cohen. He was joined by Juliana Day and Lyman Wynne and later by Roger Shapiro and John Zinner. This group produced a series of well-known papers introducing such concepts as *pseudomutuality* (Wynne, Ryckoff, Day, & Hirsch, 1958), *role stereotyping* (Ryckoff, Day, & Wynne, 1959), *trading of dissociations* (Wynne, 1965), and *delineations* (Shapiro, 1968). But perhaps their most important clinical contribution was the application of the concept of *protective identification* (from Melanie Klein) to the family as a group (from the work of Wilfred Bion). This group also introduced to psycho-analytic researchers the idea of seeing the family as the unit for study, and to clinicians the analytic group-interpretive approach to families (Shapiro, 1979).

In the 1960s, Ryckoff and Wynne introduced a course in family dynam-ics at the Washington School of Psychiatry, which led to a family therapy train-ing program. They were joined by Shapiro and Zinner and Robert Winer. In 1975 they recruited Jill Savege (now Scharff) and David Scharff. By the mid 1980s the Washington School of Psychiatry, under the directorship of David Scharff, had become one of the leading centers of psychoanalytic family ther-apy. The Scharffs left in 1994 to form their own institute. What characterizes the Scharffs's work is its object relations focus and its frank psychoanalytic approach to families.

Among others who have incorporated psychoanalytic theory into family therapy are: Helm Stierlin (1977), Robin Skynner (1976), William Meissner

(1978), Arnon Bentovim and Warren Kinston (1991), Fred Sander (1979, 1989), Michael Nichols (1987), Nathan Epstein, Harry Grunebaum, and Clifford Sager. Another influential object relations approach to family therapy is that of Samuel Slipp (1984, 1988), whose work differs from the Scharffs's in attempting to be more of an integration of systems and psychoanalytic concepts and methods.

THEORETICAL FORMULATIONS

The practical essence of psychoanalytic theory is being able to recognize and interpret unconscious impulses and defenses against them—and, adding object relations theory, old expectations that distort current relationships.

It isn't a question of analyzing individuals instead of family interactions: it's knowing where to look to discover some of the basic wants and fears that keep those individuals from interacting in a mature way.

Psychoanalytic theory gets so complex when you get into the specifics that it's easy to get lost. Here are the basics.

Freudian Drive Psychology. At the heart of human nature are the drives—sexual and aggressive. Mental conflict arises when children learn, and mislearn, that expressing these basic impulses will lead to punishment. Conflict is signaled by unpleasant affect: anxiety or depression. Anxiety is unpleasure associated with the idea (often unconscious) that one will be punished for acting on a particular wish—for example, the anger you're tempted to express would make your partner stop loving you. Depression is unpleasure plus the idea (often unconscious) that the feared calamity *has already occurred*—for example, the anger you showed your mother long ago made her stop loving you; in fact, nobody loves you.

The balance of conflict can be shifted in one of two ways: by strengthening defenses against a conflicted wish or by relaxing defenses sufficiently to permit some gratification.

Self Psychology. The essence of *self psychology* (Kohut, 1971, 1977) is that human beings crave appreciation. If, when we're young, our parents demonstrate their appreciation, we internalize this acceptance in the form of strong and self-confident personalities. But to the extent that our parents insufficiently demonstrate admiring appreciation and acceptance, then our craving for it is retained in an archaic manner. As adults we alternately suppress the desire for attention and then allow it to emerge unmodified whenever we're in the presence of a receptive audience.

Object Relations Theory. Drive psychology and the psychology of the self describe the basic motives and fears of human nature—and the resultant conflict. Psychoanalysis is primarily the study of individuals and their elemental motives (drives and the need for attachment), and family therapy is the study of social relationships; the bridge between the two is *object relations theory*. While the details of object relations theory can be quite complicated, its essence is simple: We relate to people in the present partly on the basis of expectations formed by early experience. The residue of these early relationships leaves *internal objects*—mental images of self and other, and self in relation to others, built from experience and expectation. The unconscious remnants of those internalized objects form the core of the person—an open system developing and maintaining its identity through social relatedness, present *and* past.

Freud's original focus was on bodily appetites, particularly sex. While these appetites obviously involve other people, they are primarily biological needs, and the relationships they involve are secondary matters. Sex cannot be divorced from object relations, but on the other hand sexual relations can be more physical than personal. This is less true of aggression (to which Freud turned his interest in later years), because aggression is not an organic appetite. As Guntrip (1971) put it, aggression is a personal reaction to "bad" object relations. Therefore as Freud's interest shifted from sex to aggression, the interpersonal, object-relational side of his thinking came to the fore. Eventually he ceased to regard anxiety as dammed-up sexual tension and considered it to be the ego's reaction to danger—often, loss of love or rejection.

Subsequently Melanie Klein's observations of the role of aggression in infancy led her to think about object relations. She combined Freud's psychobiological terms and concepts with her own brilliant insights into the mental life of little children to develop psychodynamic object-relational thinking.

Klein's theory (Segal, 1964) stemmed from her observations of the infant's developing relationship with the first significant object, namely, the mother. According to Klein, an infant doesn't form impressions of mother based solely on real experience, but instead sifts experience through an already rich fantasy life. The infant's innate makeup contains forces of love and hate, which are experienced before the real objects themselves. From the start, perception of real objects is filtered through the distortions of an already formed inner world. The infant doesn't develop impressions of a "bad" mother from actual experience; he projects his own aggressive fantasies onto her. The child then reintrojects—that is, internalizes—those objects that cause pain, which leads to a cruel superego and severe anxiety. The environment confirms but does not originate the baby's primary anxieties and inner conflicts (Segal, 1964).

The infant's first internalized objects are fragmented; that is, they are experienced as *part-objects,* and as either "good" or "bad." In place of Freud's instinctual maturational phases—oral, anal, phallic, and genital—Klein postulated two developmental positions which depend on the role of object relations. Introjection of bad objects, such as a dry breast or the angry face of mother, generates anxiety and fear, which leads the baby into what Klein (1946) called the *paranoid position.* If the child also has sufficient positive experiences, the introjection of these good objects helps to alleviate anxieties and fears.

At about the time of weaning, the infant begins to experience the mother as a whole person, with both good and bad qualities. In addition, the infant discovers that he has the capacity to hurt the ones he loves. In consequence, the baby is depressed at becoming ambivalent toward mother and feels guilty about the capacity to inflict pain on her. This leads to the *depressive position,* which in turn is instrumental in the development of the oedipal conflict beginning in the second year of life.

Klein has been criticized for her failure to follow her own observations to their logical conclusion—namely, that object relations are more relevant than instincts to personality development. Ronald Fairbairn went much further than Klein in the direction of object relations and away from drive psychology. His radical version of object relations theory stressed the ego as object-seeking and downplayed the role of instincts—making love more important than sex.

Because internal object relations are developed from the earliest and most primitive forms of interpersonal interaction, it's not surprising that the major advances in this field have been made by people like Klein and Fairbairn who treated and studied very young children and disturbed adults. In the late 1930s and 1940s, based on his work with schizoid patients (1952), Fairbairn elaborated the concept of *splitting*. Freud originally mentioned splitting as a defense mechanism of the ego; he defined it as a lifelong coexistence of two contradictory positions that do not influence each other.

Fairbairn's view of splitting is that the ego is divided into structures which contain (a) part of the ego; (b) part of the object; and (c) the affect associated with the relationship. The external object is experienced in one of three ways: (1) an ideal object that is just right, which leads to feelings of satisfaction; (2) a rejecting object that frustrates, which leads to anger; or (3) an exciting object that excites needs, which leads to longing. As a result of internalizing split objects, the resulting structure of the ego is: (1) a *central ego,* conscious, adaptable, satisfied with its ideal object; (2) a *rejecting ego,* unconscious, inflexible, frustrated by its rejecting object; or (3) an *exciting ego,* unconscious, inflexible, in a state of longing for a tempting but unsatisfying object. To the degree that splitting is not resolved, object relations retain a kind of "all good" or "all bad" quality.

The primitive ego uses splitting to keep positive and negative images separate, at first because positive and negative experiences happen separately, and later on as a way to avoid anxiety. Splitting, which prevents the anxiety associated with negative (aggressive) images from being generalized throughout the ego, usually disappears in the second year of life as positive and negative images are integrated. If it's excessive, however, splitting interferes with integration of these images and leads to the dramatic shifts from calm to upset of borderline personalities.

Internalization of object relations starts on a relatively primitive level and, as the child grows, becomes more sophisticated. *Introjection* is the earliest and most primitive form of internalization. The child reproduces and fixates its interactions with the environment by organizing memory traces which include images of the object, the self interacting with the object, and the associated affect. Included are good and bad internal objects, each with images of the object and the self. Thus, if mother yells, images of a bad mother and an unworthy self are stored. Introjection is a crude and global form of taking in, as if those fragments of self-other interaction were swallowed whole.

Identification, a higher level of internalization, involves the internalization of a role. In the earliest introjections, object- and self-images are not clearly differentiated; in identification they are. The result of identification is that the child takes on certain roles and behaves in the same way the parents do. Notice, for example, how two-year-olds love to dress up like mommy or daddy.

Ego identity (Erikson, 1956) represents the most sophisticated level of internalization. It is the overall organization of synthesized identifications and introjections. Ego identity involves a consolidation of inner structures, which provides a sense of coherence and continuity of the self. Ego identity includes a consolidated self-concept and a consolidated world of object representations. At the highest level of development, according to Kernberg (1976),

> A harmonious world of internalized object-representations, including not only significant others from the family and immediate friends but also a social group and a cultural identity, constitute an ever growing internal world providing love, reconfirmation, support, and guidance within the object relations system of the ego. Such an internal world, in turn, gives depth to the present interaction with others. In periods of crisis, such as loss, abandonment, separation, failure, and loneliness, the individual can temporarily fall back on his internal world; in this way, the intrapsychic and the interpersonal worlds relate to and reinforce each other. (p.73)

In their observations of infants and young children, Rene Spitz and John Bowlby emphasized the child's profound need for physical *attachment* to a single and constant object. If this primitive need is denied, the result will be *anaclitic depression* (Spitz & Wolf, 1946), a turning away from the world and withdrawal into apathy. According to Bowlby (1969), attachment is not simply a secondary phenomenon, resulting from being fed, but a basic need in all (including human) animals. We must have a secure and loving human attachment in infancy if we are to become secure adults. Those who do not have this experience are excessively vulnerable to even the slightest lack of support, and become chronically overdependent. This, in psychoanalytic terms, explains the genesis of *enmeshed* families.

Margaret Mahler observed infants and young children and described the essential role of a process of *separation-individuation*. For the first month of life, which Mahler described as the *autistic phase,* infants are concerned primarily with their own bodily needs and sensations. The second, or *symbiotic phase,* lasts from approximately two to six months, during which the good mother relieves the baby's tension by feeding, changing, holding, and smiling. The more adequate the care given during this phase, the higher the child's self-esteem will be. After this the child begins a gradual process of separation from the mother, progressively renouncing symbiotic fusion with her. The result of successful separation and individuation is a well-differentiated and internally integrated organization of the self (Mahler, Pine, & Bergman, 1975). Failure to achieve separation and individuation undermines the development of a cohesive sense of self and a differentiated sense of identity, resulting in an overly intense emotional attachment to the family. Depending upon the severity of the failure to separate, crises are liable to develop when the child reaches school age, enters adolescence, or prepares to leave home as an adult.

The shift in emphasis from drives to object relations can also be seen in the work of Americans such as Karen Horney, Erich Fromm, and Harry Stack Sullivan, whose level of analysis was more social and cultural than depth analytic. In his theory of interpersonal psychiatry, Harry Stack Sullivan (1953) emphasized that individuals interact with each other on the basis of past relations with others. Sullivan pointed out the crucial importance of the early mother-child interaction on the *self-system* or *self-dynamism.* The nature of these interactions leads to three types of personifications which determine the nature of the self-system. When the mother is warm and nurturing, the child feels good; when the mother rebuffs or frustrates the child's need for tenderness, the child feels bad; and when the child is exposed to extreme pain or frustration, he dissociates to escape anxiety which would otherwise be intolerable. These experiences create the self-dynamisms: *good me, bad me,* and *not me,* which then become part of the person's response to future interpersonal situations.

In Sullivanian theory, the child searches for *security* and *satisfaction,* and develops a self-system derived from interpersonal relations with the parents by repudiating those actions which cause the parents anxiety. Thus, the extent of the parents' anxiety sets the limits on the child's healthy growth and development.

More recently Erik Erikson (1956, 1963) has theorized that introjections and identifications, along with social roles, form the basis of *ego identity.* Erikson never abandoned the instinctual basis of Freudian theory. He recognizes the influence of sexual and aggressive drives, and accepts the importance of the oral stage of development; however, he stresses the importance of *basic trust.* In order for basic trust to develop, the infant needs physical comfort and protection from undue anxiety, frustration, and rejection. Armed with basic trust, the growing person can face new situations with confidence and equanimity; without it, new experiences bring fear and apprehension.

To understand object relations theory, it's essential to bear in mind that it isn't objects that are in the psyche, but fantasies of objects. As Edith Jacobson (1964) pointed out, the object is never perceived exactly as it is; what is perceived is a representation that reflects the subjective experience of the object. Thus object relations are determined not only by how the object behaves toward the subject but also by how the subject perceives and then integrates that behavior. In *The Brothers Karamazov,* Dostoyevsky, speaking through the monk Zossima, makes exactly this point.

> From the house of my parents I have brought nothing but pleasant memories, for there are no memories more precious than those of one's early childhood in one's own home, and that is almost always so, if there is any love and harmony in the family at all. Indeed, precious memories may be retained even from a bad home so long as your heart is capable of finding anything precious.

The internal world of object relations never exactly corresponds to the actual world of real people. It is an approximation, strongly influenced by the earliest object images, introjections, and identifications. This inner world gradually matures and develops, becoming progressively synthesized and closer to reality. The individual's internal capacity for dealing with conflict and failure is intimately related to the maturity and depth of the internal world of object relations. Trust in one's self and one's goodness is based on the confirmation of love from internalized good objects.

Although the application of his ideas will be developed in subsequent sections, we cannot leave theory without mentioning Heinz Kohut. Not since Freud's drive psychology has there been as significant an impact on psychoanalysis as Kohut's *psychology of the self.* Kohut believed that at the heart of human desires is a longing for admiring attention. The child lucky enough to grow up with appreciative parents will be secure, able to stand alone as a center of initiative, and able to love. The unhappy child, cheated out of loving affirmation, will move through life forever craving the attention he or she was denied. As we shall see, Kohut's ideas have enormous practical application.

NORMAL FAMILY DEVELOPMENT

The distinction between normal and abnormal development is less clearly drawn by psychoanalytic writers than by family therapists in other schools. Following Freud, they take clinical phenomena and psychopathological developments as starting points from which to retrace the development of personality, normal and abnormal. Bear in mind, therefore, that many of the processes described in this section as normal family development have the potential to produce behavior disorders, and that most of the processes described as behavior disorders also have normal counterparts.

The psychoanalytic model of normal development contains concepts drawn from object relations theory, attachment theory, and theories of the self—all of which are modifications and additions to Freud's psychology of drives. The first stage of object relations is an objectless stage. Freud called this *primary narcissism;* Mahler called it *autistic.* The newborn's responses are limited to conditioned reflexes. Gradually, sensation, perception, and memory develop, shaping the infant's experience and encoding the influence of other people. Thereafter the entire process of growth depends upon the ego's relations with objects, at first as actual interactions with real objects, and later as unconscious residues of these first interactions. According to Freudian models, psychological well-being depends upon: (a) gratification of instincts; (b) realistic control of primitive drives; and (c) coordination of independent psychic structures. According to object relations theory, achieving and preserving psychic wholeness through good object relations is the key to psychological adjustment.

The child's innate potential does not mature in sublime indifference to the interpersonal world. The infant needs a facilitating environment in order to thrive. This environment does not have to be an unattainable ideal; an *average expectable environment* featuring *good-enough mothering* (Winnicott, 1965a) is sufficient. Tender, responsive parents first accept the infant's total dependence;

but as time goes on, they support the child's growing autonomy, and eventually ratify the child's finding a life of his own through personal relations with others.

The parents' capacity to provide good-enough mothering and sufficient security for the baby's developing ego depends upon whether they themselves feel secure. To begin with, the mother must be secure and selfless enough to channel most of her energy into supporting and caring for her infant. She drains interest from herself and her marriage and focuses it on the baby. As the baby comes to need less, mother gradually recovers her self-interest, which allows her to permit the child to become independent (Winnicott, 1965b). At the same time she also redevelops an interest in the marital relationship.

If the early relationship with mother is secure and loving, the infant will gradually be able to give her up, while retaining her loving support in the form of a good internal object. In the process, most little children adopt a *transitional object* (Winnicott, 1965b) to ease the loss—a soft toy or blanket that the child begins to cling to during the period when he or she starts to realize that mother is a separate object and can go away. The toy that Mommy gives reassures her anxious baby; it is a reminder that stands for her and keeps alive the mental image of her until she returns. When Mommy says, "Goodnight," the child hugs the teddy bear until morning when Mommy reappears.

The outcome of good object relations in infancy is the emergence of a secure and successfully differentiated identity. The little child who has been cared for by consistently loving and reliably supportive parents develops a sense of *libidinal object constancy* (Kernberg, 1966). The well-loved child feels worthwhile. This sense of worth endows the child with a capacity to delay gratification, tolerate frustration, and achieve competent ego functioning; he or she has a coherent and cohesive sense of self, and is able either to be with others or to be independent. The child with a backlog of good object relations matures with the ability to tolerate closeness as well as separateness.

The child's identity is continually enriched and revised, especially at nodal points of development such as the oedipal period, puberty, and adolescence. But the search for identity does not end with adolescence (Erikson, 1959); the sense of identity continues to be shaped by experiences in adulthood, especially social relations, career development, and family life (Levinson, 1978; Nichols, 1986). Although popular culture treats the search for identity as a narcissistic quest (Lasch, 1978), for Erikson it means finding one's identity in relation to social groups, including the family.

The early attachment between mother and child has been shown to be a critical aspect of healthy development (Bowlby, 1969). Close physical proximity and *attachment* to a single maternal object are necessary preconditions for healthy object relations in childhood and adulthood. The infant needs a state of total merging and identification with the mother as a foundation for future growth of a strongly formed personal self.

After passing through the normal autistic and symbiotic phases, the child enters a long *separation-individuation period* at approximately six months (Mahler, Pine, & Bergman, 1975). First efforts at separation are tentative and brief, as symbolized playfully in the game of peekaboo. At about eight months, the child begins to experience *stranger anxiety* (Spitz, 1965). (The normalness of stranger anxiety has recently been called into question by Daniel Stern's research, to be discussed shortly.) Exaggerated stranger anxiety is a sign that the child is not secure in separating from mother; absence of stranger anxiety indicates that the child has not established a firm bond to mother as a primary object.

Soon the child begins to creep and then crawl, first away from and then back to mother. What enables the child to practice separating is the awareness that mother is constantly there for assurance, like a safe harbor.

The necessary and sufficient condition for successful completion of separation-individuation is the reliable and loving support of a good mother. "Predictable emotional involvement on the part of the mother seems to facilitate the rich unfolding of the toddler's thought processes, reality testing and coping behavior . . . " (Mahler, Pine, & Bergman, 1975, p. 79). A *good-enough mother* is physically and emotionally present; her support of separation-individuation results in the child's achieving a firm sense of identity and a lifelong capacity for developing nonsymbiotic object relations.

Recently, Otto Kernberg and Heinz Kohut have brought theories of the self to center stage in psychoanalytic circles. According to Kernberg (1966), the earliest introjections occur in the process of separating from mother. If separation is successful and securely negotiated, the child establishes himself or herself as an independent being. When the introjective process is positive and constructive, the child absorbs part of the mother's personality for constructive use. Ideally, part of what the child internalizes is conflict-free and independent of drive pressures and defensive needs.

The mother must have a capacity to tolerate separation and withdrawal in order to accept the child's growing independence. If the child is excessively dependent and clings in fear of separation, or if the mother is made anxious by the loss of the symbiotic relationship, or is excessively rejecting, the process is subverted. In the normal outcome, loving parents are the objects of selective and partial identifications, in which only those features that are in harmony with the image of the self are internalized. As Kernberg (1966) says,

> Actually the enrichment of one's personal life by the internal presence of such selective, partial identifications representing people who are loved and admired in a realistic way without indiscriminate internalization, constitutes a major source of emotional depth and well-being. (p. 243)

Normal ego development reaches a stage where positive and negative introjections are synthesized to provide a realistic and balanced view both of others and of the self in relation to others.

In Kohut's (1971, 1977) self psychology, the formation of a strong and cohesive sense of self depends upon the availability of parental *self-objects* who respond with approval to the child's grandiose fantasies, thereby relieving feelings of helplessness. The child, who is thus able to overcome feelings of helplessness, is able to recognize that he or she and mother are separate persons, each with their own needs. In this way the child is able to tolerate separation from the mother and to develop a sense of goodness and strength. Moreover, if mother remains warm and loving during the process of separation, the little child retains a sense of lovableness while achieving individuality and strength. The child who sees approval and acceptance in the mirror of parental eyes develops a strong self, capable of tolerating victory and defeat, as well as acceptance or rejection, throughout adult life.

Unquestionably the most significant recent contribution to the psychoanalytic study of normal family development is the work of Daniel Stern (1985). Stern, a psychoanalyst and infant researcher, has painstakingly traced the development of the sense of self through detailed observations of infants and small children. The infant's *emergent sense of self* begins in the first two months of life as a sense of physical cohesion and continuity in time. Already at this age, the infant has a sense of himself as a person—a distinct and integrated body, an initiator of actions, an experiencer of feelings, and a communicator. From two to six months, infants consolidate the sense of a *core self* as a separate, cohesive, bounded physical unit, with confidence in their own agency and worth. At first the sense of self is a physical self, then somewhere between the seventh and ninth month infants start to develop a second organizing perspective, *intersubjective relatedness*. The most revolutionary of Stern's findings is that child development is *not* a gradual process of separation and individuation. Rather, Stern's meticulous observations reveal that infants differentiate themselves almost from birth, and then progress through increasingly complex modes of relatedness. From *attunement* (reading and sharing the child's affective state) to *empathy*, attachment, trust, and dependency are needs throughout life.

Michael Kahn has begun to establish a theoretical and clinical framework for understanding sibling relationships across the life span (Bank & Kahn, 1982). Since the sibling subsystem comes in so many combinations and variations, Kahn has found concepts of birth order and fixed roles character of each child in the family to be insufficient and reductionistic. He views siblings as existing within a dialectical framework, identifying with and differentiating from one another, influenced by the projections and expectations of their parents, having a secret subsystem in which intensive behaviors and feelings are unleashed. Depending on their stage in the life cycle, Kahn sees siblings drawing closer or more distant, requiring therapists to be skillful in bringing them together as a viable resource group (Kahn & Lewis, 1988). Sibling relationships are a previously underutilized but rich resource system, particularly in light of the strain on parental resources in contemporary two-paycheck households.

From the psychoanalytic perspective, the fate of family development is largely determined by the early development of the individual personalities that make up the family. If the spouses are mature and healthy adults, then the family will be healthy and harmonious. According to Skynner (1976) the characteristics of optimally well-developed families are as follows: affiliative, open, reaching out to others; respect for separateness and individuality; open, clear communication; firm parental coalitions, sharing of power, flexible control by negotiation, spontaneous interactions, with humor and wit; initiative and the encouragement of uniqueness; and lively, strong character development.

Some of the most interesting and productive psychoanalytic ideas are contained in descriptions of the psychodynamics of marriage. In the 1950s, the marital bond was described as a result of unconscious fantasy (Stein, 1956).

We marry a blurry blend of real partners and hoped-for partners. But more recently, and more interestingly, psychoanalysts have described the overlapping and interlocking of fantasies and projections (Blum, 1987; Sander, 1989). Some authors have described this as "mutual projective identification" (Zinner, 1976; Dicks, 1967), others as "neurotic complementarity" (Ackerman, 1966), "marital collusion" (Dicks, 1967), "mutual adaptation" (Giovacchini, 1958, 1961), and "conscious and unconscious contracts" (Sager, 1981). In 1989 one of the most thoughtful contemporary psychoanalytic family therapists, Fred Sander, summed up the analytic position this way:

> Thus, we are noting explicitly what earlier authors from Freud on implicitly noted: the shared participation in neurotic conflicts. The threats of object loss, loss of love, castration, and superego disapproval—the calamities of childhood in all ages and cultures—continue to affect our relations to others, especially those with whom we live and work. The repression of such universal childhood experiences and conflicts leads to their repetition with important others who reciprocally enact similar or complementary unconscious conflicts. (pp. 165–166)

Among psychodynamic family therapists, few have made contributions as important as Ivan Boszormenyi-Nagy's "contextual therapy" which emphasizes the ethical dimension of family development. Nagy considers relational ethics—both within the family and between the family and the larger society—to be a fundamental dynamic force, holding families and communities together through reliability and trustworthiness. In a field that often seeks refuge in the illusion of clinical neutrality, Nagy reminds us of the importance of decency and fairness between people. According to Nagy, loyalty and trust provide the glue that holds families together.

For marital partners, Nagy's criterion of health is a balance between rights and responsibilities. Depending on their integrity and the complementarity of their needs, marital partners can develop a trustworthy give and take (Boszormenyi-Nagy, Grunebaum, & Ulrich, 1991). When needs clash, negotiation and compromise are necessary and must be fair.

DEVELOPMENT OF BEHAVIOR DISORDERS

Nonpsychoanalytic family therapists locate problems in the interactions *between* people; psychoanalytic therapists identify problems *within* the interacting people. According to classical psychoanalytic conflict theory, symptoms are attempts to cope with unconscious conflicts and the anxiety that signals the emergence of repressed impulses. Structurally, these conflicts are between the id and the ego: an instinctual drive seeks expression in a struggle against an opposing restraint (Fenichel, 1945). While agreeing with this basic formulation, object relations theorists added the notion that not only behavior but also psychic structure evolves out of early experiences with others. Therefore, psychopathology is seen as reflecting the consequences of untoward early object relations.

As psychoanalytic thinkers shifted their emphasis from instincts to object relations, infantile dependence and incomplete ego development became the core problems in development, in place of the oedipal complex and repressed instincts. Fear-dictated flight from object relations, which begins in early childhood, is now considered the deepest root of psychological problems.

Psychoanalysts trace the roots of behavior disorders to the earliest months of life when parents first begin interacting with the infant. One important reason for psychopathology is that the child develops distorted perceptions by attributing qualities belonging to one person to someone else. Freud (1905) discovered this phenomenon and called it *transference* when his patient Dora displaced her feelings for her father and a family friend onto him, and terminated treatment abruptly just as it was on the threshold of success. Others have observed similar phenomena and called them by other names "scapegoating" (Vogel & Bell, 1960); "trading of dissociations" (Wynne, 1965); "merging" (Boszormenyi-Nagy, 1967); "irrational role assignments" (Framo, 1970); "delineations" (Shapiro, 1968); "symbiosis" (Mahler, 1952); and "family projective process" (Bowen, 1965). Regardless of name, all are variants of Melanie Klein's (1946) concept, *projective identification.*

Projective identification is a process whereby the subject perceives an object as if the object contained elements of the subject's personality *and* evokes behavior and feelings from the object that conform to these projected perceptions. Unlike projection, projective identification is a truly interactional process. Not only do parents project anxiety-provoking aspects of themselves onto their children, the children collude and behave in a way that fulfills their parents' fears. By doing so, they may be stigmatized or scapegoated, but they also gratify aggressive impulses, as, for instance, in delinquent behavior (Jacobson, 1964); they realize their own omnipotent fantasies; they receive subtle reinforcement from their families; and they avoid the terrible fear of rejection for not conforming (Zinner & Shapiro, 1972). Meanwhile the parents are able to avoid the anxiety associated with having certain impulses; experience vicarious gratification of the projected impulses through their children; and still punish the children for expressing them. In this way, an intrapsychic, structural conflict becomes externalized, with the parent acting as the superego, punishing the child for acting on the dictates of the parental id. That's one reason parents overreact: They're afraid of their own impulses.

> The J. family sought help controlling 15-year-old Paul's delinquent behavior. Arrested several times for vandalism, Paul seemed neither ashamed of nor able to understand his compulsion to strike out against authority. As therapy progressed, it became clear that Paul's father harbored a deep but unexpressed resentment of the social conditions which made him work long hours for low wages in a factory, while the "fat cats didn't do shit, but still drove around in Cadillacs." Once the therapist became aware of Mr. J.'s strong but suppressed hatred of authority, they also began to notice that he smiled slightly whenever Mrs. J. described Paul's latest exploits.

The descriptions of disturbed family relations made by psychoanalytically trained observers during the 1950s and 1960s focused on identifying features of the family environment conducive to the development of schizophrenia. For the most part these theorists dealt with dyadic concepts—"emotional divorce" (Bowen, Dysinger, & Basamania, 1959), "marital schism" and "marital skew" (Lidz, Cornelison, Fleck, & Terry, 1957); and they emphasized adult roles and communication—"role reciprocity" (Mittlemann, 1948); and "pseudomutuality" (Wynne, Ryckoff, Day, & Hirsch, 1958).

More recent descriptions either suggest or are explicitly based on arrested ego development and pathological early object relations. Skynner (1981) listed the following major features of disturbed families: diffuse interpersonal boundaries, unclear identities, satisfaction from fantasy as opposed to reality, difficulty coping with separation and loss, attempts to preserve past states of relationships—often fantasied—and attempts to manipulate others into rigidly held views of them. Many of these concepts are clearly related to the developmental tasks described above.

From an object relations point of view, inadequate separation and individuation as well as introjection of pathological objects are critical determinants of poor adult adjustment. Whether premature or delayed, difficulty in separating creates lasting problems. Guntrip (1969) described how separation anxiety weakens the ego, as follows:

> However caused, the danger of separation, whether by desertion or withdrawal, is that the infant, starting life with a primitive and quite undeveloped psyche, just cannot stand the loss of his object. He cannot retain his primitive wholeness for more than a short period in the absence of mother and cannot go on to develop a strong sense of identity and selfhood without an object-relation. Separation-anxiety then is a pointer to the last and worst fear, fear of the loss of ego itself, of depersonalization and the sense of unreality. (p. 128)

Failure to develop a cohesive sense of self and a differentiated identity causes a prolonged and intensely emotional attachment to the family. This dependent attachment to parents handicaps a person's ability to develop a social and family life of his or her own. This, in object relations terms, explains the enmeshment that characterizes so many symptomatic families (Minuchin, 1974).

The parents' own failure to accept the fact that their children are separate beings can take extreme forms, leading to the most severe types of psychopathology. Several investigators have remarked that anorexia nervosa is a problem that results from inadequate separation and individuation (Bruch, 1978; Masterson, 1977). Often the parents' own serious personality disorders prevent them from understanding and accepting their children's need for independence. Such parents cannot tolerate separation or deviation from their rules, and respond to independent ventures with extreme overcontrol. The result is that the children do not differentiate their own needs from those of their parents; and they become overly compliant, "perfect" children. Lidz (Lidz, Cornelison, & Fleck, 1965) described a mother of identical twins who, when she was constipated, would give her two sons an enema or laxative.

The compliant facade, or "false self" (Winnicott, 1965b), of these children is adaptive only as long as they remain at home with their parents. That's why poorly differentiated children usually face a crisis in adolescence, a time when developmental pressures for independence conflict with infantile family attachments. The outcome may be continued dependence or a violent adolescent rebellion. But the teenager who rebels as a reaction against strong unresolved dependency needs is ill-equipped for mature social relations—not to mention marriage. Behind a facade of proud self-reliance, such individuals harbor deep longings for dependence and tend to be extremely emotionally reactive. When they marry, they may seek constant approval, or automatically reject control and influence, or both.

> In their first couples therapy session, Mr. and Mrs. B.'s complaints were mirror images. He claimed she was "bossy and demanding," while she said that he "had to have everything his own way and wouldn't listen to anybody." An exploration of Mr. B's history revealed that he was the youngest child in a closely-knit family of five. He described his mother as warm and loving, but said she tried to smother him, and that she discouraged all his efforts to be independent. Subjected to these same pressures, his two older sisters conformed and still remain unmarried, living with their parents. Mr. B., however, rebelled against his mother's domination and left home to join the Marines at 17. As he related his experience in the Marine Corps and successful business ventures, it was clear that he was fiercely proud of his independence.
>
> Once the story of Mr. B.'s success in breaking away from his overcontrolling mother was brought out into the open, both Mr. and Mrs. B. had a clearer understanding of his tendency to overreact to anything he perceived as controlling. Deeper analysis subsequently revealed that while Mr. B. staunchly rejected what he called "bossiness," he nevertheless was terribly concerned with securing praise and approval. Apparently, he had learned to fear his deep-seated dependency needs, and he protected himself with a facade of "not needing anything from anybody." Nevertheless, the needs were still there, and had in fact been a powerful determinant of his choice of wife.

Much of the current psychoanalytic thinking about the effects of pathological object relations has come from Otto Kernberg's and Heinz Kohut's studies of borderline character disorders and narcissistic personalities. While the majority of persons seeking family therapy are not so severely disturbed, a great many people suffer from similar dynamics.

In treating borderline personality disorders, Kernberg (1966) was struck by the fact that his patients alternately expressed complementary sides of a conflict, one minute expressing libidinal or aggressive impulses, the next minute behaving defensively in just the opposite manner. He deduced that their behavior was the result of marked compartmentalization of ego states due to a *splitting of the ego*.

The essence of Kernberg's position is that borderline pathology is an object relations disorder. Excessive rage is its cause, and splitting is the defense against it. Borderline patients are liable to sudden outbursts of anger, then equally suddenly will change to warm, friendly, and dependent behavior. When provoked to rage, their image of the hated person corresponds to an early image of mother; their self-image is as a rejected or attacked little child.

Kohut (1971, 1977) described the development of narcissistic pathology, which can take extreme forms as in narcissistic personality disorders, but in less severe forms is one of the most significant and widespread problems in human nature. The child whose needs for *mirroring* and *idealization* are not adequately met goes through life forever hungering to be admired. This hunger may be manifest in the showy exhibitionism most people associate with the term "narcissistic," but it is equally likely to be seen as a childlike craving for appreciation. The child who hungered in vain for praise becomes an adult who alternately suppresses the longing for attention, then lets it break through in an all-or-none form in the presence of anyone who seems to be responsive. If selfishness means unconcern with others, narcissistic personalities are just the opposite. They are obsessed with the opinion of others—and have an inordinate need to be loved and admired.

The more starved for appreciation the child is, the less likely the adult will ever be satisfied. The reason is that the under-responded-to child does not modify the *grandiose self* into realistic goals and ambitions, but represses it, where it remains as an impossible standard of unconscious ambition.

To the extent that pathogenic introjections form the core of the self, there is a propensity for projection. Meissner (1978) described this as the *paranoid process;* split-off and repressed parts of the self are externally displaced, distorting object relations. Pathological introjects not only create a poor self-image, they contaminate relations with others as well. This process causes transference reactions, and it seriously affects marital choices and, ultimately, the dynamics of family life.

When it comes to marital choice, psychoanalysts assure us, love is blind. Freud (1921) wrote that the overvaluation of the loved object when we fall in love leads us to make false judgments based on *idealization*. The "fall" of "falling in love" reflects an overflow of narcissistic libido, so that the object of our love becomes a substitute for our own unattained ego ideal. Naturally our own identity glows in an ideal light. It is particularly when we have dark doubts that we seem to need this special lighting.

Psychoanalysts point out that marital choice is based partially on the desire to find an object who will complement and reinforce unconscious fantasies (Dicks, 1963). Depending upon the nature of these fantasies, some people expect their partners always to gratify them, and others expect their partners never to gratify them. Moreover, people tend to seek mates with complementary needs (Meissner, 1978); this point is illustrated in those marriages where one partner is dominant and the other submissive. Such relationships may be both stable and functional; beginning therapists are therefore well advised not to impose their own values, or try to "save" women from doll's-house marriages, or rescue men from being dominated by their wives—unless they ask for such help.

Further complicating marital choice is the fact that we learn early to hide some of our real needs and feelings in order to win approval. Children who are insecure tend to develop an outward appearance of being good, and to deny and repress impulses and feelings they fear may lead to rejection. Winnicott (1965a) dubbed this phenomenon the *false self*—children behave as if they were perfect angels, pretending to be what they are not. But because they are only acting, their emotional responses lack depth and genuineness. Such children don't trust people to accept their unbridled selves, and use false selves to protect fragile self-esteem.

In its most extreme form, the development of a false self leads to schizoid behavior (Guntrip, 1969); even in less severe manifestations it affects the choice of a marital partner. During courtship both partners are eager to please and, therefore, present themselves in the best possible light. Powerful dependency needs, narcissism, and unruly impulses may be submerged before marriage; but once married, the spouses reveal themselves without camouflage—warts and all.

Marital choice is heavily influenced by the mutual fit of the two partners' projective systems. Typically each wants the other to be an idealized parent. But since this need was frustrated in childhood, it is defended against, and neither directly felt nor revealed. The honeymoon may therefore turn out to be no honeymoon at all, as a woman realizes that the tower of strength she thought she married is in fact not her father, but a callow young man with dependency needs of his own. Likewise, a new husband may discover that he is now the target of those angry hysterics he had previously seen directed only against his wife's mother.

In addition to feeling freer to be themselves after marriage, many spouses actually regress to an earlier stage of development. While they are teenagers living with their parents, most people react to stress and frustration in immature ways, such as pouting or attacking angrily. Such behavior is not likely to be accepted by peers, so people tend to suppress it outside their families, while they are living on their own. However, after they marry, so that they are once again in a family situation, many people begin again to act like adolescents. Consequently the first few months of marriage can be very trying.

Families as well as individuals experience fixation and regression. Most families function adequately until they are overtaxed, at which time they become "stuck" in rigid and dysfunctional patterns (Barnhill & Longo, 1978). When faced with too much stress, families tend to decompensate to earlier levels of development. The amount of stress a family can tolerate depends upon its level of development and the type of fixations its members may have.

Like individuals, families may pass through one developmental stage and on to the next without having fully resolved the issues of the transition. Thus there may be partial fixations at one or more stages of the family life cycle. When stressed, the family not only reexperiences old conflicts, but also falls back on old patterns of coping. Consequently, family therapists need to identify fixation points and regressive patterns of coping, as well as current difficulties.

Psychiatrists, and especially psychoanalysts, have been criticized (Szasz, 1961) for absolving people of responsibility for their actions. To say that someone has "acted-out" "repressed" sexual urges through an extramarital affair is to suggest that he or she is not to be held accountable for infidelity. One writer, however, Ivan Boszormenyi-Nagy, stresses the idea of ethical account-ability within families. Good family relationships include behaving ethically with other family members and considering each member's welfare and inter-ests. Nagy believes that family members owe one another *loyalty,* and that they acquire *merit* by supporting each other. To the degree that parents are fair and responsible, they engender loyalty in their children; however, parents create loyalty conflicts when they ask their children to be loyal to one parent at the expense of loyalty to the other (Boszormenyi-Nagy & Ulrich, 1981).

Pathological reactions may develop from *invisible loyalties.* These are un-conscious commitments that children take on to help their families, to the detriment of their own well-being. For example, a child may get sick to unite parents in concern. Invisible loyalties are problematic because they are not subject to rational awareness and scrutiny. The similarity between invisible loyalties and object relations concepts is not surprising; many of Nagy's con-cepts redescribe traditional psychoanalytic concepts in the language of rela-tional ethics. Another example is his (1967, 1972) concept of *interlocking need templates,* essentially the same as protective identification.

Nagy believes that symptoms develop when the trustworthiness of rela-tionships breaks down because caring and accountability are absent. But while emphasizing such ethical and transactional considerations, Nagy does not ne-glect the subjective experience and unconscious dynamics of individual family members (Boszormenyi-Nagy & Ulrich, 1981).

> There is no theoretical parsimony in trying to invalidate the significance of drives, psychic development, and inner experience. On the contrary, it appears that the intensive, in-depth relational implications of psycho-analytic theory need to be explored, expanded, and integrated with the other contextual dimensions. (p. 160)

While most psychoanalytic thinkers would agree that it's appropriate and necessary to consider individual rights and responsibilities within the family, some have pointed out that individual boundaries are blurred by un-conscious connections with other family members. Kernberg (1975), for ex-ample, writes that blurring of boundaries between the self and others is a result of projective identification, since part of the projected impulse is still recognized within the ego.

Marriage, on the surface, appears to be a contract between two respon-sible people; at a deeper level, however, marriage is a transaction between hidden internalized objects. Contracts in marital relations are usually described using the terms of behavioral or communications theories; but Sager's (1981) treatment of marital contracts also considers unconscious factors: Each contract has three levels of awareness: (1) verbalized, though not always heard; (2) conscious but not verbalized, usually because of fear of anger or disapproval; and (3) un-conscious. Each partner acts as though the other ought to be aware of the terms of the contract, and is hurt and angry if the spouse doesn't live up to these terms. Spouses who behave like this don't accept each other's real personality and identity; each wants the other to conform to an internalized role model, and punishes the other when these unrealistic expectations are disappointed (Dicks, 1963). Even when such behavior is overtly resisted, it may at the same time be unconsciously colluded with. It is valid and useful to emphasize individual rights and responsibilities in real relationships (Boszormenyi-Nagy, 1972), but it is also true that at an unconscious level a marital pair may represent a single personality, with each spouse playing the role of half self and half the other's projective identifications. This is why people tend to marry those with needs complementary to their own (Meissner, 1978).

A similar dynamic operates between parents and children. Even before they're born, children exist as part of their parents' fantasies (Scharff & Scharff, 1987). The anticipated child may represent, among other things, a more devoted love object than the spouse, someone to succeed where the parent has failed, or a peace offering to reestablish loving relations with grandparents.

Zinner and Shapiro (1972) coined the term *delineations* for parental acts and statements that communicate the parents' images to their children. Pathogenic delineations are based more on parents' defensive needs than on realistic perceptions of the children; moreover, parents are strongly motivated to maintain defensive delineations despite anything the children actually do. Thus it is not uncommon to see parents who insist upon seeing their children as bad, helpless, and sick—or brilliant, normal, and fearless—regardless of the truth.

Any and all of the children in a family may suffer from such distortions, but usually only one is identified as "the patient" or the "sick one." He or she is chosen because of some trait that makes him or her a suitable target for the parents' projected emotions. These children should not, however, be thought of as helpless victims. In fact, they collude in the projected identification in order to cement attachments, assuage unconscious guilt, or preserve their parents' shaky marriages. Often the presenting symptom is symbolic of the denied parental emotion. A misbehaving child may be acting out her father's repressed anger at his wife; an overly dependent child may be expressing his mother's fear of leading an independent life outside the home; and a bully may be counterphobically compensating for his father's projected insecurity.

Intrapsychic personality dynamics are obscured by psychological defenses, which mask the true nature of an individual's feelings, both from himself and from others. *Family myths* (Ferreira, 1963) serve the same function in families, simplifying and distorting reality. Stierlin (1977) elaborated on Ferreira's view of family myths and developed the implications for family assessment and therapy. Myths protect family members from facing certain painful truths, and also serve to keep outsiders from learning embarrassing facts. A typical myth is that of family harmony, familiar to family therapists, especially those who have worked with conflict-avoiding families. In the extreme, this myth takes the form of "pseudomutuality" (Wynne, Ryckoff, Day, & Hirsch, 1958) found in schizophrenic families. Often the myth of family harmony is maintained by the use of projective identification; one family member is delegated to be the bad one, and all the others insist they are happy and well-adjusted. This bad seed may be the identified patient or sometimes a deceased relative.

Families often view outsiders, especially family therapists, as intruders who want to stir up painful and embarrassing memories. The more they fear such inquiries, the more they cling to family myths. Therapists must neither be fooled by these myths, nor make the mistake of attacking them prematurely.

GOALS OF THERAPY

The goal of psychoanalytic family therapy is to free family members of unconscious restrictions so that they will be able to interact with one another as whole, healthy persons on the basis of current realities rather than unconscious images of the past. Plainly this is an ambitious task and often therapists will accept less. Families in crisis are treated with understanding and support to help them through their immediate difficulty. Once the crisis is resolved, the psychoanalytic family therapist hopes to engage the family in long-term reconstructive psychotherapy. Some families accept, but many do not. When the family is motivated only for symptom relief, the therapist should support its decision to terminate, lest the family members drop out and feel that they have failed. Some psychoanalytic family therapists deliberately plan short-term treatment. In these cases, just as in individual short-term dynamic psychotherapy (e.g., Sifneos, 1972), it is considered essential to narrow the field of exploration by selecting a specific focus for treatment. A notable exponent of short-term psychoanalytic family therapy is Christopher Dare, at the Maudsley Hospital in London. Although it is not common, some psychoanalytic family therapists also engage in explicitly crisis-oriented family therapy (Umana, Gross, & McConville, 1980).

When psychoanalytic family therapists opt for crisis resolution with symptom-reduction as the only goal, they function much like other family therapists. Hence, they focus more on supporting defenses and clarifying communication than on analyzing defenses and uncovering repressed needs and impulses. In general, however, behavioral changes that in other therapy models would be seen as goals of treatment (e.g., getting a school-phobic child to attend class) are seen by psychodynamic family therapists as by-products of the resolution of underlying family conflicts. The fundamental changes sought include basic reorganization of the family and transformation of the personalities of its members.

It is easy to say that the goal is personality change; it is rather more difficult to specify precisely what is meant by "change." The kind of change most commonly sought after is described as separation-individuation (Katz, 1981) or differentiation (Skynner, 1981); both terms emphasize the growth and independence of individuals from their families of origin, and thus reflect the prominent influence of object relations theory. (Perhaps an additional reason for emphasizing separation-individuation is the fact that enmeshed families are more likely to seek and to remain in treatment than are isolated or disengaged families.) Individual therapists often think of individuation in terms of physical separation. Thus adolescents and young adults may be treated in isolation from their families in order to help them become more independent. Family therapists, on the other hand, believe that emotional growth and autonomy are best achieved by *working through* the emotional bonds within the family. Rather than remove individuals from their families, psychoanalytic family therapists convene families to help them learn how to let go of one another in a way that allows each individual to be independent as well as related. Individuation neither requires nor is achieved by severing relationship bonds. The following extended example illustrates how the goals of psychoanalytic family therapy were implemented with a particular family.

> Three months after he went away to college, Barry J. had his first psychotic break. A brief hospital stay made it clear that Barry was unable to withstand separation from his family without decompensating; therefore, the hospital staff recommended that on discharge he should live apart from his parents with only minimal contact, in order to help him become an independent adult. Accordingly, he was discharged to a supportive group home for young adults and seen twice weekly in individual psychotherapy. Unfortunately, he suffered a second breakdown, and within two months was once again hospitalized.
>
> As the time for discharge from this second hospitalization approached, the ward psychiatrist decided to convene a meeting of the entire family in order to discuss plans for Barry's post-hospital adjustment. During this meeting it became painfully obvious that powerful forces within the family were binding Barry and impeding any chance for genuine separation. Barry's parents were both pleasant and effective people who separately were most engaging and helpful. Toward each other, however, they displayed an icy hatred. During those few moments in the interview when they spoke to each other, rather than to Barry, their hostility was palpable. Only their concern for and involvement with Barry, their youngest, prevented their relationship from becoming a battleground—a battleground on which Barry feared one or both of them might be destroyed.
>
> At the staff conference following this interview two plans for disposition were advanced. One group, recognizing the powerful pathological influence of the family, recommended that Barry be removed as far as possible from the family and treated in individual psychotherapy. Only by isolating Barry from his parents, they argued, was there hope that he could mature into an independent person. Others on the staff disagreed, arguing that only by treating the family conjointly could the collusive bond between Barry and his parents be resolved. After lengthy discussion the group reached a consensus to try the latter approach.
>
> Most of the early family meetings were dominated by the parents' anxious concern about Barry: about the apartment complex where he lived, about his job, about his friends, about how he was spending his leisure time, about his clothes, about his grooming—in short, about every detail of his life. Gradually, with the therapist's support, Barry was able to limit how much of his life was open to his parents' scrutiny. As he did so, and as they were less able to preoccupy themselves with him,

they began more and more to focus on their own relationship. As Barry became more successful at handling his own affairs, his parents became openly combative with each other.

Following a session during which the parents' marital relationship was the primary focus, the therapist recommended that the parents come for a few separate sessions in addition to the regular family meetings. In these separate sessions, unable to divert their attention to Barry, the J.s fought viciously, leaving no doubt that theirs was a seriously destructive relationship. Rather than getting better in treatment, their relationship got worse.

After two months of internecine warfare—during which time Barry continued to improve—Mr. and Mrs. J. sought a legal separation. Once they were separated, both parents seemed to become happier, more involved with their friends and careers, and less worried about Barry. As they further released their stranglehold on their son, both parents began to develop a warmer and more genuine relationship with him. Even after the parents divorced they continued to attend family sessions with Barry.

In place of the original tensely symbiotic bond, a more balanced relationship between Barry and his parents gradually emerged. Resolution of hidden conflicts, and working through of unconscious loyalties, led to genuine autonomy of separate persons—enjoying but no longer needing each other—an outcome far better than isolation.

In Nagy's contextual therapy the goal is a balance of fairness in the burdens and benefits of adult life. The growth of the individual is seen to include giving and caring. Taking into account conflicts that have led to past injustices and acknowledging and redressing them is considered essential to, not in competition with, enhanced self-worth.

Nagy shares with other psychoanalytic family therapists the assumption that growth and relief of symptoms occur through facing avoided emotional processes. Contextual therapy considers the therapeutic implications of responsibility for imposing one's projections onto others. But the reintegration of avoided aspects of the self cannot be an isolated or selfish pursuit. Self-discovery often necessitates, and also frequently makes possible, the courageous renegotiation of avoided or inequitable relationships (Boszormenyi-Nagy, Grunebaum, & Ulrich, 1991).

The goals of contextual therapy include a balance between autonomy and mutuality. Family members are helped to face and overcome irrational, unproductive guilt and to claim their own entitlements. However, facing realistic guilt and to claim their own entitlements. However, facing realistic guilt —based on actual harm done to others, deliberately or inadvertently—is seen as essential to expanding accountability within families. Thus, each person works toward self-fulfillment by asserting his or her rights and by living up to his or her obligations. Although helping people to give more generously in family relations may sound like a luxury for the well-adjusted, it is not. The added benefits of caring about the ethical implications of relationships actually help to strengthen a weak ego.

CONDITIONS FOR BEHAVIOR CHANGE

As any student knows, psychoanalytic therapy achieves personality change and growth through insight; but the idea that insight cures is a misleading oversimplification. Insight is necessary, but not sufficient, for successful psychoanalytic treatment. In psychoanalytic family therapy, family members expand their insight by learning that their psychological lives are larger than their conscious experience, and by coming to understand and accept repressed parts of their personalities. Just as in individual therapy, interpretations, to be effective, should be limited to preconscious material—that which the patient is almost aware of; interpretations of unconscious material arouse anxiety, which means they will be rejected. Whatever insights are achieved, however, must subsequently be *worked through* (Greenson, 1967)—that is, translated into new and more productive ways of behaving and interacting.

Some (Kohut, 1977) have even suggested that psychoanalytic treatment works not as much by insight as by reducing defenses—patients simply experience and express repressed parts of themselves. From this point of view, it may be more important for family members to express their unconscious needs than to learn to understand them. Regardless of which position is taken, most therapists work to do both—that is, foster insight and encourage expression of repressed impulses (Ackerman, 1958).

Analytic therapists foster insight by penetrating beneath the surface of behavior to the hidden motives below. In individual therapy, dreams and free associations are considered to be *manifest content*, not to be taken at face value. Likewise, manifest family interactions are thought to be disguised versions of the latent feelings hidden behind them. Nonanalytic family therapists accept the meaning of the family's manifest interactions; analytic family therapists attempt to uncover other material, especially that which is hidden, unconscious, and from the past. According to Framo (1970), "The family cannot undergo deep or meaningful change if the therapist deals only with current, immediate interactions among the members" (p. 158).

Naturally, families defend against exposing their innermost feelings. After all, it is a great deal to ask of anyone to expose old wounds and embarrassing emotions. Psychoanalysts deal with this problem by creating a climate of trust and by proceeding very slowly. But the risk of exposure is far greater in family therapy. Not only do family members have to acknowledge painful feelings, they are asked to do so in front of the very people they most want to hide them from. A therapist might offer as an interpretation the idea that a man hates his wife because he blames her for depriving him of the freedom of his lost youth. In individual treatment, the patient may acknowledge this fairly readily, wonder why he has suppressed his feelings, and begin to explore the roots of his reactions. But imagine how much more difficult it is to admit its truth and acknowledge his feelings in front of his wife.

Since patients in family therapy are likely to be concerned about public exposure as well as self-protection, therapists must offer them a great deal of security. Such security is necessary both for uncovering material for analysis, and also for working through this material in family interaction. Once an atmosphere of security is established, the analytic family therapist can begin to identify projective mechanisms and bring them back into the marital relationship. Then the spouses can reinternalize parts of themselves that they projected onto their mates. Once they no longer need to rely on projective identification, they can acknowledge and accept previously split-off, guilt-ridden libidinal and aggressive parts of their own egos. The therapist helps spouses resolve introjects of their parents, so they can see how their present difficulties emerged from unconscious attempts to perpetuate old conflicts from their families of origin. This work is painful and cannot proceed without the continual security offered by a competent and supportive therapist. Nichols (1987) emphasizes the need for *empathy* to create a "holding environment" for the whole family.

Any form of family therapy derived from psychoanalytic principles must establish a climate of sufficient safety to expose and analyze object-relational images internalized at an early age. Moreover, in order to work through these insights, secure social interactions must be nurtured in family treatment sessions so that unfinished developmental tasks can be uncovered and surmounted. Speaking to this point, Guntrip (1971) wrote that analysts who emphasize instinct theory can blame treatment failures on the great strength of their patients' sexuality and aggression. But from an object-relations perspective, such failures are more likely to be seen as the therapist's failure to make treatment relationships secure. For the therapist, this means listening without becoming overly intrusive; for family members, it means learning to hear each other's complaints as statements of feelings and requests for change, rather than as attacks that threaten their ego integrity.

To some, the idea of *transference* seems relevant only to individual therapy, where in the absence of a real relationship most of the patient's feelings toward the therapist must be inspired by fantasy. What need is there to think of transference in family therapy when the "real" relationships are actually present? In fact, transference is ubiquitous in all emotionally significant relationships. By reexperiencing and acting out repetitious past patterns—toward the therapist, or other family members, or both—a person can begin to view these interactions objectively and, with a therapist's help, begin to break up repetitious pathological cycles. According to Nagy (1972) family therapy offers an even more fertile field of utilizing transference than does individual therapy.

> Beginning family therapists are soon struck with a different climate for therapeutic transference as they begin to see families rather than isolated individuals. The chief reason for this is the fact that family relationships themselves are embedded in a transference context and the family therapist can enter the ongoing transference relationship system rather than having to recreate it as a new relationship in the privacy of an exclusive therapist-patient work relationship. (p. 378)

Elsewhere, Nadelson (1978) wrote,

> Since marital conflict may be viewed as a result of the mutual projection, by each partner, of early internalized objects, and thus may become the battle-ground for past conflict, the therapist must be aware of each spouse's

transference projection onto the partner as well as onto the therapist. (p. 123)

When two or more generations of family members are present in treatment it often becomes painfully obvious how certain distortions in one relationship are rooted in repetitions of previous experiences. Here psychoanalytic family therapists have great information, and the leverage to rework developmental experiences in such a way as to modify pathological introjects. In describing the interrelations among family members' pathology, Ackerman (1966) coined the felicitous phrase, "a cluster of interpenetrating illnesses."

By gathering whole families for treatment, the psychoanalytic therapist broadens the number of transference reactions, but mutes their intensity. Transference to the therapist exists, but because the family is present, it is less intense than in individual therapy. As Nagy (1972) has observed, "parentification" of the therapist is antithetical to existing family ties. Both the real and the transference reactions to other family members divert a good deal of emotional energy that otherwise might be focused on the therapist.

The field of observation is enlarged for the psychoanalytic therapist, who can see not only the real relationship among the generations that are assembled but also the vestiges of previous generations and past interactions encoded as object images and manifested as transference. As in individual therapy, the family therapist ignores transference at his peril. But although awareness of transference, as well as resistance and projection, must guide the therapist's interventions, these reactions need not always, or only, be interpreted. Some psychoanalytically inspired therapists prefer to offset interactions based on transference rather than to interpret them (Boszormenyi-Nagy & Ulrich, 1981).

Two of the major considerations in family therapy are who should be included in the treatment and on whom should the help be focused. Some approaches, as, for instance, strategic and behavioral, focus on helping the identified patient, even though the family may be seen conjointly. Most psychoanalytic family therapists seem to agree that the commitment should be to all family members; however, they are more likely to mean helping individuals to grow and mature, than helping the family as an organic whole. According to Blanck (1967), "To help an individual or couple in marital conflict one must help each partner move towards a higher level of personality development" (p. 160).

The nature of this "higher level of personality development" has been defined in both structural and object-relations terms. For example, Nadelson (1978) emphasized the structural aim of bringing instinctual drives under the dominion of the ego when she wrote,

The ultimate aim of interpretation and working through in psychoanalytically oriented marital therapy is the neutralization and integration of aggressive and libidinal needs so that behavior is motivated more in the service of the ego and less by impulse and intrapsychic conflict. (p. 146)

When aggressive and libidinal impulses are interpreted and experienced, they become conscious. Once they become aware of such impulses, family members are better able to integrate them into their lives and thus overcome their pathological, controlling power.

The personal growth aimed for in psychoanalytic treatment can also be sought in terms of improved object relations. For family members to overcome pathological attachments to each other, they must be helped to become whole individuals. As Guntrip (1971) put it, "Psychotherapy is the reintegration of the split-ego, the restoration of lost wholeness" (p. 94). The split ego, which developed from bad object relations early in life, is resolved by good object relations, first in psychotherapy and subsequently in interactions within the family.

TECHNIQUES

For all the complexity of psychoanalytic theory, psychoanalytic technique is relatively simple—not necessarily easy, but simple. In psychoanalytic family therapy there are four basic techniques: listening, empathy, interpretation, and maintaining analytic neutrality. Two of these—listening and analytic neutrality—may not sound terribly profound or different from what other family therapists do, but they are.

Listening is a strenuous but silent activity, rare in our culture. Most of the time we're too busy waiting to get in a word edgewise to listen more than superficially. This is especially true in family therapy where therapists feel a tremendous pressure to do something to help the troubled and troubling families they treat. And this is where the importance of maintaining analytic neutrality comes in. To establish an analytic atmosphere it is essential to aim for listening and understanding without worrying about whether or what the family changes. Change may come about as a by-product of understanding, but the analytic therapist suspends anxious involvement with outcomes. It is impossible to overestimate the importance of this frame of mind in establishing a climate of analytic exploration.

The psychoanalytic therapist resists the temptation to be drawn in to reassure, advise, or confront families in favor of a sustained but silent immersion in their experience. When analytic therapists do intervene, they express empathic understanding in order to help family members open up, and they make interpretations to clarify hidden and confusing aspects of experience. While there is no way to specify the optimal mix of listening and intervening, most therapists talk too much. There are many reasons and twice as many rationalizations for this excess activity, but they have a common result: The therapist remains overly central. Psychoanalytic therapists concentrate instead on careful listening, which, incidentally, also adds power to the infrequent interpretations they do make.

In classical psychoanalysis, therapeutic change is achieved by analysis: confrontation, clarification, interpretation, and working through (Greenson, 1967). Even when modifications are made, as in psychodynamic psychotherapy where cathartic techniques, suggestion, and manipulation are employed (Bibring, 1954), interpretation remains the decisive technique. This holds true for psychoanalytic family therapy as well. However, psychoanalytic clinicians doing family therapy are more inclined to include other, not strictly analytic, techniques because in family treatment the patients can begin to use awareness and start to behave differently in their families without having to leave the treatment room.

Before the therapist can attempt to change families, he or she must formulate an understanding of them. Here, psychoanalytic therapists are particularly well equipped because they have a comprehensive theory of personality and behavior. Moreover, as some authors (Dare, 1979) have pointed out, psychoanalytic understanding is useful for developing a comprehensive picture of family dynamics even when treatment techniques are drawn from other approaches. Thus the early psychoanalytic family therapists used psychoanalytic concepts for understanding families, but resorted to other methods, especially facilitating communication, for treatment.

What distinguishes psychoanalytic from most other diagnostic formulations of families is that, as we discussed above, they understand the individual family members' intrapsychic dynamics; in fact, the majority of psychoanalytic concepts are about individuals or dyads. But since psychoanalytic family therapists must also deal with larger relationship systems, they also must consider the family's interpersonal dynamics as well as the intrapsychic lives of its members.

The following is an abbreviated sketch of an initial psychoanalytic evaluation of a family.

After two sessions with the family of Sally G., who was suffering from school phobia, the therapist made a preliminary formulation of the family's dynamics. In addition to the usual descriptions of the family members, the presenting problem, and their history, the formulation included assessments of the parents' object relations and the collusive, unconscious interaction of their marital relationship.

Mr. G. had been initially attracted to his wife as a libidinal object who would fulfill his sexual fantasies, including his voyeuristic propensities. Counterbalancing his sexual feelings was a tendency to idealize his wife, the dynamic reaction of his libidinal impulses. Thus he was deeply conflicted and intensely ambivalent in his sexual relations with her.

At another level, Mr. G. had unconscious expectations that she would be the same long-suffering, self-sacrificing kind of person that his mother was. Thus, he longed for motherly consolation from her. However, these dependent longings were threatening to his sense of masculinity, so he behaved outwardly as though he were tough, self-sufficient, and needed no one. That he had a dependent inner object inside himself was shown by his tender solicitude towards his wife and children when they were ill. But they had to be in a position of weakness and vulnerability to enable him to overcome his defenses enough for him to gratify his own infantile dependency needs vicariously.

Mrs. G. expected marriage to provide her with an ideal father, someone who would be loving, nurturing, and supportive. Given this unconscious expectation, the very sexuality that attracted men to her was also a threat to her wish to be treated like a little girl. Like her husband, she too was highly conflicted about sexual relations. Raised as an only child, she always expected to come first. She was even jealous of her husband's warmth toward Sally, and attempted to maintain distance between father and daughter by her own intense attachment to Sally.

At the level of her early self-object images, she was a jealous, greedy, demanding little girl. Her introjection of her mother provided her with a model of how to treat a father figure. Unfortunately, what worked for her mother with her father did not work for her with her husband.

Thus, at an object-relations level, both spouses felt themselves to be deprived little children, each seeking automatic gratification of wishes, each wanting to be taken care of without having to ask. When these magical wishes were not granted, both of them seethed with angry resentment. Eventually they reacted to trivial provocations with the underlying rage, and horrible quarrels erupted.

When Sally witnessed her parents' violent altercations, she became terrified that her own hostile and murderous fantasies might come true. Although her parents hated their own internalized bad parent figures, they seemed to act them out with each other. Further enmeshing Sally in their conflict was the fact that the ego boundaries between herself and her mother were blurred. It was almost as though mother and daughter shared one joint personality.

Dynamically, Sally's staying home from school could be seen as a desperate attempt to protect her mother-herself from her father's attacks, and to defend both her parents against her own, projected, murderous fantasies.

Nonanalytic clinicians tend to focus their evaluations on overt communications and interactions, as well as on conscious hopes and expectations. From a psychoanalytic perspective such descriptions only scratch the surface. Unconscious forces constitute the core of family life. However, this doesn't mean that psychoanalytic clinicians deal only with the psychology of individual personality defects. Family dynamics are more than the additive sum of individual dynamics. Individuals may bring impaired object relations to family life, but it is the unconscious fit between family members that essentially determines adjustment.

Applying object relations theory to family evaluation, Dicks (1967) proposed three levels on which to assess the marital relationship: (1) cultural values and norms—race, religion, education, and values; (2) central egos—personal norms, conscious judgments and expectations, habits, and tastes; and (3) unconscious forces that are repressed or split off, including drives and object-relations needs. If a couple is in harmony on any two of these three levels, Dicks believed they will stay together, even in the face of constant conflict. However, if they are incompatible on two or more levels, the marriage will probably end in divorce.

Dicks's analysis helps to explain why many couples seem to remain together despite constant fighting, and why other couples who seem content enough suddenly split up. Presumably the battling couples who cleave together fit each other's unconscious needs, and their object-images dovetail. In discussing one such couple, Dicks (1967) wrote,

> At the level of social value judgment, I would have no hesitation in rating the marriage of Case Ten as more living, deeper and "truer" than the conventional whited sepulchres in which no sleeping dog is permitted to raise his head, let alone bark. (p. 119)

Analysts do not postpone treatment until they have made an exhaustive study of their cases; on the contrary, psychoanalytic therapists may not complete their evaluations, may not even arrive at a final diagnosis, until the end of treatment.

However, although analytic clinicians may continue to elaborate and refine their understanding of dynamics over the course of treatment, effective therapy cannot proceed without some focused dynamic formulation. Beginning therapists—who lack theory as well as experience—sometimes proceed on the assumption that if they merely sit back and listen, understanding will emerge. This is rarely true in individual therapy and almost never true in family therapy. The therapist needs a hypothesis.

An excellent model for developing a psychodynamic focus is the work of Arnon Bentovim and Warren Kinston in Great Britain (Bentovim & Kinston, 1991), who offer a five-step strategy for formulating a focal hypothesis:

1. How does the family interact around the symptom, and how does the family interaction affect the symptom?
2. What is the function of the current symptom? (In the L. family they suspected that if the parents didn't draw together and exclude their son, the result would be severe conflict between the parents.)
3. What disaster is feared in the family that keeps them from facing their conflicts more squarely? (Why, for example, in the L. family is marital conflict avoided?)
4. How is the current situation linked to past trauma?
5. How would the therapist summarize the focal conflict in a short memorable statement? (The L. family is excluding the child so as to overcome a marital breakup, which occurred in the family of origin due to a competing parent-child relationship.)

After the preliminary psychodynamic assessment, the therapist must decide who to include in treatment. Psychoanalytic family therapists today work with every possible combination of family members. Perhaps most common, however, is treatment of married couples; most psychoanalytic clinicians will prefer to emphasize the adult nucleus of the family because it is consistent with their own verbal and intellectual level.

From an object relations point of view (Dicks, 1963), marriage is a transaction between hidden, internalized objects. These internal objects, which reflect the parenting and marital relationships in the spouses' original families, are brought into awareness by interpretation of the unconscious bases for the couple's interactions. Frequently, couples are found to have dominant *shared internal objects* (Dicks, 1967), based on unconscious assimilation of parent figures. Such couples do not relate to each other as real persons, but as angry or loving parents, to be tormented or idealized. (See Sander [1989] for a recent version of this view.)

Some aspects of internalized objects are conscious, readily expressed, and easily examined. These are based upon direct identification with consciously perceived parental models, or overcompensation against negative images. A bullying husband may be overcompensating for feeling weak, like his father. His behavior seems to say, "I won't be pushed around the way my father was." Such consciously held object images will emerge regardless of therapeutic technique; however, in order to get unconscious images to emerge, psychoanalytic clinicians rely upon a nondirective exploratory style.

Psychoanalytic patients are taught to *free associate*—that is, express their thoughts as they occur spontaneously, without planning or censorship. This technique is the best way to bring unconscious material to the surface. While the patient free-associates, the analyst occasionally asks clarifying questions, but mostly listens with silent interest. Eventually, the analyst begins to interpret material, particularly resistance and transference.

Psychoanalytic family therapists generally follow this basic approach. To begin with, family members are invited to speak freely about their concerns with very little interruption or guidance from the therapist. This may not sound different from what other family therapists do, but psychoanalytic family therapists are far more nondirective than practitioners of other schools. This nondirectiveness comes out in both obvious and subtle ways. Strategic therapists ask pointed questions about behavior sequences surrounding symptoms; structuralists direct family members to engage in extended dialogues; psychoanalytic therapists just listen. This is not to say that they don't ask questions or that their interest is not selective. The point is that they are convinced that the spontaneous flow of their patients' thoughts and feelings provides important clues to their underlying concerns; their free associations also reveal patterns of family interaction. Once a family starts discussing its problems, psychoanalytic therapists refrain from comments or questions until the spontaneous flow of the family's dialogue subsides (Dicks, 1967).

Not only do they avoid directing what their patients say, psychoanalytic therapists are also careful not to be drawn into offering advice. Most other family therapists also deny or minimize the amount of advice they give; but some do so frequently, however inadvertently—as in the following case.

> Summarizing her fourth session with the Z. family, a psychology intern reported that they had responded quite well to an important interpretation. She then proceeded to review the detailed process notes of the session with her supervisor.
>
> Midway through the session, Mr. Z. described an argument with his wife that took place during the week. He had come home late from work, and his wife began to nag and scold him. Previously when this happened Mr. Z. would feel terribly hurt, and go off sulking and thinking how cruel and unfair his wife was to him. This time, however, her nagging provoked him to fight back, and they had a terrific row. At this point in the narrative, the therapist intervened, saying, "So, this time

you stood up for yourself. And afterwards you felt better, didn't you?" Mr. Z. said yes, he did feel better afterwards, and then fell silent.

Listening to this material, the supervisor realized that although Mr. Z.'s fighting back was a step in the right direction, the therapist's intervention was not an interpretation, but a thinly veiled manipulation; furthermore, it closed off exploration of the couple's interaction. Certainly Mr. Z. was aware that his pouty withdrawal in the face of criticism from his wife was not an adaptive response. What he didn't understand were the unconscious reasons for his doing so—what awful consequences he anticipated in his fantasy, who it was his wife reminded him of, and what her conscious and unconscious feelings were about arguing with a man. By simply giving Mr. Z. a verbal pat on the back, the therapist helped to seal off these crucial data.

The following are examples of advice-giving and persuasion passing as interpretations. Notice that the interventions are statements of widely held beliefs and personal opinions—therapeutic clichés—rather than uncovering comments based on specific material revealed by unique persons.

A husband reported that after feeling anxious and depressed at the office all day, he had stopped on the way home and bought a bouquet of flowers for his wife. She, pleased with the gift, was especially warm and friendly that evening, and the husband felt reassured. The therapist commented, "That's good; you have to give to get."

After several sessions in which he was silent and depressed, a teenage boy finally began to argue with his mother, angrily accusing her of not understanding him and playing favorites with his brother and sister. Just as the mother was about to respond, the therapist intervened, saying, "That's good. It's good to let your feelings out. If you'd express your anger more you wouldn't get so depressed."

In the first example, the therapist, by delivering a hackneyed bit of advice, missed an opportunity to explore the husband's anxiety and the reason he was reluctant to tell his wife that he was unhappy. In the second, the therapist's "interpretation" precluded an exploration of what the youngster imagined would happen if he asked for more attention from his mother. Moreover, it also obscured the mother's response and took it out of the session. If she responds to her son's complaints in an angry or rejecting fashion after the session, even if it is reported, the interaction will not be directly available in the session for therapeutic intervention. Thus the advantage of being able to work through and integrate the boy's new behavior was lost.

Psychoanalytic family therapy is certainly more active than classical psychoanalysis; nevertheless, it remains a nondirective uncovering technique. The discipline involved in learning to interfere minimally and to scrutinize one's responses to eliminate unessential or leading interventions is a critical part of psychoanalytic technique, with individuals or with families. Interpretations should neither reassure nor direct people; they should facilitate the emergence of new material, forgotten or repressed, and mobilize feelings previously avoided (Dicks, 1967).

In addition to limiting interpretations to specific material revealed by their patients, psychoanalytic therapists also limit the number of interpretations they make. Two or three per session is typical. Most of the rest of the analytic therapist's activity is devoted to eliciting material without becoming overly directive. Sessions typically begin with the therapist inviting family members to discuss current experiences, thoughts, and feelings. In subsequent meetings, the therapist might begin either by saying nothing or perhaps, "Where would you like to begin today?" The therapist then leans back and lets the family talk, with minimal direction or interference with the spontaneous flow of their communication. Questions are limited to requests for amplification and clarification. "Could you tell me more about that?" "Have the two of you discussed how you feel about moving to Chicago?"

When the initial associations and spontaneous interactions dry up, the psychoanalytic therapist probes gently, eliciting history, people's thoughts and feelings, and their ideas about family members' perspectives. "What does your father think about your problems? How would he explain them?" This technique underscores the analytic therapist's interest in assumptions and projections.

Although we have repeatedly emphasized the nondirective nature of psychoanalytic technique, it is far from a passive approach. While family members are speaking about whatever is on their minds, the therapist is actively analyzing what is being said for derivatives of drives, defenses, ego states, and manifestations of transference. Psychoanalytic therapists, more than most others, order the raw data of family dialogues by fitting them to their theory. The bare facts are always ambiguous; psychoanalytic theory organizes them and makes them meaningful.

In addition to fitting the raw data to theory, the psychoanalytic therapist also directs it by pursuing the past. Particular interest is paid to childhood memories of and associations to interactions with parents. The following vignette shows how transitions are made from the present to the past.

> Among their major disappointments in each other, Mr. and Mrs. S. both complained bitterly that the other one "doesn't take care of me when I'm sick, or listen to my complaints at the end of the day." Not only did they share the perceptions of the other one's lack of "mothering," they both steadfastly maintained that *they* were very supportive and understanding. Mrs. S.'s complaint was typical: "Yesterday was an absolute nightmare for me. The baby was sick and fussy, and I had a miserable cold. Everything was twice as hard for me and I had twice as much to do. All day long I was looking forward to John's coming home. But when he finally did, he didn't seem to care about how awful I felt. In fact he only listened to me for a minute before he started telling some dumb story about his office." Mr. S. responded by telling a similar story, but with the roles reversed.
>
> At this point the therapist intervened to ask both spouses to describe their relationships with their mothers. What emerged were two very different but very revealing histories.

Mr. S.'s mother was a child of the Depression, for whom self-reliance, personal sacrifice, and unremitting struggle were paramount virtues. Though she loved her children, she withheld warmth, affection, and nurturance lest they become "spoiled and soft." Nevertheless, Mr. S. craved his mother's attention and constantly sought it. Naturally, he was often rebuffed. A particularly painful memory for him was of a time he came home in tears after getting beaten by a bully in the school yard. But instead of the loving comfort he hoped for, his mother scolded him for "acting like a baby," and told him he had to learn to fight his own battles. Over the years he learned to protect himself from these rebuffs by developing a rigid facade of independence and strength.

With the second significant woman in his life, his wife, Mr. S. maintained his rigid defensiveness. He never talked about his problems, but since he continued to yearn for compassionate understanding, he resented his wife bitterly for not drawing him out. His own failure to risk rejection by asking for support served as a self-fulfilling prophecy, confirming his expectation, "She doesn't care about me."

Mrs. S.'s background was quite different from her husband's. Her parents were indulgent and demonstrative. They doted on their only child, communicating their love by expressing constant, anxious concern for her well-being. When she was a little girl, the slightest bump or bruise was the occasion for lavish expressions of solicitous concern. She came to marriage used to talking about herself and her problems. At first Mr. S. was enchanted. *Here is someone who really cares about my feelings,* he thought. But when he discovered that she didn't ask him to talk about his own concerns, he became resentful and progressively less sympathetic. This convinced her, *He doesn't care about me.*

After the historical roots of current family conflicts have been uncovered, interpretations are made about how family members continue to reenact past, and often distorted, images from childhood. The data for such interpretations come from transference reactions to the therapist or to other family members, as well as from actual childhood memories. Even more so than in individual therapy, psychoanalytic therapists who work with families deal less with recollections of the past than with reenactments of its influence, manifest as transference. For this reason it is considered essential to create and maintain a milieu in which patients feel safe enough to relive some of their crucial unresolved conflicts, and to reactivate their early relationship images.

The following case demonstrates how a therapist's permissive acceptance enables family members to gradually shed their outer defenses and to reveal their basic conflicts and object images, which provide the material for mutative interpretations.

The H.'s were a wealthy, highly educated family, who were concerned with their oldest child's listlessness, irritability, and poor performance in school. Despite the fact that the boy showed all the signs of a mild depressive episode, the therapist insisted on seeing the whole family.

In the first few sessions, the family was very polite and dignified, with each one playing a recognizable role. Alex, the identified patient, described his discouragement and lack of interest in school, while his parents expressed their concern, alternately supportively and critically. Alex's younger sister Susan, a lively and robust child, showed little concern for her brother, and generally spoke much more about her life outside the family than her brother did.

At first the family was so composed and collected that the therapist began to experience reality as they did: namely, that nothing was wrong in the family, except for Alex. After a time, the parents voiced a few disagreements about how to respond to Alex, but they quickly submerged them. Gradually, however, as they felt safer in therapy—safer than they did alone together at home—Mr. and Mrs. H. began to argue more and more openly. During this process the therapist made no interpretations, but concentrated her efforts on accepting the couple's arguing, while gently blocking their efforts to detour their conflict. Because they felt protected by the therapist, the spouses allowed the full fury of their feelings to be expressed, and their arguments became increasingly vituperative.

By uncovering the hidden conflict in the marriage, and blocking the scapegoating of the identified patient, the therapist was following the same course that most nonanalytic therapists would pursue. At this point, she did not simply stay with the couple's conflict, but instead began to explore their separate childhood histories. In short, having uncovered their conflict, she sought to trace its genetic sources.

What emerged from Mr. H.'s portrait of his childhood was a picture of a boy who had learned to appease his hypercritical mother by not openly challenging her. Moreover, since he did not expect much positive reaction from her, he generally avoided her company as much as possible.

For her part, Mrs. H. described her close relationship with a dominant mother and a lifelong disdain for her father, a man who was very successful professionally, but played only a marginal role in her upbringing.

Only after extensive exploration of these early object relations did the therapist begin to interpret the couple's conflictual behavior. Mr. H., she pointed out, believed that he had to mollify his wife (like his mother), but didn't expect any understanding or support from her, so he withdrew from her and lavished his affection on his children. In their early married years, Mrs. H. struck back in self-defense; she demanded that he spend more time with her, talk more, be more attentive. Eventually, however, she accepted his withdrawal (as she had seen her mother do with her father), and redirected her angry disappointments to her son. In short, these two apparently sophisticated adults were behaving, unconsciously, like children; he like a frightened child hiding from a harsh, critical mother, and she like a spoiled daughter hopelessly enraged at the lack of a relationship with her husband.

In this case the therapist analyzed and interpreted the unconscious object representations that played a large part in the family's conflict. In addition, her acceptance of the couple's loud arguments provided them with a tolerant superego figure to be incorporated in the holding environment. Psychoanalytic family therapists are aware that their influence is not confined to rational analysis, but also includes a kind of reparenting. Thus therapists may act in a more controlling or permissive fashion depending on their assessment of the particular needs of the family.

One psychoanalytic family therapist who was acutely aware of his personal influence on families was Nathan Ackerman. His recommendations on technique (Ackerman, 1966) were designed to penetrate family defenses in order to surface hidden conflicts over sex and aggression. To begin with, he advocated a deep personal commitment and involvement with families. His own style was intimate and provocative. Unlike the traditionally reserved and aloof analyst, Ackerman related to families in a very open and personal manner. In this regard he wrote (1961):

> It is very important at the outset to establish a meaningful emotional contact with all members of the family, to create a climate in which one really touches them and they feel they touch back. (p. 242)

After making contact, Ackerman encouraged open and honest expression of feeling by being open and honest himself. His spontaneous self-disclosure of his own thoughts and feelings made it hard for family members to resist doing likewise.

Ackerman certainly made full use of his warm and charismatic personality, but did more than simply "be himself" and "let it all hang out" in family sessions. He also made conscious and deliberate use of confrontive techniques to ease family secrets and conflicts from behind their defensive facades. His own memorable phrase to describe this was "tickling the defenses." Always aware of people's tendency to avoid what is painful or embarrassing, he teased, cajoled, and provoked family members to open up and say what was really on their minds.

Naturally, psychoanalytic family therapists emphasize that much of what is hidden in family dialogues is not consciously withheld, but rather repressed into unconsciousness. The approach to this material is guarded by resistance, and when it is manifest it is often in the form of transference. In fact, it is fair to say that the goal of any form of psychoanalytic psychotherapy is to overcome resistance and to work through the past in the transferences of the present.

Resistance is any conscious or unconscious behavior that blocks or impedes therapy. In families, resistance is collusive and more often manifest in overt behavior than it is in private therapy. Frank discussions of problems within the family are often painful, and most people go to great lengths to avoid them. Some of the common forms of resistance include seeking individual therapy or separate sessions to avoid facing family problems; persistently talking to the therapist instead of to other family members; avoiding conflictual topics; scapegoating; becoming depressed to avoid the danger of angry confrontations; and steadfastly refusing to consider one's own role in problematic interactions.

Most psychoanalytic family therapists deal with resistance by interpreting it early in its appearance. The family technique for interpreting resistance is different from that used in individual therapy. In individual therapy the aim is primarily to foster insight into the nature and meaning of resistance; therefore, resistances are generally not interpreted until they become obvious to the patient. Moreover, the most effective interpretations are elicited from the patient, rather than given by the therapist. For example, in individual psychotherapy a psychoanalytic therapist would wait for three or four recurrences before discussing a patient's lateness. Confronting lateness on its first occurrence is merely liable to make the patient defensive, and thus impede understanding of the reason he or she is tardy. After the lateness (or other form of resistance) has become a recognized pattern, the therapist will ask the patient to consider its meaning.

By contrast, family therapists interpret resistance more directly and sooner. The reason for this is that resistance in family therapy is more likely to take the form of acting-out, so that family therapists have to meet resistance with confrontation very early on. The following vignette illustrates the interpretation of resistance.

> Mr. and Mrs. Z. had endured ten years of an unrewarding marriage, with an unhappy sexual relationship, in order to preserve the fragile security that being married offered them. Mrs. Z.'s totally unexpected and uncharacteristic affair forced the couple to acknowledge the problems in their marriage, and so they consulted a family therapist.
>
> Although they could no longer deny the existence of conflict, both spouses exhibited major resistance to confronting their problems openly. Their resistance represented personal reluctance to acknowledge certain of their feelings, and a joint collusion to avoid frank discussions of their relational problems.
>
> In the first session, both partners said that married life had been "more or less okay"; that Mrs. Z. had some kind of "midlife crisis"; and that it was she who needed therapy. This request for individual therapy was seen as a resistance to avoid the painful examination of the marriage, and the therapist said so. "It seems, Mr. Z., that you'd rather blame your wife than consider how the two of you may both be contributing to your difficulties. And you, Mrs. Z., seem to prefer accepting all the guilt in order to avoid confronting your husband with your dissatisfaction and anger."
>
> Accepting the therapist's interpretation and agreeing to examine their marriage together deprived the couple of one form of resistance, as though an escape hatch had been closed to two reluctant combatants. In the next few sessions both spouses attacked each other vituperatively, but they talked only about her affair and his reactions rather than about problems in their relationship. These arguments were not productive because whenever Mr. Z. felt anxious he attacked his wife angrily, and whenever she felt angry she became depressed and guilty.
>
> Sensing that their fighting was unproductive, the therapist said, "It's clear that you've put each other through a lot of unhappiness and you're both quite bitter. But unless you get down to talking about specific problems in your marriage, there is little chance that you'll get anywhere."

Thus focused, Mrs. Z. timidly ventured that she'd never enjoyed sex with her husband, and wished that he would take more time with foreplay. He snapped back, "Okay, so sex wasn't so great, is that any reason to throw away ten years of marriage and start whoring around!" At this, Mrs. Z. buried her face in her hands and sobbed uncontrollably. After she regained her composure, the therapist intervened, again confronting the couple with their resistance: "It seems, Mr. Z., that when you get upset, you attack. What is it that makes you so anxious about discussing sex?" Following this the couple was able to talk about their feelings about sex in their marriage until near the end of the session. At this point, Mr. Z. again lashed out at his wife calling her a whore and a bitch.

Mrs. Z. began the following session by saying that she had been extremely depressed and upset, crying off and on all week. "I feel so guilty," she sobbed. "You *should* feel guilty!" retorted her husband. Once again, the therapist intervened. "You use your wife's affair as a club. Are you still afraid to discuss specific problems in the marriage? And you, Mrs. Z., cover your anger with depression. What is it that you're angry about? What was missing in the marriage? What did you want?"

This pattern continued for several more sessions. The spouses who had avoided discussing or even thinking about their problems for ten years used a variety of resistances to veer away from them in therapy. The therapist persisted in pointing out their resistance, and urged them to talk about specific complaints.

Psychoanalytic family therapists endeavor to foster insight and understanding; they also urge families to consider what they are going to do about the problems they discuss. This effort—part of the process of working through—is more prominent in family therapy than in individual therapy. Nagy, for example, considers that family members must not only be made aware of their motivations, but also held accountable for their behavior. In contextual therapy, Nagy (1987) points out that the therapist must help people face the intrinsically destructive expectations involved in invisible loyalties, and then help them find more positive ways of making loyalty payments in the family ledger. What this boils down to is developing a balance of fairness among various family members.

Ackerman too stressed an active working through of insights by encouraging families to constructively express the aggressive and libidinal impulses uncovered in therapy. In order to alleviate symptoms, impulses must become conscious; but an emotional experience must be associated with increased self-awareness in order for lives to change. To modify thinking and feeling is the essential task of psychoanalytic therapy, but family therapists are also concerned with supervising and analyzing changes in behavior.

EVALUATING THERAPY THEORY AND RESULTS

Too many family therapists neglect psychoanalytic theory in general and psychoanalytic family therapy in specific. Regardless of what other approaches a therapist uses, the writings of psychoanalytically informed clinicians are a rich resource. Every therapist would profit from knowing something about self psychology and object relations theory (the latter may be more intellectually stimulating, but the former may be more useful clinically).

Having said this, however, we also wish to make a cautionary point. Doctrinaire psychoanalytic family therapies are powerful in the hands of trained psychoanalysts. However, many family therapists who get discouraged with the usual contentious family dialogues, gravitate to psychoanalytic methods as a way to break through the defensive wrangling that some families can't seem to get past. Interrupting a family's arguments to explore the feelings of individual family members is an excellent way to block defensive squabbling. But if therapists make themselves overly central (by directing all conversation through themselves) and if they overemphasize individuals and neglect family interactions, then the power of family therapy—addressing relationship problems directly at their source—may be lost. Interrupting defensive sparring to get to the authentic feelings and hopes and fears that lie beneath the usual arguments is all to the good. But unless these interrogatories are followed by extensive and free-flowing interchanges among family members themselves, these explorations may only produce the illusion of change as long as the therapist is present to act as detective and referee.

Psychoanalytic therapists have generally been opposed to attempts to evaluate their work using empirical standards. Since symptom reduction is not the goal, it cannot serve as the measure of success. And since the presence or absence of unconscious conflict is not apparent to family members or outside observers, whether or not an analysis can be considered successful has to depend on the subjective clinical judgment of the therapist. Psychoanalytic clinicians, of course, consider that the therapist's observations are entirely valid as a means of evaluating theory and treatment. The following quotation from the Blancks (1972) illustrates this point. Speaking of Margaret Mahler's ideas, they wrote,

> Clinicians who employ her theories technically question neither the methodology nor the findings, for they can confirm them clinically, a form of validation that meets as closely as possible the experimentalist's insistence upon replication as criterion of the scientific method. (p. 675)

Another example of this point of view can be found in the writing of Robert Langs. "The ultimate test of a therapist's formulation," says Langs (1982), "lies in the use of the therapist's impressions as a basis for intervention" (p. 186). What then determines the validity and effectiveness of these interventions? Langs does not hesitate; the patient's reactions, conscious and unconscious, constitute the ultimate litmus test. "True validation involves responses from the patient in both the cognitive and interpersonal spheres."

Is the ultimate test of therapy then the patient's reactions? Yes and no. First, the patient's reactions themselves are open to various interpretations—especially since validation is sought not only in direct manifest responses but also in unconsciously encoded derivatives. Moreover, this point of view does not take into account the changes in patients' lives that occur outside the office or consulting room. Occasionally therapists report on the outcome of psychoanalytic family therapy, but mostly as an uncontrolled case study. One such unsubstantiated report is Dicks's (1967) survey of the outcome of psychoanalytic couples therapy at the Tavistock Clinic, in which he rated as having successfully treated 72.8 percent of a random sample of cases.

SUMMARY

Psychoanalytically trained clinicians were among the first to practice family therapy. However, when they began treating families, most of them traded in their ideas about depth psychology for those of systems theory. The result was most often an eclectic mix of psychoanalytic and systems concepts, rather than a true integration.

Since the mid 1980s, there has been a resurgence of interest in psychodynamics among family therapists, an interest dominated by object relations theory and self psychology. In this chapter we have sketched the main points of these theories, and shown how they are relevant to a psychoanalytic family therapy which integrates depth psychology and systems theory. A few practitioners (e.g., Kirschner & Kirschner, 1986; Nichols, 1987; Slipp, 1984) have combined elements of both; some have developed more frankly psychoanalytic approaches (notably Scharff & Scharff, 1987; Sander, 1989); none has achieved a true synthesis.

REFERENCES

Ackerman, N. W. 1958. *The psychodynamics of family life.* New York: Basic Books.

Ackerman, N. W. 1961. The emergence of family psychotherapy on the present scene. In *Contemporary psychotherapies,* M. I. Stein, ed. Glencoe, IL: The Free Press.

Ackerman, N. W. 1966. *Treating the troubled family.* New York: Basic Books.

Bank, S., and Kahn, M. D. 1982. *The sibling bond.* New York: Basic Books.

Barnhill, L. R., and Longo, D. 1978. Fixation and regression in the family life cycle. *Family Process. 17:*469–478.

Bentovim, A., and Kinston, W. 1991. Focal family therapy. In *Handbook of family therapy.* vol. II, A. S. Gurman and D. P. Kniskern, eds. New York: Brunner/Mazel.

Bibring, E. 1954. Psychoanalysis and the dynamic psychotherapies. *Journal of the American Psychoanalytic Association.* 2:745–770.

Blanck, G., and Blanck, R. 1972. Toward a psychoanalytic developmental psychology. *Journal of the American Psychoanalytic Association. 20:*668–710.

Blanck, R. 1967. Marriage as a phase of personality development. *Social Casework. 48:*154–160.

Blum, H. P. 1987. Shared fantasy and reciprocal identification: General considerations and gender disorder. In *Unconscious fantasy: Myth and reality,* H. P. Blum et al., eds. New York: International Universities Press.

Boszormenyi-Nagy I. 1967. Relational modes and meaning. In *Family therapy and disturbed families,* G. H. Zuk and I. Boszormenyi-Nagy, eds. Palo Alto: Science and Behavior Books.

Boszormenyi-Nagy, I. 1972. Loyalty implications of the transference model in psychotherapy. *Archives of General Psychiatry.* 27:374–380.

Boszormenyi-Nagy, I. 1987. *Foundations of contextual therapy.* New York: Brunner/Mazel.

Boszormenyi-Nagy, I., and Framo, J., eds. 1965. *Intensive family therapy: Theoretical and practical aspects.* New York: Harper & Row.

Boszormenyi-Nagy, I., and Spark, G. 1973. *Invisible loyalties: Reciprocity in intergenerational family therapy.* New York: Harper & Row.

Boszormenyi-Nagy, I. and Ulrich, D. N. 1981. Contextual family therapy. In *Handbook of family therapy,* A. S. Gurman and D. P. Kniskern, eds. New York: Brunner/Mazel.

Boszormenyi-Nagy, I. Grunebaum, J., and Ulrich, D. 1991. Contextural therapy. In *Handbook of family therapy.* vol. II, A. S. Gurman and D. P. Kniskern, eds. New York: Brunner/Mazel.

Bowen, M., Dysinger, R. H., and Basamania, B. 1959. The role of the father in families with a schizophrenic patient. *American Journal of Psychiatry.* 115:1017–1020.

Bowen, M. 1965. Family psychotherapy with schizophrenia in the hospital and in private practice. In *Intensive family therapy,* I. Boszormenyi-Nagy and J. L. Framo, eds. New York: Harper & Row.

Bowen, M. 1966. The use of family therapy in clinical practice. *Comprehensive Psychiatry.* 7:345–374.

Bowlby, J. 1949. The study and reduction of group tension in the family. *Human Relations.* 2:123–128.

Bowlby, J. 1969. *Attachment and loss.* vol. 1: *Attachment.* New York: Basic Books.

Broderick, C. B., and Schrader, S. S. 1981. The history of professional marriage and family therapy. In *Handbook of family therapy,* A. S. Gurman and D. P. Kniskern, eds. New York: Brunner/Mazel.

Bruch, H. 1978. *The golden cage.* Cambridge, MA: Harvard University Press.

Burlingham, D. T. 1951. Present trends in handling the mother-child relationship during the therapeutic process. *Psychoanalytic study of the child.* New York: International Universities Press.

Dare, C. 1979. Psychoanalysis and systems in family therapy. *Journal of Family Therapy.* 1:137–151.

Dicks, H. V. 1963. Object relations theory and marital studies. *British Journal of Medical Psychology.* 36:125–129.

Dicks, H. V. 1967. *Marital tensions.* New York: Basic Books.

Dostoyevsky, F. 1958. *The Brothers Karamazov.* New York: Penguin Books.

Erikson, E. H. 1956. The problem of ego identity. *Journal of the American Psychoanalytic Association.* 4:56–121.

Erikson, E. H. 1959. Identity and the life cycle. *Psychological Issues.* 1:1–171.

Erikson, E. H. 1963. *Childhood and society.* New York: Norton.

Fairbairn, W. D. 1952. *An object-relations theory of the personality.* New York: Basic Books.

Fenichel, O. 1945. *The psychoanalytic theory of neurosis.* New York: Norton.

Ferreira, A. 1936. Family myths and homeostasis. *Archives of General Psychiatry.* 9:457–463.

Flugel, J. 1921. *The psychoanalytic study of the family.* London: Hogarth Press.

Framo, J. L. 1970. Symptoms from a family transactional viewpoint. In *Family therapy in transition,* N. W. Ackerman, ed. Boston: Little, Brown.

Freud, S. 1905. Fragment of an analysis of a case of hysteria. *Collected papers.* New York: Basic Books, 1959.

Freud, S. 1909. Analysis of a phobia in a five-year-old boy. *Collected papers,* vol. III. New York: Basic Books, 1959.

Freud, S. 1921. Group psychology and the analysis of the ego. *Standard edition,* 17:1–22. London: Hogarth Press, 1955.

Freud, S. 1923. The ego and the id. *Standard edition.* 19:13–66. London: Hogarth Press, 1961.

Friedman, L. 1980. Integrating psychoanalytic object relations understanding with family systems interventions in couples therapy. In *Family therapy: Combining psychodynamic and family systems approaches,* J. Pearce and L. Friedman, eds. New York: Grune & Stratton.

Giovacchini, P. 1958. Mutual adaptation in various object relations. *International Journal of Psychoanalysis. 39*:547–554.

Giovacchini, P. 1961. Resistance and external object relations. *International Journal of Psychoanalysis. 42*:246–254.

Greenson, R. R. 1967. *The theory and technique of psychoanalysis.* New York: International Universities Press.

Guntrip, H. 1961. *Personality structure and human interaction.* London: Hogarth Press.

Guntrip, H. 1969. *Schizoid phenomena, object relations theory and the self.* New York: International Universities Press.

Guntrip, H. 1971. *Psychoanalytic theory, therapy, and the self.* New York: Basic Books.

Gurman, A. 1981. Integrative marital therapy. In *Forms of brief therapy,* S. Budman, ed. New York: Guilford Press.

Jackson, D. D. 1967. The individual and the larger context. *Family Process. 6*:139–147.

Jacobson, E. 1964. *The self and the object world.* New York: International Universities Press.

Johnson, A., and Szurek, S. 1952. The genesis of antisocial acting out in children and adults. *Psychoanalytic Quarterly. 21*:323–343.

Kahn, M. D., and Lewis, K. G., eds. 1988. *Siblings in therapy: Life span and clinical issues.* New York: Norton.

Katz, B. 1981. Separation-individuation and marital therapy. *Psychotherapy: Theory, Research and Practice. 18*:195–203.

Kernberg, O. F. 1966. Structural derivatives of object relationships. *International Journal of Psychoanalysis. 47*:236–253.

Kernberg, O. F. 1975. Countertransference. In *Borderline conditions and pathological narcissism,* O. F. Kernberg, ed. New York: Jason Aronson.

Kernberg, O. F. 1976. *Object-relations theory and clinical psychoanalysis.* New York: Jason Aronson.

Kirschner, D., and Kirschner, S. 1986. *Comprehensive family therapy: An integration of systemic and psychodynamic treatment models.* New York: Brunner/Mazel.

Klein, M. 1946. Notes on some schizoid mechanisms. *International Journal of Psycho-Analysis. 27*:99–110.

Kohut, H. 1971. *The analysis of the self.* New York: International Universities Press.

Kohut, H. 1977. *The restoration of the self.* New York: International Universities Press.

Langs, R. 1982. *Psychotherapy: A basic text.* New York: Jason Aronson.

Lasch, C. 1978. *The culture of narcissism.* New York: Norton.

Levinson, D. J. 1978. *The seasons of a man's life.* New York: Ballantine Books.

Lidz, T., Cornelison, A., Fleck, S. 1965. *Schizophrenia and the family.* New York: International Universities Press.

Lidz, T., Cornelison, A., Fleck, S., and Terry, D. 1957. The intrafamilial environment of schizophrenia patients; II: Marital schism and marital skew. *American Journal of Psychiatry. 114*:241–248.

Mahler, M. S. 1952. On child psychosis and schizophrenia: Autistic and symbiotic infantile psychoses. *Psychoanalytic Study of the Child,* vol. 7.

Mahler, M., Pine, F., and Bergman, A. 1975. *The psychological birth of the human infant.* New York: Basic Books.

Martin, P. A., and Bird, H. W. 1953. An approach to the psychotherapy of marriage partners. *Psychiatry. 16*:123–127.

Masterson, J. F. 1977. Primary anorexia nervosa in the borderline adolescent and object-relations view. In *Borderline personality disorders: The concept, the syndrome, the patient,* P. Hartocollis, ed. New York: International Universities Press.

Meissner, W. W. 1978. The conceptualization of marriage and family dynamics from a psychoanalytic perspective. In *Marriage and marital therapy*, T. J. Paolino and B. S. McCrady, eds. New York: Brunner/Mazel.

Minuchin, S. 1974. *Families and family therapy*. Cambridge, MA: Harvard University Press.

Minuchin, S. 1989. Personal communication. Quoted from *Institutionalizing madness*, J. Elizur and S. Minuchin, eds. New York: Basic Books.

Mittlemann, B. 1948. The counterpart analysis of married couples. *Psychoanalytic Quarterly*. 17:182–197.

Modell, A. H. 1968. *Object love and reality*. New York: International Universities Press.

Nadelson, C. C. 1978. Marital therapy from a psychoanalytic perspective. In *Marriage and marital therapy*, T. J. Paolino and B. S. McCrady, eds. New York: Brunner/Mazel.

Nichols, M. P. 1986. *Turning forty in the eighties*. New York: Norton.

Nichols, M. P. 1987. *The self in the system*. New York: Brunner/Mazel.

Oberndorf, C. P. 1938. Psychoanalysis of married couples. *Psychoanalytic Review*. 25:453–475.

Ryckoff, I., Day, J., and Wynne, L. 1959. Maintenance of stereotyped roles in the families of schizophrenics. *AMA Archives of Psychiatry*. 1:93–98.

Sager, C. J. 1981. Couples therapy and marriage contracts. In *Handbook of family therapy*, A. S. Gurman and D. P. Kniskern, eds. New York: Brunner/Mazel.

Sander, F. M. 1979. *Individual and family therapy: Toward an integration*. New York: Jason Aronson.

Sander, F. M. 1989. Marital conflict and psychoanalytic therapy in the middle years. In *The middle years: New psychoanalytic perspectives*, J. Oldham and R. Liebert, eds. New Haven: Yale University Press.

Scharff, D., and Scharff, J. 1987. *Object relations family therapy*. New York: Jason Aronson.

Scharff, J., ed. 1989. *The foundations of object relations family therapy*. New York: Jason Aronson.

Segal, H. 1964. *Introduction to the work of Melanie Klein*. New York: Basic Books.

Shapiro, R. L. 1968. Action and family interaction in adolescence. In *Modern psychoanalysis*, J. Marmor, ed. New York: Basic Books.

Shapiro, R. L. 1979. Family dynamics and object relations theory. In *Adolescent psychiatry*, S. C. Feinstein and P. L. Giovacchini, eds. Chicago: University of Chicago Press.

Sifneos, P. E. 1972. *Short-term psychotherapy and emotional crisis*. Cambridge, MA: Harvard University Press.

Skynner, A. C. R. 1976. *Systems of family and marital psychotherapy*. New York: Brunner/Mazel.

Skynner, A. C. R. 1981. An open-systems, group analytic approach to family therapy. In *Handbook of family therapy*, A. S. Gurman and D. P. Kniskern, eds. New York: Brunner/Mazel.

Slipp, S. 1984. *Object relations: A dynamic bridge between individual and family treatment*. New York: Jason Aronson.

Slipp, S. 1988. *Technique and practice of object relations family therapy*. New York: Jason Aronson.

Spitz, R. E. 1965. *The first year of life*. New York: International Universities Press.

Spitz, R., and Wolf, K. 1946. Anaclitic depression: An inquiry into the genesis of psychiatric conditions early in childhood. *Psychoanalytic Study of the Child*. 2:313–342.

Stein, M. 1956. The marriage bond. *Psychoanalytic Quarterly*. 25:238–259.

Stern, D. N. 1985. *The interpersonal world of the infant*. New York: Basic Books.

Stierlin, H. 1977. *Psychoanalysis and family therapy.* New York: Jason Aronson.

Sullivan, H. S. 1953. *The interpersonal theory of psychiatry.* New York: Norton.

Szasz, T. S. 1961. *The myth of mental illness.* New York: Hoeber-Harper.

Umana, R. F., Gross, S. J., and McConville, M. T. 1980. *Crisis in the family: Three approaches.* New York: Gardner Press.

Vogel, E. F., and Bell, N. W. 1960. The emotionally disturbed as the family scapegoat. In *The family,* N. W. Bell and E. F. Vogel, eds. Glencoe, IL: Free Press.

Winnicott, D. W. 1965a. *The maturational process and the facilitating environment.* New York: International Universities Press.

Winnicott, D. W. 1965b. *The maturational process and the facilitating environment: Studies in the theory of emotional development.* New York: International Universities Press.

Wynne, L. C. 1965. Some indications and contradictions for exploratory family therapy. In *Intensive family therapy,* I. Boszormenyi-Nagy and J. L. Framo, eds. New York: Harper & Row.

Wynne, L. C. 1971. Some guidelines for exploratory family therapy. In *Changing families,* J. Haley, ed. New York: Grune & Stratton.

Wynne, L., Ryckoff, I., Day, J., and Hirsch, S. 1958. Pseudomutuality in the family relations of schizophrenics. *Psychiatry.* 21:205–220.

Zinner, J. 1976. The implications of projective identification for marital interaction. In *Contemporary marriage: Structure, dynamics, and therapy,* H. Grunebaum and J. Christ, eds, Boston: Little, Brown.

Zinner, J., and Shapiro, R. 1976. Projective identification as a mode of perception and behavior in families of adolescents. *International Journal of Psychoanalysis.* 53:523–530.

Experiential Family Therapy

An experiential branch of family therapy emerged from the humanistic psychology of the 1960s that, like the individual humanistic therapies, emphasized immediate, *here-and-now* experience. The quality of ongoing experience was both the criterion of psychological health and the focus of therapeutic interventions. Experiential family therapists consider feeling-expression to be the medium of shared experience and the means to personal and family fulfillment.

Experiential therapy was most popular when family therapy was young, when therapists talked about systems change, but borrowed their techniques from individual and group therapies. Experiential family therapists drew heavily from Gestalt therapy and encounter groups. Other expressive techniques, such as *sculpting* and *family drawing,* bore the influence of the arts and of psychodrama. Because experiential treatment emphasizes sensitivity and feeling-expression, it wasn't as well suited to family therapy as were approaches that deal with systems and action; consequently, the experiential approach has lately been used less and some of its early exponents, such as Peggy Papp, have adopted systems concepts and methods. Nevertheless, the approach remains vital in the hands of such people as Carl Whitaker, followers of the late Virginia Satir, Walter Kempler, August Napier, David Keith, Leslie Greenberg and Susan Johnson, and Fred and Bunny Duhl; they and other experiential family therapists have introduced a number of expressive techniques that any family therapist may find useful.

SKETCHES OF LEADING FIGURES

Two giants stand out as leaders of experiential family therapy: Carl Whitaker and Virginia Satir. Whitaker is the dean of experiential family therapy, the leading exponent of a freewheeling, intuitive approach aimed to puncture pretense and liberate family members to be themselves. He was among the first in the field to do psychotherapy with families, and he has steadily grown in stature to become one of the most admired therapists in family therapy. Iconoclastic, even outrageous at times, Whitaker has, nevertheless, retained the respect and admiration of the family therapy establishment. He may be their Puck, but he's one of them.

Carl Whitaker grew up on an isolated dairy farm in Raymondville, New York. Rural isolation may have bred shyness and a touch of sadness, but, perhaps, also conditioned Whitaker to be less hemmed in than most of us by social convention. After college in Syracuse and medical school and a residency in obstetrics and gynecology, Whitaker went into psychiatry where he immediately became fascinated by the psychotic mind. Unfortunately—or fortunately—back in the 1940s Whitaker couldn't rely on neuroleptic drugs to blunt the hallucinatory fantasies of his patients; instead he listened and learned to understand thoughts crazy but human, thoughts that the rest of us keep buried.

After working at the University of Louisville College of Medicine and the Oakridge Hospital, Dr. Whitaker accepted the chairmanship of Emory University's Department of Psychiatry, where he remained from 1946 to 1955, building a first-rate program. In the face of mounting pressure to make the department more psychoanalytic, Whitaker and his entire faculty finally resigned to form the Atlanta Psychiatric Clinic, a productive and creative group, including Thomas Malone, John Warkentin, and Richard Felder. Experiential psychotherapy was born of this union, and the group produced a number of highly provocative and challenging papers (Whitaker & Malone, 1953). In 1965 Whitaker went to the University of Wisconsin Medical School, and also conducted a private practice in Madison. Since his retirement in the late 1980s, Whitaker has traveled frequently to share his wisdom, experience, and himself at conventions and workshops. Among Whitaker's most well-known associates are August Napier, now in private practice in Atlanta, and David Keith, now at the State University of New York in Syracuse.

The other major charismatic figure among experiential family therapists was the late Virginia Satir. Satir, who was one of the well-known members of the early MRI group in Palo Alto, emphasized communication as well as emotional experiencing, and so her work must be considered in both the communications and experiential traditions.

Social worker Virginia Satir began seeing families in private practice in 1951. In 1955 she was invited to set up a training program for residents at the Illinois State Psychiatric Institute. (One of her students was Ivan Boszormenyi-Nagy.) In 1959 Don Jackson invited Satir to join him at MRI, where she became the first director of training and remained until she left MRI in 1966 to become the director of Esalen Institute in Big Sur, California.

Satir was the prototypical nurturing therapist in a field enamored with experience-distant concepts and tricky strategic maneuvers. Her warmth and genuineness gave her a tremendous appeal and impact as she traveled all over the country leading demonstrations and workshops. Her ability to move large audiences in experiential exercises made her a legend as family therapy's most celebrated humanist.

In the 1970s Satir's influence waned and she received less recognition than she deserved as one of the innovators of family therapy. This was very painful for her. In Venezuela, in 1974, at a *Family Process* board meeting there was a debate between Salvador Minuchin and Satir about the nature of family therapy. Minuchin argued that it was a science that required skills rather than just warmth and faith, and that the main job was to fix broken families; Satir stuck to her belief in the healing power of love, and spoke out for the salvation for humankind through family therapy. It turned out that Minuchin was speaking for the field, and Satir felt out of step. After this she drifted away from the family therapy establishment and, instead, became a world traveler and spokesperson for her evangelical approach. Satir died of pancreatic cancer in 1988.

Another Californian who has written a great deal about experiential family therapy is Walter Kempler, who brings many of the ideas and techniques of Gestalt and other emotive therapies to his work with families. He describes procedures commonly found in encounter groups and existential-humanistic individual therapies, which demonstrate the roots of experiential family therapy.

Fred and Bunny Duhl, former codirectors of the Boston Family Institute, have introduced a number of expressive techniques into experiential family therapy. They use nonverbal means of communication, such as *spatialization* and *sculpting* (Duhl, Kantor, & Duhl, 1973), as well as *roleplaying* and *family puppets* (Duhl & Duhl, 1981). Their approach, which they call "integrative family therapy," is an amalgam of elements from numerous sources, including psychodrama, experiential psychotherapy, cognitive psychology, structural family therapy, and behavioral psychotherapy. The Duhls are included in this chapter because of their technical contributions, rather than because their work fits neatly into this, or any other, conceptual scheme.

Cofounder of the Boston Family Institute in 1969, along with Fred Duhl, was David Kantor, who brought with him a background in psychodrama and helped emphasize the "family as theater" metaphor in family therapy (Kantor & Lehr, 1975).

Among the most recent experiential approaches to family therapy is the "emotion-focused couples therapy" of Leslie Greenberg and Susan Johnson, which draws on Perls, Satir, and the MRI group (Greenberg & Johnson, 1985, 1986, 1988).

We group such unclassifiable individualists as Virginia Satir and Carl Whitaker together in this chapter because they are united by their investment in spontaneity, creativity, and risk-taking. While they share a commitment to freedom, individuality, and personal fulfillment, experientialists are otherwise relatively atheoretical. The hallmark of this approach is the use of techniques to open individuals to their inner experience and to unfreeze family interactions. Having reached their greatest popularity in the 1960s (Nichols & Zax, 1977), experiential approaches have been largely displaced by new developments in more systems-oriented therapies. Once feeling expression occupied center stage in psychological therapies; today that place is held by behavior and cognition. Psychotherapists have discovered that people think and act; but that doesn't mean we should ignore the immediate emotional experience that is the main concern of experiential family therapy.

THEORETICAL FORMULATIONS ——————————————

Carl Whitaker may have best expressed the experientialists' position on theory in his "The Hindrance of Theory in Clinical Work" (Whitaker, 1976a). In this article Whitaker described what he considered the chilling effect of theory on intuition and creativity in psychotherapy. Theory may be useful for beginners, Whitaker says, but his advice is to give up theory as soon as possible in favor of just being yourself. He quotes Paul Tillich's existential aphorism, "being is becoming," to support his own contention that psychotherapy requires openness and spontaneity, not theory and technique; and he cites the fact that technical approaches usually don't work for second-generation therapists (as many people found out when they tried to imitate the "simple" steps of Minuchin's structural family therapy). Perhaps we hamper our own creative efforts by trying to copy our mentors. Although Whitaker doesn't make this point, it may also be that the theories of clinical innovators are only secondary elaborations—afterthoughts and rationalizations—of intuitive methods that express their own personal styles.

Whitaker says that therapists who base their work on theory are likely to substitute dispassionate technology for caring, and goes on to imply that theory is a refuge from the anxiety-provoking experience of sharing a family's life stress. Instead of having the courage just to "be" with families and help them grapple with their problems, theoretically inclined clinicians use theory to create distance in the name of objectivity.

Most people consider psychotherapy to be a mixture of art and science; for experiential therapists, art is 90 percent, science 10 percent. The search for theory, according to this viewpoint, arises from an attempt to escape the tension and anxiety of being openly empathic with unhappy families. Whitaker says therapists don't need theories to handle stress and anxiety; what they need are supportive cotherapists and helpful supervisors. In short, it isn't technique, but personal involvement that enables therapists to do their best. By avoiding theory, Whitaker believes that he forces families to establish their own theoretical way of living. David Keith (1988) echoes this conviction, saying that he often leaves families stewing in ambiguity rather than oversimplifying life by pointing them in a particular direction. This is a therapeutic pattern modeled after benevolent parenting, which carries a deep respect for people's ability to discover their own directions in life.

No theory is, of course, itself a theory. To say that therapy shouldn't be constrained by theory is to say that it should be loose, creative, open, and spontaneous. Therapists should share feelings, fantasies, and personal stories, if that's what they feel like doing, and if that's what it takes to help families become more aware and sensitive. Despite Whitaker's disdain for theory, however, experiential family therapy is very much a child of the existential, humanistic, and phenomenological tradition.

Philosophers like Edmund Husserl and Martin Heidegger (1963) began to work out the implications for clinical practice contained in existential thought. Their ideas were assimilated and developed by Ludwig Binswanger (1967) who formulated a new theory of psychotherapeutic process, but remained tied to the psychoanalytic method. The same may be said of Medard Boss (1963), the developer of "Daseinanalysis," which also differed from psychoanalysis more in theory than in practice. Much of the theorizing of these existential psychologists was in reaction to perceived shortcomings of psychoanalysis and behaviorism. In place of *determinism,* the existentialists emphasized *freedom* and the necessity to discover the essence of one's *individuality* in the immediacy of experience. Instead of being pushed by the past, they saw people as pulled toward the future, impelled by their *values* and *personal goals.* Where psychoanalysts posited a structuralized model of the mind, existentialists treated persons as wholes. Finally, existentialists substituted a positive model of humanity for what they believed was an unduly pessimistic psychoanalytic model. They believed that people should aim at personal fulfillment, rather than settle for partial resolution of their neuroses.

These new ideas—which Maslow (1968) called the "Third Force Psychology"—were translated into practice by Victor Frankl, Charlotte Buhler, Fritz Perls, Rollo May, Carl Rogers, Eugene Gendlin, Sidney Jourard, R. D. Laing, Carl Whitaker, and others. The most influential of these approaches were Frankl's (1963) *Logotherapy,* Perls's (1961) *Gestalt Therapy,* Rogers's (1951) *Client-Centered Therapy,* and Gendlin's (1962) *Experiencing.* Incidentally, it was probably Whitaker and Malone (1953) who first used the term "experiential psychotherapy."

The conceptual writings of experiential psychotherapists generally consist of a series of loosely connected constructs and statements of position. Most of them are melioristic, and often the language is more colorful and stagy than clear and precise. Take, for instance, the following sample from Whitaker and Keith (1981).

> Metacommunication is considered to be an experiential process, an offer of participation that implies the clear freedom to return to an established role security rather than be caught in the "as if" tongue-in-cheek microtheater. That trap is the context that pushes son into stealing cars or daughter into incest with father while mother plays the madame. The whimsy and creativity of the family can even be exaggerated to where family subgroups or individuals are free to be nonrational or crazy. (p. 190)

According to Virginia Satir (1972), "So many of the words professional people use to talk about human beings sound sterile and lack life-and-breath images," (p. 21) that she preferred folksy and concrete images. Consequently much of the writing done by experientialists is more evocative than elucidative.

Despite the paucity of elegant theoretical statements, there are a number of basic theoretical premises that define the experiential position on families and their treatment—a basic commitment to individual awareness, expression, and self-fulfillment. Whitaker emphasizes that self-fulfillment depends upon family cohesiveness, and Satir stressed the importance of good communication with other family members; but the basic commitment seems to be to individual growth. Moreover, while there was some talk about family systems (Satir, 1972), the early experiential model of families was more like a democratic group than a system with structure and a hierarchy. (This is less true of more recent work by Whitaker and the highly sophisticated efforts of Gus Napier and David Keith.) Still there is great emphasis on flexibility and freedom with respect to family roles and the distribution of power. Roles are thought to be reciprocal. If one spouse is a quiet, private person, the other is apt to be sociable and outgoing. Treatment is generally designed to help individual family members find fulfilling roles for themselves, without an overriding concern for the needs of the family as a whole. This is not to say that the needs of the family system are denigrated, but they're thought to follow automatically on the heels of individual growth. At times the family was even portrayed as the enemy of individual freedom and authenticity (Laing & Esterson, 1970).

After reading the previous paragraph, David Keith (in a personal letter) helped put into perspective the experiential position about the claims of the individual versus the claims of the family, as follows:

> Our thinking is individually focused to the extent that I am very clear that I am the only one inside my skin. No one knows how I feel or how I think. Likewise I am unable to know how anyone else feels or thinks. There is a dialectical tension between the individual and the family—between dependence and independence. To overemphasize either individuality or family connectedness is to distort the human condition. This tension is transcended only by experience, not by thinking or theory. One of my basic assumptions in working with families is that, for better or worse, the family is in charge of itself. A corollary to that idea is that I am suspicious of families in that I know that families will sacrifice members in order to preserve the whole, or to shield certain members.

Theories of families as systems are translated into techniques that facilitate communication and interaction. The emphasis on altering interactions implies an acceptance of whatever level of individual experience and understanding is already present. This is where experiential theory differs (as does psychoanalytic theory) from most systems approaches. Here the emphasis is on expanding experience. The assumption is that such expansion on the individual level is prerequisite to breaking new ground for the family group, and the consequent new material and increased awareness will, almost automatically, stimulate increased communication and sharing of feelings among family members. Families will talk more when their members become more aware of what they have to say.

Underlying much of the work of experiential family therapy is the premise, seldom mentioned, that the best way to promote individual and family growth is to liberate affects and impulses. Efforts to reduce defensiveness and unlock deeper levels of experiencing rest on this basic assumption.

NORMAL FAMILY DEVELOPMENT

Experiential family therapists subscribe to the humanistic faith in the natural goodness and wisdom of unacculturated human feelings and drives. Left alone, people tend to flourish, according to this point of view. Problems arise because this innate tendency toward *self-actualization* (Rogers, 1951) runs afoul of social (Marcuse, 1955) and familial (Laing & Esterson, 1970) counterpressures. Society enforces repression in order to tame people's instincts to make them fit for productive group living. Unhappily, socially required self-control is achieved at the cost of "surplus repression" (Marcuse, 1955) and emotional devitalization. Families add their own additional controls to achieve peace and quiet, perpetuating outmoded *family myths* (Gehrke & Kirschenbaum, 1967) and using *mystification* (Laing, 1967) to alienate children from their experience.

In the ideal situation, these controls aren't excessive, and children grow up in an atmosphere of support for their feelings and creative impulses. Parents listen to their children, accept their feelings, and validate their experience, which helps the children develop healthy channels for expressing their emotions and drives. Affect is valued and nurtured; children are encouraged to experience things passionately and to express the full range of human emotions (Pierce, Nichols, & DuBrin, 1983).

Mental health is viewed as a continuous process of growth and change, not a static or homeostatic state. "The healthy family is one that continues to grow in spite of whatever troubles come its way" (Whitaker & Keith, 1981, p. 190). Furthermore, the healthy family deals with stress by pooling its resources and sharing problems, not dumping them all on one family member.

Experiential therapists describe the normal family as one which supports individual growth and experience. In so doing, clinicians may unwittingly foster a dichotomy between the individual and the family: "bad" families repress people, "good" ones leave them alone. Neither Carl Whitaker nor Virginia Satir falls into this trap, although Whitaker seems ambivalent about accepting the necessity for an organized family structure. At times he speaks of the need for hierarchy and generational boundaries, while at other times he emphasizes creative flexibility. The following quotation (Whitaker & Keith, 1981) shows his vacillation on this point.

> The healthy family maintains a separation of the generations. Mother and father are not children and the children are not parents. The two generations function in these two separate role categories. Members of the same generation have equal rank. However, there is a massive freedom of choice in periodic role selection and each role is available to any member. Father can be a five-year-old, mother can be a three-year-old, the three-year-old can be a father, the father can be a mother, depending upon the situation, with each family member protected by an implicit "as if" clause. (p. 190)

In any case, Whitaker sees the family as an integrated whole, not a confederation of separate individuals. Other experientialists often seem to think of the whole as less than the sum of its parts. Kempler (1981), for example, emphasizes *personal responsibility,* which he defines as each person maximizing his or her own potential. Some call this narcissism (Lasch, 1978), but experientialists assume that enhanced personal commitment automatically leads to greater commitment to others.

Satir (1972) described the normal family as one that nurtures its members. Individual family members listen to and are considerate of each other, enabling them to feel valued and loved. Affection is freely given and received. Moreover, family members are open and candid with each other. "*Anything* can be talked about—the disappointments, fears, hurts, angers, criticisms as well as the joys and achievements" (Satir, 1972, p. 14).

Satir also considered flexibility and constructive problem-solving as characteristic of a healthy family. Nurturing parents, she says, realize that change is inevitable; they accept it and try to use it creatively. Her description of the "nurturing family" brings to mind the world portrayed by Norman Rockwell on the covers of *The Saturday Evening Post:* warm and pleasant, but not quite true to life. Perhaps Satir's (1972) idealized version of family life is better taken as a prescription for, rather than a description of, healthy family living.

In general, experiential family therapists describe the family as a place of sharing experience. The functional family supports and encourages a wide range of experiencing; the dysfunctional family resists awareness and blunts responsiveness. The vitality of each person's individual experience is the ultimate measure of sanity. Healthy people accept the truth and richness of their experience in each moment. This enables them to stand up for who they are and what they want—and to accept the same from others. Functional families are secure enough to be passionate; dysfunctional families are frightened and bloodless. Neither problem-solving skills nor particular family structures are considered to be nearly as important as expanding open, natural, and spontaneous experiencing. The healthy family offers its members the freedom to be themselves, and supports privacy as well as togetherness.

DEVELOPMENT OF BEHAVIOR DISORDERS

From the experiential perspective, denial of impulses and suppression of feelings are the root of family problems. Dysfunctional families are rigidly locked into self-protection and avoidance (Kaplan & Kaplan, 1978). In Sullivan's (1953) terms, they seek *security,* not *satisfaction.* They're too busy trying not to lose to ever dare to win.

Such families function automatically and mechanically, rather than through awareness and choice. Their presenting complaints are many, but the basic problem is that they smother emotion and desire. Laing (1967) described this as the *mystification* of experience, and he held parents responsible. Parents are, of course, not the villains. The process is circular. Kempler (1981) also speaks of family pressure for loyalty and cohesion as interfering with individuals' loyalties to themselves. The untested premise in these unhappy families is that assertiveness or confrontation would lead to emotional chaos. The sad result is that feelings are never acknowledged.

According to Whitaker (Whitaker & Keith, 1981), there's no such thing as a marriage—merely two scapegoats sent out by their families to perpetuate themselves. Each is programmed to recapitulate the family of origin; together they must work out the inherent conflict in this situation. Feeling helpless and frustrated, they cling even more to what is familiar, intensifying, rather than alleviating their problems. Each resists the other's way of doing things. When couples present in this struggle for control, one may appear sicker than the other. But, according to Whitaker (1958), the degree of disturbance in spouses almost always turns out to be similar, even if at first they appear different.

Couples who remain together eventually reach some kind of accommodation. Whether it's based on compromise or unilateral concession, it lessens the previous conflict. Dysfunctional families, terrified of conflict, cling rigidly to the structures and routines that they work out together. Having experienced being different—and not liking it—they now cling to togetherness. Once again alternatives are dismissed or blocked from awareness.

What distinguishes dysfunctional families is that the flow of their behavior is clogged with unexpressed emotion, robbing them of flexibility and vitality. Clinicians see fixed triangles and pathological coalitions; anyone can see their rigidity.

Avoidance of feelings is described as the cause and effect of family dysfunction. Kempler (1981) lists a number of devices commonly used to avoid feelings: asking questions, instead of stating opinions; using the editorial we ("*We* are worried about Johnny"); and changing subjects. The attention paid to these protective conversational devices, used to avoid intimacy, reflects the experientialists' concern with relatively minor forms of psychic difficulty.

Experiential family therapists believe that a climate of emotional deadness leads to symptoms in one or more family members. However, because they are as concerned with positive health as with clinical pathology, experientialists point to the "normal" casualties that others might overlook. Whitaker (Whitaker & Keith, 1981) speaks of "the lonely father syndrome," "the battle fatigue mother syndrome," "the infidelity syndrome," and "the parentified child syndrome." These "normal" problems concern experiential family therapists just as much as do the symptoms of the identified patient. Experiential family therapists also look for culturally invisible pathologies, such as obesity, heavy smoking, and overwork. These symptoms of family trouble are "invisible," because they're regarded as normal.

Systems-oriented family therapists (see Chapters 5, 9, 10, 11) generally look no deeper than interactions between family members to explain psychopathology. But, experientialists, like psychoanalysts, are concerned as much with individuals as with systems, and consider intrapsychic problems when explaining psychopathology. For example, Kaplan and Kaplan (1978) speak of projection and introjection and intrapsychic defenses which lead to interpersonal problems in the family. Members of such families disown parts of themselves and fit together by adopting complementary but rigidly limiting roles. One person's "strength" is maintained by the other's "weakness." The ongoing, patterned interactions in such families are described as "confluent," meaning ritualized playing out of roles. The majority of clinical examples from the experiential literature are about families with a depressed or critical wife and a reasonable but ineffectual husband. Moreover, unlike other family therapists, experientialists describe patterns of family dysfunction using the individual or a dyad as the unit of analysis. Kempler (1981), typical of the Gestalt-and-encounter wing of experiential therapists, describes dyadic patterns of avoiding intimacy with clever names, such as "pouter-shouter," "crier-shrieker," and "shrew and mouse."

Dysfunctional families are made up of people incapable of autonomy or real intimacy. They don't know themselves and they don't know one another. The root cause is *alienation* from experience, what Kempler (1981) calls "astigmatic awareness." Their communication is restricted because their awareness is restricted. They don't say much to each other because they don't feel much. They don't really experience their own experience, much less share it with other family members.

Many of the experientialists' descriptions of disordered behavior are based on concepts borrowed from other orientations. Perls's notion of *unfinished business* is frequently referred to (e.g., Kempler, 1965). Whitaker, who has worked with almost all of the major figures in family therapy, uses Minuchin's concepts of *enmeshment* and *disengagement* (Whitaker & Keith, 1981), as well as many of Bowen's notions about *triangles* and *emotional cutoffs* from the extended family (Napier & Whitaker, 1978). He also uses the concept of *projective identification,* although not so named (Whitaker & Keith, 1981).

> If a mother is guilty about her early sex life, she may pressure the oldest son to be a priest or the oldest daughter to be a nun. If mother was frustrated in her effort to go to medical school, she may pressure son to become a family doctor. (p. 196)

Whitaker also speaks of family pathology as arising from an impasse in a transition in the life cycle or in the face of changing circumstances. While this is anything but novel, it's certainly consistent with the experientialists' emphasis on the need for change and flexibility. Not to change in the face of changing circumstances can be equally problematic as doing something actively destructive. In this model, the covert is often seen as more dangerous than the overt.

In her portrayal of troubled families, Satir (1972) emphasized the atmosphere of emotional deadness. Such families are cold; they seem to stay together merely out of habit or duty. The adults don't enjoy their children, and the children learn not to value themselves or care about their parents. In consequence of the lack of warmth in the family, these people avoid each other, and preoccupy themselves with work and other activities outside the family.

It's important to notice that the "dysfunction" Satir described isn't the kind of pathology found in diagnostic manuals. Satir, like others in the experiential camp, was just as concerned with "normal" people who lead lives of quiet desperation as with the more blatantly disturbed people who usually present themselves to clinics. As Satir (1972) put it,

> It is a sad experience for me to be with these families. I see the hopelessness, the helplessness, the loneliness. I see the bravery of people trying to cover up—a bravery that can still bellow or nag or whine at each other. Others no longer care. These people go on year after year, enduring misery themselves or in their desperation, inflicting it on others. (p. 12)

Satir stressed the role of destructive communication in smothering feeling, and said that there were four wrong ways people communicate: *blaming, placating*, being *irrelevant*, and being *super reasonable*. What's behind these patterns of dishonest communication? Low self-esteem. If we feel bad about ourselves, it's hard to tell the truth about our feelings—and threatening to let others tell us, honestly, what they feel.

GOALS OF THERAPY

Growth, not stability, is the goal of experiential family therapy. Symptom relief, social adjustment, and work are considered important, but secondary to increased personal integrity (congruence between inner experience and outer behavior), greater freedom of choice, less dependence, and expanded experiencing (Malone, Whitaker, Warkentin, & Felder, 1961). The painful symptoms that families present with are regarded as tickets of admission (Whitaker & Keith, 1981); the real problem is emotional sterility. The aim is for individual family members to become sensitive to their needs and feelings, and to share these within the family. In this way, family unity is based on lively and genuine interaction, rather than on repression and self-abnegation.

Some experiential therapists have a tendency to focus on individuals and their experience more than on family organization. In Kempler's (1981) case the commitment to the individual is acknowledged: "I consider my primary responsibility to people—to each individual within the family—and only secondarily to the organization called family" (p. 27). This emphasis on the individual over the family is *not* true of the more systems-wise experiential family therapists, such as Carl Whitaker, David Keith, and Gus Napier.

In common with others in the existential-humanistic tradition, experiential therapists believe that the way to emotional health is to uncover deeper levels of experiencing—the potential for personal fulfillment locked inside all of us. It's what's inside that counts. Virginia Satir (1972) stated the goals of family therapy in this way:

> We attempt to make three changes in the family system. First, each member of the family should be able to report congruently, completely, and honestly on what he sees and hears, feels and thinks, about himself and others, in the presence of others. Second, each person should be addressed and related to in terms of his uniqueness, so that decisions are

made in terms of exploration and negotiation rather than in terms of power. Third, differentness must be openly acknowledged and used for growth. (p. 120)

When experiential methods are applied to treating family systems (rather than to individuals who happen to be assembled in family groups), the goal of individual growth is merged with the goal of achieving a strengthened family unit. Carl Whitaker's work nicely embodies this dual goal. According to him, personal growth requires family integration, and vice versa. A sense of belongingness and the freedom to individuate go hand in hand. In fact, it's often necessary to bring parents emotionally closer together to enable their children to leave home, since many children can't leave unless they sense that their parents can be happy without them.

In addition to the general goal of increasing the creativity of the family and its members, experiential therapists also try to help every family work out its own particular problems. But this work is done with minimal systematic conceptualization or advanced planning. In fact many of the goals may be unconscious during therapy and can only be acknowledged in retrospect (Napier, 1977). Experiential therapy includes rational and nonrational elements. The former are designed to promote conscious awareness and understanding, the latter are to increase spontaneity and sincerity. Conscious experience of inner potentials (affects, fantasies, impulses) deprive them of their pathogenic influence and liberate their life force. The result of this increased awareness is a reintegration of repressed or disowned parts of the self.

Most experientialists emphasize the feeling side of human nature: creativity, spontaneity, and the ability to play. Whitaker advocates "craziness," nonrational, creative experiencing and functioning, as a proper goal of therapy. If they let themselves become a little crazy, he believes, families will reap the rewards of zest, emotionality, and spontaneity.

When writing about their treatment goals, experiential clinicians emphasize the value of experience for its own sake. Whitaker (1967), for example, sees all therapy as a process of expanding experience, which he believes leads to growth.

New experience for family members is thought to break down confluence, disrupt rigid expectancies, and unblock awareness—all of which promotes individuation (Kaplan & Kaplan, 1978). Bunny and Fred Duhl (1981) speak of their goals as a heightened sense of competence, well-being, and self-esteem. In emphasizing *self-esteem,* the Duhls echo Virginia Satir (1964, 1988) who believed that low-self esteem, and the destructive communication responsible for it, were the main problems in unhappy families. Expanded awareness of self and others is thought to promote flexible behavior, in place of automatic, stereotyped habits. Because they emphasize behavior change as a consequence of enhanced experiencing, the Duhls define explicit behavioral goals in collaboration with their patients.

Most family therapists consider increased sensitivity and growth in individuals as serving the broad aim of enhanced family functioning. Some experiential family therapists keep the family-systems goal implicit and devote relatively few of their interventions to promote it; others perceive individual growth as explicitly linked to family growth, and so devote more of their attention to promoting family interactions. The Duhls (1981) espouse "new and renewed integration" within and between family members as mutually reinforcing goals of treatment. Whitaker (1976a) presumes that families come to treatment because they're unable to be close, and therefore unable to individuate. By helping family members recover their own potential for experiencing, he believes he's also helping them recover their ability to care for one another.

CONDITIONS FOR BEHAVIOR CHANGE

Among the misconceptions of those new to family therapy is that families are fragile and therapists must be cautious to avoid breaking them. A little experience teaches that the opposite is true. Most families are so rigidly structured that it takes therapeutic dynamite to change them. Effective family therapy requires powerful interventions—and for experiential family therapists that power comes from emotional experiencing.

Experiential clinicians use evocative techniques and the force of their own personalities to create personal therapeutic encounters, regression, and intimate disclosure. The vitality of the therapist as a person is one major force in therapy; the vitality of the *encounter* is another. This powerfully personal experience is thought to help establish caring, person-to-person relationships among all family members. Gus Napier (Napier & Whitaker, 1978) wrote, in *The Family Crucible,* a nice description of what experiential therapists think causes change. Breakthroughs occur when family members risk being "more separate, divergent, even angrier" as well as "when they risk being closer and more intimate." Outbursts of anger are often followed by greater intimacy and warmth, because the unexpressed anger that keeps people apart also keeps them from loving one another.

Because feeling-expression and intimate experience within sessions are believed to be crucial, anxiety is stimulated and prized. (The opposite is true with more cerebral approaches to family therapy such as Murray Bowen's.) Experiential therapists are alternately provocative and warmly supportive. In this way they help families dare to take risks. This permits them to drop protective defenses and really open up with each other.

Existential encounter is believed to be the essential force in the psychotherapeutic process (Kempler, 1973; Whitaker, 1976a). These encounters must be reciprocal; instead of hiding behind a professional role, the therapist must be a genuine person who catalyzes change using his or her personal impact on families. As Kempler (1968) said:

> In this approach the therapist becomes a family member during the interviews, participating as fully as he is able, hopefully available for appreciation and criticism as well as he is able to dispense it. He laughs, cries and rages. He feels and shares his embarrassments, confusions and helplessness. He shares his fears of revealing himself when these feelings are a part of his current total person. He sometimes cannot share himself and hopefully he is able to say at least that much. (p. 97)

Virginia Satir said it this way:

> Some therapists think people come into therapy not wanting to be changed; I don't think that's true. They don't think they *can* change. Going into some new, unfamiliar place is a scary thing. When I first begin to work with someone, I am not interested in changing them. I am interested in finding their rhythms, being able to join with them, and helping them go inside to those scary places. Resistance is mainly the fear of going somewhere you have not been. (quoted in Simon, 1989, pp. 38–39)

For Satir, demonstrating caring and acceptance was the key to helping people overcome their fear, open up to their experience, and open up to each other. It's a willingness to understand and accept people—rather than an anxious eagerness to change them—that enables experiential therapists to help people discover and acknowledge deeply held, but poorly understood fears and desires.

Therapists are advised to attend to their own responses to families. Are they anxious, angry, or bored? Once noted, these reactions are to be shared with the family. Whitaker and his colleagues at the Atlanta Psychiatric Clinic (Whitaker, Warkentin, & Malone, 1959) pioneered the technique of spontaneously communicating their feelings *fully* to patients. These therapists often seemed highly impulsive, even falling asleep and reporting their dreams. According to Kempler (1965), "By being, as nearly as possible, a total person, rather than playing the role of therapist, the atmosphere encourages all members to participate more fully as total personalities" (p. 61). He translates this into action by being extremely self-disclosing, even in his opening statements to families. At times, this seems more self-indulgent than provocative. For example, he says (Kempler, 1973), "If the therapist is hungry he should say so: 'I'm getting hungry. I hope I can make it until lunchtime' " (p. 37).

The belief is that by being a "real person," open, honest, and spontaneous, the therapist can teach family members to be the same. As Whitaker (1975) said, if the therapist sometimes gets angry, then patients can learn to deal with anger in others and in themselves. While this is a compelling point of view, its validity rests on the assumption that the therapist is a worthwhile model—not only a healthy, mature person, but also one whose instincts are trustworthy and useful to families. Experiential therapists have great faith in themselves as valid barometers against which family members can measure themselves.

This is an attractive idea, and one that seems to work in the hands of experienced practitioners like Carl Whitaker. However, younger and less experienced therapists would be wise not to overestimate the salutary effects of their personal disclosures, nor to underestimate the potential for countertransference in their emotional reactions to families.

Experiential family therapists share the humanistic faith that people are naturally healthy and if left to their own devices will be creative, zestful, loving, and productive (Rogers, 1951; Janov, 1970; Perls, Hefferline, & Goodman, 1951). The main task of therapy is therefore seen as unblocking defenses and opening up experience.

Some experiential therapists pay more attention to resistance to feeling within family members than to resistance of family systems to change. For example, Kempler's conception of interlocking family patterns is that they are easily resolved by the therapist's pointing them out. "Often in families, merely calling attention to the pattern is sufficient for one or more members to stop their part in it, thereby eliminating the possibility of continuing that inter-locking behavior" (Kempler, 1981, p. 113). Kempler believes the objective of experiential therapy is to complete interpersonal encounters. He tries to pro-mote this objective by simply pushing family members through impasses. But, just as is true with encounter groups (Lieberman, Yalom, & Miles, 1973), these changes will probably not be sustained without being repeated and worked through.

Dysfunctional families have strong conservative (homeostatic) predilec-tions; they opt for safety rather than satisfaction. Since needs and passions are messy, unhappy families are content to submerge them; experiential thera-pists are not. Clinicians like Whitaker believe that it is important to be effec-tive, not safe. Therefore he deliberately aims to generate enough stress to destabilize the families he works with.

Just as stress opens up family dialogues and makes change possible, therapeutic regression enables family members to discover and reveal hidden aspects of themselves. Once these personal needs and feelings emerge, they become the substance of progressively more intimate, interpersonal encoun-ters within the family.

What sets experiential family therapy apart from most other family treat-ments is the belief that promoting family interaction is not a sufficient vehicle for change. Most other approaches begin with an interpersonal focus; their aim is to help family members tell each other what's on their minds. But this means that they'll only be sharing what they're conscious of feeling. They'll have fewer secrets from each other, but they'll continue to have secrets from themselves, in the form of unconscious needs and feelings. Experiential thera-pists, on the other hand, believe that increasing the experience levels of indi-vidual family members will lead to more honest and intimate family interactions. The following example demonstrates this "inside out" process of change.

> After an initial, information-gathering session, the L. family was discuss-ing ten-year-old Tommy's misbehavior. For several minutes Mrs. L. and Tommy's younger sister took turns cataloging all the "terrible things" Tommy did around the house. As the discussion continued, the thera-pist noticed how uninvolved Mr. L. seemed to be. Although he dutifully nodded agreement to his wife's complaints, he seemed more depressed than concerned. When asked what was on his mind, he said very little, and the therapist got the impression that, in fact, very little *was* on his mind—at least consciously. The therapist didn't know the reason for his lack of involvement, but she did know that it annoyed her, and she de-cided to say so.
>
> **THERAPIST:** (To Mr. L.) You know what, you piss me off.
>
> **MR. L.:** What? (He was shocked; people; he knew; just didn't speak that way.)

THERAPIST: I said, you piss me off. Here your wife is concerned and upset about Tommy, and you just sit there like a lump on a log. You're about as much a part of this family as that lamp in the corner.

MR. L.: You have no right to talk to me that way (getting angrier by the minute). I work hard for this family. Who do you think puts bread on the table? I get up six days a week and drive a delivery truck all over town. All day long I have to listen to customers bitching about this and that. Then I come home and what do I get? More bitching. *"Tommy did this, Tommy did that."* I'm sick of it.

THERAPIST: Say that again, louder.

MR. L.: I'm sick of it! I'm sick of it!!

This interchange dramatically transformed the atmosphere in the session. Suddenly, the reason for Mr. L.'s disinterest became clear. He was furious at his wife for constantly complaining about Tommy. She, in turn, was displacing much of her feeling for her husband onto Tommy, as a result of Mr. L.'s emotional unavailability. In subsequent sessions, as Mr. and Mrs. L. spent more time talking about their relationship, less and less was heard about Tommy's misbehavior.

Following her own emotional impulse, the therapist in the example above increased the affective intensity in the session by attacking a member of the family. The anxiety generated as she did so was sufficient to expose a hidden problem. Once the problem was uncovered, it didn't take much cajoling to get the family members to fight it out.

Although the reader may be uncomfortable with the idea of a therapist attacking a family member, it's not unusual in experiential therapy. What makes this move less risky than it may seem is the presence of other family members. When the whole family is there, it seems safer for therapists to be provocative with less risk of hurting or driving patients away than is true in individual treatment. And as Carl Whitaker (1975) points out, families will accept a great deal from a therapist, once they're convinced that he or she genuinely cares about them.

While experiential family therapists emphasize expanded experiencing for individuals as the vehicle for therapeutic change, they are now beginning to advocate inclusion of as many family members as possible in treatment. As experientialists, they believe in immediate personal experiencing; as family therapists, they believe in the interconnectedness of the family. The family may be likened to a team in which none of the players can perform adequately without the unity and wholeness of the group.

Carl Whitaker (1976b) believes that it's important to work with three generations. He pushes for at least a couple of meetings with the larger family network, including parents, children, grandparents, and divorced spouses. Inviting these extended family members is an effective way to help them support treatment, instead of opposing and undermining it.

Whitaker believes that children should always be included, even when they aren't the focus of concern. He finds it difficult to work without children, who, he believes, are invaluable for teaching parents to be spontaneous and honest. In order to overcome possible reluctance to attend, Whitaker invites extended family members as consultants, "to help the therapist," not as patients. In these interviews grandparents are asked for their help, for their perceptions of the family (past and present), and sometimes to talk about the problems in their own marriage (Napier & Whitaker, 1978). Parents may begin to see that the grandparents are different from the images of them they introjected twenty years before. The grandparents, in turn, may begin to see that their children are now adults.

In addition to the increased information available when the extended family is present, small changes in the large family group may have more powerful repercussions than large changes in one subsystem. Since family therapy is based on the premise that changing the system is the most effective way to change individuals, it follows that a cross-generational group holds the greatest potential for change. (In fact it may be that the real reason many family therapists don't include the extended family is that they lack the nerve or the leverage to bring them in.)

TECHNIQUES

According to Walter Kempler (1968), in experiential psychotherapy there are no techniques, only people. This epigram neatly summarizes the experientialists' emphasis on the curative power of the therapist's personality. It isn't so much what therapists do that matters, but who they are. If the therapist is rigid and uptight, then the treatment is likely to be too cool and professional to generate the intense emotional climate deemed necessary for experiential growth. If, on the other hand, the therapist is an alive, aware, and fully feeling person, then he or she will be able to awaken these potentials in families.

Carl Whitaker also endorses this position, and is himself the paradigmatic example of the spontaneous and creative therapist. The point is: therapists who would foster openness and authenticity in their patients, must themselves be open and genuine. However, this point is at least partly rhetorical. Whoever they *are*, therapists must also *do* something. Even if what they do isn't highly structured or carefully planned, it can nevertheless be described. Moreover, experiential therapists tend to do a lot; they're highly active and some (including Kempler) use quite a number of techniques.

In fact, experiential therapists can be divided into two groups with regard to therapeutic techniques. On the one hand, some employ highly structured devices such as *family sculpting* and *choreography* to stimulate affective intensity in therapy sessions; on the other hand, therapists like Carl Whitaker rely on the spontaneity and creativity of just being themselves with patients. Whitaker hardly plans more than a few seconds in advance; and he certainly does not use structured exercises and tactics. However, underlying both these strategies is a shared conviction that therapy should be an intense, moving experience in the here-and-now.

Virginia Satir had a remarkable ability to communicate clearly and perceptively. Like many great therapists, she was a vigorous and dynamic person who engaged clients authoritatively from the first session onward. Where she led, clients followed. But she did not rely merely on spontaneity and personal disclosure. Rather, she worked actively to clarify communication, turned people away from complaining about the past toward finding solutions, supported every member of the family's self-esteem, pointed out positive intentions (long before "positive connotation" became a strategic device), and showed by example the way for family members to touch and be affectionate (Satir & Baldwin, 1983). She was a loving but forceful teacher.

Satir actively elicited emotion by asking questions about feelings and perceptions that weren't being expressed clearly, and by asking family members to shift positions and enact roles. Her shifting voice tone, tempo, and volume, and her facial and hand gestures were powerful nonverbal elements that created responsiveness in family members. Few people could be in her presence and not be moved.

One of the hallmarks of Satir's work was her use of touch. Hers was the language of tenderness. She often began by making physical contact with the children, as evidenced in her case "Of Rocks and Flowers." This was the case of a blended family with a history of severe physical abuse. Bob, a recovering alcoholic, was the father of two boys, Aaron (four) and Robbie (two), whose mother had abused them repeatedly—pushing them down stairs, burning them with cigarettes, and tying them up under the sink. At the time of the interview, she was under psychiatric care and did not see the children. Bob's new wife, Betty, was abused by her previous husband who was also an alcoholic. She was pregnant and afraid that the boys would abuse the baby. The boys had already been expressing the anger and violence they'd been exposed to—slapping and choking other children. Bob and Betty, acting out of frustration and fear, responded to the boys roughly, which only increased their violence.

Throughout the session, Satir showed the parents how to touch the children tenderly and how to hold them firmly, yet protectively, when they wanted to stop the children from doing something. She demonstrated the difference between this gentle firmness and grabbing the boys roughly in anger.

When Bob started to tell Aaron something from a distance, Satir insisted on adding proximity and touch. She sat Aaron down directly in front of his father and asked Bob to take the little boy's hands and speak directly to him.

The following fragments from the session are taken from Andreas (1991).

> Those little hands know a lot of things; they need to be reeducated. OK. Now, there is a lot of energy in both these youngsters, like there is in both of you. And I am going to talk to your therapist about making some room for you to have some respite (from the children). But use every opportunity you can to get this kind of physical contact. And what I would also recommend that you do is that the two of you are clear about what you expect.
>
> And if you (Bob) could learn from Betty how to pay attention (to the kids) more quickly. I would like you to be able to get your message without a "don't" in it, without a "don't"—and that your strength of your

arms when you pick them up—I don't know if I can illustrate it to you, but let me have your arm for a minute (reaching for Bob's forearm). Let me show you the difference. Pick up my arm like you were going to grab me. (Bob grabs her arm). All right. Now when you do that, my muscles all start to tighten, and I want to hit back. (Bob nods.) Now pick up my arm like you wanted to protect me. (Bob holds her arm). All right. I feel your strength now, but I don't feel like I want to pull back like this. (Bob says, "yeah.")

And what I'd like you to do is to do *lots* and lots of touching of both of these children. And when things start (to get out of hand), then you go over—don't say anything—go over to them and just take them (demonstrating the protective holding on both of Robbie's forearms) but you have to know in your inside that you're not pulling them (Aaron briefly puts his hands on top of Virginia's and Robbie's arms) like this (demonstrating), but you are taking them in a strong way (stroking Bob's arm with both hands), like you saw the difference. I'll demonstrate it to you (Bob), too. First of all I am going to grab you (demonstrating) like that. (Bob says, "yeah.") You see you want to pull back. All right. Now, at this time what I am going to do is give you some strength (demonstrating holding his arm with both hands. Robbie pats Virginia's hand). But I am not going to ask you to retaliate. Now this is the most important thing for you to start with.

(Virginia turns to Betty and offers her forearm.) OK. Now I'd like to do the same with you. So, take my arm really tight, just (Betty grabs Virginia's arm, and Aaron does, too.) Yeah, that's right, like you really wanted to give me "what for." OK. All right. Now give it to me like you want to give me support, but you also want to give me a boundary. (Aaron reaches toward Betty's hand and Virginia takes Aaron's free hand in her free hand.) It's a little bit tight, a little bit tight.

So the next time you see anything coming, what you do is you go and make that contact (Virginia demonstrates by holding Aaron's upper arm) and then let it go soft. (Virginia takes Aaron's hands and begins to draw him out of Betty's lap.) Now, Aaron, I'd like you to come up here so I could demonstrate something to your mother for a minute. (Aaron says, "OK.") Now, let's suppose some moment I'm not thinking and I take you like that (grabbing Betty's arms suddenly with both hands.) You see what you want to do? (Betty nods.) All right. Now I am going to do it another way. I am giving you the same message (Virginia holds Betty's arm firmly with both hands, looking directly into her eyes, and starts to stand up), but I am doing it like this. And I am looking at you, and I'm giving you a straight message. OK. Now your body at that point is not going to respond negatively to me. It is going to feel stopped, but not negative. And then I will take you like this. (Virginia puts one arm around Betty's back and the other under her upper arm.) Just like this (Virginia puts both arms around Betty and draws her close) and now I will hold you. I will hold you like that for a little bit.

Following this session, Satir commented on her technique:

There had been so many things happening, and the fear was so strong in relation to these children that if you thought of one image it was like they were monsters. So one of the things that I wanted to do was also to see that they had the capacity to respond with a touch, using myself in that regard by having them put their hands on my face—that was a kind of mirror for the family itself, the people in the family. And then allowing them, and encouraging them to do that with their own parents. See, touch, that comes out of the kind of ambience which was there at the time, says things no words can say.

Just as experiential therapists are theoretically eclectic, many of their techniques are also borrowed from a variety of sources. For example, the theatrical and psychodramatic origins of *family sculpting* and *choreography* are quite evident. Similarly, Whitaker's work with the extended family seems to derive from Murray Bowen's work. Experiential family therapists have also drawn on encounter groups (Kempler, 1968), Gestalt therapy techniques (Kaplan & Kaplan, 1978), psychodrama (Kantor & Lehr, 1975), and art therapy (Bing, 1970; Geddes & Medway, 1977).

Although all the therapists considered in this chapter employ evocative techniques, they differ sharply with regard to how self-consciously they do so. Some plan sessions around one or more well-practiced techniques, while others are deliberately unstructured; they emphasize *being with* the family rather than *doing* something, and say that techniques shouldn't be planned, but allowed to flow from the therapist's personal style and spontaneous impulses. Principal speaker for the latter view is Carl Whitaker. Techniques, Whitaker believes (Keith & Whitaker, 1977), are a product of the therapist's personality and of the cotherapy relationship. His own numerous published case studies reveal a playful, nonstructured approach. When children are present, Whitaker is a model parent, alternately playing with the kids in an involved, loving manner, and disciplining them with firmness and strength. Patients learn from being with Carl Whitaker to become more spontaneous and open, and to feel more worthwhile.

Since he favors a personal and intimate encounter over a theory-guided or technique-bound approach, it's not surprising that Whitaker's style is the same with individuals, couples, or groups (Whitaker, 1958). He assiduously avoids directing real-life decisions, preferring instead to open family members up to their feelings and join them in sharing their experience. This may sound trite, but it's a powerful and important point. As long as therapists (or anyone else for that matter) are anxious to change people, it's hard, very hard, to help them feel and understand their fears and desires—and it's impossible to really empathize with them.

A comparison between Whitaker's early work (Whitaker, Warkentin, & Malone, 1959; Whitaker, 1967) and his later reports (Napier & Whitaker, 1978) shows that he changed over years of seeing families. He started out as deliberately provocative and outlandish. He might fall asleep in sessions and then report his dreams; he wrestled with patients; he talked about his own sexual fantasies. Today he is much less provocative—this seems to be what happens to therapists as they mature: they have less need to impose their own direction and more willingness to understand and sympathize. Indeed, reading some of Whitaker's early reports makes one wonder how much was genuinely spontaneous and how much a studied pose; how much was for the relationship, how much for himself, and how much for the titillation of observers.

Because Whitaker's treatment is intense and personal, he believes it essential that two therapists work together. Having a cotherapist to share the emotional burden and to interact with keeps the therapist from being totally absorbed in the emotional field of the family. All family therapy tends to activate the therapist's own feelings toward types of family members. A detached, analytic stance minimizes such feelings; intense involvement maximizes them. The trouble with countertransference is that it tends to be unconscious. Therapists are more likely to become aware of such feelings after sessions are over. Easier still is to observe countertransference in others. Consider the example of Dr. Fox. Dr. Fox is a married man who specializes in individual therapy, but occasionally sees married couples in distress. In 75 percent of such cases, Dr. Fox encourages the couple to seek a divorce, and his patients have a high rate of following his advice. Perhaps if Dr. Fox were happier in his own marriage or had the courage to change it, he'd be less impelled to guide his patients where he fears to go.

Whitaker and his Atlanta Psychiatric Clinic colleagues wrote an excellent treatise on countertransference in family therapy (Whitaker, Felder, & Warkentin, 1965), suggesting that therapists should be emotionally involved —"in" the family, but not "of" the family. The therapist who's emotionally involved in the family should be able to identify with each of the family members. Thinking about experiences you've had that are similar to the family member's or asking yourself, "What would I like or need if I were that person?" facilitates the process of identification.

In order to minimize potential destructive acting out of countertransference feelings, Whitaker recommends sharing feelings openly with the family. If feelings are expressed to the family they are less likely to be lived out than if they remain hidden. At times, however, even the therapist may be unaware of such feelings. This is where a cotherapist is important. Very often the cotherapist recognizes such feelings in a colleague and can discuss them after a session, or counteract them during the session. A strong investment in the cotherapy relationship (or treatment team) keeps therapists from being *inducted* (drawn into families). Therapists who see families without a cotherapist may bring in a consultant to help achieve the emotional distancing necessary to stay objective.

Young therapists are especially likely to be critical of parents and sympathetic toward the kids; the best prevention for such countertransference reactions is maturity. A mature person has the freedom to enter intense relationships, personal and professional, without becoming enmeshed or reacting as though to his or her own parents. Adequate training, experience, and supervision also immunize therapists against taking sides. In addition, having a strong and rewarding family life minimizes the likelihood of the therapist seeking ersatz gratification of personal needs with patients.

Because of their interest in current thoughts and feelings, most experientialists eschew history-taking and formal assessment. Kempler (1973) once stated his disdain for diagnosis: "Diagnoses are the tombstones of the therapist's frustration, and accusations such as defensive, resistant, and secondary gain, are the flowers placed on the grave of his buried dissatisfaction" (p. 11). The point of this flowery remark seems to be that the objective distance necessary for formal assessment removes the therapist from a close emotional interaction with families; moreover, since diagnostic terms tend to be pejorative, they may serve to discharge hostility while masquerading as scientific objectivity.

For most experientialists, assessment takes place automatically as the therapist gets to know the family. In the process of getting acquainted and developing an empathic relationship, the therapist learns what kind of people he or she is dealing with. Whitaker begins by asking each family member to describe the family and how it works. "Talk about the family as a whole." "What is the family like; how is it structured?" In this way, he gets a composite picture of individual family members and their perceptions of the family group. Notice also that by directing family members toward the structure of the family as a whole, he shifts attention away from the identified patient and his or her symptoms.

Kempler, who conducts family therapy much like an encounter group, often begins by sitting and saying nothing. This device generates anxiety and helps create an atmosphere of emotional intensity. There is, however, something paradoxical about opening like this; it seems nondirective and it seems to be a way of decentralizing the therapist, but it's neither. In fact, by not saying anything, the therapist calls attention to himself, and is in a very controlling position. Any pretense that this opening device signals a nondirective approach is quickly dispelled by reading the transcripts of encounter-group-style family therapists (Kempler, 1981). Whether they open with silence or by inquiring into specific content areas, they soon become extremely active and directive, asking questions, directing conversations, and actively confronting evasive or defensive family members.

Whitaker's first sessions (Napier & Whitaker, 1978) are fairly structured, and they include the taking of a family history. For him, the first contacts with families are opening salvos in "the battle for structure" (Whitaker & Keith, 1981). He labors hard to gain enough control to be able to exert maximum therapeutic leverage. He wants the family to know that the therapists are in charge, and he wants them to accept the idea of family therapy. This begins with the first telephone call. Whitaker (1976b) insists that the largest possible number of family members attend; he believes that three generations are necessary to ensure that grandparents will support, not oppose, therapy, and that their presence will help correct distortions. If significant family members won't attend, Whitaker may refuse to see the family. Why begin with the cards stacked against you?

Experiential therapists tend to push and confront families from the outset (Kempler, 1973). Their interventions tend to be creative and spontaneous, and are described as letting the unconscious operate the therapy (Whitaker, 1967). Many seem to develop genuine and personal attachments to patients, and don't hesitate to side with first one family member, then another.

Among experiential, if not all family therapists, Carl Whitaker is the most outspoken proponent of therapists using their own personalities to effect change. For Whitaker, the therapist's personal adequacy, ability to be caring, firmness, and ability to be unpredictable are far more effective tools than any therapeutic techniques. He believes that a therapist's wisdom, experience, and creativeness will guide his or her interventions better than any preconceived plan or structure. (This probably works better for therapists who are wise, experienced, and creative than for those who are not.)

Experiential family therapists help families to become more real, direct, and alive by modeling this behavior for them. They don't just point the way, they lead the way. Most are very provocative. Whitaker (Napier & Whitaker, 1978), for example, in one session asked a teenage daughter if she thought her parents had a good sex life. Kempler (1968) describes the therapist as a catalyst and as an active participant in family interactions. As a catalyst, he makes suggestions and gives directives. Typical directives include telling family members to look at each other, speak louder, repeat certain statements, or rephrase a remark to make it more emotional. He (Kempler, 1968) cites an example of telling a husband that he whimpers at his wife and whimpers at the therapist. Moreover, this was said in a sarcastic tone, deliberately designed to arouse the man's anger, "Tell her to get the hell off your back—and mean it!" The decision to become an active participant in family encounters depends largely on the therapist's own emotions. If he gets upset or angry, he's liable to say so. "I can't stand your wishy-washy answers!" The avowed purpose of such bluntness is to teach—by example—the use of "I-statements." As Kempler (Kempler, 1981) remarks, "The expressed experiential 'I' ness of the therapist is the epitome of experiential intervention" (p. 156). He frequently challenges and even argues with family members, while freely acknowledging that this largely has to do with his own frustration.

Although they can be blunt, these therapists also limit how far they push people. Kempler (1968) says that therapists should be spontaneous, but not impulsive; and most experientialists agree that only a very warm and supportive therapist can afford to risk being pushy and provocative. Napier and Whitaker (1978) also espouse setting limits on the "let it all hang out" credo that sometimes is used to justify permitting family members to engage in destructive fights. Trying to emulate Whitaker's provocativeness without his warmth and power to restrain can lead to disaster.

Whether they are provocative or supportive, experiential family therapists are usually quite active and directive. Instead of being left to work out their own styles of interaction, family members are frequently told, "Tell him (or her) what you feel!" or asked, "What are you feeling now?" Just as the best way to get a school teacher's attention is to misbehave, the best way to get an experiential therapist's attention is to show signs of feeling, without actually expressing it.

Therapists observe nonverbal signs of feeling; they notice how interactions take place; they notice whether people are mobile or rigid; and they try to identify suppressed emotional reactions. Then they try to focus awareness (Kaplan & Kaplan, 1978). By directing attention to what a person is experiencing at the moment, the therapist may induce a breakthrough of affect or a revelation of previously withheld material. When family members appear to be blocked or disrupted, the therapist focuses on the ones who seem most energized.

THERAPIST: I see you looking over at Dad whenever you ask Mom a question, what's that about?

JOHNNY: Oh, nothing—I guess.

THERAPIST: It must mean *something*. Come on, what were you feeling?

JOHNNY: Nothing!

THERAPIST: You must have been feeling something. What was it?

JOHNNY: Well, sometimes when Mommy lets me do something, Dad gets real mad. But instead of yelling at her, he yells at me (crying softly).

THERAPIST: Tell him.

JOHNNY: (Angrily, to the therapist,) Leave me alone!

THERAPIST: No, it's important. Try to tell your Dad how you feel.

JOHNNY: (Sobbing hard) You're always picking on me! You never let me do anything!

Experiential therapists use a great number of expressive techniques in their work. With some, this amounts to a kind of eclectic grab bag, as the following remark from Bunny and Fred Duhl (1981) suggests.

For us, we feel free to choose a particular technique or methodology as one chooses a tool from a tool box—that is, the appropriate tool for the specific job—in order to achieve the goal of a changed system interaction in a manner that fits all participants, goals, and processes. (p. 511)

Among the techniques available in the experiential family therapy tool box are *family sculpture* (Duhl, Kantor, & Duhl, 1973), *family puppet interviews* (Irwin & Malloy, 1975), *family art therapy* (Geddes & Medway, 1977), *conjoint family drawings* (Bing, 1970), and *Gestalt therapy techniques* (Kempler, 1973). Included among the accoutrements of experiential therapists' offices are toys, doll houses, clay, teddy bears, drawing pens and paper, and batacca bats. Although these props are commonly used for play therapy, experiential therapists don't limit their use to children.

In *family sculpture*, originated by David Kantor and Fred Duhl, the therapist asks each member of the family to arrange the others in a meaningful tableau. This is a graphic means of portraying each person's perceptions of the family, in terms of space, posture, and attitude. This was also a favorite device of Virginia Satir, who frequently used ropes and blindfolds to dramatize the constricting roles family members trap each other into (Satir & Baldwin, 1983).

The following example of sculpting occurred when a therapist asked Mr. N. to arrange the other members of the family into a scene typical of the time when he comes home from work.

MR. N.:   When I come home from work, eh? Okay (to his wife) honey, you'd be by the stove, wouldn't you?

THERAPIST: No, don't talk. Just move people where you want them to be.

MR. N.:   Okay.

He guided his wife to stand at a spot where the kitchen stove might be, and placed his children on the kitchen floor, drawing and playing.

THERAPIST: Fine, now, still without any dialogue, put them into action.

Mr. N. then instructed his wife to pretend to cook, but to turn frequently to see what the kids were up to. He told the children to pretend to play for awhile, but then to start fighting, and complaining to Mommy.

THERAPIST: And what happens, when you come home.

MR. N.:   Nothing. I try to talk to my wife, but the kids keep pestering her, and she gets mad and says to leave her alone.

THERAPIST: Okay, act it out.

As the family mimed the scene that Mr. N. had described, each of them had a powerful awareness of how he felt. Mrs. N. acted out trying to cook and referee the children's fights. The children, who thought this a great game, pretended to fight, and tried to outdo each other getting Mommy's attention. When Mr. N. "came home," he reached out for his wife, but the children came between them, until Mrs. N. finally pushed them all away.

Afterwards, Mrs. N. said that she hadn't realized her husband felt pushed away. She just thought of him as coming home, saying hello, and then withdrawing into the den with his newspaper and bottle of beer.

Family sculpture, choreography, or *spatializing* (Jefferson, 1978) is also used to illuminate scenes from the past. A typical instruction is, "Remember standing in front of your childhood home. Walk in and describe what typically happened." With this technique, the idea is to make a tableau using people and props to portray one's perceptions of family life. It's a useful device to sharpen sensitivity, and it provides useful information to the therapist. It's probably most useful if it suggests changes, which are then acted upon. "Do you like it that way? If not, change it to be the way you want it to be. And if you really care, then do something about it between sessions."

Another structured expressive exercise is *family art therapy.* Kwiatkowska (1967) instructs families to produce a series of sequentially ordered drawings, including a "joint family scribble," in which each person makes a quick scribble and then the whole family incorporates the scribble into a unified picture. Bing (1970) has families draw a picture of a themselves as a family. Rubin and Magnussen (1974) ask for joint murals, as well as two- or three-dimensional family portraits.

Elizabeth Bing (1970) describes the *conjoint family drawing* as a means to warm families up and free them to express themselves. In family drawings the basic instruction is, "Draw a picture as you see yourselves as a family." The resulting pictures may disclose perceptions that haven't previously been discussed, or may stimulate the person drawing the picture to realize something that he or she had never thought of before.

> A father once drew a picture of the family that showed him off to one side, while his wife and children stood holding hands. Although he was portraying a fact well known to his wife and himself, they hadn't spoken openly of it. Once he produced his drawing and showed it to the therapist, there was no avoiding discussion. In another case, when the therapist asked each of the family members to draw the family, the teenage daughter was quite uncertain what to do. She had never thought much about the family, or her role in it. When she started to work, her drawing just seemed to emerge. After she finished, she was somewhat surprised to discover that she'd drawn herself closer to her father and sisters than to her mother. This provoked a lively discussion between her and her mother about their relationship. Although the two of them spent time together, the daughter didn't feel close, because she thought her mother treated her like a kid, never talking about her own concerns, and showing only superficial interest in the daughter's life. For her part, the mother was surprised, and not at all displeased, that her daughter felt ready to establish a relationship on a more equal, sharing basis.

Another projective technique designed to increase expressiveness is the *symbolic drawing of family life space* (Geddes & Medway, 1977). First the therapist draws a large circle. Then he or she instructs the family that everything inside the circle is to represent what is inside the family. Persons and institutions thought not to be part of the family are to be placed outside in the environment. Each person in the family is to draw a small circle, representing himself or herself, and place it inside the family circle in a position meaningfully related to the others. As the family complies with these instructions, the therapist reflects their apparent perceptions. "Oh, you feel you are on the outside, away from everyone else." "It looks like you think your sister is closer to your parents than you are."

In *family puppet interviews,* Irwin and Malloy (1975) ask one of the family members to make up a story using puppets. This technique, originally used in play therapy with small children, is supposed to be a vehicle for expression and for highlighting conflicts and alliances. In fact, its usefulness is probably limited to working with small children. Most adults resist expressing anything really personal through such a childlike medium. Even a frightened eight-year-old knows what's up when a therapist says, "Tell me a story."

Roleplaying is another favorite device of experimental therapists. Its use is based upon the premise that experience, to be real, must be felt and exposed in the present. Recollection of past events and consideration of hoped-for or feared future events can be made more immediate by roleplaying them in the immediacy of the session. Kempler (1968) encourages parents to fantasize and roleplay scenes from childhood. A mother might be asked to roleplay what it was like when she was a little girl, or a father might be asked to imagine himself being a boy caught in the same dilemma as his son is.

Most of the experiential family therapists frequently break off family dialogues to work with individuals. At times this may be to explore emotional blocks, investigate memories, or even analyze dreams. "The individual intrapsychic work may require a few minutes or it may take an entire session. In some instances it has taken the better part of several sessions" (Kempler, 1981, p. 203). The reason for the individual work is the belief that an individual's unfinished business prevents him or her from authentically encountering others in the family.

When someone is mentioned who isn't present in the session, therapists may introduce Gestalt *there-and-then* techniques (Kempler, 1973). If a child talks about her grandfather, she may be asked to speak to a chair, which is supposed to personify grandfather. These techniques have proven very useful in individual therapy (Nichols & Zax, 1977) to intensify emotional experiencing by bringing memories into focus and by acting out suppressed reactions. Whether or not such devices are necessary or useful in family therapy is open to question. In individual treatment patients are isolated from the significant figures in their lives, and roleplaying may be useful to approximate being with those people. But since family therapy is conducted with at least some of the most significant people present, it seems doubtful that roleplaying or other means of fantasy are necessary. If emotional action is wanted, plenty is available simply by opening the dialogue between family members.

Whitaker (1975) uses a similar roleplaying technique, which he calls "psychotherapy of the absurd." This consists of augmenting the unreasonable quality of a patient's response to the point of absurdity. It often amounts to calling a person's bluff, as the following example illustrates:

PATIENT: I can't stand my husband!

THERAPIST: Why don't you get rid of him, or take up a boyfriend?

At other times this takes the form of sarcastic teasing, such as mock fussing in response to a fussy child. The hope is that patients will get objective distance by participating in the therapist's distancing; the danger is that patients will feel hurt at being made fun of.

EVALUATING THERAPY THEORY AND RESULTS

If you noticed that most of the references in this chapter were from the 1970s and inferred from this that experiential techniques were popular in the early days of family therapy, you'd be right. Most contemporary family therapists stick closer to the family's reality, and focus less on individuals and their emotional experience than on narrative, interaction, and the organization of the family. Structured exercises (such as drawing, sculpting, and roleplaying) can be evocative and compelling, and they allow therapists to control what goes on in the session. But anything more than occasional use of such devices may rob therapy of the inherent power of working directly with family dialogues, which get at how family members actually think and interact with each other.

Emotional experiencing for its own sake is probably more suited to encounter groups than to family therapy.

However, having expressed reservations about a therapy designed primarily around techniques to elicit feelings, let us add that two elements in experiential therapy are very useful and relevant. Although the extreme provocativeness of the young Carl Whitaker or Walter Kempler seem more suitable to the 1960s than to the 1990s, many family therapists would do well to be more honest and direct with the people they treat. For too many therapists, the unwritten first principle seems to be: whatever you do, don't ever say anything that might possibly make somebody mad at you. This apprehension, sometimes rationalized as respect, holds many therapists back from honestly confronting family members about what they're doing that isn't working.

A second lesson family therapists might take from their experiential colleagues is shifting to the individual and his or her experience as a way of breaking through defensive squabbling between family members. Usually when family members argue, they lead with their defenses. Instead of saying, "*I'm* hurt," they say, "*You* make me mad"; instead of admitting that they're afraid, they criticize the other's behavior. An effective way to interrupt the unproductive escalation of arguments that lead nowhere is to take time to explore the affect of the participants, one at a time. By talking to individuals about what they're feeling—and the roots of such feelings—family members can be helped to get past the defensiveness that keeps them apart, and to reconnect at a more genuine level.

Experiential family therapists have shown a general lack of interest in verifying their theories of their results. That emotional expression and interaction produce change is more or less taken for granted. Even Alvin Mahrer (1982), one of the most productive researchers and scholars among experiential therapists, believes that outcome studies of psychotherapy are essentially useless. His position is that studies of outcome might be of interest to administrators or insurance companies, but they will have little impact on practitioners. Instead, he recommends studying "in-therapy outcomes": what therapeutic interventions lead to desired consequences on patients' behavior?

Although Mahrer (1982) and others (Nichols & Zax, 1977) have begun to examine such "in-therapy outcomes" in individual treatment, there are as yet no empirical studies of experiential family therapy. What is offered instead as verification consists of anecdotal reports of successful outcome (Napier & Whitaker, 1978; Duhl & Duhl, 1981) and descriptions of techniques which were observed to be effective in catalyzing emotional expression within sessions (Kempler, 1981).

Experiential family therapists aim to provide a useful experience for the families they treat, but they don't seem to believe that every family member must change overtly to validate their efforts. Moreover, change is believed to frequently come in small ways, which may be difficult to measure. If, as a result of experiential therapy, a family is able to make more direct contact with a schizophrenic son, this would be considered a success.

Whitaker (Whitaker & Keith, 1981) claims little empirical evidence of the success of his approach, but cites the goodwill of the community, referrals from previous patients, and the satisfaction of families after treatment as evidence of success. He also mentions his own satisfaction as a therapist, stating that when therapy is unsuccessful therapists become burned out and bitter.

SUMMARY

Experiential family therapy is designed to change families by changing family members, reversing the direction of effect usually envisioned by family therapists. Among experientialists, families are conceived of and treated as groups of individuals more than as systems. Enhanced sensitivity and expanded awareness are the essential aims of treatment.

In addition to focusing on *intra*personal change, experiential family therapy is also distinguished by a commitment to growth as opposed to problem-solving. Personal growth and self-fulfillment are seen as innate human tendencies, which naturally emerge once interference and defensiveness are reduced. Treatment is therefore aimed at reducing defenses within and between family members. Experientialists challenge and question the familiar and the automatic. In order to introduce novelty and enhance immediate experiencing, therapists use their own lively personalities as well as numerous structured, expressive techniques. Like encounter group leaders, experiential family therapists act as *agents provocateur* for intense emotional awareness and expression. Therapy is viewed as an existential encounter, conducted by therapists who participate fully and spontaneously. Interventions are said to arise out of the therapist's aliveness and creativity. At various times these interventions take the form of self-disclosure, teasing, sarcasm, humor, personal confrontation, paradoxical intention, and modeling.

These freewheeling responses may seem intimidating, but the risk is minimized by the presence of other family members (and frequently, cotherapists). Nevertheless, any therapy that features personal disclosure from the therapist has the potential to make the therapist—his or her experience, needs, values, and opinions—more important than the patients. The following is an example of "therapeutic candor" from a prominent experiential family therapist. "I'm almost ready for you people. I'm still thinking about the previous session which was quite moving" (Kempler, 1977, p. 91). Such a remark seems oblivious to the needs of the family. The rationale offered for such dumping is that it enables the therapist to be more completely focused on the present. Perhaps so, but it seems equally likely to divert family members from their experience to his.

Experiential therapy derives from existential, humanistic, and phenomenological thought, from which comes the idea that individual freedom and self-expression can undo the devitalizing effects of culture. Beyond this, however, experiential family therapy tends to be relatively atheoretical. The result is an approach with little basis for systematically conceptualizing family dynamics, and instead simply borrows concepts and techniques from other approaches.

The essential vitality of this approach lies in its techniques for promoting and expanding intense experience. As they grow up, most people learn to blunt the full range of their experiencing. Indeed, defensive avoidance of anxiety may be the most prominent motivating force in people's lives. Experiential therapy takes families who have become refractory to emotional experience and puts some of the oomph back in their lives.

At its best, experiential therapy helps people uncover their own aliveness. Experience is real. Therapy conducted on the basis of putting people in touch with their own genuine experience has an undeniable validity. Moreover, when this personal discovery is conducted in the context of the family, there is a good chance that family relations can be revitalized by authentic interaction among people who are struggling with becoming themselves.

In order to reduce defensiveness and heighten emotional experience, experiential therapists can be highly active. Unfortunately, it's difficult to be active without also becoming directive. Even the best of those in this tradition (Napier & Whitaker, 1978) find it difficult to resist telling people what they should be, rather than simply helping them find out who they are. Moreover, provocative directions such as, "Tell her to get the hell off your back and mean it!" (Kempler, 1968), often seem to produce compliant shows of feeling, rather than genuine emotional responses. When emotional resistance is truly reduced, feelings will emerge, without the direction of a therapist.

In experiential therapy the emphasis is on experience, not understanding. Nevertheless, experiential practitioners seem ambivalent in their attitudes about the utility of insight and understanding. Most, like Whitaker (Whitaker, Felder, & Warkentin, 1965), emphasize the nonrational forces in treatment, so that the intellectual side of human nature is subordinated to the feeling side. Whitaker's (Whitaker & Keith, 1981) statement that insight doesn't work—recognition isn't change—is typical. Elsewhere his treatment is described (Napier, 1977) as providing a complex emotional experience, not "intellectual nagging." However, case studies of experiential family therapy are filled with examples of advice-giving and interpretation. It seems that psychotherapists—of all persuasions—are as prone as the rest of humankind to offer advice and render judgment, and experiential family therapists do so no less often than members of other schools. The Duhls (Duhl & Duhl, 1981), for example, recognize the need for insight to support emotional change, and have criticized what they call "intervention without education."

Once, the idea that families are systems was both novel and controversial; today it is the new orthodoxy. Now that the pendulum has swung so far in the direction of systems thinking, individuals and their private joys and pains are rarely mentioned. Surely one of the major contributions of experiential family therapy is to remind us not to lose sight of the person in the system.

REFERENCES

Andreas, S. 1991. *Virginia Satir: The patterns of her magic.* Palo Alto, CA: Science and Behavior Books.

Bartlett, F. H. 1976. Illusion and reality in R. D. Laing. *Family Process. 15:*51–64.

Bing, E. 1970. The conjoint family drawing. *Family Process. 9:*173–194.

Binswanger, L. 1967. Being-in-the-world. In *Selected papers of Ludwig Binswanger,* J. Needleman, ed. New York: Harper Torchbooks.

Boss, M. 1963. *Psychoanalysis and Daseinanalysts.* New York: Basic Books.

Duhl, B. S. 1983. *From the inside out and other metaphors.* New York: Brunner/Mazel.

Duhl, B. S., and Duhl, F. J. 1981. Integrative family therapy. In *Handbook of family therapy*, A. S. Gurman and D. P. Kniskern, eds. New York: Brunner/Mazel.

Duhl, F. J., Kantor D., and Duhl, B. S. 1973. Learning, space and action in family therapy: A primer of sculpture. In *Techniques of family psychotherapy*, D. A. Bloch, ed. New York: Grune & Stratton.

Frankl, V. E. 1963. *Man's search for meaning.* New York: Washington Square Press.

Geddes, M., and Medway, J. 1977. The symbolic drawing of family life space. *Family Process. 16*:219–228.

Gehrke, S., and Kirschenbaum, M. 1967. Survival patterns in conjoint family therapy. *Family Process. 6*:67–80.

Gendlin, E. T. 1962. *Experiencing and the creation of meaning.* New York: Macmillan.

Greenberg, L. S., and Johnson, S. M. 1985. Emotionally focused couple therapy: An affective systemic approach. In *Handbook of family and marital therapy*, N. S. Jacobson and A. S. Gurman, eds. New York: Guilford Press.

Greenberg, L. S., and Johnson, S. M. 1986. Affect in marital therapy. *Journal of Marital and Family Therapy. 12*:1–10.

Greenberg, L. S., and Johnson, S. M. 1988. *Emotionally focused therapy for couples.* New York: Guilford Press.

Heidegger, M. 1963. *Being and time.* New York: Harper & Row.

Irwin, E., and Malloy, E. 1975. Family puppet interview. *Family Process. 14*:179–191.

Janov, A. 1970. *The primal scream.* New York: Dell.

Jefferson, C. 1978. Some notes on the use of family sculpture in therapy. *Family Process. 17*:69–76.

Kantor, D., and Lehr, W. 1975. *Inside the family.* San Francisco: Jossey-Bass.

Kaplan, M. L., and Kaplan, N. R. 1978. Individual and family growth: A Gestalt approach. *Family Process. 17*:195–205.

Keith, D. V. 1988. The family's own system: The symbolic context of health. In *Family transitions: Continuity and change over the life cycle*, C. J. Falicov, ed. New York: Guilford Press.

Keith, D. V., and Whitaker, C. A. 1977. The divorce labyrinth. In *Family therapy: Full-length case studies*, P. Papp, ed. New York: Gardner Press.

Kempler, W. 1965. Experiential family therapy. *The International Journal of Group Psychotherapy. 15*:57–71.

Kempler, W. 1968. Experiential psychotherapy with families. *Family Process. 7*:88–89.

Kempler, W. 1973. *Principles of Gestalt family therapy.* Oslo, Norway: Nordahls.

Kempler, W. 1981. *Experiential psychotherapy with families.* New York: Brunner/Mazel.

Kwiatkowska, H. Y. 1967. Family art therapy. *Family Process. 6*:37–55.

Laing, R. D. 1967. *The politics of experience.* New York: Ballantine.

Laing, R. D., and Esterson, A. 1970. *Sanity, madness and the family.* Baltimore: Penguin Books.

Lasch, C. 1978. *The culture of narcissism: American life in an age of diminishing expectations.* New York: Norton.

Lieberman, M. A., Yalom, I. D., and Miles, M. B. 1973. *Encounter groups: First facts.* New York: Basic Books.

Mahrer, A. R. 1982. *Experiential psychotherapy: Basic practices.* New York: Brunner/Mazel.

Malone, T. P., Whitaker, C. A., Warkentin, J., and Felder, R. E. 1961. Rational and nonrational psychotherapy. *American Journal of Psychotherapy. 15*:212–220.

Marcuse, H. 1955. *Eros and civilization.* New York: Beacon Press.

Maslow, A. H. 1968. *Toward a psychology of being.* 2nd ed. Princeton, NJ: Van Nostrand.

Napier, A. Y. 1977. Follow-up to divorce labyrinth, In *Family therapy: Full-length case studies*, P. Papp, ed. New York: Gardner Press.

Napier, A. Y., and Whitaker, C. A. 1978. *The family crucible.* New York: Harper & Row.

Neill, J. R., and Kniskern, D. P., eds. 1982. *From psyche to system: The evolving therapy of Carl Whitaker.* New York: Guilford Press.

Nichols, M. P., and Zax, M. 1977. *Catharsis in psychotherapy.* New York: Gardner Press.

Papp, P. 1976. Family choreography. In *Family therapy: Theory and practice,* P. J. Guerin, ed. New York: Gardner Press.

Perls, F. S. 1961. *Gestalt therapy verbatim.* Lafayette, CA: Real People Press.

Perls, F. S., Hefferline, R. E., and Goodman, P. 1951. *Gestalt therapy.* New York: Delta.

Pierce, R., Nichols, M. P., and DuBrin, J. 1983. *Emotional expression in psychotherapy.* New York: Gardner Press.

Rogers, C. R. 1951. *Client-centered therapy.* Boston: Houghton Mifflin.

Rubin, J., and Magnussen, M. A. 1974. A family art evaluation. *Family Process. 13*:185–200.

Satir, V. M. 1964. *Conjoint family therapy.* Palo Alto, CA: Science and Behavior Books.

Satir, V. M. 1971. The family as a treatment unit. In *Changing families,* J. Haley, ed. New York: Grune & Stratton.

Satir, V. M. 1972. *Peoplemaking.* Palo Alto, CA: Science and Behavior Books.

Satir, V. M. 1988. *The new peoplemaking.* Palo Alto, CA: Science and Behavior Books.

Satir, V. M., and Baldwin, M. 1983. *Satir step by step: A guide to creating change in families.* Palo Alto, CA: Science and Behavior Books.

Simon, R. 1989. Reaching out to life: An interview with Virginia Satir. *The Family Therapy Networker. 13*(1):36–43.

Simon, R. M. 1972. Sculpting the family. *Family Process. 11*:49–51.

Sullivan, H. S. 1953. *The interpersonal theory of psychiatry.* New York: Norton.

Whitaker, C. A. 1958. Psychotherapy with couples. *American Journal of Psychotherapy. 12*:18–23.

Whitaker, C. A. 1967. The growing edge. In *Techniques of family therapy,* J. Haley and L. Hoffman, eds. New York: Basic Books.

Whitaker, C. A. 1975. Psychotherapy of the absurd: With a special emphasis on the psychotherapy of aggression. *Family Process. 14*:1–16.

Whitaker, C. A. 1976a. The hindrance of theory in clinical work. In *Family therapy: Theory and practice,* P. J. Guerin, ed. New York: Gardner Press.

Whitaker, C. A. 1976b. A family is a four-dimensional relationship. In *Family therapy: Theory and practice,* P. J. Guerin, ed. New York: Gardner Press.

Whitaker, C. A., Felder, R. E., and Warkentin, J. 1965. Countertransference in the family treatment of schizophrenia. In *Intensive family therapy,* I. Boszormenyi-Nagy and J. L. Framo, eds. New York: Harper & Row.

Whitaker, C. A., and Keith, D. V. 1981. Symbolic-experiential family therapy. In *Handbook of family therapy,* A. S. Gurman and D. P. Kniskern, eds. New York: Brunner/Mazel.

Whitaker, C. A., and Malone, T. P. 1953. *The roots of psychotherapy.* New York: Blakiston.

Whitaker, C. A., Warkentin, J., and Malone, T. P. 1959. The involvement of the professional therapist. In *Case studies in counseling and psychotherapy,* A. Burton, ed. Englewood Cliffs, NJ: Prentice Hall.

Behavioral Family Therapy

Behavioral family therapists started out using learning theory techniques devised for treating individuals and applying them to problems encountered by families; but in the twenty years since its inception, the technology of behavioral family therapy has become increasingly sophisticated and its practitioners increasingly aware that families are more complicated than individuals. Behavior therapists have developed a variety of powerful, pragmatic techniques that they administer to a variety of family problems, but most of the emphasis remains on parent training, behavioral marriage therapy, and treatment of sexual dysfunctions.

The distinctive methods of behavioral family therapy are derived from classical and operant conditioning. Target behavior is precisely specified in operational terms; operant conditioning, classical conditioning, social learning theory, and cognitive strategies are then used to produce change. As behavior therapists have built up experience treating family problems, they have begun to address such traditionally nonbehavioral concerns as the therapeutic alliance, the need for empathy, the problem of resistance, communication, and problem-solving skills. However, even when dealing with such mainstream issues, behaviorists are distinguished by their methodical and directive approach. More than by any technique, behavioral therapy is characterized by careful assessment and evaluation. Analysis of behavioral sequences prior to treatment, assessment of therapy in progress, and evaluation of its final results are the hallmarks of behavioral therapy.

When behavioral therapists apply their techniques to families, they are explicit and direct; and they measure their results. This is consistent with the credo of behavior therapy, namely, that behavior is determined more by its consequences than its antecedents.

SKETCHES OF LEADING FIGURES

Behavior therapy is a direct descendent of the laboratory investigations of Ivan Pavlov, the Russian physiologist whose work on conditioned reflexes led to the development of *classical conditioning*. In classical conditioning, an *unconditioned stimulus* (UCS), such as food, which leads to a reflex *unconditioned response* (UCR), like salivation, is paired with a *conditioned stimulus* (CS), such as a bell. The result is that the conditioned stimulus begins to evoke the same response. Pavlov published the results of his laboratory work with animals and also reported on the application of his techniques to abnormal behavior in humans (Pavlov, 1932, 1934). Subsequently John B. Watson applied classical conditioning principles to experimentally induce a phobia in "Little Albert" (Watson & Raynor, 1920), and Mary Cover Jones successfully resolved a similar phobia in the case of "Peter" (Jones, 1924).

In the 1930s and 1940s extensions and elaborations of Pavlov's conditioning theory were applied to numerous clinical problems. Nevertheless classical conditioning was still viewed as having limited practical utility. Then, in 1948, Joseph Wolpe introduced *systematic desensitization*, with which he achieved great success in the treatment of phobias and generated enormous interest in behavioral treatment. According to Wolpe (1948) anxiety is a persistent response of the autonomic nervous system acquired through classical conditioning. Systematic desensitization deconditions the anxiety through *reciprocal inhibition*, by pairing responses that are incompatible with anxiety to the previously anxiety-arousing stimuli. For example, if Indiana Jones was frightened of snakes, Wolpe would first teach Dr. Jones how to relax deeply, and then have him imagine approaching a snake in a graded hierarchy of stages. Each time Indy became anxious, he would be told to relax. In this way the anxiety evoked by imagining snakes would be systematically extinguished by reciprocal inhibition.

Systematic desensitization has proven to be a very powerful technique for reducing anxiety, which is even more effective when it includes actual practice in gradually approaching the feared object or situation (*in vivo desensitization*).

The application of classical conditioning methods to family problems has been primarily in the treatment of anxiety-based disorders, including agoraphobia and sexual dysfunctions, pioneered by Wolpe (1958) and later elaborated by Masters and Johnson (1970) at Washington University. Effective behavioral treatments for enuresis have also been developed using classical conditioning (Lovibond, 1963).

By far the greatest influence on behavioral family therapy came from B. F. Skinner's *operant conditioning*. The term *operant* refers to voluntary behavioral responses, as opposed to involuntary or reflex behavior. The frequency of operant responses is determined by their consequences. Those responses that are *positively reinforced* will occur more frequently; those that are *punished* or ignored will be *extinguished*. In 1953 Skinner published an enormously influential book, *Science and Human Behavior*, in which he presented a behaviorist approach to all human behavior.

The operant conditioner carefully observes target behavior, and then quantifies its frequency and rate. Then, to complete a *functional analysis* of the behavior, the experimenter or clinician notes the consequences of the behavior to determine the *contingencies of reinforcement*. For example, someone interested in a child's temper tantrums would begin by observing when they occurred and what their consequences were. A typical finding might be that the child threw a tantrum whenever his parents denied his requests, and that the parents frequently gave in if the tantrums were prolonged. Thus the parents would be discovered to have been reinforcing the very behavior they least wanted. To eliminate the tantrums, they would be taught to ignore or punish them. Moreover they would be told that giving in, even occasionally, would maintain the tantrums, because behavior that is partially or *intermittently reinforced* is the most difficult to extinguish. If the child were aware of the contingencies, he might think, "They're not giving me what I want now, but if I keep fussing they will eventually give in; if not this time, then the next."

Skinner, who first used the term "behavior therapy," argued convincingly that behavior problems can be dealt with directly, not merely as symptoms of underlying psychic conflict. The first professional journal in this field, *Behavior Research and Therapy*, started in 1963, elicited a flood of studies demonstrating dramatic and impressive behavior change. A key question that arose in those early days was, "How permanent were the behavior changes?" Yes, behavior therapists could shape new sequences of behavior; but would such changes last? In learning theory terms, this is a problem of *generalization,* a problem crucial to any form of therapy. Behavior therapists consider this a problem to be solved, rather than a question to be debated. Behavioral family therapists have worked to generalize their results by moving from the consultation room to natural settings (home and school), using naturalistic reinforcers, using family members as therapists, and by *fading* (gradually decreasing) external contingencies. Generalization is now programmed rather than hoped for or lamented.

Among the first reports of effective behavior therapy for family problems was Williams's (1959) successful intervention to reduce bedtime tantrums in a young child. The parents were instructed to put the child to bed in an affectionate manner, to close his bedroom door, and ignore his subsequent protestations. The key principle here is *extinction.*

Operant conditioning is particularly effective with children, because parents have considerable control over their reinforcers and punishments. Boardman (1962) trained parents in the effective use of a punishment paradigm to deal with the aggressive antisocial behavior of their five-year-old. Wolpe (1958) described how to employ spouses as cotherapists in anxiety management. Risley and Wolf (1967) trained parents in the operant reinforcement of speech in their autistic children. In technical terms, these parents and spouses were trained to eliminate the contingencies that maintained the deviant behavior and to employ different contingencies to prompt and support more desirable behavior patterns that were incompatible with the deviant behavior (Falloon, 1991). In plain English, they were taught to ignore inappropriate and to reward appropriate behavior.

Although no single charismatic figure was responsible for the development of behavior family therapy, three leaders played a dominant role: a psychologist, Gerald Patterson, a psychiatrist, Robert Liberman, and a social worker, Richard Stuart.

Gerald Patterson, at the University of Oregon, was the most influential figure in developing the field of behavioral parent training. Patterson and his colleagues realized that observation of family interactions in a laboratory or consulting room was far removed from the behavior in the natural environment of the home. As a result, they developed methods for sampling periods of family interaction in the home, trained parents in the principles of social learning theory, developed programmed workbooks (e.g., Patterson, 1971b), and worked out careful strategies for eliminating undesirable behavior and substituting desirable behavior. Among others prominent in this field are Anthony Graziano, Rex Forehand, Daniel and Susan O'Leary, and Roger McAuley in Belfast, Ireland.

The second major figure in the development of behavioral family therapy was Robert Liberman. In his 1970 paper, "Behavioral Approaches to Family and Couple Therapy," he outlined the application of an operant learning framework to the family problems of four adult patients with depression, intractable headaches, social inadequacy, and marital discord. In addition to employing contingency management of mutual reinforcers, Liberman introduced the use of *role rehearsal* and *modeling* concepts of Bandura and Walters (1963) to family therapy.

The third major influence on behavioral family therapy was the contingency contracting approach of Richard Stuart (1969). Rather than focus on how the undesired behavior of one family member could be modified, Stuart focused on how the exchange of positive behavior could be maximized. Thus he introduced the principle of *reciprocity*.

In his first efforts, Stuart (1969) transferred operant principles, used to modify children's behavior, to couples in distress. He applied a reciprocal reinforcement paradigm in which couples learned to: (a) list the behavior they desired from each other; (b) record the frequency with which the spouse displayed the desired behavior; and (c) specify exchanges for the desired behavior. In this early work, tokens were used for reinforcers. Mutual exchanges were based on written contracts.

The early work in behavioral family therapy depended almost entirely on applications of operant conditioning and appeared most successful where behavioral problems could be defined in terms of relatively straightforward stimulus-response exchanges.

Ed Katkin (1978) reported success with *charting* in the treatment of a paranoid and jealous wife. In charting, the patient is asked to keep an accurate record of the problem behavior. Katkin's ploy was to ask the wife to record the frequency of her irrational accusations. This approach illustrates the early attempts to approach family problems through the treatment of individuals. It also illustrates the adaptation of nonbehavioral techniques—in this case, paradoxical intention.

Other early applications of behavior therapy to couples included teaching spouses how to shape positive behavior in one another (Liberman, 1970) and having them analyze the consequences of their behavior and learn to interrupt negative interaction chains (Friedman, 1972). Mutual behavior change efforts were given even more structure by introducing behavioral contracts, written agreements to exchange desired behavior (Rappaport & Harrell, 1972).

During the 1970s behavioral family therapy was developed into three major packages: parent training, behavioral marital therapy, and sexual therapy. At present the leading figures in behavioral marital therapy include Robert Weiss, Neil Jacobson, Richard Stuart, Michael Crowe, Ian Falloon, Norman Epstein, and Gayola Margolin. Weiss took over the development of marital therapy from Gerald Patterson and was particularly influential in establishing a substantial body of research in the assessment and treatment of marital discord.

Two additional developments have further increased the popularity and influence of behavior therapy. First, many nonbehavioral family therapists selectively include behavioral interventions in their work. A good example of this was Minuchin's (Minuchin, Rosman, & Baker, 1978) use of operant conditioning in his work with anorexia nervosa. Second, there has recently been a rapprochement between stimulus-response conditioning models and cognitive theories (e.g., Mischel, 1973; Barton & Alexander, 1981; Epstein, Schlesinger, & Dryden, 1988). Now many behavioral therapists are beginning to consider the role of various "internal" processes such as attitudes, thoughts, and feelings. In addition, family systems theory is having an increasing impact on behavioral family therapists. Gerald Patterson, once a pure operant behaviorist, studied systems theory with Salvador Minuchin; as first illustrated in an article published in *Family Process* by Spinks and Birchler (1982), dealing with resistance has become a major concern in behavioral family therapy; and recent books on the state of the art in behavior family therapy (e.g., Falloon, 1988) are very sophisticated in their handling of family systems dynamics.

THEORETICAL FORMULATIONS

Those approaching behavior therapy for the first time are often confused by references to *learning theory, behavior modification, behavior therapy,* and *social learning theory.* Are these terms synonymous or do they mean different things? Although sometimes used interchangeably, each of these expressions has its own meaning. *Learning theory* refers to the general body of principles discovered in laboratory experiments on learning and conditioning. These laws are the scientific foundation upon which behavioral treatment rests. *Behavior modification* and *behavior therapy* have been used interchangeably, although some distinctions have been made between them. Lazarus (1971) suggested that *behavior modification* refers to strict operant procedures, while *behavior therapy* is associated with counterconditioning methods for treating anxiety. *Behavior modification* has lately been less often used and seems to conjure up an image of mindless control among the public, who sometimes confuse the ends of behavior control with the efficiency of methods used to achieve it. Because the term *behavior therapy* is now commonly used to refer to all operant and nonoperant behavioral treatments, we will follow this usage. *Social learning theory* is a broad approach to human behavior, integrating principles from social, developmental, and cognitive psychology along with those principles of learning derived from experimental psychology. In social learning theory, environmental influences are still the primary concern, but private thoughts and feelings are also used to understand behavior. This framework takes into account the pervasive effects of social influences on behavior. *Cognitive-behavior therapy* refers to those approaches inspired by the work of Aaron Beck (1976) and Albert Ellis (1962) that emphasize the need for attitude change to promote and maintain behavior change.

The central premise of behavior therapy is that *behavior is maintained by its consequences.* It follows from this that behavior will resist change unless more rewarding consequences result from new behavior (Patterson, 1971b). Elaborating the consequences of behavior as well as the cues that elicit it requires an understanding of *stimuli* and *reinforcements*.

Four different stimulus functions are described by learning theorists: eliciting stimuli, discriminative stimuli, neutral stimuli, and reinforcing stimuli. *Eliciting stimuli* are aspects of a situation that reliably produce a response. These are particularly relevant to classical conditioning, where certain eliciting stimuli are known to produce reflexlike responses. *Discriminative stimuli* signal the occasions when a particular response will be followed by a certain consequence. Because they have been associated with those consequences in the past, discriminative stimuli have acquired a cuing function making particular responses more probable. Children, for example, quickly learn to detect certain discriminative stimuli that indicate their parents "really mean it" when they say something. *Neutral stimuli* have no direct relationship to behavior, but conditioning can establish a link between a previously neutral stimulus and a response. Thus Pavlov's dogs responded to a bell only after it had been paired with feeding. *Reinforcing stimuli* are consequences of behavior that affect the probability of future responses. They are cues that reinforcement will follow.

Responses are usually defined as *respondent* or *operant.* Respondents are those that are under the control of eliciting stimuli, and their consequences do not usually affect their frequency of occurrence. Operants are behaviors that are not automatically elicited by some stimulus, but whose occurrence is affected by their consequences. From a systems point of view, the distinction between respondents and operants is problematic. Operants are causes, while respondents are effects. From a linear viewpoint this is a useful distinction, but when we think in terms of circular causal chains, the usefulness of this distinction breaks down. With a nagging wife and a withdrawing husband, what is cause and what is effect? Is the nagging an operant or a respondent behavior? (Both spouses can give you the answer—and both answers will be different.)

Some responses may not be recognized as operants—something done to get something—just because people aren't aware of the reinforcing payoffs.

For example, whining is usually reinforced by attention, although the people providing the reinforcement may not realize it. In fact, a variety of unpleasant behaviors, including nagging and temper tantrums, are reinforced by attention. Even though the attention may be unpleasant—yelling—it may be the most social interaction that the nagging spouse or tantruming child receives. Thus, responses are often maintained under conditions that are counterintuitive.

Reinforcements are consequences that affect the rate of behavior, either accelerating or decelerating it. Consequences that accelerate behavior are called *reinforcers,* while those that decelerate behavior are known as *punishers.* Within the class of reinforcers there are: (a) *positive reinforcers,* positive or rewarding consequences; and (b) *negative reinforcers,* aversive consequences terminated by a response. Thus, parents can positively reinforce their child's cleaning her room by rewarding her after she does it, or negatively reinforce her by nagging until she does it.

Punishment can take the form of (a) *aversive control,* such as yelling or spanking, or (b) *withdrawal of positive consequences,* such as having to sit in the corner or being "grounded" for a week. Punishment and negative reinforcement are often confused, but do have distinctly different meanings.

Reinforcement and punishment may be either primary or secondary. *Primary reinforcers* are natural or biological outcomes, including sex and food; *primary punishments* might be physical pain or loud noises. *Secondary reinforcers* are ones that have acquired a positive meaning through social learning, like praise or eye contact, while *secondary punishers* include criticism or withdrawal of attention. Because attention has such a powerful influence on behavior, focusing attention on undesirable behavior often provides unintended social reinforcement.

Extinction occurs when no reinforcement follows a response. Inattention, as many people know, is often the best response to behavior that you don't like. The reason many people fail to credit this is because withholding response rarely leads to *immediate* cessation of unwanted behavior. This is because most behavior has been partially or intermittently reinforced, and therefore takes time to extinguish.

The relationship between a response and its consequences defines the *contingencies* governing that response. *Reinforcement schedules* describe the relationship between responding and the occurrence of consequences. When reinforcement occurs at irregular intervals, the response becomes more resistant to extinction. Perhaps you can think of a reinforcement schedule with such regular contingencies of reinforcement that even a few occurrences of nonreinforcement would be sufficient to convince you that no further reinforcement is forthcoming.

While it's easy to see how simple responses can be reinforced, it may be less clear how more complicated responses, including responses not yet in someone's repertoire, can be learned. One way for this learning to occur is by successive approximation, or *shaping.* For example, parents can shape a child's learning to play soccer by paying attention to and praising the child's gradual development of the component skills of the game. Negative behavior can also be shaped, as in those families where children only get attention for progressively more angry and destructive behavior. (Children and recalcitrant spouses can also shape yelling by refusing to respond until the volume gets turned way up.)

In addition to shaping, *modeling* is also used to teach complex or new behavior (Bandura, 1969). People often learn by emulating others, particularly if the models are perceived as successful or prestigious, and if their behavior is seen to lead to reinforcing consequences (Bandura & Walters, 1963). Modeling can be used by a therapist or a family member who exhibits a desired behavior which is then imitated by another member of the family. The amount of learning that takes place during modeling depends upon the degree to which the target family member pays attention, has the capacity to understand and rehearse the new behavior, and can reproduce the behavior. Modeling has been found to be an effective way to short-cut the long and tedious process of trial-and-error learning. (Imagine trying to teach someone how to be pleasant without showing them how.)

To many people, behavior therapy seems mindless and mechanistic. With all their talk about "schedules of reinforcement" and "controlling behavior," behavior therapists seem to ignore thoughts and feelings. While this may have been true of early behaviorists, it is less true today. Behavior therapists are increasingly aware that people not only act but also think and feel. And behaviorists are becoming increasingly aware of complications with simply reeducating patients about their behavior. The most frequent form this recognition takes is in efforts to integrate pure stimulus-response behaviorism (Skinner, 1953) and cognitive theories (Mahoney, 1977). Inner events such as cognitions, verbalizations, and feelings are now recognized as events which function as stimuli in controlling behavior.

As behavior therapists shifted their attention from individuals in isolation to family relationships, they came to rely on Thibaut and Kelley's (1959) *theory of social exchange*. According to social exchange theory, people strive to maximize "rewards" and minimize "costs" in relationships. When applied to marriage, this behavioral economics provides a basis for understanding the reciprocity that develops between spouses. In a successful marriage both partners work to maximize mutual rewards, while minimizing costs. By contrast, in unsuccessful marriages the partners are too busy trying to protect themselves from being hurt to consider ways to make each other happy. Each person can trim the costs of relating by giving less value (e.g., by withdrawing) or by shifting to negative reinforcement and punishment. According to Thibaut and Kelley, behavior exchanges follow a norm of reciprocity over time, so that aversive or positive stimulation from one person tends to produce reciprocal behavior from another. Pleasantness begets pleasantness; nastiness begets nastiness.

In its early days behavior therapy tended to focus on individuals rather than relationships. This focus is reflected in the early reports of behavioral marital therapy in which therapists treated spouses separately in individual sessions (Goldiamond, 1965) or treated only one spouse. For example, in two of three marital therapy cases reported by Lazarus (1968) only the wife was treated. Typically, wives were offered desensitization and assertiveness training to help them establish a more balanced and effective relationship with their husbands. Other therapists taught wives the principles of reinforcement and extinction so that they could modify their husbands' behavior (Goldstein, 1971; Goldstein & Francis, 1969).

Asked to treat children, behaviorists initially began seeing them individually. Later, like systems theorists, they began to consider other people in the children's environments as part of the problem. But unlike systems theorists, many behaviorists continue to operate with a linear point of view. The parents' behavior is seen as *causing* the children's behavior. Moreover, despite disclaimers to the contrary (Gordon & Davidson, 1981; Liberman, 1970), the unit of behavioral analysis is *dyadic* rather than *triadic*. The focus is on changing interactions between a parent (usually the mother) and a child, or between one spouse and another. Little or no attention is paid to how these relationships are affected by others in the family. Gordon and Davidson (1981) acknowledge that deviant child behavior may be related to other problems in the family, but suggest that this is much exaggerated by systems theorists.

> Clinical experience indicates that deviant child behavior occurs in families with *and without* marital discord. The simple presence of marital discord in these families may or may not be causally related to the child's problems. (p. 522)

From a systems point of view, such a statement seems naive; the authors apparently fail to recognize that *overt* marital discord may be absent precisely *because* the spouses have triangulated their conflict onto a child.

NORMAL FAMILY DEVELOPMENT

Behaviorists de-emphasize historical data in favor of analyses of current sequences of behavior. As a result, behavioral family therapists have little to say about the development of normal or abnormal behavior. Instead they focus their attention on descriptions of the current state of affairs. Moreover, most of their descriptions of healthy family relationships are extrapolated from descriptions of distressed families. However, in recent years, behavioral investigators have begun to delineate the characteristics of successful marriages directly (Jacobson, Waldron, & Moore, 1980; Markman, 1981; Wills, Weiss, & Patterson, 1974).

According to the behavior exchange model (Thibaut & Kelley, 1959), a good relationship is one in which giving and getting are balanced. Another way of stating this is that there is a high ratio of benefits relative to costs. Put as generally as this, little is added to everyday common-sense notions of family satisfaction. But behaviorists have begun to spell out, in empirical studies, some of the details of what makes for relationship satisfaction. For example, Weiss and Isaac (1978) found that affection, communication, and child care are the most important behaviors leading to marital satisfaction. Earlier, Wills, Weiss, and Patterson (1974), in a pioneering behavioral analysis of satisfaction in marriage, found that affectional and instrumental *dis*pleasures were more important than pleasures in determining marital satisfaction. They found that the exchange of displeasurable responses reduced marital satisfaction significantly more than pleasurable responses increased it. A good relationship, then, is one in which there is an exchange of pleasant behavior and, even more important, minimal unpleasant behavior. Another way of putting this is that good relationships are under positive reinforcing control.

Since satisfaction and persistence in a relationship depend on maintaining a high level of rewards relative to costs, success will depend on a couple's coping successfully with numerous obstacles to the maximization of this ratio (Holtzworth-Munroe & Jacobson, 1991). Maintaining a high ratio isn't much of a problem during the early stages of a relationship, when reinforcing value is at its peak and few of the costs inherent in a long-term commitment have yet been encountered. In time, however, spouses begin to experience each other in new roles, not all of which are rewarding; commitment requires each to accommodate to the other. Something more easily said than done.

Because behaviorists focus on overt behavior, they have tended to look at the benefits of family life in terms of manifest and tangible events. Thus they tend to overlook the fact that unconscious benefits are among the most important sources of satisfaction and stability in family life. Moreover, the behavior exchange model posits a *comparison level* or evaluation of cost/benefit reward ratio offered by the partner as compared with possible relationships outside the family. Here the behavioral bias may underestimate the importance of one's own self-evaluation of worth. Some people may be satisfied with a low benefit to cost ratio, because they feel that they "don't deserve any better." Furthermore, your own evaluation of the benefits of family life is also influenced by previous models (especially parents), and by images of an ideal partner. Clinical experience demonstrates that some people are dissatisfied despite being married to partners who behave in a very rewarding fashion. Perhaps for these people internal images of what married life "should be" are more important than the overt behavior of their spouses. Put in terms of social learning theory, there is a need to consider not only the stimuli provided by other family members, but also the way these stimuli are perceived. An increasing attention to cognitive variables will allow behavior therapists to take such ideas into account.

Communication skill level—the ability to talk, especially about problems—is considered by behaviorists *the* most important feature of good relationships (Gottman, Markman, & Notarius, 1977; Jacobson, Waldron, & Moore, 1980). (It is also the feature of relationships that is most obvious and easily observed.) Good communication increases the rewards and pleasures of relating by leading to effective stimulus control over behavior. Clear communication enables family members to discriminate among and between behavioral events, and enhances their ability to be understanding and to give support. Communication skills also predict later marital satisfaction levels (Markman, 1981).

In time all couples run into conflict, and therefore a critical skill in maintaining family harmony is skill in conflict resolution (Gottman & Krokoff, 1989). Families in treatment often express the desire to be free of problems, and many look to therapists to solve their problems for them. Unfortunately, problems are part of life. Therefore healthy families are not problem-free, but have the ability to cope with problems when they arise. Recognizing this, behavioral family therapists stress the need for problem-solving skills and the ability to resolve conflicts as criteria for successful marriages (Jacobson & Margolin, 1979).

In a good relationship the partners are able to speak openly and directly about conflicts. They focus on issues and keep them in perspective, and they discuss specific behaviors that are of concern to them. They describe their own feelings and request changes in the behavior of others, as opposed to just criticizing and complaining. "I've been kind of lonely and I wish you and I could go out and do things more often" is more likely to get a positive response than, "You never care what I want! All you care about is yourself!" In addition to expressing their concerns as requests rather than attacks, successful family members listen to other family members' points of view and attempt to understand what is being said.

When problems arise or when circumstances change, families need the skills to change behavior. Some behaviorists consider communications skills to be the most powerful determinant of marital success (Markman, 1979), while others emphasize sexual gratification (Masters & Johnson, 1970).

Many people assume that good family relationships will occur naturally if people are well matched and if they love each other. Behaviorists, on the other hand, consistently emphasize the need to develop relationship skills. Good marriages, they believe, are not made in heaven, but are a product of learning effective coping behavior. Jacobson (1981) described a good relationship as one in which the partners maintain a high rate of rewards.

> Successful couples adapt effectively to the requirements of day-to-day intimacy. In particular, they expend their reinforcement power by frequently acquiring new domains for positive exchange. Spouses who depend on a limited quantity and variety of reinforcers are bound to suffer the ill effects of satiation. As a result, over time their interaction becomes depleted of its prior reinforcement value. Successful couples cope with this inevitable reinforcement erosion by varying their shared activities, developing new common interests, expanding their sexual repertoires, and developing their communication to the point where they continue to interest one another. (p. 561)

Like others, behaviorists emphasize the capacity for adaptability, flexibility, and change; they stress that these are not personality traits but skills that can be learned, most easily in relationships that are under the stimulus control of rules and where there is a consensus about what the rules are (Weiss, 1978). Moreover, the rules should be comprehensive and flexible rather than narrow or rigid (Jacobson & Margolin, 1979). In these happy relationships awards exceed costs; social reinforcement is dispensed equitably and at a high rate. Moreover, these relationships are built upon positive control, rather than negative reinforcement, punishment, and coercion (Stuart, 1975).

DEVELOPMENT OF BEHAVIOR DISORDERS

Behaviorists view symptoms as learned responses, involuntarily acquired and reinforced. Unlike their nonbehavioral colleagues, they don't look for underlying meaning in symptoms, nor do they posit conflict in or between spouses as leading to problems in the children. Instead they concentrate their attention on the symptoms themselves and look for environmental responses that reinforce the problem behavior.

At first glance it would seem unlikely that family members reinforce undesirable behavior. Why, for example, would parents reinforce temper tantrums in their children? Or why would a wife reinforce her husband's withdrawal, when it appears to cause her so much pain? The answer is not to be found in some kind of convoluted motive for suffering, but in the simple fact that people often inadvertently reinforce precisely those responses that cause them the most distress.

Naturally it's easier to see how *other* people cause their own problems. How many times have you seen parents threaten their children with punishment they don't carry out? And most of us still remember how our own parents failed to reward us for certain skills and achievements. The local shopping mall, American family life's public stage, is a good place to observe how harried parents fail to punish misbehavior and reward good behavior in their children. And while it's a little harder, it's also possible to begin observing yourself and discovering how often you use reinforcement to shape the behavior of people in your own social context.

It's also possible to notice that "punishments" may have the opposite effect from what is intended. Consider the following scenario.

> Five-year-old Sandy is playing quietly while her father reads the newspaper. After a few minutes, she knocks the Tinker Toys off the table and onto the floor. Her father puts down the paper and tells her to be quiet. A little later she starts singing; again her father tells her to quiet down. Finally, she begins making so much noise that her father slams down the paper, storms into the room where she's playing, and gives her a long lecture on the virtues of playing quietly and not disturbing her parents.

What is Sandy apt to learn from this episode? That if she makes enough noise she'll get her father's attention.

Parents usually respond to problem behavior in their children by scolding and lecturing. These reactions may seem like punishment, but they may in fact be reinforcing, because attention—even from an angry parent—is an extremely powerful *social reinforcer* (Skinner, 1953). The truth of this is reflected in the sound advice to "Ignore it and it will go away." The problem is that most parents have trouble ignoring undesirable behavior in their children. Notice, for example, how quickly children learn that certain words get a big reaction from their parents. Moreover, even when parents do resolve to ignore some misbehavior, they usually don't do so consistently. This can make things even worse, because *intermittent reinforcement* is the most resistant to extinction (Ferster, 1963).

In addition to countless behavior problems unwittingly maintained by parental attention, others persist because many parents are unaware of how to make effective use of punishment. Parents make threats that they don't follow through on; they punish so long after the fact that the child doesn't associate the punishment with the bad behavior; they use punishments so mild as to have no effect; or they use punishments so severe as to cause fear and anxiety instead of discriminative learning.

Systems thinkers would find the previous discussion wanting, because it's based on a linear view of causality: Children continue to misbehave *because* their parents use ineffective contingencies of reinforcement. While it's true that most behavioral family therapists do operate with a linear model, some have attempted to offer a more complex model. For example, Liberman (1972) has described the family as a system of *interlocking reciprocal behaviors;* Gerald Patterson has described patterns of *reciprocal reinforcement* in families. Consider the behavior of a mother and daughter in the supermarket.

> The little girl asks her mother for a candy bar; the mother says, "No." The child begins crying and complaining, and the mother says, "If you think I'm going to buy you candy when you make such a fuss you have another think coming, young lady!" But the child escalates her tantrum, getting louder and louder. Finally, the exasperated and embarrassed mother gives in, saying, "All right, if you'll quiet down first, I'll buy you some cookies."

Obviously, the child has been reinforced for throwing a temper tantrum. Not so obviously, but also true, the mother has been reinforced for giving in—by the child's quieting down after being promised cookies. Thus a spiral of undesirable behavior is maintained by reciprocal reinforcement.

Behavioral family therapists have described a number of defective patterns of reinforcement in cases of marital discord. Azrin, Naster, and Jones (1973) listed the following causes of marital discord:

1. Receiving too little reinforcement from the marriage.
2. Too few needs given marital reinforcement.
3. Marital reinforcement no longer provides satisfaction.
4. New behaviors are not reinforced.
5. One spouse gives more reinforcement than he or she receives.
6. Marriage interferes with extramarital sources of satisfaction.
7. Communication about potential sources of satisfaction is not adequate.
8. Aversive control predominates over positive reinforcement.

The use of *aversive control* is often cited as the major determinant of marital unhappiness. In dysfunctional marriages, spouses react to problems with attempts at aversive control—nagging, crying, withdrawing, or threatening. Rarely do these couples think to shape positive alternatives. So, as a result, the spouses feel more and more negatively about each other. If someone yells at you to stop doing something, you will probably feel upset and anxious; you may understand what the person wants you to do, but you certainly won't feel like going out of your way to please that person. You may not even understand; you may be too anxious or bitter.

In distressed marriages there are fewer rewarding exchanges and more punishing exchanges, verbal and instrumental (Stuart, 1975). Spouses typically reciprocate their partners' use of punishment, and a vicious circle develops (Patterson & Reid, 1970). Partners enter marriage expecting that the rewards of being married will exceed the rewards of remaining single. Marriage provides countless opportunities for rewarding exchanges, and well-functioning couples exchange many benefits. However, when there is a failure to exchange benefits, the reward system shifts from positive to aversive control. The wife whose generosity toward her husband is neither acknowledged nor reciprocated begins to demand her share of exchanged rewards. Unfortunately, as Weiss (1978) observed, "Forced rewards, like solicited compliments, lose their value" (p. 189).

People in distressed family relationships also have poor problem-solving skills (Vincent, Weiss, & Birchler, 1975; Weiss, Hops, & Patterson, 1973). When they discuss a problem, they frequently change the subject; they phrase wishes and complaints in vague and critical ways; and they respond to complaints with countercomplaints. The following exchange demonstrates sidetracking, cross-complaining, and name-calling, all typical of distressed marriages.

"I'd like to talk about all the sweets you've been giving the kids lately." "What sweets! Talk about me, you're always stuffing your face. And what do you ever do for the kids? You just come home and complain. Why don't you just stay at the office! The kids and I get along better without you."

According to Patterson and Reid (1970), reciprocity also exists between parents and children: Parents who behave aversively toward their children get the same in return. This also holds true for negative reinforcement. Children as well as parents develop patterns of reinforcement which exert a powerful controlling effect. If the children are consciously aware of these contingencies, they may be called "manipulative," but often they are as oblivious to the consequences of their responses as are their parents.

Most behavioral analyses point to the lack of reinforcement for adaptive strivings in distressed families. The old adage, "The squeaky wheel gets the grease," seems to apply in such families. Depressions, headaches, and temper tantrums tend to elicit concern and therefore more attention than prosocial behavior. Because this process is unwitting, family members are often mystified about their role in maintaining maladaptive behavior. Behavior therapists believe that since abnormal behavior is learned and maintained by the same processes as normal behavior, it can therefore be treated directly, without reference to underlying causes.

GOALS OF THERAPY

The goals of behavioral therapy are quite specific and limited: modifying specific behavior patterns to alleviate the presenting symptoms. There is little concern with systems change or with growth and development. Symptom change is not thought to lead to symptom substitution, but to inaugurate a positive spiral of behavior, and is dealt with by techniques designed to substitute desirable alternative behaviors.

The behavioral family therapist tailors treatment to fit each family; the goal is to eliminate undesirable behavior or increase positive behavior as defined by the family (Azrin, Naster, & Jones, 1973). Sometimes it may be necessary to redefine a family's goal of decreasing negative behavior in terms of increasing positive and incompatible behavior (Umana, Gross, & McConville, 1980), or to one that is interpersonal rather than centered on one individual. But these changes are essentially strategies to solve the presenting problem and not related to developing broader goals.

Couples often state goals of reducing aversive behavior, but this pain-avoidance strategy only reduces dissatisfaction without increasing positive feelings (Weiss, 1978). Therefore behavioral couples therapists also help spouses increase their satisfaction by accelerating positive behavior. "The goal of behavioral marital counseling is to provide couples with behavior change operations based upon positive control procedures" (Weiss, 1978, p. 206).

The general goals of behavioral therapy are to increase the rate of rewarding interactions by fostering positive behavior change; to decrease the rate of coercion and adversive control; and to teach more effective communication and problem-solving skills (Gurman & Knudson, 1978).

Some of the goals of behavioral family therapy may be shaped by the clientele and setting in which it is practiced. Behavior marital therapy, for example, is most frequently practiced in university teaching clinics. The therapists are often graduate students, and much of the treatment is conducted on an experimental basis. Clients in these settings tend to be relatively young and advantaged; and clients and therapists are often close to each other in age, outlook, and values. Not surprisingly, therapy in such a context often becomes a collaborative effort between people who feel each other to be peers, and a fair amount of teaching goes on. In case studies of behavioral family therapy, many of the interventions take the form of interpretations designed to foster conscious insight. For example, Liberman (1972) reported on his treatment of a couple in which the wife got her husband's attention only when she had headaches. Liberman explained the dynamics of this to the couple; thereafter the husband started paying attention to the appropriate wifely and motherly behavior, while ignoring the headaches. Sounds simple, doesn't it?

What this demonstrates is that behavioral family therapists aim not only to alleviate symptoms, but also to teach skills and foster understanding so that families will be able to solve their own problems in the future. This point is also supported by Robert Weiss (1978) who suggests that many forms of behavioral family therapy are more concerned with prevention than with cure.

CONDITIONS FOR BEHAVIOR CHANGE

The basic premise of behavior therapy is that behavior will change when the contingencies of reinforcement are altered. Behavioral family therapy aims to change specific targeted family problems through the identification of behavioral goals, social learning theory techniques for achieving these goals, and the use of natural or contrived social reinforcers to facilitate this process. Significant others are trained to use contingency management techniques to influence behavior of other family members and to provide appropriate consequences for desired behavior.

The hallmarks of behavioral family therapy are: (1) careful and detailed assessment, to determine the baseline frequency of problem behavior, to guide therapy, and to provide accurate feedback about the success of treatment; and (2) specific strategies designed to modify the contingencies of reinforcement in each unique client family.

To begin with, a *functional analysis of behavior* is required to identify the antecedents and consequences of the target behavior. Once this is complete, a specific approach is designed for specific problems. First, behavioral family therapists specify family problems in concrete, observable—and measurable—terms. Second, they plan specific strategies based on an empirical theory of behavior change. And third, their efforts are subjected to empirical analysis of their effects in achieving specified behavioral goals. Thus, each family is treated as a unique case, whose therapy program is conceived of as a single-subject experiment.

Careful observation is considered a prerequisite to attempts to control behavior. Great emphasis is placed on measurement and scientific methodology. The first task of the therapist is to observe and record the frequency and duration of problem behavior, as well as the stimulus conditions that precede it and the reinforcement that follows it. This enables the therapist to design an individually tailored treatment program.

Moving out of the playroom and the office into the natural world of the home and classroom enabled behavior therapists to discover that some of their previous notions about child aggression were fundamentally erroneous. Contrary to Skinner's assumptions, punishment *does* have long-term effects. The data show that reinforcement of positive behaviors, such as cooperation and compliance, do not lead to reductions in antisocial behavior. Introducing punishment (time out, point loss) produces long-term reductions in antisocial behavior (Patterson, 1988).

Furthermore, behavioral family therapists now realize that the manner in which problems are reinforced in families is often a complex process (Falloon, 1991). In addition to the reinforcing responses that immediately follow a specific problem behavior, more remote reinforcers may play a part in creating support for problem behavior. These may include tacit approval of aggressive behavior, particularly by men in the family, often accompanied by modeling of this behavior. Spanking children for fighting demonstrates by example the violence that a parent may wish to discourage. In addition, behavior that is approved of by peers or other groups outside the family may be extremely difficult to modify at home—especially if the therapist fails to take this wider context into account.

The primary approach in behavioral family therapy is operant rather than classical conditioning (with the exception of treating sexual dysfunctions), and the focus is on changing dyadic interactions (parent-child or spouse-spouse). This dyadic focus differs from the triadic approach of systems-oriented family therapists. Although some behavioral family therapists (Liberman, 1970; Falloon & Lillie, 1988) have disputed this distinction, we believe this is a major difference between behavioral and nonbehavioral family therapists.

Although behavior change remains the primary focus, more and more behavioral family therapists are recognizing the critical role of cognitive factors in developing and resolving relationship problems. Barton and Alexander (1981), for example, maintain that family members' behavior toward each other will only change if their views of themselves and each other change. And Jacobson and Margolin (1979) point out that the establishment of a collaborative attitude in distressed spouses often is a prerequisite for efforts toward positive behavior change.

Barton and Alexander, who call their approach *functional family therapy* (Barton & Alexander, 1981; Morris, Alexander, & Waldron, 1988), point out that members of unhappy families tend to attribute their problems to negative traits (laziness, irresponsibility, poor impulse control) in other members. Such views block therapeutic change by projecting blame in a way that makes it impossible for anyone to change. Such inaccurate, negative, and incomplete views of what's going on leave family members with a limited sense of control over their lives together. Unless such rigid views can be challenged, family members may continue to feel powerless. After all, what can one person do to change another person's "laziness," "irresponsibility," or "poor impulse control"?

Cognitive behavior therapists believe that attributional shifts are necessary to make behavior change possible, but that, in turn, behavior change is necessary to reinforce new and more productive attributions.

In general, behaviorists de-emphasize the "art" of therapy, treating it instead as a technical procedure dependent largely upon the application of learning theory. Some behavioral writers have argued that change will occur if current behavioral principles are applied regardless of the individual personality or style of the therapist (Stuart, 1969; Hawkins, Peterson, Schweid, & Bijou, 1966). But contemporary behavior therapists now realize that successful treatment requires complex skills and great tact. According to Ian Falloon (1991), the supportive therapeutic alliance essential for effective treatment is maintained by displaying respect for the family, reliably adhering to the agreed-on time and place and focus of therapy (this means not shifting from parenting to marital problems without the explicit agreement of the couple), and appreciating that family members are doing the best they can. "The role of the therapist is not to confront the inadequacies of these best efforts, but to facilitate efforts to overcome manifest deficit and to improve the efficiency of the family members' responses" (Falloon, 1991, p. 85). Falloon advises that confrontation, coercion, and criticism be minimized and that therapists concentrate instead on validating the efforts family members are making.

Traditionally, behaviorists have been little concerned with resistance, despite the fact that systems theorists have established that any ongoing social system resists change, either from within or without. Although behavioral family therapists have lately recognized the importance of resistance (Birchler, 1988), most have tended to assume that people seeking psychotherapy are capable of rational, collaborative effort to change. As Spinks and Birchler (1982) put it:

Most behaviorists view so-called resistance phenomena as the results of ineffective case management. That is, resistance is a sign that the treatment model or the therapist have been unsuccessful, not that the clients inherently resist change, or will not change. (p. 172)

Cognitive behavior therapists have become more concerned with resistance (Birchler, 1988), but their view of it differs from systemic family therapists in two ways. First, they see resistance as primarily a property of individuals, rather than a homeostatic tendency in systems. Second, they assume that although family members may have beliefs or expectancies that interfere with change, these beliefs are relatively straightforward—easily reexamined and reevaluated. Once an individual's concerns are addressed, therapy can continue for the group. While this happy optimism seems preferable to those systemic therapists who assume family members are blindly driven by mechanical forces they are powerless to resist, it also seems a little naive.

As their experience with families increased in the 1970s and 1980s, behavioral family therapists began to incorporate more principles and techniques from systems theory into their work. Gerald Patterson, for example, studied Minuchin's structural family therapy, and Gary Birchler integrated systems theory and behavioral marital therapy (Birchler & Spinks, 1980; Spinks & Birchler, 1982). According to Birchler, straight behavioral family therapy is overly structured and fails to deal with underlying relationship dynamics.

A major tenet of behavioral family treatment is that behavior change is better achieved by accelerating positive behavior than by decelerating negative behavior. Although, as we've seen, there may be a need to introduce punishment to eliminate antisocial behavior in aggressive children, behavior therapists generally try to minimize coercion by aversive control or extinction. It is believed that most distressed families already use these approaches to excess. Therefore only positive reinforcement is consistently and widely used in behavioral family therapy.

Behavioral family therapists directly manipulate contingencies of reinforcement in the families they treat, and may provide reinforcement themselves when the family members comply with their instructions. Once new behaviors are established, therapists counsel family members to use intermittent positive reinforcement and then to fade out material reinforcements in favor of social ones. Following this direct control, therapists teach family members how to observe and modify their own contingencies of reinforcement to maintain their initial gains using self-control procedures.

Learning theory may have been developed by observing white rats in laboratory mazes, but applying learning theory to families is quite a different matter. In behavioral family therapy it is important not to make simplistic assumptions about what may be rewarding and what may be punishing. Instead, it is critical to examine the interpersonal consequences of behavior. The therapist must find out what is reinforcing for each person and each family, rather than assume that certain things are universally rewarding. Moreover, a variety of different behaviors may be aimed at the same payoff. For example, a child might throw tantrums, whine, or drop things at various times, but all of these may be reinforced by parental attention. Therefore, in order to understand how to help families change, the therapist must shift attention from the behavior *(R)* to the consequences *(KC)*.

TECHNIQUES

Since behavioral family therapy is usually practiced as either parent training, marital therapy, or treatment of sexual dysfunction, we shall describe each of these approaches separately.

Behavioral Parent Training

The process of psychotherapy begins with the therapist redefining the client's conception of the nature of the problem and of the appropriate solution. Most family therapists begin with the assumption that the family, not the individual, is the problem, so that the whole family should be convened to solve it. Behavioral therapists, on the other hand, accept the parents' view that the child is the problem, and generally meet with only one parent (guess which one) and the child, although some behaviorists (Gordon & Davidson, 1981) recommend that both parents and even older siblings be included.

Clients also expect therapy to be a kind of education, and behavior therapists tend to operate as educators (Liberman, 1972). Thus, from the outset, behavioral family therapists employ a model which accords with the typical parents' view of the nature of their problems and the sort of solutions that would be helpful.

The early work of Patterson, Risely, Wolf, and others working with disturbed children was packaged in a diverse array of educationally oriented programs to train parents in the application of behavioral skills. With the aid of instruction and programmed workbooks, parents were taught the application of social learning principles to temper tantrums, bed-wetting, autistic behavior, homework, hyperactivity, toilet training, disobedience, phobias, and aggressive behavior. The advantage of these educational efforts was bringing a knowledge of how behavior is reinforced to bear on a large number of problems. The disadvantage is that when therapy is reduced to teaching, therapists fail to uncover and resolve conflicts that are responsible for maintaining problems and bringing them about in the first place. Moreover, as Falloon and Lillie (1988) observed:

> Many of these training programs were conducted in workshops attended by large numbers of parents and presented by professionals with limited therapeutic skills and understanding of behavior therapy principles. As a result, the cornerstone of behavior therapy, the behavioral analysis and evaluation of specific goals, was frequently overlooked. (p. 10)

Thus the advantage of behavior therapy—being a straightforward approach with simple strategies—became a disadvantage in the hands of therapists who wrongly assumed that if the principles of reinforcement were simple then therapy, too, could be simple. It isn't.

Behaviorists say that what distinguishes them is not so much a set of techniques, but the fact that they apply principles from experimental and social psychology to clinical problems, and that they carefully verify the results of their procedures. Liberman (1972) expressed this by referring to therapeutic tactics as "behavioral change experiments," and the literature is replete with a variety of behavioral techniques, together with empirical demon-strations of their utility. In fact behavioral parent training has been successfully applied to almost every type of behavioral problem in children (Graziano, 1977; O'Dell, 1974; McCauley, 1988). Graziano (1977) classified these problems in six categories: (1) somatic symptoms (seizures, eating problems, toilet training); (2) complex syndromes (brain damage, retardation, psychosis); (3) negativistic and aggressive behavior (hyperactivity, fighting, physical and verbal abuse); (4) fears and phobias (school phobia, fear of loud noises); (5) language and speech disorders (elective mutism); and (6) common behavior problems in the home (bedroom cleaning, persistent whining, getting dressed).

The many techniques developed to address these various problems can be grouped in three major categories: operant conditioning, respondent conditioning, and cognitive/affective techniques. By far the most commonly used approach is operant conditioning, where the reinforcers employed may be tangible or social. In fact, smiling, praise, and attention have been found to be as effective as money or candy (Bandura, 1969). Operant techniques may be further divided into *shaping, token economies, contingency contracting, contingency management,* and *time out. Shaping* (Schwitzgebel & Kolb, 1964) consists of reinforcing change in small steps that gradually approximate the desired goals. *Token economies* (Baer & Sherman, 1969) use a system of points or stars to reward children for successful behavior. In this very popular approach, children collect a reward once they have accumulated a sufficient number of tokens. *Contingency contracting* (Stuart, 1971) involves agreements by the parents to make certain changes following changes made by their children. *Contingency management* (Schwitzgebel, 1967) consists of giving and taking away rewards and punishments based upon the children's behavior. *Time out* (Rimm & Masters, 1974) is a punishment where children are made to sit in the corner or sent to their rooms.

Respondent conditioning techniques involve modification of physiological responses. Most common of these are systematic desensitization (Wolpe, 1969), assertiveness training (Lazarus, 1971), aversion therapies (Risley, 1968), and sex therapies (Masters & Johnson, 1970). Most of these (particularly the last one) are primarily used with adults but have also been applied to training parents to use with their children. Some commonly used cognitive/affective techniques include thought-stopping (McGuire & Vallance, 1964), rational emotional therapy (Ellis, 1962), modeling (Bandura, 1969), reattribution (Kanfer & Phillips, 1970), and self-monitoring (Rimm & Masters, 1974). Although behaviorists proudly point to the incorporation of cognitive therapy into their procedures, little of this approach is widely used in the field of behavioral parent training. Parents have been trained individually and in groups, through lectures, assigned readings, programmed materials, discussions, modeling, and direct coaching. Practitioners begin by deciding what responses to modify and which techniques to employ. Research literature provides some guidelines, but here as elsewhere clinicians tend to favor the approach they are most familiar with.

In common with other forms of behavioral family therapy, parent training begins with an extensive assessment procedure. While the exact procedure varies from clinic to clinic, most assessments are based upon Kanfer and Phillips's (1970) *SORKC* model of behavior: *S* for stimulus, *O* for the state of the organism, *R* for the target response, and *KC* for the nature and contingency of the consequences. The following example illustrates how this assessment model is applied.

> In the case of parents who complain that their son pesters them for cookies between meals and throws tantrums if they don't give him any, the tantrums would be considered the target behavior, *R*. *O*, the state of the organism, might turn out to be mild hunger or, even more likely, boredom. The stimulus, *S*, might be the sight of cookies in the cookie jar; and the nature and contingency of the consequences, *KC*, might be that the parents give in by feeding the boy cookies occasionally, and especially if he makes enough of a fuss.

Like any useful diagnostic scheme, the *SORKC* model begins to suggest solutions as soon as it is applied.

In simple cases, such as the one above, applying the *SORKC* model is straightforward, but it quickly becomes more complex with families, where there are long chains of interrelated behavior, and therapists must examine the mutual impact of behavior on each family member. Consider the following.

> Mr. and Mrs. J. complain that their two small children whine and fuss at the dinner table. A home observation reveals that when Mr. J. yells at the children for misbehaving they start to whine and stand by their mother's chair.

Given this sequence it is not difficult to apply the *SORKC* model. Imagine, however, that the above sequence is only part of a more complex picture.

> In the morning, Mr. J. makes a sexual overture to his wife, but she, tired from taking care of the children, rolls over and goes back to sleep. Mr. J. is hurt and leaves for work after making some unkind remarks to his wife. She, feeling rejected by her husband, spends the entire day playing with the children for solace. By the time she has to cook dinner, Mrs. J. is exhausted and exasperated with the children. Mr. J. comes home after a difficult day at the office and tries to make up with his wife by hugging her. She responds but only perfunctorily because she is busily trying to cook. While she's at the stove, the children and Mr. J. vie for her attention, each one wanting to tell her something. Finally, she blows up—at her husband—"Can't you see I'm busy!" He goes into the den and sulks until dinner is ready. Just as his wife finds it difficult to express her anger at the children and takes it out on him, Mr. J. has trouble directing anger at his wife and so tends to divert it onto the children. At the dinner table he yells at them for the slightest infraction, at which they whine and turn to their mother. She lets one sit on her lap while she strokes the other's hair.

In this longer, but not atypical sequence, what is stimulus and what response? Obviously these definitions become circular, and their application depends upon the perspective of the observer.

Assessment in behavioral parent training entails defining, observing, and recording the frequency of the behavior that is to be changed, as well as the events that precede it and those that follow it. Interviews, usually with the mother, are designed to provide basic information, such as a definition of the problem and a list of potential reinforcers. Observations may be conducted behind a one-way mirror or during a home visit. Baseline data, collected prior to the initiation of therapy, may be recorded by therapists or by one or more family members. Typically, parents are trained to pinpoint problem behavior, to observe and record its occurrence, and to note the occurrence and frequency of various events which might serve as stimuli and reinforcers.

Parents generally find it difficult to pinpoint specific problem behavior; instead their complaints are phrased by attributing the cause and effect of problems to personality traits. "The problem with Johnny is that he's lazy—shy, hostile, hyperactive, or disrespectful." Therapists respond by probing for descriptions with concrete behavioral referents, and by developing a picture of the interactions between the parents and child. The question, "What does Johnny *do* that indicates his laziness?" helps pinpoint the problem. When this is followed by an inquiry such as, "And what do you do when he does that?" a picture of the interaction emerges. Asking for detailed descriptions elicits information about the frequency, intensity, duration, and social consequences of the problem behavior. Behaviorally oriented checklists and questionnaires are also administered. These provide information that may have been omitted or overlooked in interviews. The final product of this stage of the assessment is the selection of target behaviors for modification.

The measurement and functional analysis stage consists of actually observing and recording the target behavior, as well as its antecedents and consequences. This may be done by the parents at home or by the therapists in the clinic—and, now, more and more, by therapists in the natural setting (Arrington, Sullaway, & Christensen, 1988).

In the next stage the therapist designs a specific treatment package to match the particular needs of the family. Among the factors considered are the degree to which environmental control is possible; whether or not serious interpersonal problems between the parents may preclude their working together collaboratively; possible psychological problems in either parent which might interfere with parent training; and whether or not other forms of treatment might be more effective or economical.

The second consideration, possible conflict between the parents, is usually assumed to be of critical importance by nonbehavioral therapists. Behavioral therapists vary considerably in the degree to which they consider parental conflict to be a problem. Most minimize the role of conflict between the parents, as the following quotation (Gordon & Davidson, 1981) illustrates.

> On several occasions we have observed parents whose marriage is characterized by extreme dislike for each other who have, nevertheless, been able to put aside their differences in order that they may work together in a constructive fashion to help their child. (p. 526)

Once the assessment is complete, the therapist decides which behaviors should be increased and which decreased. To accelerate behavior, the *Premack principle* (Premack, 1965) is applied; that is, high probability behavior (particularly pleasant activities) is chosen to serve as a reinforcer for behavior with a low probability of occurrence. Where once it was thought that reinforcers must satisfy some basic drive, such as hunger or thirst, it is now known that behaviors chosen more frequently (given a wide variety of choices) can serve as reinforcers for those chosen less frequently. The following example shows how the Premack principle can be applied in parent training.

> Mrs. G. stated that she couldn't get her five-year-old son Adam to clean up his room in the morning. She went on to say that she had already tried rewarding him with candy, money, and toys, but "Nothing works!" A functional analysis of Adam's behavior revealed that, given his choice of things to do, the most probable behaviors were watching television, riding his bicycle, and playing in the mud behind his house. Once these activities were made contingent upon tidying his room he quickly learned to do so.

A variety of material and social reinforcers have been employed to accelerate desired behaviors, but as the Premack principle demonstrates, to be effective, reinforcers must be popular with the particular child in question. While money or candy seem like powerful rewards, they may not be as effective as a chance to play in the mud for some children.

Once effective rewards are chosen, parents are taught to shape the desired behavior by reinforcing successive approximation to the therapeutic goals. They are also taught to raise the criteria for reinforcement gradually, and to present reinforcement immediately contingent upon the desired behavior. Once the child is regularly performing the desired response, reinforcement becomes intermittent in order to increase the durability of the new behavior.

Interestingly, although parents are taught to apply operant conditioning principles to their children, behavioral therapists generally do not apply these same principles to the parents whom they are training. Instead they rely on the assumption that the process of training is inherently reinforcing. There are exceptions to this, however, as the following (Rinn, 1978) illustrates.

> It is advisable that the clinician be as reinforcing as possible (e.g., praise, smiles, excited voice) whenever the family carries out homework assignments and procedures. Therapists who are not particularly enthusiastic about the importance of data collection have a tendency to reinforce low rates of data presentation from families. (p. 378)

Deceleration techniques apply contingent punishment and extinction. The most common technique for decelerating behavior is *time out* from positive reinforcement. This means ignoring or isolating the child after he or she misbehaves. This procedure has been shown to be effective with a wide variety of child problems (Forehand & MacDonough, 1975). Studies have shown that a duration of about five minutes is the most effective (Pendergrass, 1971). Children are first warned, to give them a chance to control their own behavior, before they are put into time out. Other techniques used to decelerate behavior include verbal reprimand, ignoring, and isolation. Simply repeating commands to children has been shown to be a most ineffective way to change their behavior (Forehand, Roberts, Doleys, Hobbs, & Resnick, 1976). Response-contingent aversive stimulation (LeBow, 1972) is little used with families, although it has been used effectively working directly with children (Jacobson & Martin, 1976).

Because of the inconvenience of reinforcing behavior immediately after it occurs, token systems have been very popular with parent trainers. Points are earned for desirable behavior and lost for undesirable behavior (Christophersen, Arnold, Hill, & Quilitch, 1972). The principles of behavioral parent training described above are exemplified and more clearly delineated in the following case study.

> Mrs. F. is a twenty-five-year-old housewife and mother of two small children who came to the clinic complaining of headaches and crying spells. The intake interviewer found her to be mildly depressed and, although she had symptoms of a passive dependent personality disorder, concluded that the depression was primarily a reaction to her difficulty coping with her children. Suzie, age five, was a shy child who rarely played with other children and had frequent temper tantrums. Robert, who was eight, was more outgoing and sociable, but did very poorly in school. Between them the children were a handful, and Mrs. F. felt helpless and resentful in her dealings with them.
>
> A functional analysis of behavior revealed that Suzie's shyness resulted in her getting a great deal of extra attention from her anxious mother. Whenever Suzie declined an invitation to play with other children, her mother spent a great deal of time talking with her and doing special things to make her feel better. The therapist selected social behavior (not shyness) as the first target response, and instructed Mrs. F. to reinforce all efforts at socializing and to ignore Suzie when she avoided social contact. Thereafter, whenever Suzie made any attempt to socialize with other children, Mrs, F. would immediately reinforce her with attention and praise. When Suzie chose to stay home rather than play with other children, her mother ignored her, instead busying herself with her own activities. In three weeks, Mrs. F. reported that Suzie had made remarkable changes and "seemed to have gotten over her shyness."
>
> Following this initial successful experience the therapist felt it was time to help Mrs. F. tackle the more difficult problem of Suzie's temper tantrums. Since the temper tantrums were unlikely to occur while the family was at the clinic or during a home visit, the therapist instructed Mrs. F. to make observational notes for a week. These notes revealed that Suzie generally had her tantrums when either of her parents denied her requests for a treat or some special indulgence, such as staying

up an extra half an hour to watch television. Moreover, tantrums were especially likely to occur at the end of the day when Suzie (and her parents) were tired. As for how the parents responded to these maddening temper tantrums, Mrs. F. reported that "We've tried everything. Sometimes we try to ignore her, but that's impossible, she just screams and shrieks until we can't stand it anymore. Then we sometimes spank her, or sometimes give her what she wants—just to shut her up. Sometimes after we spank her she cries so much that we let her stay up and watch television until she calms down. That usually works to quiet her down."

After listening to this description, the therapist explained as gently and carefully as she could how Mr. and Mrs. F. had inadvertently been reinforcing the tantrums, and told them what they would have to do to stop them. For the next week, the F.'s were instructed to ignore temper tantrums whenever they occurred. If they occurred at bedtime, Suzie was to be put in her bed; if she continued to cry and scream, she was to be left alone until she stopped. Only when she stopped were her parents to talk with her about what was on her mind. The following week Mrs. F. reported that the temper tantrums had indeed decreased, except for one night when they took on a new and more troubling form. When Suzie was told that she would not be able to stay up late to watch television she began to yell and cry as usual. Instead of relenting, Mrs. F. put Suzie in her room and told her to get ready for bed. However, realizing that her parents were going to ignore her, as they had earlier in the week, Suzie began to scream and smash things in her room. "It was awful, she was completely out of control. She kicked and struck out at everything in sight, even smashing the little dog-shaped lamp I bought her. We didn't know what to do, so just that once we let her stay up." Again the therapist described the consequences of such behavior, and explained to Mrs. F. how, should Suzie again become destructive, both parents should hold her until the tantrum subsided.

At the next session, Mrs. F. described how Suzie did "get out of control again." This time, instead of giving in, the parents held her as they had been told. Mrs. F. was amazed at the fury and duration of the resulting tantrum. "But we remembered what you said—there was no way we were going to give in!" It took twenty minutes, but Suzie finally calmed down. This, it turned out, was the last time Suzie ever became so violent during a temper tantrum. Nevertheless she did continue to have an occasional tantrum during the next few weeks of therapy. According to Mrs. F., the few tantrums that did occur seemed to take place in different settings or under different conditions than the usual episodes at home (which Suzie had now learned would not be reinforced). For example, one episode took place in a supermarket, when Suzie was told she could not have a candy bar. By this time, however, Mrs. F. was thoroughly convinced of the necessity of not reinforcing the tantrums, and so she didn't. Because she was embarrassed at all the noise her daughter was making in public, she did find it necessary to take her out of the store. But she made Suzie sit in the car and took pains not to let it be a pleasant experience for her. Very few tantrums followed this one.

Next the therapist turned her attention to the problem of Robert's poor performance at school. A careful assessment revealed that Robert rarely brought assignments home from school and when asked usually denied that he had any homework. After checking with Robert's teacher the therapist discovered that the children generally did have homework, and that they were expected to work between thirty minutes and an hour a night. Mrs. F. selected a high probability behavior, watching television, and made it contingent upon Robert's having first completed his homework assignment. For the first two weeks of this regimen, Mrs. F. found it necessary to call the teacher every night to verify the assignments. But soon this was no longer necessary. Doing homework fairly quickly became a habit for Robert and his grades increased from Ds and Cs to Bs and As by the end of the school year. At this point, everyone was happier, and Mrs. F. felt the family no longer needed help.

A follow-up session in the fall found things continuing to go well. Suzie was now much more sociable and had not had any temper tantrums in months. Robert was doing well in school, although he had begun to neglect some of his more difficult assignments. To address this, the therapist explained to Mrs. F. how to institute a token system, and she was able to use it with excellent results in a short space of time.

The preceding example illustrates a form of behavioral parent training in which the therapist meets with the mother and instructs her in the use of operant conditioning principles. Another format is to observe parent and child interacting behind a one-way mirror in the clinic. In this way, the therapist can get a first-hand look at what actually transpires. With this approach, parents can be taught how to play with their children, as well as how to discipline them, and how to negotiate with them. Sometimes the observing therapist may communicate to the parents through a remote microphone, called a "bug in the ear."

The techniques that have been described are particularly effective with small children and preadolescents. With teenagers the use of *contingency contracting* (Alexander & Parsons, 1973; Rinn, 1978) is a more widely used procedure. Contracting is introduced by the therapist as a way for everybody in the family to get something by compromising. Both parent and teenager are asked to specify what behavior they would like the other to change. These requests form the nucleus of the initial contract. In order to help family members arrive at contracts, the therapist models, prompts, and reinforces: (a) clear communication of content and feelings; (b) clear presentation of demands; leading to (c) negotiation, with each person receiving something in exchange for some concession.

Alexander and Parsons (1973) recommend starting with easy issues while the family is learning the principles of contingency contracting. Success in dealing with minor issues will increase the family's willingness to deal with more difficult problems. Some parents are reluctant to negotiate with their children to "do things that they *should do anyway,* without being bribed." In fact, these parents have a legitimate point, and they should be helped to understand the difference between rules (which are nonnegotiable) and privileges (which can be negotiated).

Behavioral parent training is also conducted in general child training programs, which are designed for preventive education. The content of these programs varies from general principles of operant behavior to specific techniques for dealing with specific problems. They usually begin with an introduction to social learning theory. Following this, parents are instructed how to pinpoint behaviors and to select one or two for modification. After being taught to analyze the antecedents and consequences of the target behavior, parents learn to monitor the frequency and duration of the responses. Many of these programs include instruction in charting, or graphing, the target behavior. Parents are also taught how to state and enforce rules, and the necessity for being consistent. Usually, techniques for accelerating desired behavior are used concomitantly. Training in the use of positive reinforcement includes helping the parents to increase the frequency and range of reinforcers that they apply. In addition to increasing behavior that their children are already engaging in, the parents are taught to develop new behaviors through shaping, modeling, instructing, and prompting.

Behavioral Marriage Therapy

Most forms of psychotherapy begin as art and move toward science; behavioral marriage therapy did the reverse, beginning as science and moving toward art. Early reports in the literature (Goldiamond, 1965; Lazarus, 1968) consisted of relatively straightforward application of learning theory principles to problems of married couples. A strictly operant conditioning approach was common (Goldstein, 1971), and therapists were relatively naive about the interpersonal dynamics of families. Since that time behavioral marriage therapy has become increasingly popular and increasingly sophisticated.

As in other forms of behavioral therapy, marriage therapy begins with an elaborate, structured assessment process. This process usually includes clinical interviews, ratings of specific target behaviors, and standard marital assessment questionnaires. Most widely used of the latter is the Locke-Wallace Marital Adjustment Scale (Locke & Wallace, 1959), which is a twenty-three-item questionnaire, covering various aspects of marital satisfaction including communication, sex, affection, social activities, and values. Rating scales are used to describe and quantify couples' most troublesome problems. Weiss and his colleagues at the Oregon Marital Studies Program ask couples to record their spouse's "pleasing" and "displeasing" behavior during the week.

Assessments are designed to reveal the strengths and weaknesses of the marital relationship and the manner in which rewards and punishments are exchanged. Several relationship skills are evaluated, including the ability to discuss relationship problems, current reinforcement value for one another, skill in pinpointing relevant reinforcers in the relationship, competencies in sex, childrearing, financial management, distribution of roles, and decision-making.

Interviews are used to specify and elaborate target behaviors first revealed on the structured assessment devices. Some attempt is also made during interviews to understand the etiology of the problems that couples describe as well as to discover problems other than those noted by the spouses themselves. In general, however, behavioral marital therapists deemphasize interviews (Jacobson & Margolin, 1979) in favor of written questionnaires and direct observation of couples' interactions. Jacobson (1981) offers an outline for pretreatment assessment which is paraphrased in Table 8.1 (see pages 348–349).

After completing the assessment, the behavioral clinician presents the couple with an analysis of their relationship in social learning terms. In doing so, therapists take pains to accentuate the positive, striving to maintain positive expectancies and a collaborative set (Jacobson, 1981). Married partners tend to state their goals negatively, in terms of decelerating aversive behavior: "I want less arguing from him"; or "She nags too much." Most have difficulty describing behavior that they want their spouses to accelerate. To help them do so, some therapists (Azrin, Naster, & Jones, 1973) assign a homework task asking the spouses to make a list of pleasing things their partners do during the week. Reviewing these lists in the following session provides the opportunity to emphasize the importance of giving positive feedback.

Since disturbed marital interaction is viewed as resulting from low rates of positive reinforcement exchanged by couples (Stuart, 1969; Patterson & Hops, 1972), a major treatment strategy is to increase positive control while decreasing the rate of aversive control. This strategy is promoted both while the couple is interacting in the clinic, and by assigning them homework to alter their pattern of interaction at home. A second major strategy is to improve communication, which in turn facilitates couples' abilities to solve problems. Stuart (1975) lists five intervention strategies which summarize the behavioral approach to treating troubled marriages. First, couples are taught to express themselves in clear, behavioral descriptions, rather than in vague and critical complaints. Second, couples are taught new behavior exchange procedures, emphasizing positive in place of aversive control. Third, couples are helped to improve their communication. Fourth, couples are encouraged to establish clear and effective means of sharing power and making decisions. Fifth, couples are taught strategies for solving future problems, as a means of maintaining and extending gains initiated in therapy.

In his initial efforts Stuart (1969) employed the operant method of exchanging tokens as rewards for targeted desired behaviors. In this way one person could build up a "credit balance" by performing a high frequency of behaviors desired by other family members, which could later be exchanged when he or she was the recipient of rewarding behavior from others. Refinements of this approach dispensed with tokens. Mutual exchanges were based on written contracts. Although much of Stewart's work has been devoted to marital discord, his contingency contracting and principles of enhancing the mutual positive reinforcement potential of family members has been used widely by behavioral family therapists (Patterson, 1971b).

Behavior exchange procedures are taught to help couples increase the frequency of desired behaviors. Couples are advised to express their wishes

TABLE 8.1 Jacobson's Pretreatment Assessment for Marital Therapy

A. *Strengths and skills of the relationship*

What are the major strengths of this relationship?

Specifically, what resources do these spouses have to explain their current level of commitment to the relationship?

What is each spouse's current capacity to reinforce the other?

What behaviors on the part of each spouse are highly valued by the other?

What shared activities does the couple currently engage in?

What common interests do they share?

What are the couple's competencies and skills in meeting the essential tasks of a relationship: problem-solving, provision of support and understanding, ability to provide social reinforcement effectively, sexual capabilities, childrearing and parenting skills, ability to manage finances, household responsibilities, interpersonal skills regarding interaction with people outside the relationship?

B. *Presenting problems*

What are the major complaints, and how do these complaints translate into explicit behavioral terms?

What behaviors occur too frequently or at inappropriate times from the standpoint of each spouse?

Under what conditions do these behaviors occur?

What are the reinforcers that are maintaining these behaviors?

What behaviors occur at less than the desired frequency or fail to occur at appropriate times from the standpoint of each spouse?

Under what conditions would each spouse like to see these behaviors occur?

What are the consequences of these behaviors currently, when they occur?

How did the current problems develop over time?

How are current lines of decision-making authority drawn?

Is there a consensus on who makes important decisions in regard to various areas of the relationship?

What kinds of decisions are made collectively as opposed to unilaterally?

C. *Sex and affection*

Are the spouses physically attracted to one another?

Is either currently dissatisfied with rate, quality, or diversity of sex life together?

If sex is currently a problem, was there a time when it was mutually satisfying?

What are the sexual behaviors that seem to be associated with current dissatisfaction?

Are either or both partners dissatisfied with the amount or quality of nonsexual physical affection?

TABLE 8.1 *Continued*

Are either or both partners currently engaged in an extramarital sexual relationship?

If so, is the uninvolved partner aware of the affair?

What is the couple's history regarding extramarital affairs?

D. *Future prospects*

Are the partners seeking therapy to improve their relationship, to separate, or to decide whether the relationship is worth working on?

What are each spouse's reasons for continuing the relationship despite current problems?

What steps has each spouse taken in the direction of divorce?

E. *Assessment of social environment*

What are each person's alternatives to the present relationship?

How attractive are these alternatives to each person?

Is the environment (parents, relatives, friends, work associates, children) supportive of either continuance or dissolution of present relationship?

Are any of the children suffering from psychological problems of their own?

What would the probable consequences of relationship dissolution be for the children?

F. *Individual functioning of each spouse*

Does either spouse exhibit any severe emotional or behavioral problems?

Does either spouse represent a psychiatric history of his/her own? Specify.

Have they been in therapy before, either alone or together? What kind of therapy? Outcome?

What is each spouse's past experience with intimate relationships?

How is the present relationship different?

Adapted from: Jacobson, N. S. 1981. Behavioral marital therapy. In Handbook of Family Therapy, A. S. Gurman and D. P. Kniskern, eds. (pp. 565–566) New York: Brunner/Mazel.

and annoyances specifically and behaviorally. A typical device is to ask each spouse to list three things that he or she would like the other to do more often. These can provide the basis for a trade, or *quid pro quo*. While explicitly exchanging "strokes" in this way, spouses are implicitly learning ways of influencing each other through positive reinforcement. An alternative tactic is to ask each partner to think of things the other might want, do them, and see what happens. Weiss and his associates direct couples to have "love days," where one spouse doubles his or her pleasing behaviors toward the other

(Weiss & Birchler, 1978). Stuart (1976) has couples alternate "caring days," where one spouse demonstrates caring in as many ways as possible.

The major intent of these procedures is to help couples establish *reinforcement reciprocity,* based on rewarding behavior, in place of coercion. Positive control is doubtless more pleasant and effective than aversive control. However, the concept of reinforcement reciprocity implies a symmetrical relationship. While this pattern may characterize some couples seen in university clinics, it surely does not apply to all; and it certainly does not apply to the majority of couples seen in other settings. Unfairness and inequality in marriage is one of the knottiest problems in American families. Assuming that husbands and wives can nicely negotiate agreements about who does what seems a little like assuming that rich nations will bargain in good faith with poor ones.

Behavioral marriage therapists try to help spouses learn to ask for what they want, rather than to expect the other to intuit it. In fact, the whole field has moved from stressing patterns of reinforcement to working on communication and problem-solving (Weiss, 1978). Unlike some other marital therapists, however, behavior therapists emphasize communication that is agreement-oriented rather than expression-oriented. The stress is always more on negotiating agreements than on expressing feelings. Because of this, some critics (Gurman & Kniskern, 1978) have suggested that behavioral marriage therapists try to eliminate arguing and expressions of anger, in the pursuit of dispassionate problem-solving. Indeed, Jacobson (1981) recommends that couples not try to solve a problem while they are fighting about it, but postpone the discussion to a prearranged problem-solving session. "Couples report that if they postpone the discussion to the next scheduled problem-solving session, by the time the session occurs the problem seems trivial" (Jacobson, 1981, p. 579). Perhaps, but it also seems likely that the postponement allows for the reconstitution of defensiveness and, further, that the feelings involved are suppressed, not resolved. Angry feelings are part of being alive; to suppress them is to deaden oneself—and stultify one's relationships.

In a carefully designed longitudinal study Gottman and Krokoff (1989) found that disagreement and angry exchanges, which have often been considered destructive to relationships, may not be harmful in the long run. These patterns were correlated with immediate dissatisfaction, but they were predictive of improved marital satisfaction after three years. Defensiveness, stubbornness, and withdrawal from conflict, on the other hand, *did* lead to long-term deterioration in marriages. Passive compliance may create a facade of harmony, but it doesn't work in the long run—as many dominating partners with compliant mates discover when their partners, who "used to be so agreeable," suddenly become "so critical."

Conflict engagement may make couples uneasy, but it's often an essential prelude to facing and solving problems. The anger that accompanies direct expression of dissatisfaction may be painful but it may also be healthy. Gottman and Krokoff conclude (1989): "If the wife must introduce and elaborate disagreements in marriages, our data suggest that, for the sake of long-term improvement in marital satisfaction, she may need to do this by getting her husband to confront areas of disagreement and to openly vent disagreement and anger" (p. 51). In other words, confrontation is effective only if it doesn't make the partner defensive. It isn't just honesty that counts, but honesty expressed in a way the partner can tolerate.

Training in communications skills may be done in a group format (Ely, Guerney, & Stover, 1973; Hickman & Baldwin, 1971; Pierce, 1973) or with individual couples. The training includes instruction, modeling, role playing, structured exercises, behavior rehearsal, and feedback (Jacobson, 1977; Patterson, Hops, & Weiss, 1973; Stuart, 1976). Couples are taught to be specific, phrase requests in positive terms, respond directly to criticism instead of cross-complaining, talk about the present and future rather than the past, listen without interruption, minimize punitive statements, and eliminate questions that sound like declarations (O'Leary & Turkewitz, 1978).

After explaining these principles, therapists invite couples to incorporate them in their discussions, during which the therapists provide feedback. Many therapists recommend that couples replay previous arguments during therapy, and ask the spouses to paraphrase each other's remarks before replying to them.

Once a couple has been taught to communicate in ways that are conducive to problem-solving, they are introduced to the principles of *contingency contracting*. Contingency contracting means changing something contingent on the partner making changes. There are two forms of contract negotiation used in behavioral family therapy. The first of these is the *quid pro quo* contract (Knox, 1971; Lederer & Jackson, 1968), where one spouse agrees to make a change after a prior change by the other. Contracting is highly structured and the agreements are usually written down. Each spouse specifies desired behavior changes, and with the therapist's help they negotiate agreements. At the end of the session a written list is made and each spouse signs it. According to Rappaport and Harrell (1972) written agreements act as references, obviating the need to rely on memory, they can be easily modified, they act as cues (discriminative stimuli) reminding spouses of their agreements, and they symbolize the couple's commitment to change. Such a contract might take the following form:

Date _____

This week I agree to:

(1) Come home from work by 6 P.M.
(2) Play with the children for half an hour after supper.

_____
Husband's signature

Contingent on the above changes, I agree to:

(1) Go bowling once a week with my husband.
(2) Not serve leftovers for supper on weeknights.

_____
Wife's signature

This form of contracting substitutes positive for aversive control and ensures that changes in one spouse are immediately reinforced by the other (Eisler & Hersen, 1973). Therapists guide the couple's choices of reinforcement so that the rewards desired by one spouse are not aversive to the other, and contracts for sexual behavior are avoided (O'Leary & Turkewitz, 1978).

Jacobson and Martin (1976) have argued that *quid pro quo* contracts are more efficient and less time-consuming than other forms. However, the *quid pro quo* arrangement requires one spouse to be the first to change. In an atmosphere of mistrust and animosity neither may be willing to do so. An alternative form of contracting is the *good faith* contract, in which both spouses agree to make changes that are not contingent upon what the other does (Weiss, Hops, & Patterson, 1973). Each spouse's independent changes are independently reinforced. In the example cited above, the husband who comes home each night by 6 P.M. and plays with the children after supper might reward himself by buying a new shirt at the end of the week, or be rewarded by his wife with a back rub. Stuart (1980) emphasizes training couples to negotiate exchanges in a "two-winner" context, rather than the "win-lose" orientation that typifies many distressed relationships. Knox (1973) has suggested a combined form of contracting, using *good faith* contracts until appropriate changes are initiated and then switching to *quid pro quo* contracts once an atmosphere of trust and confidence is established.

Problem-solving training is used to deal with problems that are too conflictual or complicated for simple exchange agreements. The key to successful problem-solving is developing a collaborative set between the spouses. Negotiations are preceded by a careful and specific definition of problems. Only when the spouses agree on the definition of a problem can they effectively begin to discuss a solution. Discussions are limited to only one problem at a time. Each spouse begins by paraphrasing what the other has said, and they are taught to avoid making inferences about the other's motivation—especially inferences of malevolent intent. They are also encouraged to avoid verbal abuse and other aversive responses. When defining a problem it is most effective to begin with a positive statement; instead of saying, "You never . . . ," spouses are taught to say, "I appreciate the way you . . . and, in addition I want . . ."

Behavior therapists are very active in these discussions, teaching structured procedures for problem-solving and giving feedback. The discussions are frequently punctuated by such therapist comments as "You just interrupted him"; "As soon as she makes a request, you change the subject"; or "When you blamed her for the problem, the two of you started arguing instead of discussing the issue at hand."

The trouble with the activity and directiveness of behavioral marriage therapists is that couples may learn what they're doing wrong, but without having sufficient independent practice to correct it. There is a real danger that such a directive approach will tie couples into a long-term relationship in which they are dependent upon the therapist to referee their fights and tell them how to solve their disagreements. To avoid fostering such dependent relationships most nonbehavioral family therapists remain sufficiently decentralized to promote independent self-sufficiency on the part of their clients

(Minuchin, 1974; Ables & Brandsma, 1977; Guerin, Fay, Burden, & Kautto, 1987). Behavioral therapists emphasize the need to resolve dependency by gradually tapering off treatment, so that the therapist's influence can be faded out.

As we move further into the 1990s the methods employed by most behavioral marital therapists differ little from those described by Stuart (1969) and Liberman (1970). The contingency contract remains the mainstay of treatment, both in enhancing the quality and quantity of mutually pleasing transactions and diminishing the frequency of negative communication sequences and arguments. The most significant advance in behavioral treatment is the increasing use and sophistication of cognitive-behavioral methods (Epstein, Schlesinger, & Dryden, 1988).

The cognitive mediation model (Beck, 1976) posits that emotions and actions are mediated by specific cognitions. Understanding these cognitions (*beliefs, attributions,* and *expectancies*) makes it possible to identify factors that trigger and maintain the dysfunctional emotional and behavioral patterns that families bring to treatment. In Barton and Alexander's (1981) "functional family therapy," it is assumed that members of disturbed families tend to attribute their problems to negative traits; and therefore the therapist's goal is to provide family members with new information that will impel them to new emotional and behavioral reactions in order to maintain cognitive consistency. In practice this boils down to repeatedly ferreting out and confronting negative assumptions that keep people stuck.

Treatment of Sexual Dysfunction

It's often difficult to decide whether to focus directly on sexual problems or to treat them as a symptom of underlying problems in the relationship. At times it may be possible to resolve sexual problems indirectly, by working on the interpersonal relationship (Gill & Temperley, 1974). On the other hand, what appear to be intractable interpersonal problems can sometimes be resolved with improvement in a couple's sexual relationship (Kaplan, 1974). After all, sex and affection provide a bond that helps couples endure the inevitable hurts and slights that come into every relationship. In all cases, the decision as to whether or not to treat sexual dysfunction directly should be based upon informed clinical judgment, not ignorance of the techniques available.

Prior to the publication of Masters and Johnson's *Human Sexual Inadequacy* in 1970, the prevailing treatment for sexual dysfunction was a combination of analytic discussion and common-sense suggestions. For example, men suffering from premature ejaculation were often advised to think distracting, nonsexual thoughts during intercourse. For women who failed to reach orgasm the most common advice was to fake it.

Wolpe's (1958) introduction of *systematic desensitization* led to major advances in the treatment of sexual dysfunction. According to Wolpe most sexual problems are the result of conditioned anxiety. His therapy consists of instructing couples to engage in a graded series of progressively more intimate encounters, avoiding thoughts about erection or orgasm. A second behavioral approach that frequently proved effective was *assertive training* (Lazarus, 1965; Wolpe, 1958). In assertive training, socially and sexually inhibited persons were encouraged to accept and express their needs and feelings.

While these behavioral remedies were often helpful, the real breakthrough came with the publication of Masters and Johnson's (1970) approach. This was followed by a number of others who applied and extended Masters and Johnson's basic approach (Lobitz & LoPiccolo, 1972; Kaplan, 1974, 1979).

Although the specific details vary, there is a general approach to treatment followed by most sex therapists. As with other behavioral approaches, the first step is a careful and thorough assessment. Included in the assessment is a complete medical examination to rule out organic problems, and extensive interviews to determine the nature of the dysfunction as well as to establish goals for treatment. In the absence of organic problems, cases involving lack of information, poor technique, and poor communication in the sexual area are most amenable to sexual therapy. Moreover, those people suffering from premature ejaculation, vaginismus, or orgasmic dysfunction generally respond well to brief treatment (five to twenty sessions); cases of ejaculatory incompetence, erectile failure, and longstanding lack of sexual desire are generally more difficult to resolve (Heiman, LoPiccolo, & LoPiccolo, 1981).

Therapists following Masters and Johnson tended to lump sexual problems into one category—anxiety that interfered with couples' ability to relax into arousal and orgasm. Helen Singer Kaplan (1979) pointed out that there are three stages of the sexual response and, hence, three types of problems: disorders of desire, arousal disorders, and orgasm disorders. Disorders of desire range from "low sex drive" to sexual aversion. Treatment of these problems is often successful, with motivated clients. Treatment focuses on (a) deconditioning anxiety, and (b) helping clients identify and stop negative thoughts that interfere with sexual desire. Arousal disorders include decreased emotional arousal and difficulty achieving and maintaining an erection or dilating and lubricating. These problems are often helped with a combination of relaxation techniques and teaching couples to focus on physical sensations involved in touching and caressing, rather than worrying about what comes next. Orgasm disorders include the timing of orgasm (e.g., premature or delayed), the quality of the orgasm, or the requirements for orgasm (e.g., some people only have orgasm during masturbation). Problems with orgasm can also be either chronic or situational. Premature ejaculation usually responds well to sex therapy; lack of orgasm in women may respond to sex therapy, usually involving teaching the woman to practice on her own and learning to fantasize.

Following the assessment, clients are presented with an explanation of the role of conditioned anxiety in problems with sex, and they are told how anxiety developed and is being maintained in their sexual relationship. Insight and attitude change are thus a fundamental part of this "behavioral" therapy. Not only may a couple's ignorance be creating problems, but they may also harbor attitudes about sex that are incompatible with the aims of treatment. John Bancroft, who uses a behavioral approach to treat sexual problems, noted (1975) that, "Changing attitudes is an essential part of treatment which has been sadly neglected by behavior therapists" (p. 149). Kaplan

(1974) makes extensive use of psychodynamic theory and technique to deal with attitudinal resistance. Attitudes may be changed by confronting clients with discrepancies between their attitudes and reality; by subtly fostering behavior change (sometimes, where the body goes the heart follows); and by facilitating the cathartic expression of feelings.

Although sex therapy must be tailored to specific problems, most treatments are initiated with *sensate focus*. In this phase of treatment couples are taught how to relax and enjoy touching and being touched. They are told to go home and find a time when they are both reasonably relaxed and free from distraction, and then get in bed together naked. Then they take turns gently caressing each other. The person being touched is told to simply relax and concentrate on the feeling of being touched. Later the one being touched will let the partner know which touch is most pleasing and which is less so. At first couples are told not to touch each other in the sensitive breast or genital areas, in order to remove undue anxiety.

After they learn to relax and exchange gentle, pleasant caressing, couples are encouraged to gradually become more intimate—but to slow down if either should feel anxious. Thus sensate focus is a form of *in vivo desensitization*. Couples who are highly anxious and fearful of "having sex" (which many people reduce to a hectic few minutes of poking and panting) learn to overcome their fears through a gradual and progressively more intimate experience of mutual caressing. As anxiety drops and desire mounts, they are encouraged to engage in progressively more intimate exchanges. In the process, couples are also taught to figure out and communicate to each other what they like and don't like. So, for example, instead of enduring something unpleasant until she finally gets so upset that she snaps at her partner or avoids sex altogether, a woman might be taught how to gently but quickly show him, "No, not like that, like this." Sex therapists also emphasize the need to become comfortable with initiating and refusing sexual contact. Couples are taught how to initiate sex without the ambiguity or poor timing that leads to a history of tension, anxiety, and, eventually, dread.

Once sensate focus exercises have gone smoothly, the therapist initiates specific techniques to deal with specific problems. Among women the most common sexual dysfunctions are difficulties with orgasm (Kaplan, 1979), and frequently these problems are rooted in lack of information. The woman and her partner may be expecting her to have orgasms reliably during intercourse without additional clitoral stimulation. In men, the most common problem is premature ejaculation, for which part of the treatment is the *squeeze technique* (Semans, 1956), in which the woman stimulates the man's penis until he feels the urge to ejaculate. At that point, she squeezes the frenulum (at the base of the head) firmly between her thumb and first two fingers until the urge to ejaculate subsides. Stimulation begins again until another squeeze is necessary.

Techniques to deal with erectile failure are designed to reduce performance anxiety and increase sexual arousal. These include desensitization of the man's anxiety; discussions in which the partners describe their expectations; increasing the variety and duration of foreplay; the *teasing technique* (Masters & Johnson, 1970), in which the woman alternately starts and stops stimulating the man; and beginning intercourse with the woman guiding the man's flaccid penis into her vagina.

Successful sex therapy usually ends with the couple's sex life much improved, but not as fantastic as frustrated expectations had led them to imagine—expectations that were part of the problem in the first place. As in any form of directive therapy, it's important for sex therapists to gradually fade out their involvement and control. Therapeutic gains are consolidated and extended by reviewing the changes that have occurred; by anticipating future trouble spots; and by planning in advance to deal with problems according to principles learned in treatment.

EVALUATING THERAPY THEORY AND RESULTS

Behavior therapy was born and bred in a tradition of research, and so it's not surprising that behavioral family therapy is the most carefully studied form of family treatment. Almost all reports of behavioral family therapy are accompanied by some assessment of outcome, and there are hundreds of reports of successful parent training, couples' treatment, and sex therapy. However, the majority of these are single case studies, both anecdotal and experimental. They do help substantiate the efficacy of the behavioral approach to problems in family living, but such case reports are probably better considered demonstrations than investigations. In addition, there are also a host of controlled experimental studies of behavior family therapy. Gordon and Davidson (1981) summarized studies of the effectiveness of behavioral parent training, and found that the majority of measures yielded positive results in the majority of cases. They reported hundreds of documented successes with a wide variety of problem children. The outcome criteria in studies of parent training are usually based on parents' and observers' frequency counts of prosocial and deviant behavior. Researchers have found that more advantaged families show distinctly better results from behavior parent training (O'Dell, 1974). This is not surprising, considering the heavy emphasis on theory and education in this approach.

A typical finding is that targeted behavior improves; only marginal changes, however, can be seen for nontargeted problem behavior. Apparently the specific focus on presenting problems in this approach lends leverage to resolving focal complaints, but only minimally generalizes to overall family functioning. Moreover, improvements do not generalize from home to other settings, such as school (Gurman & Kniskern, 1978). Finally, there is a tendency for therapeutic gains to decrease sharply between termination and follow-up.

The behavioral literature also contains a large number of empirical studies of marital therapy. These studies are usually done on brief treatment (approximately nine sessions) and the most common criteria of success are observers' ratings and couples' self-reports. In 1978 Gurman and Kniskern (1978) reported on eight controlled analogue studies; two showed behavioral couples therapy to be significantly better than no treatment; in five controlled analogue studies behavioral couples therapy was found to be more effective than alternative forms of treatment in only one case. In the same survey, Gurman and Kniskern found that six of seven naturalistic comparative studies favored behavioral couples therapy. These findings provide support for the efficacy of this approach; however, as the authors noted, behavioral therapy is still relatively untested on couples with severe marital problems. When they updated their survey in 1981, Gurman and Kniskern (1981) found similar results, and concluded that behavioral marriage therapy appears to be about as effective for mild to moderate marital problems as are nonbehavioral approaches.

Several studies have shown that the most effective ingredient in any form of marital therapy is increasing the couple's communication skills (Jacobson, 1978; Jacobson & Margolin, 1979). Jacobson's studies strongly support his approach, based on observational measures of communication and self-reported marital satisfaction. Liberman and his colleagues (Liberman, Levine, Wheeler, Sanders, & Wallace, 1976) found that on objective measures of marital communication, behavioral marriage therapy in a group setting was more effective than insight-oriented couples groups. However, the two approaches did not differ in effecting increased marital satisfaction. O'Leary and Turkewitz (1979) have shown that behavior exchange procedures are effective, especially with young couples; older couples tend to respond more favorably to communications training.

Despite the tremendous growth of public and professional interest in sex therapy, there are still few well-controlled studies of its effectiveness. In a careful review, Hogan (1978) found that most of the literature consists of uncontrolled, clinical case studies. These reports are little more than box scores of successes and failures. Absent are pre- and post-measures, detailed specification of techniques, points of reference other than the therapists, and follow-up data. Moreover, since most of these reports come from the same handful of therapists, it is impossible to discern what is being evaluated—the techniques of sex therapy or the skill of these particular therapists. This state of the research hadn't changed much by 1990, according to more recent summary reports (Crowe, 1988; Falloon & Lillie, 1988).

The greatest success rates with sexual therapy have been found in treating vaginismus, orgasmic dysfunction, and premature ejaculation. Vaginismus, the spastic contraction of vagina muscles, has been successfully treated in 90 to 95 percent of cases (Fuchs, Hoch, Paldi, Abramovici, Brandes, Timor-Tritsch, & Kleinhaus, 1973). Eighty-five to 95 percent of the women who had never previously achieved orgasm did so after treatment. Success rates are lower, 30 to 50 percent, when limited to those who had previously reached orgasm during coitus (Heiman, LoPiccolo, & LoPiccolo, 1981). The reported success rates for treatment of premature ejaculation using the squeeze technique (Masters & Johnson, 1970) are uniformly high, 90 to 95 percent.

For men who had never had erectile functioning, the success rates are between 40 and 60 percent—though, as Michael Crowe (1988) has noted, this problem turns out to be medically related more often than we used to think. For those who once had adequate erectile functioning and then developed difficulty, success rates average 60 to 80 percent (Heiman, LoPiccolo, & LoPiccolo, 1981). Retarded ejaculation or failure to ejaculate is relatively uncommon; consequently there are fewer reported treatment cases. Among this small sample, reported success rates range from 50 to 82 percent (Heiman, LoPiccolo, & LoPiccolo, 1981). Treatment of individuals with very low levels of interest in sex is relatively new (Kaplan, 1979) and there are as yet few statistics, but apparently such cases respond well to treatment (LoPiccolo & LoPiccolo, 1978).

The fact that there are relatively few published studies should not obscure the fact that sex therapy appears to be an effective procedure for some very vexing problems. Most observers (Gurman & Kniskern, 1981) agree that it should be considered the treatment of choice when there is an explicit complaint about a couple's sex life.

Currently there are three areas of research in family intervention that seem to be ready to move to a more advanced stage of development. These areas are: conduct disorders in children (Patterson, 1986; Morris, Alexander, & Waldron, 1988), marital conflict (Follette & Jacobson, 1988), and schizophrenic adults (Falloon, 1985).

SUMMARY

Although behavior therapists have begun to apply their techniques to family problems, they have done so, for the most part, within a linear frame of reference. Behavioral problems are regarded as *caused* by dysfunctional patterns of reinforcement between parents and children, or between spouses. Therefore, behavioral family therapy is used to teach parents how to apply learning theory to control their children; to help couples substitute positive for aversive control; and to decondition anxiety in partners with sexual problems. Behavioral family therapists give very little consideration to complex and circular family interactions.

Family symptoms are treated as learned responses, involuntarily acquired and reinforced. Treatment is generally time-limited and symptom-focused. The behavioral approach to families is based on social learning theory, which is a complex and sophisticated model, according to which behavior is learned and maintained by its consequences, and can be modified by altering those consequences.

Behaviorists' systematic analysis of behavior and their insistence on technically sound interventions make it clear that a therapist's personality is not all that's needed to help people change. Behaviorists don't believe that therapists have to *be* something—warm, self-disclosing, forceful—rather, they have to *do* something. Personal skills are required, not personal style; to treat behavioral problems you need to understand behavioral theory.

An essential adjunct to social learning theory is Thibaut and Kelley's exchange theory, according to which people strive to maximize interpersonal "rewards" while minimizing "costs." Social behavior in a relationship is maintained by a high ratio of rewards to costs, and by the perception that alternative relationships offer fewer rewards and more costs (comparison level of alternatives). In this view, marital and family conflicts occur when optimal behavior-maintaining contingencies do not exist, or when dysfunctional behavior change methods are applied. In unhappy families, coercion replaces reciprocity.

The general goals of behavioral family therapy are to increase the rate of rewarding exchanges; to decrease aversive exchanges; and to teach communication and problem-solving skills. Specific techniques are applied to target behaviors; in the process, families are also taught general principles of behavior management.

The behaviorists' focus on modifying the consequences of problem behavior accounts for some of the strengths and weaknesses of behavioral family therapy. By concentrating their attention on presenting problems, behaviorists have been able to develop an impressive array of effective techniques. Even such relatively intractable problems as delinquent behavior in children and severe sexual dysfunctions have yielded to behavioral technology. On the other hand, behavior is only part of the person, and the problem person is only part of the family. Any form of therapy must deal with the whole person, who not only acts but also thinks and feels. Different therapies may concentrate on only one of these three human functions—psychoanalysts concentrate on thinking, just as behaviorists concentrate on action—but to be successful a therapy must affect all three. You can't simply teach people to change if unrecognized conflict is keeping them stuck.

Unhappiness may center around a behavioral complaint, but resolution of the behavior may not resolve the unhappiness. Treatment may succeed with the symptom but fail the family. Attitudes and feelings may change along with changes in behavior, but not necessarily. And teaching communication skills may not be sufficient to resolve real conflict. Mere behavior change may not be enough for family members whose ultimate goal is to feel better. "Yes, he's doing his chores now," a parent may agree. "But I don't think he *feels* like helping out. He still isn't really part of our family." Behavior isn't all that family members in distress are concerned about, and to be responsive to all their needs behavioral family therapists need to deal with cognitive and affective issues, as well as behavioral.

Although behavioral family clinicians recognize the need to modify interpersonal interactions, they generally limit their attention to units of two, and they tend to accept the family's definition of one person (or couple) as *the* problem. Virtually no consideration is given to the role of marital problems in behavioral treatment of children, and behavioral couples therapists rarely discuss the role that children or extended family members play in marital distress.

Behaviorists hardly ever treat whole families. Instead they bring in only those subsystems that they consider central to the targeted behaviors. Unfortunately, failure to include—or even consider—whole families in treatment may be disastrous. A therapeutic program to reduce a son's aggressiveness toward his mother can hardly succeed if the father wants an aggressive son, or if the father's anger toward his wife is not more directly addressed. Moreover, if the whole family is not involved in change, new behavior may not be reinforced and maintained.

Despite these shortcomings, behavioral family therapy offers impressive techniques for treating problems with children and troubled marriages. Furthermore, its weaknesses can be corrected by broadening the focus of conceptualization and the scope of treatment to include whole families as systems. Although some behavior therapists may be naive about circular interactions and systemic structure, there is nothing inherently limiting in the usefulness of their technology.

Perhaps the greatest strength of behavior therapy is its insistence on observing what happens and then measuring change. Behaviorists have developed a wealth of reliable and valid assessment methods and applied them to initial evaluation, treatment planning, and monitoring progress and outcome. A second important advance has been the gradual movement from eliminating or reinforcing discrete "marker" behaviors to the teaching of general problem-solving, cognitive, and communicational skills. A third major advance in current behavioral family therapy is modular treatment interventions organized to meet the specific and changing needs of the individual and the family.

REFERENCES

Ables, B. S., and Brandsma, S. J. 1977. *Therapy for couples.* San Francisco: Jossey-Bass.

Alexander, J. F., and Barton, C. 1976. *Behavioral systems therapy with families.* In Treating relationships, D. H. Olson, ed. Lake Mills, IA: Graphic Publishing.

Alexander, J. F., and Parsons, B. V. 1973. Short-term behavioral intervention with delinquent families: Impact on family process and recidivism. *Journal of Abnormal Psychology. 51*:219–225.

Anderson, C. M., and Stewart, S. 1983. *Mastering resistance.* New York: Guilford Press.

Arrington, A., Sullaway, M., and Christensen, A. 1988. Behavioral family assessment. In *Handbook of behavioral family therapy,* I. R. H. Falloon, ed. New York: Guilford Press.

Azrin, N. H., Naster, J. B., and Jones, R. 1973. Reciprocity counseling: A rapid learning-based procedure for marital counseling. *Behavior Research and Therapy. 11*:365–383.

Baer, D. M., and Sherman, J. A. 1964. Reinforcement control of generalized imitation in young children. *Journal of Experimental Child Psychology. 1*:37–49.

Bancroft, J. 1975. The behavioral approach to marital problems. *British Journal of Medical Psychology. 48*:147–152.

Bandura, A. 1969. *Principles of behavior modification.* New York: Holt, Rinehart & Winston.

Bandura, A., and Walters, R. 1963. *Social learning and personality development.* New York: Holt, Rinehart & Winston.

Barton, C., and Alexander, J. F. 1975. Therapist skills in systems-behavioral family intervention: How the hell do you get them to do it? Paper presented at the annual meeting of the Orthopsychiatric Association, Atlanta.

Barton, C., and Alexander, J. F. 1981. Functional family therapy. In *Handbook of family therapy,* A. S. Gurman and D. P. Kniskern, eds. New York: Brunner/Mazel.

Beck, A. T. 1976. *Cognitive therapy and the emotional disorders.* New York: International Universities Press.

Birchler, G. R. 1988. Handling resistance to change. In *Handbook of behavioral family therapy,* I. R. H. Falloon, ed. New York: Guilford Press.

Birchler, G. R., and Spinks, S. H. 1980. Behavioral-systems marital therapy: Integration and clinical application. *American Journal of Family Therapy. 8*:6–29.

Boardman, W. K. 1962. Rusty: A brief behavior disorder. *Journal of Consulting Psychology. 26*:293–297.

Christophersen, E. R., Arnold, C. M., Hill, D. W., and Quilitch, H. R. 1972. The home point system: Token reinforcement procedures for application by parents of children with behavioral problems. *Journal of Applied Behavioral Analysis. 5*:485–497.

Crowe, M. 1988. Indications for family, marital, and sexual therapy. In *Handbook of behavioral family therapy*, I. R. H. Falloon, ed. New York: Guilford Press.

DiGiuseppe, R. 1988. A cognitive-behavioral approach to the treatment of conduct disorder children and adolescents. In *Cognitive-behavioral therapy with families*, N. Epstein, S. E. Schlesinger, and W. Dryden, eds. New York: Brunner/Mazel.

Eisler, R. M., and Hersen, M. 1973. Behavior techniques in family-oriented crisis intervention. *Archives of General Psychiatry. 28*:111–116.

Ellis, A. 1962. *Reason and emotion in psychotherapy*. New York: Lyle Stuart.

Ely, A. L., Guerney, B. G., and Stover, L. 1973. Efficacy of the training phase of conjugal therapy. *Psychotherapy: Theory, Research and Practice. 10*:201–207.

Epstein, N., Schlesinger, S. E., and Dryden, W., eds. 1988. *Cognitive-behavioral therapy with families*. New York: Brunner/Mazel.

Falloon, I. R. H. 1985. *Family management of schizophrenia: A study of the clinical, social, family and economic benefits*. Baltimore: Johns Hopkins University Press.

Falloon, I. R. H., ed. 1988. *Handbook of behavioral family therapy*. New York: Guilford Press.

Falloon, I. R. H. 1991. Behavioral family therapy. In *Handbook of family therapy*, vol. II, A. S. Gurman and D. P. Kniskern, eds. New York: Brunner/Mazel.

Falloon, I. R. H., and Liberman, R. P. 1983. Behavioral therapy for families with child management problems. In *Helping families with special problems*, M. R. Textor, ed. New York: Jason Aronson.

Falloon, I. R. H., and Lillie, F. J. 1988. Behavioral family therapy: An overview. In *Handbook of behavioral family therapy*, I. R. H. Falloon, ed. New York: Guilford Press.

Ferster, C. B. 1963. Essentials of a science of behavior. In *An introduction to the science of human behavior*, J. I. Nurnberger, C. B. Ferster, and J. P. Brady, eds. New York: Appleton-Century-Crofts.

Follette, W. C., and Jacobson, N. S. 1988. Behavioral marital therapy in the treatment of depressive disorders. In *Handbook of behavioral family therapy*, I. R. H. Falloon, ed. New York: Guilford Press.

Forehand, R., and McDonough, T. S. 1975. Response-contingent time out: An examination of outcome data. *European Journal of Behavioral Analysis and Modification. 1*:109–115.

Forehand, R., Roberts, M. W., Doleys, D. M., Hobbs, S. A., and Resnick, P. A. 1976. An examination of disciplinary procedures with children. *Journal of Experimental Child Psychology. 21*:109–120.

Friedman, P. H. 1972. Personalistic family and marital therapy. In *Clinical behavior therapy*, A. A. Lazarus, ed. New York: Brunner/Mazel.

Fuchs, K., Hoch, Z., Paldi, E., Abramovici, H., Brandes, J. M., Timor-Tritsch, I., and Kleinhaus, M. 1973. Hypnodesensitization therapy of vaginismus: Part 1. "In vitro" method. Part 11. "In vivo" method. *International Journal of Clinical and Experimental Hypnosis. 21*:144–156.

Gill, H., and Temperly, J. 1974. Time-limited marital treatment in a foursome. *British Journal of Medical Psychology. 47*:153–161.

Goldiamond, I. 1965. Self-control procedures in personal behavior problems. *Psychological Reports. 17*:851–868.

Goldstein, M. K. 1971. Behavior rate change in marriages: Training wives to modify husbands' behavior. *Dissertation Abstracts International. 32*(18):559.

Goldstein, M. K., and Francis, B. 1969. Behavior modification of husbands by wives. Paper presented at the National Council on Family Relations, Washington, DC.

Gordon, S. B., and Davidson, N. 1981. Behavioral parent training. In *Handbook of family therapy*, A. S. Gurman and D. P. Kniskern, eds. New York: Brunner/Mazel.

Gottman, J. and Krokoff, L. 1989. Marital interaction and satisfaction: A longitudinal view. *Journal of Consulting and Clinical Psychology. 57:*47–52.

Gottman, J., Markman, H., and Notarius, C. 1977. The topography of marital conflict: A sequential analysis of verbal and nonverbal behavior. *Journal of Marriage and the Family. 39:*461–477.

Graziano, A. M. 1977. Parents as behavior therapists. In *Progress in behavior modification,* M. Hersen, R. M. Eisler, and P. M. Miller, eds. New York: Academic Press.

Guerin, P. J., Fay, L., Burden, S. L., and Kautto, J. B. 1987. *The evaluation and treatment of marital conflict: A four-stage approach.* New York: Basic Books.

Gurman, A. S., and Kniskern, D. P. 1978. Research on marital and family therapy: Progress, perspective and prospect. In *Handbook of psychotherapy and behavior change: An empirical analysis,* S. L. Garfield and A. E. Bergin, eds. New York: Wiley.

Gurman, A. S., and Kniskern, D. P. 1981. Family therapy outcome research: Knowns and unknowns. In *Handbook of family therapy,* A. S. Gurman and D. P. Kniskern, eds. New York: Brunner/Mazel.

Gurman, A. S., and Knudson, R. M. 1978. Behavioral marriage therapy: A psychodynamic-systems analysis and critique. *Family Process. 17:*121–138.

Hawkins, R. P., Peterson, R. F., Schweid, E., and Bijou, S. W. 1966. Behavior therapy in the home: Amelioration of problem parent-child relations with a parent in the therapeutic role. *Journal of Experimental Child Psychology. 4:*99–107.

Heiman, J. R., LoPiccolo, L., and LoPiccolo, J. 1981. The treatment of sexual dysfunction. In *Handbook of family therapy,* A. S. Gurman and D. P. Kniskern, eds. New York: Brunner/Mazel.

Hickman, M. E., and Baldwin, B. A. 1971. Use of programmed instruction to improve communication in marriage. *The Family Coordinator. 20:*121–125.

Hogan, D. R. 1978. The effectiveness of sex therapy: A review of the literature. In *Handbook of sex therapy,* J. LoPiccolo and L. LoPiccolo, eds. New York: Plenum Press.

Holtzworth-Munroe, A., and Jacobson, N. S. 1991. Behavioral marital therapy. In *Handbook of family therapy,* vol. II, A. S. Gurman and D. P. Kniskern, eds. New York: Brunner/Mazel.

Jacobson, N. S. 1977. Problem solving and contingency contracting in the treatment of marital discord. *Journal of Consulting and Clinical Psychology. 45:*92–100.

Jacobson, N. S. 1978. Specific and nonspecific factors in the effectiveness of a behavioral approach to the treatment of marital discord. *Journal of Consulting and Clinical Psychology. 46:*442–452.

Jacobson, N. S. 1981. Behavioral marital therapy. In *Handbook of family therapy,* A. S. Gurman and D. P. Kniskern, eds. New York: Brunner/Mazel.

Jacobson, N. S., and Margolin, G. 1979. *Marital therapy: Strategies based on social learning and behavior exchange principles.* New York: Brunner/Mazel.

Jacobson, N. S., and Martin, B. 1976. Behavioral marriage therapy: Current status. *Psychological Bulletin. 83:*540–556.

Jacobson, N. S., Waldron, H., and Moore, D. 1980. Toward a behavioral profile of marital distress. *Journal of Consulting and Clinical Psychology. 48:*696–703.

Jones, M. C. 1924. A laboratory study of fear: The case of Peter. *Journal of Geriatric Psychology. 31:*308–315.

Kanfer, F. H., and Phillips, J. S. 1970. *Learning foundations of behavior therapy.* New York: Wiley.

Kaplan, H. S. 1974. *The new sex therapy: Active treatment of sexual dysfunctions.* New York: Brunner/Mazel.

Kaplan, H. S. 1979. *Disorders of sexual desire and other new concepts and techniques in sex therapy.* New York: Brunner/Mazel.

Katkin, E. S. 1978. Charting as a multipurpose treatment intervention in family therapy. *Family Process. 17:*465–468.

Keefe, F. J., Kopel, S. A., and Gordon, S. B. 1978. *A practical guide to behavior assessment.* New York: Springer.

Kimmel, C. and Van der Veen, F. 1974. Factors of marital adjustment in Locke's Marital Adjustment Test. *Journal of Marriage and the Family, 36:*57–63.

Knox, D. 1971. *Marriage happiness: A behavioral approach to counseling.* Champaign, IL: Research Press.

Knox, D. 1973. Behavior contracts in marriage counseling. *Journal of Family Counseling. 1:*22–28.

Lazarus, A. A. 1965. The treatment of a sexually inadequate male. In *Case studies in behavior modification,* L. P. Ullmann and L. Krasner, eds. New York: Holt, Rinehart & Winston.

Lazarus, A. A. 1968. Behavior therapy and group marriage counseling. *Journal of the American Society of Medicine and Dentistry. 15:*49–56.

Lazarus, A. A. 1971. *Behavior therapy and beyond.* New York: McGraw-Hill.

LeBow, M. D. 1972. Behavior modification for the family. In *Family therapy: An introduction to theory and technique,* G. D. Erickson and T. P. Hogan, eds. Monterey, CA: Brooks/Cole.

Lederer, W. J., and Jackson, D. D. 1968. *The mirages of marriage.* New York: Norton.

Liberman, R. P. 1970. Behavioral approaches to family and couple therapy. *American Journal of Orthopsychiatry. 40:*106–118.

Liberman, R. P. 1972. Behavioral approaches to family and couple therapy. In *Progress in group and family therapy,* C. J. Sager and H. S. Kaplan, eds. New York: Brunner/Mazel.

Liberman, R. P., Levine, J., Wheeler, E., Sanders, N., and Wallace, C. 1976. Experimental evaluation of marital group therapy: Behavioral vs. interaction-insight formats. *Acta Psychiatrica Scandinavia* Supplement.

Lobitz, N. C., and LoPiccolo, J. 1972. New methods in the behavioral treatment of sexual dysfunction. *Journal of Behavior Therapy and Experimental Psychiatry. 3:*265–271.

Locke, H. J., and Wallace, K. M. 1959. Short-term marital adjustment and prediction tests: Their reliability and validity. *Journal of Marriage and Family Living. 21:*251–255.

LoPiccolo, J., and LoPiccolo, L. 1978. *Handbook of sex therapy.* New York: Plenum.

Lovibond, S. H. 1963. The mechanism of conditioning treatment of enuresis. *Behavior Research and Therapy. 1:*17–21.

Mahoney, M. J. 1977. Reflections on the cognitive learning trend in psychotherapy. *American Psychologist. 32:*5–13.

Markman, H. J. 1979. Application of a behavioral model of marriage in predicting relationship satisfaction of couples planning marriage. *Journal of Consulting and Clinical Psychology. 47:*743–749.

Markman, H. J. 1981. Prediction of marital distress: A 5-year follow up. *Journal of Consulting and Clinical Psychology. 49:*760–762.

Masters, W. H., and Johnson, V. E. 1970. *Human sexual inadequacy.* Boston: Little, Brown.

McCauley, R. 1988. Parent training: Clinical application. In *Handbook of behavioral family therapy,* I. R. H. Falloon, ed. New York: Guilford Press.

McGuire, R. J., and Vallance, M. 1964. Aversion therapy by electric shock: A simple technique. *British Medical Journal. 1:*151–153.

Meichenbaum, D. 1977. *Cognitive behavior modification.* New York: Plenum.

Minuchin, S. 1974. *Families and family therapy.* Cambridge, MA: Harvard University Press.

Minuchin, S., Rosman, B. L., and Baker, L. 1978. *Psychosomatic families.* Cambridge, MA: Harvard University Press.

Mischel, W. 1973. On the empirical dilemmas of psychodynamic approaches: Issues and alternatives. *Journal of Abnormal Psychology.* 82:335.

Morris, S. B., Alexander, J. F., and Waldron, H. 1988. Functional family therapy. In *Handbook of behavioral family therapy,* I. R. H. Falloon, ed. New York: Guilford Press.

Morton, T. L., Twentyman, C. T., and Azar, S. T. 1988. Cognitive-behavioral assessment and treatment of child abuse. In *Cognitive-behavioral therapy with families,* N. Epstein, S. E. Schlesinger, and W. Dryden, eds. New York: Brunner/Mazel.

O'Dell, S. 1974. Training parents in behavior modification: A review. *Psychological Bulletin.* 81:418–433.

O'Leary, K. D., O'Leary, S., and Becher, W. C. 1967. Modification of a deviant sibling interaction pattern in the home. *Behavior Research and Therapy.* 5:113–120.

O'Leary, K. D., and Turkewitz, H. 1978. Marital therapy from a behavioral perspective. In *Marriage and marital therapy,* T. J. Paolino and B. S. McCrady, eds. New York: Brunner/Mazel.

O'Leary, K. D., and Wilson, G. T. 1975. *Behavior therapy: Application and outcome.* Englewood Cliffs, NJ: Prentice Hall.

Patterson, G. R. 1971a. Behavioral intervention procedures in the classroom and in the home. In *Handbook of psychotherapy and behavior change: An empirical analysis,* A. E. Bergin and S. L. Garfield, eds. New York: Wiley.

Patterson, G. R. 1971b. *Families: Application of social learning theory to family life.* Champaign, IL: Research Press.

Patterson, G. R. 1986. The contribution of siblings to training for fighting; A microsocial analysis. In *Development of antisocial and prosocial behavior: Research, theories, and issues,* D. Olweus, J. Block, and M. Radke-Yarrow, eds. Orlando, FL: Academic Press.

Patterson, G. R. 1988. Foreword. In *Handbook of behavioral family therapy,* I. R. H. Falloon, ed. New York: Guilford Press.

Patterson, G. R., and Hops, H. 1972. Coercion, a game for two. In *The experimental analysis of social behavior,* R. E. Ulrich and P. Mountjoy, eds. New York: Appleton-Century-Crofts.

Patterson, G. R., Hops, H., and Weiss, R. L. 1973. A social learning approach to reducing rates of marital conflict. In *Advances in behavior therapy,* R. Stuart, R. Liberman, and S. Wilder, eds. New York: Academic Press.

Patterson, G. R., and Reid, J. 1970. Reciprocity and coercion; two facets of social systems. In *Behavior modification in clinical psychology,* C. Neuringer and J. Michael, eds. New York: Appleton-Century-Crofts.

Patterson, G. R., Weiss, R. L., and Hops, H. 1976. Training in marital skills: Some problems and concepts. In *Handbook of behavior modification and behavior therapy,* H. Leitenberg, ed. Englewood Cliffs, NJ: Prentice Hall.

Pavlov, I. P. 1932. Neuroses in man and animals. *Journal of the American Medical Association.* 99:1012–1013.

Pavlov, I. P. 1934. An attempt at a physiological interpretation of obsessional neurosis and paranoia. *Journal of Mental Science.* 80:187–197.

Pendergrass, V. E. 1971. Effects of length of timeout from positive reinforcement and schedule of application in suppression of aggressive behavior. *Psychological Record.* 21:75–80.

Pierce, R. M. 1973. Training in interpersonal communication skills with the partners of deteriorated marriages. *The Family Coordinator.* 22:223–227.

Premack, D. 1965. Reinforcement theory. In *Nebraska symposium on motivation,* D. Levine, ed. Lincoln, NB: University of Nebraska Press.

Rappaport, A. F., and Harrell, J. A. 1972. A behavior-exchange model for marital counseling. *Family Coordinator. 21:*203–213.

Rimm, D. C., and Masters, J. C. 1974. *Behavior therapy: Techniques and empirical findings.* New York: Wiley.

Rinn, R. C. 1978. Children with behavior disorders. In *Behavior therapy in the psychiatric setting,* M. Hersen and A. S. Bellack, eds. Baltimore: Williams & Wilkins.

Risley, T. R. 1968. The effects and side effects of punishing the autistic behaviors of a deviant child. *Journal of Applied Behavior Analysis. 1:*21–34.

Risley, T. R., and Wolf, M. M. 1967. Experimental manipulation of autistic behaviors and generalization into the home. In *Child development: Readings in experimental analysis,* S. W. Bijou and D. M. Baer, eds. New York: Appleton.

Romanczyk, R. G., and Kistner, J. J. 1977. The current state of the art in behavior modification. *The Psychotherapy Bulletin. 11:*16–30.

Schwitzgebel, R. 1967. Short-term operant conditioning of adolescent offenders on socially relevant variables. *Journal of Abnormal Psychology. 72:*134–142.

Schwitzgebel, R., and Kolb, D. A. 1964. Inducing behavior change in adolescent delinquents. *Behaviour Research and Therapy. 9:*233–238.

Semans, J. H. 1956. Premature ejaculation: A new approach. *Southern Medical Journal. 49:*353–357.

Skinner, B. F. 1953. *Science and human behavior.* New York: Macmillan.

Spinks, S. H., and Birchler, G. R. 1982. Behavior systems marital therapy: Dealing with resistance. *Family Process. 21:*169–186.

Stuart, R. B. 1969. An operant-interpersonal treatment for marital discord. *Journal of Consulting and Clinical Psychology. 33:*675–682.

Stuart, R. B. 1971. Behavioral contracting within the families of delinquents. *Journal of Behavior Therapy and Experimental Psychiatry. 2:*1–11.

Stuart, R. B. 1975. Behavioral remedies for marital ills: A guide to the use of operant-interpersonal techniques. In *International symposium on behavior modification,* T. Thompson and W. Docken, eds. New York: Appleton.

Stuart, R. B. 1976. An operant interpersonal program for couples. In *Treating relationships,* D. H. Olson, ed. Lake Mills, IA: Graphic Publishing.

Stuart, R. B. 1980. *Helping couples change: A social learning approach to marital therapy.* New York: Guilford Press.

Thibaut, J., and Kelley, H. H. 1959. *The social psychology of groups.* New York: Wiley.

Umana, R. F., Gross, S. J., and McConville, N. T. 1980. *Crisis in the family: Three approaches.* New York: Gardner Press.

Vincent, J. P., Weiss, R. L., and Birchler, G. R. 1975. A behavioral analysis of problem solving in distressed and nondistressed married and stranger dyads. *Behavior Therapy. 6:*475–487.

Watson, J. B., and Raynor, R. 1920. Conditioned emotional reactions. *Journal of Experimental Psychology. 3:*1–14.

Weiss, R. L. 1978. The conceptualization of marriage from a behavioral perspective. In *Marriage and marital therapy,* T. J. Paolino and B. S. McCrady, eds. New York: Brunner/Mazel.

Weiss, R. L., and Birchler, G. R. 1978. Adults with marital dysfunction. In *Behavior therapy in the psychiatric setting,* M. Hersen and A. S. Bellack, eds. Baltimore: Williams & Wilkins.

Weiss, R. L., Hops, H., and Patterson, G. R. 1973. A framework for conceptualizing marital conflict, a technology for altering it, some data for evaluating it. In *Behavior change: Methodology, concepts and practice,* L. A. Hamerlynch, L. C. Handy, and E. J. Marsh, eds. Champaign, IL: Research Press.

Weiss, R. L., and Isaac, J. 1978. Behavior vs. cognitive measures as predictors of marital satisfaction. Paper presented at the Western Psychological Association meeting, Los Angeles.

Williams, C. D. 1959. The elimination of tantrum behavior by extinction procedures. *Journal of Abnormal and Social Psychology.* *59:*269.

Wills, T. A., Weiss, R. L., and Patterson, G. R. 1974. A behavioral analysis of the determinants of marital satisfaction. *Journal of Consulting and Clinical Psychology.* *42:*802–811.

Wodarski, J., and Thyer, B. 1989. Behavioral perspectives on the family: An overview. In *Behavioral family therapy,* B. Thyer, ed. Springfield, IL: Charles Thomas.

Wolpe, J. 1948. An approach to the problem of neurosis based on the conditioned response. Unpublished M.D. thesis. University of Witwatersrand, Johannesberg, South Africa.

Wolpe, J. 1958. *Psychotherapy by reciprocal inhibition.* Stanford, CA: Stanford University Press.

Wolpe, J. 1969. *The practice of behavior therapy.* New York: Pergamon Press.

Bowenian Family Therapy

The pioneers of family therapy recognized that people are products of social context, but usually limited their attention to the nuclear family. They had the same kind of fervor as the first behavior therapists, who discovered the power of reinforcement to modify behavior, and they had the same kind of narrowness. Yes, our actions are powerfully influenced by what goes on in our immediate families, and often one person's symptoms can be resolved by altering interactions in the nuclear family. But what about the forces, past and present, that generate those patterns? What makes a husband distance himself from the emotional demands of family life? And what makes a wife neglect her own life to manage her children's lives? Murray Bowen sought answers—and solutions—to such questions in the larger network of family relationships.

Bowenian family therapy has by far the most comprehensive view of human behavior and human problems of any approach to family treatment. It extends the focus deeper—into the hearts and minds of family members—and broader—into the wider family context that shaped, and continues to shape, the life of the family.

While no one doubts the formative influence of family on molding personality, many people imagine that once they leave home they are grown up: independent adults, free at last of their parents' influence. Some people prize individuality and take it as a sign of growth to separate from their parents; others wish they could be closer to their families but find visits home too painful, and so they stay away to protect themselves from disappointment and hurt. Once out of range of the immediate conflict, they forget and deny the discord. But as Bowen discovered, the family remains within us. Wherever we go, we carry unresolved emotional reactivity to our parents, in the form of vulnerability to repeat the same old patterns in every new intense relationship we enter into. As we shall see, unresolved relationships with our original families are the most important unfinished business of our lives.

SKETCHES OF LEADING FIGURES

Bowenian family systems therapy is a theoretical-clinical model that evolved directly from psychoanalytic principles and practice. Murray Bowen, its originator and major contributor, has been a dominant force in the family therapy movement since the early 1950s. His preeminent position is due not only to the fact that he was one of the parent figures in the field, but also to the innovative and comprehensive nature of his ideas.

Bowen was the oldest child in a large, cohesive family living in rural Tennessee. After medical school and internship, he served for five years in the military. There he saw widespread psychopathology, matched by equally widespread ignorance about how to deal with it, which inspired him to seek a career in psychiatry. Here, Bowen felt, he could chart a course through largely unknown territory.

Once in psychiatry Bowen turned his attention to the enigma of schizophrenia. Thoroughly trained in psychoanalysis, including undergoing thirteen years of personal analysis, Bowen, not surprisingly, sought to apply psychoanalytic concepts to schizophrenia. He began by expanding his focus from the schizophrenic patient to the mother-child dyad. The goal of this work was to further the understanding of "mother-child symbiosis." These studies began at the Menninger Clinic where Bowen trained and remained on staff until 1954. From Menninger he moved to the National Institute of Mental Health (NIMH) where he became the first director of the Family Division. One of the major observations to come out of the "mother-child symbiosis" research was the observation of repetitive relationship patterns: alternating cycles of closeness and distance, exquisitely sensitive to shifts in emotional tension within either mother or child, or the relationship between them. Separation anxiety coupled with incorporation anxiety was believed to be the underlying dynamic. From these observations Bowen focused on the notion of "anxious attachment," a pathological form of attachment driven by anxiety and emotionality that subverted reason and self-control. Anxious attachment is the opposite of "functional attachment," which is a central aspect of *differentiation*.

When Bowen moved to NIMH he expanded the scope of his studies to include fathers, and began to work out the concept of *triangles* as the central building block of relationship systems. From NIMH Bowen moved to Georgetown University's Department of Psychiatry in 1959. His plan was to transfer the NIMH family research team to Georgetown in order to continue and expand their work. Unfortunately the chairman of psychiatry who recruited Bowen, George Raines, died in 1959, and the team never got the chance to join Bowen. During the NIMH days Bowen had begun two additional projects. One was the development of a model of family psychotherapy for use with a less disturbed population; the second was the application of his newly discovered concepts to the study of his own family. Now at Georgetown, but without his research team, he concentrated on theory building, personal family study, and teaching and supervision of psychiatric residents.

During his thirty-one years at Georgetown Bowen developed his comprehensive theory of family therapy, inspired an entire generation of students, and became an internationally renowned leader of the family therapy movement. He died after a long illness in October 1990.

Among the most prominent and influential of Bowen's students are Philip Guerin and Thomas Fogarty. Both trained by Bowen, they joined together on the faculty of the Einstein Family Studies Section where Israel Zwerling and Andrew Ferber attempted to bring together a faculty representative of the diversity of thinking and practice in the field of family therapy. While at Einstein they trained Betty Carter, Monica McGoldrick (then Orfanidis), Ed Gordon, Eileen Pendagast, and Katherine Guerin, all of whom, along with Peggy Papp, joined Guerin and Fogarty in 1973 to form the Center for Family Learning in New Rochelle, New York. Under Guerin's leadership, the Center for Family Learning has become one of the major centers of family therapy training and practice.

While working on her M.S.W. at Hunter College, Elizabeth (Betty) Carter was unable to find a field placement in group therapy and so settled for something new called "family therapy" at the Ackerman Clinic. There, with fellow student Olga Silverstein, she learned about technique from Nathan Ackerman, but not much about how families function. Then she read Murray Bowen and felt a whole new world of understanding open up. From that moment she became an avid student of Bowen's approach, attending as many workshops as she could find, and then studying with Phil Guerin and Marilyn Mendelsohn at Einstein.

In 1977 Carter left the Center for Family Learning to become the founding director of the Family Institute of Westchester. She was joined by Monica McGoldrick, Fredda Herz, Ken Terkelson, and others. An ardent and articulate feminist, she is also Codirector of the Women's Project in Family Therapy with Peggy Papp, Olga Silverstein, and Marianne Walters. Today, in addition to being a respected leader in the field of family therapy and a popular teacher, Betty Carter is an active clinician who specializes in marital therapy and therapy with remarried couples.

Monica McGoldrick is another therapist in the Bowenian tradition who, like her friend and colleague Betty Carter, has become one of the most respected voices in the field. McGoldrick is the founding director of the Family Institute of New Jersey and Associate Professor of Psychiatry, UMDNJ-Robert Wood Johnson Medical School. She is a popular teacher and writer, and a leader in the field of family therapy. Among her clinical special interests are ethnicity, genograms, family therapy with one person, remarried families, and dual-career families.

Many of Bowen's students continued to work with him for a long time, among them Michael Kerr, Edward Beal, Edwin Friedman, Jack Bradt, Joseph Lorio, Charles Paddock, and Daniel Papero. Each is an important representative of the extended family systems tradition, and all have helped transmit Bowen's ideas in their teaching and through papers presented at the annual George-town Family Symposium.

Edwin Friedman, who works in the Washington, D.C. area, is both a rabbi and a family therapist. Trained by Murray Bowen, he brings an extended family systems perspective to bear on religious life. One of his most important con-tributions has been introducing a sophisticated understanding and compe-tence in family systems theory to ancillary professionals, especially pastoral counselors.

Michael Kerr, M.D., has been a long-time student and colleague of Bowen's, and since 1977 the director of training at the Georgetown Family Center. Kerr is probably the most scholarly, informed, and faithful to the original theory of all Bowen's students, as his brilliant account of Bowen theory in the book *Family Evaluation* (Kerr & Bowen, 1988) richly demonstrates.

Finally, we should mention James Framo, for many years one of the lead-ing figures in family therapy. Although Framo is often thought of either as an independent practitioner or as a colleague of Ivan Boszormenyi-Nagy, he in-corporates many of Murray Bowen's ideas in his own work. Framo is perhaps most well-known for his steadfast advocacy of couples groups.

Several key publications over the years are markers in the development of Bowenian family systems theory. Bowen's first major paper outlining the concepts of his new theory was "The Use of Family Theory in Clinical Prac-tice," published in 1966. A year later at a Philadelphia conference organized by James Framo, Bowen delivered his first organized presentation of the ap-plication of his theory to his own personal family system (Anonymous, 1972). In 1976 Guerin edited a classic anthology of original papers, one of the most valuable books in the family therapy literature (Guerin, *Family Therapy: Theory and Practice*). In 1978 Bowen assembled all of his own papers from various professional journals and published them in *Family Therapy in Clinical Practice*. In 1987 Guerin and his colleagues at The Center for Family Learning's "marital project," Judith Kautto, Susan Burden, and Leo Fay, published *The Evaluation and Treatment of Marital Conflict*, one of the best and most useful books ever written in family therapy. In the following year Carter and McGoldrick (1988) published a revised edition of their acclaimed book on the family life cycle. Finally, the publication of Family Evaluation by Michael Kerr and Murray Bowen in 1988 represents the mature and comprehensive flowering of Bowen's ideas.

THEORETICAL FORMULATIONS

Most of the early family therapists were pragmatists, more concerned with action than insight, and more interested in technique than theory. Murray Bowen was the exception to this rule. Bowen, among the most cerebral of all family therapists, has always been more committed to family as an orientation rather than a method, and more interested in theory than technique. From his point of view most mental health professionals are too caught up in nar-row questions of technique to ever fully grasp what systems theory is all about. Bowen's own theory is among the most carefully worked out and influential of family systems.

Although Bowenian theory has evolved and expanded, it has always centered around two counterbalancing life forces: those that bind personalities in family *togetherness,* and those that fight to break free toward *individuality.* Ideally these two forces are in balance. Unbalance in the direction of togetherness is called variously "fusion," "stuck-togetherness," and "undifferentiation" (Kerr & Bowen, 1988). *Differentiation,* the capacity for autonomous functioning, helps people avoid getting caught up in reactive polarities. Otherwise emotional reactivity results in polarized positions: *pursuer-distancer, overfunctioning-underfunctioning,* and so on. The concepts Bowen has used to express this central tension of the human condition have evolved from *mother-child symbiosis,* to *undifferentiated family ego mass,* to *fusion/differentiation.* However phrased, the central premise is that unresolved emotional attachment to one's family must be resolved, rather than passively accepted or reactively rejected, before one can differentiate a mature, healthy personality.

Bowen articulated the core concepts of his theory in two major papers: "The Use of Family Theory in Clinical Practice" (1966) and "Theory in the Practice of Psychotherapy" (1976). In the 1966 paper Bowen cited six interlocking concepts that make up his theory: *differentiation of self, triangles, nuclear family emotional process, family projection process, multigenerational transmission process,* and *sibling position.* He added two additional concepts in the 1970s (Bowen, 1976): *emotional cutoff* and *societal emotional process.*

Differentiation of Self

Differentiation of self, the cornerstone of Bowen's theory, is both an intrapsychic and interpersonal concept. Intrapsychic differentiation is the ability to separate feeling from thinking. Undifferentiated people hardly distinguish thoughts from feelings; their intellects are so flooded with feelings that they are almost incapable of objective thinking. Their lives are governed by an accretion of feelings from those around them, either blindly adhered to or angrily rejected. The differentiated person, on the other hand, is not a cold fish who only thinks and never feels. Instead, he or she is able to balance thinking and feeling: capable of strong emotion and spontaneity, but also capable of the restraint and objectivity that comes with the ability to resist the pull of emotional impulses.

Lack of differentiation between thinking and feeling occurs in concert with lack of differentiation between oneself and others. Because they are less able to think clearly, undifferentiated people react emotionally—positively or negatively—to the dictates of family members, or other authority figures. These people have little autonomous identity. Instead they tend to be fused with others. They find it difficult to separate themselves from others, particularly on important issues. Asked what they think, they say what they feel; asked what they believe, they echo what they've heard. They either conform or assume pseudo-independence through counter-conformity. In contrast, differentiated people are able to take definite stands on issues because they are able to think things through, decide what they believe, and then act on those beliefs. This enables them to be in intimate contact with others without being reflexively shaped by them.

Guerin defines differentiation as the process of partially freeing oneself from the emotional chaos of one's family. Getting free takes analyzing one's own role as an active participant in relationship systems, instead of blaming problems on everyone but oneself (Guerin, Fay, Burden, & Kautto, 1987). Guerin uses the concept of *adaptive level of functioning* to define and evaluate the ability to continue functioning in the face of stress. Adaptive level of functioning is the capacity to make the conscious effort to be objective and behave rationally in the face of pressures of emotionality.

Triangles

Take a minute to think about the most difficult relationship in your family. Actually, that relationship is almost certainly between the two people you thought of and one or more third parties. Virtually all emotionally significant relationships between people are shadowed by a third—a relative, a friend, even a memory.

To understand triangles, it's helpful to remember that relationships are not static. Any two people in a relationship go through cycles of closeness and distance; it's when they're distant that triangles are most likely to develop. These cycles reflect not only good times and bad in relationships, but also people's needs for autonomy and connectedness. Guerin describes two basic processes that operate in the formation of marital triangles. In the first, the spouse experiencing the most discomfort connects with someone else as a way of gaining an ally. Thus, a wife upset with her husband's distance may increase her involvement with one of the children. In the second process, a third person (perhaps a friend or a child), who is sensitized either to one spouse's anxiety or to the conflict between them, moves in to offer reassurance or calm things down. "For example, an older daughter may attempt to reduce intense marital conflict by talking individually to each parent or to the parent with whom she has the most influence. Meanwhile, her younger brother may absorb the tension of his parents or handle it by acting in an antisocial way. The acting-out behavior also serves the function of pulling the parents together to try to solve the common problem of the son's acting out" (Guerin, et al., 1987, p. 62).

Many forms of triangulation seem so innocent that we hardly notice their destructive effect. Most parents who have pretty good relationships with their children can't seem to resist complaining to them once in a while about their spouses. "Your mother's *always* late!" "Your father *never* lets anyone else drive!" These interchanges seem harmless enough. But whenever you hear a story in which one person is victim and the other villain, you're being invited into a triangle.

When we listen too long or too often to someone complaining about someone else, the flattering feeling of being confided in gives way to a nagging suspicion that maybe we should give the two people back to each other. Similarly, when we gripe to one friend about another's unfairness, we know we should talk to the person with whom we have the conflict. And we would, too, except—well, it's too awkward. The average person is about as able to resist emotional triangles as the average cat is able to resist birds.

If something's really bothering you and you're afraid to talk about it—afraid you won't be listened to—the urge to confide in someone else is overwhelming. Unburdening yourself to a friend will make you feel better. It will also lessen the likelihood that you'll engage the problem at its source. Triangulation lets off steam, but it freezes conflict in place. The trouble with triangles isn't so much that complaining or seeking solace is wrong, but rather that many triangles become chronic diversions that corrupt and undermine family relationships.

Most family problems are triangular, which is why working only on a twosome may have limited results. Teaching a mother better techniques for disciplining her son won't resolve the problem that she is overinvolved with the boy as a result of her husband's emotional distance.

Nuclear Family Emotional Process

This concept deals with the emotional forces in families that operate over the years in recurrent patterns. Bowen originally used the term "undifferentiated family ego mass" to describe emotional oneness or fusion in families. Lack of differentiation in the family of origin leads to an emotional cutoff from parents, which in turn leads to fusion in marriage. The less the differentiation of self prior to marriage, the greater the fusion between spouses. Since this new fusion is unstable, it tends to produce one or more of the following: (1) reactive emotional distance between the spouses; (2) physical or emotional dysfunction in one spouse; (3) overt marital conflict; or (4) projection of the problem onto one or more children. The intensity of these problems is related to the degree of undifferentiation, extent of emotional cutoff from families of origin, and level of stress in the system.

Family Projection Process

This is the process by which parents transmit their immaturity and lack of differentiation to their children. Emotional fusion between spouses creates tension which leads to marital conflict, emotional distance, or reciprocal over- and under-functioning. A common case is one in which the husband, who is cut off from his family of origin, relates only in a very cool and distant way to his wife. This predisposes her to a relatively intense focus on the kids. Kept at arm's length by her husband, she devotes her emotional energy to the children, usually with the greatest intensity toward one particular child. This child may be the oldest son or daughter, the youngest son or daughter, or perhaps one who looks like one of the parents. Projection is different from caring concern; it's anxious, enmeshed concern.

The child who is the object of the projection process becomes the one most attached to the parents (positively or negatively) and the one with the least differentiation of self. Since it relieves his own anxiety, the husband supports the wife's overinvolvement with the children. He may do so directly, or indirectly by virtue of his own lack of involvement.

The emotional fusion between mother and child may take the form of a warm, dependent bond, or an angry, conflictual struggle. As the mother focuses her anxiety on the child, the child's functioning is stunted. This under-development enables the mother to overcontrol the child, distracting her from her own anxieties but crippling the child emotionally. Thus infantilized, the child eventually develops symptoms of psychological impairment, necessitating further parental concern and solidifying the family pattern.

Multigenerational Transmission Process

This concept describes the transmission of the family emotional process through multiple generations. In every generation the child most involved in the family's fusion moves toward a lower level of differentiation of self, while the least involved child moves toward a higher level of differentiation.

We like to think that after we leave home we will marry someone who will make us happy. We expect to keep the good stuff from our families and get rid of the bad. It doesn't work that way. We may fight against our inheritance, but it catches up with us.

Bowen's multigenerational transmission concept takes emotional illness not only beyond the individual to the family, but also beyond the nuclear family to several generations. The problem in the identified patient is a product of the relationship of that person's parents, which is a product of the relationship of their parents, continuing back for several generations. The problem doesn't reside in the child and it's not the child's fault; nor are the parents to blame. Instead the problem is the result of a multigenerational sequence in which all family members are actors and reactors.

Sibling Position

This concept is similar to Toman's (1969) ten personality profiles of children who grow up in different sibling positions. Bowen concurs that children develop certain fixed personality characteristics based on the sibling position in their families. So many variables are involved that prediction is complex, but knowledge of general characteristics plus specific knowledge of a particular family is helpful in predicting what part a child will play in the family emotional process, and in predicting family patterns in the next generation.

Bowenian theory offers an interesting perspective with which to reconsider the familiar notion of sibling rivalry by recognizing the triangular complications of the siblings' relationship with their parents. Say that a mother is anxious that her children should never feel jealous and that she takes responsibility for ensuring that they feel equally loved. (As though she had reason to worry that the truth might be otherwise.) Her anxiety is translated into action by making a show of treating them exactly equally—an attempt at perfect fairness that usually betrays the anxiety behind it. In response, the siblings grow up feeling that their mother *is* responsible for making them feel equally important and for alleviating any fears of inequality. Each child then becomes highly sensitive to the amount of attention he or she receives in her relation to his or her siblings. This can result in the siblings continually fighting and resenting one another—just what the mother tried to prevent. Moreover, since the mother is anxious to control how the children feel, she may step in to settle their fights, thus depriving them of the opportunity to do so, and giving them additional reason to feel unequally treated by her. ("How come *I* have to go to my room? *He* started it!")

Thus, sibling conflict, which is often explained as an outcome of inevitable rivalry (as though rivalrousness were the only natural relationship between brothers and sisters), is actually just one side of a triangle. (Of course the intensity of a mother's preoccupation with her children is related to other triangles—the quality and satisfaction of her relationships with her friends, career, and husband.)

Support for this triangular way of looking at sibling relationships comes from studies by Frits Boer and his colleagues at the University of Leiden in the Netherlands. They found that: siblings were aware of partiality not only toward their siblings, but also toward themselves; first-born children reported more positive behavior toward themselves from their second-born siblings than did second-born children with regard to their older siblings; siblings with brothers reported more competition than did siblings with sisters, regardless of their own sex; and perception of parental care by the children was highly correlated with their perception of the sibling relationship—a more negatively judged parent-child relationship coincided with a more negatively judged sibling relationship (Boer, 1990).

Emotional Cutoff

Emotional cutoff describes the way people manage undifferentiation (and emotional intensity associated with it) between the generations. The greater the emotional fusion between generations, the greater the likelihood of cutoff. Some people seek distance by moving far away from their parents; others do so emotionally by, for example, avoiding personal subjects of conversation or always insulating themselves with the presence of third parties.

Mike Nichols (1986) describes how some people mistake emotional cutoff for emotional maturity: "We take it as a sign of growth to separate from our parents, and we measure our maturity by independence of family ties. Yet many of us still respond to our families as though they were radioactive and capable of inflicting great pain. Only one thing robs Superman of his extraordinary power: kryptonite, a piece of his home planet. A surprising number of adult men and women are similarly rendered helpless by even a brief visit to or from their parents" (p. 190).

Societal Emotional Process

This is a concept Kerr and Bowen discuss in their 1988 book, *Family Evaluation*. But they don't discuss it much. The term refers to the fact that the emotional process in society influences the emotional process in families—like a background influence affecting all families. The concept of social emotional process describes how a prolonged increase in social anxiety can result in a gradual lowering of the functional level of differentiation in families. Kerr and Bowen cite the example of the high crime rate that results in communities with great social pressure. Bowen acknowledges that sexism and class and ethnic prejudice are examples of unhappy social emotional process, but he tends to downplay the importance of these concerns for family evaluation and therapy. Feminists don't agree; they believe passionately that sexism is a societal emotional process that infects families—and one that should be fought, and fought hard.

Fogarty (1976a) has described individuals as having four dimensions, and relating to others in three channels. The four dimensions of self are: depth, movement toward objects, movement toward persons, and time. The depth dimension includes much that we generally think of as intrapsychic, including thoughts, feelings, dreams, and aspirations. In addition to these attributes of personality, people vary according to the nature and degree of their proclivity for involvement with things—such as possessions, work, or games—as opposed to other people. Finally, Fogarty says, people vary in being fast or slow to think, act, and feel, and in being committed to the status quo or to change. This is the time dimension.

Fogarty's four-dimensional people are linked to one another by three systems: the thinking system, the emotional system, and the operating system. The thinking system of facts, judgments, and opinions functions in proportion to knowledge and information; it dysfunctions in proportion to which fact is confused with feeling. The emotional system provides color and vitality to relationships. Neither good nor bad, right nor wrong, the emotional system either works effectively or it does not. The third system by which people are connected is the operating system. This defines the ways in which people communicate their thoughts and feelings. Silence, withdrawal, talking, or yelling may all be used to convey essentially the same thought or feeling.

To the theoretical concerns of Bowenian therapists, Monica McGoldrick and Betty Carter have added gender and ethnicity. Their point is that to open closed systems it isn't possible to ignore gender inequalities without ignoring some of the primary forces that keep men and women trapped in inflexible roles. Moreover, they might point out that the previous sentence itself is naive in implying that men and women alike are victims of gender bias. Women live with limiting social conditions *and* with men who perpetuate them—men who may not notice their advantage or feel powerful with their wives and mothers, but who live with and take for granted social conditions that make it easier for men to get ahead in the world.

McGoldrick has also been a leader in calling attention to ethnic differences in families. Her book *Ethnicity and Family Therapy* (McGoldrick, Pearce, & Giordano, 1982) was a landmark in family therapy's developing sensitivity to this issue. Without understanding how cultural norms and values differ from one ethnic group to the next, the danger is of therapists imposing their own ways of looking at things on families whose perspectives are not "dysfunctional" but legitimately different. Some readers might be concerned that lengthy descriptions of how families of various ethnic groups differ (e.g., McGoldrick, Preto, Hines, & Lee, 1990: "Trying to talk the Irish out of their sense of guilt and need to suffer is a futile effort") fosters ethnic stereotyping. McGoldrick believes that it's important to sensitize family therapists to ethnic diversity, and that the most important thing is not to learn what characterizes one group or another, but rather to be open to differences.

NORMAL FAMILY DEVELOPMENT

In Bowen's system there is no discontinuity between normal and abnormal family development. When he began studying normal families in the late 1950s, he discovered many of the same mechanisms he had previously observed in schizophrenic families. This convinced him that there are no discrete categories of families (schizophrenic, neurotic, or normal), but that all families vary along a continuum from emotional fusion to differentiation. The fact that most of Bowen's clinical contact in later years was with families of professionals probably reinforced his belief that families are more alike than different.

Optimal family development is thought to take place when family members are relatively differentiated, when anxiety is low, and when the parents are in good emotional contact with their own families of origin. Most people leave home right in the midst of transforming relationships with their parents from an adolescent to an adult basis. Thus the transformation is incomplete, and most of us, even as adults, continue to react with adolescent sensitivity to our parents—and anyone else who pushes the same buttons. Normally, but not optimally, people reduce contact with their parents and siblings to avoid the anxiety and conflict of dealing with them. Once out of contact with their families, people assume they've put the old difficulties behind them. However, they carry around unfinished business in the form of unresolved sensitivities that flare up in intense relationships wherever they go. Having learned to ignore their own role in family conflicts, they are unable to prevent recurrences in new relationships. Therefore people with greater differentiation who remain in contact with previous generations are more stable than people from enmeshed or splintered families. Although problems may not surface immediately in cut-off families, they will eventually occur in future generations.

Another heritage from the past is that the emotional attachment between spouses comes to resemble that which each had in the family of origin. People who were relatively undifferentiated in their original families will continue to be undifferentiated when they form a new family. Those who handled anxiety by distance and withdrawal will do the same in their marriages. Therefore Bowen is convinced that differentiation of autonomous personalities, accomplished primarily in the family of origin, is both a description of normal development and a prescription for therapeutic improvement. This inescapable link to the past, stressed more strongly in Bowen's approach than in any other, is the prevailing feature of functional family development.

In "Systems Concepts and the Dimensions of Self," Fogarty (1976a) elaborates the characteristics of well-adjusted families: (1) They are balanced and can adapt to change; (2) Emotional problems are seen as existing in the whole group, with components in each person; (3) They are connected across generations to all family members; (4) They use a minimum of fusion and a minimum of distance to solve problems; (5) Each dyad can deal with problems between them; (6) Differences are tolerated, even encouraged; (7) Each person can deal on thinking and emotional levels with the others; (8) They are aware of what each person gets from within and from others; (9) Each person is allowed his or her own emptiness; (10) Preservation of a positive emotional climate takes precedence over doing what is "right" or what is popular; (11) Each member thinks it's a pretty good family to live in; and (12) Members of the family use each other as sources of feedback and learning, not as emotional crutches.

In Bowen's system the hallmark of the well-adjusted person is rational objectivity and individuality. A differentiated person is able to separate thinking from feeling, and remain independent of, though not out of contact with, the nuclear and extended family. The degree of differentiation of self depends largely on the course of one's family history, which is a relatively deterministic position. However, as we shall see, it is possible to achieve higher levels of differentiation through the process of family treatment.

Betty Carter and Monica McGoldrick have done as much as anyone in family therapy to study and disseminate information about normal family development (Carter & McGoldrick, 1980). They are also in the vanguard of those calling for sensitivity to and corrective action for the inequality between men and women in American families (Carter & McGoldrick, 1988). Like others in the Bowenian tradition, Carter and McGoldrick stress that to understand the family it is necessary to understand what's going on in at least three generations. This is the operative emotional field at any one time.

Following up on the work of Rodgers (1960), Hill (1970), Solomon (1973), and Duvall (1977), Carter and McGoldrick have described the *family life cycle* as a process of expansion, contraction, and realignment of the relationship system to support the entry, exit, and development of family members in a functional way. Transitions from one stage of the family life cycle to the next require *second-order change*—change in the system itself—while problems within stages can usually be handled with *first-order change*—rearranging without restructuring the system.

In the *leaving home stage* the primary task for young adults is to separate from their families without cutting off or fleeing reactively to a substitute emotional refuge. This is a time to become an autonomous self before joining with another person to form a new family. In the *joining of families through marriage* stage the primary task is commitment to the new couple, but it is not simply a joining of two individuals; it is rather a changing of two entire systems and an overlapping to develop a third. While problems in this stage may seem to be primarily between the couple, they may also reflect a failure to separate from families of origin or an extreme cutoff that puts too much pressure on the twosome. *Families with young children* must adjust to make space for children, cooperate in the tasks of parenting, keep the marriage from being submerged in parenting, and realign relationships with the extended family. Both parents are challenged to fulfill the children's needs for nurture and control—and they are challenged to work together as a team. As anyone who's been through it knows, this is an extremely stressful stage, especially for young mothers, and it is the life cycle phase with the highest divorce rate.

The reward for those parents who survive the preceding stages is to have their children turn into adolescents. *Adolescence* is a time when children no longer want to be like Mommy and Daddy; they want to be themselves. They struggle to become autonomous individuals, and they struggle to open family boundaries. And they struggle however much it takes. Parents with lives of their own and a certain amount of flexibility welcome (or at least tolerate) the fresh (pun intended) air that blows through the family at this time. Those who insist on controlling their children as though they were still little ones, provoke painful escalations in the rebelliousness that is normal for this period. In the *launching children and moving on* stage, parents must let their children go, and they must take hold of their own lives. This may be a liberating time of fulfillment, but it is also notoriously the time of the *midlife crisis* (Nichols, 1986). Parents must not only deal with changes in their children's and their own lives, but also with changes in their relationship with their own parents who may need increasing support—or at any rate don't want to act like parents anymore. *Families in later life* must adjust to retirement, which not only means a sudden loss of vocation but also a sudden gain in proximity of the couple. With both husband and wife home all day, the house may suddenly seem a lot smaller. Later in life families must cope with declining health, illness, and then death, the great equalizer.

The one major variation in the life cycle, too common to still be considered a deviation, is *divorce.* With the divorce rate at 50 percent and the rate of redivorce at 61 percent (Glick, 1984), divorce now strikes the majority of American families. The major tasks of the divorcing couple are to end the marriage but maintain cooperation as parents. Some post-divorce families become single-parent families—consisting in the majority of cases of mothers and children, and in the vast majority of those cases facing terrible financial strain. The other alternative is remarriage and the formation of stepfamilies, in which, often, loneliness is swapped for conflict.

Carter and McGoldrick's work on the life cycle bridges Bowen's emphasis on multigenerational emotional processes and various ahistorical approaches to the family (e.g., structural and strategic) which emphasize the developmental stage of the moment. Guerin's clinical model emphasizes stress more than stages of development. Life cycle changes within individuals, dyadic relationships, and the family as a whole are seen as producing an increasing demand on both functioning and vulnerability. For purposes of clinical work Guerin suggests that developmental stress be viewed as "transition times." Transition times are defined as any addition, subtraction, or change in status of a family member. In this paradigm, a piling up of transition times is "cluster stress." Periods of cluster stress are by their nature times of increased vulnerability for individual family members and the family as a whole. It is during these times that symptom formation is most likely to occur.

DEVELOPMENT OF BEHAVIOR DISORDERS

In the Bowenian system, symptoms are thought to result from stress that exceeds a person's ability to handle it. The ability to handle stress is a function of differentiation: The more well-differentiated the person, the more resilient he or she is and the more flexible and sustaining his or her relationships. The less well-differentiated the person, the less stress it takes to produce symptoms.

If "differentiation" were oversimplified to "level of maturity," the Bowenian formula for symptom development wouldn't differ from the usual diathesis-stress model that says disease develops when an individual's predisposition is sufficiently taxed. The difference is that differentiation isn't just a quality of individuals, but of relationships. Thus a relatively immature person who manages to create a reasonably healthy marriage will be at less risk than an equally immature person who is alone or in an unhealthy relationship. Symptoms develop when the level of anxiety exceeds the *family system's* ability to bind or neutralize it.

But even the quality of two-person relationships is insufficient to explain symptom-development, because when anxiety builds in the twosome, the relationship will automatically involve a third person. If the third person stays in contact with the twosome but remains neutral, anxiety will be reduced and symptom-development will be less likely. However, if the third person does become emotionally involved—taking sides (which prevents the twosome from working out their difficulties) or becoming the focus of displaced emotion (which results in an overload of anxiety)—the likelihood of symptom development increases.

The most vulnerable individual (in terms of isolation and lack of differentiation) is most likely to develop symptoms or be at the center of relationship conflict. The mechanism for this selectivity is the multigenerational transmission process. For example, a child of ten who presents with a conduct disorder is considered in the context of a three-generational genogram. From the theory it is assumed that the symptomatic child is the most triangled child in the family and, thereby, the one most emotionally caught up in the tension between the parents or affected most by the external tension in a particular parent. The multigenerational process behind this symptom complex is viewed as a byproduct of the parental level of differentiation from their families of origin, played out and exacerbated first within the marriage, then transmitted through the relationship between the parents (according to Bowen, usually the mother) and symptomatic child.

The clinical methodology tied to this formulation calls for: (1) increasing the parents' ability to manage their own anxiety and thereby being better able to handle their child's problematic behavior; and (2) fortifying the parents' level of emotional functioning by increasing their ability to operate with less anxiety in their families of origin. In this approach the child may or may not be seen. Calming down the parents and coaching them to deal more effectively with the problem was the primary approach taken by Bowen.

In the modification of these methods taken by Guerin and Fogarty, more emphasis is put on establishing a relationship with the symptomatic child, and working with the dysfunctional struggle and reactive emotional process in the nuclear family triangles. Extended family work is put off unless it is directly and explicitly linked to symptom formation and maintenance. In other words, where Bowen generally went straight for the family of origin, second-generation Bowenians pay more attention to the nuclear family, and are likely to wait to institute work on the family of origin as a way to reinforce gains and to enhance individual and family functioning.

Behavior disorders in adults—such as repeated job loss, uncontrollable anger, and compulsions of substance, sex, or acquisition—are viewed in the context of either dysfunctional spouse- or adult-child triangles, and clinical interventions are planned accordingly.

According to Bowen, behavior disorders, mild or severe, result from *emotional fusion* transmitted from one generation to the next. Emotions flood the intellect, impairing rational functioning and competence. The greater the degree of fusion, the more life is programmed by primitive emotional forces, despite rationalizations to the contrary (Bowen, 1975). Furthermore the greater the fusion between emotions and intellect, the more one is fused to the emotional reactions of other people. Emotional fusion consists of anxious attachment, overtly expressed or reactively rejected. Both the clinging, dependent person and the aloof, isolated one are equally caught up in emotional fusion; they merely manifest it in different ways. As long as they are emotionally stuck in the positions they occupied in their families of origin, their personal growth is stunted.

Emotional fusion is the reciprocal of differentiation. The fused person has few firmly held convictions and beliefs; he or she seeks acceptance and approval above any other goal, and makes decisions based primarily on feelings rather than rational thought. The undifferentiated person may have few or many opinions, but in either case the opinions are received, not thought out. Creating a good impression is all important, and the undifferentiated person is likely to be either dogmatic or compliant, but rarely able to calmly state his or her own beliefs without trying to inflate self or attack others.

Symptoms are a product of emotional reactivity, acute or chronic. They can be generated by an anxiety-driven togetherness pressure to conform, or by disruption of a fused relationship that has sustained someone's functioning (Kerr & Bowen, 1988). In undifferentiated people, symptoms can be relieved (though not necessarily resolved) by retreat to the safety of a dependent relationship, or by fleeing intimacy through distancing. The symptom patterns that develop from emotional fusion are: unhappy marriages, either combative or emotionally distant; dysfunction in one of the spouses (with reciprocal overfunctioning in the other); or projection of problems onto one or more children. The following clinical vignette illustrates how emotional fusion in the family of origin is transmitted.

> After his father died, Mr. Klein and his older sister were reared by their mother. This woman was a relatively mature and thoughtful person, but following the death of her husband she increasingly devoted all her attention to her children. They were her chief preoccupation, and shaping their lives became the major project of her life. Throughout their childhood she insisted that they conform to her standards; she was persistent in correcting their manners, energetic in demanding high performance in school, and highly critical of anything they sought to do outside the home. She discouraged contact with neighbors and school

friends, who were engaged in such "frivolous" pastimes as playing ball or going to school dances.

In late adolescence Mr. Klein began to realize the powerful control his mother exerted over him and his sister. The sister was never able to break free from her mother's influence and remained single, living with her mother for the rest of her life. Mr. Klein, however, was determined to leave home and become independent. Since he had always been told what to think, where to go, and how to behave, it was difficult to move out and be on his own. However, he was strong-willed and energetic; finally, in his mid twenties, he left home and turned his back on his mother. He moved to a distant city, started working, and eventually married.

The woman he married, Liza, came from a large, closely knit, and affectionate family. She and her four sisters were very much attached to each other and remained best friends throughout their lives. Their relationship with their parents was warm and close; none of the sisters ever questioned this model of family structure.

After she graduated from high school, Liza announced to the family that she wanted to go to college. This was contrary to the family norm that daughters remain at home and prepare themselves to be wives and mothers. Hence a major battle ensued between Liza and her parents; they were struggling to hold on, and she was struggling to break free. Finally she left for college, but she was ever after estranged from her parents. They had forgiven, but not forgotten, her violation of the family tradition.

When Liza and Mr. Klein met, they were immediately drawn to one another. Both were lonely and cut off from their families. After a brief, passionate courtship, they married. The honeymoon didn't last long. Never having really differentiated himself from his domineering mother, Mr. Klein was exquisitely sensitive to any effort to direct him. He became furious at his wife's slightest attempt to change his habits or get him to accommodate to her way of doing things. After years of grating against his dictatorial mother, his patience for control had long since worn thin. Mrs. Klein, on the other hand, sought to reestablish in her new marriage the closeness she had in her family. But in order to be close, she and her husband had to do things together and share similar interests and routines. When she moved toward him, suggesting that they do something, he was angry and resentful, feeling his individuality impinged upon. After several months of conflict and argument, the two settled into a period of relative equilibrium. Mr. Klein put most of his energy into his work, where he felt free and autonomous, leaving his wife to adjust to the distance between them. A year later their first child, David, was born.

Both parents were delighted to have a baby, but what was for Mr. Klein a pleasant addition to the family was for Mrs. Klein the means to fulfill her desperate need to be close to someone. The baby meant everything to her. While he was an infant she was the perfect mother, loving him tenderly and caring for his every need. When he was hungry she fed him; when he was wet she changed him; and when he cried—whenever he cried—she held him. When Mr. Klein tried to become involved with his infant son, his wife hovered about making sure he didn't do anything "wrong" with her precious baby. Naturally this infuriated Mr. Klein, and after a few bitter arguments he gradually left David more and more in his wife's care.

As he learned to walk and talk, David got into mischief, as all little children do. He grabbed things that he wasn't supposed to, refused to stay in his playpen, and fussed whenever he didn't get his way. His crying was unbearable to his mother. She found herself unable to set limits or establish control on this precious baby whose love she needed so badly. When she put him in his crib for a nap, he cried. Although she desperately needed some time by herself, and little David also needed his nap, she was so unable to stand the crying that after five minutes she went and brought him downstairs. This was the beginning of a lifelong pattern.

David grew up with a distant father and a doting mother, thinking he was the center of the universe. Whatever he wanted, he expected to get; whenever he was frustrated, he threw a tantrum until he got what he wanted. Bad as things were at home, at least the family existed in a kind of equilibrium. Dad was cut off from his wife and son, but he had his work. Mother was cut off from her husband, but she had her baby. Although he was willful and disobedient, he gave her the affection she craved. David's difficulties began when he went off to school. Used to getting his own way, he found it impossible to share with other children, or to abide by the rules. His disobedience and tantrums did nothing to endear him to his schoolmates or teachers. The other children avoided him, and he grew up having few friends. With teachers he acted out his father's battle against any efforts to control him. When Mrs. Klein heard complaints about David's failure to conform to the school's demands, she sided with her son and saw these complaints as resulting from a failure to recognize David's specialness. ("These people just don't know how to deal with a creative child.") So she moved him from school to school. But everywhere the conflicts were the same.

David grew up with a terrible pattern of adjustment to school and friends, but retained his extremely close relationship with his mother. The crisis came with adolescence. Like his father before him, David tried to develop independent interests outside the home. However, he was far less capable of separating than his father had been, and his mother was equally incapable of letting him go. The result was the beginning of chronic conflicts between David and his mother. Even as they argued and fought, though, they remained centered on each other. David spent more time battling his mother than doing anything outside the family.

Although he eventually left home at twenty-five, David remained a severely limited person. He hadn't learned the knack of looking after himself, and so had to settle for a series of unrewarding and uninteresting jobs. Never having learned to compromise or adjust to other children, he found it extremely difficult to make friends. He spent the rest of his life as a lonely, isolated, and marginally adjusted person. Worst of all, he didn't even have the consolation of the warm relationship with his mother.

David's history illustrates the components of Bowen's theory of behavior disorder. Both of his parents grew up relatively undifferentiated in emotionally fused families. As dictated by their own emotional needs, Mr. and Mrs. Klein's parents held their children too close, too long. This fusion sharply limits independent thinking and acting. Smothered by parents, it's hard to do other than reflexively accept or oppose them.

As Betty Carter explains it (personal communication), problems break out when the "vertical" problems of anxiety and toxic family issues, that come down through the generations, intersect with the "horizontal" stresses that come at transition points in the family life cycle. Thus David's time of greatest vulnerability came when the unresolved fusion he inherited from his mother intersected with the stress of his adolescent urge for independence.

Except in unusual cases, even emotionally fused children reach a point where they try to break away. But breaking away in such instances tends to be accomplished by emotional cutoff rather than by mature resolution of family ties. In childhood we relate to our parents as children. We depend on them to take care of us, we uncritically accept many of their attitudes and beliefs, and we behave in ways that are generally effective in getting our way with them. This usually means some combination of being good, patiently waiting to be rewarded, and being upset and demanding. A good deal of this childish behavior just doesn't work in the adult world. However, most of us leave home before changing to an adult-to-adult pattern with our parents. We—and they—only begin to change before it's time to leave.

A meek, patient child may become a bit more assertive and demanding in adolescence. Predictably, parents react with disappointment and anger. But instead of weathering the storm and patiently persisting with an adult stance, most people get hurt and withdraw. This is the *emotional cutoff.* Instead of persisting long enough to transform the relationship to an adult basis, most people decide that the only way to deal with their parents is to move away. Unhappily, this only gives the illusion of independence.

The girl who didn't get past meek patience with her parents will probably adopt a similar stance outside the home. When it doesn't work, she may react with temper—which also won't work. Those who cut themselves off from their parents to minimize tension carry with them their childish ways, which break out to spoil intimacy.

According to Bowen, people tend to choose mates with equivalent levels of undifferentiation. They may be manifest in quite different ways—perhaps extreme dependence in one, with extreme independence in the other—but, underneath, the level of immaturity is the same. Observations of sharp increases in problems after nuclear families cut off from extended families (Kerr, 1971) tend to corroborate Bowen's view. When inevitable conflict develops, each spouse will be aware of the contribution of emotional immaturity—in the other one. Each will be prepared for change—in the other one. He will discover that her treating him like a father entails not only clinging dependence, but also emotional tirades and temper tantrums. She will discover that he withdraws the closeness she found so attractive in courtship as soon as she makes any demands. He fled from his parents because he needs closeness but cannot handle it. Faced with conflict, he again withdraws. Sadly, what turned them on to each other carries the switch that turns them off.

What follows is marital conflict, dysfunction in one of the spouses, debilitating overconcern with one of the children, or various combinations of all three. When families come for help, they may present with any one of these problems. Whatever the presenting problem, the dynamics are similar; undifferentiation in families of origin is transferred to marital problems, which are in turn projected onto a symptomatic spouse or child. Thus the problems of the past are visited on the future.

GOALS OF THERAPY

Most people can accept that unresolved family problems, passed down through the generations, continue to plague us here in the present. But most people also get hopelessly confused trying to ferret out the basic pattern of those problems. They take elaborate genograms and discover that Great Uncle Fred was this and Great Grandmother Harriet did that. So?

Tracing the pattern of family problems means paying attention to two things: process and structure. These are also the keys to therapy from a Bowenian perspective. Process refers to patterns of emotional reactivity; structure refers to patterns of interlocking triangles.

The goal of Bowenian therapy is to decrease anxiety and increase differentiation of self—nothing else lasts. Genuine change in the family system requires reopening of closed family ties and detriangulation, which creates the conditions for individual autonomy and growth. Symptoms are de-emphasized in a treatment that resembles *in vivo* psychoanalysis. Problems are presumed to inhere in the system, not the person; and change in the self is sought through changing in relationship to others. In order to change the system, and enable family members to achieve higher levels of differentiation, modification must take place in the most important triangle in the family—the one that involves the marital couple. To accomplish this the therapist creates a new triangle, with himself or herself and the two primary members of the family. If the therapist stays in contact with the spouses, while remaining emotionally neutral, then the spouses can begin the process of detriangulation and differentiation which will profoundly and permanently change the family system.

Defining specific goals for therapy seems to become progressively more vague as the unit of treatment gets larger. Changes sought in individuals need to be spelled out in rather specific detail (cf., Ford & Urban, 1963); goals for nuclear families are somewhat less specific. When Bowen describes goals for the extended family (as opposed to the individual goal of differentiation) it seems enough for him to speak of developing one-to-one relationships and avoiding triangles. The point is not that the goals of extended family work are naive or less well thought-out than those for individuals, but that they are relatively self-evident. Once the point is conceded that people are embedded in a larger social context, it seems obvious what needs to be done; open the system.

Guerin's sophisticated clinical approach has led to a more differentiated set of therapeutic goals. These goals are derived from highly articulated clinical models developed to deal with problems of children and adolescents, marital conflict, and dysfunctional adults. Guerin's goals are both general and specific. General goals are: (1) placing the presenting problem in the context of the multigenerational system by doing a thorough and accurate genogram; (2) connecting with key family members and working with them to calm their own anxiety and level of emotional arousal and, thereby, lower anxiety throughout the system; and (3) define the parameters of the central symptomatic triangle, as well as important interlocking triangles. More specific goals are determined by the presenting problem and which unit of the family (mother and child, nuclear family, marital couple, individual) is the primary clinical focus.

In working with marital conflict, Guerin and his colleagues (1987) evaluate the progress of their work by looking for specific areas of improvement. The areas evaluated correspond to the criteria used by Guerin to measure the severity of conflict. These criteria are divided into: family system criteria, which include emotional climate, cluster stress, and intensity of triangulation; marital dyad criteria, which include communication, "critical index," "credibility index," relationship time and closeness, pursuer-distancer synchrony, and tracking of the interactional sequence; and individual criteria, which include degree of projection versus self-focus, and neutralization of resentment and bitterness. In working with individuals, using a family systems format, the goals proposed by Guerin are management of anxiety and depression, with an increase in functional attachment and operational freedom throughout the multigenerational unit.

Monica McGoldrick, speaking from a feminist perspective, argues that it isn't enough to approach marital relationships with neutrality—to help couples negotiate compromises with each other in their own terms. As long as marital relationships are based on inherent imbalances, conscientious therapists must be aware of inequality and actively work to redress it. That means introducing the subject of gender inequality, even if it isn't an active part of a couple's agenda:

> Most men have trouble with intimacy. It's part of how they were socialized. We've got to admit it to ourselves, and help men change. We need to help them see the detrimental impact of the dominant value system that makes it difficult for them to relate effectively to their families. At the same time we need to help women to become effective in the areas where they are lacking: dealing with money, anger, and effective participation in the world of paid work and success. (McGoldrick, 1990)

McGoldrick believes that economic inequality between men and women is a powerful and neglected context of marriage, making it harder for women to insist on change because it's harder for them to be financially self-sufficient. Money means options. McGoldrick therefore believes that it's important to encourage women to develop their earning power. In short, "gender-sensitive therapy" extends the goals of treatment beyond the expressed complaints of families to include the context within which these complaints develop. This means attending to the wider family context *and* to inequalities of gender and class:

If the wife is not in an economically viable position, marital therapy may be impossible. If she does not have the power to negotiate the relationship from a position of equality, the pretense of negotiation may be a farce. Beware of urging her to leave before having some awareness of the limitations and her options.

HIS therapy may involve attention to his dreams, keeping a journal, learning to be intimate with his children or his friends.

HER therapy may involve focusing on her resume, a Dale Carnegie course, or a consultation with a financial planner, and taking a vacation from family responsibilities. (McGoldrick, 1990)

Betty Carter puts the case for gender sensitivity in therapists this way: "Marital therapy that ignores sexism is like rearranging the deck chairs on the Titanic."

CONDITIONS FOR BEHAVIOR CHANGE

Increasing the ability to distinguish between thinking and feeling within the self and others and learning to use that ability to direct one's life and solve problems is the guiding principle of Bowenian therapy. Detriangling—keeping third parties from interfering in one's relationships and avoiding interfering in theirs—is the most important mechanism of change.

Bowen believes that change occurs when anxiety is low, and that understanding, not behavior, is the critical vehicle for change. Strategic and structural therapists believe that behavior change, not understanding, is critical, and that such change is most likely to occur when anxiety is high and conflicts are allowed to surface. Bowen, on the other hand, believes that anxiety breeds emotional fusion, and that lasting change requires understanding and differentiation in a calm, unheated atmosphere.

Bowenian therapists lessen emotional reactivity by lowering anxiety. Therapists must learn to tolerate the inevitable emotionality in families, *without becoming reactive themselves*. "The learning depends on having the courage to engage emotionally intense situations repeatedly and to tolerate the anxiety and internal emotional reactivity associated with that engagement. This is anxiety associated with trying to become more of a self, an anxiety of progression rather than regression" (Kerr & Bowen, 1988, pp. 130–131). Therapists must avoid automatically accommodating or rebelling, dominating, submitting, or scapegoating. In other words, just as family members must learn to overcome emotionally driven automatic reactions—appeasing, controlling, or shifting focus—so must therapists.

Guerin suggests that if a family comes in during a crisis they should be encouraged to discuss it until their agitation is relieved. He calls this "cooling down the affective overload" (Guerin & Pendagast, 1976). Beginners often make the mistake of trying too quickly to divert families from their initial concerns to those with more theoretical interest to the therapist. If they do this too bluntly or abruptly, they may cause families to drop out prematurely.

Bowen also differs from most systems therapists in believing that meaningful change does not require the presence of the entire family. Instead he believes that change is initiated by individuals or couples who are capable of affecting the rest of the family. His program of treatment can be described as proceeding from inside to out. Differentiation of self, which begins as a personal and individual process, is the vehicle for transforming relationships and the entire family system. For most family therapists treating individuals doesn't make much sense; after all, their fundamental premise is that individuals are products of their social context. Although he also believes this, Bowen's work is predicated on the idea that well-motivated individuals are more capable of change than are larger family groups. The therapeutic process is a cycle in which the individual differentiates a self, which transforms the family system, which in turn leads to further differentiation in the individual.

Therapy may not require the presence of the entire family, but it *does* require an awareness of the entire family. Looking at the nuclear family isn't enough. Bowen stresses the importance of a broad assessment, saying, for example, "A family therapist may treat two parents and their schizophrenic son, but not attach much importance to the fact that the parents are emotionally cut off from their families of origin. The parents' cutoff from the past undermines their ability to stop focusing on their son's problems; once again, the therapy will be ineffective" (Kerr & Bowen, 1988, p. vii).

Part of the process of differentiating a self is to develop a personal relationship with everyone in the extended family. The power of these connections may seem mysterious at first—particularly for people who don't think of their strength or well-being as dependent on family ties. A little reflection reveals that increasing the number of important relationships will enable an individual to spread out his or her emotional energy. Instead of concentrating all emotional energy in one or two family relationships, it is defused into several. Freud had a similar notion on an intrapsychic level. In "The Project for a Scientific Psychology," he described his neurological model of the mind. The immature mind has few outlets ("cathexes") for channeling psychic energy and, hence, little flexibility or capacity to delay responding. The mature mind, on the other hand, has many channels of response, which permits greater flexibility. Bowen's notion of increasing the emotional family network is like Freud's model writ large.

Since we learn to relate to the family during childhood, we learn to relate as children. Because most of us leave home before we have established adult personalities, we continue to react childishly to our parents, brothers, and sisters. Furthermore, we react similarly in any new relationship that restimulates our unmodified sensitivities. Returning to the family—as adults— enables us to understand and modify old habits. This in turn frees us from acting out childish reactions in future relationships.

Bowen maintains that his treatment approach follows from his theory rather than from his personal style (Anonymous, 1972). Yes and no. Undoubtedly his highly reasoned and self-disciplined approach has its roots in the core of Bowen's personality. But be that as it may, his techniques of treatment do follow from theory more than other approaches in the field. The theory postulates fusion in grandparents transmitted to parents and projected onto children; the therapy prescribes differentiation, reversing this process in overlapping stages. Opening closed relationships and resolving triangles in the extended family results in greater differentiation, which then leads to a reduction in problems in the nuclear family. This emphasis on the extended family is one of the unique and defining features of Bowen's system.

Unresolved tensions in families are described as leading to a series of overlapping triangles (Andres, 1971). Conflict between two people is detoured to a third person who is triangled in. With additional tension, a fourth person may be brought in, leaving out the third. In a family with a great deal of tension and an equivalent tendency toward emotional cutoff, the available triangles will eventually be exhausted and the family will triangle in an outsider. The outsider may be a friend, minister, colleague, or psychotherapist. If a stranger comes into contact with two parts of the triangle (for instance, a mother and father), the stranger will either become triangulated or withdraw (Bowen, 1976). If the stranger is a family therapist, he or she can remain in contact with the twosome, but avoid becoming emotionally triangulated.

Therapy with couples is based on the premise that tension in the dyad will dissipate if they remain in contact with a third person (in a stable triangle)—if that person remains neutral and objective rather than emotionally entangled. This therapeutic triangle can reverse the insidious process of problem-maintaining triangulation. Furthermore, change in any one triangle will change the entire family system.

Family therapy with individuals is based on the premise that if one person in the family achieves a higher level of differentiation of self, this will enable (or cause) other members of the family to do the same. Bowen teaches individuals about triangles, and then coaches them to return to their families of origin where they work to detriangle themselves, develop greater objectivity, and thus achieve a permanent reduction in their emotional reactiveness. This in turn has a therapeutic impact on all systems of which these individuals are a part.

TECHNIQUES

Bowenian therapists believe very strongly that understanding how family systems operate is far more important than this or that technique. In fact, Bowen speaks of "technique" with disdain, especially eclecticism uninformed by theory. While it is obviously true that, regardless of how involved with theory they are, every therapist must *do* something—that is, all therapists use techniques—Bowenians insist that it is important not to become preoccupied with specific techniques, not to look for the magic bullet.

If there *were* a magic bullet in Bowenian therapy—one essential technique—it would be asking questions. The questions are designed to help clients think about, rather than react to, their dilemmas, and discover how to modify their own role in troubled relationships. Bowen himself was a very laid-back therapist: all he did was ask questions. (Incidentally, Bowen's questions were always circular questions: questions designed to tease out patterns of relationship.)

Those who have followed Bowen ask questions, too, but also move in occasionally to challenge, confront, and explain. Betty Carter, for example, asks questions designed to help couples understand their situation, but then tries to intensify the process and speed it up a little by explaining what works or doesn't work and by assigning tasks. Most of the tasks she assigns are calculated to move people out of triangles. She might, for example, encourage a wife to visit her mother-in-law, or a husband to begin calling his own mother on the phone. Another favorite device of Carter's is to encourage people to write letters, addressing unresolved issues in the family. One way to prevent such letter writing from degenerating into telling people off is to have clients bring in the letters and then help them edit out the anger and emotional reactivity.

Guerin, perhaps more than any other Bowenian, has worked to develop clinical methodologies and models of intervention that feature specific techniques. His categorizing marital conflict into four stages of severity with detailed suggestions for treating each stage (Guerin, Fay, Burden, & Kautto, 1987) is the most elaborate demonstration of his well-worked-out technique.

Bowen advocates a variety of methods all aimed at the same goals. Whether treatment involves nuclear families, couples, individuals, or multiple family groups, the effort is directed at modifying the family system.

Family Therapy with Couples

Whenever possible, Bowen prefers to work with both parents or spouses. When the therapist joins the couple, a therapeutic triangle is formed. If the therapist avoids being emotionally triangulated, the couple will be forced to deal with each other. The emotional tone of sessions should be lively enough to be meaningful, but cool enough to be objective. This is accomplished by asking more, and less, provocative questions, and by regulating the amount of interaction between the spouses. When things are calm, feelings can be dealt with more objectively, and the spouses can talk rationally with each other. But when feeling outruns thinking, it's best to ask questions which get the spouses to think more and feel less, and to talk to the therapist rather than to each other. Couples who have argued for years about the same subject are often amazed to discover that the first time they ever really hear the other's position is when they listen as the other talks to the therapist. It's so much easier to hear when you aren't busy planning your own response. If all else fails to cool things down, Fogarty (1976b) recommends seeing the spouses in separate sessions.

Contrary to popular belief, couples don't solve problems just by talking about them. Left to their own devices they tend to argue unproductively, project all responsibility onto the other one, and attack instead of negotiate. Change requires talk *and* willingness to listen, so that each can begin to change personally rather than endlessly demand change of the other. Because of the universal tendency to see only others' contributions to problems, special techniques are required to help family members see the process, not just the content, of interactions; to see their part in the process, instead of just blaming others; and finally to change.

Guerin (1971) recommends the "displacement story" as a device for helping family members achieve sufficient distance to see their own roles in the family system. The displacement story is about other families with similar problems. For example, a couple too busy attacking to listen to each other might be told: "It must be terribly frustrating not getting through to each other. Last year I saw a couple who just couldn't seem to stop arguing long enough to listen to each other. Only after I split them up and they blew off steam for several sessions individually with me did they seem to have any capacity to listen to what the other one was saying."

Guerin also uses films as displacement materials. If the proper aesthetic distance is maintained, people can become emotionally involved with a movie so that it has an impact but at the same time remain sufficiently removed to be objective. Underdistancing, in therapy sessions or in some highly provocative movies, results in an emotional experience devoid of reflection. Overdistancing, such as may occur in a lecture or uninteresting film, may lead to a lack of involvement and impact. Guerin selects films like *Kramer Versus Kramer, The War of the Roses, I Never Sang for My Father, Scenes from a Marriage*, and *Breaking Away* to use as displacement materials for teaching family dynamics to trainees and to families in therapy.

Armed with a knowledge of triangles, the therapist endeavors to remain neutral and objective. This requires an optimal level of emotional distance, which Bowen says (1975) is the point where the therapist can see both the tragic and the comic aspects of the couple's interactions. Keeping detriangled requires a calm tone of voice and talking about facts more than feelings. This calm objectivity on the part of Bowenian therapists is expressed and enhanced by the use of process questions—questions aimed to get through emotional reactivity and make contact with family members' reasonableness.

As the spouses talk, the therapist concentrates on the process of their interaction, not on the details under discussion. Becoming overly concerned about the content of the discussion is a sign that the therapist is emotionally entangled in the couple's problems. It may be hard to avoid being drawn in by issues as controversial as money, sex, or discipline of children, but the therapist's job is not to settle disputes—it is to help the couple do so. The aim is to get husband and wife to express ideas, thoughts, and opinions to the therapist in the presence of the other spouse. Should one break down in tears, the therapist remains calm and inquires about the thoughts that touched off the tears. If the couple begins arguing, the therapist becomes more active, calmly questioning one, then the other, and focusing on their thoughts.

Although strict neutrality is considered essential by Bowen, those of his followers with feminist convictions believe that it's important to address problems of sexual inequality, even if couples don't bring them up. Betty Carter, for example, introduces issues of gender inequality by asking questions about who does what in the family, and how much time each parent spends with the kids. She asks each spouse how much money they make. And when the usual discrepancy emerges, she asks, "What role do you think this plays in the decision-making process?"

Descriptive labels are helpful devices for seeing the process underlying the content of family interactions. For example, Fogarty (1976b) has described the "pursuer-distancer" dynamic among couples. The more one pursues, and asks for more communication, time, and togetherness, the more the other distances—watches TV, works late, or goes off with the kids. Frequently, spouses alternate pursuing and distancing in different areas. Husbands commonly distance themselves emotionally, but pursue sexually. The trick, according to Fogarty, is, "Never pursue a distancer." Instead, help the pursuer explore his or her own inner emptiness. "What's in your life other than the other person?" It is also important that the therapist not pursue the distancer. When no one is chasing, the distancer will be able to move toward the family.

To underscore the need for objectivity and emotional neutrality, Bowen speaks of the therapist as a "coach" or "consultant." He does not mean to imply coldness or indifference on the therapist's part, but rather to emphasize the calm rationality required to avoid triangulation. In traditional terms this is known as "managing transference and countertransference reactions." And just as analysts are analyzed themselves so they can recognize their own countertransference, so Bowen considers differentiating a self in one's own family necessary to avoid being emotionally triangled by couples. Guerin suggests that the best way to develop a genuine understanding of family concepts is to try them out in your own family (Guerin & Fogarty, 1972).

In order to help each spouse define a position as a differentiated self, it's useful for the therapist to establish an "I-position" (Guerin, 1971). The more the therapist defines an autonomous position in relation to the family, the easier it is for family members to define themselves to each other. Gradually family members learn to calmly state their own beliefs and convictions, and to act on them without attacking others or becoming overly upset by their responses. When one partner begins differentiating, the other is discomfited and presses for a return to the status quo (Carter & Orfanidis, 1976). If this emotional counterreaction is weathered calmly, with neither one giving in to opposition or becoming hostile, then both partners move toward a higher level of differentiation. The process takes place in small steps, with spouses alternating between separateness and togetherness. Eventually, when each has a sufficiently well-articulated self, they can come together in mutual caring and respect, rather than in clinging dependency.

After sufficient harmony has been purchased with progress toward self-differentiation, Bowen teaches the couple how emotional systems operate, and encourage them to explore their own families of origin (Bowen, 1971). He prepares them for this by first making occasional references to their families of origin. Once they begin to recognize the relevance of their prior family experience to their current problems, transition to the focus on their families of origin will be smooth. Kerr (1971) suggests that when relationship problems in the nuclear family are being discussed, therapists should occasionally ask questions about similar patterns in the family of origin. If they can see that they are repeating earlier patterns, family members are more likely to recognize their own emotional reactivity. Recently, one of us (M. P. N.) saw a couple who were unable to decide what to do with their severely disturbed teenaged daughter. Although the daughter was seriously disturbed and virtually uncontrollable, her mother found it very difficult to consider hospitalization. When she was asked what her own mother would have done, without hesitating she replied that her long-suffering mother would have been too guilt-ridden ever to consider placement, no matter how much she and the rest of the family might suffer. Little more needed to be said.

More didactic teaching occurs in the transition from brief to long-term therapy. Knowledge of family systems theory enables family members to analyze their own problems, and gives them a framework in which they can continue to change. Such information is useful when tensions have abated, but trying to impart it can be risky during periods of conflict and anxiety. At such times battling family members are liable to distort any statements about how families function as support for one or the other opposing position. So primed are warring spouses to make the other "wrong" in order for them to be "right," that they "hear" much of what the therapist says as being for them or against them. But when they are calm, they abandon the idea that if one is right the other must be wrong, and they can profit from didactic sessions. As they learn about systems theory, both spouses are sent home for visits, to continue the process of differentiation in their extended families. During this phase of treatment—coaching—Bowen believes that infrequent sessions are not only possible, but desirable (1976). Meeting with the therapist only once a month or so forces families to become more responsible and resourceful. It also dissolves a great deal of dependency on the therapist.

Family Therapy with One Person

Bowen's personal success at differentiating himself from his family convinced him that a single, highly motivated person can be the fulcrum for changing an entire family system (Anonymous, 1972). Subsequently he made family therapy with one person a major part of his practice. He uses this method with one spouse when the other refuses to participate, or with single adults who live far from their parents or whose parents won't come for treatment. Aside from these cases, in which Bowen has made a virtue out of necessity, he uses this approach extensively with trainees and other mental health professionals. Extended family work with spouses is also the focus of couples treatment after the presenting anxiety and symptoms subside.

The goal of working with individuals is the same as working with larger units: differentiation. With individuals the focus is upon resolving neurotic emotional relationships in the extended family. This means developing person-to-person relationships, seeing family members as people rather than emotionally charged images, learning to observe one's self in triangles, and finally, detriangling one's self (Bowen, 1974).

The extent of unresolved emotional attachment to parents defines the level of undifferentiation. More intense levels of undifferentiation go hand in hand with more extreme efforts to achieve emotional distance, either through internal mechanisms or physical distance. A person may handle mild anxiety with parents by remaining silent or avoiding personal discussions; but when anxiety rises he or she might find it necessary to walk out of the room or even leave town. However, the person who runs away is as emotionally attached as the one who stays home and uses psychological defenses to control the attachment. The one who runs away needs closeness but can't handle it. In marriage and other intense relationships, when tension mounts the person will again withdraw.

Two sure signs of this emotional cutoff (Bowen, 1974) are denial of the importance of the family, and an exaggerated facade of independence. Cutoff people boast of their emancipation and infrequent communication with their parents. The opposite of emotional cutoff is an open relationship system, in which family members have genuine, but not confining emotional contact. Bowen's therapy is designed to increase the frequency and intimacy of emotional contact with the extended family. In fact, Bowen finds the results of extended family work superior to working directly on the nuclear family (Bowen, 1974).

Prerequisites to differentiating a self in the extended family are: (1) some knowledge of how family systems function; and (2) strong motivation to change. It's difficult to sustain the energy to work on the family in the absence of current distress, and many people often work only in spurts from one crisis to the next (Carter & Orfanidis, 1976). When things are calm they relax, and only when problems arise again do they continue their efforts to change.

The actual process of change is begun by learning about one's larger family—who made up the family, where they lived, what they did, and what they were like. Most people are surprisingly ignorant of their family's history. A basic working knowledge of family, as far back as grandparents, is an adequate beginning. A useful device for organizing this material is the *genogram.*

Genograms are schematic diagrams of families, listing family members and their relationships to one another. Included are ages, dates of marriage, deaths, and geographical locations. Men are represented by squares and women by circles, with their ages inside the figures. Horizontal lines indicate marriages with dates written on the line, and vertical lines connect parents and children. (For more detailed suggestions see McGoldrick & Gerson, 1985.) Let us say, in constructing a typical genogram, that I (M. P. N.) am forty-eight (actually, I'm ninety-seven, but let's say forty-eight), my wife is fifty, and we were married in 1968 (Figure 9.1).

The next diagram shows that we have two children—a daughter aged eighteen and a son aged sixteen, and that we live in Albany, New York (Figure 9.2).

Next the genogram is expanded to include the extended family, beginning with my family of origin (see Figure 9.3). My father, aged seventy-eight, and my mother, aged seventy-five, live in Washington, D.C.; my brother and his wife live in Ridgefield, Connecticut, and they have three children.

My wife's family of origin, shown in Figure 9.4 on page 396, consists of her parents, who live in Chicago, and her brother who lives in New Jersey. The

FIGURE 9.1

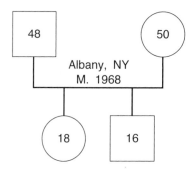

FIGURE 9.2

double slash in the line joining her brother and his ex-wife indicates that they are divorced; she remarried in 1988 and is living in Philadelphia; he is living with his fiance who has a twenty-five-year-old daughter by a previous marriage.

Dates of important events such as deaths, marriages, and divorces deserve careful study. These events send emotional shock waves throughout the family, which may open lines of communication and foster personal contact, or may close off channels; in the latter case issues may get buried and family members progressively more cut off. A divorce may bring the family together or divide it. In some cases, news of the divorce reminds the family that the people divorcing are separate individuals with emotional needs, rather than a self-sufficient unit. Furthermore, family members may discover that it's easier to be with the divorcing spouses one at a time, when they are freed from the chronic tension of being together. In other cases, families take sides after a

FIGURE 9.3

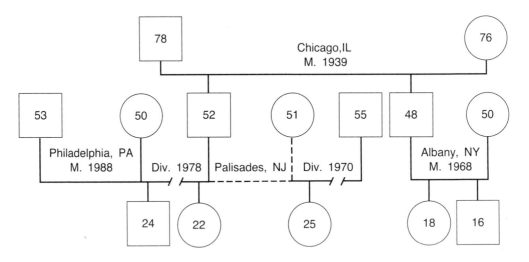

FIGURE 9.4

divorce. One side is "right," the other is "wrong"; the divorce between two people becomes a divorce between two segments of the family.

Another significant piece of information on the genogram is the geographical location of various groups in the family system. Clusters of family groups in one location suggest strong family bonds. In more explosive families, the emotional cutoff is graphically illustrated by extreme distances separating family subunits. Of course it's possible to live in the same community and be separated by emotional distance. Also, many people choose to live where there are career opportunities, a reason that has little to do with family feeling. Nevertheless, the geographical spread of the family is a good clue of underlying emotional patterns.

Filling out the genogram is not an end in itself, nor is it a simple matter. The genogram is only a skeleton which must be fleshed out with important information about the family. In order to put meat on the skeleton's bones, it is necessary to know what to look for. Dates, relationships, and localities are the framework for exploring emotional boundaries, fusion, cutoffs, critical conflicts, amount of openness, and the number of current and potential relationships in the family.

Family members may know some of these things, but not all. For, as recent work by Nisbett and Wilson (1977) suggests, people's reports about their experience often reflect their personal theories of attribution (what's *supposed to be*) rather than accurate observation (what *is*). Sometimes a "good relationship" with parents turns out to be one in which fusion and tension are managed by distancing tactics, such as infrequent contact, superficial conversation, or gossiping about other family members. Therefore it's important to ask for descriptions of family relationships, rather than conclusions about them. Not "Do you have a good relationship with your parents?" but "Where do your parents live? How often do you see them, write, or call? What do you and your mother talk about when you're alone together? Do you ever go out to lunch, just you and your dad?" This more detailed inquiry reveals the nature of personal relationships and the existing triangles in the system.

Other kinds of information that help to explain the family include cultural, ethnic, and religious affiliations; educational and economic levels; relationships with the community and social networks; and the nature of the work that family members do. Just as an individual cut off from his extended family is liable to be fused in his nuclear family, a family cut off from social and community ties is liable to be enmeshed in its own emotions, with limited outside resources for dissipating anxiety and distress.

The person who embarks on a quest of learning more about his or her family usually knows where to look. Most families have one or two members who know a great deal about the family—perhaps a maiden aunt, a patriarch, or a cousin who is very family-centered. Phone calls, letters, or, better yet, visits to these family archivists, will yield much information, some of which will produce startling surprises.

Gathering information about the family is also an excellent vehicle for the second step in the differentiation project, which is establishing person-to-person relationships with as many family members as possible. This means getting in touch with people and speaking personally with them, not about other people or impersonal topics. If this sounds easy, try it. Few of us can spend more than a few minutes talking personally with certain family members without getting anxious. When this, happens, we're tempted to withdraw physically or emotionally, or triangle in another person. Gradually extending the time of real personal conversation will improve the relationship and help differentiate a self.

There are profound benefits to be derived from developing person-to-person relationships with members of the extended family, but they have to be experienced to be understood. In the process of opening and deepening personal relationships you will learn about the emotional forces in the family. Some of the family triangles will immediately become apparent; others will emerge only after more careful examination. Usually we notice only the most obvious triangles because we're too emotionally engaged to be rational and astute observers. Few people can be objective about their parents. They are either comfortably fused or uncomfortably reactive. Making frequent short visits will help control emotional reactiveness so that you can become a better observer.

Many of our habitual emotional responses to the family impede our ability to understand and accept others; worse, they make it impossible for us to understand and control ourselves. It's perfectly natural to get angry and blame people when things go wrong. The differentiated person, however, is capable of stepping back, controlling emotional responsiveness, and reflecting on the best strategies for improving things. Bowen (1974) calls this "getting beyond blaming and anger," and says that, once learned in the family, this ability is useful for handling emotional snarls throughout life.

Ultimately, differentiating a self requires that you identify interpersonal triangles you participate in, and detriangle from them. The goal is to relate to the other people without gossiping or taking sides, and without counterattacking or defending yourself. Bowen suggests that the best time to do this is during a family crisis, but it can be begun at any time.

A common triangle is between one parent and a child. Suppose that every time you visit your folks your mother takes you aside and starts complaining about your father. Maybe it feels good to be confided in. If you're a mental health professional, maybe you'll have fantasies about rescuing your parents—or at least your mother. In fact, the triangling is destructive to all three relationships: you and Dad, Dad and Mom, and, yes, you and Mom. In triangles, one pair will be close and two will be distant (Figure 9.5). Sympathizing with Mom alienates Dad. It also makes it less likely that she will do anything about working out her complaints with him.

Finally, although this triangle may give you the illusion of being close to your mother, it is at best an ersatz intimacy. Nor is defending your father a solution. That only moves you away from Mom towards Dad, and widens the gulf between them. As long as the triangulation continues, personal and open one-to-one relationships cannot develop.

Once the triangle is recognized for what it is, you can make a plan of action so you stop participating in it. The basic idea is to do something, anything, to get the other two people to work out their own relationship. The simplest and most direct approach is to suggest that they do so. In the example just given you can suggest that your mother discuss her concerns with your father, *and* you can refuse to listen to more of her complaints. Less direct, but more powerful, is to tell Dad that his wife has been complaining about him, and you don't know why she doesn't tell him about it. She'll be annoyed, but not forever. A more devious ploy is to overagree with Mom's complaints. When she says he's messy, you says he's a complete slob; when she says he's not very thoughtful, you say he's a monster. Pretty soon she'll begin to defend him. Maybe she'll decide to work out her complaints with him; or maybe she won't. But either way you will have removed yourself from the triangle.

Once you become aware of them, you'll find that triangles are ubiquitous. Some common examples include griping with colleagues about the boss; telling someone that your spouse doesn't understand you; undercutting your spouse with the kids; and watching television to avoid talking to your family. Breaking free of triangles may not be easy, but the rewards are great. Bowen believes that differentiating an autonomous self requires opening relationships in the extended family, and then ceasing to participate in triangles. The payoff comes not only from enriching these relationships, but also from enhancing your ability to relate to anyone—friends, fellow workers, patients, and your spouse and kids. Furthermore, if you can remain in emotional contact, but change the part you play in the family—and maintain the change in

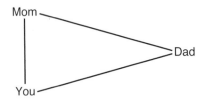

FIGURE 9.5

spite of family pressure to change back—the family will have to change to accommodate to your change.

Some degree of rejection is expectable when one embarks on a direction for oneself that is not approved of by spouses, parents, colleagues, or others. The rejection, which is triggered by the threat to the relationship balance, is designed to restore the balance (Kerr & Bowen, 1988).

Some useful guidelines to resisting the family's attempts to get you to change back to unproductive but familiar patterns of the past have been enumerated by Carter and Orfanidis (1976), by Guerin and Fogarty (1972), and by Herz (1991). You can read about how to work on family tensions by resolving your own emotional sensitivities in two marvelous books by Harriet Lerner: *The Dance of Anger* (Lerner, 1985) and *The Dance of Intimacy* (Lerner, 1989).

Although differentiation in the family can be accomplished on your own, it is best to work with a coach who has successfully guided others through the process. If you do attempt this work, an important rule of thumb is to keep your own counsel. A professional coach can give neutral and objective advice; family members and friends cannot. Keep in mind that the changes you make are for yourself. Arm yourself with a plan to handle the family's counterreactions. As you move in and out of the family system, distinguish between planned and reactive distance. Distance is useful when you want to think, but interpersonal problems are never resolved at a distance.

When a problem arises in the family, examine your own behavior. Problem behavior is an expression of a family process, and you have responsibility for part of that process. The only change anyone can really make is change in oneself. If you're confused about what you're doing to maintain the status quo, try simply reversing what you were doing. Instead of pleading with your mother to visit you, try ignoring her. Instead of yelling at the kids, back off and let your spouse do it. Such reversals often have an immediate and dramatic impact on the system. But to see any real results, you may have to persist in the face of the family system's resistance to change.

Reentry into your family of origin is necessary to open the closed system. Sometimes all that's required is visiting. Other times, buried issues must be raised, activating dormant triangles by stirring up emotions in the system. If you can't move directly toward your father without his withdrawing, move toward other people with whom he is close, thus activating a triangle. If your father is tense about being alone with you, spend some time alone with your mother. This is likely to make him want to have equal time.

In reentry, it's advisable to begin by opening closed relationships before trying to change conflictual ones. Don't start by trying to resolve the warfare between yourself and your mother. Begin by looking up a sibling or cousin with whom you've been out of touch. In all contacts deal with personal issues, but avoid stalemated conflicts. If your contacts with some sections of the family are routine and regular, make them more irregular and unpredictable.

Those who continue working on their family relationships beyond the resolution of a crisis, or beyond the first flush of enthusiasm for a new academic interest, can achieve profound changes in themselves, in their family systems, and in their own clinical work. Extended family systems therapy is never finished. Coaching sessions may be spaced at more infrequent intervals, but even when these sessions are discontinued, it is usually with the understanding that the client will continue applying the principles in family, social, and work relations. If the client feels stuck or faces a new crisis, the process can always be renewed.

EVALUATING THERAPY THEORY AND RESULTS

What makes Bowen's theory so useful and important is that it describes and explains the emotional forces within us that regulate how we relate to other people. The single greatest impediment to understanding one another is our tendency to become emotionally reactive and respond defensively instead of listening and hearing each other. Like all things about relationships, this emotionality is a two-way street: some speakers express themselves with such emotional pressure that listeners inevitably react to that pressure rather than hearing what the speaker is trying to say. Bowenian theory describes this reactivity, explains its origins in the lack of differentiation of self, and explains how to reduce emotionalism and move toward mature self-control—by cultivating relationships widely in the family and learning to listen without becoming defensive or untrue to one's own beliefs.

In Bowenian theory, anxiety is the all-purpose explanation (for why people are dependent or avoidant and why they become emotionally reactive), reminiscent of Freudian conflict theory (which explains all symptoms as the result of anxiety that stems from conflicts over sex and aggression). The second all-purpose concept in the Bowenian system is, of course, differentiation. Since differentiation is roughly synonymous with maturity, students might ask, to what extent is the proposition that more differentiated people function better a circular argument? In respect to the Bowenian tradition of asking questions rather than imposing opinions, we'll let this stand as an open question for your consideration.

The major shortcoming of the Bowenian approach to treatment is that in concentrating on individuals and their extended family relationships, it neglects the power of working directly with the nuclear family. In many cases the most direct way to resolve family problems is to bring together everyone in the same household and encourage them to face each other and talk about their conflicts. These discussions may turn noisy and unproductive, but a skilled therapist can help family members realize what they're doing that's unproductive and guide them toward understanding. There are times when couples or families are so hostile and defensive that these direct dialogues must be interrupted to help individuals get beyond defensiveness to the hurt feelings underneath. At such times, it is useful, perhaps imperative, to block family members from arguing with each other. But an approach, such as Bowen's, that encourages therapists to speak to individual family members one at a time probably underutilizes the power of working directly with nuclear families in action.

The status of extended family systems therapy and theory rests not upon empirical research but upon the elegance of Murray Bowen's theory, clinical reports of successful treatment, and the personal profit experienced by those who have worked at differentiating a self in their families of origin.

Bowen's original research with schizophrenic families was more clinical observation than controlled experimentation. In fact, Bowen was decidedly cool to empirical research (Bowen, 1976), preferring instead to refine and integrate theory and practice. The little empirical work that has been done in the field is reported at the annual Georgetown Family Symposia. There, evaluations of various programs and occasional research reports have been presented. One of these, a study by Winer, was of sufficient interest to be published in *Family Process* (Winer, 1971). Winer reported on observations of four families in multiple family therapy led by Murray Bowen. Over the course of treatment, the experimenter tracked the ratio of self references to other references, and the number of differentiated-self references. Statements considered as differentiated-self references included: speaking for self without blaming, dealing with change or desired change in self rather than in others, distinguishing thoughts from feelings, and showing awareness and goal-directedness. There were two significant findings, both of which supported Bowen's position. First, in early sessions there were fewer self statements; the greatest number referred to "we" and "us," indicating that the spouses did not differentiate separate positions. Second, there was an evolution toward more differentiated I-statements over the course of treatment. Initially these occurred less than half the time, but after a few sessions differentiated statements predominated.

Although it does support the effectiveness of Bowen's therapy in increasing differentiation, the Winer study did not test the premise that differentiation of self is synonymous with positive therapeutic outcome. In fact that is an article of faith with Bowen, and it points to a certain circularity in this theory: symptoms indicate emotional fusion, and fusion is demonstrated by the presence of symptoms (Bowen, 1966).

Bowen repeatedly stresses the importance of theory in clinical practice (Bowen, 1976), and so invites judgment on the basis of his theory. Therefore, it should be noted that although his theory is thorough, consistent, and useful, it is largely a series of constructs based on clinical observation. The basic tenets are not supported by empirical research and, in fact, are probably not amenable to confirmation or disconfirmation in controlled experimentation. Bowen's theory, like psychoanalysis, is probably best judged not as true or false, but as useful or not useful. On balance, it seems eminently useful.

Evidence for the effectiveness of extended family systems therapy rests largely on personal experience and clinical reports. Bowenian therapists apparently do at least as well as the standard figures; that is, one-third of the patients get worse or no better; one-third of the patients get somewhat better; and one-third get significantly better.

People who develop systems of therapy are influenced by their personal and emotional experiences, and Bowen is more aware and candid than most about this (Anonymous, 1972). His family was middle-class, symptom-free, and relatively enmeshed; and his techniques seem most relevant for this sort of family. Like Bowen, most of the other therapists considered in this chapter also work in private practice with primarily middle-class patients.

Phil Guerin and Tom Fogarty have made notable contributions, not only in keeping alive and teaching Bowenian theory, but also in refining techniques of therapy. Both are master therapists. Betty Carter and Monica McGoldrick have made more of a contribution in studying how families work: the normal family life cycle, ethnic diversity, and the pervasive role of gender inequality. Because they are students of the family as well as therapists, some of their interventions have a decidedly educational flavor. In working with stepfamilies, for example, Betty Carter takes the stance of an expert and teaches the stepparent not to try to assume an equal position with the biological parent. Stepparents have to earn moral authority; meanwhile what works best is supporting the role of the biological parent. Just as Bowen's approach is influenced by his personal experience, it seems that both Carter and McGoldrick infuse their work as family therapists with their own experience as career women and their own convictions about the price of inequality.

All these therapists are fine clinicians; and they and their students have the advantage of working with theories that are sufficiently specific to provide clear strategies for treatment. Particularly now when family therapy is so fashionable, most people who see families use an eclectic hodgepodge of unrelated concepts and techniques; they are not apt to have a clear theory or a consistent strategy. The unhappy result is that most family therapists are drawn into the families' emotional processes and absorbed in content issues. The treatment that results tends to be haphazard and ineffectual.

Second-generation family therapists, like Guerin and Fogarty, are well-grounded enough in a theoretical system (for them, Bowen's) that they are able to diverge from it and add to it without losing focus. However, third-generation family therapists (students of students) are often left with no clear theoretical underpinning, and their work suffers from it. Interestingly, students of the pioneer family therapists have not been particularly innovative. None of them has surpassed their teachers. These observations underscore the plight of graduate students who are exposed to a variety of approaches, often presented with more criticism than sympathetic understanding. Consequently they are left with no single coherent approach. Probably the best way to become an effective clinician is to begin as a disciple of one particular school. Apprentice yourself to an expert—the best you can find—and immerse yourself in one system. After you have mastered that approach and practiced it for a few years, then you can begin to modify it, without losing focus and direction.

SUMMARY

Bowen's conceptual lens is wider than most family therapists', but his actual unit of treatment is smaller. His concern is always with the multigenerational family system, even though he usually meets with individuals or couples. Since he first introduced the "three-generational hypothesis" of schizophrenia, he has been aware of how interlocking triangles connect one generation to the next—like threads interwoven in a total family fabric. Although Bowenian therapists are unique in sending patients home to repair their relationships with parents, the idea of intergenerational connections has been very influential in the field.

According to Bowen, the major problem in families is emotional fusion; the major goal is differentiation. Emotional fusion grows out of an instinctual need for others, but is an unhealthy exaggeration of this need. Some people manifest fusion directly as a need for togetherness, while others mask it with a pseudo-independent facade. The person with a differentiated self need not be isolated, but can stay in contact with others and maintain his or her own integrity. Similarly, the healthy family is one that remains in viable emotional contact from one generation to another.

In Bowenian theory the triangle is the universal unit of analysis—in principle and in practice. Like Freud, Bowen stresses the pivotal importance of early family relations. The relationship between the self and parents is described as a triangle and considered the most important in life. Bowen's understanding of triangles is one of his most important contributions and one of the central ideas in family therapy.

For Bowen, therapy is a logical extension of theory. Before you can make any significant inroads into family problems, you must have a thorough understanding of how family systems operate. The cure is to go backwards, to visit your own parents, grandparents, aunts, and uncles, and learn to get along with them.

Bowen's theory espouses a balance between togetherness and independence, but the practice has a distinctly intellectual character. He sees anxiety as a threat to psychic equilibrium, consequently his approach to treatment often seems dispassionate. Bowen moves away from the heat of family confrontations in order to contemplate the history of family relationships. Like moving from the playing field into the stands, patterns become more visible, but it may be more difficult to have an immediate impact.

Bowen's model defocuses on symptoms in favor of systems dynamics. The treatment discourages therapists from trying to "fix" relationships, and instead encourages clients to begin a lifelong effort at self-discovery. This is not, however, merely a matter of introspection, but of actually making contact with the family. Clients are equipped for these journeys of self-discovery with cognitive tools for understanding their own patterns of emotional attachment and disengagement.

Seven techniques are most prominent in the practice of Bowenian family systems therapy:

1. *Genogram.* From his earliest NIMH days, Bowen used what he termed a "family diagram" to collect and organize important data concerning the multigenerational family system. In a 1972 publication Guerin renamed the family diagram the "genogram," a name that stuck. The main function of the genogram is to organize data during the evaluation phase and to track relationship processes and key triangles over the course of therapy. The most comprehensive guide to working with genograms is Monica McGoldrick's and Randy Gerson's book, *Genograms in Family Assessment* (McGoldrick & Gerson, 1985).

2. *The Therapy Triangle.* This technique is based on the theoretical assumption that conflictual relationship processes within the family have activated key symptom-related triangles in an attempt to reestablish stability; and the family will automatically attempt to include the therapist in the triangling process. If they succeed, therapy will generally be stalemated. On the other hand, if the therapist can remain free of reactive emotional entanglements—in other words, stay detriangled—the family system and its members will calm down to the point where they can begin to work out solutions to their dilemmas.

In the treatment of couples, each spouse is asked in turn a series of process questions aimed at toning down anxiety and emotional arousal, and fostering objective observation and thought. Some effort is made to slow down the overfunctioner in the dyad, while engaging and making it safe for more distant underfunctioners to open up and get involved. This same technique can be used with child-centered families by having the therapist place himself or herself at the point of a potential triangle with the symptomatic child and each parent, as well as between the parents. (Notice how similar this is to structural family therapists' attempts to get enmeshed mothers to pull back, and disengaged fathers involved. See Chapter 5.)

3. *Relationship Experiments.* Relationship experiments are carried out around structural alterations in key triangles. The goal is to help family members become aware of systems processes—and learn to recognize their own role in them. Perhaps the best illustration of such experiments are those developed by Fogarty for use with emotional pursuers and distancers. Pursuers are encouraged to restrain their pursuit, stop making demands, and decrease pressure for emotional connection—and to see what happens, in themselves and in the relationship. This exercise isn't designed to be a magic cure (as some people have hoped), but to help clarify the emotional processes involved. Distancers are encouraged to move toward the other person and communicate personal thoughts and feelings—in other words to find an alternative to either avoiding or capitulating to the other's demands.

4. *Coaching.* Coaching allows therapists to work openly and directly to help patients work on their family problems. Coaching is the Bowenian alternative to a more personal and emotionally involved role common to most other forms of therapy. By acting as coach, the Bowenian therapist hopes to avoid taking over for patients or becoming embroiled in family triangles. Coaching doesn't mean telling people what to do. It means asking process questions designed to help clients figure out family emotional processes and their role in them. The goal is increased understanding, increased self-focus, and more functional attachments to key family members.

5. *The "I-Position."* Taking a personal stance—saying what you feel, instead of what others are "doing"—is one of the most direct ways to break cycles of emotional reactivity. It's the difference between saying "You're lazy" and "I wish you would help me more"; or between "You're always spoiling the children" and "I think we should be stricter with them." It's a big difference.

Bowenian therapists not only encourage clients to take I-positions, they also do so themselves. An example would be when after a family session the mother pulls the therapist aside and confides that her husband has terminal cancer, but she doesn't want him or the children to know. What to do? Take an I-position: Say to the mother: "I believe your husband and children have a right to know about this." What she does, of course, is still up to her.

Another assumption in Bowenian therapy is that confrontation increases anxiety and decreases the ability to think clearly and see options. Therefore, displacing the focus, making it less personal and less threatening, is an excellent way to increase objectivity. This forms the basis for two related techniques, multiple family therapy and displacement stories.

6. *Multiple Family Therapy.* In his version of multiple family therapy, Bowen works with couples, taking turns focusing on first one then another and minimizing interaction. The idea is that one couple may learn more about emotional process by observing others—others in whom they are not so invested as to have their vision clouded by feelings. James Framo uses a similar approach.

7. *Displacement Stories.* This is Guerin's technique, showing films and videotapes and telling stories, to teach family members about systems functioning in a way that minimizes their defensiveness.

Finally, although students of family therapy are likely to evaluate different approaches according to how much sense they make and how useful they promise to be, Bowen himself considered his most important contribution to be showing the way to make human behavior a science. Far more important than methods and techniques of family therapy, Murray Bowen made profound contributions to our understanding of how we function as individuals, how we get along with our families, and how these are related.

REFERENCES

Andres, F. D. 1971. An introduction to family systems theory. In *Georgetown Family Symposium*, vol. 1, F. Andres and J. Lorio, eds. Washington, DC: Department of Psychiatry, Georgetown University Medical Center.

Anonymous. 1972. Differentiation of self in one's family. In *Family interaction*, J. Framo, ed. New York: Springer.

Boer, F. 1990. *Sibling relationships in middle childhood.* Leiden, the Netherlands: DSWO Press.

Bowen, M. 1966. The use of family theory in clinical practice. *Comprehensive Psychiatry.* 7:345–374.

Bowen, M. 1971. Family therapy and family group therapy. In *Comprehensive group psychotherapy*, H. Kaplan and B. Sadock, eds. Baltimore: Williams and Wilkins.

Bowen, M. 1972. Being and becoming a family therapist. In *The book of family therapy*, A. Ferber, M. Mendelsohn, and A. Napier, eds. New York: Science House.

Bowen, M. 1974. Toward the differentiation of self in one's family of origin. In *Georgetown Family Symposium*, vol. 1, F. Andres and J. Lorio, eds. Washington, DC: Department of Psychiatry, Georgetown University Medical Center.

Bowen, M. 1975. Family therapy after twenty years. In *American handbook of psychiatry*, vol. 5, S. Arieti, ed. New York: Basic Books.

Bowen, M. 1976. Theory in the practice of psychotherapy. In *Family therapy: Theory and practice*, P. J. Guerin, ed. New York: Gardner Press.

Carter, B., and McGoldrick, M. 1980. *The family life cycle.* New York: Gardner Press.

Carter, B., and McGoldrick, M. 1988. *The changing family life cycle: A framework for family therapy.* 2nd ed. Boston: Allyn and Bacon.

Carter, E., and Orfanidis, M. M. 1976. Family therapy with one person and the family therapist's own family. In *Family therapy: Theory and practice*, P. J. Guerin, ed. New York: Gardner Press.

Duvall, E. M. 1977. *Marriage and family development.* 5th ed. Philadelphia: Lippincott.

Fogarty, T. F. 1976a. Systems concepts and dimensions of self. In *Family therapy: Theory and practice*, P. J. Guerin, ed. New York: Gardner Press.

Fogarty, T. F. 1976b. Marital crisis. In *Family therapy: Theory and practice*, P. J. Guerin, ed. New York: Gardner Press.

Ford, D. H., and Urban, H. B. 1963. *Systems of psychotherapy.* New York: Wiley.

Glick, P. 1984. Marriage, divorce and living arrangements. *Journal of Family Issues. 5* (1):7–26.

Guerin, P. J. 1971. A family affair. *Georgetown Family Symposium*, vol. 1, Washington, DC.

Guerin, P. J. 1972. We became family therapists. In *The book of family therapy*, A. Ferber, M. Mendelsohn, and A. Napier, eds. New York: Science House.

Guerin, P. J., ed. 1976. *Family therapy: Theory and practice.* New York: Gardner Press.

Guerin, P. G., Fay, L., Burden, S., and Kautto, J. 1987. *The evaluation and treatment of marital conflict: A four-stage approach.* New York: Basic Books.

Guerin, P. J., and Fogarty, T. F. 1972. Study your own family. In *The book of family therapy*, A. Ferber, M. Mendelsohn, and A. Napier, eds. New York: Science House.

Guerin, P. J., and Pendagast, E. G. 1976. Evaluation of family system and genogram. In *Family therapy: Theory and practice*, P. J. Guerin, ed. New York: Gardner Press.

Herz, F., ed. 1991. *Reweaving the family tapestry.* New York: Norton.

Hill, R. 1970. *Family development in three generations.* Cambridge, MA: Schenkman.

Kerr, M. 1971. The importance of the extended family. *Georgetown Family Symposium*, vol. 1, Washington, DC.

Kerr, M., and Bowen, M. 1988. *Family evaluation.* New York: Norton.

Lerner, H. G. 1985. *The dance of anger: A woman's guide to changing patterns of intimate relationships.* New York: Harper & Row.

Lerner, H. G. 1989. *The dance of intimacy: A woman's guide to courageous acts of change in key relationships.* New York: Harper & Row.

McGoldrick, M., 1982. Through the looking glass: Supervision of a trainee's trigger family. In *Family therapy supervision*, J. Byng-Hall and R. Whiffen, eds. London: Academic Press.

McGoldrick, M. 1990. Gender presentation. Article in progress.

McGoldrick, M., and Gerson, R. 1985. *Genograms in family assessment.* New York: Norton.

McGoldrick, M., Pearce, J., and Giordano, J. 1982. *Ethnicity in family therapy.* New York: Guilford Press.

McGoldrick, M., Preto, N., Hines, P., and Lee, E. 1990. Ethnicity in family therapy. In *The handbook of family therapy.* 2nd ed., A. E. Gurman and D. P. Kniskern, eds. New York: Brunner/Mazel.

Nichols, M. P. 1986. *Turning forty in the eighties.* New York: Norton.

Nichols, M. P., and Zax, M. 1977. *Catharsis in psychotherapy.* New York: Gardner Press.

Nisbett, R. E., and Wilson, T. D. 1977. The halo effect: Evidence for unconscious alteration of judgments. *Journal of Personality and Social Psychology. 35*:250–256.

Papero, D. 1990. *Bowen family systems theory*. Boston: Allyn and Bacon.

Rodgers, R. 1960. Proposed modification of Duvall's family life cycle stages. Paper presented at the American Sociological Association Meeting, New York.

Solomon, M. 1973. A developmental conceptual premise for family therapy. *Family Process*. *12*:179–188.

Toman, W. 1969. *Family constellation*. New York: Springer.

Winer, L. R. 1971. The qualified pronoun count as a measure of change in family psychotherapy. *Family Process*. *10*:243–247.

Strategic and Systemic
Family Therapies

The strategic and systemic schools of family therapy are models that tried to apply most directly Gregory Bateson's ideas to family treatment. This endeavor resulted in a set of creative ways to generate change and manipulate resistance in families that were viewed as cybernetic systems. The apparent power of these methods captured the imagination of the field during the 1970s and early 1980s, and therapists became attracted to the creativity, optimism, and economy of these approaches.

But in the 1990s, as family therapy moved away from the position of therapist-as-expert-manipulator and toward therapist-as-collaborator, many aspects of these models fell out of favor. As we shall see, however, it is important to understand these approaches for more than historic reasons. They contain elements of sophisticated understanding of family complexities and powerful techniques that may be getting lost in our rush to embrace a kinder, gentler form of family therapy. In addition, some have evolved in ways that address these recent concerns.

In this chapter we will look most closely at three models: (1) the *Mental Research Institute* (MRI) group, (2) the strategic approach of *Jay Haley* and *Cloe Madanes,* and (3) the *Milan model.* These approaches share a systemic (circular) view of problem-maintenance and a strategic (planned) orientation to change. They organize therapy around creative strategic interventions designed to bypass resistance, and to do so as quickly as possible. They focus on resolving problems through interaction, without worrying about the intrapsychic lives of individual family members.

Haley (1973) coined the term "strategic therapy" when describing Milton Erickson's work. In many ways, the strategic approaches of both the MRI group and Haley can be seen as different applications of Erickson's methods to work with families. To make this translation to family interaction, these theorists added cybernetics and, in Haley's later work, the structural framework.

SKETCHES OF LEADING FIGURES

Among the leading strategic family therapists are: Jay Haley and Cloe Madanes in Washington, D.C.; and members of the Mental Research Institute (MRI) in Palo Alto, including Paul Watzlawick, John Weakland, and Richard Fisch.

Haley's development is unique among family therapists in that he learned from and with the three people who had the most influence on the evolution of family therapy: Milton Erickson, Gregory Bateson, and Salvador Minuchin. The impact of each of these pioneers is apparent in Haley's model which, more than any other in this chapter, integrated divergent trends as family therapy developed.

In 1967 Haley left MRI to join Minuchin and Braulio Montalvo at the Philadelphia Child Guidance Clinic. For approximately ten years he was director of family therapy research there, as well as a clinical member of the University of Pennsylvania's Department of Psychiatry. His association with Minuchin was productive for both men. Minuchin credits Haley for helping him articulate many of the principles elaborated in *Families and Family Therapy* (Minuchin, 1974), and Haley gives Minuchin credit for helping him understand the structure of families. Since Haley's first description of his approach in *Problem Solving Therapy* (Haley, 1976), he has used the structural view of family organization as the context within which to apply his strategic techniques. Haley's example may serve to help bridge the gap between competing approaches in the field.

In the early 1970s Haley left Philadelphia for Washington, D.C., to join the faculty of the University of Maryland Medical School and to establish his own family therapy clinic with Cloe Madanes. Madanes, known as one of the most creative therapists in the field, started at MRI in 1966 as a research assistant. In 1971 she was hired as a supervisor at the Philadelphia Child Guidance Clinic, where she worked with Haley, Minuchin, and Montalvo. In 1974, Haley and Madanes opened the Family Therapy Institute of Washington, D.C., now one of the major training institutes in the country. In addition, many therapists have been exposed to Haley and Madanes' ideas by attending one of their many workshops across the country.

The Mental Research Institute (MRI) led the way in research and training in family therapy's first decade. MRI began in 1959 when its founding director, Don Jackson, who was a consultant to the Bateson project, assembled an energetic and creative staff interested in communication, therapy, families, and schizophrenia. Among them were Jules Riskin, Virginia Satir, Jay Haley, John Weakland, Paul Watzlawick, and Janet Beavin. Haley and Weakland brought to MRI both the exciting cybernetic ideas of Bateson and the revolutionary clinical ideas of Erickson, with whom they were studying periodically in Phoenix.

This group started one of the first formal training programs in family therapy, conducted some of the first family interaction research, and made some of the most important early contributions to the family therapy literature, including Satir's (1964) *Conjoint Family Therapy*, Watzlawick, Beavin, and Jackson's (1967) *Pragmatics of Human Communication,* and Haley's (1963) *Strategies of Psychotherapy.*

Later, MRI was also home to several other influential strategic writers, including Carlos Sluzki, its director for several years and editor of *Family Process* through much of the 1980s, James Coyne who used the model to understand and treat depression, and Steve deShazer, who expanded on the original MRI model to create his solution-focused approach (described in Chapter 11).

In 1967 the Brief Therapy Center of MRI opened under the directorship of Richard Fisch. The staff included John Weakland, Paul Watzlawick, and Arthur Bodin. Their mission was to develop the briefest possible treatment for psychiatric disorders. What emerged was an active approach, focused on the presenting symptoms, and limited to ten sessions. This approach, come to be identified as the MRI model, was described in Watzlawick, Weakland, and Fisch's (1974) book, *Change: Principles of Problem Formation and Problem Resolution,* which popularized strategic therapy, and later in a follow-up volume, *The Tactics of Change: Doing Therapy Briefly* (Fisch, Weakland, & Segal, 1982).

The MRI model and Haley's work had a major impact on the Milan Associates, Mara Selvini Palazzoli, Luigi Boscolo, Gianfranco Cecchin, and Guiliana Pata, who developed the influential Milan model.

Selvini Palazzoli was a prominent Italian psychoanalyst, specializing in eating disorders, when, out of frustration with the results of her individual orientation (Selvini Palazzoli, 1981), she began exploring the writings of many of the theorists mentioned above, and began to develop her own approach to families. In 1967 she led a group of eight psychiatrists who originally tried to apply psychoanalytic ideas to working with families. Later they turned to the ideas of Bateson, Haley, and Watzlawick, which, in 1971, led the systemic faction of the group (Selvini Palazzoli, Boscolo, Cecchin, and Prata) to form the Center for the Study of the Family in Milan, where they developed the "Milan model."

In 1980 the Milan Associates underwent another split, with Boscolo and Cecchin moving in the direction of training and Selvini Palazzoli and Prata more interested in research. Each, group formed separate centers with new staffs, and their approaches also diverged; the men becoming increasingly less strategic and more interested in changing family belief systems through a process of asking questions, and the women pursuing their interest in understanding and interrupting the destructive games they believe severely disturbed families are caught up in.

In addition to these primary developers of the strategic and Milan models, there are other people who have contributed to both. Lynn Hoffman's evolution as a therapist parallels that of the strategic-systemic branch of family therapy. In the 1960s she collaborated with Haley and, in 1977, joined the Ackerman Institute in New York where she experimented with strategic approaches and later became a major proponent of the Milan model in the United States (Hoffman, 1981). Subsequently, she left Ackerman for Amherst, Massachusetts, and left the Milan model for a "second-order" approach based on social constructionist, narrative principles (see Chapter 11).

The Ackerman Institute has been an incubator for both the strategic and Milan models. Prominent contributors from the Ackerman faculty include: Peggy Papp (1980, 1983), who has been a creative force in the strategic school; Joel Bergman (1985), who developed many original strategies for dealing with difficult families; Peggy Penn (1982, 1985), who elaborated on the Milan innovation of circular questioning; and Olga Siverstein, who is known for her clinical artistry.

Karl Tomm (1984a, 1984b, 1987a, 1987b), a psychiatrist in Calgary, Canada, had been the most prominent interpreter and elaborator of the Milan model in North America, but recently, with the influence of Michael White's work (see Chapter 11), has been developing his own ideas about the impact of the therapist on families.

Joseph Eron and Thomas Lund (1993, 1994), in Kingston, New York, have tried to bring strategic therapy up to date by integrating it with narrative approaches, based on their common constructionist principles.

Finally, Richard Rabkin (1977), a literate and eclectic social psychiatrist practicing in New York City, was influenced by and influenced all the developers of strategic therapy.

THEORETICAL FORMULATIONS

Strategic therapists are more interested in generating changes in behavior than changes in understanding; consequently, they write more about technique than theory. The hallmark of the strategic approaches is designing novel strategies for solving problems. Like most clinicians, their theories are simpler and more pragmatic than those of scholars and academicians. Haley has often remarked that clinicians need simple maps to guide their action, while researchers can entertain complex ones because they have the luxury of not having to change things.

Because Milton Erickson's work had such a strong impact on the thinking of the strategic theorists, we will present first the aspects of Ericksonian theory that were incorporated into strategic formulations. Erickson boldly broke with the prevailing psychiatric traditions of his time, which were based on elaborate theories for explaining and categorizing human behavior but provided little direction for how to change it. Unlike psychoanalysts, who held that symptoms shouldn't be focused on because they were only the tip of the intrapsychic iceberg, Erickson was highly symptom- or problem-focused. He sought to discover details regarding the impact and context of symptoms in order to find leverage for changing them (Haley, 1981).

Rather than viewing the unconscious mind as a seething caldron of dangerous and aggressive impulses, Erickson saw it as a source of wisdom and creativity that, if unfettered by conscious inhibition, could solve problems and heal symptoms. Thus he found little value in traditional attempts to foster insight through interpretation, or in historical fishing expeditions, because the conscious minds of therapist and client were doing the interpreting and the fishing. He assumed that deep down patients knew what to do; they just didn't have access to that wisdom. One way to get access was to break out of habitual patterns of behavior or thinking, so Erickson developed many ways of getting people to simply do something different in the context of the old behavior, or to do the old behavior in a new context.

In addition, at a time when therapy was considered a laborious, multi-year proposition, Erickson's experience as a hypnotherapist convinced him that people could change quickly, and he tried to make therapy as brief as possible. He also took responsibility for changing his patients rather than assuming that patients had to take that responsibility for themselves. Thus, failures shouldn't be explained away as being due to the patient's resistance, because Erickson saw his job as finding ways to bypass or use "resistance." Many of what have been called paradoxical techniques came out of Erickson's application of hypnotic principles to avoid creating resistance in patients or to use their resistance to benefit therapy (Haley, 1981). For example, to induce trance, a hypnotherapist learns not to point out how a client is fighting going under but, instead, might tell the client to keep his or her eyes open until they become unbearably heavy.

Erickson initiated the revolution in understanding and treating people that strategic family therapy elaborated and made popular. He believed that people had the resources to change quickly once a therapist could get the process started. He eschewed interpretation and focused on changing action and context. Through Haley and Weakland's translations of Erickson's work, these assumptions about rapid change became theoretical underpinnings of strategic family therapy. These radical ideas about the nature of therapy and change were combined with the cybernetic concepts that Bateson introduced to the remarkable group of theorist-clinicians who were in Palo Alto during the late 1950s and 1960s.

From cybernetics, strategic theorists borrowed the concept of the *positive feedback loop,* and applied it to problematic family interaction (see Chapter 2 for more on cybernetics and family therapy). For the MRI group (particularly Watzlawick, Weakland, Fisch, and Bodin) that translated into a simple yet powerful principle of problem formation. They concluded that all families encounter many difficulties over the course of their lives, but whether or not a difficulty becomes a "problem" (that needs intervention) depends on how family members respond to it (Watzlawick, Weakland, & Fisch, 1974).

That is, families often make common-sensical but misguided attempts to solve their difficulties and, upon finding that the problem persists or gets worse, often apply more of the same attempted solutions. This only produces an escalation of the problem that provokes more of the same, and so on—in a vicious cycle. For example, Johnny feels threatened by the arrival of his baby sister and so he becomes temperamental. His father thinks he is being defiant and self-centered and tries to get him to act his age by punishing and criticizing him. Father's harshness confirms Johnny's belief that his parents love his sister more than him, so he acts even younger. Father, in turn, becomes more critical and punitive, and Johnny becomes increasingly sullen and alienated from the family. This is an escalating positive feedback loop: The family system is reacting to a deviation in the behavior of one of its members with feedback designed to dampen that deviation (*negative feedback*), but it actually has the effect of amplifying the deviation (*positive feedback*).

What's needed is to get father to reverse his attempted solution. If he could comfort rather than criticize Johnny and help him see that he wasn't being displaced, then Johnny might calm down. The system is governed, however, by unspoken rules that allow for only one interpretation of Johnny's behavior—as being disrespectful. For father to reverse his attempted solution, this rule would have to change.

Thus, MRI theorists, Don Jackson in particular, also borrowed from cybernetics an interest in *family rules*—underlying premises that govern the operation of family systems. A thermostat, as an example of a cybernetic system, has settings (rules) that govern the range of deviation the system will tolerate before negative feedback in the form of heating or air conditioning is activated. In most families, there are unspoken rules governing all sorts of behavior, most of which serve them well. Where a rule promotes the kind of rigid attempted solutions described above, it isn't just the behavior (father's critical discipline), but the rule governing that behavior (father's *interpretation* of Johnny's behavior) that must change. When only behavior or interactions within a system change, this is *first-order change*, as opposed to *second-order change*, which occurs when the rules of the system that govern those interactions change (Watzlawick, et al., 1974). How does one change the rules? One way is the technique of *reframing*—that is, changing father's interpretation of Johnny's behavior from disrespect to fear of displacement; from bad to sad.

Thus, the MRI approach to problems is quite simple: first, identify the more of the same, positive feedback loops that maintain problems; second, the rules (or frames) that support those interactions; and third, find a way to change those rules, Their interest, then, is limited to problem-centered, short-term sequences of interaction; they don't look beyond these sequences at other potential problems in a family, unless the family identifies them as problems. With this minimalistic ethic, the MRI group, unlike Haley or the Milan team, doesn't speculate about the function a family member's symptoms may be serving for the family or about problematic family boundaries or coalitions.

Haley, on the other hand, added a functionalist (see Chapter 2) emphasis to the Ericksonian and cybernetic influences, with his interest in the interpersonal and system-wide payoff of behavior. Later, he added many structural concepts picked up in the years he spent working with Minuchin in Philadelphia. Haley lengthened the duration of sequences he considered important in understanding problems from those immediately surrounding a problem, often involving only two people, to sequences involving at least three people and lasting longer periods of time. For example, Haley might notice that whenever Johnny and his father fight, mother protects Johnny by criticizing father for being so harsh. He might also see Johnny becoming more agitated when mother criticizes father, trying to get his parents' attention off their conflicts and onto him.

From this interest in larger and longer sequences, Haley also considers a different level of rules that govern them. He believes that the rules around the *hierarchy* in the family are crucial and finds a malfunctioning family hierarchy lurking behind most problems. Indeed, Haley (1976) suggests that, "an individual is more disturbed in direct proportion to the number of malfunctioning hierarchies in which he is embedded" (p. 117). It may be obvious that Johnny's parents don't work together effectively to discipline and nurture Johnny, and so Johnny is embedded in one malfunctioning hierarchy, but it may also be the case that Johnny's grandparents undermine his father too. In this case, two generational boundaries would be violated. More recently, Haley's position has shifted from seeing dysfunctional hierarchies as necessarily causing problems to avoiding etiological speculation and bolstering parental authority as a common part of the cure, regardless of the cause.

Haley (1980) also identified long-term sequences within families of troubled young adults. In these sequences, which might take place over months or years, the parents start to argue, which distresses the young adult to the point that he or she becomes symptomatic; the parents unite to try to deal with the strange symptoms and, perhaps, hospitalize the now identified patient; the patient gets better in the hospital and begins to take steps toward autonomy; without being able to focus on the patient, the parents are distressed and begin to argue; so the patient's symptoms return; and so on and on. The rule governing this disabling sequence is that the parents' marriage can't survive if they are left alone to face each other. Haley tried to change this rule by showing parents that if they work together they can control and help their troubled child. The good feeling produced by successfully improving the family hierarchy sets the stage for challenging their belief that they can't face the differences between them.

Thus, Haley's assessment and his goals are structural: to improve the family's hierarchy and boundary problems that support dysfunctional sequences. It is his calculated approach and step-by-step tactics that are strategic.

Along these lines, the book *Problem-Solving Therapy* contains one of Haley's (1976) unique contributions: the idea that families can't simply move from a dysfunctional structure directly to a functional one. Instead he believes that families must proceed through several stages, some of which may be less than ideal, before reaching a healthy structure—much as a broken arm must remain in a cast for a period of time and then be exercised before it can heal. For example, Haley might suggest that before Johnny's parents feel good about each other and work together to deal with him, the family may have to go through a stage in which father and son get closer and exclude mother from their relationship. Or, the parents may need to go through a stage in which they work only on cooperating on discipline, putting aside their marital resentments, before reaching a stage in which they can address those issues.

Haley's approach could be called "plan-ahead therapy." He helped therapists consider the importance of developing strategies for the overall course of therapy, as well as anticipating a family's reaction to events in their lives, and in therapy. He also encouraged the planning of each session and developed a how-to model of a first session with families that consisted of several stages (Haley, 1976).

Finally, Haley differed from his MRI colleagues, who avoided imputing motives to the behavior they observed, because he viewed human interactions as interpersonal struggles for control and power. He kept a functionalist eye on family patterns, looking for the purpose problems might serve for the individual or for the family. To counter the problem's payoff, he often borrowed Erickson's technique of prescribing an ordeal so that the price for keeping a symptom came to outweigh that of giving it up. To illustrate this technique, consider Erickson's famous maneuver of prescribing that an insomniac set his alarm every night to wake up and wax his kitchen floor for several hours. Haley tried to explain all therapy as based on ordeals, suggesting that people change to avoid the many ordeals inherent in remaining a client (Haley, 1984).

Cloe Madanes (1981 1984) also emphasized this function-of-the-symptom aspect of problems, particularly the *incongruous hierarchy* created when children use their symptoms to try to help their parents. For example, when a daughter sees her mother looking depressed, the daughter can provoke a fight that prods the mother from being sad and helpless to acting strong and competent. Much of Madanes's approach involved finding creative ways for symptomatic children to help their parents openly and directly so that they wouldn't have to resort to symptoms as the only way to help their parents.

In her most recent book, Madanes's (1990) formulations have become more elaborate. As an overview, she states, "All problems brought to therapy can be thought of as stemming from the dilemma between love and violence" (p. 5), and the rest of the book describes strategies for transforming violence into love. She categorizes family problems according to four basic intentions of the family members involved. First is the desire *to dominate and control,* and Madanes sees symptoms like delinquency and behavioral problems as related to this kind of motivation. The second intention is *to be loved,* and she associates psychosomatic symptoms, depression, anxiety, and eating disorders with this motive. The third desire is *to love and protect others;* related symptoms include suicide threats, abuse and neglect, obsessions, and thought disorders. The final category of intention is *to repent and forgive,* and she finds that these families have problems like incest, sexual abuse, and sadistic acts.

For each of these categories of families, Madanes recommends certain strategies for helping them change. For example, for the first category of domination and control, she suggests that therapists get parents to work together to take charge of their problem children, whereas if the problem was more related to the third category, love and protection, the children might be asked to find a different way to protect or care for their parents. In generating these guidelines, Madanes offers a more comprehensive framework for using strategic interventions than has been previously available.

Mara Selvini Palazzoli and her associates in Milan (1978) had read the work of Bateson, the MRI group, and Haley, and were working with families of schizophrenic and anorexic patients. Like Haley, they focused on the power-game aspect of family interactions and, relatedly, on the protective function that symptoms served for the whole family. The Milan Associates (Selvini Palazzoli, Gianfranco Cecchin, Luigi Boscolo, and Guiliana Prata) extended the length of family sequences that therapists considered in their assessments even beyond the months-long sequences that Haley (1980) described in *Leaving Home.* They interviewed families about their history, sometimes over several generations, searching for evidence to confirm their hunches about how the children's symptoms came to be necessary. These hypotheses often involved elaborate networks of covert family alliances and coalitions, including extended family. They usually concluded that the patient had to use her symptoms to protect one or more other family members so as to maintain the delicate network of family alliances.

It appears that while the various strategic or systemic models had some theoretical elements in common, each model covered a different range of family phenomena and focused on a different length of family sequence (Breunlin & Schwartz, 1986). The MRI model focused exclusively on the brief, more of the same, interactions surrounding the problem and had little concern for structural formulations. Haley included those short sequences but was also interested in longer ones that last months or years and reflect chronic structural problems. The Milan Associates were interested in some of those longer sequences but also in the way that families evolved over generations which led to the network of alliances that necessitated symptoms.

NORMAL FAMILY DEVELOPMENT

The MRI group was vehemently opposed to setting up standards of normality, and instead adopted what they called a "nonnormative" stance. "By nonnormative, we mean that we use no criteria to judge the health or normality of an individual or family. As therapists, we do not regard any particular way of functioning, relating, or living as a problem if the client is not expressing discontent with it" (Fisch, 1978). Thus, by limiting their task to eliminating problems presented to them, the MRI group avoids taking any position regarding how families *should* behave. This relativism has deep roots. As early as 1967, Don Jackson wrote an essay called "The Myth of Normality" in which he argued that because there is no one model of health or normality, it's a mistake to impose one on clients.

Despite their disdain for normative goals, it's clear that MRI therapists believe that healthy families are flexible enough to modify attempted solutions that don't work. This flexibility is needed not only with everyday difficulties, but also to navigate transitional points in the family's development (Weakland et al., 1974). In addition, it's implied that successful families will not overreact or underreact to difficulties, and will avoid the kind of utopian thinking that makes people try to fix things that don't need fixing—like the "generation gap."

The Milan associates also adopted a nonnormative stance (Selvini Palazzoli et al., 1978). Their hypotheses about systems of relationships that maintained problems usually involved any number of covert, cross-generational alliances; so one could infer that they believed families should have clear generational boundaries. (Normality isn't the converse of abnormality, however, so one can't always make that extrapolation.)

They also, however, strove to maintain an attitude that was originally called "neutrality" (Selvini Palazzoli et al., 1980) and later came to be known as "curiosity" (Cecchin, 1987) regarding families. Therapists who adopt this attitude don't apply preconceived goals or normative models to families. Instead, by raising questions that help a family examine itself and that expose hidden power games, they trust that the family will reorganize on it's own in a better way, even if that way doesn't conform to some normative map.

In contrast to the relativism of these other two approaches, Haley's thinking about families was based on assumptions about normal (or at least functional) family functioning. His therapy was designed to help families re-organize dysfunctional structures into what he considered to be functional ones (Haley, 1976). The normative map that he uses in this endeavor is basically the same one that Minuchin and the structuralists use, with its clear generational boundaries and hierarchy (see Chapter 5). Haley (1973) also emphasized the impact of life cycle stages on a family's structure.

DEVELOPMENT OF BEHAVIOR DISORDERS

In strategic and systemic models there are three basic explanations for the way problems develop. The first is cybernetic: Difficulties are turned into chronic problems by the persistence of misguided attempted solutions, forming positive feedback escalations (Watzlawick et al., 1974). The second is structural: Problems are the result of flaws in a family's hierarchy or boundaries. The third is functional: Problems result when people try to protect or control one another indirectly, such that their problems come to serve a function for the system. The MRI group limited itself to the first explanation, while the other strategic or systemic models embraced all three, although each model emphasized one explanation over the others. Haley and Madanes include aspects of both structural and functional thinking. The Milan Associates also considered both structural and functional ideas in their hypothesizing.

To clarify these differences, consider the following example: sixteen-year-old Tommy recently began refusing to leave the house. An MRI therapist might ask his parents about how they had been trying to get him to venture out. This therapist would focus on the parents' attempted solutions, believing that these were maintaining Tommy's refusal, and on the parents' explanation or "frame" for Tommy's behavior, believing that the parents' frame for Tommy's problem may be maintaining their attempted solutions.

A Haley-style strategic therapist might be interested in the parents' attempted solutions, but would also search for information about: the parents' marriage, the ways in which Tommy was involved in struggles between his parents or other family members, or the protective nature of Tommy's problem. This therapist would be acting on the assumption that Tommy's behavior was probably part of a dysfunctional triangle, consisting of mother, father, and Tommy, that was maintaining Tommy's symptoms. This therapist might further assume that this triangular sequence was fueled by unresolved conflicts between the parents. A Madanes-style strategic therapist might also be interested in this triangle, but, in addition, would be curious about how Tommy's behavior might be protecting one or the other parent from having to face some threatening issue. This protecting would be seen as the problem-maintaining dynamic.

A Milan-style, systemic therapist wouldn't focus so much on attempted solutions but, instead, would ask questions about a variety of past and present relationships in the family. In so doing, the Milan therapist would be trying to uncover an elaborate network of power alliances, often running across generations, that constituted the family's "game." Such a game left Tommy in the position of having to use his symptoms to protect another family member or to help that member win. Through this process the family might disclose, for example, that if Tommy were to grow up and leave home, mother would be sucked back into a power struggle between her parents, which she had avoided only by having a child on whom to focus. Also, by not succeeding in life, Tommy might be protecting his father from the shame of having a child who exceeded him in accomplishment, just as he had done with his father.

From the above discussion we can see that, while all of these approaches view problems as embedded in interactional sequences among family members, they differ in terms of the number of family members included and the duration of the sequences in which they are interested, beginning with the MRI model, in which the focus is on short, present-day sequences involving only a few family members, and ending with the Milan model, which examines long-term, historical sequences involving many family members. Haley and Madanes fall between these two positions, taking into account both short and some longer sequences and involving at least three family members.

GOALS OF THERAPY

For all strategic and systemic therapies, the primary goal is the resolution of the presenting problem. They differ considerably, however, on how best to achieve this goal, how much must happen for the changes in the problem to last, and how much responsibility the therapist should take for creating these changes.

The MRI group is proudly minimalist in goals. Once the presenting problem is resolved to the client's satisfaction, therapy is concluded. Even where other problems are apparent to the therapist, if the family doesn't ask for help with those problems, they aren't targeted. MRI therapists justify this minimalist position by asserting that, because they view people who have problems as stuck rather than sick, their job is to simply help people get unstuck and moving again, not to change their personalities or family structures.

They disdain more open-ended forms of family therapy in which the goals are less clear. Fisch and colleagues (1973) wrote sarcastically of such therapies: "By no means should the therapist encourage any discussion about concrete goals of treatment, since the family would then know when to stop treatment" (p. 601). In contrast, MRI therapists pride themselves on helping families define clear and reachable goals so that everyone knows when treatment has concluded—and how successfully. They often find that much of the therapy takes place simply in the process of pushing clients to set such clear, behavioral goals, because in doing so clients are forced to clarify vague ambitions and dissatisfactions. Also, in getting clients to define achievable goals, MRI therapists help people let go of the utopian goals with which they often enter therapy and, thereby, diminish their sense of frustration or hopelessness.

Like behaviorism, which dominated psychology at the time the MRI model was developing, the MRI model is behavioral in both its goals and its primary assessment of observable patterns of interaction, preferring not to speculate about intrapsychic states or intentions. In trying to achieve the larger goal of problem-resolution, the immediate goal is to change the behavioral responses of people to their problems. More specifically, as described earlier, MRI therapists try to interrupt (often to reverse) more of the same vicious feedback loops. To achieve this behavioral change they may try to "reframe the problem," and, in that sense, aren't strictly behavioral. But any cognitive change still is in the service of the primary goal of behavior change.

Recently, in response to the perception that strategic therapists ignore emotions, Trudy Kleckner and her colleagues (1992) suggested that,

> It is not that strategic therapists don't deal with feelings—it's just that they don't talk about it with each other, write about it in the literature, or teach it to trainees . . . strategic therapists do not spend significant amounts of time merely talking about feelings or getting clients to recognize and own feelings; they concentrate instead on getting clients to express their feelings in ways that are more likely to lead to client satisfaction in daily life. (p. 49)

Again, the emphasis is on using the expression of emotion pragmatically, in the service of changing behavioral patterns.

Haley's approach is also quite behavioral (though he also uses reframes) and, even more than the MRI group, he downgrades the importance of insight or awareness as a goal. He has always been scornful of therapies that helped clients understand why they did things but did little to get them to do something different.

Haley's ultimate goal often is a structural reorganization of the family, particularly its hierarchy and generational boundaries, but since he approaches therapy in stages, he has intermediate goals along the way. Unlike structural family therapy, however, all of these structural goals are directly connected to the presenting problem. For example, to improve the relationship between the polarized parents of a rebellious teenager, a structural family therapist might get the parents to talk to each other about their marital issues, where Haley would have them talk instead about their difficulty working together to deal with their rebellious son. Only after the problems with their son had improved would Haley allow their discussions to shift to their marriage.

Unlike the MRI group, who focused exclusively on the presenting problem because that was all they wanted to change, Haley's problem-focus was a strategy. He shared strategic therapists' general goal to avoid having to deal directly with client resistance. He found that if therapists make the presenting problem the center of their interventions, a family's motivation to change the problem will keep them engaged even while they change their structure.

To continue contrasting structural and strategic approaches, structural therapists don't shy from and sometimes deliberately provoke conflict or tension in sessions, and rely on their personal relationship with each family member to keep them engaged. Strategic therapists rely on strategies rather than their personalities to minimize resistance or conflict while people change. One of these strategies is to focus on the problem until it's resolved and then explore other, often more threatening, family issues, after the family has more trust in the therapist and in each other because of their previous success. Unlike the MRI group then, Haley doesn't necessarily believe that therapy should end with the resolution of the presenting problem, but instead therapy should continue until the structural problems that produced it are resolved.

Haley's inclination to divide therapy into stages extended to individual sessions. Haley (1976) recommended that therapists follow a clear first-session format that included several stages: a social stage in which the goal is to make the family feel comfortable, a stage in which the problem is defined and family members' opinions about it are solicited, and a stage in which family members interact about the problem.

Haley's interest in stages and his formulaic approach reflects the strategic therapist's ethic that responsibility for change rests with the therapist rather than the client. They believe therapists shouldn't blame treatment failures on their clients' lack of readiness, but instead should find ways to motivate them. With this conviction comes the responsibility on strategic theorists like Haley to develop and clearly describe specialized techniques for all kinds of problems or resistances, as well as the steps and stages of therapy. Thus, the writing of strategic therapists tends to be short on theory and long on technique.

Recently, Madanes (1990) has expanded the goals of her version of strategic therapy well beyond the problem-focused or even the structural goals to include growth-oriented objectives like balance, harmony, and love. She states that, "A goal of therapy is to bring harmony and balance into people's lives. To love and to be loved, to find fulfillment in work, to play and enjoy: All are part of a necessary balance" (p. 13). Despite the fact that her practice of therapy is still quite strategic, this is a big departure from the standard goals of strategic therapy and brings Madanes closer to the goals of people like Satir and other experientalists. Indeed, the name of her therapy has shifted to "strategic humanism" to emphasize its softer aspects.

It is in the area of goals and responsibility for therapy that strategic and systemic therapies eventually diverged. The early work of the Milan group (Selvini Palazzoli, Boscolo, Cecchin, & Prata, 1978) was heavily influenced by the MRI and Haley models. The Milan associates, as described above, expanded the network of people involved in maintaining the problem, but were still primarily interested in finding powerful techniques to interrupt family games. The techniques they developed differed from those of the strategic schools in that they were less behavioral and, instead were designed to expose games and reframe motives for strange behavior. Thus, while being less problem-focused and more interested in changing a family's awareness or beliefs than strategic therapists, the original Milan approach was no less manipulative: the responsibility for change rested on the therapist whose job it was to outwit resistance.

When the Milan associates split into two groups in the early 1980s, a strategic emphasis remained in the work of Selvini Palazzoli and the groups she subsequently formed. She, however, took a low profile during the 1980s while she researched her hypotheses and developed a new strategic approach (Selvini Palazzoli, 1986). The goal of that therapy was to disrupt and expose the "dirty games" that severely disturbed family members play with each other. More recently, she abandoned brief, strategic models altogether and now does long-term therapy with more focus on insight for the individual patient (Selvini, 1993).

After the breakup, Luigi Boscolo and Gianfranco Cecchin moved in a different direction, away from strategically manipulating families and toward collaborating with them to form systemic hypotheses about their problems. For this branch of the Milan group, therapy became more of a research expedition which the therapist entered without specific goals or strategies, trusting that this process of self-examination would allow families to better choose whether or not they wanted to keep their problems. The therapist was released from responsibility for any certain outcome and took an attitude of curiosity (Cecchin, 1987) toward families, rather than the interventive attitude of strategic therapists.

In moving in this direction, Boscolo and Cecchin took a position relative to therapist goals and attitude directly opposite to that of their strategic predecessors. This illustrates the pendulum-swinging process described in Chapter 2; it also echoes the polarization around the issue of power and control that existed in the original Bateson group. Bateson, the anthropologist, wanted to understand families but was strongly opposed to tampering with them, whereas Haley and the others influenced by Erickson thought that this systemic wisdom should be used to find the most effective ways to fix families. The strategic schools remain committed to that belief while Boscolo and Cecchin have tried to translate the spirit of Bateson's noninterventionist ethic into therapy.

CONDITIONS FOR BEHAVIOR CHANGE

As we have discussed, for the MRI strategic school the primary condition for resolving problems is to change the behavior associated with them. It is believed that through seeing the results of altering rigid behavioral responses, clients will become more flexible in their problem-solving strategies. When this happens, clients will achieve second-order change—a change in the rules governing their response to problems.

For example, Jill argues with her father about her curfew and father grounds her. She then runs away and stays with a friend. A first-order intervention at this point might be to help father find a more effective punishment to tame this out-of-control child. A second-order strategic intervention might be to direct father to act distracted and sad around his daughter and to imply to her that he has given up trying to control her. This shifts Jill from feeling trapped by her father to feeling concerned about him, and she becomes more reasonable. Father learns that when attempted solutions aren't working, try something different. This change is second-order in that it is a change in the rules governing the way father and daughter interact.

Clients may not need to be educated about their problems or to have insight into why they have needed them or how they arose. Families may not need to reorganize their relationships—especially those not directly involved in the presenting problem. They may simply need to try something different, even if it runs against common sense, as did the strange advice given Jill's father. Second-order change in families often seems to arise out of apparently illogical new solutions. This is because many logical or common sense solutions have already been tried by families before they come to treatment. What families don't need is more of the same. What they do need is flexibility.

Effective therapists must sometimes be able to convince clients to try something completely different. To achieve this, strategic therapists give directives that clients are to follow between sessions. To get clients to comply, since these directives are often counterintuitive, therapists must be able to maximize motivation and minimize resistance.

Along these lines, MRI therapists try to figure out who is the "customer" in the family—that is, who has the most motivation for things to change. Often the customer isn't the person with the problem, and sometimes isn't even in the family. Frequently they will work primarily, or even exclusively, with the customer, believing that it is most efficient to work with the most motivated person in the system, and that frequently problems will clear up even if only one person in the system changes.

On many of these points, Haley would agree. Haley (1976) believed that telling people what they're doing wrong doesn't help them change, it only mobilizes resistance. The same is true, Haley believed, of cathartic expression of feeling. He claimed that changes in behavior alter feelings and perceptions, rather than the other way around. Madanes (1980) said, "If a problem can be solved without the family's knowing how or why, that is satisfactory" (p. 79). It may seem curious, then, that Madanes, Haley, and the MRI group have relied heavily on the technique of reframing, in which the therapist tries to change the way clients perceive or understand their problems. The strategic theorist's response to this inconsistency is likely to be that reframing is in the service of behavior change, which is what really changes client perception or feeling. According to Haley, until people have a different experience with a problem, they won't be able to see it differently.

Over time, the Milan group turned behaviorism on its head. From the beginning they were more interested in getting a family to *see* things differently (through a reframing technique called "positive connotation" to be discussed later) than in getting family members to *behave* differently. Increasingly, they (Boscolo and Cecchin, in particular) moved toward a meaning-changes-behavior position as they found that helping people examine the systemic evolution of their problems allowed them to relate differently. This led to a style of therapy that contained few directives and mostly involved asking questions designed to help family members reexamine their predicaments. This shift from behavior to meaning set the stage for the constructivist movement (Chapters 3 and 11).

TECHNIQUES

Strategic therapy is the most technique-driven of all family therapies. Strategic therapists have maintained Erickson's tradition of tailoring interventions to the idiosyncrasies of person and problem. As a result, rather than presenting a general method to be adapted to different contexts, the strategic literature is full of unique interventions, customized to fit specific problems. For example, in surveying the strategic literature up to 1980, Duncan Stanton (1981) found references that describe interventions for over forty different syndromes or types of problems, covering everything imaginable, from adolescent problems to schizophrenia to thumb-sucking. The flow of problem-specific strategic interventions still hasn't slowed, even though fewer of these articles appear in mainstream family therapy journals. With the emergence of their own journal, the *Journal of Strategic and Systemic Therapies,* (recently renamed the *Journal of Systemic Therapies*), strategic and systemic writers, while no less productive, have become more insular and reach a smaller audience.

While this parade of articles and books describing customized techniques has continued since the basic strategic theory and techniques were described in the mid-1970s (most notable among these: Fisch, Weakland, & Segal, 1982; Papp, 1983; Coyne, 1987; Coyne, Kahn, & Gotlib, 1987; Haley, 1984; Madanes, 1984; Stanton & Todd, 1982), there haven't been major (second-order) shifts in strategic concepts or method since then. We will describe the basic methods of the MRI, Haley, and Milan models.

The MRI Approach

Members of the MRI's Brief Therapy Center follow a six-step treatment procedure:

1. Introduction to the treatment setup
2. Inquiry and definition of the problem
3. Estimation of the behavior maintaining the problem
4. Setting goals for treatment
5. Selecting and making behavioral interventions
6. Termination

Upon arrival, clients fill out a form covering basic demographic data. Next, the therapist explains that sessions are recorded and observed, and points out the advantages of having several professionals involved in the case. The therapist also explains that treatment is conducted within a maximum of ten sessions, thereby setting up a powerful expectation of change.

Once the preliminaries are concluded, the therapist asks for a clear definition of the major problem. The MRI group believe that clients must be able to define a single major problem for therapy to succeed. When the problem is stated in vague terms, such as "We just don't seem to get along," or in terms of presumptive causes, "Dad's job is making him depressed," the therapist helps translate it into a clear and concrete goal, asking questions like "What will be the first small sign that things are getting better?"

When the problem and goals are defined clearly and behaviorally, MRI therapists begin to ask about the clients' attempted solutions that may be maintaining the problem. For example, the husband who nags at his wife to spend more time with him may succeed only in driving her further away; the parents who criticize their son in an attempt to get him to quit fighting with his sister may perpetuate his sense that they like her better; or the husband who does everything his wife asks to reassure her of his love may feel so resentful that he begins to hate her.

In general, the solutions that tend to perpetuate or exacerbate problems fall into one of three categories:

1. The solution is simply to deny that a problem exists; action is necessary, but not taken. For instance, parents do nothing despite growing evidence that their teenage son is heavily involved with drugs.

2. The solution is an effort to solve something that isn't really a problem; action is taken when it shouldn't be. For example, parents severely punish a child for masturbating.

3. The solution is an effort to solve a problem within a framework that makes a solution impossible; action is taken, but at the wrong level. A husband, for instance, buys increasingly expensive gifts for his unhappy wife, when what she wants is his affection (Watzlawick, Weakland, & Fisch, 1974).

Each of these three classes of problem-maintaining attempted solutions imply therapeutic strategies: in the first, clients need to act; in the second, to stop acting; and in the third, to act in a different way. Once the therapist conceives of a strategy for changing the problem-maintaining sequences, the clients must be convinced of the value of following this strategy. To sell their directives to clients, MRI therapists will reframe the problem (provide a new meaning for problem behaviors) to increase the likelihood of compliance. Thus, MRI reframes are different from psychodynamic interpretations in that the goal of a reframe isn't to produce insight or to educate, but instead to induce compliance or to change perspective. Traditionally, the MRI therapist wasn't constrained to use reframes he or she believed to be true. Instead, these pragmatists felt free to use any plausible rationale that might bolster their directives. Thus a therapist might tell an angry, disengaged teen that when his father calls him worthless and locks him out of the house, it's the only way father knows how to show love to him. This cavalier, "anything goes" kind of reframing that is imposed on families has been criticized (Flaskas, 1992). Many strategic therapists now pay closer attention to their clients' beliefs and try to be more sensitive in the way they construct and present their reframes.

> Believing in the absence of any absolute "truth" is not synonymous with ignoring or riding roughshod over the "subjective truths" of others. The usefulness of any "truths" used in the proposing of different frames for a client's or family's consideration rests primarily on how these frames are viewed from the subjective perspectives of those involved. . . . To do this helpfully and respectfully clearly means listening at all times with profound levels of care and attention to what family members are saying. (Cade & Hudson O'Hanlon, 1993, p. 116)

As we described earlier, in order to change problem-maintaining sequences, strategic therapists often try to get family members to do or believe things that run opposite to common sense. Such counterintuitive techniques have been called *paradoxical interventions* because it seems paradoxical that people must sometimes do things that are in apparent opposition to the goals of therapy in order to reach those goals (Frankl, 1960; Haley, 1973, 1976; Hare-Mustin, 1975; Watzlawick, Weakland, & Fisch, 1974).

For example, Watzlawick and his colleagues (1974) described a young couple who were bothered by their parents' tendency to treat them like children by doing everything for them. Despite the husband's adequate salary, the parents continued to send money and to lavish gifts on them, refused to let them pay even part of a restaurant check, and so on. The strategic team helped the couple solve their difficulty with their doting parents by having the couple become less rather than more competent. Instead of trying to show the parents that they didn't need help, the couple was told to act helpless and dependent, so much so that the parents got disgusted and finally backed off. This form of paradox is an *outpositioning* strategy (Rohrbaugh et al., 1981) in the sense that the couple forced the sequence to change by taking their parent's position—that they were dependent—and exaggerating it to an absurd extreme.

The techniques most commonly thought of as paradoxical are symptom prescriptions in which the family is told to continue or expand the behavior they complain about. In some contexts, such a prescription might be made with the hope that the family will try to comply with it, and thereby be forced to reverse their attempted solutions. If sad Johnny is told to try to become depressed several times a day and his family is asked to encourage him to be sad, then they will no longer try ineffectively to cheer him up and he won't feel guilty for not being happy. Michael Rohrbaugh and his colleagues (1981), in their useful taxonomy of paradoxical techniques, called this a *compliance-based* paradox because the therapist wants the family to comply with the directive.

At other times, a therapist may prescribe the symptom, while secretly hoping that the clients rebel against this directive. The therapist may encourage Johnny to continue to be depressed because, in doing so, he's helping his brother (with whom Johnny is competitive) feel superior. This is called a *defiance-based* intervention because the therapist wants the client to defy the directive, and reframes the reason for the directive in terms that will maximize Johnny's defiance.

Still other times the therapist may *prescribe the symptom* with the hope that in doing so the network of family relationships that maintain the problem will be exposed. The therapist says that Johnny should remain depressed because that way he can continue to keep his mother's attention, which will keep her from looking to father for affection, since father is still emotionally involved with his mother, and so on. Since Rohrbaugh didn't include this category, we will call it an *exposure-based* paradox, which is most frequently associated with the Milan, rather than the MRI, model.

From this discussion, we can see that the reframe or rationale that accompanies the paradoxical directive is quite important. It will include different content and use different language depending on whether the therapist wants to maximize compliance, defiance, or exposure.

Rohrbaugh described another class of paradoxical directives that is also designed to manipulate resistance. Most families enter therapy with a certain amount of ambivalence regarding the problem and the changes required to improve it. When the therapist encourages the family to make these changes, family members are likely to respond with the fearful side of their ambivalence and increase their resistance. If the therapist, instead, were to preempt these fears by warning the family of the dangers of change and restraining them from trying to change too fast, the family may react with the side of their ambivalence that wants the changes. Thus, MRI therapists will frequently use such *restraining techniques* as asking about the negative consequences of change and warning family members to go slow, or to worry about the relapse when improvements occur.

While paradoxical techniques are still used by some strategic therapists, others, because of the deception involved in their use, have abandoned them or present them humorously and are honest about their intent. As Cade and Hudson O'Hanlon (1993) comment,

> We now find ourselves rarely, if ever, using covert and deceptive interventions. However, we here intend no sanctimonious, "holier-than-thou" comments on erstwhile paradoxical therapists. After all, we have been numbered among their ranks. It is just that our ideas about therapy have evolved over time. Along with the majority of our colleagues, we no longer see therapy in the same adversarial way that we used to. (p. 157)

Haley and Madanes Approach

In many ways, Jay Haley's work is a cross between the MRI approach and the structural approach of Minuchin and his colleagues. In terms of the actual moves in a session, Haley tends to be strategic and may use many of the paradoxical techniques described above. His goals, however, are usually structural, with an emphasis on the family hierarchy. Haley (1976) believes that if therapy is to end well, it must begin properly. Therefore, he devotes a good deal of time and attention to the opening moves of treatment. Regardless of who is presented as the official patient, Haley begins by interviewing the entire family, or as much of it as can be assembled. His approach to this initial interview is highly structured and regularly follows four stages: a social stage, a problem stage, an interaction stage, and finally a goal-setting stage. These stages, with clear-cut instructions for each, provided a secure structure for a generation of novice family therapists who wanted to know just what to do in their first session.

Families are often quite uncomfortable and defensive when they come to therapy for the first time. Family members often don't know why they are there or what to expect, and fear that the therapist will blame them for the problem. Therefore, Haley has therapists use the initial minutes of a first session to help everyone relax. He makes a point of greeting every family member and trying to make sure they are comfortable. He acts as though he were a host, making sure that his guests feel welcome. While making small talk, Haley observes how each family member behaves and how they all interact.

After this brief *social stage,* Haley gets down to business in the *problem stage.* Before asking for the family's position, he introduces himself, repeats what he knows about the family, and explains why he has asked the entire family to come—that is, because he wants everyone's opinions and ideas. Haley then asks each person to give their perspective on the problem. His clear and practical suggestions even address such specific questions as whom to speak to first. Since mothers are usually more central and fathers less involved, Haley recommends that the therapist speak first to the father in order to increase his concern and involvement. This suggestion nicely illustrates Haley's strategic maneuvering, which begins with the first contact and characterizes the course of all subsequent meetings.

Haley listens carefully to the way each family member defines the problem and their involvement in it, making sure that no one interrupts until each has had a turn. During this phase, Haley is observing the reactions of each family member for clues to the family's triangles and hierarchy, but he discourages therapists from making any interpretations or comments regarding these observations that might make the family defensive. Instead, these observations are filed away, awaiting further confirmation and providing the basis for further interventions. He does "interactionalize" problems that are presented as belonging only to one member. For example, mother says that Johnny is just a depressed person. In listening to everyone's report, Haley noticed that the parent's disagreed regarding the best way to help Johnny, so he can list this disagreement, which certainly doesn't help Johnny, as another aspect of the problem.

Once everyone has had a chance to talk, Haley encourages them to discuss their various points of view among themselves. In this, the *interactional stage,* the therapist can observe, rather than just hear about, the sequences that surround the problem. As they talk, Haley looks for alliances between family members against others. How functional is the hierarchy? Do the parents work well together or do they undercut each other? How does the patient respond to conflict between others? During this stage, the therapist is like an anthropologist, watching for patterns in the family action.

Sometimes Haley ends the first session by directing the family to carry out a task. In subsequent sessions, directives play a central role in his problem-solving therapy. Effective directives don't take the form of simple advice. Advice is rarely helpful, unless clients happen to be ignorant of some piece of information, or unless problems are minor. As Haley says, advice generally doesn't help because people don't have rational control over what they do.

To design an effective directive, the therapist has to learn what solutions have already been tried and failed. To persuade family members to do a task, they must be convinced that each one will gain something by cooperating with the therapist. They also need to see themselves as competent to try something new, so therapists are well advised to find ways to boost their self-concepts (Madanes, 1990).

The following two tasks are taken from Haley's *Problem-Solving Therapy*. A couple who were out of the habit of being affectionate with each other were told to behave affectionately in order to teach their child how to show affection. In another case, a mother who was unable to control her twelve-year-old son had decided to send him away to military school. Haley suggested that since the boy had no idea how tough his life would be at military school, it would be a good idea for the mother to help prepare him. They both agreed. Haley directed her to teach him how to stand at attention, be polite, and wake up early every morning to make his bed. The two of them followed these instructions as if playing a game, with mother as sergeant and son as private. But after two weeks the son was behaving so well that his mother no longer felt it necessary to send him away,

Madanes (1981) has used the observation, illustrated by the second case above, that people will often do something they wouldn't ordinarily do if it is framed as play or pretend, to develop a whole range of *pretend techniques*. One such strategy is to ask a symptomatic child to pretend to have the symptom, and encourage the parents to pretend to help. The child can give up the actual symptom now that pretending to have it is serving the same family function. The following two case studies summarized from Madanes (1981) illustrate the pretend technique.

In the first case, a mother sought therapy because her ten-year-old son had night terrors. There were also two older daughters and a baby brother. Madanes suspected that the boy was concerned about his mother, who was poor, spoke little English, and had lost two husbands.

Since the boy had night terrors the therapist asked all the members of the family to describe their dreams. Only the mother and the son had nightmares. The mother's nightmare was that someone would break into the house, and the boy's was that he was being attacked by a witch. When Madanes asked what the mother did when the boy had nightmares, she said that she took him into her bed and told him to pray to God. She explained that she thought his nightmares were the work of the devil.

The treatment team's conjecture was that the boy's night terrors were both a metaphorical expression of the mother's fears, and an attempt to help her. As long as the boy was afraid, his mother had to be strong in order to help him; thus she could not be afraid herself. Unfortunately, while she tried to protect him, she frightened him further by talking about God and the devil. Both mother and child were helping each other in unproductive ways.

The family members were told to pretend that they were home and mother was afraid that someone might break in. The son was asked to protect his mother. In this way the mother had to pretend to need the child's help instead of really needing it. At first the family had difficulty playing the scene because the mother would attack the make-believe thief before the son could help. Thus she communicated that she was capable of taking care of herself; she did not need the son's protection. After the scene was performed correctly, with the son attacking the thief, they all discussed the performance. The mother explained that it was difficult for her to play her part because she was a competent person who could defend herself. Madanes sent the family home with the task of repeating this dramatization every evening for a week.

If the son started screaming during his sleep, his mother was to wake him up and play the scene again. They were told that this was important to do no matter how late it was or how tired they were. The son's night terrors completely disappeared.

In the second case, a mother sought psychiatric treatment for her five-year-old son because he had uncontrollable temper tantrums. After talking with the family for a few minutes Madanes asked the son to pretend to have a tantrum to show her what it was like. The boy said, "Okay, I'm the Incredible Hulk!" He puffed out his chest, flexed his muscles, made a monstrous face, and started screaming and kicking the furniture. Madanes then asked the mother to do what she usually did in such circumstances. The mother responded by telling her son, in a weak and ineffective way, to calm down. She tried to pretend to send him to another room as she tried to do at home with little success. Next, Madanes asked the mother if the boy was doing a good job of pretending. She said that he was.

Madanes asked the boy to repeat the scene. This time he was Frankenstein and his tantrum was performed with a more rigid body posture and a face more appropriate to Frankenstein's monster. Then Madanes talked with the boy about the Incredible Hulk and Frankenstein and congratulated the mother for rearing such an imaginative child.

Following this discussion, mother and son were told to pretend that he was having a tantrum while she was walking him to his room. The boy was told to act like the Incredible Hulk and to make lots of noise. Then they were told to pretend to close the door and hug and kiss. Next Madanes instructed the mother to pretend that she was having a tantrum, and the boy was to hug and kiss her. Madanes instructed mother and son to perform both scenes every morning before school, and every afternoon when the boy came home. After every performance the mother was to give the boy milk and cookies if he did a good job. Thus the mother was moved from a helpless position to one of superiority in which she was in charge of rewarding his make-believe performance. The next week the mother called to say that they did not need to come for therapy because the boy was behaving very well and that his tantrums had ceased.

Both of these cases contain the hallmarks of strategic therapy: tracking the sequences around the problem and giving directives that change those sequences. Like Haley, Madanes is primarily interested in the sequences that relate to the family's hierarchy. Unlike Haley, however, her directives are usually aimed less at getting parents back in control through power plays and more through structuring new, enjoyable opportunities for parents and children to care for or protect each other.

Haley's preference is often to get parents to work together to control their out-of-control children. This preference is clearly illustrated in the strategies he recommends for dealing with severely disturbed young adults in the book *Leaving Home*. Parents are to put aside their personal resentments and collaborate in planning and implementing a highly structured, rather authoritarian, regime of discipline for their young adult, treating him or her younger-than-age until the child is back on track toward normality. Haley speculates that by forcing the parents to cooperate for the good of their child, he is interrupting the sequence in which the tension from their marital conflicts precipitates their child's crazy behavior as a way to distract them.

While Haley believed that a problematic marriage often lurks behind a child's problem, he also warned therapists to not target these marital issues too soon or, in some cases, at all. He believed that families were often protective of and threatened by disturbances in that relationship. Instead, by getting parents to work together to help their child, the couple may make simultaneous changes in their relationship without it ever being overtly addressed. If marital issues do come up, the parents will feel less fear of dealing with them if they have had success in cooperating to help their child. All of this reinforces Haley's commitment to remain focused on the presenting problem until it improves.

Later, Haley (1984) returned to his strategic, Ericksonian roots in a book called *Ordeal Therapy,* a collection of case studies in which ordeals were prescribed that made the clients' symptoms more trouble than they were worth. Haley's general approach is based on this premise: "If one makes it more difficult for a person to have a symptom than to give it up, the person will give up the symptom" (p. 5). For example, a standard ordeal is for a client to have to get up in the middle of the night and exercise strenuously whenever he or she had symptoms during that day. Another example might be for the client to have to give a present to someone with whom he or she has a poor relationship—for example, a mother-in-law or ex-spouse—each time the symptoms occur. As these examples illustrate, the ordeal should be something that clients don't want to do, but would be good for them or would improve their health or relationships. In constructing ordeals, clients should feel like they are making a deal with themselves rather than with the therapist.

Since Haley also subscribed to structural goals in therapy, he also used ordeals to restructure families. For example, a sixteen-year-old boy put a variety of items up his behind and then expelled them, leaving his stepmother to clean up the mess, while his father remained peripheral. Haley (1984) arranged that, after each such episode, the father had to take his son to their backyard and have the boy dig a hole three feet deep and three feet wide, in which he was to bury all the things he was putting up his rear end. After a few weeks of this, Haley reported that the symptoms stopped, the father became more involved with his son, and the stepmother became closer to the father.

As we mentioned earlier in this chapter, Madanes (1990) has developed a classification system for families that provides guidelines describing which strategic techniques to use with which kind of family. In this system she suggests when to use her own favorite methods, like pretend techniques or finding ways that children can be appropriately helpful to their parents; when to use Haley's ordeals or hierarchical techniques; and when to use techniques more associated with the MRI, like prescribing the symptom.

In addition, she developed a sixteen-step model for the reparation of families in which there has been sex abuse. Many of these steps revolve around getting the abuser to apologize on his knees to the victim, getting the family also to apologize for not protecting the victim, and making sure that the abuse doesn't recur. Working with victims and perpetrators of sex abuse is a difficult and complex process. It is good to have a model but to also be aware that its formula may not fit every case.

The current form of Haley/Madanes therapy, called strategic human-ism, still involves giving directives based on hypotheses the therapist gener-ates. In this, strategic humanism is not in step with the contemporary trend in family therapy toward collaborative approaches. The directives they deliver, however, are more oriented toward increasing family members' abilities to soothe and love than to gain control over one another. This represents a major shift and is in sync with family therapy's shift away from the power elements of hierarchy and toward finding ways to increase harmony. The ex-pression of emotions like repentance, sorrow, love, and empathy is a much larger part of this new form of strategic therapy than existed in former ver-sions. The strategic therapist has also been humanized in this revision. The expression of empathy for clients is given as much weight as the ability to design effective directives.

The Milan Model

The techniques of the Milan model are difficult to summarize because there were several very different Milan models.

The original model was highly strategic and formulaic. Families were treated by male-female cotherapists, while being observed by other members of a therapy team. Sessions were held, on the average, once a month and, in-itially, were limited to ten, in emulation of the MRI model. The monthly ses-sions were an artifact of the long distances many families had to travel to the center in Milan; however, the team came to believe that the long interval between sessions was beneficial. If families were seen weekly, the effects of the previous session's paradoxical prescription might be diminished because families seemed to take longer to fully react.

The standard session format had five parts: the presession, the session, the intersession, the intervention, and the postsession discussion. As Boscolo, Cecchin, Hoffman, and Penn (1987) describe:

> During the presession the team came up with an initial hypothesis about the family's presenting problem. . . . During the session itself, the team members would validate, modify, or change the hypothesis. After about forty minutes, the entire team would meet alone to discuss the hypothe-sis and arrive at an intervention. The treating therapists would then go back to deliver the intervention to the family, either by positively connot-ing the problem situation or by a ritual to be done by the family that commented on the problem situation and was designed to introduce change. . . . Finally, the team would meet for a postsession discussion to analyze the family's reactions and to plan for the next session. (p. 4)

As indicated in that description, the main intervention was either a ritual or a positive connotation.

The *positive connotation* was the most distinctive innovation to emerge from this original Milan model. Derived from the MRI technique of reframing the symptom as serving a protective function for the family—for example, Johnny needs to continue to be depressed to distract his parents from their marital issues—the positive connotation eliminated the implication inherent in such reframes that some family members wanted or benefited from the patient's symptoms. This implication made for resistance that the Milan team found could be circumvented if the patient's behavior was construed not as protecting specific people or relationships, but as preserving the family's homeostasis or rigid rules. Indeed, every family member's behavior was often connoted in this system-serving way.

In this way, through a session the treatment team would hypothesize about the way that the patient's symptom fit into the family system, and after the mid-session break the therapists would turn this hypothesis into a statement and give it to the family, along with the injunction that the situation should not change. Johnny should continue to sacrifice himself by remaining depressed as a way to reassure the family that he will not become an abusive man like his grandfather. Mother should also maintain her overinvolvement with Johnny as a way to make him feel valued while he sacrifices himself. Father should continue to criticize mother and Johnny's relationship so that mother will not be tempted to abandon Johnny and become a wife to her husband.

Rituals were used to engage the whole family in a series of actions that run counter to, or exaggerate, rigid family rules and myths. For example, one family of four was highly enmeshed with their large extended family. They were told to hold family discussions behind locked doors every other night after dinner during which each family member was to speak for fifteen minutes about the family. Meanwhile they were to redouble their allegiance and courtesy to the other members of the clan. By exaggerating the family's loyalty to the extended family while simultaneously breaking that loyalty rule by meeting apart from the clan and talking about it, the family could examine and break the loyalty rule that perpetuated their dysfunctional system.

Rituals were also used to dramatize the positive connotation. For example, each family member might have to express their gratitude each night to the patient for having his or her problem (Boscolo et al., 1987). The Milan group also devised a set of rituals based on an "odd and even days" format (Selvini Palazzoli et al., 1978b). For example, a family in which the parents are deadlocked over parental functions might be told that on even days of the week father will be in charge of the patient's behavior and mother is to act as if she was not there. On odd days, mother's in charge and father's to stay out of the way. Here, again, the family's rigid sequences are interrupted and they must react differently to each other.

These positive connotations and rituals are powerful and provocative interventions. To keep families engaged while using such methods, the therapist-family relationship becomes crucial. Unfortunately, the Milan team originally portrayed therapy as a struggle for power between therapists and families. Their main advice to therapists was to remain neutral in the sense of avoiding the appearance of taking sides with one family member or another. This *neutrality* was often interpreted by practitioners of the model as distance, so that therapists often delivered these dramatic interventions while seeming aloof and, not surprisingly, families often became angry or didn't return.

In the late 1970s and early 1980s, the original Milan team began to split around the nature of therapy. Selvini Palazzoli maintained the model's strategic and adversarial bent, although she stopped using paradoxical interventions. Instead she and Guiliana Prata and some new colleagues experimented with a specific kind of ritual called the *invariant prescription,* which they assigned to every family they treated.

Selvini Palazzoli (1986) believed that psychotic or anorexic patients are caught up in a *"dirty game"*; a power struggle originally between their parents that these patients are pulled into and, ultimately, wind up using their symptoms in an attempt to defeat one parent for the sake of the other. Her invariant prescription method begins in much the same way the original Milan model did, using circular questions to build hypotheses. But this time the questioning and hypothesizing center around the family's presupposed dirty game.

At the end of the third assessment session, by which time a sense of the family's game should be established, the invariant prescription begins (Gelcer & Schwartzbein, 1989). The parents are directed to tell their children and select members of the extended family that they have a secret. They are also supposed to observe and record the reactions of family members to their keeping a secret. During ensuing sessions, the therapist and the parents meet to discuss the family's reaction and the parents are instructed to not only continue keeping the secret but to go out together for varying periods of time, and to do so mysteriously, without warning other family members. Therapy continues this way until the patient's symptoms abate.

This invariant prescription can be seen as a variant of structural or Haley-style strategic therapy in that by getting parents to share a secret and go out together, the therapist is shoring up the boundary around their subsystem. Plotting together and mysteriously eloping adds a sense of playfulness and connectedness to a stultified marriage, which might ease the power struggle underlying a dirty game. Children or other family members who watch the parents keeping a secret and eloping may initially fear and try to break this new alliance between the parents but, if they are unsuccessful, may feel relieved to see an end to the parents' chronic cold war and to be out of the middle of it. In addition, as the parents carefully observe, record, and discuss the family's reactions to their new behavior, they become more aware of the network of dysfunctional family alliances and more aware of the process of change in those patterns.

As seems to be Selvini Palazzoli's wont, she recently reinvented her therapy once more, this time abandoning any form of strategic, short-term therapy (invariant prescription included) for long-term therapy with patients and their families (Selvini, 1993). Thus, she has come full circle, beginning with psychodynamic roots, then abandoning any concerns with the individual to focus on family patterns, and now returning to a long-term therapy that emphasizes insight and focuses again on the individual. This new therapy revolves around understanding the denial of family secrets and suffering over generations. In this way it is linked conceptually, if not technically, to her former models.

Boscolo and Cecchin also have moved away from strategic intervening, but they have moved toward a collaborative style of therapy. This therapy grew from their increasing impression that the value in the Milan model wasn't so much in the directives (positive connotations or rituals), which had been the model's centerpiece, but in the interview process itself. Their therapy came to center around *circular questioning*, an interviewing technique aimed to elicit family members opinions regarding differences of several kinds:

> . . . differences in perception of relationships ("Who is closer to Father, your daughter or your son?"); questions about differences of degree ("On a scale of one to ten, how bad do you think the fighting is this week?"); now/then differences ("Did she start losing weight before or after her sister went off to college?"); and hypothetical or future differences ("If she had not been born, how would your marriage be different today? If you were to divorce, which parent would the children stay with?"). (Boscolo, Cecchin, Hoffman, & Penn, 1987, p. 11)

By asking about differences like these, the circular nature of problems becomes apparent as family members are lifted out of their limited and linear perspectives. Circular questions have been further refined and catalogued by Penn (1982, 1985) and Tomm (1985a, 1985b). Boscolo (Boscolo & Bertrando, 1992) remains intrigued with their potential.

As an example, let's return to Johnny's family and imagine the following conversation (adapted from Hoffman, 1983):

QUESTION: Who is most upset by Johnny's depression?

ANSWER: Mother.

QUESTION: How does mother try to help Johnny?

ANSWER: She talks to him for hours and tries to do things for him.

QUESTION: Who agrees most with mother's way of trying to help Johnny?

ANSWER: The psychiatrist who prescribes his medication.

QUESTION: Who disagrees?

ANSWER: Father. He thinks Johnny shouldn't be allowed to do what he wants.

QUESTION: Who agrees with father?

ANSWER: We all think Johnny is babied too much. And grandma too. Grandpa would probably agree with mother but he died.

QUESTION: Did Johnny start to get depressed before or after grandfather's death?

ANSWER: Not long after, I guess.

QUESTION: If grandfather hadn't died, how would the family be different now?

ANSWER: Well, mother and grandma probably wouldn't fight so much because grandma wouldn't be living with us. And mother wouldn't be so sad all the time.

QUESTION: If mother and grandma didn't fight so much and mother wasn't so sad, how do you think Johnny would be?

ANSWER: Well, I guess he might be happier too. But then he'd probably be fighting with father again.

Just by asking questions, the frame for Johnny's problem gradually shifts from a psychotic one to being symptomatic of difficult changes in the family structure.

Boscolo and Cecchin became aware that the spirit in which these questions are asked determined the usefulness of this technique. If a therapist maintains a strategic mind-set—uses the questioning process to strive for a particular outcome—the responses of family members will be constrained or inhibited by their sense that the therapist is after something. If, on the other hand, the therapist asks circular questions out of genuine curiosity (Cecchin, 1987), as if joining the family in a research expedition regarding their problem, an atmosphere can be created in which the family can arrive at new understandings of their predicament on their own.

More recently, Cecchin (Cecchin, Lane, & Ray, 1993) has suggested that, in addition to remaining curious, the therapist should maintain an attitude of "irreverence." By irreverence is meant not becoming too attached to any model or belief and helping families become more irreverent toward the beliefs that constrain them. In this way, Cecchin joins the skeptical postmodernist movement described in Chapter 3.

Other Contributions

Up to this point we have described the techniques developed by the major schools of strategic or systemic therapy: the MRI group; Haley and Madanes; and the Milan Associates. There are many other people who have added innovations.

Strategic therapy has pioneered the *team approach* to therapy. Originally, the MRI group used teams behind one-way mirrors to help brainstorm strategies, as did the Milan group. Peggy Papp (1980) and her colleagues at the Ackerman Institute brought the team more directly into the therapy process by turning the observers into a kind of "Greek chorus" that reacted to events in the therapy session. For example, the team might, for strategic purposes, disagree with the therapist. In witnessing this staged debate between the team and their therapist over whether a family should change, family members might feel that both sides of their ambivalence were appreciated and represented in the therapy session. Having the team interact openly with the therapist or even with the family during sessions paved the way for later approaches in which the team might enter the treatment room and discuss the family while the family watched (Andersen, 1987).

Jim Alexander was a behaviorist who, out of frustration with limits of his exclusively behavioral orientation, incorporated strategic ideas. The result is *functional family therapy* (Alexander & Parsons, 1982) which, as the name implies, is concerned with the function that family behavior is designed to achieve (see also Chapter 8). Functional family therapists assume that most family behaviors are attempts to become more or less intimate and through "relabeling" (another word for reframing) help family members see each other's behaviors in that benign light. They also help family members set up behavioral contingency management programs to help them get the kind of intimacy they want more directly. Functional family therapy, then, represents an interesting blend of strategic and behavioral therapies and, unlike many strategic schools, retains the behaviorist ethic of basing interventions on sound research.

Carlos Sluzki has made a number of contributions to strategic theory and technique, including an innovative approach to marital therapy, a topic rarely addressed by strategic writers (Sluzki, 1978). He provided a series of concrete guidelines such as: "If A and B concur in defining A as victim and B as victimizer, then find a way of reversing the roles/labels and state the reversal forcefully" (p. 368). For example, Sluzki was treating a couple who were locked in a relationship in which the wife's nagging, complaining negativism was complemented by the husband's appeasing optimism. Both of them agreed that she was the victimizer and he was the victim. Sluzki praised her for taking on the burden of being the villain, but added that making her husband good while she remained the "mean one" must have given her some satisfaction. But he said, there are no kicks like being the "good guy," and he selfishly monopolizes this role.

Then Sluzki assigned them the following task: He told the husband to respond to any of his wife's statements by being as pessimistic as possible, regardless of his true feelings. Sluzki then directed the wife to remain as pessimistic as always, "in order to make the task more difficult for her husband."

The task served the following purposes: (1) the prescription acknowledged that he could be genuinely pessimistic; (2) her habitual behavior was being relabeled as a gesture of good will; (3) if they followed instructions, they would quite quickly reach a deadlock that would force her to extricate the positive side of the matter; (4) nobody—but the therapist—would be blamed for any escalation into pessimism between them, totally eliminating any label of victim and victimizer; and (5) they were being granted a humorous way out of confrontations, which they continued to use thereafter on occasions. In fact, both expressed a remarkable reduction of the conflicts and a general improvement in the relationship from then on, while Sluzki, in typical MRI form, expressed concern about their unexplainable and too dramatic change.

Some authors have combined the strategic and structural approaches. Duncan Stanton (1981) begins with straightforward structural techniques and resorts to strategic interventions only when a family strongly resists his restructuring attempts. After the often paradoxical strategic interventions have reduced resistance, he returns to the structural approach. Maurizio Andolfi (1979, Andolfi & Zwerling, 1980; Andolfi, Angelo, & di Nichilo, 1989) does it the other way, starting strategically and ending structurally. He restrains severely dysfunctional families from changing until the identified patient improves and the family members are more accessible to him, at which point he becomes more structural. Unlike other strategic therapists, however, Andolfi gets very personally and actively involved. His freewheeling and provocative interventions are reminiscent of his mentor, Carl Whitaker, and it is this high-intensity style that has drawn many American family therapists to study with him in Rome.

EVALUATING THERAPY THEORY AND RESULTS

The strategic family therapies reached the height of their popularity in the early 1980s. They were clever, prescriptive, and systematic—qualities appreciated by therapists who often felt overwhelmed by the chaos and emotion of families in treatment. Then in the mid-1980s a reaction set in, and people began criticizing the manipulative and calculating aspects of strategic therapy. What the field came to reject was a mechanistic view of families, as though they were puppets of a system they were too blind to see, and a hierarchical view of therapy, as though only an oh-so-clever therapist could pull the strings.

Midway through the 1990s, the strategic approaches described in this chapter have lost much of their popularity. However, even as we move away from an overreliance on technique and manipulation, and toward therapy done *with* not *to* families, we shouldn't lose sight of valuable aspects of strategic therapy. These include having a clear therapeutic goal, anticipating ways that families will react to interventions, understanding and tracking sequences of interaction, and the creative use of directives.

Most of the small amount of research regarding the effectiveness of strategic therapy isn't rigorous. More than any of the other models in this book, information about strategic therapy is exchanged through the case report format. Nearly all of the hundreds of articles and books on strategic therapy include at least one description of a successful technique or therapy outcome. Thus, strategic therapy appears to have a great deal of anecdotal support for its efficacy (although people tend not to write about their cases that fail).

Some strategic groups have tracked their outcome a little more systematically. In the book *Change* that launched the MRI model, Watzlawick and colleagues (1974) conducted follow-up phone interviews with 97 consecutive cases three months after treatment was terminated. Interviewers asked clients whether their complaints were relieved, if they had sought additional treatment elsewhere, and if any new problems had developed. To minimize the possibility that patients might exaggerate the benefits of treatment to please their therapists, all interviews were conducted by members of the team who were not involved in treatment. With an average length of treatment of seven sessions, 40 percent reported complete relief, 32 percent reported considerable but not complete relief, and 28 percent reported no change. In none of the complete relief cases were there any signs of symptom substitution.

When Haley (1980) reported on the outcome of his "leaving home" model with schizophrenic young adults, he used rehospitalization as his only criterion. Fourteen such patients, each of whom had been hospitalized for the first time, were treated by different therapists for an average of 14 sessions. The therapists of these patients followed up on their treatment between two and four years after terminating. In that time, three of the fourteen had been rehospitalized, while another patient had committed suicide.

There are some studies of the outcome of family therapies that are based on, or are similar to, the methods of strategic therapy. In their classic study, Langsley, Machotka, and Flomenhaft (1971) studied the effectiveness of their family crisis therapy, which has some similarities with both the MRI and Haley models. Patients who were seen as needing hospitalization were randomly assigned to either a psychiatric hospital or a crisis family therapy condition on an outpatient basis. Eighteen months later, the group who received family therapy had spent less than half the number of days in the hospital than the group who had previously been hospitalized. Furthermore, the cost of treatment during this period was six times as high for the hospitalized group.

In another carefully controlled study, Alexander and Parsons found their functional family therapy (described earlier in this chapter) to be more effective in treating a group of delinquents than a client-centered family approach, an eclectic-dynamic approach, or a no-treatment control group (Parsons & Alexander, 1973). Recidivism was cut in half by the functional approach, in contrast to the other three groups which did not differ significantly from each other. Furthermore, a three-year follow-up showed that the incidence of problems in the siblings was significantly lower for the functional treatment.

Stanton, Todd, and their associates (1981) demonstrated the effectiveness of an approach combining structural and Haley's strategic family therapies for treating heroin addicts. The results of this study were impressive because family therapy resulted in twice as many days of abstinence from heroin than a methadone maintenance program.

The Milan group's early work was filled with anecdotal case reports of amazing outcomes with anorexia nervosa, schizophrenia, and delinquency (Selvini Palazzoli, Boscolo, Cecchin, & Prata, 1978, 1980). Later, however, members of the original team expressed reservations about the model and implied that it wasn't as effective as they originally suggested (Selvini Palazzoli, 1986; Selvini Palazzoli & Viaro, 1988; Boscolo, 1983).

Some who have studied the Milan model more systematically concur with these less enthusiastic impressions (Machal, Feldman, & Sigal, 1989). In discussing their disappointing results with the Milan model, the authors of both of these studies cited clients' negative reactions to the therapist or team. Families frequently felt that the therapists were cold and distant and the team was impersonal. It seems that the attitude of adversarial strategizing recommended in *Paradox and Counterparadox* showed through the therapists' attempts to positively connote family members. We seem to have to learn the same lesson over and over: people have trouble changing if they don't feel cared about.

These studies question the effectiveness of the original Milan model. The fact that none of the founders of this model continues to practice it also indicates that, despite its initial appeal and popularity, it had problems.

There is a lesson in family therapy's initial infatuation and later disillusionment with the Milan model. We need to study outcome carefully and thoroughly before declaring our therapies successful. The world will always confirm the assumptions one has about it, if one doesn't look too closely. Quick phone calls to families asking how things are going don't qualify as looking closely.

Although some forms of strategic therapy seem to have had some impact on certain populations, it is difficult to generalize these results too far because the number of rigorous studies is small and because strategic therapy is far from a homogeneous approach. The forms of therapy used in these different studies differ considerably from each other.

SUMMARY

Derived from a combination of Ericksonian hypnotherapy and Batesonian cybernetics, strategic therapy has developed a body of powerful procedures for treating psychological problems. Strategic approaches vary in the specifics of theory and technique, but share a problem-centered, pragmatic focus on changing behavioral sequences, in which therapists take responsibility for the outcome of therapy. Insight and understanding are eschewed in favor of directives designed to change the way family members relate to each other. Because strategic therapists prefer to circumvent rather than deal directly with resistance, their directives are often paradoxical, although there is now less tolerance for deceiving clients than once was true.

There are currently two main strategic camps: the MRI group on the West Coast, and Haley and Madanes on the East. The MRI model tries to remain strictly interactional—observing and intervening into sequences of interaction surrounding a problem rather than speculating about the feelings or intentions of the interactants. Haley and Madanes are interested in motives—Haley mainly in the desire to control others, and Madanes in the desire to love and be loved. In addition, unlike the MRI group, Haley and Madanes incorporate many structural concepts in their model and don't limit their goals to simple problem resolution. They believe successful treatment often requires structural change, with an emphasis on improving family hierarchy.

Like Haley, the Milan Associates originally saw power in the motives of family members and tried to understand the elaborate multigenerational games that surrounded symptoms. They designed powerful interventions—positive connotations and rituals—to expose or disrupt these games, and to change the meaning of the problem. Later the original group split, with Selvini Palazzoli and new colleagues going through several transformations until settling on their current long-term approach based on family secrets. Cecchin and Boscolo moved away from the power of single interventions, became more interested in the questioning process as a way to help families to new understandings, and in so doing paved the way for family therapy's current interest in conversation and narrative.

Strategic therapists are trying to keep their approach vital by learning from past mistakes. As Cade and Hudson O'Hanlon (1993) report,

Beginners will often overconcentrate on technique, on devising "clever" interventions, paying insufficient attention to respect, understanding, and validation. This may be, to some extent, the fault of writers on brief/strategic approaches, including ourselves, who may at times have over-concentrated on techniques and interventions and underplayed the importance of basic attitudes and values, and of wisdom, integrity, and restraint. . . . Brief/strategic therapists have also not been very good at demonstrating the patient, painstaking, and sometimes exhaustive groundwork that often precedes the "brilliant" interventions, nor the many cases in which steady, competent work rather than dramatic "fireworks" has brought about significant changes. (p. 18)

They are also integrating other ideas and keeping up with the postmodern spirit of the 1990s. For example, in 1993 Haley and Madanes met in a large conference with Minuchin to discuss the integration of structural and strategic approaches. Haley also released a book of conversations about therapy between him and an associate in which the evolution of his thinking is apparent (Grove & Haley, 1993). In addition, some authors have integrated MRI strategic concepts with narrative approaches (Eron & Lund, 1993, 1994). They incorporate strategic's emphasis on clear therapeutic goals and strategies with the collaborative therapist's stance and the breadth of scope of narrative therapy. It is good to see that strategic thinking is evolving because even in this era of the nonexpert therapist, there is still room for thoughtful problem-solving strategies and therapeutic direction.

REFERENCES

Alexander, J., and Parsons, B. 1973. Short-term behavioral intervention with delinquent families: Impact on family process and recidivism. *Journal of Abnormal Psychology. 81:*219–225.

Alexander, J., and Parsons, B. 1982. *Functional family therapy.* Monterey, CA: Brooks Cole.

Andersen, T. 1987. The reflecting team: Dialogue and meta-dialogue in clinical work. *Family Process. 26:*415–417.

Andolfi, M. 1979. *Family therapy: An international approach.* New York: Plenum Press.

Andolfi, M., Angelo, C., and di Nichilo, M. 1989. *The myth of Atlas.* New York: Brunner/Mazel.

Andolfi, M., and Zwerling, I., eds. 1980. *Dimensions of family therapy.* New York: Guilford Press.

Bergman, J. 1985. *Fishing for barracuda: Pragmatics of brief systemic therapy.* New York: Norton.

Boscolo, L. 1983. Final discussion. In *Psychosocial intervention in schizophrenia: An international view.* H. Stierlin, L. Wynne, and M. Wirsching, eds. Berlin: Springer-Verlag.

Boscolo, L., Cecchin, G., Hoffman, L., and Penn, P. 1987. *Milan systemic family therapy.* New York: Basic Books.

Boscolo, L., and Bertrando, P. 1992. The reflexive loop of past, present, and future in systemic therapy and consultation. *Family Process. 31:*119–133.

Breunlin, D., and Schwartz, R. 1986 Sequences: Toward a common denominator of family therapy. *Family Process. 25:*67–87.

Cade, B., and Hudson O'Hanlon, W. 1993. *A brief guide to brief therapy.* New York: Norton.

Cecchin, G. 1987. Hypothesizing, circularity and neutrality revisited: An invitation to curiosity. *Family Process. 26:*405–413.

Cecchin, G., Lane, G., and Ray, W. 1993. From strategizing to nonintervention: Toward irreverence in systemic practice. *Journal of Marital and Family Therapy.* 19:125–136.

Coleman, S. 1987. Milan in Bucks County. *Family Therapy Networker. 11:42–47.*

Coyne, J. 1987. Depression, biology, marriage and marital therapy. *Journal of Marital and Family Therapy. 13:393–408.*

Coyne, J., Kahn, J., and Gotlib, I. 1987. Depression. In *Family interaction and psychopathology,* T. Jacob, ed. New York: Plenum Press.

Eron, J., and Lund, T. 1993. An approach to how problems evolve and dissolve: Integrating narrative and strategic concepts. *Family Process. 32:291–309.*

Eron, J., and Lund, T. 1994. *Strategy in narrative therapy: From magic to method.* New York: Guilford Press.

Fisch, R. 1978. Review of problem-solving therapy, by Jay Haley. *Family Process. 17:107–110.*

Fisch, R., Watzlawick, P., Weakland, J., and Bodin, A. 1973. On unbecoming family therapists. In *The book of family therapy,* A. Ferber, M. Mendelsohn, and A. Napier, eds. Boston: Houghton Mifflin.

Fisch, R., Watzlawick, P., Weakland, J., and Bodin, A. 1973. On unbecoming family therapists. In *The book of family therapy,* A. Ferber, M. Mendelsohn, and A. Napier, eds. Boston: Houghton Mifflin.

Fisch, R., Weakland, J., and Segal, L. 1982. *The tactics of change.* San Francisco: Jossey-Bass.

Flaskas, C. 1992. A reframe by any other name: On the process of reframing in strategic, Milan and analytic therapy. *Journal of Family Therapy. 14:145–161.*

Frankl, V. 1960. Paradoxical intention: A logotherapeutic technique. *American Journal of Psychotherapy. 14:520–535.*

Gelcer, E., and Schwartzbein, D. 1989. A Piagetian view of family therapy: Selvini-Palazzoli and the invariant approach. *Family Process. 28:439–456.*

Grove, D., and Haley, J. 1993. *Conversations on therapy.* New York: Norton.

Haley, J. 1963. *Strategies of psychotherapy.* New York: Grune & Stratton.

Haley, J. 1973. *Uncommon therapy.* New York: Norton.

Haley, J. 1976. *Problem-solving therapy.* San Francisco: Jossey-Bass.

Haley, J. 1980. *Leaving home: The therapy of disturbed young people.* New York: McGraw-Hill.

Haley, J. 1981. *Reflections on therapy.* Chevy Chase, MD: The Family Therapy Institute of Washington D.C.

Haley, J. 1984. *Ordeal therapy.* San Francisco: Jossey-Bass.

Hare-Mustin, R. 1975. Treatment of temper tantrums by a paradoxical intervention. *Family Process. 14:481–485.*

Hoffman, L. 1981. *Foundations of family therapy.* New York: Basic Books.

Hoffman, L. 1983. A co-evolutionary framework for systemic family therapy. In *Diagnosis and assessment in family therapy,* J. Hansen and B. Keeney, eds. Rockville, MD: Aspen Systems.

Jackson, D. 1967. The myth of normality. *Medical Opinion and Review. 3:28–33.*

Kleckner, T., Frank, L., Bland, C., Amendt, J., and duRee Bryant, R. 1992. The myth of the unfeeling strategic therapist. *Journal of Marital and Family Therapy. 18:41–51.*

Langsley, D., Machotka, P., and Flomenhaft, K. 1971. Avoiding mental hospital admission: A follow-up study. *American Journal of Psychiatry. 127:1391–1394.*

Machal, M., Feldman, R., and Sigal, J. 1989. The unraveling of a treatment program: A follow-up study of the Milan approach to family therapy. *Family Process, 28:457–470.*

Madanes, C. 1980. Protection, paradox and pretending. *Family Process. 19:73–85.*

Madanes, C. 1981. *Strategic family therapy.* San Francisco: Jossey-Bass.

Madanes, C. 1984. *Behind the one-way mirror.* San Francisco: Jossey-Bass.

Madanes, C. 1990. *Sex, love, and violence: Strategies for transformation.* New York: Norton.

Minuchin, S. 1974. *Families and family therapy.* Cambridge, MA: Harvard University Press.

Papp, P. 1980. The Greek chorus and other techniques of paradoxical therapy. *Family Process.* 19:45–57.

Papp, P. 1983. *The process of change.* New York: Guilford Press.

Parsons, B., and Alexander, J. 1973. Short term family intervention: A therapy outcome study. *Journal of Consulting and Clinical Psychology.* 41:195–201.

Penn, P. 1982. Circular questioning. *Family process.* 21:267–280.

Penn, P. 1985. Feed-forward: Further questioning, future maps. *Family Process.* 24:299–310.

Rabkin, R. 1977. *Strategic psychotherapy.* New York: Basic Books.

Rohrbaugh, M., Tennen, H., Press, S., and White, L. 1981. Compliance, defiance, and therapeutic paradox: Guidelines for strategic use of paradoxical interventions. *American Journal of Orthopsychiatry.* 51:454–466.

Satir, V. 1964. *Conjoint family therapy.* Palo Alto, CA: Science and Behavior Books.

Selvini, M., ed. 1988. *The work of Mara Selvini Palazzoli.* Northvale, NJ: Aronson.

Selvini, M. 1993. Major mental disorders, distorted reality and family secrets. Unpublished manuscript.

Selvini Palazzoli, M. 1981. *Self-starvation: From the intrapsychic to the transpersonal approach to anorexia nervosa.* New York: Aronson.

Selvini Palazzoli, M. 1986. Towards a general model of psychotic games. *Journal of Marital and Family Therapy.* 12:339–349.

Selvini Palazzoli, M., Boscolo, L., Cecchin, G., and Prata, G. 1978a. A ritualized prescription in family therapy: Odd days and even days. *Journal of Marriage and Family Counseling.* 4:3–9.

Selvini Palazzoli, M., Boscolo, L., Cecchin, G., and Prata, G. 1978b. *Paradox and counterparadox.* New York: Jason Aronson.

Selvini Palazzoli, M., Boscolo, L., Cecchin, G., and Prata, G. 1980. Hypothesizing—circularity—neutrality: Three guidelines for the conductor of the session. *Family Process.* 19:3–12.

Selvini Palazzoli, M., and Prata, G. 1983. A new method for therapy and research in the treatment of schizophrenic families. In *Psychosocial intervention in schizophrenia: An international view.* H. Stierlin, L. Wunne, and M. Wirsching, eds. Berlin: Springer-Verlag.

Selvini Palazzoli, M., and Viaro, M. 1988. The anorectic process in the family: A six-stage model as a guide for individual therapy. *Family Process.* 27:129–148.

Sluzki, C. 1978. Marital therapy from a systems theory perspective. In *Marriage and marital therapy: Psychoanalytic, behavioral and systems therapy perspectives,* T. J. Paolino and B. S. Mc Crady, eds. New York: Brunner/Mazel.

Stanton, D. 1981. Strategic approaches to family therapy. In *Handbook of family therapy,* A. Gurman and D. Kniskern, eds. New York: Brunner/Mazel.

Stanton, D., Todd, T., and Associates. 1982. *The family therapy of drug abuse and addiction.* New York: Guilford Press.

Tomm, K. 1984a. One perspective on the Milan systemic approach: Part I. Overview of development, theory and practice. *Journal of Marital and Family Therapy.* 10:113–125.

Tomm, K. 1984b. One perspective on the Milan systemic approach: Part II. Description of session format, interviewing style and interventions. *Journal of Marital and Family Therapy.* 10:253–271.

Tomm, K. 1987a. Interventive interviewing: Part I. Strategizing as a fourth guideline for the therapist. *Family Process. 26:*3–13.

Tomm, K. 1987b. Interventive Interviewing: Part II. Reflexive questioning as a means to enable self-healing. *Family Process. 26:*167–184.

Watzlawick, P., Beavin, J., and Jackson, D. 1967. *The pragmatics of human communication.* New York: Norton.

Watzlawick, P., Weakland, J., and Fisch, R. 1974. *Change: Principles of problem formation and problem resolution.* New York: Norton.

Weakland, J., Fisch, R., Watzlawick, P., and Bodin, A. 1974. Brief therapy: Focused problem resolution. *Family Process. 13:*141–168.

Emergent Models
of the Nineties

In the last decade, family therapy has been transformed. The early emphasis on behavior and the overwhelming power of family systems has evolved into the recognition that systems are influential but not determinative, that syndromes are not always caused by and, instead, can cause family problems, and that individual family members not only act and interact but also have hearts and minds. The original models—structural, strategic, Bowenian—remain vital, but a number of newer approaches are capturing the field's imagination with fresh ideas and methods.

These models include: the *solution-focused* model developed by Steve de Shazer and colleagues and expanded by Bill O'Hanlon and Michele Weiner-Davis; the *collaborative, conversational* models developed by Harlene Anderson, the late Harry Goolishian, Lynn Hoffman, and Tom Andersen; Michael White's *deconstruction* model; the *psychoeducational* and *medical family therapy* models pioneered by Carol Anderson, John Rolland, and others; and Richard Schwartz's *internal family systems* model.

SOLUTION-FOCUSED THERAPY

The solution-focused model grew out of the soil of strategic therapy (particularly from the MRI model) and yet it also represents a departure from that tradition. It maintains the strategic school's de-emphasis on history and underlying pathology, and commitment to brevity, but it moves away from the focus on problems. Where strategic family therapists talk with clients about the interactions that surround problems—with an eye toward discovering attempted solutions that aren't working—solution-focused therapists get clients to concentrate on solutions that *have* worked or might work. At first glance, this shift may seem trivial, but it isn't.

Most of the leading figures in this movement worked together at one time or another at the Brief Family Therapy Center in Milwaukee. This private training and treatment institute was started in the late 1970s when a group within a Milwaukee community agency who were drawn to the MRI model became dissatisfied with the agency's constraints and broke out on their own. The initial group included the married couple of Steve de Shazer and Insoo Berg. De Shazer, who had worked earlier in Palo Alto with the MRI group, devoted much of his time to researching, theorizing, and writing, while Berg pursued her interest in training therapists.

Other notable clinician/theorists associated with this center include Eve Lipchik, who was particularly interested in the development of therapeutic questions, and Michele Weiner-Davis, who converted another agency in Woodstock, Illinois, to the solution-focused model. Both of these women are currently in private practice and present the solution-focused approach in workshops around the country. Bill O'Hanlon, who practices in Omaha, Nebraska, was never formally associated with the Milwaukee center but, having been trained by Milton Erickson and having become a prominent translator of Erickson's ideas, the step toward the solution-focused approach was an easy one. He and Weiner-Davis (O'Hanlon & Weiner-Davis, 1989) have collaborated to expand on the groundwork laid by de Shazer.

Because solution-focused therapists set their sights on solutions rather than problems, they have little to say about how problems arise. One of the defining characteristics of family therapy has always been its focus on the present, where problems are maintained, not on the past that "caused" them. Solution-focused therapists prefer to focus on the future, where problems can be solved. They contend that therapists don't need to know a great deal about the nature of the problems that bring people to therapy. Instead, they need to know about the nature of solutions that can apply across people (de Shazer, 1985).

Like the MRI model, they believe that people are constrained by their narrow, pessimistic views of their problems or their lives which generate rigid sequences of more-of-the-same attempted solutions. As O'Hanlon and Weiner-Davis (1989) put it:

> So, the meanings people attribute to behavior limit the range of alternatives they will use to deal with a situation. If the methods used do not produce a satisfactory outcome, the original assumption about the meaning of the behavior is generally not questioned. If it were, new meanings might be considered, which in turn might prompt a different, perhaps more effective, approach. Instead, people often redouble their efforts to solve the problem in an ineffective way, thinking that by doing it more, harder or better (e.g., more punishments, more heart-to-heart talks, and so on) they will finally solve it. (p. 48)

Solution-oriented therapists also take a strong position against the idea that problems serve ulterior motives, or that people are ambivalent about their problems. They assume that clients *really do* want to change. De Shazer (1984), in fact, has declared the death of resistance as a concept, suggesting that when clients don't follow directives, it's their way of "cooperating" by teaching the therapist the best way to help them.

Solution-focused therapists also believe that people are quite suggestible, and that therapists may, unwittingly, create or maintain problems that, to solution-focused therapists, do not exist (O'Hanlon & Weiner-Davis, 1989):

> If the client walks into a behaviorist's office, he or she will leave with a behavioral problem. If clients choose psychoanalysts' offices, they will leave with unresolved issues from childhood as the focus of the problem. If a client seeks help from a Jungian analyst, he or she is likely to get a problem that can be treated most effectively by examining symbolism in the client's dreams. (p. 54)

Thus, much of the work for solution-focused therapists lies in the negotiation of a goal that is achievable, and isn't related to the therapist's preconceptions about what lies behind the problem.

With this orientation, then, there is no model of normal family or individual development. Solution-focused therapists borrow from constructivists the idea that there is no absolute reality, so therapists shouldn't impose what they think is normal on clients. In addition, the search for the structural flaw that characterizes most other forms of psychotherapy is rejected. As de Shazer (1991) writes, "Structuralist thought points to the idea that symptoms are the result of some underlying problem, a psychic or structural problem such as incongruent hierarchies, covert parental conflicts, low self-esteem, deviant communication, repressed feelings, 'dirty games', etc." The solution-focused therapist dispenses with such speculations and instead is interested only in language—the way people describe themselves and their problems.

> Rather than looking behind and beneath the language that clients and therapists use, we think that the language they use is all that we have to go on. . . . What we talk about and how we talk about it makes a difference, and it is these differences that can be used to make a difference (to the client) . . . we have come to see that the meanings arrived at in a therapeutic conversation are developed through a process more like negotiation than the development of understanding or an uncovering of what it is that is "really" going on. (Berg & de Shazer, 1993, p. 7)

Thus, changing language is powerful because "as the client and therapist talk more and more about the solution they want to construct together, they come to believe in the truth or reality of what they are talking about. This is the way language works, naturally" (Berg & de Shazer, 1993, p. 9). This is why the therapy can be so brief—it is a lot easier to get clients to use different language about their problems than it is to produce major changes in behavior patterns or intrapsychic structure.

Therapy, then, is highly relativistic. The therapist should be concerned only with the complaints that clients present and shouldn't impose values by suggesting that clients address other, unpresented, problems.

> Solution-oriented therapist don't believe that there is any single "correct" or "valid" way to live one's life. We have come to understand that what is unacceptable behavior in one family or for one person is desirable behavior in another. Therefore, clients, not therapists, identify the goals to be accomplished in treatment. (O'Hanlon & Weiner-Davis, 1989, p. 44)

Thus, like MRI therapists, the goals of solution-focused therapy are to resolve the presenting complaints by helping a client do or think something different so as to become more satisfied with his or her life. More than MRI therapists, however, solution-focused therapists trust and use the resources of clients to help them reach their goals. They believe that people already have the skills to solve their problems but, often, have lost sight of these abilities because the problems loom so large to them that their strengths are crowded out of the picture. Sometimes a simple shift in focus from what's not going well to what they are already doing that works can remind them of, and expand their use of, these resources. Other times, people may have to search for abilities that they aren't currently using and bring those dormant skills to bear on their problems.

The orientation toward solutions, then, is an attempt to create an atmosphere in which people's strengths can move out of the shadows and into the foreground. De Shazer (1985, 1986) found these strengths lurking in the spaces between problems—in the "behaviors, perceptions, thoughts, feelings, and expectations that are outside the complaint's constraints. These exceptions . . . can be used as building blocks in the construction of a solution . . . solutions involve determining what 'works' so that the client can do more of it" (de Shazer, 1986, p. 48).

To illustrate this process, de Shazer (1986) uses the metaphor of a man whose problem is that he wants to leave Chicago. To solve this problem much of the following information has little relevance: how he got to Chicago, how long he's been there, what's kept him from leaving earlier, or the nature of Chicago. Instead, the traveler need only focus on where he wants to go, and on the resources at his disposal for getting there.

It may be, however, that in discussing his desires, he remembers some good days in Chicago, and that while these exceptions had seemed insignificant, in thinking about what made them exceptional, he realizes that those were days when he was having fun with other people. He decides that he doesn't really have to leave Chicago after all, and instead directs his energy toward spending more time with people he enjoys. It is this focus on goals, resources, and exceptions to the problem that characterizes solution-focused models. With that focus people will either find a solution to their original problem (leaving Chicago) or decide that their problem is something else (not enough time with friends) and find a solution to it.

In the early 1980s, de Shazer's team began experimenting with this orientation toward solutions by giving all clients the same assignments, which they called "formula tasks." Some of these assignments seemed to be universally effective regardless of the problem. One of these tasks, given in the first session, was to ask clients to observe what happens in their life or relationships that they want to continue (de Shazer, 1985). They found that this assignment helped reorient clients from focusing on the bad things in their lives to thinking about and expecting the good. They also found that this shift in perspective seemed to build on itself—to create a more positive outlook that led to better interactions, which in turn reinforced and expanded that positive outlook.

With the success of these formula tasks, it began to dawn on the team that the process of change could be initiated without much knowledge of the problem or the personalities of those suffering from it. They began to focus on ways to initiate and maintain this problem-solving faculty in people, which they believed was inhibited by a focus on problems and deficits. This thinking led to the development of the "miracle question" and the "exception question," two mainstays of the solution-focused approach (de Shazer, 1985, 1988).

The *miracle question* is: "Suppose one night, while you were asleep, there was a miracle and this problem was solved. How would you know? What would be different?" This question activates a problem-solving mind-set in people by giving them a clear vision of their goal, perhaps in the same way that visualization of the perfect serve helps a tennis player. It also helps clients look beyond the problem to see that what they really want may not simply be the elimination of the problem, but instead to be able to do things that the problem is obstructing. When this is the case, the therapist can encourage them to begin doing those things despite the problem and, suddenly, the problem doesn't loom as large. For example, Mary, who suffers from bulimia, says that if not for her symptoms she'd get closer to people and have more fun. If, with her therapist's encouragement, Mary begins to take interpersonal risks and has more fun, then her bulimia may become less of a problem, less of an obstacle in her life, which might also increase her ability to control it.

The *exception question* ignores the picture of the problem that clients hold up and, instead, directs their attention to the negative of that image—to times in the past when they didn't have the problem. By exploring these times and what was different about them, clients find clues to what they can do to expand those exceptions. In addition, clients may find that in light of the fact that they were able to change or eliminate the problem sometimes, their outlook towards it changes. It seems less oppressive and omnipresent, more controllable.

Mary remembers several times the previous week when she had the urge to binge and purge but didn't. She discovers that at those times she was away from her parents and didn't feel as if she was disappointing them. She decides that it's time to become more independent. "Thus, a solution is a joint product of therapist and client talking together about whatever it is that the problem/complaint is not" (Berg & de Shazer, 1993, p. 21).

Lately, *scaling questions* have become prominent in the solution-focused literature. Berg and de Shazer (1993) write that "scaling questions were first developed to help therapist and client talk about nonspecific topics like depression and communication" (p. 22), where it is difficult to identify concrete behavioral changes and goals. The therapist asks the depressed client, for example, "on a scale of zero to ten, with zero being how depressed you felt when you called me, and ten being how you feel the day after the miracle, how do you feel right now?" The client might say 2 and the therapist might say, "so you feel a little better than when you called. How did you achieve this improvement?" Or the therapist might ask, "what do you think you need to do to achieve a 3?" In this way, the therapist and client can recognize and nurture small changes toward the goal rather than being stuck in the "I'm either depressed or I'm not" kind of thinking that typifies such problems.

Solution-focused therapists hold that if both client and therapist can reorient themselves in the direction of strengths—exceptions to the problem, clarified goals, and strategies to achieve them—then therapy can be quite brief. Two assumptions justify this belief. The first draws once again from constructivism and the power of expectation or suggestion. As O'Hanlon and Weiner-Davis (1989) explain,

> Since what you expect influences what you get, solution-oriented therapists maintain those presuppositions that enhance client-therapist cooperation, empower clients, and make our work more effective and enjoyable. We hold assumptions which focus on strengths and possibilities; fortunately, these assumptions also help create self-fulfilling prophecies. (p. 34)

If one perspective is as valid as the next, then why not assume that solutions can be found easily and quickly?

The second assumption is borrowed from the MRI model—that a small change is usually all that is needed because it can snowball into bigger changes. O'Hanlon and Weiner-Davis (1989) state,

> Once a small positive change is made, people feel optimistic and a bit more confident about tackling further changes. Couples seeking treatment often provide clear examples of this phenomenon. Blaming and withholding typically characterize these relationships. However, when person A undertakes one small gesture which pleases person B, person B reciprocates, which in turn stimulates person A to respond in kind, and so on. (p. 42)

With these two assumptions about change, the solution-focused theorists have fashioned a collection of questions and tasks that are designed to foster optimism and start the snowball rolling. They not only have drawn many assumptions and techniques from the MRI group, but they also back up their claims with the same kind of research.

In 1988, David Kiser followed the outcome of 164 clients treated at the Brief Family Therapy Center for 6, 12, and 18 months after therapy (Wylie, 1990). He used a questionnaire similar to the one used by the MRI group in 1974, where they reported that about 75 percent of their cases had at least some relief from their presenting complaint (Watzlawick, Weakland, & Fisch, 1974). Kiser found even better results.

Of 69 cases receiving 4 to 10 sessions, 64 clients, or nearly 93 percent, felt they had met or made progress on their treatment goal (about 77 percent of the 64 met the goal, and more than 14 percent made progress). At the 18-month follow-up, of all 164 clients (94 percent of whom had had 10 or fewer sessions), about 51 percent reported the presenting problem was still resolved, while about 34 percent said it was not as bad as when they had initiated therapy. In other words, about 85 percent of the clients reported full or partial success. (Wylie, 1990, pp. 34–35)

While this kind of research isn't rigorously scientific, it does indicate that solution-focused therapists may have a sizable number of satisfied customers.

The solution-focused movement epitomizes several trends in family therapy. Its growing popularity is related, in part, to the increasing pressure from managed care companies and mental health administrators for therapy to be brief. In contrast to other brief models, shifting the focus from problems to solutions creates a more optimistic and proactive form of therapy that may help therapists avoid burnout. In addition, solution-oriented therapy is clear-cut and easy to apply; so much so that de Shazer and his team have devised a computer program that can tell therapists exactly what to do depending on a client's response.

This approach, like the others in this chapter, reflects the field's shift away from searching for the cause of problems to empowering people to improve their lives. With an increased trust in clients' abilities comes an increased emphasis on the use of questions to elicit them, a trend begun by the Milan model and shared with Michael White's approach. Finally, this solution-orientation seems a logical extension of the field's interest in relativistic constructivism, the idea that people create their own realities. If all realities are merely interpersonal constructions, then why not coconstruct with people a reality in which their problems are solvable?

Judging by the number of workshop attendees and books and articles, solution-focused is clearly one of the most popular current approaches. The last several years have produced a remarkable spate of books: on the model itself (de Shazer, 1988, 1991b; O'Hanlon & Weiner-Davis, 1989; Walter & Peller, 1992; Furman & Ahola, 1992; Cade & O'Hanlon, 1993; O'Hanlon & Martin, 1992), on the model applied to couples (Weiner-Davis, 1992; Hudson & O'Hanlon, 1992), and applied to alcoholism (Berg & Miller, 1992).

Critics of the solution-focused approach have challenged its simplicity, brevity, and the credibility of its outcome claims (Wylie, 1990). While at times the approach has been portrayed modestly—as a way to start therapy on a positive note, with the option to switch to other methods if the problem perseveres (de Shazer, 1987; O'Hanlon, 1990)—other statements convey the impression that almost any problem can be treated successfully with a few solution-focused sessions. Such claims raise the concern that, in some cases, the therapist's need for clients to think positively may induce denial or minimizing of problems.

If people are as suggestible as solution-focused advocates seem to think, what prevents therapists, caught up in their enthusiasm for quick cures, from suggesting away problems that should be addressed? In a recent critique, Efran and Schenker (1993) write, "solution-focused therapists can be accused of whitewashing anything negative . . . what assurance is there that clients of solution-focused therapists haven't simply learned to keep their complaints to themselves in the presence of the therapists?"

Are these merely the grumblings of a family therapy establishment protecting its assumptions and influence? Recently solution-focused therapists themselves have begun expressing reservations about the model's injunction to remain constantly upbeat (Storm, 1991; Lipchik, 1992, 1993; Efron & Veenendaal, 1993). As Cheryl Storm (1991) reports, "I have found that being relentlessly solution-focused is a mismatch for some clients. These individuals insist on talking about the problem in detail and, if ignored, fire the therapist. I thought I was misapplying the approach but now believe I . . . overemphasized change." Others (Efron & Veenendaal, 1993) echo these sentiments, "Our experiences do not permit us to completely accept the enthusiastic positiveness of the solution-focused model. . . . When we attempt to use these models and stances exclusively, we build up a sense of wrongness and futility, as if we were somehow pulling the wool over the eyes of clients and ourselves" (p. 17). Eve Lipchik (1993) has even begun including discussions of clients' feelings in therapy (a major breech of solution-focused orthodoxy) because "I sense within all my clients . . . the desire to be loved and affirmed by a significant other or others" (p. 27).

Perhaps it isn't the solution-focused techniques themselves that have created this kind of disillusionment, but the rigid, formulaic ways they have come to be applied. Among the questions asked by critics are: Is the therapist really having a respectful conversation, in the postmodern sense, with a client when the therapist only praises, searches for exceptions, and defines goals? Do such insistently optimistic dialogues have the effect of silencing people's doubts and their pain? (Perhaps before anything else, people need a witness to, rather than a filter for, their feelings.) Can the solution-focused therapist find a way to honor client perceptions that don't fit into the formula? Can clients trust the feedback of someone who constantly strives to find things to praise and never challenges or questions them? Can clients be honest regarding the outcome of their therapy with someone who seems to want so much for them to feel better about things?

While these are important challenges, there are other questions that highlight the model's strengths. For example: Isn't it important for therapists to have clear, concrete guidelines so therapy doesn't become vague and directionless? Isn't it more empowering to help people envision their goals and focus on their strengths rather than to dwell on their problems and deficits? If people's experience is tied to the way they think and talk about it, then isn't it better to use language to lead people out of pain than to ruminate on it?

It may be that the formulaic quality and immodest outcome claims critics complain about are because the model is in a groundbreaking stage and these problems will correct with time. Indeed, we suspect that, as is the case with many models, the solution-focused leaders are less rule-bound in their practice than in their preaching. Michele Weiner-Davis (1993) recently confessed that sometimes she lets clients focus on their problems rather than always pushing them for exceptions. " . . . my clients cry and express pain, anger, disappointment and fears just as they might in any other therapist's office. And I respond with compassion . . . my therapy story [what she presents in workshops] is not the total picture of how I do therapy" (p. 157). We hope students will keep this difference between practice and pronouncement in mind while learning the orthodox versions of all these models.

COLLABORATIVE, CONVERSATIONAL APPROACHES

Among the evolving and influential approaches to family therapy in the 1990s are those of Harlene Anderson, the late Harry Goolishian, Lynn Hoffman, and Tom Andersen. United in their opposition to the cybernetic model and its mechanistic influence, these postmodernists focus more on caring rather than curing, as Thomas Moore (1992) espoused in *The Care of the Soul*.

Like de Shazer, and Roy Schafer in psychoanalysis, these theorists have become taken with the narrative metaphor—with the power of language and the stories people hold about themselves. Unlike de Shazer, however, they moved away from preordained techniques that try to manipulate language and, instead, hold empathetic conversations out of which emerge new meanings. As Harlene Anderson (1992) recently wrote:

> In this concept of therapy, the therapist is not a narrative editor of the client's story, someone who uses language as a rhetoric-like editing tool. Rather, the therapist is in language with the client . . . [which implies] a therapy that is less hierarchical, more egalitarian, mutual, respectful, and human, a therapy which allows a therapist to be aware of the depth, existence, and experiences of the individual . . . (p. 21)

The major commitment of these theorists is to move the therapist out of the expert-in-charge stance to form a more egalitarian partnership with clients. In doing this they hope to empower families and turn therapy into a mutual search for new options and understanding.

Because these theorists downplay technique, their approach is difficult to describe; it's more of an attitude or philosophy than a particular method. Consequently, the leaders of this movement write far more about their point of view than about what they do in therapy. These leaders include: Harlene Anderson (director of the Galveston Family Institute), who collaborated with Harry Goolishian for many years until his death in 1991. Together they have been in the vanguard of the movement away from the cybernetic metaphors and toward the postmodern focus on language and interaction.

Lynn Hoffman, who works with a team in Northhampton, Massachusetts, has a long career of championing new developments in family therapy. Beginning as a strategic therapist, she was smitten by the Milan model, and now has followed Anderson and Goolishian into this collaborative territory with equal enthusiasm. Tom Andersen, a Norwegian psychiatrist, is another veteran of the Milan movement who grew tired of the hierarchical, interventive emphasis of that and other family therapy models. In what he calls reflecting processes, he levels the therapy playing field by hiding nothing from his clients, so that he and his team discuss openly their reactions to what the family says. This *reflecting team* (Andersen, 1991) approach has become a widely used aspect of the collaborative model's therapy by consensus. In this method, observers come out from behind the one-way mirror to discuss the session while the family and therapist watch and listen. Then the family is asked to react while the team watches. This process produces a supportive, honest environment in which the family feels part of a larger team—and the team feels more empathy for the family from interacting directly with them.

What these theorists share is the conviction that too often clients aren't heard because therapists are doing therapy to them rather than with them. As Tom Andersen (1993) admits, " . . . what I myself found important, but extremely difficult, to do was to try to listen to what clients say instead of making up meanings about what they say. Just listen to what they say" (p. 321). Harlene Anderson (1993) recommends that therapists take a position of "not knowing" that leads to a genuine conversation with clients in which "the therapist's pre-experiences and pre-knowledges do not lead. In this process both the therapist's and the client's expertise are engaged to dissolve the problems" (p. 325).

They distinguish these conversations from the nondirective, Rogerian style because the collaborative therapist doesn't just reflect but also offers ideas and opinions, though always tentatively. As in the other postmodern approaches, questions are primary. As Anderson (1993) explains,

> Conversational questions come from a position of not knowing and are the therapist's primary tool. They involve responsive or active listening, which requires attending to the clients' stories in a distinct way, immersing oneself in clients' conversations, talking with them about their concerns, and trying to grasp their current story and what gives it shape . . . the questions are not formed by the therapist's preconceived theories of what the story should be . . . Conversational questions are, therefore, not generated by technique, method, or a preset template of questions . . . Each question . . . comes from an honest, continuous therapeutic posture of not understanding too quickly, of not knowing. (pp. 330–331)

The paragraph above contains elements that make this conversational approach the closest application of skeptical postmodernism to family therapy thus far. It conveys the disdain for grand theories (Hoffman, for example, advances the idea that there are no patterns intrinsic to human affairs) and the reluctance to claim expertise or value any perspective over another, which are the hallmarks of that philosophical tradition. As Anderson remarks, this approach "suggests that the therapist's knowledge, experience, and values are no truer than the client's—nor more final" (Hoffman-Hennessay & Davis, 1993, p. 343).

The most widely cited conceptual influence on these theorists is postmodern psychologist Kenneth Gergen (1985, 1991), whose social constructionist theory portrays people as being shaped entirely by interactions with others. Since the fluid, plastic self is created by conversations, it makes sense that it would also be changed through conversation. It also makes sense that whatever new meaning emerged from a conversation that made the client feel better or "dissolved" the problem is fine. As Hoffman (1993) says, ". . . we are not attached to any particular outcome, only to one that would remove or diminish the reason people came to talk to us" (Hoffman-Hennesay & Davis, 1993, p. 371).

Describing this approach is difficult because there is no formula and published descriptions are rare (de Shazer, 1991). Recently, Harlene Anderson (1993) reported a case that we will summarize, bearing in mind that it only illustrates what she did on that particular day. She consulted with a therapist who felt stuck because her thirteen-year-old client Anna was repeatedly running way from home and having physical battles with her mother and older sister. Initially Anderson talked with Anna, her mother, and the therapist together, asking what they were concerned about. By asking clients to discuss their concerns or problems, Anderson's approach is clearly different from de Shazer's immediate focus on exceptions or solutions. She believes that therapists should "make room for the familiar," that is, show curiosity and appreciation for the client's usual reality which then brings forth the client's curiosity.

Both Anna and her mother gave their views on Anna's running away and other problems while Anderson followed along, asking for clarification and elaboration, occasionally broadening the focus. Predictably, Anna and her mother interrupted and argued with each other, to the point where Anna began to cry. Anderson then suggested that she speak with mother while Anna and the therapist watched from behind the mirror. Mother told her story of personal struggle: getting into drugs, being a single-parent with two children, losing her job, having a "breakdown," and losing custody of her kids for nine months. She reported that during much of this time Anna was on the streets and that since gaining such independence, Anna won't give it up.

Throughout this conversation, Anderson made empathetic comments and asked questions. She told the mother, "So you're kind of three gutsy ladies. Is that hereditary?" She then asked what Anna might be like if many of those difficult things hadn't happened and what it would take for her to have more peaceful encounters with Anna. After mother responded that she wanted to enjoy the girls more and that she and Anna were both adventurous, Anderson said "So in a way, it's how to maintain this spirit of adventure, this spirit of independence, while at the same time not being self-destructive or dangerous."

Anderson then talked to Anna while mother watched from behind the mirror. Anna described her reasons for running away and Anderson asked her to put herself in her mother's place and imagine what she would do. Anna was able to do this and also talked of her many worries and issues. Anderson ended the interview without giving any advice and thanked them for coming. The therapist reported months later that the consultation had a variety of positive effects.

In reviewing this session, it's apparent that what Anderson did isn't radically different from what many good therapists might do: reflect, empathize, offer a positive reframe here and there—in other words, give clients the feeling that their story has been heard and help them hear one another's story. What's different is that many therapists wouldn't think this was enough. At some point when they thought they had the information they needed, they would intervene more forcefully, they would leave the not-knowing stance and become the expert. Perhaps the most difficult aspect of this approach is the discipline it takes to care, not cure.

There are, of course, questions and concerns about this approach as well. As discussed in Chapter 3, its relativism regarding the kinds of stories that emerge from these conversations raises concerns that one can inadvertently collude with families to deny or minimize their problems. For example, Anna repeatedly voiced concern about an episode in which she "blacked out," that is, dissociated, during a fight with her mother, and feared that in the middle of a future episode she might kill someone. Anderson didn't explore this episode which would raise red flags for therapists familiar with the effects of abuse. For social constructionists a focus on these red flags might lead to the kinds of pathologizing conversations that therapists should avoid. Collaborative therapists don't have to worry about these issues because even if Anna had been abused, her personality will be reconstituted by the new meaning emerging from these collaborative conversations.

On the other hand, these theorists are bringing family therapy in from the cold. For too many years the field's infatuation with technology hardened its heart. Anderson, Goolishian, Hoffman, and Andersen are giving us permission to be human again, which means to be compassionate, humble, and honest. The fact that this represents a big shift isn't something about which the field should be proud.

MEDICAL AND PSYCHOEDUCATIONAL FAMILY THERAPY

Traditionally, family therapy has been oriented toward curing symptoms and solving problems. Over the past decade a new conception of family therapy has emerged. Rather than curing medical or psychiatric syndromes, the goal of this group is to maximize the functioning and coping abilities of ill or disabled patients and their families. This represents a shift from the idea that families cause problems to the idea that problems, like natural disasters, sometimes happen to families.

This movement has two related sources. One, called *psychoeducational family therapy*, came from working with schizophrenic patients and their families. The other, *medical family therapy*, developed from helping families struggle with chronic illnesses such as cancer, diabetes, and heart disease.

Like the other models in this chapter, the medical and psychoeducational approaches don't subscribe to the idea that families cause these syndromes, so the family members they work with do not feel blamed. These approaches share the belief, however, that families can have a powerful effect on the course of these syndromes and try to collaborate with them to maximize adjustment and minimize disruption to the family.

Psychoeducation and Schizophrenia

As described in Chapter 1, it was the search to find a cause and cure for schizophrenia within families that launched the field of family therapy in the 1950s. Ironically, thirty years later it is the psychoeducational model, which doesn't attempt to find a cause or cure, that may help schizophrenics the most.

The psychoeducational model was born of dissatisfaction with both traditional family therapy and psychiatric approaches to schizophrenia. As Carol Anderson, Douglas Reiss, and Gerald Hogarty (1986) lament,

> We have blamed each other, the patients themselves, their parents and grandparents, public authorities, and society, for the cause and for the too often terrible course of these disorders. When hope and money become exhausted, we frequently tear schizophrenic patients from their families, consigning them to the existential terror of human warehouses, single room occupancy hotels, and more recently to the streets and alleys of American cities. (p. vii)

Family therapists, in their attempts to get at the putative function of the schizophrenic's symptoms or to get family members to express bottled-up feelings, created sessions full of highly charged emotion which often generated blame and defensiveness. After noticing the frequent decline in functioning of patients and increased anxiety in their families after such sessions, Anderson and her colleagues (1986) "began to wonder if most 'real' family therapy was in fact antitherapeutic" (p. 2).

Psychiatry, on the other hand, had put all its eggs in the medication basket and hardly bothered with the patient's family. Psychiatrists believed that the high relapse rate for schizophrenics was due mainly to patients discontinuing their medication. As studies of relapse rates emerged, demonstrating that compliance with medication regimens did not necessarily prevent relapse, the patient's environment was reconsidered. Several studies concluded that the schizophrenic patients who fared best after being hospitalized were those who returned to the least stressful households. A British group including George Brown, John Wing, Julian Leff, and Christine Vaughn had focused on what they called "expressed emotion" (EE) in the families of schizophrenics—particularly criticism, hostility, and emotional overinvolvement (Brown et al., 1962, 1972). Studies suggested that patients returning to high EE households had much higher rates of relapse than those returning to low EE homes (Brown et al., 1972; Vaughn & Leff, 1976; Vaughn et al., 1984).

These observations indicated that schizophrenia was a thought disorder involving a biological vulnerability of unknown origin that makes people highly reactive to and easily overwhelmed by stress in their environment. Apparently when family members are hypercritical or intrusive, the schizophrenic patient cannot process these communications adequately and becomes overloaded, leading to decompensation.

With this view in mind, three different groups in the late 1970s and early 1980s began experimenting with ways to reduce stress in the most common environments for schizophrenic patients, their parents' homes. Michael Goldstein led a group at UCLA (Goldstein et al., 1978) who designed a brief, structured model focused on anticipating the stresses the family was likely to face and reducing conflict around the patient. The Goldstein group demonstrated that this family program, in combination with medication, could achieve an impressive decrease in relapse rates. Following the Goldstein study, groups headed by Ian Falloon at USC (whose model is highly behavioral) and Carol Anderson at the Western Psychiatric Institute in Pittsburgh experimented with psychoeducational models. Rather than trying to describe all these models, we will focus on Anderson's because it is clearly articulated and, despite the psychoeducational antipathy for what family therapists have done to schizophrenics and their families, it contains many concepts and methods derived from family therapy.

Anderson and her colleagues (1986) focus on the devastating impact of schizophrenia on family systems, rather than on the possible effects of preexisting family characteristics on either the onset or maintenance of the syndrome. They see the isolation and enmeshment of many families of schizophrenics as an inevitable consequence of the embarrassment, frustration, and concern that family members feel.

> During an acute illness in any family member, of course, it is necessary for the rest of the family to focus their attentions and their energies on the patient. However, in any long-term illness (like diabetes, heart disease, *or* schizophrenia), patients must learn to live with their limitations and life must go on for those around them. If this does not happen, the impact of illness can become debilitating to families. (p. 125)

Thus, while family members may be contributing to a less than optimal course of their child's schizophrenia, it isn't because their system needs symptoms; it's because the illness has drained the family's resources and generated dysfunctional patterns both within the families and with those whose attempts to help are making things worse.

Thus, psychoeducators try not only to help families change their ideas about and interactions with patients but also to reverse the damage that may have been done to families by the insensitive professionals. Instead of providing the information, support, structure and sense of control that these families need when in crisis, many mental health professionals ignore family members except to gather information about the patient and the family—information about what went wrong. The implications of this line of questioning add to the sense of guilt, shame, and confusion that family members already feel. It's no wonder that many families either give up and hand their patients over to these authoritarian professionals, or get into antagonistic battles with them.

Instead, psychoeducators seek to establish a collaborative partnership in which family members feel empathized with, supported, and also empowered to deal with the patient. Families should leave their contacts with professionals with a sense of their importance in the treatment process but also a sense that they are not alone—that a caring group is involved with them. To achieve this kind of partnership, Anderson and colleagues find that they must reeducate professionals to give up ideas that the family caused or wants the schizophrenia, to scan for and emphasize family strengths rather than deficits, and to share what information exists about schizophrenia rather than keeping families in the dark,

It is this information-sharing that constitutes the education of psycho-education. Anderson and her colleagues believe that information about the nature and course of schizophrenia helps family members develop a sense of mastery—a way to understand and anticipate the often chaotic and apparently uncontrollable process. Too often in the past, this information was withheld out of neglect of or antagonism toward families, or because schizophrenia's less than rosy prognosis might discourage them. Since families are usually the principle caretakers, however, it makes sense that they should be the most, rather than the least, informed members to the team.

In a one-day "survival-skills workshop" Anderson and her colleagues teach groups of family members the history and epidemiology of schizophrenia, and current information about its etiology, prognosis, psychobiology, and treatment. They discuss in some depth the EE findings regarding the impact of the social environment on patients, and they suggest how families can reorganize to deal with these special needs. Research demonstrating the importance of medication in preventing relapse is also presented.

The goal of these workshops is to translate what's known about schizophrenia into a framework that allows family members to understand and not feel bad about their behavior, the patient's behavior, and the behavior of professionals. Family members are also given the sense that they are part of a turning point in psychiatric history when schizophrenics and their families are treated with compassion and understanding. They are given hope that life can be better, although psychoeducators are careful not to give what they consider to be the false hope of a complete cure.

Families are encouraged to provide an atmosphere of low stimulation and expectation, but not without structure or limit-setting. While patients are to be given a lot of latitude regarding their desire to withdraw from stimulation or other idiosyncrasies, they aren't to be allowed to engage in strange or irritating behavior that upsets others in the house. Family members are to minimize conflict and criticism among themselves and toward the patient, so that when parents set limits they are to do so in a matter-of-fact, rather than angry, manner. If necessary, they are to set up chores and rules around the house as they might for a younger child so that the patient has the structure he or she might need.

One of psychoeducation's key interventions is to lower expectations, to reduce pressure on the patient to perform normally. For example, the goals for the first year following an acute episode are primarily the avoidance of a relapse and the gradual taking on of some responsibilities in the home. Family members are to view the patient as they might someone who's had a serious physical illness and needs a long recuperation. Patients may need an excessive amount of sleep, solitude, and limited activity for some time following an episode, and may seem restless, with trouble concentrating. By predicting these developments, psychoeducators try to prevent conflict between the patient and family members due to impatience or frustration with lack of movement toward unrealistic goals.

These recommendations are in sharp contrast to the traditional family therapy attitude of "treat people as if they are normal and they will behave normally." Haley's (1981) *Leaving Home* model encouraged parents to expect normal behavior from schizophrenics and to work together to get the patient to pursue a normal life as soon as possible. The Milan Associates (Selvini Palazzoli et al., 1978) implied that schizophrenics could be cured after a few sessions. As we shall see, Michael White (1989) gets families and patients to fight against, rather than to expect, the schizophrenic person's "in-the-corner lifestyle." The psychoeducational shift in goals away from cure and toward coping is a radical and difficult one for family therapists, and represents one of the biggest and most controversial departures from the family therapy mainstream.

Anderson and her group (1986) point to the results of these workshops in responding to criticism of their methods.

> Whether it is the information itself, the decreased sense of blame and guilt that is communicated by the absence of an emphasis on family etiology, the conveying of respect and equality, or the increase in hope generated by a new approach, the response to these workshops has been dramatic. The climate between staff and families seems to become less polarized, less tense, and resistant family members become more cooperative. Family and professionals both become less isolated, and less subject to burnout. (p. 131)

This workshop and the initial meetings with the family that may have preceded it are only part of the psychoeducational regimen. Regularly scheduled outpatient family sessions and crisis support are likely to last for a year or more after an acute episode. These sessions include assigning small tasks to the patient and monitoring their performance. But it's in these later sessions that the Anderson group allows the focus to stray from the patient and on to problems in the family's structure, which may have arisen as a result of the schizophrenia, or even to problems that family members are facing that aren't directly related to the patient.

That is, from this point on, Anderson's psychoeducational approach looks very much like structural family therapy, except that the family's structural flaws are construed as the *result* of rather than the *cause* of the presenting problem.

> During the chronic course of a schizophrenic illness, generational and interpersonal boundaries within families often become blurred. When the patient is an adolescent or young adult, one or both parents may become involved with the patient to the detriment of their relationship with one or another of the children. Wives or husbands come to treat their ill spouses as children, and children come to perform parental roles to fill in for ill parents. Often, the patient's illness dominates the household, so that all decisions and plans are made on the basis of what the patient needs, wants, or will tolerate. This, in effect, puts the patient in control of the rest of the family. These confused generational bounda-

ries are a problem for everyone, as is the central position the patient occupies within the family. The familial structure becomes skewed in such a way that the normal needs of its members cannot be satisfied or attended to properly. (p. 173)

Thus, much of the therapy follows the familiar themes of reinforcing generational boundaries by encouraging parents to work together on discipline and moving children out of parental roles, opening up the family's boundary to the outside world and developing support networks, urging parents to re-invest in their marriage, and getting family members to not speak or do for the patient.

In addition, as we mentioned, the Anderson model doesn't shy away from dealing with problems in family members' lives that aren't obviously related to the schizophrenia. They find that marital conflict, problems with the patient's siblings, and depression are common and can interfere with the family's ability to reorganize to help the patient. They are careful, however, to address these problems only when the family asks for help with them, or when such problems are clearly impeding the patient's progress. The danger in going after problems without an invitation from the family is that they may feel blamed and defensive—as if the therapist suspected that those problems were behind the schizophrenia. Anderson et al. (1986) report that frequently these other problems improve without direct attention as the family reorganizes to help the patient.

Is the psychoeducational model effective? The answer to that question depends on one's definition of success. By psychoeducational standards of lowering relapse rates for the first year following an acute schizophrenic episode, all psychoeducational studies show comparably dramatic success. For example, in the Anderson et al. (1986) study,

Among treatment takers (n = 90), 19% of those receiving family therapy alone experienced a psychotic relapse in the year following hospital discharge. Of those receiving the individual behavioral therapy, 20% relapsed, but *no* patient in the treatment cell that received both family therapy and social skills training experienced a relapse. These relapse rates constitute significant effects for both treatments when contrasted to a 41% relapse rate for those receiving only chemotherapy and support. (p. 24)

Other studies have shown equally impressive results (Falloon et al., 1982; Leff et al., 1982). There seems to be little question that psychoeducation can delay relapse and readmission to a hospital better than other approaches to schizophrenia that have been studied. The question for family therapists is whether they are willing to settle for that kind of limited goal.

If, as is true of other family therapy models (e.g., Haley, 1981; Selvini Palazzoli et al., 1978), one's goal is to return the patient to normal functioning through the resolution of family problems that are hypothesized to maintain the need for the schizophrenic symptoms, then the psychoeducators' success in delaying relapse would be interpreted differently. Psychoeducators would be seen as stabilizing dysfunctional families by helping them focus on their child as the sick one and, thereby, continue to avoid issues that maintain their dysfunctional system and the need for symptoms.

This criticism is less relevant for the Anderson model because the kinds of structural family problems that might create a need for symptoms are dealt with as they emerge. Indeed, families are more likely to ask for help with those kinds of scary issues if they don't think the therapist sees them as responsible for the schizophrenia.

In this sense, then, Anderson's version of psychoeducation can be seen as a nonantagonistic, less intense, form of structural family therapy. The consistent message to families that they are in no way responsible for the patient's illness, and the consistent empathy and support for the family's struggle with that illness, creates a nondefensive, collaborative therapeutic atmosphere in which the therapist can help families address structural problems without having to attack or blame them for it. Whether the structural problems predate the schizophrenia or were caused by it seems irrelevant as long as they are addressed.

Anderson and her colleagues (1986) suggest that this model need not be limited to the treatment of schizophrenia, but may be applied to any chronic problem, and Anderson (1988) has also described its application to depression. Much of the work with addictions based on Alcoholics Anonymous or on the Adult Children of Alcoholic models can be seen as fitting this psychoeducational mold. Alcoholism is viewed as a disease, families are educated, empathized with, and supported regarding its effects on them (Steinglass, Bennett, Wolin, & Reiss, 1987).

Medical Family Therapy

If one considers schizophrenia a chronic disease, then psychoeducational family therapy can be seen as a specialized form of medical family therapy. Medical family therapists work with families struggling with any kind of chronic illness or disability in much the same way as was described above for families of schizophrenics. This work is less controversial within family therapy than psychoeducation, however, because fewer people would assert that illnesses like MS, diabetes, and stroke are caused by family patterns, should not be medicated, or could be cured by family therapy. Thus, the families that medical family therapists work with are less ashamed and defensive to begin with, and less polarized with helping professionals than families of schizophrenics.

Medical family therapy was pioneered by Don Bloch, who started the journal *Family Systems Medicine* in 1982 with the goal of connecting the psychosocial and the biomedical aspects of health care. A decade later, the field seems to be coming of age, with three recent books setting the pace (McDaniel, Hepworth, & Doherty, 1992; Ramsey, 1989; Rolland, 1994).

Medical family therapists work in close collaboration with pediatricians, family practitioners, and rehabilitation specialists. They advocate that near the time of diagnosis, families should receive a routine consultation to explore their resources relative to the demands of the illness or disability. They cite the growing body of research suggesting a strong relationship between family dynamics and the clinical course of many medical conditions (Campbell, 1986) as evidence that such consultation and collaboration may be highly preventative.

Just as family therapy was taken to task for not recognizing the impact on families of issues like gender, ethnicity, and race, medical family therapists say that the field has ignored the impact of chronic illness. For example:

> A woman with multiple sclerosis, hospitalized for depression, was seen by a family therapist in sessions with her husband and their three daughters. The family therapist slid by the issue of the woman's multiple sclerosis and focused on the true underlying problem, which she decreed was the overinvolvement of the patient's daughters with their mother. (McDaniel, Hepworth, & Doherty, 1993, p. 23)

As a result, two of the daughters withdrew support, leaving the youngest, who was already consumed by her own family obligations, as the sole support of her struggling parents.

Chronic illness often has a devastating impact. It can take over the patient's and the family's lives, ravaging health, hope, and peace of mind. As Peter Steinglass says, "it can be like a terrorist, who has appeared on the doorstep, barged inside the home, and demanded everything the family has" (quoted in McDaniel et al., 1993, p. 21).

How can we help families cope with this terrible impact? John Rolland (1984, 1987, 1988, 1993, 1994) has constructed a helpful framework that clarifies how qualities of an illness or disability will interact with qualities of a family. He points out that illness can vary according to several qualities: *onset* (sudden or gradual), *course* (stable, progressive deterioration, or unpredictable relapsing), *degree of incapacitation* (from none to severe), and *outcome* (whether it will affect longevity or possibly result in sudden death). Different illnesses have different combinations of these qualities and, depending on the combination, place varying demands on a family. For example, if, because of an accident, a family member goes blind, there is a sudden crisis followed by a stable course which doesn't shorten life expectancy and isn't totally incapacitating. On the other hand, if a person is found to be HIV positive, the family faces a gradual onset and a progressive, highly incapacitating course resulting in death.

These demands of the illness interact with qualities of the family, such as the family's life cycle stage and the role the stricken family member plays; the family's leadership resources and degree of isolation; and their beliefs about serious illness and who should help, derived from their ethnicity and history with illness. With an awareness of these factors, therapists can help families prepare to deal with an illness, or where it has been with them for years, gain perspective on their resulting polarizations and enmeshments. The therapist helps families reorganize their beliefs and resources to keep the illness from dominating them.

In conclusion, psychoeducational and medical family therapy approaches share many elements with the other models in this chapter which together represent a significant trend: a strong move away from an antagonistic relationship with families, toward a collaborative partnership. Therapists now are encouraged to look for a family's strengths rather than deficits, and find ways to lift families out of the guilt and blame that accompany their problems. Medical family therapy represents a natural and important collaboration among therapists, physicians, and families that is likely to shape family therapy's future.

MICHAEL WHITE

The work of Michael White contains elements that are remarkably similar to aspects of both the solution-focused and the psychoeducational/medical approaches. Like them, White doesn't assume that symptoms serve functions in families—in fact, he believes that people are oppressed by their problems—and he forms collaborative, empowering therapy relationships. Like the medical family therapists, he focuses on the effect that problems have on families. Like the solution-focused therapists, he gets families to explore and expand times where the problem didn't dominate the family—the effect that people have had on their problems—that de Shazer calls *exceptions* and White calls *unique outcomes.*

Michael White is a family therapist living in Adelaide, Australia. He and Cheryl White are based at the Dulwich Center, out of which comes training, clinical work, and publications related to Michael White's approach. White has had a powerful impact on the family therapy scene in Australia and New Zealand for many years and, since he has been travelling internationally over the past several years, his influence has become widespread in Europe and in this country. He has collaborated closely with New Zealander David Epston who has contributed a narrative emphasis to their work (White & Epston, 1990). Recently, Karl Tomm, who has been an advocate and translator of the Milan model, has expanded that role to include White's work.

In his early writing, White's view of people and their problems drew heavily from Bateson. More recently the late philosopher Michel Foucault (1965, 1973, 1980, 1984) has had the strongest impact. With Foucault's influence, White has constructed a model designed to free people from the oppression of their problems, much as a populace might be freed from an oppressive state. To do this, White has increasingly turned towards the narrative metaphor (and away from systems thinking), seeing people's problems as related to the stories they have about themselves, which in turn often reflect oppressive cultural practices.

White (1989) isn't interested in what causes problems, but he is interested in the evolving effects of problems on families over time. His belief is that people with problems often develop what he calls "problem-saturated descriptions" of their lives: The negative events in their lives and negative aspects of their personalities are constantly in the foreground, making them feel powerless and, consequently, easy prey of problems. As family members try and fail to solve their problems, this story of failure comes to dominate the family (White, 1989).

> Although the problem was usually defined as internal to the child, all family members were affected by it, and often felt overwhelmed, dispirited and defeated. In various ways they took the ongoing existence of the problem, and their failed attempts to solve it, as a reflection on themselves, each other and/or on their relationships (p. 5).

Therapy helps people "locate, generate or resurrect alternative stories . . . " (p. 7) that offer a different sense of self and a different relationship to problems.

Note White's similarity to the constructionist thinking of the second-order theorists like Harlene Anderson and Harry Goolishian (1988), who also try to change families' stories through conversation. One of White's differences is in the way he uses language to achieve this "re-storying." Rather than having free-flowing, nondirective conversations with families in hopes that a new and better story will emerge, White has a specific type of story that he wants people to adopt. This new story highlights the person's or family's past, present, and future agency over the course of their lives and problems. People, not problems, are in charge.

The first step in constructing a new story is to get distance from the old one. To separate people from their problem-saturated stories, White *externalizes* their problems: He speaks of the problem as if it were a separate entity, existing outside of any family member—an entity with a will of its own, which is to dominate the person or family. This externalizing helps family members see that it isn't the person or the family relationships that are the problem. Rather, it's the problem, or the person's relationship with it, that's the problem.

With the problem externalized, White can ask a series of questions regarding family members' relationship with it. As people separate themselves from their problem and examine their relationship with it, they can see that, perhaps, there have been times when they had some control over it—times that White calls *unique outcomes*—successes that had been obscured by their problem-saturated story. Once family members stop blaming one another for the problem, they can work together to fight it. Like an exorcist, White helps families cast their devilish problems out, and then helps them reorganize to fight them.

White's therapy is a series of questions. One set of questions examines the influence the problem has had over family members' lives; a second set maps the influence family members have had over the problem (the unique outcomes, e.g., "Can you recall an occasion when you/your son/your relationship/etc., could have given in to the problem but didn't?"). These questions not only introduce a new story by helping the family see that they haven't been as dominated by the problem as they thought, but such questions also reinforce the externalizing process because, in answering, family members have to talk about the problem as separate from themselves.

In relying on questioning, White follows the tradition in family therapy begun by Bowen, taken up by the Milan Associates, and expanded by others such as Karl Tomm (1987a, 1987b). There is one major difference, however, between the circular questioning those theorists developed and White's use of questions. Circular questions are asked without a particular outcome in mind so that the family isn't constrained in their responses by the agenda of the therapist (Cecchin, 1987). The idea is to use circular questions to loosen up family discussions and focus them on the level of relationship, which allows families to examine themselves and reorganize in any way they want.

White's questions, on the other hand, are rhetorical, designed to help people realize that: (1) they are separate from their problems, (2) they have power over their problems, and (3) they are not who they thought they were. Thus, White unabashedly leads people to certain stories, with the trust that, rather than being constrained, they will be liberated from their previous stories and recognize a far greater range of alternatives.

Due perhaps to the influence of Foucault who analyzes contemporary society through a lens of power (wherein the state oppresses people by keeping them divided and making them think they're responsible for their own problems), White's metaphors consistently depict the relationship between people and their problems as a struggle for control—as if the problem were a living adversary. The problem takes advantage of the family's divisiveness and hopelessness to oppress and "feed off" of them. Gradually, they begin refusing to submit to it, and instead, begin to undermine, turn the tables on, or "starve it." White suggests that the problem is dependent on its effects for its survival, so that by not allowing it to effect them in the old way, clients cut off the problem's "life support system."

As people begin to perceive their relationship with the problem differently and begin to come out from under its oppression, White asks questions regarding how this change affects their stories about themselves and each other (e.g., "What does this tell you about yourself/your relationship/your son/ etc., that is important for you to know?"). This ties the subjugation of the problem to the larger goal of the "reauthoring" of the client's self or family story.

White's therapy comes to life in his case descriptions, so we present excerpts below from his (1989, pp. 10–11) description of a family with an encopretic child that illustrates many of these concepts and methods.

> When mapping the influence of family members in the life of what we came to call "Sneaky Poo," we discovered that:
>
> 1. Although Sneaky Poo always tried to trick Nick into being his playmate, Nick could recall a number of occasions during which he had not allowed Sneaky Poo to "outsmart" him. These were occasions during which Nick could have cooperated by "smearing," "streaking," or "plastering," but he declined to do so. He had not allowed himself to be tricked into this.
>
> 2. There was a recent occasion during which Sneaky Poo could have driven Sue into a heightened sense of misery, but she resisted and turned on the stereo instead. Also, on this occasion, she refused to question her competence as a parent and as a person.
>
> 3. Ron could not recall an occasion during which he had not allowed the embarrassment caused by Sneaky Poo to isolate him from others. However, after Sneaky Poo's requirements of him were identified, he did seem interested in the idea of defying these requirements . . .

4.   . . . it was established that there was an aspect to Sue's relationship with Nick that she thought she could still enjoy, that Ron was still making some attempts to persevere in his relationship with Nick, and that Nick had an idea that Sneaky Poo had not destroyed all of the love in his relationship with his parents.

After identifying Nick's, Sue's, and Ron's influence in the life of Sneaky Poo, I introduced questions that encouraged them to perform meaning in relation to these examples, so that they might "reauthor" their lives and relationships.

How had they managed to be effective against the problem in this way? How did this reflect on them as people and on their relationships? . . . Did this success give them any ideas about further steps that they might take to reclaim their lives from the problem?

In response to these questions, Nick thought that he was ready to stop Sneaky Poo from outsmarting him so much, and decided that he would not be tricked into being its playmate any more . . .

White met with the family two weeks later and found that Nick had fought Sneaky Poo valiantly, having only one minor episode, and he seemed happier and stronger. Sue and Ron had also done their parts in the battle. In her effort to not cooperate with Sneaky Poo's requirements for her to feel guilty, Sue had begun to "treat herself" when Sneaky Poo was getting her down and Ron had fought Sneaky Poo's attempts to keep him isolated by talking to friends about the problem.

I encouraged the family to reflect on and to speculate about what this success said about the qualities that they possessed as people and about the attributes of their relationships. I also encouraged them to review what these tacts suggested about their current relationship with Sneaky Poo. In this discussion, family members identified further measures that they could take to decline Sneaky Poo's invitations to them to support it. (p. 11)

White reports that the family expanded these efforts in the interim and by the third session they felt confident that Sneaky Poo had been defeated. At a six-month follow up they were still doing well.

We aren't aware of any systematic efforts to study the outcome of White's approach. In nearly all of his writing, he sprinkles descriptions of successful cases, like the one above. White (1989) has applied his model to such difficult problems as anorexia nervosa, schizophrenia, uncontrolled children and adolescents, encopresis and enuresis, and mourning and loss. In each of these areas he has developed innovative twists of his technique to accommodate to the problem's idiosyncrasies and we are given the impression that his approach works quite well.

The issue of outcome is an elusive one, however. For example, if we examine White's writing on schizophrenia and compare it to the psychoeducation of Anderson et al. (1986), described above, we find that despite many apparent contradictions between the two models, including the kind of outcome families struggling with schizophrenia should expect, there are remarkable similarities in both technique and expected outcome.

The most striking contradiction between these models is that, unlike Anderson and her colleagues, who accept the psychiatric definition of schizophrenia, White (1989) believes that the medical understanding of schizophrenia limits people's ability to counter it. "If schizophrenia constructs rigid and implicit beliefs about chronicity and deterioration; if scientific classification produces docile subjects; . . . then the socially constructed nature of schizophrenia must exert a powerful influence on its course" (p. 48).

As he does with other problems, White externalizes schizophrenia, or what he calls the "in-the-corner lifestyle" that it produces, thereby reducing the guilt and recrimination that surrounds it and uniting family members to fight it. The Anderson model, by calling schizophrenia a disease, also externalizes it and fosters a comparable atmosphere of collaboration,

Maybe the difference is in what's expected of the patient in terms of the pace at which he or she can return to normal functioning. Do psychoeducators inadvertently collaborate with the "in-the-corner lifestyle" by telling family members to let the patient withdraw when he or she wants to, and by suggesting that change will be extremely slow? Like the psychoeducators, White (1989) doesn't claim that his model can cure schizophrenia; only that it can help alter the "in-the-corner lifestyle" (that the whole family submits to) and thus reduce relapse rates.

He also has learned to lower family members' expectations for quick change. "Throughout this process, the therapist's stance remains mildly conservative. S/he is enthusiastic about the successful steps that family members take in their escape from the in-the-corner lifestyle, but always encourages them to consider shortening future steps and to take them one at a time" (p. 55). With questions like, "Do you think you have let ambition push you into doing too much too soon?" White restrains families and patients from expecting too much of the patient, much as the psychoeducators do.

In juxtaposing Anderson and White we were struck by the similarity of the two approaches in practice, in contrast to the major contradictions in their views of schizophrenia. It seems that sensitive therapists take similar lessons from the families they treat and adjust their theories accordingly. If the two approaches achieve comparable results, this would imply that the power of both lies in their ability to counter the cycles of blame and recrimination in families and pull them together.

In conclusion, Michael White has constructed an approach that has much in common with other emergent models of the 1990s, yet he presents a unique and powerful view of (and language about) problems and people that has great appeal. He uses constructivism (or what he, after Foucault, calls constitutionalism) to explain how people can reauthor their life stories, but instead of leading him to the relativistic extremes we criticized in Chapter 3, White, with Foucault's influence, retains strong values for helping people organize to escape the oppression of problems or other people.

> . . . those developments I refer to as constitutionalism do not introduce a form of relativism that might suggest that "one description of reality is

as good as any other," or that "experiences are only traumatic because reality is described in that way" . . . this constitutionalist position confronts therapists with demands for action in relation to their value position . . . I am thinking of a commitment to action against the abuses of power: against neglect, against cruelty, against injustice, and against the subjugation of alternative knowledges. (White, 1993)

These convictions produce a highly focused and methodical therapy with specific techniques (in the form of a sophisticated process of questioning) and goals.

THE INTERNAL FAMILY SYSTEMS MODEL

As we've discussed, family therapists originally focused on action—on behavioral sequences—and then, in the 1980s, the field became interested in the belief systems that drove people's actions. As therapists became more interested in meaning, one might expect that intrapsychic processes would be reexamined using the systemic principles and techniques that have been applied so effectively to families. For much of family therapy such an exploration was resisted by the field's traditional aversion to intrapsychic speculation—what might be called its "psyche-phobia"—and by its adoption of constructivism and focus on language which attended only to consciously held beliefs.

In the early 1980s, however, Richard Schwartz (1987, 1988, 1992, 1994) did begin this kind of systemic exploration of internal process. Schwartz has been with the Institute for Juvenile Research in the Department of Psychiatry at the University of Illinois at Chicago for the past fourteen years, where he conducts training and research. His doctorate is in marital and family therapy so that, not being steeped in traditional intrapsychic models, he entered the world of internal process relatively naively, with few preconceptions as to what he would find.

While conducting an outcome study of structural-strategic family therapy with bulimia that, overall, achieved good results (Schwartz, Barrett, & Saba, 1985), Schwartz worked with some clients for whom family therapy alone didn't seem to be enough. Frustrated with the limits imposed by the exclusion of internal process, he broke this tradition by asking clients about what went on inside them before, during, and after a binge.

He discovered that each client described a similar sequence of interaction among what they called internal "voices" or "parts" of them. "A part of me attacks me for being so fat, then another part feels hurt and lonely, and then still another takes over and makes me binge. . . . " Their descriptions made it seem as if these parts or voices were more than just habitual thought patterns or feeling states—as if they were autonomous internal personalities. Schwartz wondered if the same systemic principles and techniques that had been effective with families might also apply to his clients' internal systems. He continued to interview clients, tracking the interplay among their competing voices, trying to understand the relationships among them, and experimenting with ways to intervene systemically in this inner ecology.

Schwartz found that not only did systemic principles apply to internal processes, but when they were applied, family members began to understand themselves and each other in ways that allowed them to change more easily than other intrapsychic models predicted. With these techniques clients were able to tap into previously obscured inner resources and change their relationship with the various parts of themselves.

Schwartz also found that the language of the model itself was a powerful tool for helping family members understand one another and their problems. It's easier to consider changing a small part of yourself than to have to change your whole personality.

Despite being the only model in this chapter that explores internal process, Schwartz's internal family systems (IFS) model, like the other emergent models of the 1990s, fosters a collaborative relationship with clients and a blame-free atmosphere for family sessions. Like Anderson's psychoeducation and White's externalization, the IFS model unites family members to counter the conditions contributing to the problem. By extending systems thinking to the level of internal process, however, the IFS affords a richer understanding of people and their problems than models that exclude internal systems, and broadens the therapist's ability to move fluidly between internal and external levels, allowing an understanding of each level to inform the work with the other.

The IFS model rests on relatively simple basic assumptions that, although developed independently, correspond with some of the assumptions of other models that have explored this subpersonality phenomena (Assagioli, 1965; Jung, 1956; Hillman, 1975; Stone & Winkelman, 1985; Watkins & Watkins, 1979; Watanabe, 1986).

The first of these assumptions is that the mind consists of a multitude of specialized sub-minds, each with unique talents and intentions, and a certain range of emotion and expression. Schwartz found that these subpersonalities (or what he calls "parts," a term people seem to be comfortable with), interact internally like members of a tribe or large family. They organize into alliances, vie for control, and, at times, go to war against each other.

To understand how this process works, consider a time in your life when you were facing a difficult decision. You probably experienced internal debates among conflicted thoughts or feelings regarding the right move to make. If you had focused exclusively on one of those thoughts or feelings, and asked it questions, you might find that it was more than just a transient thought or feeling. You might find that it had a lot to say, that it had been saying similar things to you all of your life, and that it commonly fought with the same parts it was fighting with at that point.

In tracking the sequences among these parts, Schwartz found that they often protect or distract one another much as happens in distressed families. He also found that most people habitually favor and listen to some parts while disliking and shutting out others. From these observations, he became interested in the parallels between a person's internal system and their external family system.

Take the example of Jane who grew up in a family that strongly feared overt expressions of anger and taught girls to take care of others and neglect themselves. Jane, like most of us, has a part of her that wants to help her stand up and assert herself, but because of her family background she was cut off from that part of her. Instead, she listened to her fearful and selfless parts' warnings that bad things would happen if she stood up for herself.

Since Jane's assertive part was forced to watch helplessly while people continuously exploited her, it became extremely angry. On the rare occasions when Jane couldn't contain this angry part, it seized control and made her fly into a rage, surprising and scaring people around her who were used to her passivity. These outbursts only confirmed to her fearful and selfless parts how dangerous the assertive part was, increasing their conviction to keep it silent, which, of course, made it angrier, and so on. Thus, Schwartz found that the same positive feedback loops that characterize escalations among family members occurred in the polarizations within "internal families" as well.

He also found that often when these internal positive feedback sequences were reversed, the formerly polarized parts quickly returned to their natural state, which was always valuable—just as happens when polarizations among family members are reversed. To achieve this kind of depolarization among a person's parts, Schwartz gained access to the person's inner system with Gestalt therapy's "open-chair" technique or through guided imagery, and then he began experimenting with a variety of family therapy techniques. He found that by using a simple boundary-making technique from structural family therapy he could help people get their polarized parts to deal with each other while blocking the interference of other parts. During this experimenting, Schwartz found that when he tried to get a client to interact with one part (call it part A), frequently another part or parts that were polarized with A would interfere by making the client feel something extreme about part A—perhaps fear, anger, envy, or hopelessness. To counter this, Schwartz asked clients to find the interfering parts and get them to stop interfering, much as a family therapist urges interfering family members to respect a boundary around a family subsystem. Most clients could do this, and when they did, their perception of part A, which had been extreme, suddenly shifted to compassion for or curiosity about part A.

For example, when Jane, using imagery, first saw her angry part, she felt frightened by it and it looked like a monster. After she moved her fearful and selfless parts into imaginary rooms and asked them to not interfere, she suddenly felt sorry for the angry part, which now looked younger and less fierce. She could listen to it describe how it felt isolated and abandoned by her. At that point, she could negotiate a new relationship with this part—she would try to listen to and speak for it more, and, in return, it would not try to take over. The more Jane used her assertive part, the less she was exploited by people, and the less extreme the part became. In this way, internal changes create external changes, and vice versa.

Schwartz also tried guiding clients to separate from, not just a few, but all the parts they could identify. He consistently discovered that, when separated from their parts, everyone had a similar experience described variously as feeling calm, lighthearted, confident, and "in the present." He found, in addition, that once they had achieved this state, people could change their relationships with their parts with relative ease. He called this differentiated entity the *Self*, and discovered that while in this Self-mind, people could lead their internal families quite effectively.

In the IFS model, then, the Self is not a passive, observing state of mind but an active internal leader. In this leadership role the Self listens to each part and what it really wants, nurtures or comforts some parts, helps change the role of others, and negotiates with polarized parts to resolve their differences. For example, the Self may comfort and soothe frightened or sad parts, calm rageful defenders, or get striving achiever parts to compromise with parts that demand more relaxation. In this sense, the person's Self becomes a therapist to their internal family.

Schwartz found that once he helped a person differentiate their Self from their parts, they could do a great deal of work on their own, between sessions. In doing that work, people achieved new insights or perspectives regarding themselves and their problems on their own, without interpretations by the therapist. Thus, the IFS therapist is taken out of the position of having to construct and sell new realities. The therapist creates an environment in which people change themselves and, consequently, feel less dependent on therapists.

Schwartz (1987) used the metaphor of an orchestra, in which the parts were analogous to the musicians and the Self to the conductor. A good conductor values each musician's talents and knows their limitations. Each musician, despite wanting to spotlight his or her own talent or have the piece played in a way that emphasizes his or her contributions, respects the conductor's judgement and follows the conductor's direction.

If each were to choose its own tempo, phrasing, or volume, the result would be cacophonous; sections would compete, and no one would be happy. Similarly, one part of a person might insist that he or she get to work, while another demands a playful diversion, and still another pleads for intimacy with a lover. Without a respected leader who will eventually see that their needs are met, the parts would fight for control and sabotage one another, resulting in constant internal conflict or in the domination of one part and the oppression of others.

In working with a family, the goal is for the Self of each family member to be in the lead when they interact with one another. When someone in a family has a problem that frustrates others, usually parts of one family member struggle to change parts of another, leading to positive feedback loop escalations between parts of different family members, and also within each family member.

For example, Tony has been fighting at school and rebelling at home. The therapist asks about the parts that make him do that, and Tony describes a conflict between a rebellious part of him and a part that worries about displeasing his parents and criticizes him for rebelling. He thinks things might go better for him if he could resolve this internal conflict, but he doesn't know how. The therapist asks father what parts of him are activated by Tony's rebellion. Father describes a frustrated and furious part, and agrees that things don't get better when this part of him takes over; he feels ashamed afterward, but he can't seem to control this "temper." Mother says that father's temper triggers scared parts of her that try to protect Tony from father's temper.

The therapist asks each family member to describe the parts of them that are involved in the problem and asks questions like: How difficult is it for them to control their parts? How might the problem be affected if they could stay their Selves rather than letting their parts take over? And how do they want to change their relationship with these parts that interfere in their life? (Admitting that a little part of yourself contributes to the problem feels less shameful and overwhelming than implicating your whole personality.)

Instead of having a rebellious, disrespectful child, the parents find they have a son who has some trouble with a few of his parts, but also has a Self that wants to work on those parts. Father is transformed from a raging tyrant to a good man struggling with his angry part. The view of mother is likewise changed by this multiplicity perspective of personality, which is more benevolent and holds more potential for change than the idea that people have unitary and fixed personalities.

An IFS therapist who encounters "resistance" believes he or she has inadvertently activated protective parts of family members. Since the therapist expects parts of a person, family, or any ecology to react protectively when threatened, the therapist views this as a natural reaction.

Rather than trying to overpower or to outwit resistance, the therapist respects those protective parts as holding important information regarding the therapist's impact on this delicate ecology, and may suggest that clients ask their parts what they are upset about. Once protective parts disclose their fears, therapist and clients can negotiate ways to accommodate or reassure those parts.

Schwartz and his colleagues have gradually learned about common relationship patterns among peoples' parts, so that they are better able to avoid triggering these protective reactions. For example, many people are like fifteen-year-old Ben who grew distant and defensive when, in an early session, the therapist asked him if he ever felt sad about his parents' divorce. The therapist later learned that, like many people, Ben feared and avoided his sad part because it had overtaken him in the past, making him feel helpless and fragile. Many other parts of Ben had organized to keep him away from the sad part, and had to be convinced that Ben could approach that sad part without being overcome by it before they would allow his Self any access to it.

In his recent work with adult survivors of childhood sexual abuse, Schwartz (1992, 1994; Goulding & Schwartz, in press) has identified three different sets of roles that parts commonly adopt when a person has been hurt. One group, called the *exiles*, are those parts of us that contain the pain, fear, sadness, memories, and sensations resulting from past hurtful experiences. Because these exiles make us vulnerable to being hurt again, another group of parts, the *managers*, try to keep them locked away, out of our consciousness. These managers organize our lives in ways that minimize the activation of the exiles—making us withdraw from relationships or strive for perfection or power so we are always in control. Despite these managerial efforts, exiles will become activated and threaten to take over. When that happens, a third group of parts called *firefighters* take action to put out the growing fire of feeling emerging from the exiles by dousing them with something—food, drugs, alcohol, etc.—or by distracting us through activities like sex, self-mutilation, or work. Understanding this three-group system has allowed IFS therapists to work safely with clients who have been extremely abused and, as a result, seem severely disturbed.

The techniques of the IFS have been refined over the past ten years and are well-defined but also quite involved. They are described comprehensively in a new book (Schwartz, 1994). Even without extensive knowledge of IFS technique, however, therapists will find that by simply using the language of parts, the tone of therapy improves dramatically. The therapist asks about the problem, and then asks each family member what they say to themselves about it. In reiterating any family member's response to that question, the therapist might ask "So a part of you says _____ about the problem, is that right?" And then, "How do you think the problem would be affected if this part of you didn't take over?"; "What's that part afraid would happen if it let you lead in this area?"; "Ask the part to let your Self lead the discussion about the problem this time and see how it goes."

Through this process, people become increasingly aware of when their parts are interfering, and then increasingly able to lead with their Selves. Families then can find their own solutions because the full resources of each family member are available to the group rather than being squandered in rigid polarizations within and between family members. When a person is able to remain his or her Self in the face of extreme parts of another person, the other person's Self gradually emerges and their interaction becomes more productive. (This is similar to Bowen's technique of getting people to remain differentiated in the face of their family's emotional field.)

Aspects of IFS therapy are similar to Bowenian and structural family therapies as well as other models covered in this chapter, and the IFS provides an alternative understanding of how those models are effective. With the absence, at this point, of more than anecdotal documentation of its effectiveness, however, the IFS model's acceptance is based on its intuitive appeal. To remedy this, Schwartz and his colleagues are designing outcome studies, one of which is with conduct disordered adolescents.

In family therapy the appeal of the IFS model will also be limited by the field's long-standing reluctance to consider intrapsychic process. For example, structural family therapist Jorge Colapinto (1993) recently complained that the IFS model's notion that we all have a core Self was turning family therapy back toward acontextual, individual psychotherapy.

> Under Schwartz's proposal, the main role of the therapist is to help the client take distance from his or her family and turn towards his or her Self . . . . As in traditional psychotherapy, the strength of the client must grow in isolation from significant others . . . . From an ethics of interdependency, one can challenge Schwartz's emphasis on the Self as a denial of connectivity. (pp. 53, 55)

It is true that therapists can become so preoccupied with a client's fascinating inner world, particularly as they are just learning the model, that they ignore or underestimate the resources of the client's family. Therapists using the IFS model need to be aware of this tendency and must consciously maintain focus at the family level.

Colapinto's reaction can also be seen in light of the challenge the IFS model presents to the fundamental premise of family therapy: that people are dependent on their context to the point that for them to change, their families must change. The IFS model's assertion that people have inner resources that, if necessary, can help them transcend the influence of their family takes issue with this premise. This question of how autonomous or context-dependent people are is one with which every clinician grapples. The way it is answered determines much of how therapy is practiced.

CONCLUSIONS

The four models presented in this chapter, plus the constructivist movement and the feminist movement (see Chapter 3), represent the wave that is carrying family therapy into the twenty-first century. Despite their differences, these models and movements share an ethic of collaborating with, rather than directing or coercing, people. This common interest in collaboration is no accident—it reflects the maturing of the field.

The pioneers saw families as powerful, resistant adversaries, in part, because they themselves felt weak; they lacked the conceptual frameworks and techniques that could give them confidence while working with highly distressed families. It's taken family therapists time to develop these concepts and methods, and as therapists felt stronger relative to the families they treated, their need to control or outwit families has diminished. Family therapists have learned that they don't have to *make* families change. Indeed, therapists are finding that when they don't try to make families change but instead create a climate in which problems can be explored in less defensive or polarized ways, families are able to change themselves.

This shift in the therapist-family relationship shouldn't make inactive observers of therapists. Therapists can still be leaders in therapy, even as their style of leadership shifts from the authoritative director who points out or reframes problems, to the confident partner who elicits strengths.

In this regard, we worry that the notion of therapist as nonexpert might be interpreted to mean that therapists needn't study how family problems develop and how they can be resolved. There are ways to have and convey expertise without becoming authoritarian. There are times when a therapist may need to confront or teach and there are ways to do so without becoming a bully. What's important is that therapists have and convey an underlying respect for clients, not that they are always sympathetic and agreeable.

Despite these concerns, it's clear that the role of the therapist is shifting in family therapy. These emergent models of the 1990s are the harbingers of a new era in which therapists search for ways to help people discover their own resources, instead of trying to impose solutions.

REFERENCES

Andersen, T. 1991. *The reflecting team.* New York: Norton.
Andersen, T. 1993. See and hear, and be seen and heard. *The new language of change,* S. Friedman, ed. New York: Guilford Press.

Anderson, C. M. 1988. Depression and families. In *Chronic disorders and the family,* F. Walsh and C. Anderson, eds. New York: Haworth Press.

Anderson, H. 1993. On a roller coaster: A collaborative language systems approach to therapy. In *The new language of change,* S. Friedman, ed. New York: Guilford Press.

Anderson, H., and Goolishian, H. A. 1988. Human systems as linguistic systems: Preliminary and evolving ideas about the implications for clinical theory. *Family Process.* 27:371–393.

Anderson, C. M., Reiss, D., and Hogarty, B. 1986. *Schizophrenia and the family.* New York: Guilford Press.

Assagioli, R. 1965. *Psychosynthesis.* New York: Penguin Books.

Berg, I. K., and de Shazer, S. 1993. Making numbers talk: Language in therapy. In *The new language of change,* S. Friedman, ed. New York: Guilford Press.

Berg, I. and Miller, S. 1992. *Working with the problem drinker: A solution-focused approach.* New York: Norton.

Breunlin, D., Schwartz, R., and MacKune Karrer, B. 1992. *Metaframeworks.* San Francisco: Jossey-Bass.

Brown, G. W., Birley, J. L. T., and Wing, J. K. 1972. The influence of family life on the course of schizophrenic disorders: A replication. *British Journal of Psychology.* 121:241–258.

Brown, G. W., Monck, E. M., Carstairs, G. M. and Wing, J. K. 1962. Influence of family life on the course of schizophrenic illness. *British Journal of Preventive and Social Medicine.* 16:55–68.

Cade, B. and O'Hanlon, W. 1993. *A brief guide to brief therapy.* New York: Norton.

Campbell, T. 1986. Family's impact on health: A critical review and annotated bibliography. *Family Systems Medicine.* 4:135–148.

Cecchin, G. 1987. Hypothesizing, circularity, and neutrality revisited: An invitation to curiosity. *Family Process.* 26:405–413.

Colapinto, J. 1993. Superman and the Self. *American Family Therapy Academy Newsletter,* Spring, 52–56.

de Shazer, S. 1984. The death of resistance. *Family Process.* 23:11–21.

de Shazer, S. 1985. *Keys to solutions in brief therapy.* New York: Norton.

de Shazer, S. 1986. An indirect approach to brief therapy. In *Indirect approaches in therapy,* S. de Shazer and R. Kral, eds. Rockville, MD: Aspen.

de Shazer, S. 1987. Minimal elegance. *Family Therapy Networker.* September/October, 59.

de Shazer, S. 1988. *Clues: Investigating solutions in brief therapy.* New York: Norton.

de Shazer, S. 1991a. Muddles, bewilderment, and practice theory. *Family Process.* 30:453–458.

de Shazer, S. 1991b. *Putting difference to work.* New York: Norton.

de Shazer, S., Berg, I. K., Lipchik, E., Nunnally, E., Molnar, A., Gingerich, W., and Weiner-Davis, M. 1986. Brief therapy: Focused solution development. *Family Process.* 25:207–222.

Efran, J., and Schenker, M. 1993. A potpourri of solutions: How new and different is solution-focused therapy? *Family Therapy Networker.* 17(3):71–74.

Efron, D. and Veenendaal, K. 1993. Suppose a miracle doesn't happen: The nonmiracle option. *Journal of Systemic Therapies.* 12:11–18.

Foucault, M. 1965. *Madness and civilization: A history of insanity in the age of reason.* New York: Random House.

Foucault, M. 1973. *The birth of the clinic: An archaeology of medical perception.* London: Tavistock.

Foucault, M. 1980. *Power/knowledge: Selected interviews and other writings.* New York: Pantheon Books.

Foucault, M. 1984. *The history of sexuality*. Great Britain: Peregrine Books.

Furman, B., and Ahola, T. 1992. *Solution talk. Hosting therapeutic conversations*. New York: Norton.

Gergen, K. 1985. The social constructionist movement in modern psychology. *American Psychologist*. 40:266–275.

Gergen, K. 1991. *The saturated self*. New York: Basic Books.

Gergen, M. M., and Gergen, K. J. 1984. The social construction of narrative accounts. In *Historical social psychology*, K. J. Gergen and M. M. Gergen, eds. New Jersey: Erlbourn Associates.

Goffman, E. 1961. *Asylums: Essays in the social situation of mental patients and other inmates*. New York: Doubleday.

Goldstein, M. J., ed. 1981. *New developments in interventions with families of schizophrenics*. San Francisco: Jossey-Bass.

Goldstein, M. J., Rodnick, E. H., Evans, J. R., May, P. R., and Steinberg, M. 1978. Drug and family therapy in the aftercare treatment of acute schizophrenia. *Archives of General Psychiatry*. 35:1169–1177.

Goolishian, H., and Winderman, L. 1988. Constructivism, autopoiesis and problem-determined systems. *The Irish Journal of Psychology*. 9:130–143.

Goulding, R., and Schwartz, R. C. *Mosaic mind*. New York: Norton. in press.

Haley, J. 1981. *Leaving home*. San Francisco: Jossey-Bass.

Hillman, J. 1975. *Re-visioning psychology*. New York: Harper & Row.

Hoffman, L. 1986. Beyond power and control: Toward a second-order family systems therapy. *Family Systems Medicine*. 4:381–396.

Hoffman, L. 1990. Constructing realities: An art of lenses. *Family Process*. 29:1–12.

Hoffman-Hennessay, L., and Davis, J. 1993. Tekka with feathers: Talking about talking. In *The new language of change*, S. Friedman, ed. New York: Guilford Press.

Hudson, P. and O'Hanlon, W. H. 1992. *Rewriting love stories: Brief marital therapy*. New York: Norton.

Jung, C. 1956. *Two essays on analytical psychology*. Cleveland, OH: Meridian.

Lipchik, E. 1986. Purposeful Interview. *Journal of Strategic and Systemic Therapies*. 5:88–99.

Lipchik, E. 1992. Interview. *Journal of Strategic and Systemic Therapies, 11*(4).

Lipchik, E. 1993. "Both/and" solutions. In *The new language of change*, S. Friedman, ed. New York: Guilford Press.

McDaniel, S., Hepworth, J. and Doherty, W. 1992. *Medical family therapy*. New York: Basic Books.

McDaniel, S., Hepworth, J., and Doherty, W. 1993. A new prescription for family health care. *Family Therapy Networker*. 17:18–29, 62–63.

Moore, T. 1992. *The care of the soul*. New York: Harper Collins.

O'Hanlon, W. and Martin, M. 1992. *Solution oriented hypnosis: An Ericksonian approach*. New York: Norton.

O'Hanlon, W. H. and Weiner-Davis, M. 1989. *In search of solutions: A new direction in psychotherapy*. New York: Norton.

Ramsey, R. N., ed. 1989. *Family systems in medicine*. New York: Guilford Press.

Rolland, J. S. 1984. Toward a psychosocial typology of chronic and life-threatening illness. *Family Systems Medicine*. 2:245–263.

Rolland, J. S. 1987. Chronic illness and the life cycle: A conceptual framework. *Family Process*. 26:203–221.

Rolland, J. S. 1988. Family systems and chronic illness: A typological model. In *Chronic disorders and the family*, F. Walsh and C. Anderson, eds. New York: Haworth Press.

Rolland, J. S. 1993. Mastering family challenges: Serious and chronic illness. In *Normal family processes*, 2nd ed., F. Walsh, ed. New York: Guilford Press.

Rolland, J. S. 1994. *Helping families with chronic and life-threatening disorders*. New York: Basic Books.

Schwartz, R. 1987. Our multiple selves. *Family Therapy Networker. 11*:25–31, 80–83.

Schwartz, R. 1988. Know thy selves. *Family Therapy Networker. 12*:21–29.

Schwartz, R. 1992. Rescuing the exiles. *Family therapy networker. 16*, 33–37, 75.

Schwartz, R. 1994. *Internal family systems therapy.* New York: Guilford Press.

Schwartz, R., Barrett, M. J., and Saba, G. 1985. Family therapy for bulimia. In *The handbook of psychotherapy for anorexia nervosa and bulimia,* D. Garner and P. Garfinkel, eds. New York: Guilford Press.

Selvini Palazzoli, M., Boscolo, L., Cecchin, G., and Prata, G. 1978. *Paradox and counterparadox.* New York: Aronson.

Steinglass, P., Bennett, L., Wolin, S., and Reiss, D. 1987. *The alcoholic family.* New York: Basic Books.

Steinglass, P. and Horan, M. E. 1988. Families and chronic medical illness. In *Chronic disorders and the family,* F. Walsh and C. Anderson, eds. New York: Haworth Press.

Stone, H. and Winkelman, S. 1985. *Embracing ourselves.* Marina del Rey, CA: Devross & Co.

Storm, C. 1991. The remaining thread: Matching change and stability signals. *Journal of Strategic and Systemic Therapies. 10*:114–117.

Tomm, K. 1987a. Interventive interviewing: Part I. Strategizing as a fourth guideline for the therapist. *Family Process. 26*:3–14.

Tomm, K. 1987b. Interventive interviewing: Part II. Reflexive questioning as a means to enable self-healing. *Family Process. 25*:167–184.

Vaughn, C. E. and Leff, J. P. 1976. The influence of family and social factors on the course of psychiatric illness. *British Journal of Psychiatry. 129*:125–137.

Vaughn, C. E., Snyder, K. S., Jones, S., Freeman, W. B., and Falloon, I. R. H. 1984. Family factors in schizophrenic relapse: Replication in California of British research on expressed emotion. *Archives of General Psychiatry. 41*:1169–1177.

Walter, J., and Peller, J. 1992. *Becoming solution-focused in brief therapy.* New York: Brunner/Mazel.

Watanabe, S. 1986. Cast of characters work. *Contemporary Family Therapy. 8*:75–83.

Watkins, J., and Watkins, H. 1979. Ego states and hidden observers. *Journal of Altered States of Consciousness. 5*:3–18.

Watzlawick, P., Weakland, J., and Fisch, R. 1974. *Change.* New York: Norton.

Weiner-Davis, M. 1992. *Divorce-busting.* New York: Summit Books.

Weiner-Davis, M. 1993. Pro-constructed realities. In *Therapeutic conversations,* S. Gilligan and R. Price, eds. New York: Norton.

White, M. 1989. *Selected papers.* Adelaide, Australia: Dulwich Center Publications.

White, M. 1993. *The histories of the present.* In Therapeutic conversations. S. Gilligan, ed. New York: W. W. Norton.

White, M., and Epston, D. 1990. *Literate means to a therapeutic ends.* New York: Norton.

Wylie, M. S. 1990. Brief therapy on the couch. *Family Therapy Networker. 14*:26–34, 66.

Comparative Analysis

The exponential growth of family therapy has crowded the field with competing schools, every one of which has made important contributions. This diversity has produced a rich and varied literature, which bears witness to the vitality of the field. But these different approaches also constitute a confusing array of concepts and techniques, creating a dilemma: with the bewildering variety of family therapies, how is one to choose among them?

A therapist's theoretical orientation is no accident. The choice is overdetermined and rooted in personal experience. For some the choice of which approach to follow is dictated by what is available from their teachers and supervisors. Others pick and choose concepts and techniques from here and there, hoping to mold their own eclectic approach. Unfortunately, with no anchor to ensure coherence, this strategy may be intellectually satisfying, but clinically ineffective. Finally, there are those who pledge allegiance to a single approach; this provides them with a consistent, but often incomplete model.

In this chapter we will offer a comparative analysis of systems of family therapy to sharpen the reader's appreciation of the separate approaches, and to serve as a guide to understanding the similarities and differences among the systems. Each system proclaims a set of truths, yet despite some overlap there are notable conflicts among these "truths." This chapter will highlight the conflicts and examine the competing positions. Our aim is to examine different solutions to some of the most significant problems of family therapy.

THEORETICAL PURITY AND
TECHNICAL ECLECTICISM

Systems of family therapy are most clearly distinguished by their conceptual positions. Whether they claim to be based entirely on theory (behavioral family therapy) or to be atheoretical (experiential family therapy), each of the systems is supported by a set of beliefs about families and how to change them. Moreover, these theories relate to practice in a circular and mutually reinforcing manner. Practice generally precedes theory; thereafter progress in theory and practice proceeds in leapfrog fashion: Developments in one lead to developments in the other.

The systematizers of family therapy were methodologists first, theoreticians second. The facts of their clinical observations and experience came before the hypotheses and speculations of their theories. Originally these theories were like maps drawn by explorers of new territories; but for those who came afterwards, students and colleagues, the theories offered preset guidelines for viewing the terrain.

Because they offer a preset way of looking at clinical data, theories have a biasing effect on observation. Students undoubtedly "see" what the theories they've studied prepare them to see. This is easily demonstrated by showing a videotape of the opening minutes of a family therapy session to a group of students. Even if the family conducts itself in a perfectly unremarkable fashion, students will "see" evidence of pathology, phrased in terms of whatever concepts they have learned.

Theories can bias perceptions, but they also bring order out of chaos. They enable us to organize our observations and to make sense out of what families are doing. Instead of seeing a "blooming, buzzing confusion," we begin to see patterns of interaction. Moreover, these patterns are organized in conceptual categories that are directly relevant to therapeutic intervention.

Theories also serve a political purpose. They demarcate one system from the others, and announce their unique points of view. For this reason, theoretical positions tend to be stated in doctrinaire terms that maximize their distinctions. While this makes interesting reading, it is somewhat misleading. The truth is that the different systems of family therapy are more alike in practice than their theories suggest. Moreover, each new approach tends to become more eclectic over time. Practitioners start out as relative purists, but eventually discover the value of concepts from other approaches and the usefulness of other people's techniques. The result is that, with increasing experience, most family therapists gradually become more eclectic.

Practice is the expected consequence of theory, but it doesn't always work out that way. Theory is molded by the requirements of logical consistency and elegance, and often reflects a desire to be seen as original and clever. Practice is molded in the pragmatic arena of clinical treatment; it's shaped by encounters with real people, who often turn out to be more complicated than abstract models. Clinicians trained in one school are often forced by the complexity of the task to incorporate methods from other schools. In everyday practice the schools of family therapy tend to become synthetic and integrative. Therapists from technique-oriented schools, which focus on small sequences of interaction (behaviorists and strategists), have begun to adopt the organizing frameworks of schools with more comprehensive understanding of family dynamics (Bowenian and structural). At the same time, certain techniques that have proven their potency have been adopted by many of the schools of family therapy. Family therapists of all persuasions are now likely to clarify communications, direct enactments, and express skepticism about some clients' ability to change, no matter what their approach.

FAMILY THERAPIST—ARTIST OR SCIENTIST? _____

Expertise requires a body of operative knowledge, but it is not synonymous with expertness. Accomplished therapists begin with a grounding in theory; beyond that they must learn to extemporize. The therapist is not the system. Just because Minuchin cures anorexia nervosa doesn't mean that anyone can, simply by joining, unbalancing, and boundary-making.

The phrase, "the art and science of psychotherapy," implies that the therapist assumes a dual role, that of artist and scientist (Jasnow, 1978). On the surface, this seems innocuous, even banal. We all agree that a practitioner is first required to master the general principles and proven techniques in the field. Later these principles and techniques must be applied skillfully in a way that's appropriate to each case and in a manner that's congruent with the therapist's personality. There is, however, much room for disagreement about the degree to which the family therapist is more like an artist or more like a scientist.

Techniques do not make a family therapist. The therapist's personal qualities, respect for patients, and reverence for life are also important. Techniques are the tools, but human qualities are the supreme qualification of the good psychotherapist. Compassion—a deeply felt understanding of other people's sufferings—and sensitivity—an appreciation of people's inner world—can be lost in preoccupation with theoretical concepts. Without understanding and respect for individuals, family therapy remains a technical operation, instead of becoming a living human experience.

Behavioral and strategic therapists emphasize the technical role of the therapist, while experiential and constructivist therapists stress the artistic side of the person. We believe that the best way to become an effective family therapist is to first learn to be a "scientist" and then become an "artist." A beginner should concentrate on learning theory and technique, and subject himself or herself to a tutorial program of supervision. During this training it is reasonable, even wise, to adopt or copy outright technique, style, and even language from one's mentors. Furthermore, it may be necessary to identify and modify or subdue certain types of responses that come naturally.

> Mr. C. was a straight-A student in a psychiatric social work program who came to a well-known family therapy institute with very strong references. His previous supervisors rated him as an outstanding young therapist, and stressed his warmth and ability to empathize with clients. When

he began to see families it was immediately apparent that he had a natural gift for understanding and communicating his acceptance of people. His families liked him and they tended to remain in treatment with him.

Unhappily, his natural warmth and compassion for people made him respond to family problems by expressing sympathy and then taking over. Although many of his families were happy to become dependent upon him, they failed to learn how to solve their own problems. Moreover, since they experienced no pressure to resolve their own problems, the therapist was left with very little leverage to influence them in significant ways.

In supervision Mr. C. was helped to recognize and restrain his well-meaning but counterproductive tendency to rescue his clients. The immediate result was a long and painful period of self-imposed restraint, but this eventually enabled him to become a better therapist.

Listening harder and intervening less made Mr. C. more aware of family dynamics. Instead of just being sympathetic, he began to see how his families were getting stuck, and instead of taking over for them, he began to see what they needed to do to take over for themselves. He learned, too, that his rescuing tendencies had partly to do with his own difficulty tolerating the anxiety of listening to unhappy feelings without acting precipitously to deny or expunge them. Like a tennis player who takes professional lessons, he went through a period of feeling awkward and constrained, but that may be part of the process of learning the science of one's field.

Most young therapists come equipped not only with some innately helpful qualities but also with a number of nontherapeutic impulses. Common among these are: assuming an overly central and controlling position with families; paying more attention to family members' feelings (or behavior, or thinking) than to other aspects of their experience; taking on the families' dilemmas as problems to be solved by the therapist; getting angry at resistant families; and identifying only with adolescents (or small children, or parents). Because most of these tendencies are automatic reflexes of character, it is unlikely that young therapists will be able to identify them without supervision. The only other way to detect troublesome lack of objectivity in a therapist is to recognize repeated failures or stalemates with certain types of families. Once these clues to problems in the therapist are identified, self-analysis, consultation, or supervision will help to determine if the problem stems from inadequate skill or from unrecognized emotional reactivity.

Today in the wake of constructivism and postmodernism, as the field struggles to avoid what is perceived as the authoritarian stance of earlier approaches, the art or science question is very much with us. If, as constructivists maintain, therapy should be a nonhierarchical conversation, where is the place for professionalism and expertise? Is the good therapist really just an artist of relationships—warm and respectful, but not uniquely privileged by training? Is the science of therapy too often practiced with inadequate respect for clients' own wisdom and cultural traditions? Does an overemphasis on the scientific aspect of therapy mask power and control operations? Or, is the real danger not the science of therapy, not learning to be experts at understanding and intervening, but intervening in bossy and controlling ways? Is the current emphasis on the art of conversation a repudiation of the science of family therapy, or merely a corrective attempt to rebalance the two?

THEORETICAL FORMULATIONS

All schools of family therapy have theories. Some are elaborate (psychoanalytic), some simple (experiential); some are developed from other disciplines (behavioral), others are developed directly from family work (structural, strategic). Theories are ideas abstracted from experience and observation. Their purpose is to simplify and order the raw data of family life as an aid to understanding. In this chapter we will evaluate theories for their pragmatic function—understanding families in order to better treat them. The schools of family therapy will be compared on the basis of their theoretical positions on a sample of key conceptual dimensions: families as systems; stability and change; past or present; communication; content/process; monadic, dyadic, or triadic points of view; the nuclear family in context; and boundaries.

Families as Systems

Communications family therapists introduced the idea that families are systems. More than the sum of their parts, systems are the parts *and* the way they function together. Family group therapists also treated families as more than collections of individuals; but their idea of a superordinate group process was a more limited concept that refers to something that happens when a group of people interact, rather than to an organizing principle that governs a family's entire life.

Not believing in systems theory is like not believing in the flag, apple pie, and motherhood. Schools of family therapy vary, however, in the degree to which they actually incorporate systems thinking in their practice, and in the kind of systems thinking they use. Behavioral family therapists say very little about systems, and treat individuals as separate entities who influence each other only by acting as stimuli and reinforcers. Most of the mainstream family therapy models, on the other hand—Bowenian, communications, strategic, Milan, and structural— base their approach to families on some version of systems thinking.

Systems theory once seemed intrinsic to family therapy because it was part and parcel of understanding families as organized groups and treating them by working with their interactions. Now, however, the postmodern movement has challenged systems thinking as just another modernist framework, a metaphor taken literally, and has shifted emphasis from action to meaning and from organization of the family group to the thinking of its members. Increasingly, Michael White, Harlene Andersen, and Tom Andersen are rejecting systems thinking.

Stability and Change

Communications theorists describe families as rule-governed systems with a tendency toward stability or homeostasis (Jackson, 1965). If a family member deviates from the family's rules, this constitutes feedback, and if the family reacts to it as *negative feedback,* they try to force that person to change back. Families, like other living systems, maintain their interactions within a relatively fixed range in order to remain stable in the face of normal environmental stresses. In structural family theory the same point is made by saying that families have a relatively stable structure which enables them to function effectively as a system, with various subsystems each fulfilling part of the family's overall task.

Families must also change to adapt to changing circumstances. To do so they must be capable of revising their rules, and modifying their structure. Dysfunctional families are distinguished by their rigidity and inflexibility; when circumstances change, they do not.

The dual nature of families—homeostatic and changing—is best appreciated by family therapists from the communications, structural, and strategic schools; they expect families to come to treatment because they failed to adapt to changing circumstances. They do not presume that the families they see are inherently pathological.

Anyone who ignores this principle runs the risk of placing an undue emphasis on pathology. If a therapist sees a family that is having trouble, but fails to consider that they may be stuck at a transitional impasse, then he or she is apt to think that they need an overhaul, when a tune-up might do. The therapies that emphasize long-range goals are all susceptible to this therapeutic overkill. Although they emphasize growth rather than pathology, psychoanalytic, experiential, and extended family practitioners are inclined to assume that the families they see are basically flawed and need fundamental reorganization. Since they have the equipment for major surgery—long-term therapy—they tend to see the patient as needing it. Sometimes the patient doesn't.

The pioneers of family therapy (with the notable exception of Virginia Satir) tended to overestimate homeostatic forces in families and underestimate their flexibility and resourcefulness. This viewpoint encouraged therapists to act as provokers, controllers, and strategizers. The corollary of the family held fast by systemic forces they cannot understand was the oh-so-clever therapist who would do the understanding for them. Many of the newer approaches to family therapy (discussed in the previous chapter) are designed to elicit family resources, rather than struggle with their fears. These models encourage therapists to collaborate with families to help them work out solutions, rather than to assume they won't change unless provoked.

Past or Present

When it was inaugurated, family therapy was heralded as a treatment that emphasized the present, in contrast to individual therapies that emphasized the past. Psychoanalysis was the chief whipping boy of family therapists eager to define themselves as different in every way. Psychoanalysis was portrayed as a monadic theory which focused on past traumas as the cause of problems, and tried to cure people by helping them remember the past. While this picture accurately describes Freud's treatment in 1895, modern psychoanalysis is quite a bit more complicated.

That people are influenced by past experiences is an unarguable fact. The question is, how necessary is it to think about the past in order to understand the present? All family therapists work in the here-and-now; some see residues of the past, others do not.

Emphasis on the past is correlated with concern for individuals. Psychoanalytic practitioners view the determinants of behavior as resting with individuals. Theirs is a personality-trait model, in which family life is seen as a product of enduring dispositions, internalized from early object relations. This viewpoint affects practice, but not in the obvious way. Psychoanalytic therapists use their knowledge of past influences to inform their understanding of the present. They don't concentrate on helping people remember the past; instead they use psychoanalytic theory to help them understand what's going on in the present. The present may be understood in terms of transference and projection from the past, but it's still the present.

Surprisingly, the therapists who spend the most time talking with their patients about the past are the very ones who emphasize the here-and-now in their writings. Experiential therapists believe that unfinished business from the past interferes with full experiencing in the present. For this reason they spend a lot of time talking with patients about old preoccupations in order to help them let go of the past (Pierce, Nichols, & DuBrin, 1983). A classic example of this approach is Norman Paul's (1967) technique of *operational mourning*.

The past also plays a prominent role in Bowenian theory. Present family relationships are assumed to be products of relationships within the original family. Problems with a child, for example, are presumed to result from the parents' unresolved conflicts with their own parents. Unlike psychoanalytic therapists, who deal with the residuals of those relationships by pointing out their influence in the current family, Bowenian therapists send patients back to their families. Is this a return to the past? In practice, that's impossible; conceptually it is a return to the past.

The schools of family therapy that view the determinants of behavior as being outside—that is, between—individuals, stress the present, in theory and practice. Family group therapists, communicationists, strategists, and structuralists have little to say about the past. They're less interested in how or why problems get started than what maintains them. They often see families as stuck in transition between one developmental phase and another, but their concern is with contemporary interactions, not with events fixed in time.

Behavior therapists once explained all behavior as a result of past learning history. Pavlov's dogs salivated at the sound of a bell because they had been conditioned to do so; parents had trouble with their children because they had trained them improperly. Today behavior therapists rely on operant conditioning as the model to explain most human behavior. According to this model, behavior is maintained by its consequences. Parents have trouble with their children because of the way they respond to them in the present. Therapy derived from this model deals with how people currently reinforce maladaptive behavior. The classical conditioning model is still used to explain certain anxiety disorders, especially sexual dysfunction, but treatment is designed to relax anxiety in the present.

Most of the newer models try to strike a balance between past and present. Michael White helps families explore the historical evolution of how their problems got the upper hand over them, but then tries to empower family members to deal with those problems in the present. Richard Schwartz finds that parts of people carry outmoded or irrational beliefs and feelings from the past, but he helps clients change their relationship with these parts in the present—they learn about the past, but stop living there. Not only is Steve de Shazer not interested in the past, he is also not interested in the present maintenance of the problem. Instead, he is interested in future solutions. Harlene Anderson is interested in anything—past, present, or future—that is important to the family.

Communication

Working with communication no longer distinguishes one school of family therapy from the others. All behavior is communicative, and all family therapists deal with verbal and nonverbal behavior. But although they all think about communication, they do so in very different ways.

Family group therapists have the most straightforward and simple view of communication. For them communication is the medium of exchange through which members of families interact. Their treatment is to help transform blocked, incomplete, and covert communication into clear and open expression. They take what is conscious but unexpressed (except perhaps nonverbally) and bring it out into the open.

Behaviorists also think of communication in simple terms; for them, communication is a skill that can be taught. In addition they understand something less obvious about communication; namely that the message received may not be the one intended. They distinguish reinforcement from aversive control, and have, for example, pointed out that yelling at a child may be reinforcing, even though it's intended to be punishing. On the other hand, angrily berating a spouse for not spending more time with you may be more punishing than informing.

In psychoanalytic psychotherapy, communication is taken as metaphor, with the manifest content conveying derivatives of hidden needs and feelings. The therapist's job is to decode these latent meanings in order to help patients better understand themselves. In psychoanalytic family therapy, the therapist not only brings these hidden meanings to light but also helps family members express their latent emotions to each other. The therapist uses a knowledge of defenses, especially displacement and symbolization, to understand the unconscious content of family members' communications, and a knowledge of family dynamics to help complete these communications in the family.

Structural and strategic therapy both may be considered offshoots of communications theory (Madanes & Haley, 1977), and each emphasizes a particular aspect of communications in family relations. According to structural family theory, patterns of communications are what create family structure. Family organization develops from repeated sequences of interaction—communication; therapists detect the family's underlying structure by observing who speaks to whom and in what way. If a mother complains that she "can't communicate" with her teenaged daughter, the structural therapist will enact a sequence where they try to talk to each other in the session. If they talk for only a few moments before breaking off, the therapist will conclude that they are disengaged; if they argue back and forth like peers or siblings, the therapist may conclude that there is no hierarchical distinction, they are enmeshed; or if their conversation is repeatedly interrupted by the father, the therapist may conclude that interpersonal boundaries are blurred, and that the communication problem between the mother and daughter is a product of the father's enmeshment.

In Madanes and Haley's version of strategic therapy the main purpose of communication is to gain power in interpersonal relationships. From this point of view symptoms are perceived as communications designed to manipulate other family members. More recently, Haley and Madanes have emphasized love and protection as motives for communication. But, as we all know, much that is controlling can be done in the name of love. For instance, a child's phobic fear of going to school may be a covert way to communicate that he is afraid that his parents might separate; the symptom serves to keep them together to take care of him. Family members' responses to problems are thought to create symptoms. In this case the parents' decision to stay home to take care of the child only makes matters worse. A strategic therapist would not try to help the family understand the meaning of these symptoms, but would instead try to provoke them to relate—communicate—in a way that makes the symptoms unnecessary. If the parents, together, took the child to school and, together, helped him with his homework, the improvement of the child could be divorced from whether or not the parents stay together.

The experientialists' interest in communication is also two-layered; what they consider important are unexpressed feelings, lying beneath the surface content of family members' communications. Like psychoanalytic therapists, they consider it important to reduce defenses so that people can communicate what's really on their minds. Unlike psychoanalysts, they look in the present for relatively conscious feelings. Instead of interpreting defenses, they confront them in order to help people break out of their inhibitions. Because they work with families, they are concerned not only with uncovering feelings but also with helping family members communicate their feelings honestly and openly within the family. Satir, in particular, focused on communication style as reflective of a person's level of self-esteem. She encouraged straight talk as a way to straighten out relationships—and to make people feel better about themselves for being honest.

Extended family systems therapists foster communication as a vehicle for opening up relationships with the wider kinship group. In emotional cutoffs there is a breakdown in communication; in emotional reactivity communication comes from an undifferentiated stance in which people lose sight of their own thoughts and feelings; and in triangulated relationships communication is diverted. Therapy is designed to help people reestablish communication with extended family members, teach them to communicate "I-position" statements, and redirect communication from a triangulated third party to the person for whom it was originally intended.

The conversation-based models of the 1990s try to open channels of communication so that family members can tell their stories and be heard by the others in the family. There is less interest in teaching communication skills than in creating a communicative environment in which people can reauthor their personal and family narratives.

Content/Process

A system is the parts of a whole plus the way they function; process is the way families and groups function. Family and group therapists learn to attend to process and attempt to change it. When a mother and her teenaged daughter discuss the daughter's curfew, the mother and daughter are interested in *what* the other one says; the mother listens to when the daughter wants to come home and the daughter listens to her mother's response. A family therapist, listening to the same conversation, will be more interested in *how* the mother and daughter talk to each other. Does each state her point of view directly? Do they listen to each other? Is the mother clearly in charge? These questions have to do with the process of the conversation; they may not determine when the daughter comes home, but they reveal how the dyad functions.

When families come for treatment, they are usually focused on a content issue; a husband wants a divorce, a child refuses to go to school, a wife is depressed, and so on. The family therapist talks with the family about the content of the problem, but thinks about the process of discussion by which they try to solve it. While the family discusses what to do about a child's refusal to go to school, for instance, the therapist notices whether the parents seem to be in charge and if they support each other. If the therapist tells the parents to solve the problem by making the child go to school, then he or she is working with content, not process. The child may go to school, but the parents won't have improved the process of their decision-making.

All schools of family therapy have a theoretical commitment to working with the process of family interaction. Psychoanalytic and experiential clinicians try to reduce defensiveness and foster open expression of thoughts and feelings; family group and communications therapists increase the flow of interactions and help family members reduce the incongruence between different levels of communication; Bowenians block triangulation and encourage family members to take differentiated, "I-position" stances; strategic therapists ferret out and interdict problem-maintaining sequences of interaction; behaviorists teach parents to use positive control, and couples to eliminate coercive communication; structural therapists realign emotional boundaries and strengthen hierarchical organization.

Despite their theoretical commitment to process concepts, family therapists sometimes get distracted by content issues. Sometimes content is important. If a wife is drinking to drown her worries or a husband is molesting his daughter, a therapist needs to know and do something about it. But to the extent that therapists focus exclusively on content, they are unlikely to help families change to become better functioning systems. Psychoanalytic therapists sometimes lose sight of process when they concentrate on individual family members and their memories of the past. Similarly, experientialists are prone to becoming overly central while working with individual family members to help them overcome emotional defensiveness. The danger is that by so doing therapists will neglect the interactional processes in the family that affect individual expression.

Behavioral family therapists generally neglect process in favor of content. They do so when they isolate a particular behavioral sequence from its context in the family, ignoring the process that maintains it. They also interfere with the process of family interaction by assuming a directive, teaching role. As long as the teacher stands in front of a class and lectures, there is little opportunity to observe how the students behave on their own.

Process concepts are so central to extended family systems therapy that there is little danger that therapists in this school will forget them. Only naive misunderstanding of Bowenian therapy would lead someone to think merely of reestablishing family ties, without also being aware of processes of triangulation, fusion, and differentiation. The same is true of structural family therapy, family group therapy, and communications therapy; process issues are always at center stage.

Strategic family therapists have a dual focus—their goals are content-oriented, but their interventions are directed at process. As in behavioral therapy, the goal is in terms of content—solving the presenting problem. To understand what maintains the problem, however, strategic therapists shift their attention to process. Usually this involves discrete sequences of interaction, which they try to block by using directives. The goal, though, is not to improve the process of family functioning, but merely to interdict a particular sequence in order to resolve the content of the presenting problem.

The difference between structural and strategic interest in process is reflected in supervision styles. Structuralists rely on direct observation of family sessions through one-way mirrors and videotapes because they believe that nonverbal interactions (who sits where, who makes faces while someone talks, who looks to whom for permission to answer) are crucial. Strategic and solution-focused therapists are far more concerned with the verbal process of sessions and, consequently, are more apt to use audiotapes or therapist reports when supervising.

The newer models of family therapy, with their de-emphasis on systems thinking, have moved away from a focus on process. Narrative constructivists are less interested in changing family interaction patterns than in changing the ways family members understand their problems and themselves—less interested in changing behavior than in expanding stories.

Monadic, Dyadic, or Triadic Model

Family therapy was initiated when clinicians recognized that the identified patient's behavior is a function of the whole family; all family practitioners now subscribe to this systems viewpoint. In practice, however, family therapists sometimes think in terms of units of one, two, or three persons. Some clinicians (psychoeducational therapists, for example) think of one person in the family as the patient, and bring in the family to help deal with the patient. When these therapists work with families they emphasize the individual's thoughts and feelings. Their aim is to help family members become more aware of how they feel about and deal with the identified patient.

Psychoanalytic therapists tend to think about intrapsychic dynamics, whether they meet with people alone or with their families. They see current family relations as a product of internalized relationships with the previous family, and they are often more concerned with these mental ghosts than with flesh-and-blood families. Child behavior therapists use a monadic model when they accept a family's definition that their symptomatic child is the problem, and set about teaching the parents to change the child's behavior. Experiential therapists also work with individuals to help them uncover and express their feelings.

Actually, no living thing can adequately be understood in monadic terms. A bird's egg may be the closest thing in nature to a self-contained monad. The fetus is locked away inside its shell with all the nutrients it needs to survive. Even this view is incomplete, however, for there is an exchange of heat between the egg and the surrounding environment. Without the mother's warmth, the baby bird will die.

A dyadic model is necessary to understand the fact that people are always in relationships. Even the psychoanalytic patient, free-associating on the couch, is filtering memories and dreams through reactions to the analyst. Most of the time family therapists operate with a dyadic model; they usually work on relationships between two people at a time. Even when a large family is in treatment, the focus is usually on various pairs of family members, considered in succession.

Helping two people learn to relate better doesn't always mean that the therapist thinks in dyadic terms. Behavioral couples therapists work with two spouses, but treat them as separate individuals, each of whom is deficient in the art of communicating. A true dyadic model is based on the understanding that two people in a relationship are not separate monads interacting with each other; they each define the other. Using this model a wife's agoraphobia would be understood as a reaction to her husband and as a means of influencing him. Likewise, his decision to send her alone for behavior modification reflects his refusal to accept his role in her life.

Family therapists of all schools use some dyadic concepts; unconscious need complementarity, expressive/instrumental, projective identification, symbiosis, intimacy, quid pro quo, double bind, symmetrical, complementary, pursuer/distancer, and behavioral contract. Some terms are based on dyadic thinking even though they may involve more than two people: compliant (referring to a family's relationship to a therapist) or defiant; some seem to involve only one: countertransference, dominant, and supercompetent. Still other concepts are capable of encompassing units of three or more, but are often used to refer to units of two: boundary, coalition, fusion, and disengagement.

Too often family therapists think in dyadic terms and neglect triadic complications. Murray Bowen introduced the concept of emotional triangles into the family therapy literature, and has done more than anyone else to point out that human behavior is always a function of triadic relationships. Structural family therapists have also consistently been aware that enmeshment or disengagement between two people is always a function of reciprocal relationships with a third. Communications therapists wrote about triadic relationships, but tended to think in terms of units of two. The same is true of most strategic therapists, although Haley, Selvini Palazzoli, and Lynn Hoffman are consistently aware of triadic relationships.

The advantage of triadic thinking is that it permits a more complete understanding of behavior in context. If a boy misbehaves when his mother doesn't use firm discipline, teaching her to be firm won't work if her behavior is a function of her relationship with her husband. Perhaps she subtly encourages her child to misbehave as a way of undermining her husband's authority; or she and her husband may have worked out a relationship where her incompetence reassures him that he's the strong one.

The fact that triadic thinking permits a more complete understanding doesn't mean that family therapists must always include all parties in treatment. The issue is not how many people are in treatment, but whether or not the therapist considers problems in their full context.

The Nuclear Family in Context

Just as most family therapists espouse the ideas of systems theory, most also regard families as open systems. The family is open in that its members interact, not only with each other, but also with extrafamilial systems in a constant exchange of information, energy, and material. Family therapy is a treatment of people in context; the most significant context for most people may be the nuclear family, but even to understand the nuclear family properly it is necessary to consider its context.

Communications family therapists introduced the concept of open systems to family therapy, but actually treated families as though they were closed systems. They paid little attention to sources of stress outside the family and rarely considered the impact of friends or extended family on the nuclear unit. The first clinicians to take the extrafamilial into account (and into treatment) were Murray Bowen and Ross Speck. Bowen always stressed the critical role of extended family relationships, and Speck mobilized the patient's network of family and friends to aid in treatment.

Bowenian therapists and network therapists virtually always include people outside the nuclear family in treatment; psychoanalytic, group-oriented, behavioral, and communications therapists almost never do. Among experientialists, Whitaker has begun to routinely include members of the extended family in treatment for one or two sessions. Including extended family members or friends in treatment is often useful and sometimes essential. It is not, however, the same thing as thinking of the family as an open system. An open system is not a larger system; it is a system that interacts with its environment.

Nowhere is the idea of families as open systems better articulated than in Minuchin's (1974) *Families and Family Therapy*. Writing about "Man in His Context," Minuchin contrasts family therapy with psychodynamic theory. The latter, he says, draws on the concept of man as a hero, remaining himself in spite of the circumstances. On the other hand, "the theory of family therapy is predicated on the fact that man is not an isolate. He is an acting and reacting member of social groups" (p. 2). Minuchin credits Gregory Bateson with erasing the boundary between inner and outer space, and goes on to say that just as the boundary separating the individual from the family is artificial, so is the boundary separating the family from the social environment. "Theories and techniques of family therapy lend themselves readily to work with the individual in contexts other than the family" (p. 4).

Structural family therapists recognize that families are embedded in a social context, and they often include teachers, school administrators, and other social agents in family diagnosis and treatment. If a single mother is enmeshed with her children, a structural family therapist might help her get more involved with friends or community activities as a way of helping her loosen her grip on the children.

Strategic family therapists may not treat families as open systems, but they don't confine their search for problem-maintaining sequences to the nuclear family. Selvini Palazzoli's work illustrates that in close-knit Italian families, grandparents are often directly involved in sequences of behavior that support symptoms, and members of the MRI group often work with problem-maintaining sequences that involve someone outside the family, like a supervisor at work or a neighbor. Routinely including grandparents or friends in family therapy is useful but not essential; however, to gain a full understanding of families you must consider the forces outside the family acting and interacting with them.

Feminist therapists have challenged us to face our culture's gender inequality and to recognize reflections of this inequality in the families we treat. In addition, clinicians like Evan Imber-Black have expanded our view to include the impact of institutions and agencies, and encouraged us to deal directly with these larger systems.

The growing awareness of the impact of social and political conditions on the lives of families poses a challenge not without complications for family therapists. Ignoring racism, sexism, ethnocentrism, poverty, crime, and alienation—thinking of families as though they were self-contained units—makes about as much sense as putting your head in the sand. On the other hand, when national family therapy conventions begin to devote themselves exclusively to social and political (rather than clinical) issues, are they blurring their mission? Do family therapists have the moral authority (not to mention expertise and leverage) to redress society's ills? What is the proper role of the individual family therapist and of national family therapy associations with respect to larger issues of social injustice?

Should family therapy organizations take official positions on such issues as abortion? (The board of directors of the American Family Therapy Academy recently took an official pro-choice position on behalf of its membership.) A second question, of more practical consequence, is—given the powerful impact of social conditions on families—do family therapists have a unique role to play in politics and society, or are they, in their professional capacity at least, primarily clinicians, trained and competent to treat families for psychological problems, but having no special authority or expertise to right social wrongs? What is a therapist's responsibility for dealing with society beyond the consulting room?

Boundaries

Family practitioners study and treat people in context—individuals in context of their families, and families in context of their extended families and communities. One of the most useful concepts in family therapy is that of boundaries, a concept that applies to the relationship of all of these systems within systems in terms of the nature of their interface. The individuality and autonomy of each subsystem (individual, siblings, parents, nuclear family) is regulated by a semipermeable boundary between it and the suprasystem.

The clearest and most useful concepts of interpersonal boundaries are in the works of Murray Bowen and Salvador Minuchin. Bowen is best at describing the boundaries between individuals and their families; Minuchin is best at describing the boundaries between various subsystems within the family. In Bowen's terms, individuals vary on a continuum from fusion to differentiation, and Minuchin describes boundaries as diffuse or rigid, with resultant enmeshment or disengagement.

Bowen's thinking reflects psychoanalytic sources. Psychoanalytic theory emphasizes the development of interpersonal boundaries while describing how individuals emerge from the context of their families. Beginning with the separation and individuation from symbiosis with the mother that characterizes the psychological birth of the human infant (Mahler, Pine, & Bergman, 1975), psychoanalytic clinicians describe repeated and progressive separations that culminate first in the resolution of oedipal attachments and then eventually in leaving home.

Bowen's thinking about boundaries continues the somewhat one-sided emphasis on poorly defined boundaries between self and other. He pays little attention to the problems of emotional isolation stemming from rigid boundaries, and describes this as an artifact—a defense against a basic lack of psychological separateness. Bowen uses a variety of terms—togetherness, fusion, undifferentiation, emotional reactivity—which refer to the danger he is most concerned with, that people will lose themselves in relationships.

Minuchin offers a more balanced view of boundaries, describing the problems that result when they are either too rigid or too diffuse. Diffuse boundaries allow too much outside interference into the functioning of a subsystem; rigid boundaries allow too little communication, support, and affection between different segments of the family. Bowen describes only one boundary problem—fusion—and only one goal—differentiation; Minuchin speaks of two possibilities—enmeshment or disengagement—and his therapy is designed to fit the specific case.

Minuchin (1974) explains the function of boundaries, their reciprocal relationship, and how a knowledge of boundaries can be used to plan therapy. Boundaries protect individuals and subsystems from intrusion so that they can function autonomously. Newlyweds, for instance, need to establish a clear boundary between themselves and their parents in order to work out their own independent relationship. A diffuse boundary will leave them overly reliant on their parents, preventing them from developing their own autonomy and intimacy. If a wife calls her mother whenever she's upset, she won't learn to work things out with her husband; if she borrows money from her father whenever she wants to make a large purchase, she won't develop her own potential to earn a living.

In Bowenian theory people tend to be either emotionally fused or differentiated. Fusion is like a disease—you can have a bad case or a mild one. In structural family theory the enmeshment-disengagement distinction plays two roles. Families are described as enmeshed or disengaged; but more often families are described as made up of different subsystems with the enmeshment of some producing the disengagement of others. For example, a mother and child may be described as enmeshed (Bowen would say fused); this will be seen not in isolation but as a product of the woman's disengaged relationship with her husband. Using this understanding of the interlocking nature of subsystem boundaries, it is possible to design therapy to fit a specific family and to coordinate change among its subsystems.

Bowen's "fusion" and Minuchin's "enmeshment" both deal with the consequences of blurred boundaries, but they aren't alternate vocabularies for the same thing. Fusion is a quality of individuals and it is the counterpart of the psychoanalytic concept of individuation. Both are intrapsychic concepts for a person's *psychological* embeddedness—undifferentiation—within a relationship context. The dynamics of fusion have an impact on other relationships (especially in the form of triangulation), but fusion is *within* the person. Enmeshment is strictly a social systems concept; enmeshment is *between* people. These conceptual differences are also related to differences in treatment. Bowen coaches individuals to stay in contact and maintain an "I-position"; success is measured in individual differentiation. Minuchin joins the system and realigns coalitions by strengthening *or* weakening boundaries; success is measured by change in the whole system. Bowen's conceptualization may lead to lasting individual personality change, which may affect the whole family system; Minuchin's conceptualization permits greater leverage and quicker change. The difference is between working with individuals to change the system, and working with the system to change individuals.

With the possible exception of Bowenian theory, theoretical concepts in family therapy have been relatively simple and heuristic. Perhaps this explains why family therapists have been so captivated by theories from other disciplines. Systems concepts—feedback, circular causality, second-order change— were useful devices that helped make complex relationships predictable. But they did more as well. They gave the new discipline an aura of scientific respectability. Recent years have seen two trends in family therapy: first a fascination with abstract, esoteric theorizing, heavily laced with such wooly terms as "ecosystemic epistemology" and experience-distant concepts from the political philosophies of Michel Foucault and Jacques Derrida and from the "natural" sciences—what Nichols (1987) called an "escape to profundity"— and more recently a greater emphasis on social rather than clinical issues, especially in the two most influential journals in the field. Do we really need to bolster our enterprise with borrowed concepts from physics and biology, philosophy and French psychoanalysis, narrative and literary theory? In concentrating more on cultural and political issues, are we in danger of neglecting the study of family dynamics and treatment? By raising these questions, we don't mean to suggest simple, either-or answers. Rather, we simply want to urge students to think about how and why one discipline goes outside itself for ideas. (And incidentally, if family therapists need to enrich their observations by consulting other literatures, what about psychology, the science of human behavior?)

NORMAL FAMILY DEVELOPMENT

As a rule family therapists have less to say about developmental issues than do individual therapists. One of the distinguishing characteristics of family therapy is its focus on the here-and-now interactions that maintain family problems. Normal family development involves the past and what is healthy and, therefore, has been underemphasized.

Many family therapists have pointed out that normality and abnormality are not discrete, that there is a wide range of functional and dysfunctional behavior (Watzlawick, Beavin, & Jackson, 1967; Minuchin, 1974). This point is well taken, but it has been made often enough; it is no longer a valid excuse for failing to develop models of normal, or functional, family behavior.

Most therapists do have implicit models about what is normal, and these assumptions influence their clinical assessment and treatment. The problem is that these unarticulated models are based largely on personal experience; as long as these remain unexamined they are apt to reflect personal bias. Many people assume that healthy families are just like their own—or just the opposite. However, the fact that a therapist comes from a relatively disengaged, upwardly striving, intact nuclear family doesn't make this the only, or the best, model of family life. When it comes to setting goals for family treatment, the choice isn't between using a model of normality or having no model, but between using a model that has been spelled out and examined, or operating on the basis of ill-defined personal standards.

Among family therapists, those concerned with the past, especially members of Bowenian and psychoanalytic schools, have had the most to say about normal development. These two schools share an evolutionary, developmental perspective. Whereas most family therapists explain problems in terms of ongoing interactional difficulties, Bowen and the psychoanalysts are interested in the developmental history of problems. Although their main interest in development is to understand how problems arise, their analyses also describe normal development.

Although most schools of family therapy aren't concerned with how families get started, the Bowenian and psychoanalytic schools have a great deal to say about marital choice. Bowen speaks about differentiation, fusion, and triangles, while the psychoanalytic writers speak of unconscious need-complementarity, projective identification, and idealization; but they seem to be using different terms to describe similar phenomena. Psychodynamic therapists speak of marital choice as a result of transference from the family of origin, and of people choosing partners with the same level of maturity; Bowen says that people pick partners who replicate familiar patterns of family interaction, and select mates at the same level of differentiation.

These are descriptions of significant ways in which people marry partners with similar underlying personality dynamics. Both of these schools also discuss ways in which people choose mates who appear to be different—at least on the surface—in ways that are exciting and that seem to make up for deficiencies in the self. Obsessives tend to marry hysterics, and according to Bowen togetherness-oriented people often marry distancers. This brings up another way in which the Bowenian and psychodynamic schools are similar to each other and different from others. Both have an appreciation of depth psychology; both recognize that personalities have different strata. Both think that the success of a marital relationship depends not only on the partners' shared interests and values but also on the nature of their internal, introjected object images.

Psychoanalysts emphasize the critical importance of good object relations in early childhood. The infant's ability to develop a cohesive self-image and good internal objects depends on "good-enough mothering" in an "average expectable environment." With a cohesive sense of self the child will grow up able to be with others and to be independent; without a coherent self, being with others may feel like being engulfed, and being alone may feel like being abandoned. Early object relations aren't just memories; they actually form psychic structures of the mind, preserving early experiences in the form of self-images and object-images. These internalized object-images determine how people in the environment will later be experienced. Thus the child's future—and the future of his or her family development—is laid down at an early age.

Bowen's description of normal family development is highly deterministic. Parents transmit their immaturity and lack of differentiation to their children; emotional fusion is passed on in a multigenerational transmission process. A family's fate is a product of relationships worked out in preceding generations.

Bowenian and psychoanalytic therapists describe the triangular relationship between mother and father and child as crucial to all later development. Psychoanalytic writers describe this oedipal situation in terms of conflicting drives, and believe that their resolution affects all future relationships. Bowenians describe this triangle in terms of stabilizing unresolved emotional tension in the marital dyad, and see it as the prototype of all subsequent relationships.

Clinicians are most likely to see people from families in which the triangular family romance was not resolved, but these theories include the possibility of successful resolution. Both theories, Bowenian and psychoanalytic, hold up visions of ideal functioning toward which people can strive but which they can never fully achieve. The result can be either a utopian model which condemns patients to dissatisfaction with their lives, or a standard used to guide people toward an enriched but not perfect life.

The clearest statement of such a standard is Bowen's (1966) description of families with "moderate to good differentiation." In these families the marriage is a functioning partnership in which spouses can be intimate without losing their autonomy. They permit their children to develop autonomous selves without becoming unduly anxious or trying to mold the children to their own images. Everyone in these families is responsible for himself or herself and neither credits others for personal success nor blames them for failure. They are able to function well with other people or to be alone, as the situation requires. Their intellectual functioning is not infused with emotionality at times of stress; they are adaptable, flexible, independent, and able to cope with good times and bad.

While they do not emphasize the past, most of the other schools of family therapy have a few isolated concepts for describing processes of normal family development. For example, communications therapists speak of the *quid pro quos* (Jackson, 1965) exchanged in normal marriages. Behaviorists describe the same phenomenon in terms of social exchange theory (Thibaut & Kelley, 1959).

Although all family therapists have a few concepts for dealing with normal family development, Minuchin is one of the few (other than Bowen and the psychodynamic therapists) who say that it's important to know what is normal in order to recognize what is abnormal. According to Minuchin (1974), clinicians need to have both an intellectual and emotional appreciation of the facts of ordinary family life in order to become effective therapists. First, it's necessary to recognize that normal family life isn't a bed of roses. When two people marry they must learn to accommodate to each other; each succeeding transition in the family life cycle requires further modifications of the family structure. Clinicians need to be aware of this, and able to distinguish functional from dysfunctional structures, as well as pathological structures from structures that are simply in a transitional process. Moreover, Minuchin adds, it's hard to be truly effective as a therapist without having personally experienced some of the problems that families in treatment are struggling with. (This is a point that older and more experienced therapists are more apt to make than are young ones.)

Because structural family therapy begins by measuring the adequacy of the client family's structure, it sometimes appears to have an ideal standard. In fact, however, normality is defined in terms of functional accomplishment, and structural family therapists recognize that diverse patterns may be functional. Functional families may be somewhat enmeshed or disengaged. The clarity of subsystem boundaries is far more important than the composition of the subsystem. For example, a parental subsystem made up of a father and oldest child can function effectively if the lines of responsibility and authority are clearly drawn. Patterns of enmeshment and disengagement are viewed as preferred styles, not necessarily as indications of abnormality.

The other schools of family therapy describe concepts of normality by mentioning specific mechanisms that are missing in dysfunctional families. Strategic therapists, for example, portray dysfunctional families as creating symptoms out of normal problems by failing to adjust to the demands of changing circumstances, and then trying to solve the problem by doggedly doing more of the same.

Bowenian and psychoanalytic family clinicians have developed elaborate models of normal development partly because they have an intrinsic interest in theory building. Both schools value understanding for its own sake. But what are the practical consequences of building models of normal family development? To begin with it's important to realize that the goals of these two approaches are different from the goals of most other family therapies. They are designed not merely for solving problems but for life-long structural reorganization—intrapsychic and interpersonal. To recognize the dynamic residues of a family's past, it's necessary to have a model of how the past was—and should be—organized.

Most family therapists don't think in terms of restructuring the past, and therefore believe they have little need for models of normal family development. Instead, they intervene around specific sequences of problem-maintaining behavior, which are conceptualized in terms of function. The sequences they observe are dysfunctional; therefore, by implication, what's functional must be just the opposite. Communication therapists use discrete concepts of family functioning, like rules and metarules. That's what they think about, that's what they see, and that's what they intervene to alter.

While it may not be necessary to have a way of understanding a family's past in order to help them, it is necessary to have a way of understanding the family's organization of the present, using a model of normal behavior to set goals for treatment. Such a model should include a design for the present and for change over time. Among the ideas presented in this book the ones most useful for a basic model of normal family functioning include structural hierarchy, effective communication, and family life cycle development.

The issues involved in whether or not to hold up normative maps as goals are thorny. If therapists adhere too strongly to a normative model, they may impose it on families for whom it doesn't fit—families from other cultures, for example—and they're more likely to take an authoritarian stance regarding the proper ends of treatment. On the other hand, therapy without a model of healthy family functioning can degenerate into a directionless exercise. Any normative model should be taken as a rough guideline and used flexibly rather than taken as a Procrustean bed onto which families are forced to fit.

Ironically, at the same time that integration is breaking down the distinctions between models of family therapy, an opposite trend is taking place in American society at large. Multiculturalism has replaced the ideal of the melting pot. Surely ethnic pride and a renewed respect for the culture and traditions of various groups makes for a richer and more diverse society than the white-bread WASPy standard once aspired to by anxious immigrants. Most of us are learning that differences aren't problems; intolerance and oppression are—not just the overt and ugly kind, like the police assault on Rodney King, but also everyday, subtle acts of prejudice and disrespect. But is there a danger in the multicultural ideal of setting up an insulating pride, fostering an us-against-them attitude on behalf of America's ethnic groups? Maybe "pluralism" is a better term for celebrating the uniqueness of one's own heritage, without promoting factionalism and separatism. Perhaps minority cultures can find common cause while accepting the equality of other cultures without at the same time striving for undifferentiated likeness.

Another assumption about normal families that has been questioned is the model of the nuclear family. Almost 30 percent of American families are headed by one parent, up from about 20 percent in 1980. Although the percentage is higher in African-American families, the rate of increase in both single parenthood and illegitimacy is now higher among whites. Not only have family therapists learned to see the single-parent family a workable alternative to the two-parent model, many have questioned not only the normality but also the utility of the nuclear model.

Anyone who works extensively with African-American families learns to recognize that these families often have more fluid boundaries and that "fictive kin" (enduring relationships with people who aren't actually related by blood) may be important connections in these families. And yet the idea that the American nuclear family is in danger of disappearing, or of becoming unrecognizable, may, like a lot of other millennial prophesies, turn out to be premature. After nearly two decades of studious neutrality about different family arrangements, the two-parent model has once again become a rallying cry of family commissions, policy analysts, and social scientists. They hail it not only as the best hedge against poverty for children, but also as the most reliable prescription for their success and happiness. Maybe God invented the idea of two parents for more than merely biological reasons. What do you think? Meanwhile family therapists who are more clinicians than social critics will continue to work with a variety of families and family forms, endeavoring not to fit them to any abstract model, but to help them realize their own unique potential.

DEVELOPMENT OF BEHAVIOR DISORDERS

In the early days of family therapy, patients were seen as scapegoats on whom families projected their conflicts and whose deviance maintained family stability. Much of the literature emphasized how parents with serious but covert conflict unite in concern for their emotionally disturbed child, who then becomes the identified patient. This was a theory of how family conflict causes behavior disorders in children. Many of the concepts put forward at that time were about dysfunctional ways of keeping the peace: scapegoating, pseudo-mutuality, rubber fence, family projection process, double bind, disqualification, mystification, and so on. These mechanisms may have driven young people crazy, but they helped keep their families together.

Initially, the patterns of disturbed function observed in schizophrenic families were thought to cause schizophrenia. Eventually, etiological models gave way to transactional ones. Instead of causing schizophrenia, these disturbed family interactions came to be seen as patterns of family relationship in which schizophrenia is embedded. Neither the family nor the symptomatic member is the locus of the problem—the problem isn't *within* people, it's *between* them.

Today family therapists think less about what causes problems than about how families unwittingly maintain the problems that come their way. Each of the systems of family therapy have unique ideas about how pathological families fit together, but the following themes are useful to define some of the important differences of opinion in the field: inflexible systems, function of symptoms, underlying dynamics, and pathological triangles.

Inflexible Systems

Inflexibility is the characteristic of pathological family systems most frequently indicted. Chronic inflexibility is a striking feature of families with disturbed members; these families are so rigid that it's virtually impossible to grow up in them healthy and normal. Acute inflexibility explains why other families become dysfunctional at transitions in the life cycle; disorder breaks out in these families when they fail to modify their organization in response to growth or stress.

Early observers of schizophrenic families emphasized their rigid inflexibility. Wynne coined the term *rubber fence* to dramatize how psychotic families resist outside influence, and *pseudomutuality* to describe their rigid facade of harmony. R. D. Laing showed how parents, unable to tolerate their children's healthy strivings, used *mystification* to deny and distort their experience. Communications theorists thought that the most striking disturbance in schizophrenic families was the extreme inflexibility of their rules. According to this analysis, these families were unable to adapt to the environment because they had no mechanisms for changing their rules; they were rigidly programmed to negative feedback, treating novelty and change as deviations to be resisted. Forces of homeostasis overpower forces of change, leaving these families stable but chronically disturbed.

This tradition of viewing families of schizophrenics and other severely disturbed patients as rigidly homeostatic has been taken into the 1980s and 1990s by Selvini Palazzoli in the form of her concept of "dirty games." Carol Anderson and Michael White, on the other hand, have tried to counter this negative way of looking at families with disturbed members by suggesting that their rigidity may be the result of living with serious problems—and being blamed by mental health professionals.

Explaining family problems in terms of rigid homeostatic functioning is today one of the cornerstones of the strategic school. Strategists describe dysfunctional families as responding to problems within a limited range of solutions. Even when the attempted solutions don't work, these families stubbornly keep trying; thus the attempted solutions, rather than the symptoms, are the problem. Behaviorists use a similar idea when they explain symptomatic behavior as a result of faulty efforts to change behavior. Often when parents think they're punishing their children, they're actually reinforcing them with attention.

Psychoanalytic and experiential clinicians have identified pathological inflexibility in individuals and couples, as well as in whole families. According to these two schools, intrapsychic rigidity, in the forms of conflict, developmental arrest, and emotional suppression, are the individual's contribution to family pathology. Psychoanalysts consider pathological families as closed systems that resist change. According to this line of thought, symptomatic families treat the present as though it were the past. When faced with a need to change, dysfunctional families regress to earlier levels of development where unresolved conflicts left them fixated.

Experientialists often describe pathological families as chronically resistant to growth. The symptom-bearer is seen to be signaling a family pattern of opposition to life forces. Unfortunately this model makes the family the villain and the individual the victim. The experiential model of inflexibility is fairly simple, and is primarily useful with minor forms of psychic difficulty.

Structural family therapists locate the inflexibility of dysfunctional families in the boundaries between subsystems. Disturbed families tend to be either markedly enmeshed or disengaged. Young therapists who have trouble diagnosing family structure are at first happily surprised when confronted with a profoundly disturbed family. The structure is so easy to see. Unfortunately, families with an unmistakably clear structure are extremely deviant and very difficult to change.

Structural family therapy also identifies inflexibility in symptomatic families. Rigidity was one of the most prominent characteristics found in psychosomatic families, for example. Minuchin (1974) stresses that otherwise normal families will develop problems if they are unable to modify a previously functional structure to cope with an environmental or developmental crisis. Family therapists should be very clear on this point: symptomatic families are often basically sound, they simply need help adjusting to a change in circumstances.

The Function of Symptoms

Early family therapists described the identified patient as serving a critical function in disturbed families, detouring conflict and, thus, stabilizing the family. Vogel and Bell (1960) portrayed emotionally disturbed children as family scapegoats, singled out as objects of parental projection on the basis of traits which set them apart from other members of the family. Thereafter their deviance promotes cohesion. Communications theorists thought that symptoms were fraught with meaning—functioning as messages—and with consequences—controlling other family members.

Today many family therapists deny that symptoms have either meaning or function. Behavioral and MRI therapists don't assume that symptoms are necessary to maintain family stability, and so they intervene to block the symptom without being concerned about restructuring the family. Behaviorists have always argued against the idea that symptoms are a sign of underlying pathology or that they serve any important function. Behavioral family therapists treat problems as the uncomplicated result of faulty efforts to change behavior and lack of skills. Restricting their focus to symptoms is one of the reasons they're successful in discovering the contingencies that reinforce them; it's also one of the reasons why they aren't very successful in cases where a child's problems function to stabilize a conflicted marriage, or where a couple's arguments protect them from dealing with unresolved personal problems. MRI therapists recognize that symptoms may serve a purpose, but deny that it's necessary to consider that purpose when planning therapy. Instead of trying to figure out what function may be served by symptoms, they concentrate on understanding how the pieces of the system fit together in a coherent fashion. Members of this school take the modest position that if they help free families from their symptoms, then the families can take care of themselves.

The psychoeducational approach and that of Michael White take a strong stand against the symptoms-serve-a-purpose idea. They argue that this thinking blames the victims and that families feel oppressed by, not grateful for, the symptoms of their members. Richard Schwartz takes the position that there may sometimes be parts of family members that fear change, but the parts that want relief can often be activated without having to confront the fearful parts.

Some of the schools of family therapy continue to believe that symptoms signal deeper problems, and that they function to maintain family stability. In families that cannot tolerate open conflict, a symptomatic member may serve as a smokescreen and a diversion. Just as symptomatic behavior preserves the balance of the nuclear family, so may problems in the nuclear family preserve the balance in the extended family. In psychoanalytic, Bowenian, and structural formulations, a couple's inability to form an intimate bond may be ascribed to the fact that one or both of them are still being used to mediate the relationship between their parents. In this way symptomatic behavior is transmitted across generations, and functions to stabilize the multigenerational family system.

Many times it's possible to see how systems function to arouse a depressed or disengaged parent to become more involved with the family. Two examples will illustrate this frequent observation. The first is from Jay Haley's (1976) *Problem-Solving Therapy*. According to Haley, a child's misbehavior is often part of a repetitive cycle that serves to keep the parents involved. In a typical sequence, father becomes unhappy and withdraws; the child misbehaves; mother fails to discipline the child; father steps in, reinvolving himself with the mother through the child. The second example is from an interview conducted by Harry Aponte (a noted structural family therapist), quoted in Hoffman (1981).

> The interview is with a poor black family that fully answers to the description "multiproblem." Everybody—the mother, six grown or nearly grown children, and two grandchildren—is at risk, from breakdown, illness, nerves, violence, accident, or a combination of all these factors. In addition, the family members are noisy, disruptive, and hard to control.
>
> At a certain point Aponte asks the mother, "How do you handle all this?" The mother, who has been apathetic and seemingly unconcerned as the therapist tries to talk with the children, says, "I put on my gorilla suit." The children laugh as they describe just how terrible their mother is when she puts on her gorilla suit.
>
> An incident occurs shortly after this conversation which suggests that a circular causal sequence is at work, one of those redundancies that may have to do with family balance. Mother is still apathetic and looks tired, and the therapist begins to ask about her nerves. At first the children are somewhat quiet, listening. As she begins to admit that she has had bad nerves and that she is taking pills, they begin to act up. One boy pokes the baby; another boy tries to restrain the baby from kicking back; the baby starts to yell. The therapist asks the twenty-year-old daughter (the baby's mother) if she can control him; she says no. At this point the mother gets up and smacks her daughter's baby with a rolled-up newspaper, rising out of her lethargy like some sleeping giant bothered by a gnat. She sits the baby down with a bump, and he makes no further trouble. During this sequence the rest of the children jump and shriek with joy, causing their mother to reprimand them, after which they calm down and the mother sits back, more watchful now and definitely in control. (p. 83)

Here a mother overwhelmed by stress becomes depressed; as she describes her depression the children become anxious and misbehave; the misbehavior triggers a reaction in the mother, rousing her from withdrawal to control the chaos. The children's symptomatic misbehavior functions as cause and cure of the mother's depression, in a recurring cycle.

Underlying Dynamics

In the 1950s family therapists challenged the psychoanalytic belief that symptoms are only surface phenomena and that the real problems are inside. Instead, they showed how observations limited to the surface of family interactions were sufficient to understand and treat behavioral problems.

Today there are still many family therapists who deny that it is necessary or valid to look for underlying dynamics in order to explain or treat symptomatic behavior. These clinicians believe that it is sufficient to observe patterns of interaction in the family. Some strategic therapists, like the MRI group, confine the field of focus to interactions surrounding symptomatic behavior; others, like the Milan group, take a broader view of the whole family. Behaviorists maintain that in order to account for unwanted behavior it is necessary only to observe its reinforcing consequences.

Despite the family therapy tradition of explaining problem behavior without bringing in underlying dynamics, many family therapists believe that neither the presenting symptoms nor surrounding interactions are the real problem; the real problem is some form of underlying family pathology. When families come in, these therapists look beneath—or beyond—behavioral sequences for some hypothesized basic flaw in the family. Minuchin's concept of family structure is the leading example of such a concept. Structural family therapists listen to families describe problem behavior, but they look for underlying structural pathology to explain and resolve these problems.

Structural pathology is conceptually different from the intrapsychic conflict in psychodynamic theory. Intrapsychic conflict is an inferred psychological concept; structural pathology is an observed interactional concept. (Constructivists would disagree. They believe every "observation" about reality is really a construction of reality.) Nevertheless, in practice, structural family therapists shift their attention from the family's complaints to a different level of analysis.

Family structure is now one of the central concepts in family therapy, and the field can be divided into those who include structure in their analyses and those that do not. Haley (1980) does, and for this reason many people consider him a structuralist as much as a strategist. Selvini Palazzoli and Lynn Hoffman bring in structural concepts in terms of systemic conflict and "too richly cross-joined systems" (Hoffman, 1981). John Weakland of the MRI group emphatically denies the need to include structural concepts in family assessment, and he considers doing so a species of discredited psychodynamic theorizing. Others in the family field, including behaviorists (Patterson) and some experientialists (Whitaker), accept the utility of structural concepts; their doing so shows a growing convergence among competing systems.

The postmodern revolution, discussed in Chapter 3, is also poststructural in the sense that conceptions of an underlying structure are viewed as modernist (misguidedly absolutist) and, therefore, problematic. Postmodern family therapists like Michael White, Steve de Shazer, and Harlene Anderson all avoid structural speculations.

Neither psychoanalytic nor Bowenian therapists use Minuchin's structural family theory, but both schools have their own concepts of underlying dynamics. Psychoanalysts originated the idea of underlying dynamics; present-day psychoanalytic family therapy practitioners use this idea in concepts of intrapsychic structural conflict (id, ego, superego); developmental arrest; internal object relations; and interlocking psychopathological structures among family members. According to the psychoanalytic model, problems may develop in interactions, but it is the interacting individuals who have the basic flaws.

In Bowen's theory, fusion, family projection process, and interlocking triangles are the major concepts of underlying family dynamics. So much are these underlying issues emphasized that Bowenians probably spend less time than anyone else dealing directly with presenting symptoms or even with symptom bearers.

Bowenian theory uses a *diathesis-stress* model of mental disorder. This is a model from genetic research in which a person develops a disorder when a genetic weakness is sufficiently stressed by an event in the environment. In Bowenian theory, people who develop symptoms in the face of anxiety-arousing stress have low levels of differentiation and are emotionally cut off from support systems, especially in the extended family. The diathesis may not be genetic, but it is passed from one generation to the next.

The psychoeducational therapists have brought the diathesis-stress model into family therapy through their view of schizophrenia as a disease that is powerfully affected by environmental (family) stress. The goal becomes to reduce stressful "expressed-emotion" in families. Richard Schwartz, by extending systems thinking into the realm of internal process, offers one solution of the issue of whether internal (intrapsychic) or external (interactional) dynamics underlie problems: He sees problems embedded in imbalances at both levels, each affecting the other. Both are important and so therapists can effectively address either.

Pathological Triangles

The double bind theory was a landmark shift from an individual to a systems unit in the analysis of behavior disorder. Current concepts of pathology sometimes refer to individuals—fusion of emotion and intellect, repressed affect, developmental arrest; and sometimes to dyads—fusion in a relationship, mystification, unresolved symbiotic attachment. However, the most sophisticated thinking in the field is triadic.

Pathological triangles are at the heart of several family therapy explanations of behavior disorder. Among these, Bowen's theory is perhaps the most elegant and well known. Bowen explains how when two people are in conflict, the one who experiences the most anxiety will triangle in a third person. This model not only provides a beautiful explanation of systems pathology, but also serves warning to therapists. As long as a therapist remains fused with one party to an emotional conflict, then he or she is part of the problem, not part of the solution.

In psychoanalytic theory, oedipal conflicts are the root of neurosis. Here the triangle is stimulated by family interactions, but formed and maintained in the individual psyche. Mother's tenderness may be seductive and father's jealousy threatening, but the wish to destroy the father and possess the mother is a figment of fantasy. Pathological fixation of this conflict may be caused by developments in the outer space of the family, but the conflict is harbored in the inner space of the mind.

The psychoanalytic model of the individual is that of a divided self at war within. But psychoanalytic family practitioners treat family problems as disorders in relationships. The cause of the problem may be a function of individual personalities, but the result is in the interaction. *Pathological need complementarity* is the core psychoanalytic concept of interlocking pathology of family relationships. A person with a strong need to be submissive, for instance, will marry someone with a strong need to be dominant. These needs are based on early identifications and introjections. The husband who has a sense of himself as a victim has internalized pathogenic introjections that revolve around aggressive conflicts, but his needs are acted out in pathological relationships— that is, his unconscious need for an aggressor will lead him to select a mate who can act this role, allowing him to project his repressed or split-off aggression onto his wife. Divided selves thus become divided spouses.

Structural family theory of disorder is based on triangular configurations where a dysfunctional boundary between two people or subsystems is a reciprocal product of a boundary with a third. Father and son's enmeshment reflects father and mother's disengagement; a single mother's disengagement from her children is the counterpart of her overinvolvement outside the family. Structural family theory also uses the concept of pathological triangles to explain *conflict-detouring triads,* where parents divert their conflict onto a child. Minuchin, Rosman, and Baker (1978) have even demonstrated that physiological changes occur when parents in conflict transfer their stress to a psychosomatic child. Using this model, therapy is designed to disengage the child from the parents' struggle and to help the parents work out their conflicts directly.

Most strategic family therapists work with a dyadic model—one person's symptoms are maintained by others' (taken as a single group) efforts to resolve them. Haley and Selvini Palazzoli, however, use a triangular model in the form of *cross-generational coalitions.* These "perverse triangles," as Haley (1977) calls them, occur when a parent and child, or grandparent and child, collude to form a bastion of covert opposition to another adult. Failure to recognize these cross-generational coalitions dooms to failure any attempt to help parents resolve "their" problems with a symptomatic child. For this reason, behavioral parent training probably won't work when there is significant unrecognized conflict between the parents. Teaching a father how to reward respectful behavior from his son won't get very far if mother subtly reinforces the son's disrespect.

Triangular functioning seems less central to the newer models described in Chapter 11 because they are less focused on the way families create or even maintain problems and more on how to help them out of whatever predicaments they're in.

There's a lot of talk these days about "dysfunctional families" as a source of human unhappiness. Unfortunately, much of this amounts to little more than parent bashing. *We* suffer because of what *they* did: Our mother's drinking, our father's brutish or cold ways—these are the causes of our unhappiness. Perhaps this is an advance on stewing in guilt and shame, but it's a long way from understanding what really goes on in families. One reason for blaming family sorrows on the personal failings of parents is that it's hard, very hard, for the average person to see past individual personalities to the structural patterns that make them a family—a system of interconnected lives governed by strict but unspoken rules. People feel controlled and helpless not because they are victims of parental folly and deceit, but because they don't understand how families work—or how they get stuck, and how to get themselves unstuck.

Family therapists, who do see these connections, have lately gotten further and further away from the idea that families who seek therapy have something wrong with them. Rejecting what they see as the judgmental stance of their predecessors, many family therapists today espouse a more democratic, "nonhierarchical," form of therapy in which clients and therapists are partners in a joint enterprise. Some issues to consider are: What is gained and what is lost by avoiding thinking of families who seek therapy as having something wrong with them? Is there a difference between thinking of families as having something wrong with them versus thinking of them as *doing* something wrong—something that isn't working? How can you distinguish between a compassionate therapist who avoids blaming and one who is so anxious to be liked that he or she doesn't dare confront clients for fear that they might possibly get mad?

GOALS OF THERAPY

The goal of all psychological treatment is to help people change in order to relieve their distress. This is true of individual therapy, group therapy, and family therapy. Why then is so much written about the differing goals of various schools of therapy? Some of it has to do with differing ideas about how people change; some of it merely has to do with alternate vocabularies for describing change. When Bowenians speak of "differentiation of self" and psychoanalytic therapists speak of "increased ego strength," they mean pretty much the same thing.

If we strip away the semantic differences, there are two major dimensions of goals on which the schools of family therapy vary. First, the schools differ with respect to the form of their intermediate goals; they seek change through different aspects of personal and family functioning. Second, the schools differ in terms of how much change they seek. Some are content with symptom resolution, others aspire to transform the whole family system.

The variations in the form of intermediate goals among the systems are based on theoretical differences about which aspects of personal and family functioning it is most necessary to change. One of the goals of experiential family therapy is to help families become more emotionally expressive. Experientialists believe that emotional stagnation is a primary problem, and that increased expressiveness will make people more alive and happy. To a large extent, therefore, the differences in the form of intermediate goals among different schools reflects theoretical differences of opinion about how behavior change is best accomplished. We will discuss these distinctions more fully below in *Conditions for Behavior Change.*

The second difference in goals—how much change—has to do with the way schools differ with respect to their aims about the resolution of presenting problems or the overhauling of family systems. All family therapists are interested in resolving problems and decreasing symptomatology. But they vary along a continuum from being exclusively concerned with symptom resolution to being more concerned with ultimately changing the entire family system. Strategic and behavioral therapists are least concerned with changing the whole system; psychoanalytic and Bowenian therapists are most concerned with systems change. In addition, psychoanalysts and Bowenians are particularly interested in fundamental changes in individual personalities (intrapsychic structural change or differentiation), and they are unique among family therapists in this respect.

The goal of structural family therapy is both symptom resolution and structural change. But the structural change sought has the modest aim of reorganizing that particular part of the family that has become problematic by failing to change to meet changing circumstances. Structural family therapists do not have the more ambitious goal of remaking the whole family. Group, communications, and experiential family therapists also aim midway between symptomatic improvement and systematic family reorganization. Practitioners from these schools focus neither on presenting complaints nor on the overall family system. Instead they pay special attention to discrete processes which they think underlie symptoms: group dynamics, patterns of communication, and emotional expressivity. Improvements in these processes are thought to resolve symptoms and promote growth, but neither symptom resolution alone nor systems change per se is the goal.

In our view, one goal of family therapy must be to resolve the problems that clients come in with. If a family asks for help with a specific problem and the therapist helps them express their feelings better but doesn't help them solve the problem, then he or she has failed the family in an important way. One of the virtues of the behavioral and strategic approaches that focus narrowly on presenting complaints is that they don't fool themselves or their clients about whether or not these problems get solved. Some of the other approaches with grander aspirations run the risk of losing sight of this first responsibility of family therapists. For example, if a mother complains that her small daughter is disobedient and doesn't do well in school, and a therapist bypasses these problems to get to the "real issues," which may be defined as the woman's relationship with her parents or conflicts with her husband, there is a real danger of failing the family. If success is defined as accepting the therapist's point of view and working toward his or her conceptual goal, then therapy becomes a power struggle or an indoctrination. To some extent this happens in all therapies, but it is justified only when achieving the therapist's conceptual goals also meets the family's goals.

The advantage of working toward symptom change is that it's directly responsive to the family's request and eliminates much obfuscation about whether or not therapy is successful. The disadvantage is that working only at the level of symptomatic or symptom-maintaining behavior may produce changes that don't last. This fundamental debate about the effects of symptomatic improvement must ultimately be answered empirically. In the meantime it seems clear that changing symptom-maintaining behavior—even without worrying much about underlying family dynamics—can produce a positive spiral, increasing change that leads to increasingly satisfactory family functioning. On the other hand, there is the danger that symptom resolution will succeed but not last, especially when interventions are designed to effect monadic or dyadic change without taking into account how individuals or pairs are affected by the whole family context.

We don't agree with psychoanalysts who say that without insight into unconscious motivation, behavioral changes won't last, or with Bowenians who say that problems in the nuclear family won't change until relationships with the extended family are repaired. But it does seem that to ensure that symptom resolution will last, successful interventions must take into account triangular patterns of relationships in the nuclear family.

As a final note on goals, problem resolution or cure has been family therapy's trademark, emblematic of the optimism of its practitioners, proud problem solvers. Now, however, by embracing the disease model (Yes, Virginia, there is such a thing as schizophrenia), some family therapists, notably those who practice psychoeducation, advocate coping with serious psychopathology as a worthy goal. This modest but realistic goal has been hard for some family therapists to accept and has generated a great deal of controversy. What appears to be at stake is a question of which is more powerful: family therapy or certain entrenched conditions—some forms of psychopathology, arrested psychodynamics, poverty and despair, or even failures of nerve that make it so very difficult for some people to risk change.

CONDITIONS FOR BEHAVIOR CHANGE

Once it was necessary to contrast family therapy with individual therapy in order to establish family treatment as a distinct and legitimate approach. Family therapists used to emphasize their differences with individual therapists; today they emphasize differences among themselves. The various schools share a consensus about broad principles of change but differ on many specific issues. The core principle of family therapy is treating people in context. What divides the field into competing camps are differences of opinion about how best to bring about change. In this section we will compare and contrast models in terms of action or insight; change in the session or change at home; duration of treatment; resistance; family-therapist relationship; and paradox.

Action or Insight

One of the early distinctions between family therapy and individual therapy had to do with action and insight. Individual therapists stressed intellectual and emotional insight; family therapists stressed action. Although they emphasized action in their writing, many of the techniques of early family therapists were designed to change action through understanding. Actually, since people think, feel, and act, no form of therapy can succeed without affecting all three of these aspects of the human personality. Different approaches may concentrate on different modes of experience, but they inevitably deal with the total—thinking, feeling, and acting—person.

Action and insight are the primary vehicles of change in family therapy. Most family therapists use both mechanisms, but some schools emphasize either action (strategic) or insight (psychoanalytic).

The case for action is based on the observation that people often don't change even though they understand why and how they should. The truth of this is familiar to anyone who has ever tried and failed to lose weight, stop smoking, or spend more time with the kids. Behaviorists make the case for action by pointing out that behavior is often reinforced unwittingly; explanations, they say, don't change behavior, reinforcement does. Parents are taught to change their children's behavior by rewarding desired actions and ignoring or punishing undesirable ones. Likewise, married couples are taught that actions speak louder than words; it doesn't matter so much what you tell your spouse, what matters is that you reward pleasing behavior. Behavioral family therapists don't, however, practice what they preach. They tell clients that reinforcement is the way to change behavior, but they rely on simple explanations to bring about those changes. Action may be the message, but understanding is the medium.

Like behaviorists, strategic therapists focus on behavior, and aren't concerned with insight. However, they differ from behaviorists in one important respect—behaviorists rely on the power of rational instruction; strategic therapists eschew understanding altogether. They don't believe in insight, and they don't believe in teaching; instead they believe that the way to change behavior is through manipulation. They box stuck families into a corner, from which the only way out is to become unstuck.

The case for insight is based on the belief that if people understand themselves they will be free to act in their own best interest. Psychoanalytic clinicians believe that people are blind to their real motives and feelings. Without insight into hidden conflicts, they believe, action is self-defeating, even dangerous. Unexamined action can be self-defeating because symptomatic relief without insight fosters denial and repression; it can be dangerous if repressed impulses are acted on precipitously.

Many actions are regarded in the psychoanalytic school as symptomatic—that is, such actions are protective devices designed to bind the anxiety that signals impulses whose expression might lead to punishment. Only by understanding their impulses and the dangers involved in expressing them can people change. Moreover, since the important conflicts are unconscious, only methodical interpretation of the unconscious brings about lasting change. In psychoanalytic therapy, unanalyzed action initiated by families is called "acting out"; unanalyzed action initiated by therapists is considered manipulation. Insight can only be achieved if families verbalize their thoughts and feelings rather than act on them, and therapists interpret unconscious meaning rather than suggest or manipulate action.

Discussions of insight are often divisive, because insight is a buzzword; proponents extol it, opponents ridicule it. Advocates of insight use the concept as a pseudomedical idea—insight, like medicine, cures. Actually, insight doesn't cure anything; it's something through which cure occurs. To say that a family acquires insight means that family members learn what they intend by their actions, and also what they want from each other; how they act on their insight is up to them.

Do people change when they are propelled into action, or when they develop understanding? Both. People change for a variety of reasons; the same person may change one day because of being forced into action, and another day because of some new understanding. Some individuals may be more or less responsive to either action or insight, and these people will be more or less successful in therapies that emphasize insight or action. People change when they are ready *and* when the right stimulus is applied.

In contrast to the polar positions taken by these three schools, the other systems work with action *and* insight. In structural family therapy, change is initiated in action and then supported by understanding. According to Minuchin (Minuchin & Nichols, 1993), family structure and family beliefs support and reinforce each other; the only way to achieve lasting change is to challenge both. Action comes first because it leads to new experiences which make insight possible. In Bowenian theory, interventions also affect both levels—action and understanding—but the order of effect is reversed. Bowenians begin by calming people down, so that they'll be receptive to learning extended family systems theory. Once family members are armed with this new understanding, they are sent into action—back to their families to reestablish ties based on differentiation of self.

The Milan model and the later work of Cecchin, Boscolo, and Hoffman have elevated the importance of working with systems of meaning. Thus, systems-oriented family therapists are becoming less tied to behavioral analyses and action-oriented interventions. Further taking into account the "externalizing" technique of Michael White and David Epston, the therapy as conversation model of the late Harry Goolishian and Harlene Anderson, the popularity of social constructionism, and the reemergence of psychodynamic influence (as well as the revival of hermeneutics), the trend in the field is definitely away from action and toward if not insight, at least meaning.

A growing number of family therapists would reject the notion of insight as tied to outmoded beliefs in objective truth. Good postmodernists, they would prefer the idea of "narrative reconstruction" to "insight" and would prefer to see the therapist as helping clients construct newer and more hopeful stories rather than excavating some buried truth. However, regardless of whether we speak in declassé terms of insight or in more contemporary terms of coconstructing reality, the fact is that the contemporary interest in narrative theory and the popularity of the reflecting team (in which postsession discussions take place in the presence of the clients) are symptoms of family therapy's drift from action to insight (or meaning, if you prefer).

This contemporary emphasis on meaning is especially attractive to therapists who favor a collaborative approach, but while the individuals who make up families are certainly feeling, thinking, and acting beings, we wonder if what ties them most strongly together in creating and maintaining problems isn't that their actions are coordinated and interlocking. Helping them reconsider the way they perceive their dilemmas may help them see new ways to address them. But often, of course, seeing what we need to do somehow doesn't quite get us to do it. Perhaps working with meaning *as well as* action would be a better idea for family therapists than trading in one for the other.

Change in the Session or Change at Home

All family therapists aim to transform interactions among family members, but they differ as to where they expect these transformations to take place. In structural family therapy, transformation occurs in the session, in the present, and in the presence of the therapist. Action is brought into the consulting room in the form of enactments, and change is sought then and there. The same is true in experiential family therapy; emotional breakthrough comes in session, in response to the therapist's provocations. In both of these therapies changes wrought in the session are believed to transfer to the family's life outside.

Other family therapists promote change that they expect to occur not in the session but at home. Strategic therapists are relatively inactive in the session. They use sessions to gather information to formulate interventions, which they often deliver in the form of directives to be carried out at home. Bowenians also plan changes that will take place outside the consultation room. Family members are encouraged to return to their families of origin, and coached to respond in new and more productive ways. Most forms of behavior therapy are planned to influence interactions that take place at home. Parents are sent home to reward their children's positive behavior, and spouses are taught to please each other, or to have sex without anxiety. Some behaviorists, however, supervise parents playing with and disciplining their children in the session, usually behind a one-way mirror.

The goal of family therapy is to solve problems so that people can live better. The ultimate test of success comes at home, after therapy is over. But since therapists take on the job of creating change, utilizing the context of the session—first to promote interactions and then to observe and change them— gives maximum impact. Just as live supervision is preferred because it teaches therapists what to do while they do it, so supervised change in the session seems more effective than unsupervised change at home.

Duration of Treatment

Most family therapy is brief. (With managed care it may get briefer.) Families generally seek treatment at a time of crisis and are motivated only to solve their immediate problems. Usually they only reluctantly agree to come in as a family, and generally they aren't interested in personal growth. Because family therapists only have the leverage necessary to work with families as long as they're in distress, family treatment tends to be pragmatic and symptom-focused. This is especially true in strategic family therapy.

Some strategic therapists limit treatment to about ten sessions, and announce this at the outset as a means of motivating families to work for change. Haley (1976) says that change occurs in stages and he plans therapy accordingly, but many strategic therapists believe that change occurs in sudden shifts (Hoffman, 1981; Rabkin, 1977). Strategists don't reason with families, they give them a sudden jolt. These jolts—usually paradoxical directives—provoke families stuck in dysfunctional homeostasis to change with or without their willing cooperation. Success in this operation requires that lasting change be achieved on the impact of a few interventions, and that it can occur without any understanding on the part of the family.

Other schools of family therapy believe that lasting change requires understanding, and that it occurs gradually over the course of several months of treatment. The duration of therapy is related both to the goal of treatment and to the question of who's considered responsible for change. Strategists and behaviorists limit their goals to solving the presenting problem, and they assume responsibility for change. Psychoanalytic and experiential practitioners seek profound personal changes in their clients, and they place the responsibility for change with the clients. These therapists take responsibility only for providing a therapeutic atmosphere in their sessions; change is up to the clients.

Structural family therapists are interested in solving problems, not in personal growth; however, the problems they're most concerned with are structural. They believe that it's necessary to restructure dysfunctional families for lasting benefit to occur. MRI therapists, on the other hand, say that it's not necessary to change the whole family; all that's required is to interrupt the vicious feedback cycles that maintain present symptoms.

Bowenian therapy can be a lifelong enterprise. The goal is personal growth *and* change in the entire extended family system. Since change is the responsibility of the client and occurs during visits home, the process may take years.

If the family's goal is growth and enrichment, then therapy must be protracted; but if the goal is relief, then therapy should be brief. Problems arise when therapists try to hold on to families. The motives for doing so are many and complex, including pursuit of utopian goals, money, guilt over not having done more, and unresolved emotional attachments. For some mental health professionals, being in therapy is a way of life. These therapists may convey exaggerated expectations of improvement, with the result that family members are bound to suffer disillusionment. Fortunately, therapy is expensive, time-consuming, and stressful; this puts pressure on families to get it over with and get on with their lives.

In brief prescriptive therapy, termination is initiated by the therapist when there is a change in the presenting problem or when the agreed-on number of sessions is up. With compliant families, strategic therapists acknowledge progress and give the family credit for success; with defiant families, they express skepticism and predict a relapse. (The idea of giving families credit for success may have a hollow ring when families have no idea what they did to bring it about.) In longer, elicitory therapy, termination is initiated by the clients, either directly or indirectly. It's time to consider termination when family living becomes more enjoyable, when family members run out of things to talk about in therapy, or when they begin to complain about competing obligations. Part of successful termination is helping families accept the inevitability of the normal problems of everyday life. Successful therapy partly changes behavior and partly changes expectations. Therapy *can* go on forever, but by keeping it brief, therapists prevent families from becoming dependent on outside help and teach them to rely on their own resources.

Resistance

Families are notoriously resistant to change. In addition to the combined resistances of individual family members, the system itself resists change. Where there is resistance, therapy cannot succeed without overcoming it. Behavior therapists minimize the importance of resistance and succeed only where their clients are willing and able to follow instructions. The other schools of family therapy consider resistance the major obstacle to treatment and have devised various ways to overcome it.

Psychoanalytic practitioners believe that resistance is motivated by unconscious defenses, which first must be made manifest and then resolved through interpretation. This is an intrapsychic model but it doesn't ignore conscious and interactional resistances. Instead, psychoanalytic therapists believe that interactional problems—among family members or between the family and therapist—have their roots in unconscious resistance to basic drives. Experiential therapists have a similar model; they see resistance to emotional expression, and they blast away at it using personal confrontations and emotive exercises. Experientialists believe that breaching defenses automatically releases natural, healthy strivings; change occurs from the inside out.

People do avoid knowing painful things about themselves, but even more strenuously conceal painful truths from other members of the family. It's one thing to tell a therapist that you're angry at your spouse; it's another thing to tell your spouse. Therapies that are more interactive and systems-oriented focus on conscious withholding and on the system's resistance to changing its rules.

Minuchin's solution to the problem of resistance is straightforward: he wins families over by joining and accommodating to them. This gives him the leverage to utilize powerful confrontations designed to restructure the pattern of family interactions. Resistance is seen as a product of the interaction between therapist and family; change is accomplished by alternately challenging the family and then rejoining them to repair breaches in the therapeutic relationship.

Strategic family therapists expect resistance, but avoid power struggles by going with resistance rather than opposing it head on. They assume that families don't understand their own behavior and will oppose attempts to change it. In response, some strategic practitioners try to gain control by provoking families to resist. Once the family begins to respond in opposition to therapeutic directives, the therapist can manipulate them to change in the desired direction. In practice, this can result in either doggedly pursuing reverse psychology, or in a creative form of therapeutic jujitsu. The creative response to resistance is illustrated by the Milan group, who, for example, routinely ask a third person to describe interactions between two others ("gossip in the presence") in order to minimize defensiveness.

Steve de Shazer denies the existence of resistance, saying that it is the family's way of cooperating and that it's up to the therapist to learn from it. Richard Schwartz sees resistance as a proper reaction of protective parts of family members whose job it is to not allow anyone into the family until it's clear that the person knows what he or she is doing and won't harm or humiliate them. Schwartz goes to great lengths to respect and reassure those protective parts.

Finally, under the heading of resistance, we should consider the phenomenon of *induction*. Induction is what happens when a therapist is drawn into the family system—and abides by its rules. When this happens the therapist becomes just another member of the family; this may stabilize the system, but it reduces therapeutic mobility and prevents systems change. A therapist is inducted when he or she is sucked in to fulfill a missing family function—disciplining children when the parents can't or don't, sympathizing with a husband whose wife does not, or coaxing a reticent teenager to open up to the therapist instead of to his parents; or when the therapist does what everybody else does—avoids challenging the fragile patriarch, minimizes a drinking problem, or sees a mother as just a nag.

Minuchin describes the danger of induction and teaches structural family therapists how to recognize and avoid it (Minuchin & Fishman, 1981). Part of the value of live supervision is helping to avoid induction. Working with colleagues helps to avoid induction, either with cotherapists (Whitaker) or with a team (Selvini Palazzoli). Bowenians avoid induction by remaining calm and objective; they stay in contact but keep themselves detriangled and outside of the family projection system.

Induction is so subtle that it's hard to see, so seductive that it's hard to resist. As helpers and healers, therapists are especially prone to take over for people, doing for them what they don't do for themselves. But taking over—being inducted—precludes real change. As long as families have someone to do for them, they don't have to learn to do for themselves.

Rigidly stuck families are run by their fears, and therapists, eager to be liked, are vulnerable to those fears. Families quickly teach therapists what's safe and what's threatening: "Don't look in there"; "Don't ask *him* about *that*." The art of therapy is understanding and sympathizing with those fears, but avoiding induction enough to be able to challenge them. As in so many things, progress takes doing what you're afraid to do.

Family-Therapist Relationship

Individual psychotherapists have argued that the fundamental pillar of treatment is the patient-therapist relationship. Carl Rogers even claimed that certain qualities of the therapist were necessary and sufficient to produce successful outcomes. Family therapists tend to be more technically oriented and they de-emphasize the therapeutic relationship in their writing. Systems thinkers run the risk of losing sight of the individuals that make up the system. Furthermore, whether or not they consider the human qualities of the participants in therapy, all family therapists have an implicit model of patient-therapist relationship.

The variations of patient-therapist relationships—including subject-object, interpersonal, phenomenological, and encounter—are a function of individual practitioners, but they also tend to characterize different schools of treatment. The hallmark of the *subject-object* paradigm is the therapist's objective observation of the family. In this model the therapist is a natural scientist, who makes observations and carefully tailored interventions. Personal and emotional reactions are regarded as confounding intrusions. The assumption is that therapist and family are separate entities. This is not an attractive description, and few family therapists would describe themselves in these terms; nevertheless there are aspects of behavioral, psychoanalytic, Bowenian, strategic, and structural therapy that fit this model.

Behavioral family therapists think of themselves as objective observers and rational scientists; without a doubt they fit this paradigm. Psychoanalytic practitioners operate within this model when they think of themselves as neutral and objective, as blank screens upon whom patients project their distorted perceptions and fantasies. Although many psychoanalytic clinicians still maintain this assumption, it is not consistent with the best and latest psychoanalytic thinking. No therapist is neutral and objective; the blank screen is a metaphor and a myth. Therapists reveal themselves in a thousand ways, and patients' reactions are always influenced by the reality of the therapist's behavior as well as by personal distortions. Bowenians think of themselves as objective, even scientific, observers who act as teachers or coaches to help clients overcome their emotionality. The strategic school has produced some of the most sophisticated concepts of the intricate relationship between therapists and families (Hoffman, 1981). The subject-object paradigm is not a basic feature of this school, but it creeps in when therapists think of themselves as outsiders, locked in contest with families. The adversarial stance of some therapists in this system assumes that the therapist and family can and should be separate. The structural emphasis on mapping a family's structure can lead some therapists to see themselves as simply mapmakers, rather than mapmakers who are also part of the map.

The *interpersonal* paradigm treats therapy as a two-way interaction. This model acknowledges that therapists and families are related and that they constantly influence each other. Psychoanalytic clinicians employ this idea in their concepts of transference/countertransference, projective identification, and introjection; the model of influence here is interactive and transversal. In fact, this paradigm describes most family therapists most of the time. However, the constructivist movement in the 1980s represents an even more explicit attempt on the part of some systems-oriented family therapists to include the effects of the therapist's presuppositions and behavior on the families they treat.

The *phenomenological* paradigm is one in which the therapist tries to adopt the patient's frame of reference. It is what happens when psychoanalytic practitioners try to identify with their patients, when structuralists join families, and when therapists of any persuasion try to understand and accept that families are doing the best they can. Stanton and Todd (1981) use this concept in their technique of "ascribing noble intention" to families. This tactic fits the phenomenological model when it's done sincerely; it doesn't when it's used merely as a strategic ploy—for example, in most reframing. Selvini Palazzoli's positive connotation is far more effective when done with sincerity. (Although the idea of positive connotation seems supportive, it was often experienced as patronizing, especially when delivered by the same therapists who held secret discussions behind the one-way mirror.) Boszormenyi-Nagy's recognition that symptomatic behavior is an act of unconscious loyalty to the family is definitely sincere. Experientialists speak of accepting the patient's frame of reference, but sometimes they follow an encounter paradigm, in which they loudly proclaim their own honest feelings and challenge families to do the same.

The *encounter* paradigm is an encounter between the therapist's total personality and the client's. It involves mutual sharing, honesty, openness, and self-disclosure, and its use in family therapy is primarily restricted to experientialists. During an encounter the therapist becomes a full participant, which is something that most family therapists don't let happen. However, it is possible to let yourself go and confront a family if you do so with clear therapeutic indications and not simply because you feel like it. Minuchin engages in genuine encounters, but he shows good timing and the ability to maintain his professional objectivity. Honest encounters are perhaps useful when done occasionally, for a good reason, and by someone with enough experience and insight to keep from losing perspective.

The 1980s brought a shift in the therapist-family relationship. The field began moving away from the directive, hierarchical, adversarial position of many of the original models, and toward a *collaborative* relationship, exemplified by the models described in Chapter 11. In a collaborative relationship, the therapist not only empathizes with a family's predicament, but also empowers them to use their own strengths to find solutions, from a position of partnership, rather than as The Great Expert.

Paradox

The use of paradox is a central and controversial topic in family therapy. Paradoxical instructions encourage rather than attack symptoms and objectionable behavior. They are designed to block or change dysfunctional sequences using indirect and seemingly illogical means. Paradoxical interventions are used instead of direct attempts to introduce change by therapists who assume that families cannot or will not comply with advice or persuasion.

Paradoxical interventions were associated with the newer strategic forms of therapy in the 1970s, but they weren't confined to this group and they weren't new. Behavior therapists have used paradoxical interventions for over fifty years, as negative practice or conditioned inhibition. Dunlap (1928) advised patients who wished to get rid of certain undesirable habits to practice them. He called this "negative practice," and reported success with tics, typing errors, stammering, and thumb sucking. Learning theorists believe that negative practice works through "conditioned inhibition," which has been described as fatigue induced by mass practice (Kendrick, 1960).

Frankl's (1960) "paradoxical intention" was an early version of what communications family therapists later called "prescribing the symptom." In all of these applications the idea is the same: if you deliberately practice a symptom, it will go away. Following Milton Erickson's influence, the MRI group reasoned that since family pathology was a function of paradoxical communication, it could be cured by "therapeutic double binds." According to Haley (1963) the person with a symptom gains power by controlling those around him or her. He interpreted the effectiveness of paradoxical directives as a result of the therapist's gaining control over the symptoms by ordering them to occur on command. If symptoms are a tactic in interpersonal power struggles, the therapist can take control by prescribing them. Rabkin (1977) suggests that while some symptoms serve such devious purposes, others are simply habits reinforced by trying too hard not to do something and anxiously worrying about it. For example, worrying about being self-confident, and trying too hard to act it, may cause a lack of self-confidence. When a therapist prescribes the symptom, however, the patient may stop worrying about the problem and family members may stop trying to solve it.

Strategic therapists use paradox in two ways: as directives and as reframing, which is really interpretation and subtle direction. Reframing not only gives a new label for behavior, it also acts as an indirect message to change. Strategic therapists think of symptoms as part of self-reinforcing sequences; symptoms are maintained by attempts to suppress them. Paradoxical directives provoke change by altering the attempted solutions and thus resolving the symptoms. Hoffman (1981) cites an example of a wife whose constant jealous questioning of her husband only reinforced his reticence, which in turn reinforced her jealousy. The strategy to disrupt this sequence was to use a paradoxical directive to the wife to redouble her jealous questioning. The expected result was that the wife rebelled against the task and so solved the problem. Strategic therapists claim that it is usually unnecessary to look at the context or history of a symptom in order to resolve it.

There are two problems with provoking people to change by telling them not to. The first is obvious. This paradoxical device implies that families are oppositional; many are, but many are not. The second problem is that intervening only around a symptom neglects the broader family context. Ignoring the family context is like going to London without an umbrella; you won't get wet unless it rains. Symptoms may be maintained by attempts to suppress them, but many symptoms also serve a purpose in the family structure. Among strategic therapists, Haley and Selvini Palazzoli are the most aware that symptoms sometimes fit into the larger field of the family. The key is to be flexible, not to see symptoms as always or never playing a role in the family's psychic economy.

Minuchin's structural concepts have been carried into the strategic camp by Jay Haley, whose approach is a hybrid of structural and strategic methods. Haley (1976) recognizes that problem-maintaining sequences may be rooted in the family's dysfunctional structure. He doesn't advocate using paradoxical directives with highly disturbed families (Haley, 1980) and has become more concerned with shifting triadic sequences and with establishing appropriate hierarchical structure in families.

Selvini Palazzoli and her Milan cohorts relied on paradox as an explanatory concept and a treatment device, but they also looked beyond symptom-maintaining sequences to the context of the whole family. Since disturbed families sustain their pathology through an intricate network of paradoxes, Selvini Palazzoli (1978) reasoned that the best way to break these pathological networks was through therapeutic counterparadox. The Milan group not only prescribed the problem behavior but also the whole configuration of interactions surrounding it. Usually this took the combined form of "positive connotation" and assignment of a paradoxical family ritual. In this way, they tried to deal with the problem and its larger context at the same time. This seems to us the best and most appropriate use of therapeutic paradox. Best, because it deals with the family structure as well as with the symptom; and most appropriate, because the Milan group works with severely disturbed families. Paradoxical interventions keep the therapist distanced from the family; it's not a technique for therapists who need to be liked, but it does help to avoid the suction of families with seriously disturbed members.

Paradoxical directives can break a family pattern, but why should such changes last? They will if the change also effects a change in the total family structure. Many examples of paradoxical instructions are insulting. (Madanes's [1980] pretend techniques avoid this insulting quality, and allow the therapist to avoid emotionally distancing himself or herself from the family.) Hoffman (1981), for example, describes a therapist telling a depressed wife to become more subservient to her husband. Not surprisingly, the woman rebels to defy the therapist. According to Hoffman, this technique worked because the paradoxical directive unbalanced a complementary equilibrium, which then became symmetrical. Previously, the husband and wife were balanced in a relationship where he was one-up and she was one-down. By trying to push her further down, the therapist provoked a rebellion and the couple then established a relationship based on equality. Why that should happen is not at all clear. Why don't they simply reestablish the same complementarity they had before?

Paradoxical techniques are so appealing that they seem like a magic solution to entrenched family problems. Actually, the way to resolve problems is to understand their context. In structural terms, this means understanding the family's dysfunctional structure; in systemic terms, it means understanding the circular patterns and relational context. The real key is the understanding; whether the therapist intervenes directly or indirectly is far less important. Indeed, it's possible to make paradoxical remarks in the form of a warm and sincere skepticism about a rigid family's ability to change. "I don't know, you've been operating this way for a long time, perhaps you won't be able to change." The family who hears such a comment may try to change or may not; either way they're likely to feel understood, not manipulated.

TECHNIQUES

Comparing techniques by reading about them is difficult because clinicians often describe techniques as abstract concepts rather than as concrete actions. Modeling, for example, is a concept invoked by behaviorists for telling or showing parents how to speak to their children; by experientialists for talking about their own feelings; and by structural family therapists for speaking sharply to children who interrupt their parents. Are all these techniques modeling? Actually, modeling isn't a technique; it's a hypothetical construct to explain how people learn through observation. Often, techniques are described in the jargon of a particular school—restructuring, therapeutic double binds, differentiating—and it's not clear precisely what is meant. In this section, we will treat issues of technique as a series of practical questions about how to conduct therapy, and we will describe techniques as specific actions.

Much of what's written about the techniques of family therapy is about the middle game of treatment. This reflects a tendency among family practitioners to differentiate among themselves by describing their definitive and unique interventions; and it caters to the reader's wish to get on with therapy and get to the problem-solving part. Families come for treatment anxious and eager for direction, and they communicate their anxiety to the therapist. "Help us!" they say, and in so doing they pass on some of their anxiety to the practitioner. Because they are the most anxious, young therapists are the most eager to discharge it by acting—by doing something definitive. Although family therapy is a therapy of action, the way must be prepared for action to be effective. Before a therapist can know what's wrong with a particular family and gain the leverage to change it, he or she must make emotional contact and establish a therapeutic climate within which the family will be receptive to treatment. This involves such practical considerations as: who to invite to the first session, what kind of treatment team to use, how to enter into the family system, what sort of therapeutic stance to take, and how to assess the family.

Who to Invite

Most family therapists invite everyone living under the same roof to the first session. This reflects the belief that everyone in the family is involved in any problem (or at least can contribute to its solution), even if it is manifest in only one member. It also reflects the principle that in order to change the presenting symptom it's necessary to change the family interactions that create or sustain it.

Inviting the whole family to the first consultation is a powerful restructuring and reframing move in and of itself. Whether or not it is explicitly stated or openly acknowledged, the presence of the whole family in the assessment of a psychological problem implies that they are all involved. In many cases, the act of assembling the entire family to discuss a problem is the single most effective step toward solving it. Most experienced family practitioners are convinced of this, and they don't waste much time worrying about how to get the family in. They are positive that it is essential; they know that's how they work; and so they calmly state this to the family. When the request that the whole family attend at least once is put in a straightforward, matter-of-fact way to families, most comply. Occasionally it's necessary to explain that the therapist would like everyone to attend in order to get all their points of view, but if the therapist is comfortable with the idea, most families will also accept it.

Sometimes, however, one or two family members won't attend the consultation. When this happens most family therapists work with whoever is available. In such cases the failure of key family members to participate in treatment seems like a problem; it may be *the* problem. If a father, for instance, refuses to participate in a therapy designed to help his daughter overcome her shyness, his absence from treatment is a sign that his unavailability may be a significant element in the problem. Working with the mother and children to get him involved may be the most important step in solving the presenting problem. On this matter, sensitive family therapists are like psychoanalysts who consider resistance not as an impediment to treatment, but as the object of treatment.

Members of some schools of family therapy rarely insist on seeing the entire family. Practitioners of behavioral parent training focus on teaching the parents—usually the mother—how to deal with the identified patient. For this reason, some invite only the parents and child to the first session, while others (Gordon & Davidson, 1981) recommend interviewing both parents in the child's absence. Strategic family therapists vary in whom they include in the first session. Haley (1976) recommends seeing the whole family, but many of his MRI colleagues will see individuals, parents, or couples alone as the situation seems to require. This determination is based on who in the family is "the customer"—who asks for help and who seems to be unhappy enough to do something about the problems.

Bowenian therapists usually work with individuals or couples. If a child is presented as the problem, members of this school see the parents; if a couple complains of marital problems, Bowenian therapists will see them together; and if only one person is willing to attend, the Bowenian therapist will see that person.

Finally, most family therapists (whether they specialize in couples therapy or not) will see a marital couple without their children if the couple complains of problems in their relationship. This is not, however, universally true. Structural, experiential, and psychoanalytic therapists often ask that the children attend the first session, and exclude them only if and when the couple needs to discuss private matters, such as their sexual relationship. Milan therapists often find they get the most useful information from family members who are most peripherally involved, because they can speak the most openly.

Instead of seeing less than the whole family, some therapists insist on seeing more. Network therapists convene large groups of family and friends; some therapists routinely try to include grandparents. Inviting members of the extended family is a practice that cuts across the different schools. Many family therapists invite grandparents if they live in the household or if they seem particularly involved; some—for example, Whitaker and Selvini Palazzoli—invite grandparents as a matter of course. Another variant on the composition of therapy is seeing several families or couples together in a group. We have some reservations about the use of this procedure. Group therapy with individuals who are strangers is a useful method because it creates a naturalistic imitation of life. In family therapy there is no need to imitate life;

convening the family brings life into the treatment room. However, group therapy with couples and families can be useful after they have made progress on overcoming their difficulties—in the focused way that private therapy allows. Then, meeting with other families or couples can be useful by helping them see how others solve similar problems. Sometimes it's easier to learn something when you're watching than when you're on the hot seat.

Although each of these variations on who is initially invited into treatment is supported by a rationale, we believe that the best practice is to include all members of the same household in the initial meeting. Later there may be good reasons for meeting with a subset of the family, but at the outset it's best to see everyone. (Encouraging everyone in the family to attend doesn't, however, mean that it's necessary or useful to convert them to a family therapy point of view. In fact, it may not even be a good idea for therapists to call what they do "family therapy," a term that unnecessarily advertises what many families aren't ready to accept.) Sometimes deviations from this format may be due more to anxiety than to good clinical judgment. Families are anxious about meeting together and airing their problems, and so, naturally, many are reluctant to come as a whole group. This is understandable, and should be dealt with calmly by insisting that everyone attend. Therapists, too, are anxious about convening families, particularly when the family indicates that one of its members doesn't want to come. The therapist's anxiety is sometimes the real reason for meeting with less than the whole family; in other words, some of the variations in composition of family meetings are probably due more to countertransference than to sound principles of family treatment.

There are times when it makes sense to work with a subset of the family—when, absolutely, only some will attend, or when the therapist thinks some people should be blocked. The main thing is not to be pressured into such a decision, and certainly not to drift into it without thinking.

Treatment Team

Family therapists frequently work in groups, either with a cotherapist or with a team of observers. Family interactions are so complex that it is difficult for one person working alone to see all that goes on. Moreover, the emotional pull on therapists who work with families is so strong that it's easy to be drawn in, to take sides, and to lose balance and objectivity. Working with colleagues helps because it provides additional observations and makes any loss of perspective obvious. In general, cotherapy seems to be favored by those schools of family therapy that emphasize intense emotional involvement (especially the experiential school); observation teams are favored by those schools that emphasize tactical planning (strategic, Milan), or who train therapists through live supervision (structural).

Whitaker has taken a strong position in favor of cotherapy; Minuchin and Haley take the opposite point of view. Whitaker's brand of experiential therapy is intensely personal and interactive. Because of this, he advocates (Whitaker & Keith, 1981) using cotherapists to counterbalance one another; while one is actively involved in a freewheeling interchange with the family, the other acts to limit partiality and to counteract the intrusion of counter-transference-based interventions.

Minuchin and Haley have both argued that a solo therapist is more able to act decisively and is therefore preferable to cotherapists. Haley's position is consistent with his directive style, and it is shared by most strategic therapists (with the notable exception of the original Milan therapists who worked in mixed-gender teams of cotherapists). Minuchin, on the other hand, is controlling but less central and directive than most strategic therapists. His goal is to change families by manipulating their interactions in the session. To this end he uses family members as cotherapists. If a small child is shy, Minuchin will prod someone in the family to draw the child out; if a teenager is disobedient, Minuchin will goad the parents to become disciplinarians. By using family members as cotherapists, structural family practitioners avoid being induced to take over a function that is missing in the family.

None of the other schools of family therapy takes as clear a stand about cotherapy. Those who advocate cotherapy teams frequently cite the desire to provide male and female role models or advocates; this is especially true for sex therapists. Psychoanalytic therapists emphasize privacy and tend to work alone, as do Bowenian therapists. Network therapists work in teams of four or more simply as a matter of practical necessity, since they have to manage large groups. Behavioral therapists tend to work in cotherapy pairs while they are graduate students, and then work alone after they finish their training.

Most uses of cotherapy are probably based on economic and teaching considerations. In training settings, where there are more trainees than families, cotherapy may be a way to give everyone a chance to act as therapist. Beginners are often asked to work together as a way of helping each other. Although having a cotherapist may ease a beginner's initial anxiety, it can lead to confusion about who is in charge and where to go.

A solution favored by many family clinicians is to work alone backed up by a team of observers behind a one-way mirror. For research and training this method is invaluable; for everyday clinical practice it's a useful adjunct to the therapist's power of observation. Teams of observers are most commonly used by structural, Milan, and strategic therapists; the observers comment after a session is over, and also may enter or consult while the session is in progress. This is done programatically by the MRI group and by the Milan Associates. The advantage of this format is that observers can provide additional information, advice, and feedback. By contacting the family either by entering and speaking directly to them, or by sending a message through the therapist, observers can say something provocative or critical without the therapist's having to share responsibility for their statements. The use of the reflecting team makes this whole process more open, more collaborative, and—hopefully—more constructive.

The use of videotape adds another dimension to the treatment team. It enhances the observers' ability to see small movements and repetitive patterns, and it enables the therapist to observe himself or herself interacting with the family. Videotaping equipment is expensive and not usually found outside of training clinics; its use is thus more an economic than a theoretical or technical issue. The same is true of one-way mirrors, observers, and cotherapists, which are usually used more often in clinics and training centers than in private practice. Cotherapy is, however, not uncommon among private practitioners, and its use may be partly a way of assuaging loneliness. To some extent, then, cotherapy is a little like a marriage: it works well if the partners are well matched and flexible, but if they aren't, it can be a disaster.

Entering the Family System

Family clinicians think of the family in terms of a system—a collection of parts interacting as a single entity. Whether they realize it or not, therapists themselves are part of a larger system, one that includes the family and the therapist. This is true for therapists who keep their emotional distance (Bowenian, behavioral) as well as for those who become emotionally involved (experiential). All schools of family therapy have a more or less consistent style of making contact with families and of maintaining a particular therapeutic stance.

In structural family therapy the process of entering families is considered a critical determinant of therapeutic success and it has been described more fully by this school than by any other. Minuchin (1974) uses the terms *joining* and *accommodation* to describe how the therapist relates to a family and adjusts to accept the family's organization and style. Most families come to treatment anxious and mistrustful; they expect their viewpoint to be challenged, and they expect to be blamed for causing their own problems. Fearing criticism and worried about having to change, they are set to resist. Recognizing this, structural family clinicians begin by trying to put the family at ease: they greet each member of the family separately; ask each for his or her point of view; and accept what they have to offer, even if at first it is only angry silence. "Okay, right now you're angry and don't want to talk."

The restructuring moves that come later—often as dramatic and forceful confrontations—require a great deal of leverage; this is achieved by joining. From a structural point of view, some of the other schools that emphasize the resistant properties of families (especially the strategic school) probably do an inadequate job of joining. In addition to joining, therapists gain leverage by establishing their status as experts. Minuchin doesn't emphasize this point in writing, but when he introduces himself as Director of the Clinic he immediately establishes himself as an expert and a figure of authority. Not all therapists have impressive titles, but most make some effort to establish themselves as authorities, whether by hanging diplomas on the wall or by demonstrating competence through their actions.

Among strategic therapists, Haley has written the most about the process of entering the family system. His position (Haley, 1976) is similar to Minuchin's; he describes the therapist as a host who must make the family comfortable and put them at ease, while at the same time maintaining a businesslike demeanor. He also uses the idea of accommodating to the family's organization by suggesting that therapists speak first to the parents; but his recommendation that the less-involved parent be addressed first is not consistent with accommodating, and it is the first clue to Haley's stance as a therapist.

Like most strategic therapists, Haley is an expert manipulator. Members of this school relate to families from an emotionally distant position; they don't say what they really think and feel, but speak for a calculated effect—depending on the nature of resistance encountered. Whether they take a one-up or one-down position, their stance is that of experts who coolly assess family problems and prescribe solutions. Perhaps the best illustration of this stance is the way the Milan Associates consulted with their observers and returned to present the family with a written prescription. Members of the MRI group often adopt a one-down position; they demonstrate humility, confusion, and pessimism in order to avoid provoking resistance with optimistic pressure to change. To be successful with this strategy, therapists must be able to forgo the need to look good or be seen as in command.

In sharp contrast to the strategic approach, experiential family therapists enter fully into emotional life of the family and work from a stance that is open and close. Experientialists begin by greeting families and getting acquainted. In the process, they are likely to speak of their own feelings and attitudes and to develop a warm, empathic relationship. Such intimate emotional engagement makes it difficult to be objective; it's hard to understand the patterns in the whole family system when you're actively engaged in emotional dialogues with individual family members. This is one of the reasons why Whitaker insists on working with a cotherapist.

Psychoanalytic practitioners scrupulously refrain from active involvement with their clients. They do so by design, to avoid directing or becoming actors in a drama that they believe should unfold spontaneously. In psychoanalytic psychotherapy the therapist's stance is the most important ingredient in the method. Not interpretation, not analysis of the unconscious, but silent observation is the key to getting at hidden issues in the family.

The father of psychoanalytic family therapy, the late Nathan Ackerman, was an exception; he engaged in active dialogue with families, aggressively confronting them, "tickling their defenses," and even sharing some of his own feelings. He did so in part because he was more of a psychoanalyst inventing family therapy than a practitioner of psychoanalytic therapy with families. He followed the dictates of his own personality as much as he did his training. Perhaps this is a good place to make the point that the way therapists relate to families—whether they are more or less active, more or less emotionally close—reflects their personal styles and preferences as well as the stance favored by the systems they follow. All therapists learn that using an approach that is congenial to personal style avoids unnecessary conflict. It's also true, however, that practitioners within the various schools tend to have similar stances.

Bowenian therapists take a position midway between the emotional intimacy of experientialists and the controlled technical mastery of strategists. Their byword is objectivity; their goal is to make contact with families but to remain detriangled. Learning is thought to occur in a calm atmosphere, so the Bowenian therapist tries to reduce anxiety and create a climate of rational understanding. He or she begins by inquiring about the symptoms and their clinical course. Once this is done the therapist begins to act as a teacher, explaining family systems theory, and as a coach, encouraging family members to make contact with the rest of the family and to work toward defining a self.

Behavioral therapists take over in the role of expert. Their stance is that of teachers; they take a central position, ask questions, explain principles, and assign homework. Their centrality, activity, and directiveness make it difficult for them to observe the natural and spontaneous interactions of the families they work with. It is an approach that controls and limits the field of observation. They can thus bring a great deal of technical expertise to dealing with part of the problem, but they run the risk of isolating that part from the whole family context.

Those who treat families as though they were conducting therapy groups vary in the intensity of their emotional engagement. Some, following the Tavistock model, are disengaged observers; others, influenced by the human potential movement, are active and interactive. Whether engaged or detached, family group therapists treat families as collections of individuals; they don't join families, they conduct family meetings.

When communications family therapy began, the family was treated as an opposing team—a confused and confusing opponent whose power to destroy meaning had to be controlled from the outset. Members of this school paid a great deal of attention to the structure and management of sessions; they were afraid to let things unfold naturally, because they thought they would never be able to regain control. They began with explicit statements of their belief that the whole family was involved in the patient's symptoms, and they laid down the rules for how therapy would be conducted: "Speak for yourself"; "Don't interrupt."

As they gained experience, communications therapists realized that families tend to resist so direct an approach. They began to use more indirect means of establishing control, largely through paradoxical interventions, and so changed communications therapy into strategic therapy. But the general model is still a cerebral attempt to outwit families. Therapists are considered to be well motivated and rational; families are treated as stuck and liable to resist. The result is an emotionally distanced stance and a treatment imposed on families for their own good.

The contemporary emphasis on collaborative relationships is a reaction against this kind of manipulative distance. Narrative constructivists reject the role of expert in favor of that of a concerned conversationalist, genuinely curious and as free as possible of preconceptions.

Assessment

Systems of family therapy vary in their emphasis on assessment and in the methods they use to make assessments. Each school has a theory about families that determines where they look for problems and what they see. Some look at the whole family (Milan, structural, Bowenian); some look at individuals and dyads (psychoanalytic, experiential); and some focus narrowly on sequences that maintain symptoms (strategic, behavioral). Strategic therapists think small to keep their clients from being overwhelmed, and to help them achieve immediate success.

Behavioral family therapists place the greatest importance on assessment and use the most formal and standardized procedures. In this approach assessment is separated from treatment and is the first order of business. Behaviorists also assess the effectiveness of their interventions, so it is more proper to say that their initial diagnostic assessment is separate from treatment. The great advantage of the behavioral emphasis on assessment is that it provides clear data, definite goals, and a reliable way to determine whether or not therapy succeeds. The disadvantage is that by using standardized interviews and questionnaires, behaviorists don't see the family in natural interaction. By looking only at a part of the family (mother and child, or marital couple), they miss the total context; by structuring the assessment, they see only how the family reacts to the therapists.

Strategic family therapists also make careful assessments, but they do so in a more naturalistic fashion. They begin by inquiring about problems, and then listen to discover how the problems are maintained by attempted solutions. The critical questions in this approach are: What is the problem? Who is involved? What are they doing to make a symptom out of a problem? These questions are answered by what the family says, and what the therapist concludes; there is less emphasis on observing actual interactions than in the experiential or structural schools. On the other hand, strategic practitioners are quite sensitive to the interactions between themselves and families, and they take these interactions into account as part of their evaluation. They frequently give directives in the first session to discover whether families are compliant or resistant. This emphasis is consistent with the centrality of the patient-therapist relationship and with the limited utilization of in-session interactions among family members.

Structural family therapists also emphasize assessment, but their evaluations are based on observation of family members interacting among themselves. These interactions take place either spontaneously or at the therapist's direction. Enactments give the therapist a chance to observe patterns of enmeshment and disengagement, which are the principal components in a structural family diagnosis. The positive aspects of this school's assessment procedure are that it utilizes the family's patterns of interaction among themselves, it includes the entire family, and it is organized in simple terms that point directly to desired changes. If the therapist enacts a discussion between two parents, but they are frequently interrupted by their child, the structural family evaluation would be that the boundary around the marital subsystem is too diffuse. The goal of therapy in such a case would be to increase the parents' involvement with each other, while strengthening the boundary between the parents and the child. A potential disadvantage to structural assessment is that it may lose sight of individuals while focusing on their roles in the family. This doesn't necessarily happen, but it is an error made by many beginning family clinicians.

The Bowenian school also does an excellent job of considering the whole family in its assessment procedure. Unlike structuralists, however, Bowenians rely on what they are told instead of what they see, and they are interested in the past as well as the present. Their evaluations consist of extensive clinical interrogatories, guided by Bowenian theory. The theory says that symptoms are a function of anxiety-provoking stressors, the level of differentiation of family members, and the degree of emotional cutoff from support systems, especially the extended family.

An extended family systems assessment begins with a description and history of the presenting problem. Exact dates are noted and later checked for their relationship to events in the extended family life cycle. Next comes a history of the nuclear family, including information about when the parents met, what their courtship was like, their marriage, and childbearing. Particular attention is also paid to where the family lived and when they moved, especially in relation to where their extended families live. The next part of the evaluation is devoted to the history of both spouses' birth, sibling position, significant facts of childhood, and about the past and current functioning of their parents. All of this information is recorded on a genogram, covering at least three generations. This assessment provides a panoramic view of the whole family and its history; it also provides detailed information about the individuals in the family.

The psychoanalytic and experiential schools also pay a good deal of attention to individuals. Their assessments focus on individual family members and their dyadic relationships within the family. Evaluations in these two schools are unstructured and take place in the ongoing process of treatment. An exception to this rule is that some psychoanalytic clinicians (Nadelson, 1978) meet with each spouse separately before proceeding to evaluate the family together. As in other approaches, the data that psychoanalytic and experiential therapists examine are not always the same as those that they are ultimately interested in. Behaviorists are interested in behavior, but they accept verbal reports; psychoanalysts are interested in latent ideas and experientialists are interested in latent feelings, but they both look carefully at behavior in the sessions for clues as to what is being withheld.

Although the form of evaluation is similar in psychoanalytic and experiential therapy, the content is quite different. These two schools occupy extreme ends on a continuum of the elaborateness of theory; psychoanalytic theory is extensive and complex, experiential theory is limited and simple. The breadth of psychoanalytic theory enables practitioners in this school to theorize well ahead of their data; a little information suggests a great deal. The advantage is that the theory organizes the data and provides valuable leads to uncovering hidden meanings. The danger is that the theory may distort the data, leading the clinician to see what is not there. Experientalists don't have these advantages or disadvantages. Their evaluations are guided by a simple theory about feelings and how they are suppressed; they tend not to uncover much that is hidden, but they also tend not to see things that aren't there.

Just as there are many ways to conduct therapy, there are many assessment procedures; what works in one system may not work in another. We believe, however, that there are two general principles of assessment that are valid for all family therapists. First, it's best not to rely on formal, structured evaluation procedures. The introduction of this much structure early in treatment produces an artificial atmosphere; instead of learning how a family behaves naturally, the clinician who makes a formal assessment learns what they say and how they interact with him or her. Moreover, once a therapist becomes a formal evaluator, it's difficult to move into a decentralized position and become an observer of family dynamics. Furthermore, once a family is treated with the structure of a formal assessment, they may forever resist freely interacting in therapy.

Although it seems to contradict our first point, we also believe that most family practitioners pay too little attention to assessment. There is a tendency to treat all families the same, especially by therapists with powerful techniques but limited conceptual schemes. For example, paradoxical directives are useful but aren't necessary with compliant, well-motivated families. "Speak for yourself" is a good suggestion for enmeshed families, but not necessary for disengaged ones. Quid-pro-quo contracts may not be appropriate for couples with a complementary structure. Using pet techniques unguided by an assessment of the whole family may do some good, but without an evaluation of the family's structure such techniques are unlikely to change the basic configuration that creates and maintains family problems.

Once a therapist has assembled the family, joined with them, established a therapeutic stance, and assessed their structure and functioning, the stage is set for the powerful techniques that constitute the decisive interventions of family therapy.

Decisive Interventions

Members of every school of family therapy use a wide variety of techniques; some are dictated by the approach, others by the therapist's personality and experience. Even if we limit our attention to the techniques common to all members of each of the schools, the list would be long and confusing. Some techniques are used by virtually everyone who practices family therapy—reflecting feelings, clarifying communication; this common list has been growing as the different approaches have become more integrated. Each approach, however, relies on one or two techniques that are relatively unique and decisive. In this section we will highlight and compare these definitive interventions.

In psychoanalytic family therapy there are two decisive techniques. The first of these, *interpretation,* is well known, but not well understood. Properly used, interpretation refers to elucidating unconscious meaning. It doesn't mean statements of opinion—"You need to express your feelings to each other before you can really be close"; advice—"As long as you continue writing to him the affair isn't over"; theory—"Some of the reasons you were attracted to him are based on unconscious needs"; or confrontations—"You said you didn't care, but you were really angry." Interpretations are explicit statements of the therapist's conjecture about the unconscious meaning of certain behaviors or utterances. "You've been talking about your son's unpleasant habit of arguing with you all the time. Based on what you've said previously, I think that some of this anger is deflected from your husband. He does the same thing, but you're afraid to tell him so, and that's why you get so mad at your son."

By reframing from asking questions, giving advice, or directing what people should talk about, the psychoanalytic practitioner maintains a consistent stance of listening and fostering understanding. By limiting his or her interventions to interpretations, the therapist makes it clear that treatment is designed for learning; whether families take advantage of this atmosphere and whether they change their behavior as a result of what they learn is up to them.

The second decisive technique in psychoanalytic family treatment is *silence*. The therapist's use of silence permits him or her to discover what is on the patients' minds and to test the family's resources; it also lends force to the eventual interpretations. When the therapist is silent, family members talk, following their own thoughts rather than responding to the therapist's. If they know that the therapist won't often interrupt, they react and respond to each other. This produces a wealth of information that wouldn't otherwise emerge. If a father begins the first session by saying, "The problem is my depression," and the therapist asks, "How long have you been depressed?" he or she may not discover what thoughts are associated in the man's mind with his depression, or how the man's wife responds to his complaint.

The therapist's silence prolongs the dialogue among family members. This enables the therapist to learn more about how they talk, and it forces family members to find constructive ways to resolve their own interactional impasses. With an active therapist, families get in the habit of waiting for suggestions when they get stuck; with a silent therapist, they struggle to get themselves unstuck. The therapist's silence also enhances the impact of his or her interventions. Words weigh more when they are punctuated by long silences. (Unfortunately, with chaotic and extremely emotional families, therapists cannot always afford the luxury of silence, but must intervene actively to keep things under control.)

Many family group therapists use a number of active and manipulative techniques, including giving advice and making suggestions. The essence of this approach, however, is encouraging free and open discussions so that family members will improve their ability to communicate and learn to solve their own problems. The decisive technique in this approach is *confrontation*: family group therapists confront quiet family members and prod them to open up; they confront domineering members and encourage them to be quiet and listen.

Confrontation is also a decisive technique in experiential family therapy. In this school, confrontations are designed to provoke emotional reactions and are often aggressively blunt. It is not unusual for experiential therapists to tell clients to shut up, or to ridicule them for expressing themselves insincerely. Confrontations are often combined with *personal disclosure* from the therapist, which is the second major technique of this school. Experientialists use themselves as spontaneous, emotionally expressive, freewheeling models. Finally, most experiential therapists make use of a number of *structured exercises*. These include role-playing, psychodrama, sculpting, and a family drawing. The rationale for these techniques is that they are a quick way to provoke emotional experiencing in the session; their obvious drawback is that, because they are artificial, the reactions they provoke may be divorced from ordinary family experience. Family members may get something off their chests in a structural exercise, but may not transfer this to their everyday interactions at home.

Most people associate reinforcement with behavior therapy, but reinforcement is not a technique used in behavioral family therapy; *observation* and *teaching* are the major techniques in this approach. Behavioral family practitioners begin by observing very carefully the contingencies of reinforcement in the families they work with. Their aim is to discover the antecedents and consequences of problem behavior. Once they have completed a functional analysis of behavior, they become teachers, teaching families how they inadvertently reinforce undesirable behavior. As teachers their most useful lesson is how to use positive control. They teach parents that it's more effective to reward children for good behavior than to punish them for bad behavior; they teach married couples to substitute being nice to each other for their usual bickering.

Positive control—rewarding desirable behavior—is one of the most useful principles in family therapy. It is a valuable lesson for families and therapists. Therapists, like parents, tend to chide their charges for mistakes; unfortunately, if you're told that you're suppressing your feelings, spoiling your children, or using coercive control, you're apt to feel inadequate. Although it may be necessary to point out people's mistakes, it's more effective to concentrate on praising the positive aspects of their behavior. Among practicing family therapists this point seems to be best understood by structuralists, who speak of working with the family's strengths, and by strategists and Milan therapists, who use reframing and positive connotation to support families' efforts to do the right thing.

Extended family therapists are also teachers, but they follow a different curriculum. They teach people to be responsible for themselves and how by doing so they can transform their entire family systems. Being responsible for yourself means getting clear about what you think and feel—not what your mother says or what you read in the *New York Times* but what you really believe—and then being true to your beliefs in your dealings with other people. You don't have to change others or even wish they were different; you do have to speak for yourself and maintain your own values. The power of this position is tremendous. If you can accept that you are you, and that other people are different and themselves, then you no longer have to approach relationships with the idea that either you or the other person has to change. This enables you to be in contact with people without becoming unduly upset or emotionally reactive.

In addition to teaching differentiation, Bowenian therapists have two corollary lessons—avoiding triangulation and reopening cut-off family relationships. Taken together these three lessons enable a single person to transform the whole network of his or her family system. If your spouse nags, if your kids are disobedient, if your mother never comes to visit, *you* can create a change. Other schools of therapy exert leverage for change by including the entire family in treatment sessions; Bowenians teach individuals to be themselves, to make contact with others, and to resolve conflicts with the people they are in conflict with. This gives a person leverage for change that is portable and lasting.

Communications family clinicians contributed so much to the theoretical base of family therapy that it's difficult to separate out their techniques or to single out their principal interventions. Perhaps their greatest achievement was to point out that communication is multilayered and that often the most important things being said are said covertly. Therapy was designed to make the covert overt. Initially this was done by pointing out hidden messages; when this direct approach met with resistance, therapists began using directives to make the rules of family functioning explicit, and to provoke changes in the rules.

Strategic therapy is an offshoot of communications theory, and the techniques used by strategists are refinements of those used by communicationists. Principal among these are *reframing, directives,* and *positive connotation.* Strategic practitioners begin by getting detailed descriptions of problems and attempts to solve them. In the process, they pay particular attention to the family's language and expectations. They try to grasp the family's point of view and acknowledge it—which is positive connotation; then they use reframing to shift the family's point of view, and directives to interrupt their problem-maintaining behavior. Using this outline, members of this school plan a general method; but they tailor their intervention to fit each case.

In most cases the single most powerful intervention is probably the use of a directive. These directives are designed to break up rigid homeostatic patterns; these are assigned to be carried out when the family is at home; and they are often paradoxical. Although strategic therapists emphasize fitting the treatment to the patient, they generally assume that indirect interventions are necessary to outwit resistance. This is sometimes but not always true. It's not so much that some families are resistant and others aren't, but that resistance isn't a property *in* families; it's a quality of interaction between therapist and family. A therapist who proceeds on the assumption that families are unable and unwilling to follow advice is likely to encounter the expected resistance.

Structural family therapy is also a therapy of action, but in this approach the action occurs in the session. The decisive technique in this system is *boundary making* between family members while they are in the process of interacting. Rigid boundaries are softened when the therapist gets people to talk with each other and blocks attempts to detour or interrupt them. Likewise, diffuse boundaries are strengthened when the therapist works to realign boundaries in the whole family. Blocking a parent's intrusion into the children's functioning won't last unless that parent is helped to get more involved with the spouse.

Several promising techniques emerged in the 1980s around which whole models of therapy were built. Steve de Shazer and his colleagues expanded the technique of focusing on successful solutions to problems that family members had already tried but abandoned into a whole new approach—solution-based therapy. Michael White did the same with the technique of externalizing problems—getting families to view their problems as separate from them, and then working together to "defeat" these alien enigmas.

In reaction to the techniquism and schoolism that reached a peak in the early 1980s, family therapists today borrow freely from other approaches and de-emphasize technique in favor of a less hierarchical and more respectful quality of therapist-family relationship. Both trends are healthy, but we would like to leave this section with two questions. When is cross-fertilization enriching, and when does eclecticism rob the muscle of separate approaches by watering down their distinctive elements? And how best can family therapists get away from a mechanical and distanced emphasis on technique without losing leverage altogether by practicing a more congenial but less effective form of treatment?

CONTEXT AND APPLICABILITY OF THE SCHOOLS OF FAMILY THERAPY

The predominant influence of social context, emphasized in family therapy, also applies to family therapists themselves and to the systems of treatment they develop. The pioneers of family therapy worked in different settings and with different patient populations. They didn't set out to invent family therapy. They were working on other problems—analyzing communication, exploring the etiology of schizophrenia, treating delinquent children—and family therapy turned out to be part of the solution. But, as we have seen, "family therapy" is not one approach, it is many. The variations in setting, population, and intent of the developers combined to influence the nature of the various family therapies, and also helps to determine the type of patients that each method is most suited to. In this section we will briefly examine the context from which the different sects of family treatment emerged, and then consider which approaches are best for which problems.

The contextual roots of psychoanalytic family therapy are less easy to locate than those of other systems. Ackerman was certainly the originator of this approach, but his death in 1971 left this school without a leader. Since then contributing influences to psychoanalytic family therapy have come from many different quarters. Until recently most of the major figures in this school, including Ackerman himself, have been psychoanalytically trained clinicians who abandoned psychoanalysis for family therapy; their analytic training was reflected in their theoretical papers, but not in their clinical methods. These early psychoanalytic family practitioners worked in a variety of settings—child guidance, social welfare, and marriage and family clinics; but for the most part, the families they worked with were members of the middle class with mild to moderate problems.

Today more and more psychoanalytically trained clinicians are practicing family therapy using methods consistent with their training (Nadelson, 1978; Nichols, 1987). These practitioners tend to work in the same settings and with similar patients as do individual psychoanalytic therapists, namely, medical school outpatient clinics and private practices, with verbal, intelligent, middle-class patients who aren't seriously disturbed. Psychoanalytic treatment—individual or family—is a method of self-discovery that relies heavily on words; and it works best with verbal patients, motivated to learn about themselves. The more educated and sophisticated, the more readily they accept this approach.

The specific methods of family group therapy were developed by John E. Bell, but the general model of group therapy was used by most practitioners who treated families before family systems models of treatment were available. For this reason it isn't possible to describe a specific context in which this approach was developed. On the contrary, since this approach was developed for treating groups of strangers, it's probably more applicable to such groups than to families.

Carl Whitaker, the most prominent experiential family therapist, worked with delinquents and schizophrenics early in his career; later he shifted toward less seriously disturbed patients. This transition, from more to less serious psychopathology, tends to come with experience as a psychotherapist. Poverty and problems go together. The most seriously troubled people are often poor and are usually treated by young clinicians in public clinics.

The concepts and methods of experiential psychotherapy were developed in the human potential movement to treat people with normal problems of everyday life. The cathartic techniques of this approach may not be as useful for people struggling with serious psychopathology or chaotic living conditions, but for repressed neurotics these techniques are like an elixir that infuses new life into their days of anxiety and apathy.

Behavioral marriage therapy was developed in university departments of psychology and applied primarily to members of the academic community. These couples tend to be young educated professionals, whose relationships are symmetrical and whose problems aren't severe. They are usually well motivated and willing to follow instructions in an educational format. Behavioral parent training was also developed in academic training centers, but has been applied to seriously disturbed children in institutions as well as to mildly disturbed children in university clinics. The concrete symptomatic focus of this treatment makes it a popular approach for dealing with severely symptomatic children. For this reason, behavior therapy is often used as an adjunct to other forms of treatment for hospitalized children (Minuchin, Rosman, & Baker, 1978). In hospital settings, behavioral treatment is usually applied not by the parents but by the staff; in fact, much of the behavioral parent training is conducted by graduate students in university counseling centers and psychological training clinics.

Murray Bowen developed his ideas about family therapy while he was at NIMH, studying middle-class families with a psychotic member. This may help account for two of the main emphases in his work: differentiation of self and working with extended families. In psychotic families there's often a blurring of boundaries—what Bowen called the undifferentiated family ego mass. These families exhibit an intense clinging interdependence in which individual identities are diffused in amorphous togetherness. Bowen concluded that this lack of differentiation, or fusion, is the major source of pathology in all families. The goal of his treatment is to help family members differentiate themselves, which in turn will have a beneficial effect on the entire system. The process of differentiation begins with the therapist, who must remain emotionally neutral and avoid being drawn into the emotional quicksand of the undifferentiated family. This stance must have been necessary to avoid being engulfed by the psychotic families that Bowen started out with.

Bowen distinguished between differentiation and emotional cutoff, which is common in the middle-class suburban families he studied in Washington, D.C. Emotional cutoff is a reactive flight from fusion, masquerading as genuine independence.

Although he first developed his ideas about families while studying a psychotic population, Bowen was more successful at understanding these families than he was at treating them. He eventually gave up the idea that family therapy was effective with schizophrenic families (though Michael Kerr, who followed Bowen as director of the Georgetown Family Center, believes that family therapy is useful to reduce anxiety in *any* family), and most of his later work was with middle-class professional families. Bowenian therapy may be most useful for young couples who haven't yet successfully separated from their original families, including not only those who are obviously still dependent on their parents, but also those whose pseudoindependence is based on reactive distance. While Bowenian therapy may be ideally suited for middle-class couples in their twenties and thirties, its applicability is certainly not limited to this group. Bowen had an exquisite appreciation of triangular processes, and his therapeutic concepts are useful in any situation where two people form a coalition against a third.

Communications family therapists were scientists first, healers second. Their original intent was to study communication in schizophrenic families; only later did they decide to treat these unhappy people. At first they saw patients as victims and tried to protect them from scapegoating relatives. Later they realized that in schizophrenia there are no victims and victimizers; the whole family is stuck.

The feature of family life that captured their attention was the strange and puzzling ways families with schizophrenic members communicate. Conversation in these families is often permeated with paradoxes, disqualifications, and double binds. It's a tribute to their optimism that they thought that schizophrenia could be cured by bringing together patients with their families and somehow talking them out of their strange and destructive patterns of communication. When they found that the direct approach didn't work, they developed an indirect one. In place of interpretation they began to use manipulation. When communications therapists became strategists, they took a more emotionally distanced position, conducting therapy like generals outside the fray.

Jackson and Haley were the pivotal figures in the transition from communications theory to strategic therapy. Haley took the core concept of communications theory—that messages cannot be taken at face value because they are always qualified by other messages on different levels—and derived the notion that all communication is part of a struggle for power in relationships. This position reflects Haley's personality and the context he was working in. Haley is an intellectual and an outsider; some of his major contributions have been critiques of psychoanalysis, the human potential movement, and experiential family therapy. His therapy is about power and control—how to wrest power in order to gain control of families through ingenious manipulation. Psychiatric symptoms are seen as perversions of the normal struggle for control. Instead of openly fighting for control, families of psychiatric patients deny that there is any conflict. They don't honestly refuse to participate; they "can't" because they're "sick." Strategic therapy forces patients into a corner from which they can escape only by giving up their symptoms. Haley's concept of ordeal therapy, derived from Milton Erickson, illustrates this way of thinking.

Emotional distance, struggle for power, and manipulation—none of these sounds very nice. To understand how these positions were developed it's necessary to consider where they were developed. Communications therapists worked with acute schizophrenics whose families, they thought, were capable of driving people crazy with baffling responses and maddening double binds. Perhaps conducting therapy from a distance seemed to be the only way to avoid getting completely entangled in such families. Perhaps if therapists don't struggle for power, they will be defeated by these families; and if they don't use manipulation, they will be manipulated. Today's strategic therapists still work with seriously disturbed cases, many of whom have tried and failed with other straightforward approaches. But today's therapists are rarely as combative as in the past, and are likely to be genuinely sympathetic to the problem of living with a seriously disturbed member.

Structural family therapy was first developed with families of delinquents from the inner-city slums. These families are poor and often disorganized. Some are enmeshed—chaotic and tightly interconnected; others are disengaged—isolated and seemingly unrelated. Both types lack clear hierarchical structures. Creating functional structures by differentiating subsystems and realigning their boundaries is the object of structural family therapy.

Another characteristic of the ghetto families that Minuchin worked with at Wiltwyck is that they are outside the mainstream of American culture and feel alien in relation to middle-class helping professionals. In order to work with these families it was first necessary to get their attention and then to gain their confidence; this helps to account for Minuchin's active, directive style, and his emphasis on joining.

Structural family therapy's focus on the whole family is different from some of the other approaches that tend to work with subsets of the family. Strategic and Bowenian practitioners, for instance, move quickly to the adults, even when the presenting problem is about a child. Minuchin, however, was trained as a child psychiatrist, and he has always believed that it's important to include children in treatment.

Understanding the contexts in which the different systems of family therapy were developed makes it easier to see why they have the forms they do. However, it doesn't tell us which therapy to use with which problem. There is little hard evidence that one system is more effective than the others, nor do we know much about which is best with any particular problem.

There are, however, a growing number of researchers beginning to add hard evidence to long-standing debates, which in the past were thought to be primarily matters of opinion and personal choice. There is now a substantial and growing body of evidence about effective methods for treating schizophrenic patients and their families as well as chemically dependent persons and their families. There are numerous studies, some of which relate to specific models and others that deal with meta-analyses of family therapy clinical trials. Among the most informative discussions of the empirical literature are: Gurman, Kniskern, and Pinsof's (1986) review chapter in the third edition of the *Handbook of Psychotherapy and Behavior Change;* Hazelrigg, Cooper, and Borduin's (1987) paper "Evaluating the Effectiveness of Family Therapies: An Integrative Review and Analysis"; Burlingame et al.'s review article in the 1989 edition of the *Annual Review of Psychology;* and Kazdin's (1987) *Psychological Bulletin* article, "Treatment of Antisocial Behavior in Children: Current Status and Future Directions."

Among the most recent summaries of the research are: Henggeler, Borduin, and Mann's (1992) "Advances in Family Therapy: Empirical Foundations" in *Advances in Clinical Child Psychology;* and Kazdin's (1991) article "Effectiveness of Psychotherapy with Children and Adolescents" in the *Journal of Consulting and Clinical Psychology.* For a general discussion of research issues, see Lyman Wynne's (1988) *The State of the Art in Family Therapy Research;* and Moon, Dillon, and Sprenkle's (1990) article "Family Therapy and Qualitative Research" in the *Journal of Marital and Family Therapy.* And for a comprehensive summary of the research picture in family therapy, see Chapter 13 of this volume.

In the final analysis, the best treatment is given by the best therapist. If the best therapist in town is an experientialist, the best therapy in town is experiential.

SELECTION OF A THEORETICAL POSITION: RATIONAL AND IRRATIONAL FACTORS

How do students go about selecting a therapeutic orientation, and how should they? Deliberate choice probably exerts less influence than the personality and values of the student, or the training milieu. Having selected and been selected by a graduate program, students are pressured to conform to the models offered by their teachers and supervisors. While the idea of conformity may not be appealing, it's probably a good idea to embrace the model offered by your teachers. Learning whatever you can from every teacher or supervisor doesn't destroy your independence any more than rejecting and arguing protects it.

Except in the most homogeneous settings, students are liable to be exposed to a variety of different approaches during their graduate education; their interests are based on a series of fluid identifications with faculty members. While this may be confusing, it helps inoculate beginning clinicians against dogmatic thinking. Moreover, it provides the necessary breadth of information on which to base an informed choice of a specialty. Once you leave academic coursework to begin practical training, it's too late to shop around. During your clinical training, you should concentrate on learning one method well—that is, becoming thoroughly immersed in it. It may seem more creative to blend elements from a variety of systems in a personal integration, but this is better done after you master one single approach.

Selecting a system of family therapy to specialize in isn't simply a question of which one is best. For one thing, we still don't know which is the best form of treatment (though there have been several reports published in *The Journal of Marital and Family Therapy,* by Hetherington in 1987, Kolevzon and Green in 1982, and Kolevzon, Sowers-Hoag, and Hoffman in 1989, that deal with therapist selection of orientation). The choice depends upon what is available, what suits your clientele, and what suits you. The methods and techniques of therapy are never wholly separate from the qualities of the person applying them. Therefore, it's wise to choose an approach that's congruent with your style as a person.

Far too many people discontinue their training before they have mastered their craft. Training can be expensive; job offers beckon; and nobody wants to be a student forever. Because most people discontinue their training before they become expert, the field is filled with many so-called family therapists who are equipped with little more than a basic understanding of systems theory and a rudimentary knowledge of techniques.

After training (whether it is pursued to conclusion or prematurely terminated), there is a transition from student to full-fledged therapist. This can be a very gratifying time. Freed from the constraints of a beginner's status and removed from the watchful eyes of supervisors, practicing therapists become more spontaneous and fluid. Instead of being anxious about following a model or pleasing a supervisor, the therapist is free to get more involved with families and incorporate some of his or her natural style along with techniques that by now have become almost second nature. After you have gained experience in applying your model of therapy to the treatment of families, you are liable to experience the limitations of the model or your skill as therapist, or both. Many people then take refresher courses or look for workshops in new treatment approaches. Although we do believe strongly in mastering one particular model of therapy, we don't think it matters whether an experienced practitioner returns for a brush-up in the original model or seeks out some new ideas. Experienced practitioners will be able to—will have to—integrate whatever they learn with their personal styles.

However, being able to integrate a variety of family therapy models with your own personality only works for those who have a thorough background of training and supervision in some form of family therapy. Therapists who substitute periodic attendance at workshops and training conferences for a protracted period of indoctrination and training in one particular school of family therapy tend not to be competent family therapists. A series of workshops can stimulate and enhance the skills of experienced practitioners but cannot substitute for the necessary apprenticeship.

SUMMARY

The theme of the first edition of this book was the proliferation of competing schools, each portrayed as unique and uniquely effective. That was how family therapy entered the 1980s. Now, as family therapy moves further into the 1990s, the theme is integration. So many dedicated family therapists have been working for so long that the field has accumulated a significant number of useful ways of looking at and treating families. Today it no longer makes sense to study one and only one model and to neglect the insights of the others. Family therapists are not only cross-fertilizing across models of family therapy, they are also adding concepts and methods from psychology and individual psychotherapy.

Neither of the authors likes to use tired clichés (unless we make them up), but one familiar metaphor is that of family therapy moving out of its adolescence and into adulthood. We trot out this old chestnut because it's true. Once, like adolescents trying to define our identities, we were proud to be special and different; and we were a little snotty about the accomplishments of the older generation: individual psychotherapists. Now we seem to have less need to prove we're unique and special, and we seem to be developing more respect for those "others" who practice different versions of family therapy—and even those who practice altogether different forms of psychotherapy. Family therapy may have rediscovered psychodynamic psychotherapy in the 1980s; in the 1990s perhaps we will rediscover behavior therapy and begin to utilize its enormous technology for changing behavior.

Before we say goodbye to the family-therapy-growing-up metaphor, one more point: When the field was young we often got by on enthusiasm and promise. But that may not work in maturity. Now when we promise a therapy that works, we're expected to deliver. An important aspect of this is that empirical research demonstrating what we claim to accomplish will be one of the most important requirements in the 1990s. If family problems cause psychological problems, we should be able to demonstrate it; and, perhaps more important, if we say we can resolve problems with family therapy, we'll probably have to prove it.

Underlying each approach is a view of human nature. Differences among schools in their view of what it means to be human account for many of the differences in concepts and methods we have discussed. If people are power-game players, therapists will devise indirect strategies to outwit them. If the feelings and behavior of people depend primarily on the network of relationships (or family structure) in which they are embedded, therapists will use their relationship to restructure families. If people are undifferentiated from their irrational emotionality, therapists will use their own rationality and knowledge of how systems work to teach people how to differentiate. If people contain untapped inner resources, therapists will collaborate with them to bring out those strengths. We're pleased to see this last way of thinking gaining ground, especially, for example, in the work of the late Virginia Satir, Salvador Minuchin, Luigi Boscolo and Gianfranco Cecchin, Steve de Shazer, Bill O'Hanlon and Michele Weiner-Davis, Carol Anderson, Richard Schwartz, and Michael White.

In the past, each of the rival systems of family therapy proclaimed its unique way of understanding and treating families. However, as we have seen, the differences are more sharply drawn in theory than in practice. The success of new developments in one school often lead to their adoption by others, shrinking the gaps among the various therapeutic orientations. The trend toward convergence is the story of family therapy in the 1990s. In what follows we will offer some very subjective comments about picking and choosing some of the more useful concepts and methods that have proven themselves classics of family therapy.

Theories of family functioning have both a scientific and a practical purpose. The most useful theories treat families as systems; have concepts to describe forces for stability and change; consider the past, but concentrate on the present; treat communication as multileveled and complex; recognize the process underlying the content of family discussions; recognize the triadic nature of human relationships; remember to consider the context of the nuclear family, rather than viewing it as a closed system isolated from its environment; and recognize the critical function of boundaries in protecting the cohesiveness of individuals, subgroups, and families.

Clinicians are more concerned with pathology and change than with normality, but it's useful to have a model of normal family functioning, both to mold treatment goals and to distinguish what is pathological and needs changing from what is normal and doesn't. Some of the most useful concepts of normal family functioning are: Minuchin's structural model of families as open systems in transformation; the communications theory model of direct, specific, and honest communication in a family system with rules clear enough to ensure stability and flexible enough to allow change; the behavioral model of equitable exchange of interpersonal costs and benefits, the use of positive control instead of coercion, and mutual and reciprocal reinforcement between spouses; the family group theory which points out that groups function best when they are cohesive, when there is a free flow of communication, and when members' roles are clearly defined and appropriate to their needs; the strategic model of systemic flexibility, which allows adjustment to changing circumstances and the ability to find new solutions when old ones don't work; and the Bowenian model which explains how differentiation of self enables people to be independent at times, intimate at others.

Most family therapy concepts of behavior disorder focus on systems and interactions, but the psychoanalytic, Bowenian, Schwartz's parts model, and experiential models add intrapersonal depth to the interactional view, bridging the gap between private, inner experiences and outward public behavior. The clinical observation that many divorced people repeat the mistakes of their first marriages supports these schools' position that some of what goes on in families is a product of individual character. Some of the most valuable concepts of personality dysfunction in families are: Bowen's concept of fusion; the experiential concepts of repressed affect and stifled growth; and psychoanalytic concepts of developmental arrest, internal object relations, and instinctual conflict. These concepts of individual psychopathology are useful adjuncts, but the guiding ideas in the field explain behavior disorder in terms of systems theory. The most influential of these are about inflexible systems, too rigid to accommodate individual strivings or to adjust to changes in circumstances; symptomatic family members promoting cohesion by stabilizing the nuclear and extended families; inadequate hierarchical structure; families that are too tightly or too loosely structured; and pathological triangles.

The broad goals of family therapy are to solve presenting problems and to reorganize families. Behaviorists and strategists aim for the former, Bowenians and psychoanalysts aim for the latter; most of the other schools aim for both. As we have seen, some family practitioners expect therapy to be prolonged, while others keep it brief. These diverse strategies reflect differences of opinion about how much change families need to accomplish. In our opinion, that question should be left to the family. Therapists should accept the family's goal to solve their immediate problems, and design therapy to reorganize only that aspect of the family that has become dysfunctional. If families want more, they should say so.

Some of the specific goals of family therapy are practically universal—clarifying communication, solving problems, promoting individual autonomy—

and some are unique. Some of the schools take the presenting problem at face value, while others treat it as a metaphor and a sign. In either case, goals shouldn't be so broad as to neglect symptom resolution, or too narrow to ensure the stability of symptom resolution. Incidentally, values are seldom discussed in the family therapy literature. The one exception is Boszormenyi-Nagy, but he considers the ethical dimension only in terms of the patient. There is too little consideration of a practicing therapist's ethical responsibilities, including the possibility of conflicting responsibilities to individuals, families, and the larger community.

Some of the major differences among family therapists about how behavior is changed are focused on the following issues: action or insight; change in the session or change at home; duration of treatment; resistance; family-therapist relationship; and paradox. Even though there is a general consensus about some of these issues—for example, most family therapists believe that action is primary and insight is useful but secondary—there have always been divergent opinions on every one of these points. Strategic therapists, for example, still deny that insight is necessary or useful.

We have discussed some of the major methodological issues and tried to separate out the decisive techniques of the different systems. As is always the case when a number of variables are involved in a final result, it's not easy to know to what degree each variable contributes to that result, or how important each one is. Furthermore, the more we talk about techniques, the greater the danger of seeing family therapy as a purely technological enterprise. Studying families is like solving a riddle; the art of treating them is to relieve suffering and anguish. The job of the theoretician is to decode or decipher; it requires theory and ingenuity. The job of the therapist is to help relieve suffering; it requires theory, but also conviction, perseverance, and caring. Treating families isn't only an act of science and technology; it's also an act of love.

REFERENCES

Bowen, M. 1966. The use of family theory in clinical practice. *Comprehensive Psychiatry.* 7:345–374.

Dunlap, K. A. 1928. A revision of the fundamental law of habit formation. *Science.* 67:360–362.

Frankl, V. 1960. Paradoxical intention: A logotherapeutic technique. *American Journal of Psychotherapy. 14*:520–535.

Gordon, S. B., and Davidson, N. 1981. Behavioral parent training. In *Handbook of family therapy,* A. S. Gutman and D. P. Kniskern, eds. New York: Brunner/Mazel.

Gurman, A. S., Kniskern, D. P., and Pinsof, W. 1986. Research on the process and outcome of marital and family therapy. In *Handbook of psychotherapy and behavior change,* 3rd ed., S. L. Garfield and A. E. Bergin, eds. New York: Wiley.

Haley, J. 1963. *Strategies of psychotherapy.* New York: Grune and Stratton.

Haley, J. 1976. *Problem-solving therapy.* San Francisco: Jossey-Bass.

Haley, J. 1977. Toward a theory of pathological systems. In *The interactional view,* P. Watzlawick and J. Weakland, eds. New York: Norton.

Haley, J. 1980. *Leaving home: The therapy of disturbed young people.* New York: McGraw-Hill.

Halleck, S. 1978. *The treatment of emotional disorders.* New York: Jason Aronson.

Hazelrigg, M. D., Cooper, H. M., and Borduin, C. M. 1987. Evaluating the effective-ness of family therapies: An integrative review and analysis. *Psychological Bulletin. 101:*4228–4442.

Henggeler, S. W., Borduin, C. M., and Mann, B. J. 1992. Advances in family therapy: Empirical foundations. In *Advances in clinical child psychology,* vol. 15, T. H. Ollendick and R. J. Prinz, eds. New York: Plenum.

Hoffman, L. 1981. *The foundations of family therapy.* New York: Basic Books.

Jackson, D. D. 1965. Family rules: The marital quid pro quo. *Archives of General Psy-chiatry. 12:*589–594.

Jasnow, A. 1978. The psychotherapist—artist and/or scientist? *Psychotherapy: Theory, Research and Practice. 15:*318–322.

Kazdin, A. E. 1987. Treatment of antisocial behavior in children: Current status and future directions. *Psychological Bulletin. 102:*187–203.

Kazdin, A. E. 1991. Effectiveness of psychotherapy with children and adolescents. *Journal of Consulting and Clinical Psychology. 59:*785–798.

Kendrick, D. D. 1960. The theory of "conditioned inhibition" as an explanation of negative practice effects: An experimental analysis. In *Behavior therapy and the neuroses,* H. J. Eysenck, ed. New York: Pergamon.

Luborsky, L. 1972. Research cannot yet influence clinical practice. In *Changing fron-tiers in the science of psychotherapy,* A. E. Bergin and H. H. Strupp, eds. New York: Aldine-Atherton.

Madanes, C. 1980. Protection, paradox and pretending. *Family Process. 19:*73–85.

Madanes, C., and Haley, J. 1977. Dimensions of family therapy. *Journal of Nervous and Mental Disease. 165:*88–98.

Mahler, M. S., Pine, F., and Bergman, A. 1975. *The psychological birth of the human infant.* New York: Basic Books.

Matarazzo, J. D. 1972. Interview: J. D. Matarazzo. In *Changing frontiers in the science of psychotherapy,* A. E. Bergin and H. H. Strupp, eds. New York: Aldine-Atherton.

Minuchin, S. 1974. *Families and family therapy.* Cambridge, MA: Harvard University Press.

Minuchin, S., and Fishman, H. C. 1981. *Family therapy techniques.* Cambridge, MA: Harvard University Press.

Minuchin, S., and Nichols, M. P. 1993. *Family healing: Tales of hope and renewal from family therapy.* New York: The Free Press.

Minuchin, S., Rosman, B., and Baker, L. 1978. *Psychosomatic families: Anorexia nervosa in context.* Cambridge, MA: Harvard University Press.

Moon, S. M., Dillon, D. R., and Sprenkle, D. H. 1990. Family therapy and qualitative research. *Journal of Marital and Family Therapy. 16:*357–373.

Nadelson, C. C. 1978. Marital therapy from a psychoanalytic perspective. In *Marriage and marital therapy,* T. J. Paolino and B. S. McCrady, eds. New York: Brunner/ Mazel.

Nichols, M. P. 1987. *The self in the system.* New York: Brunner/Mazel.

Paul, W. L. 1967. The use of empathy in the resolution of grief. *Perspectives in Biology Medicine. 11:*153–169.

Pierce, R., Nichols, M. P., and DuBrin, J. 1983. *Emotional expression in psychotherapy.* New York: Gardner Press.

Rabkin, R. 1977. *Strategic psychotherapy.* New York: Basic Books.

Rogers, C. R. 1957. The necessary and sufficient conditions of therapeutic personality change. *Journal of Consulting Psychology. 21:*95–103.

Selvini Palazzoli, M., Boscolo, L., Cecchin, G., and Prata, G. 1978. *Paradox and coun-terparadox.* New York: Jason Aronson.

Selvini Palazzoli, M., Boscolo, L., Cecchin, G., and Prata, G. 1980. Hypothesizing-circularity-neutrality: Three guidelines for the conductor of family interviews. *Family Process. 19:*3–12.

Stanton, M. D., Todd, T. C., and Associates. 1981. *The family therapy of drug addiction.* New York: Guilford Press.

Thibaut, J. W., and Kelley, H. H., 1959. *The social psychology of groups.* New York: Wiley.

Vogel, E. F., and Bell, N. W. 1960. The emotionally disturbed child as the family scapegoat. In *The family,* N. W. Bell and E. F. Vogel, eds. Glencoe, IL: Free Press.

Watzlawick, P., Beavin, J., and Jackson, D. D. 1967. *Pragmatics of human communication.* New York: Norton.

Whitaker, C. A., and Keith, D. V. 1981. Symbolic-experiential family therapy. In *Handbook of family therapy,* A. S. Gurman and D. P. Kniskern, eds. New York: Brunner/Mazel,

Wynne, L. C., ed. 1988. *The state of the art in family therapy research: Controversies and recommendations.* New York: Family Process Press.

Research in Family Therapy: Trends, Issues, and Recommendations

Douglas H. Sprenkle, Ph.D.
Purdue University

Richard J. Bischoff, Ph.D.
University of San Diego

Although family therapy grew out of the pioneering research efforts of its founders (Broderick & Schrader, 1981), the rapid growth of the field was based more on the intuitive appeal of the approach than on solid research evidence of effectiveness (Henggeler, Borduin, & Mann, 1992; Nichols & Schwartz, 1991). However, in recent years as the field has increased in popularity and maturity, the amount of empirical study of family therapy has increased as well. In fact, research on family therapy has grown dramatically over the past three decades (Piercy & Sprenkle, 1990).

Early studies of family therapy focused on comparing conventional treatments (typically an inpatient, individually oriented treatment) with an outpatient family-oriented treatment. These early studies generally found family treatment superior to the conventional treatments with regard to recidivism and other important variables (e.g., Langsley, Flomenhaft, & Machotka, 1969; Langsley, Pittman, Machotka, & Flomenhaft, 1968). Although the scientific rigor of these studies may be questioned when compared with contemporary standards, they clearly helped give credence to an emerging discipline. Other early studies applied one specific model of family treatment to a specific problem area (e.g., anorexia nervosa) and found the approach to be effective (e.g., Minuchin, Baker, Rosman, Liebman, & Todd, 1975; Minuchin, Rosman, & Baker, 1978; Stanton, Steier et al., 1979; Stanton, Todd, & Associates, 1982). These positive results helped bolster support for the family therapy movement. The more recent impressive work on the family management of schizophrenia (reviewed below) is another illustration of how research has galvanized interest and respect for family therapy.

Transformations in Family Therapy Research

Much like the theoretical movements that have brought dramatic changes to the field, the domain of research has experienced major transitions as well. In fact, as both Lyman Wynne (1983) and Jay Haley (1978) pointed out over a decade ago, current research efforts scarcely resemble the investigations of the past. The first major transformation took place as the field moved from an impressionistic to a quantitative emphasis. The second transformation, currently under way, is a shift from a strict reliance on *quantitative methods* to the incorporation and acceptance of *qualitative methodologies* (Piercy & Sprenkle, 1990).

Quantitative research aims for rigorous scientific empiricism by counting, comparing, measuring, and subjecting data to statistical analysis. In the tradition of logical positivism (according to which ideas are meaningful only if they have measurable consequences), it is the approach long favored by granting agencies, journals, and dissertation committees. *Qualitative* research, on the other hand, is phenomenological and exploratory. Getting out of the laboratory and studying families in the consulting room and in their homes with in-depth interviews and thoughtful reflection is considered by many to be especially useful in a new field like family therapy where constructs are not yet clearly defined.

Quantitative investigations are deductive, with the researcher clearly specifying questions and hypotheses prior to conducting the study. The investigator attempts to place controls on the data that will limit investigator influence and allow for the most accurate explanation of the phenomena under study. Frequently used controls include randomization, detailed specification of variables and conditions, determinations of acceptable and nonacceptable data prior to study, and nonreactive measurements such as recidivism and behavioral frequency count. Designs are usually experimental in nature and emphasize prediction of cause-effect relationships and verification of hypotheses.

Qualitative investigations are inductive; rather than using experimental controls, investigators attempt to explore the richness and variety in the data in the hope that openness to discovery will lead to new insights. Strategies include selecting events that don't conform to preconceived ideas about what is in the data (theoretical selection), allowing research participants to comment on the investigator's reconstructions of the data (member checking), and bringing the data and their reconstructions of it to an uninvolved colleague for comment (peer debriefing). The goal is exploration and description, not prediction.

We welcome the trend toward valuing both types of investigation. As we will explain below, combining these two methodologies often results in more meaningful findings.

RESEARCH REVIEWS

Several comprehensive research reviews have been previously published (e.g., Baucom & Hoffman, 1986; Bednar, Burlingame, & Masters, 1988; Gurman & Kniskern, 1978; Gurman & Kniskern, 1981; Gurman, Kniskern, & Pinsof, 1986; Hazelrigg, Cooper, & Borduin, 1987; Jacobson, Follette, & Elwood, 1984; Kazdin, 1991; Markus, Lange, & Pettigrew, 1990; Todd & Stanton, 1983) as well as several others that address family therapy as it pertains to specific problem areas (e.g., Avis & Sprenkle, 1990; Beach & O'Leary, 1985; Bischoff & Sprenkle, 1993; Giblin, Sprenkle, & Sheehan, 1985; Kazdin, 1991; Robinson, Berman, & Neimeyer, 1990; Sprenkle & Storm, 1983; Tolan, Cromwell, & Brasswell, 1986; Wampler, 1982). In fact, in their decade review of marriage and family therapy, Fred Piercy and Doug Sprenkle (1990) waggishly referred to the 1980s as "the decade of marriage and family therapy research reviews."

Briefly, the extant reviews indicate that family therapy is generally effective with a wide range of problems. This has been confirmed by recent meta-analyses of the family therapy research literature (Hazelrigg et al., 1987; Henggeler et al., 1992; Markus et al., 1990). Hazelrigg et al. (1987) reviewed 20 studies meeting their methodological criteria. The authors were able to say with confidence that family treatment is more effective than no treatment. They also found suggestive evidence of the superiority of family therapy when compared to alternate treatments. Markus et al. (1990) reviewed 19 studies of conjoint family therapy that included children. They concluded that at post-treatment the average patient with family therapy was better off than 76 percent of patients with an alternate treatment, a minimal treatment, or no treatment.

Alan Gurman and his colleagues reviewed the reviews published prior to 1986 and concluded that:

> Nonbehavioral marital and family therapies produce beneficial outcomes in about two-thirds of cases, and their effects are superior to no treatment.
>
> When both spouses are involved in therapy conjointly for marital problems, there is a greater chance of positive outcome than when only one spouse is treated.
>
> Positive results of both nonbehavioral and behavioral marital and family therapies typically occur in treatment of short duration, that is, 1–20 sessions.
>
> Family therapy is probably as effective and possibly more effective than many commonly offered individual treatments for problems attributed to family conflict. (Gurman et al., 1986, p. 572)

These same authors, however, noted that there is little empirical evidence for the specific effectiveness of any of the major schools of family therapy. After cross tabulating fifteen family therapy approaches with ten clinical disorders or problems, it was found that outcome research of any sort had been conducted on only 23 percent of the 150 possible method-times-problem combinations. Suggestive evidence of effectiveness was found to be demonstrated for only 9 percent (13) of these combinations. Most importantly, only six of the treatment approaches had at least moderately positive evidence of efficacy with at least one clinical disorder or problem. Gurman et al. (1986) also noted that most of the major concepts linked to these schools (like enmeshment, triangulation, etc.) have not been adequately operationalized or empirically tested. Consequently, while we can speak with some confidence about the general effectiveness of family therapy, we must remain modest about the specifics. We agree with Fred Piercy and Doug Sprenkle's (1990) conclusion that research offers little to the clinician who must choose among competing family treatment options.

Rather than recapitulate the major works cited above. We will (1) present the important issues currently being discussed and debated in the research literature; (2) highlight some noteworthy trends in family therapy research; (3) provide a brief overview of some of the major findings derived from the existing research; and (4) suggest several recommendations for future directions.

ISSUES IN FAMILY THERAPY RESEARCH

Importance of Research to the Field

Meaningful research is extremely important to the field of marriage and family therapy. In fact, some authors have argued (as we do) that it is the ethical responsibility of those in the field to use formal research to study and legitimize the treatments being used in family intervention (e.g., Cavell & Snyder, 1991; Gurman, 1983; Liddle, 1991). Research can potentially benefit the field in three areas: (1) legitimizing the field with non-family therapy mental health professionals; (2) legitimizing the field with the larger community of government, third-party, and other funding institutions; and (3) helping the actual consumers of family therapy—the clients themselves.

Legitimization of Family Therapy with Other Clinicians. As a relative newcomer to the mental health community, family therapy is often looked down upon by non-family therapy professionals as a subspecialty of child psychiatry, clinical psychology, or social work. As such, it's not always seen as a legitimate treatment approach, or as one for which specialized training is needed. Many don't yet consider being a family therapist a substantial enough basis for one's professional identity. If the clinical effectiveness of the approach isn't validated in a rigorous way, then family therapy will never earn complete respect (Shields, Wynne, McDaniel, & Gawinski, 1994). Research can provide the evidence necessary to validate family therapy as a viable treatment modality and one that requires special skills and training.

One of the means of establishing professional legitimacy is through interdisciplinary cooperation. One example of this potential is the family systems medicine movement (McDaniel, Hepworth, & Doherty, 1992) where collaborative research with physicians and social scientists is beginning to result in increased recognition by health professionals of the value of family therapy. Unfortunately, this movement hasn't yet generated significant research support. However, it has great potential, especially with regard to demonstrating the cost-effectiveness of family therapy as an aspect of medical care.

Legitimization of Family Therapy in the Larger Community.   In this age of budget cuts, managed care, and demands for accountability, third-party funding sources are looking for proof of the effectiveness (and efficiency) of all forms of psychotherapeutic treatment. Without convincing outcome data, family therapy (or any other approach, for that matter) won't fare well in the competition for scarce resources. In our opinion, third-party payers have a right to expect evidence that therapy deserves to be reimbursed. Whatever family therapy's role in the emerging health care delivery system, there is sure to be greater demand for accountability than existing research can satisfy.

Legitimization of Family Therapy with Clients.   Probably more important than providing outcome data to other professionals and third-party payers, yet often overlooked, is the impact research can have on the consumers of family therapy themselves. As other referring professionals and the press come to have more respect for family therapy, so will clients. They will become better informed and more able to make responsible decisions about type and course of treatment.

Also, as we begin to unravel Gordon Paul's (1967) famous question about which treatment works best for which clients under which sets of circumstances, we will have the potential to alleviate human suffering in a cost-effective way. This, not statistics, publications, or the intricacies of research design, should be our ultimate concern as clinicians and researchers.

Overcoming the Gap between Research and Practice

Despite the crucial importance of research, there continues to be a great chasm between researchers and clinicians (Liddle, 1991). Although there have been a few promising efforts to bridge this gap (e.g., Barton, Alexander, & Sanders, 1985; Safran, Greenberg, & Rice, 1988), improvement is at best slow and at worst insignificant.

Interestingly, this gap didn't always exist. As evident in the introductory chapters of this book, family therapy had its roots in research. Lyman Wynne, Murray Bowen, Theodore Lidz, Gregory Bateson, Don Jackson, Jay Haley, and others all came to family therapy through their study of interactional patterns associated with problematic families (Broderick & Schrader, 1981; Wynne, 1983).

Both Jay Haley (1978) and Lyman Wynne (1983) have explained that in these early days, there was no distinction between therapists and researchers. Research attention focused on how therapeutic interventions affected the patients and their families. Lyman Wynne (1983) explained how researchers and clinicians would review audio tapes of their sessions, observe each other through one-way mirrors, and discuss "each session, formulating hypotheses and criticizing the hypotheses for many, many hours" (p. 114). Research had direct clinical relevance. Hypotheses were developed, tested, altered, and re-tested in actual clinical practice.

However, research underwent a transformation after family therapy began to gain in popularity. Researchers began to adopt more rigorous quantitative methods and to reject as unscientific the methods used by early clinician-researchers. Yet, in improving the operationalization of concepts, the reliability of measures, and the generalizability of results, the clinical applicability of the newer studies became less relevant for most practicing clinicians. This was a great price to pay for improved research quality! As a result, many clinicians have come to ignore published research findings (Barton et al., 1985; Jacobson, 1985a; Kaye, 1990; Schwartz & Breunlin, 1983) because they often do not adequately represent the complex processes of family therapy. In family therapy, each of the components (e.g., clients, therapist[s], treatment, and outcome) involves a network of interacting variables such as age, sex, intelligence, treatment model and goals, training of therapists, and so on such that controlling them is a herculean task and one that when attempted can often result in clinically meaningless findings.

The researcher and clinician have often been seen as serving different purposes and having different goals. Barton et al. (1985) explain some of the differences in how clinicians and researchers think about families and their problems. The clinician's goal is to generate and test hypotheses relatively quickly in order to help families with their dilemmas as expeditiously as possible, while the hypothesis generating and testing phases of research are much more lengthy, and the goal is typically not intervention but understanding.

Several authors (e.g., Jacobson, 1985a; Kaye, 1990; Tomm, 1986) have recently observed that research efforts are often seen by clinicians as reductionistic, "as killing the beast in trying to describe him," to use Karl Tomm's (1986) colorful phrase. Consequently, research is often prejudged by clinicians as not applying to their real-world clinical work. A result of this prejudgement is that many clinicians see the presentation of clinical case studies as more helpful than the research literature (Jacobson, 1985a; Kaye, 1990). This may be one reason for the *Family Therapy Networker*'s greater circulation over more scholarly journals such as *Family Process, The Journal of Marital and Family Therapy,* and *The Journal of Family Psychology.* Rather than being swayed by research, most clinicians prefer to judge ideas on the basis of their own experience (Atkinson, Heath, & Chenail, 1991). This is unfortunate because researchers and therapists need each other to survive (Barton et al., 1985; Gurman, 1983; Schwartz & Breunlin, 1983), even though neither camp may realize it.

Several strategies have been used over the years to bridge the gap between researchers and clinicians. Lyman Wynne (1983) spoke of early conferences focusing on dialogues between researchers and clinicians. This strategy continues to be pursued today in both the American Family Therapy Academy (AFTA) and the American Association for Marriage and Family Therapy (AAMFT) with clinician-researcher dialogues.

Another strategy attempted by researchers is to educate clinicians about the virtues of research and about how to interpret the obscure language often used in technical papers (e.g., Barton et al., 1985). Unfortunately, these attempts often fall on deaf ears or end up preaching to the already converted. More recently, calls have been made by therapists and researchers for more clinically relevant research studies (e.g., Kaye, 1990; Griffith & Griffith, 1990; Gurman, 1983; Shields, 1986a; 1986b; Tomm, 1983; 1986). But even here there is divisiveness. On the one hand, proponents of existing methodologies typically argue that satisfactory methods and instruments already exist. In fact, they argue that use of the existing methodologies is the only ethically responsible way to proceed with family therapy research (Gurman, 1983; Shields, 1986b). What's needed is for these methods to be understood, used, and interpreted appropriately (Gurman, 1983; Liddle, 1991).

On the other hand, there are also those who argue that existing methods and instruments don't (and can't) adequately capture the richness of family dynamics and therapy (Griffith & Griffith, 1990; Tomm, 1986). In reducing therapy to micro levels—which is necessary for traditional research—the meaningfulness and systemic qualities of events under study are often lost (Griffith & Griffith, 1990). What's needed are new methodologies that allow researchers to capture and maintain the richness of the therapy experience (Griffith & Griffith, 1990; Tomm, 1986).

Fortunately, methods are now beginning to be proposed that appear to be congruent with systems theory, that capture the richness of clinical experience, and that are rigorous enough to gain scientific respect. For example, Safran, Greenberg, and Rice (1988) advocate a task analytic procedure wherein the clinician/researcher moves from critical therapeutic incident, to model building, to data in a recursive fashion to flesh out and understand key clinical events. Rice and Saperia (1984) explain that this task analytic method involves four steps. First, the investigator selects a task situation that acts as a context for the study. For example, in a study conducted by one of the authors (Bischoff, 1993), the task was a 20- to 30-minute in-session discussion about the client's experience of therapy, called a self-consultation. The goal was to identify the specific components of this therapeutic procedure. Second, the investigator conducts a rational analysis or "thought experiment" that leads to an idealized performance model of the task situation. In the self-consultation study, before examining data, the investigator developed a model of the procedure based on his own ideas about what an ideal example of the task would look like. Third, the investigator engages in an intensive grounding in the data through either quantitative or qualitative means. In this study, the investigator intensively analyzed videotaped examples of the procedure using a qualitative analytic technique called constant comparison analysis. Fourth, a comparison of the client and/or therapist performances on the task is compared against the idealized model, resulting in a new idealized model of the task situation. The investigator compared the results of his analysis, including client and therapist feedback, with the original rational model. This comparison and subsequent thought experiment resulted in a new idealized performance model of the self-consultation procedure. The steps of this research procedure were subsequently repeated several times, with each iteration resulting in an increasingly refined model of the task situation.

Other research methodologies are presented by Kaye (1990) and Hoshmand (1989). Interestingly, most of these methods that have appeal to clinicians are qualitative in nature. This need not necessarily be the case. Early authors, such as David Olson (1976), made a strong case for how quantitative research can and should inform clinical work. More recently, Howard Liddle (1991) has explained that the utility of quantitative findings continues to increase as improvements are made in the conduct of quantitative studies. Consequently, results from quantitative investigations are increasingly becoming easier to integrate into clinical practice. In a recent book, Duncan, Solovey, and Rusk (1992) showed how research findings helped establish the basis for their clinical approach. They cited research on common factors in therapeutic success and explained how they incorporated this research tradition into their clinical model.

However, none of these advancements in either quantitative or qualitative research will make much of an impact on the researcher-clinician gap if family therapy trainers do not socialize therapists to look to research as a way of informing their clinical work (Liddle, 1991; 1992). Although requiring research courses and master's and doctoral level theses may aid in this socialization process, we believe trainers also need to find other ways to make research come alive to their trainees. For example, Sandra Stith and her colleagues (Stith, Rosen, Barasch, & Wilson, 1991) assisted their master's level trainees in conducting a study that had immediate clinical relevance. Because a large proportion of their clientele was made up of substance abuse and domestic violence cases, the students studied the extent to which clients who had these problems initially presented them as complaints. They found that families typically didn't acknowledge coming to therapy for these problems, but that they became prominent as the therapy progressed. Consequently, the students were able to see firsthand how their research could help them better understand the denial characteristic of these acting-out families. Of course, the ultimate value of the study wasn't its rigor and sophistication, but it's impact in socializing students to the utility of research. Other useful assignments might include encouraging trainees to turn to the research literature for guidance in choosing treatment options or having them review the research literature that pertains to a clinical problem they are currently faced with as therapists.

Bridging the Gap between Quantitative and Qualitative Methods

As was mentioned in the previous section, quantitative methods have dominated the research literature in family therapy. However, as Piercy and Sprenkle (1990) have pointed out, there appears to be a "growing awareness that while the quantitative methods are suitable for testing hypotheses (verification), they are not of much value in discovering the relationships among variables." (p. 1122) Some authors even argue that the field took a presumptuous leap into the world of quantitative methods—applying quantitative methodologies to family therapy before its concepts had been well defined and operationalized (Bednar et al., 1988).

Interestingly, the field of family therapy itself grew from qualitative roots. Bateson was a trained anthropologist who developed his cybernetic perspective from ethnographic-qualitative research among the Iatmuls of New Guinea. Other early developments in the field of family therapy have a decidedly qualitative character, such as Lyman Wynne's and Murray Bowen's research at NIMH. However, probably in an effort to conform to psychology, medicine, and some of the other more established sciences, researchers in the field began to adopt more traditional methods of data collection and analysis.

Employing qualitative methods has been suggested by some as a means for expanding and enhancing the research being done in the field of family therapy (e.g., Moon, Dillon, & Sprenkle, 1990). However, qualitative approaches haven't been universally well accepted. In fact, there has been and continues to be a great deal of debate between antagonists and proponents of qualitative methods (e.g., Atkinson et al., 1991; Cavell & Snyder, 1991; Gurman, 1983; Shields, 1986a; Tomm, 1986).

Moon et al. (1990) explain that three stances are taken in the field with regard to the quantitative/qualitative debate. First, purists believe that qualitative and quantitative research paradigms are incompatible. They argue that assumptions about the world and the nature of reality are different within the two paradigms and that therefore they have incompatible research objectives. The second group is the pragmatists. These investigators are interested in answering their research questions with the best methods possible. The pragmatists believe that there is no inherent incompatibility between qualitative and quantitative methods, and that researchers should select whatever method best answers particular research questions. The third group is the synthesists. They hold that the two methodologies are complimentary. They provide different kinds of information, both of which can contribute to a better understanding of the phenomena under study.

We see a gradual rapprochement between these two research camps (much like what's happening in the field as a whole) and a growing acceptance of the worth of both quantitative and qualitative methods (Moon & Sprenkle, 1992). Increasingly, articles and research describing qualitative methodologies are being accepted in the leading journals in the field (e.g., Gale & Newfield, 1992; Hoshmand, 1989; Moon et al., 1990; Smith, Sells, & Clevenger, in press). The American Association for Marriage and Family Therapy has begun to recognize the value of qualitative methodologies by granting its Student Research Award to qualitative investigations in 1991, 1992, and 1993.

Researchers are also coming to recognize that qualitative methods can complement their quantitative studies by providing contextual data that can enrich the interpretation of quantitative research findings (Piercy & Sprenkle, 1990). For example, Joanning, Newfield, and Quinn (1987) combined ethnographic interviews with a primarily quantitative study of the treatment of adolescent drug abusers. Another example is Jacobson, Schmaling, and Holtzworth-Munroe's (1987) two-year follow-up of a component analysis of behavioral marital therapy. This study consisted of both a controlled experiment and a structured interview. In both of these cases the qualitative findings expanded and enriched the quantitative findings.

Cohesiveness within the Field of Family Therapy

As evidenced in this volume, there is great diversity in thought within the field of marriage and family therapy. This can be confusing at best and divisive at worst. Research can have the effect of contributing to this divisiveness or of bridging the distance and confusion among approaches to family therapy.

The divisive characteristics of family therapy research were most evident in past efforts to pit one approach against another in an attempt to prove the superiority of one model—typically one's own—over others (Gurman & Kniskern, 1978; 1981). These attempts proved futile. When differences were found and investigators claimed victory, their opponents cried foul on the grounds that the defeated approach wasn't accurately represented (Mahrer, 1988; Gurman et al., 1986).

A recent example is the debate between Neil Jacobson (1991a; 1991b), Douglas Snyder and Robert Wills (1991), and others. Jacobson defended behavioral marital therapy, an approach that was found less effective to insight-oriented marital therapy in a comparative study conducted by Snyder and Wills (1989). Jacobson argued that since Snyder and Wills weren't behavioral marital therapists themselves, they couldn't adequately teach the behavioral approach to the therapists in the study nor develop a treatment manual that would fairly represent the approach. Comparative studies like this are at least potentially divisive because it's difficult to remain unbiased. Thus, comparative outcome studies usually generate more heat than light. These competitions generally exaggerate differences between approaches as typically practiced and usually convert no one.

Happily, current research efforts have moved beyond the us-against-them competitions of the past. In Gurman and Kniskern's (1978) comprehensive review of the research literature, many studies cited were global comparisons of one theoretical approach against another. However, by 1985 Neil Jacobson (1985) was urging researchers to end the global competition among the various schools of therapy. He argued that because approaches to therapy typically share a number of overlapping features, reliably significant main effects are rarely found. Jacobson urged investigators to look for interaction effects instead. In other words, investigators should try to determine which approach is more effective with a particular problem or a particular type of client. This trend was evident in Gurman et al.'s (1986) review published just one year later. Rather than trying to elucidate the relative merits of behavioral therapy over nonbehavioral therapies as Gurman and Kniskern (1978) had done in their earlier review, the authors focused on the application of specific family therapy approaches to particular problem areas (e.g., psychosomatic disorders, juvenile delinquency).

This movement away from comparative studies seems appropriate considering that few practitioners will abandon their preferred models of family therapy on account of research findings (Mahrer, 1988). Al Mahrer (1988) believes that therapists select their preferred models due to variables such as the charisma of the proponents of the model, intuition, and personality fit. Also, there is considerable evidence to suggest that common factors across therapeutic approaches have more to do with successful outcome than do the unique features of any one approach (Duncan et al., 1992; Lambert, 1986; Patterson, 1984; Todd & Stanton, 1983). Furthermore, therapist effects account for a greater proportion of outcome variance than treatment effects (Crits-Christoph, Baranackie, Kurcias et al., 1991; Crits-Christoph & Mintz, 1991; Luborsky, Crits-Christoph, McLellan et al., 1986; Luborsky, McLellan, Woody, O'Brien, & Auerbach, 1985). We are aware of instances the work of a single therapist, in a research study with multiple therapists, has made an approach look like a success or a failure. For all these reasons, it makes less and less sense to continue to pit one school of family therapy against another.

Interestingly, one of the conclusions reached by Jacobson (1991a; 1991b) in the aforementioned debate was that there are more similarities in the change-promoting characteristics of behavioral marital therapy and insight-oriented marital therapy than there are differences. This lends weight to the argument that more work needs to be done to understand the common factors that cut across various therapies. It's even possible that the field of family therapy can be drawn together by findings about non–theory–specific change processes.

We do, however, strongly support intraschool analysis of the importance of specific components that make up the various family therapy models. An excellent example is Jacobson et al.'s (1987) examination of behavioral exchange, communication, and combined approaches to behavioral marital therapy. Rather than fostering competition, such studies allow proponents to sharpen models and separate active ingredients from inert fillers.

The (Re-)Emergence of the Process Perspective

Outcome research is concerned with what happens after therapy has been completed (e.g., the number of clients achieving the goals of treatment or the effects of treatment on family functioning). Process research is concerned with what happens during therapy (e.g., changes in client levels of resistance in the course of treatment). A current trend is attempting to combine these two types of research in hopes that we can learn what specific aspects of the treatment process lead to successful outcomes.

Although the earliest family therapy research was concerned more with the process of family functioning and therapist intervention, as research became more sophisticated the focus shifted to outcome variables. Early researchers sought to validate family therapy by providing evidence of successful outcome.

The process research done in the 1970s typically averaged results on process instruments over the entire course of treatment and then related this averaged score to the outcome of the therapy. However, in using this strategy, results were often diluted and not meaningful because process variables (e.g., resistance; relationship skill) vary over the course of therapy to such an extent that the variation dilutes the conclusions. Consequently, the results of this process research had limited clinical usefulness and were often discounted as irrelevant.

However, there is currently emerging what Gurman et al. (1986) have referred to as the "new process perspective." Rather than focusing entirely on the process *or* outcome of treatment, there is a recognition that process *and* outcome go hand in hand. In fact, the final outcome of treatment—what Gurman et al. (1986) have referred to as the "big O"—is made up of a series of outcomes, or episodes in the process of therapy, that occur throughout treatment—referred to as the "little o's"—that lead to the big O. This conceptualization allows researchers to more easily link process and outcome variables.

Two of the best examples of this new process perspective have come from Gerald Patterson and his colleagues at the Oregon Social Learning Center (Chamberlain, Patterson, Reid, Cavanaugh, & Forgatch, 1984; Patterson & Chamberlain, 1988; Patterson & Forgatch, 1985) and from Leslie Greenberg and Susan Johnson in their studies of the in-session processes of emotionally focused couples therapy (Greenberg, Ford, Alden, & Johnson, 1993; Greenberg, James, & Conry, 1988; Johnson & Greenberg, 1988). In the Patterson studies, investigators examined the relationship between therapist interventions and client resistance. Rather than averaging resistance across the entire course of therapy and relating it to the general outcome of therapy, the investigators analyzed resistance separately during the beginning, middle, and concluding stages of treatment and related this to the frequency with which therapists used specific techniques during these stages of therapy. Interestingly, they found that resistance was lowest at the beginning and concluding stages of their parent skills training treatment program and highest in the middle stages. The higher levels of resistance during the middle stages of therapy were also positively correlated with the therapist's use of "teach" and "confront" interventions.

Greenberg and Johnson have used a task analytic methodology to study processes occurring within emotionally focused couples therapy. In order to contextualize therapeutic processes, these investigators carefully selected specific situations where key therapeutic processes occurred. This is in contrast to the traditional approach of averaging scores obtained through the analysis of an entire session. Through their research they found (among other things) that emotionally focused therapy promotes more affiliative behaviors in couples during the latter stages of treatment, that experiencing underlying emotions is positively associated with conflict resolution, and that one partner's intimate self-disclosure is positively associated with affiliative responsiveness in the other. They also found that clients identified the critical incidents of successful therapy to be: expressing underlying emotions, understanding one's own experience of the relationship, taking responsibility for one's own experience, and having experience and emotion validated by one's partner.

Although the new process perspective holds great promise for the field, it has as yet produced relatively few empirical studies. Mitch Dickey (1993a; 1993b) reviewed both the methodologies and substantive findings of the process studies published prior to 1992 and found only 36 empirical papers reporting on process investigations. (Interestingly, 50 percent of these papers had been published within the last five years.) There are several reasons for the relative dearth of process studies in family therapy. First, the field is still young enough that it's too early to have reached the level of sophistication necessary to conduct this type of study (Dickey, 1993a; Piercy & Sprenkle, 1990). For example, Gottman (1987) explains that the sequential analysis statistical techniques necessary to conduct quality process research are often not well understood by family therapy researchers. Second, high quality process studies are generally expensive to conduct, and funding sources are often reluctant to sponsor such projects. However, willingness to fund such studies may increase as design improvements are made (Dickey, 1993a). Finally, reliable and valid instruments specific enough to tap processes that can be related to outcome are rare (Piercy & Sprenkle, 1990) and those that do exist have been typically only used once (Dickey, 1993a; Pinsof, 1981). This may be because these instruments are typically study and setting specific and don't address the issues concerning subsequent researchers.

Nevertheless, process studies are increasing in popularity. This is fortunate because they can potentially provide a wealth of information that will make it easier to understand the processes necessary for successful family therapy and help bridge the researcher/clinician gap.

Improvements in Research Design

One of the most persistent calls over the years has been for improvements in research conceptualization and design. Great strides have been made in this regard, especially in the past 10 to 15 years (Dickey, 1993a; Gurman et al., 1986; Piercy & Sprenkle, 1990). For example, Gurman and Kniskern (1978) lamented the fact that their research review mainly consisted of methodologically inadequate studies. Since that time, however, several excellent studies have been conducted that can be used as models for future investigations of family therapy. Some of the most noteworthy include the outstanding work on the family management of schizophrenia by Falloon, Boyd, McGill et al. (1985). Another exemplary investigation is Jacobson et al.'s (1987) aforementioned component analysis of behavioral marital therapy in which the investigators broke the therapy down to its specific elements for analysis of the relative contribution of each to treatment outcome. Patterson and Chamberlain (1988) offer perhaps the best example of process research in their study of client resistance to parent management training. Also exemplary is Russell, Szmukler, Dare, and Eisler's (1987) evaluation of family therapy with anorexia nervosa and bulimia nervosa and Szapocznik, Perez-Vidal, Brickman et al.'s (1988) study of engaging teenage drug abusers and their families in treatment.

These investigations were noteworthy for more than just their careful execution and the optimum control of extraneous variables (Piercy & Sprenkle, 1990). Each of these studies also used a variety of reliable and valid measures from a number of perspectives. They included nonreactive dependent variables such as recidivism and rehospitalization. Long-term follow-up data were also a universal key ingredient.

Not only have quantitative design improvements been made, but, increasingly, consistency and rigor are being promoted in qualitative investigations as well (Moon et al., 1990). Although not as many high quality qualitative studies have been published as quantitative ones, several excellently designed studies exist that can serve as models for future investigations. Most notable is the study of the family treatment of adolescent drug abusers and their families conducted by Harvey Joanning and his colleagues (Joanning et al., 1987; Newfield et al., 1991). Although the quantitative aspects (Joanning, Quinn, Thomas, & Mullen, 1992) of this study are suspect and are of limited clinical utility, the study is noteworthy for the quality of its qualitative design. Through the qualitative portion of the study the investigators were able to provide analytic rigor while maintaining and communicating the richness of the client's experience of therapy. In this study clients were able to describe their experience of treatment, delineating what they believed were the stages through which the therapy progressed and their impressions of treatment at each of these stages. Other strong qualitative investigations include the ethnographic investigations of reflecting teams by Sell, Smith, Coe, Yoshioka, and Robbins (in press) and Smith et al. (in press); Beer's (1993) ethnographic description of marital therapy; and Gale and Newfield's (1992) conversation analysis of a solution focused marital therapy session. These studies have been particularly helpful in expanding the field's acceptance of the value of information gained through alternative research methodologies.

Statistical versus Clinical Significance

Studies of family therapy have traditionally used statistical significance as the sole criterion for evaluating treatment. However, as an evaluation of group means, statistical significance often disguises within group data. Although differences between two treatments may be statistically significant, this doesn't indicate the number of families who actually moved from a dysfunctional to a functional level. In fact, it's possible that some of those in the "improved" condition may never have actually become functional. Unfortunately, this is precisely the type of information that is most clinically meaningful (Jacobson, Follette, & Revenstorf, 1984; Piercy & Sprenkle, 1990).

In an effort to address this problem, Neil Jacobson and his colleagues (Jacobson et al., 1984; Jacobson & Revenstorf, 1989) have developed the concept of clinical significance: the degree to which the client has improved as a result of treatment (Jacobson & Revenstorf, 1989). Clinically significant results are those in which a previously dysfunctional person receives a posttest score that is more likely to belong to the functional than to the dysfunctional population. The most reliable way of determining this is by comparing the individual's score to norms of functionality on the criterion variable. In the absence of such norms, Jacobson proposes that the criterion be movement of two standard deviations (toward the functional range) from the mean.

Jacobson and his colleagues have also developed a statistical measure, the Reliable Change index (RC), which helps determine the degree to which change is a result of measurement error (Jacobson & Revenstorf, 1989). Other methods of determining client movement from dysfunctional to functional and maintenance of that change at posttest have also been proposed (Jacobson et al., 1984; Jacobson & Revenstorf, 1989). An example of the use of these procedures is found in the study by Jacobson et al. (1987) in which the clinically significant categories of "improved," "happily married," "unchanged," "deteriorated," "separated or divorced," and "relapsed" were developed. This type of categorizing proved much more informative than the sole reliance on statistical significance levels.

The application of meta-analysis to marriage and family therapy literature (Hazelrigg et al., 1987; Markus et al., 1990; Shoham-Solomon & Rosenthal, 1987; Sprenkle & Sheehan, 1985; Wampler, 1982) has also been used as a means of making study results more clinically meaningful (Piercy & Sprenkle, 1990). Meta-analysis uses standard deviation units to determine the effect size of an outcome measure (Smith, Glass, & Miller, 1980). An effect size of "plus one" means that treatment resulted in a mean score one standard deviation above the control group. This measure of change allows researchers to combine results derived from several related outcome measures and determine the magnitude of the clinical effect (Piercy & Sprenkle, 1990).

Looking to the Client for Answers

Unfortunately, most of what is known about therapy is only from the perspective of the therapist or researcher. One of the emerging trends in the field is to consider the client's experience of therapy as well. Two important preliminary studies are worth mentioning.

First, Kuehl, Newfield, and Joanning (1990; Joanning et al., 1991) asked clients who had completed a combined form of structural and strategic therapy treatment for drug abusing adolescents about their experience of the process of therapy. This ethnographic study of therapy from the client's perspective resulted in a description of six phases of therapy that closely resembled and validated the stages typically thought to occur in structural-strategic therapy.

The second study was an ethnographic exploration of the entire course of treatment (Beer, 1993). Jim Beer followed a marital therapy case from start to finish, conducting in-depth interviews separately with the clients and their therapist. The interviews took place after marital therapy sessions and included videotaped segments of the sessions to stimulate therapist and client comments and perceptions. Videotapes were also made of the video review sessions. It turned out that the clients found aspects of the therapeutic relationship (such as not taking sides, empathy, and validating the clients' experience) more helpful than specific therapeutic techniques. This study supports the general consensus in the literature that the therapeutic alliance has more impact than the theoretical orientation of the therapist (Lambert, 1986). Not surprisingly, there was a consensus among the participating clients and therapist that the research component enhanced the effect of therapy. Positive influences included the amount of time the clients spent with the researcher, the added perspective that the videotape review afforded the couple, the "different set of eyes" that the researcher offered, the egalitarian relationship that the research context implied, and the recognition of the couple's expertise (Beer, 1993).

Both of these studies challenge us to expand our thinking to include the point of view of our clients (both in research and the conduct of therapy) and also suggest alternate ways of gathering information and looking at the world.

Cost-Effectiveness of Treatment

An underlying assumption of family therapy is that individuals don't suffer problems in isolation. By giving key relationships a prominent position in the treatment, therapy should improve the functioning of all of the members of the system and save both treatment dollars and time. Although this makes intuitive sense, research in this area is sorely needed (Pike & Piercy, 1990). Connie Pike and Fred Piercy (1990) have made a strong case for the importance of cost-effectiveness research and have delineated the steps necessary to conduct it. However, researchers have yet to respond to the challenge. As Pike and Piercy (1990) put it:

> In an era where money talks, outcome research alone might not be sufficient cause for funding family therapy treatment programs since other treatment modalities may also demonstrate efficacy. However, if family therapy proves to be not only effective but cost-effective in treating certain problems or populations, such information could translate into increased government spending, research grants, and insurance coverage. Beyond this, though, such research is simply responsible and prudent. (p. 387)

OUTCOME RESEARCH: SUBSTANTIVE AREAS

As mentioned previously, research has moved away from global comparative studies toward investigating the outcomes of family therapy with specific problem areas (Gurman et al., 1986; Piercy & Sprenkle, 1990). In this section, we will highlight research pertaining to substantive areas that hold special interest and for which sufficient research has been done to begin to draw meaningful conclusions. Keep in mind, however, that empirical investigations have most generally been conducted on therapies that are more pragmatic in nature (i.e., those primarily concerned with behavior change), such as the behavioral, structural, and strategic therapies (Gurman & Kniskern, 1978; Gurman et al., 1986; Hazelrigg et al., 1987; Henggeler et al., 1992). The more "aesthetic" (Keeney & Sprenkle, 1983) therapies associated with social construction and intergenerational theories have received little empirical attention (Gurman & Kniskern, 1978; Gurman et al., 1986; Hazelrigg et al., 1987; Henggeler et al., 1992). Proponents of these therapies often eschew traditional research methods (Gurman et al., 1986). Consequently, those studies that are conducted are often not published in refereed journals or are discredited as nonscientific. In fact, reviewers of family therapy research often refuse to include investigations that don't conform to the standards of the traditional positivistic research paradigm (e.g., Dickey, 1993a; 1993b; Hazelrigg et al., 1987; Henggeler, 1992).

Authors such as Cavell and Snyder (1991) and others (e.g., Henggeler et al., 1992; Shields, 1986a) have argued that unless treatments can be operationalized to the point of lending themselves to empirical validation, they shouldn't be conducted. However, concepts and treatment issues in the aesthetic therapies are typically difficult to operationalize. Hopefully, the aforementioned qualitative methods will offer additional research options for proponents of these schools of therapy.

It should also be noted that some of the best current research has demonstrated the effectiveness of family therapy in the management or alleviation of pathologies that many believe to be biologically determined, such as schizophrenia and depression (Piercy & Sprenkle, 1990). Interestingly, family therapy hasn't typically been used in isolation in these studies. Rather, it has been paired with the use of medications or other treatments (e.g., psychoeducation). This doesn't discount the usefulness of family therapy but suggests it can be a powerful adjunct to the work of other disciplines.

Schizophrenia

In its early years family therapy held out the hope that this new way of looking at human problems might at last be the answer to that most bizarre and baffling form of madness, schizophrenia. As the years passed, however, we began to realize it was a mistake to assume that since family problems were exaggerated in families with a schizophrenic member that these problems *caused* schizophrenia. What's more, it turned out that of all the problems traditional approaches to family therapy were effective with, schizophrenia was not among them. However, in recent years investigators have discovered that family therapy does have an important role to play in the treatment of schizophrenia, though not perhaps the primary role once envisioned.

The premises on which the current research in this area is built have changed dramatically. Much of the early research focused on the belief that the etiology of schizophrenia lay in dysfunctional family communication patterns (e.g., Bateson, Jackson, Haley, & Weakland, 1956). The theory of the double bind and related communication patterns was an underlying premise for these investigations and for the therapy (Bateson, Jackson, Haley, & Weakland, 1963; Watzlawick, Beavin, & Jackson, 1967) that evolved from them. Focus was taken away from the individual symptom bearer and the onus of responsibility for the disorder was placed on the entire family unit.

In contrast, more recent research has focused on the family management of schizophrenia through psychoeducation (Anderson, Reiss, & Hogarty, 1986; Falloon et al., 1985). Etiology has been conceptualized with a vulnerability-stress model that suggests that the disorder is a result of an interaction between biological vulnerability and environmental stress (Anderson et al., 1986). Environmental stress has generally been operationalized as including a dysfunctional family emotional climate, high in "expressed emotion" (EE). High EE families are very emotionally reactive to the patient as manifested in frequent criticism, harsh tone of voice, and constant pressure. Treatment addresses both environmental stress and biological vulnerability. The latter is managed through the use of neuroleptic medication (e.g., Thorazine, Haldol, Prolixin) to control the psychotic symptomology. Environmental stress is addressed, in part, through the inclusion of the family in treatment. Families are encouraged to modify their expectations and emotional reactions to the schizophrenic member. Consequently, the family becomes a source of support rather than of aggravation. The family therapy component is usually behavioral, emphasizing problem-solving and crisis management skills (Goldstein &

Strachan, 1987). Rather than shifting all responsibility—and blame—to the family, schizophrenia is now seen as a disorder that resides in the individual but that can be exacerbated or calmed by the family's influence.

Although there have been several well-designed studies of the family management of schizophrenia (Goldstein, Rodrick, Evans, May, & Steinberg, 1978; Leff, Kuipers, Berkowitz, Eberlein-Vries, & Sturgeon, 1982; Leff, Kuipers, Berkowitz, & Sturgeon, 1985; Falloon et al., 1985; Hogarty, Anderson, Reiss et al., 1986), the study by Falloon et al. (1985) serves as a concise example of the results derived from these studies. In this investigation, Ian Falloon and his associates studied the treatment of 36 schizophrenic patients over a period of two years. Patients were randomly assigned to individual supportive therapy or to an in-home, family therapy/psychoeducation regimen. Both groups received medication. Patients receiving family based treatment scored higher on social functioning and lower on overt symptomatology throughout the project than did those receiving individual treatment. After two years, only 17 percent of patients in individual treatment hadn't had a relapse, whereas 83 percent of those in family treatment hadn't suffered a relapse.

Piercy and Sprenkle (1990) summarized the major findings of Falloon et al. (1985) and the other strong studies cited above. Their conclusions were that (1) psychosocial intervention adds significantly to the therapeutic effect of antipsychotic medications; (2) family management through psychoeducation may be superior to individual management during aftercare; (3) family management seems to enhance social functioning of the patient and eases the burden of the family; and (4) the way in which family members convey emotionally laden comments is positively associated with relapse.

Affective Disorders

Unfortunately, there have been fewer studies on the effectiveness of family therapy in the treatment of affective disorders (e.g., depression, bipolar disorder, schizoaffective disorder) than there have been on schizophrenia (Haas & Clarkin, 1988). The dearth of studies in this area is regrettable considering that affective disorders have a higher rate of occurrence than most other disorders (Beach & O'Leary, 1986; Haas & Clarkin, 1988; Wetzel, 1984). Fortunately, some authors have begun patterning studies after the excellent investigations of the treatment of schizophrenia (Clarkin, Glick, Haas et al., 1990; Florin, Nostadt, Reck, Franzen, & Jenkins, 1992; Miklowitz, Goldstein, Nuechterlein, Snyder, & Mintz, 1988; Miklowitz & Goldstein, 1990).

Preliminary findings on psychoeducational programs for affective disorders are encouraging (Henggeler et al., 1992). For example, Miklowitz et al. (1988) evaluated levels of stressful emotionality (e.g., criticism, overinvolvement) in the family of the patient. Results indicated that high levels of this construct were associated with higher relapse rates, while low levels were associated with low rates of relapse. Miklowitz and Goldstein (1990) later reported on the family treatment (through psychoeducation) of these patients following their discharge from inpatient hospitalization. Findings included that only 11 percent of those receiving the family treatment relapsed, compared with 61 percent of an untreated sample. Combining this study with those related to schizophrenia, it appears that family involvement in the treatment of major mental illness, through therapy and psychoeducation, decreases rates of relapse and recidivism. However, conclusive results related to affective disorders aren't yet available.

Psychosomatic Disorders

Another area of noteworthy findings and considerable design improvement has been the application of family therapy to the treatment of anorexia and bulimia. In general, and consistent with early findings (e.g., Minuchin et al., 1978), structural and strategic family therapies have been found to produce positive results with many anorexics, especially those younger than 18 (Dare, Eisler, Russell & Szmukler, 1990; Russell et al., 1987). However, mixed results have called into question the effectiveness of family therapy with bulimics and anorexics older than 18 (Dare et al., 1990; Russell et al., 1987).

In an excellently designed study (Dare et al., 1990; Russell et al., 1987; Szmukler, Eisler, Russell, & Dare 1985), investigators compared a structural and strategic family treatment with an individual supportive treatment of anorexics and bulimics. Eighty female patients were randomly assigned to either family or individual therapy immediately following an inpatient hospitalization. The outpatient treatments were continued for one year after discharge from the hospital. The findings suggested that family therapy is generally more effective than individual therapy when age of onset of the illness is less than 18 years. On the other hand, investigators found suggestive evidence that individual supportive therapy is more effective than family therapy when the age of onset is more than 18 years. These results held on the criteria of dropping out of treatment, weight gain, and general ratings of outcome. No significant differences were found in recidivism rates.

The successful family treatment in this study moved through a series of stages (Dare et al., 1990), beginning with a primary focus on the eating disorder, with the parents being instructed to control the child's eating. Treatment then moved to maintenance of this control in an attempt to increase body weight to within normal limits. The final phase of treatment consisted of giving control over eating and weight gain back to the child. Emphasis was also given to helping the child develop an appropriate young adult relationship with her parents, without the use of anorexic symptoms as a means of communication. Clients assigned to the family treatment condition were seen only with their family present.

Presumably family therapy was effective with younger anorexics because the restructuring of family boundaries and hierarchy was in accordance with the developmental stage of the family. Relatedly, a possible explanation for the ineffectiveness of the family therapy with older anorexics may be that the family restructuring wasn't consistent with the developmental tasks facing the anorexic. It is unclear why family treatment wasn't as effective with bulimic patients, although a small sample size and the failure to distinguish between older and younger bulimics may be a factor.

This study challenges the notion that family therapy is the treatment of choice for all anorexic and bulimic cases (Minuchin et al., 1975; Minuchin et al., 1978; Schwartz, Barrett, & Saba, 1985). The results of this study have significant implications of the importance therapists should place on flexibility in their models, taking into account each client's needs in treatment.

Drug Abuse and Alcoholism

Prior to about the 1970s, mental health professionals often assumed that they could treat alcoholism and drug abuse with whatever form of psychotherapy they usually practiced. Their thinking went something like this: People drink or use drugs because they are unhappy; therefore, if we resolve the reasons for their unhappiness, they will be able to stop abusing alcohol and drugs. The problem with this way of thinking is that alcohol and drugs have such powerful chemical effects that most people aren't able to give them up with only the support of nondirective psychotherapy. Instead, effective treatment for these virulent and tenacious problems may require a more specialized and active approach. Particularly in the area of substance abuse, family therapy has proven to be a potent component of treatment. Just as with schizophrenia, family therapy alone may not be successful, but can be when combined with detoxification, reeducation, and group support in a recovery setting.

Research support for family therapy approaches to substance abuse has been strong and consistent. In 1982, Stanton, Todd, and Associates published their landmark research on structural/strategic therapy with heroin addicts. Two family therapy conditions (paid and unpaid) were compared with a placebo condition in which families saw educational films and an unpaid treatment-as-usual condition consisting of individual counseling plus methadone. Subjects were young men under the age of 36 who had been addicted to heroin for at least two years. Family therapy led to marked improvement over the non-family therapy treatments on a variety of drug related outcome measures both at termination and at follow-up.

In 1985, the National Institute on Drug Abuse (NIDA) awarded large grants to three groups (Purdue University, Texas Tech University, and the University of California at San Francisco) to study family therapy approaches for adolescent substance abuse. At Purdue, Robert Lewis and his colleagues (Lewis, Piercy, Sprenkle, & Trepper, 1990) studied an integrated structural/strategic/behavioral model and found support for family treatment. For younger teens especially, family therapy was more successful than family drug education or individual therapy in diminishing the severity of drug use. At Texas Tech, Joanning, Quinn, Thomas, and Mullen (1992) also found a family systems approach more effective in stopping adolescent drug use than adolescent group therapy or a family drug education model. While reporting similar results in his University of California, San Francisco study, Howard Liddle found differential outcomes depending on the extent to which the therapist built strong alliances with parents and teenagers (as cited in Todd & Selekman, 1991). The research of Jose Szapocznik and his colleagues (1983; 1986; 1989) suggests that a family therapy approach can be successful even when only one person is directly involved in treatment. Szapocznik and Kurtines (1989) note that ". . . this research clarifies that what is critical in family work is not who is present in the therapy settings, but rather how the therapists conceptualize the problem and the intervention" (p. 163). It is significant that all of the aforementioned approaches utilize present-centered, problem-focused, active approaches that are relatively brief. Particularly with younger teens, with whom strong therapeutic alliances are established, such methods appear quite promising.

Sound research on family therapy approaches to alcoholism lags behind that on drug abuse. This is true in spite of the impressive literature that describes the nature of alcoholic families (Steinglass Bennett, Wolin, & Reiss, 1987; Jacob & Leonard, 1992). With few exceptions, the clinical outcome studies are pilot in nature. However, what clinical reports and controlled studies do exist favor the inclusion of family therapy in the treatment of alcoholism and offer compelling evidence that involvement of spouses in treatment programs improves the likelihood that the alcoholic will participate (Steinglass, et al., 1987) and increases the probability of a positive outcome (McGrady & Epstein, in press). The one methodologically strong study completed to date is by O'Farrell, Cutter, and Floyd (1985).

Perhaps the dearth of outcome studies on family treatment of alcoholism reflects the entrenched nature of existing alcohol treatment programs. Steinglass et al. (1987) note that there is little evidence that clinicians are approaching alcoholism with a sophisticated sense of family system principles. A dominant model of clinical practice remains the AA/Alanon philosophy of "separate but equal" treatment for spouses. It is too often the case that an alcoholic individual and his or her family are asked to fit the preconceived notions and treatment schedules of established alcoholism programs (Steinglass et al., 1987).

Child Abuse and Neglect

Despite growing concern over the seriousness of abuse and neglect within families, very little empirical work has been done in this area. This is especially true regarding the systemic treatment of spouse abuse and child sexual abuse, areas where there has been virtually no well-designed and controlled treatment research. The lack of research on these problems may in part be due to the assumptions that are generally held about the treatment of these populations. When there is danger to a child or a woman in an intimate relationship, many professionals become advocates for the victim at the expense of the larger system. This often means removing the child from the family in cases of sexual abuse or encouraging wives to leave in cases of spouse abuse. Consequently, intrafamily abuse is often seen as a protection issue and not as a family therapy issue. Effective family interventions, however, must protect victims of abuse, while at the same time supporting the family (Lipchik, 1991; Trepper & Barrett, 1989). Research on abuse is further complicated by the fact that intervention is often delegated to social control agencies, whose job it is to protect the victim, not to provide family treatment. Issues of confidentiality and workers' desire to protect victims from undue harm make it difficult to study this population. Obviously, feelings run high in such matters—with conflicting pressures to support the family or protect the child—making decisions about treatment, and research, difficult.

Fortunately, physical abuse and neglect of children have received some empirical attention. Although firm conclusions can not yet be drawn, there is suggestive evidence for the effectiveness of family therapy in the treatment of child abuse and neglect. Brunk, Henggeler, and Whelan (1987) conducted a study in which 43 families, each of whom had been investigated for child abuse or neglect, were referred by the state social services agency for treatment. The authors randomly assigned these families to one of two treatment conditions: a parent training group or a family therapy treatment using multisystemic therapy. Multisystemic therapy is a home-based family treatment that assumes problems are multidetermined and multidimensional. Each treatment is individually tailored to meet a family's needs using interventions associated with structural, strategic, and behavioral therapies.

At the conclusion of an eight-week trial, the investigators found that both treatments were associated with decreases in parent psychiatric symptomatology and family stress. There was also noticeable improvement in the family and individual problems. There was suggestive evidence that the family treatment through multisystemic therapy was more effective than the group treatment in facilitating changes that are associated with non-problem families (e.g., appropriate responsiveness to child). There was also suggestive evidence that the parent training group was more effective than multisystemic therapy at reducing social problems (e.g., social isolation). Although differential effects were found, this study provides preliminary evidence that family therapy is an effective treatment with abusing and neglectful families.

Disruptive Behavior Disorders

One of the areas where involving family members in the therapy of the identified patient has the most intuitive appeal is in the treatment of children and adolescents with conduct and oppositional disorders (e.g., arguing, whining, teasing, tantrums, and other defiant and aggressive behaviors). Even non-family therapists don't think twice about inviting parents into the treatment of the child or adolescent engaged in problem behaviors. Consequently, studies of the treatment of conduct disorders in children and adolescents cut across all mental health disciplines and number into the hundreds (Kazdin, 1991). This makes sense, considering that conduct problems in general are estimated to make up from one-third to one-half of all child and adolescent referrals (Kazdin, 1987). Unfortunately, a serious deficiency that pervades these studies severely limits their generalizability. Many, if not most, researchers have neglected to specify the type of treatment provided. Most of the studies took place in child guidance clinics and involved the parents, but it's unclear if therapy with a relational focus was the treatment under study, or if the therapists had been trained in family therapy. But, despite this limitation, psychotherapy with conduct disordered children has been found to be effective in most studies (Kazdin, 1991), and there seems to be consensus among reviewers that effective treatments should be family based (Kazdin 1987; Hazelrigg et al., 1987; Henggeler et al., 1992; Tolan et al., 1986).

One of the best known and well designed studies in this area is part of an ongoing research effort at the Oregon Social Learning Center (OSLC) (Patterson, 1974; Patterson & Chamberlain, 1988; 1992; Patterson, Chamberlain, & Reid, 1982). Gerald Patterson and Patricia Chamberlain have directed a project in which they have evaluated the effects of their family-based treatment on child functioning for over two decades. The method of treatment used in these studies is parent management training (Patterson et al., 1982), a behaviorally based treatment in which parents are taught how to implement social learning principles at home. The therapist typically works only with the parents, on the assumption that with the correct implementation of social learning principles, the child's behavior will improve.

Through the series of studies conducted at the OSLC, parent management training was compared with no treatment (Wiltz & Patterson, 1974), a placebo treatment (Walter & Gilmore, 1973), and a community based alternative treatment (Patterson et al., 1982). The results of each of these studies indicate superiority of parent management training over the alternative treatments in ratings of incidence of child behavior problems at posttest. These results have also been corroborated by other investigators (Fleishmann, 1981; Fleishmann & Szykula, 1981). In addition, the positive effects of parent management treatment have been maintained by families for up to 18 months (Fleishmann & Szykula, 1981).

Parent management training has also been found to be associated with positive effects beyond changes in the child's behavior. Alan Kazdin (1987) reports that maternal psychopathology (e.g., depression) and sibling behavior have been found to improve throughout the course of treatment, although these issues were not directly addressed during treatment.

The results of this research are instructive on several counts and can be summarized as follows: (1) parent management training has been found effective for the treatment of conduct disorders and to produce long-term results; (2) there is a system-wide impact from this type of family-oriented treatment, even though interventions were directed toward the conduct disordered child; and (3) there is evidence that successful treatment can be conducted through nonsymptomatic members.

Juvenile Delinquency

Although juvenile delinquency can be considered a subcategory of conduct disorders, we feel that it warrants separate attention in this chapter. This distinction is made mainly because juvenile delinquency refers to behavior of adolescents that has legal implications.

In general, the treatment of juvenile delinquency through psychotherapy has proven effective (Kazdin, 1987). Although many treatments of this population have emphasized isolating the offending adolescents from their families in order to proceed with treatment, these are based on an assumption that the problem is imbedded within the adolescent. With the recognition that the family environment influences adolescent behavior, most reviewers now suggest that the treatments holding most promise are those that are family based (Gurman & Kniskern, 1978; Henggeler, et al., 1992; Kazdin, 1987; Nichols & Schwartz, 1991; Tolan et al., 1986). In fact, family therapy has been found to be more effective than alternative treatments such as individual therapy, probation, and work programs in reducing rates of recidivism (Tolan et al., 1986).

Although a variety of treatment approaches have been used in the study of juvenile delinquency, in the family therapy field, behavioral and structural/

strategic family therapy or combinations of these two seem to be most common (Henggeler et al., 1982; Tolan et al., 1986). Probably most notable is a classic series of investigations by James Alexander and his colleagues (Alexander, Barton, Schiavo, & Parsons, 1977; Alexander & Parsons, 1973; Barton, Alexander, Waldron, Turner, & Warburton, 1985; Parsons & Alexander, 1973). These investigators studied the treatment of adolescents and their families referred to their facility by the probation department. The family treatment in these studies consisted of functional family therapy (FFT), incorporating components of behavioral, structural, and strategic therapies. The overall goal is to alter family interactions in such a way that family and individual needs are appropriately met, resulting in more healthy family functioning.

Alexander's first studies of FFT used adolescents of both sexes referred to treatment by the courts for behaviors identified as "soft delinquency" (e.g., running away, truancy, theft) (Alexander & Parsons, 1973; Parsons & Alexander, 1973). In one study, cases were assigned to FFT, a client-centered family group treatment, a psychodynamic family treatment, and a no-treatment condition. In the other study, cases were assigned to FFT, a placebo treatment condition, and a no-treatment control group. At the end of eight sessions, FFT was found to be superior to the alternative treatments in measures of family interaction and rates of recidivism. Interestingly, at follow-up 2-½ years after treatment, the FFT condition resulted in siblings with lower rates of court involvement (Klein, Alexander, & Parsons, 1977), a finding that speaks to the system-wide impact of the use of FFT in the treatment of juvenile delinquency.

CURRENT AND PERSISTENT ISSUES
ABOUT DIAGNOSIS AND MEASUREMENT

There are several ongoing issues related to family therapy research that have persisted throughout the history of the discipline. They are related to the difficulties inherent in conducting research in which a natural group (the family or its subsystems) is seen in treatment. These issues are (1) tensions around individual diagnosis and utilizing changes in the individual as a criteria or *the* criteria for improvement and (2) problems in measuring change at the dyadic and family systems levels.

Individual versus Family Systems Diagnosis and Change Criteria

Many researchers (ourselves included) agree with Gurman and Kniskern (1981) that since marital and family therapy typically seeks to improve the functioning of all family members and their interactions, change should be assessed at the individual, dyadic, and family systems levels.

Individual assessment, however, remains controversial. Many family therapy researchers have avoided individual assessment because they believe it puts undue emphasis on the identified patient (IP). Few would disagree that if IP status were to be the *sole* criterion for change, no conclusions could be drawn about changes on the dyadic or family system levels (Wynne, 1988; Gurman & Kniskern, 1981). In fact, a major impetus for the development of family therapy in the first place was that hospitalized schizophrenics who improved in treatment often regressed when they returned to their families. It is crucial to determine the relationship between IP and broader system change. To ignore the individual as a unit for research, however, may be as shortsighted as relying on IP change exclusively.

Another criticism of individual assessment is the philosophical argument that diagnoses pathologize persons and create self-fulfilling prophecies. The widely used individual diagnostic system, the Diagnostic and Statistical Manual of the American Psychiatric Association (DSM-IV), is based on the assumption that mental disorders exist within the individual. It gives people labels like "paranoid schizophrenic" or "borderline personality disorder" and tends to objectify problems as ingrained characteristics of the human psyche. These diagnostic categories have specific descriptive requirements that may lead to the belief that these symptoms are inherent in the individual. The result is that people often believe they are fundamentally flawed, they (or their families allow them to) renounce responsibility, and the label exacerbates the very problems therapy is supposed to help resolve (Tomm, 1990).

However, there are also advantages to individual diagnoses and outcome measures. First, IP dysfunctions tend to be more straightforwardly defined than are systemic symptoms. For example, weight gain, rehospitalization, arrests, school grades, and the like are much more easily operationalized than triangulation, detouring, collusion, and other systemic concepts. Second, IP problems allow for reasonably reliable selection criteria for a research sample. One can, for example, select families with teenage subjects 30 percent under expected body weight much more accurately than, say, families who are enmeshed. Without reliable selection criteria, it's nearly impossible to determine the variance within research samples. For this reason, and because none of the proposed alternate systemic diagnostic categories (e.g., Beavers, Hampton, & Hulgus, 1985; Olson, Bell, & Postner, 1985) has proven satisfactory, some commentators assert that the only responsible way to proceed with current research efforts is with the use of established (individual) diagnostic categories (e.g., Henggeler et al., 1992; Dickey, 1993b). They argue that whatever the limits of the DSM-IV nosology, most diagnoses can be coded reasonably reliably. Furthermore, one can frame the DSM-IV diagnostic criteria as a "snapshot" of an IP's behavior at a point in time without reifying the diagnosis as intrinsic to the person's character (Duncan et al., 1992).

In any event, more studies are being conducted and published in which individual diagnoses are used. This may be due to a greater appreciation of the importance of biological factors in individual and family functioning. It may also relate to the growing appreciation of the individual as a subsystem within the family. Finally, it may have something to do with the respect for several excellently designed studies (reviewed above) that used traditional diagnostic labels and subject selection criteria. As long as efforts are made to avoid sharing pejorative labels with research subjects, and as long as change in the IP isn't used as the *sole* criteria, we welcome this trend.

Problems in Measurement of Dyadic and Family Systems Concepts

As noted in the previous section, there are enormous problems with the measurement of systems concepts. Several schools of family therapy haven't even tried to operationalize the key elements of their theories; hence, criteria for improvement remain elusive. Even conscientious efforts have produced modest payoffs. One only has to look at the difficulties David Olson and his colleagues (Olson et al., 1985) have encountered in trying to develop a reliable and valid typology to classify families and measure change.

Olson's Circumplex Model offers a parsimonious way of classifying families according to two dimensions believed to be most salient in describing healthy versus unhealthy functioning. "Family cohesion" represents the emotional bond that family members feel toward each other. "Family adaptability" represents the family's ability to change in accordance with changing circumstances. The model hypothesizes that both dimensions have a curvilinear relationship with family health. That is, either too much or too little cohesion or adaptability is problematical. Healthy families will be balanced on both of these dimensions.

While Olson's Circumplex Model is intuitively appealing, the results of the first three versions of a self-report instrument, FACES, designed to operationalize the model, haven't found the hypothesized curvilinear relationship between family wellness and the two principle variables in the model—family cohesion and adaptability. While an observational rating scale (Thomas & Olson, 1993) does seem to fit the model better, it will take years to ascertain if the family categories described are meaningful ways to categorize families and are sensitive to change.

Florence Kaslow (1993) described the monumental task facing the consortium of family oriented groups who came together as the Coalition on Family Diagnosis. This group took on the mission of introducing the concept of "relational diagnosis" in the recent revision of the Diagnostic and Statistical Manual (DSM-IV). She notes progress was slower than hoped:

> It has proven extraordinarily difficult, for example, to conceptualize what are the objective characteristics (descriptors) of particular relationship diagnoses, and to find a terminology for these patterns that could elicit consensus among coalition participants. (p. 257)

A major concern raised by the American Psychiatric Association's DSM-IV task force is that there is insufficient research on relational problems and disorders to set thresholds of severity that would enable clinicians to determine what is a "case" meriting a diagnosis—"a necessary component if one is to operate within the parameters of a DSM-type diagnostic system" (Kaslow, 1993, p. 258).

Even those systems concepts that *can* be operationalized with some degree of reliability and validity, like marital adjustment, are typically measured with instruments administered separately to individuals such as the Dyadic Adjustment Scale (Spanier, 1976). It's even questionable if the widely used

Family Adjustment Device (Epstein, Baldwin, & Bishop, 1983) is truly a relational instrument since it only asks individuals to describe *their perceptions* of what goes on in their families. The reality is that "most 'family' data are really data generated from individuals who also happen to be family members" (Fisher, Kokes, Ransom, Phillips, & Rudd, 1985, pp. 213–214). While individuals' perceptions about marital and family interaction aren't without value (in fact, we have argued that family members' perceptions are important to research), it is questionable if the instruments measure interactional or systemic properties. The measurement of these properties typically requires inferences by trained professional coders or therapists—a complex and time-consuming process (Gurman & Kniskern, 1981).

For these and other reasons, it's not surprising that few marriage and family therapists in the trenches use standardized assessment instruments. In spite of the fact that a number of books have catalogued, critiqued, and discussed marriage and family therapy assessment instruments and their application to clinical and research use (Corcoran & Fisher, 1988; Grotevant & Carlson, 1989; Touliatos, Perlmutter, & Straus, 1990), a relatively small percentage of clinicians bother to use them. In a random sample of AAMFT clinical members, Boughner, Hayes, Bubenzer, and West (in press) found that only 20 percent, 29 percent, and 13 percent of subjects, respectively, used at least one standardized instrument for premarital, marital, and family therapy. Furthermore, the most widely used instruments in each of these three categories were not marriage and family instruments, but combinations of the Myers-Briggs Type Indicator (MBTI), the Minnesota Multiphasic Personality Inventory (MMPI), and the Taylor-Johnson Temperment Analysis (TJTA). While these results may also reflect deficiencies in training, the hassles of administering and scoring tests, and the antiresearch and evaluation bias of many family therapists, they also reflect the clinicians' beliefs concerning the dubious value and utility of many marriage and family therapy assessment instruments.

THE FUTURE OF FAMILY THERAPY RESEARCH

Despite improvements in family therapy research that have been and continue to be made, no review would be complete without recommendations for future investigations. The following are our suggestions.

1. *Increase the specificity of treatment variables.* A common characteristic of the best and most useful studies is that they have clearly specified the treatments offered. Regrettably, most investigations do not (Piercy & Sprenkle, 1990). Greater attention needs to be given to preparing treatment manuals and to ensuring that the treatment specified is the treatment provided. Not only will this increase the generalizability and interpretability of findings, but it will also reduce extraneous variance, such as therapist and treatment model effects. Also, researchers with allegiance to and current expertise in the treatment approach under investigation should be those who write the treatment manual and evaluate the therapy being provided (Jacobson, 1991b). As Piercy and Sprenkle (1990) note, within-school component analysis of a particular therapy will be most credible.

2. *Increase the attention given to therapist variables.* Two recommendations are proposed here. First, Bednar et al. (1988) and others (e.g., Gurman et al., 1986; Jacobson, 1991b; Piercy & Sprenkle, 1990) have pointed out that a therapist's allegiance to a particular approach becomes a significant factor not only in representing the approach fairly and accurately, but also in producing positive outcomes. Other things being equal, better results will be achieved by adherents to an approach. However, this factor hasn't been adequately addressed in family therapy studies. Future comparative research should use different therapists, matched on allegiance, experience, and skill. If this isn't possible, therapist bias should be examined and discussed in the interpretation of findings (Piercy & Sprenkle, 1990).

Second, investigators should consider the differential effects produced by therapists—even within the same school of therapy (Crits-Christoph et al. 1991; Crits-Christoph & Mintz, 1991; Martindale, 1978). There is a growing body of evidence suggesting that therapist effects account for a large proportion of variance, especially in studies with fewer controls (Crits-Christoph & Mintz, 1991; Luborsky et al., 1986). Controlling other sources of variability (e.g., using treatment manuals, ensuring equal difficulty of cases) can help. Another strategy is to increase the number of therapists used in comparative outcome studies (Crits-Christoph et al., 1991). More deliberate attempts to measure therapist effects should be included in both process and outcome studies of family therapy.

3. *Increase the attention given to client variables.* Researchers need to do a better job of describing what is unique about their samples and how this distinctiveness affects the generalizability of results. As previously mentioned, the clients' experience of therapy also needs to be studied more. As it is, we know very little, aside from conjecture, about what clients believe makes a difference in therapy. Yet, this knowledge is crucial to meet their needs and to assess the services we provide.

Calvert and Johnston (1990) explain that treatment acceptability refers to the degree to which the actual consumers see the treatment procedures as appropriate. They recommend that acceptability of treatment should be examined from three points of reference: (1) society, (2) mental health professionals, and (3) the consumer or client. We also see this as an important research direction. As we learn more about treatment acceptability, we should experience fewer dropouts, greater client compliance, and greater client satisfaction with treatment.

Second, increased attention needs to be given to finding reliable and valid ways of describing and classifying families and couples (Piercy & Sprenkle, 1990). As was mentioned previously, past attempts have been met with mixed acceptance, especially by researchers. Continued attention needs to be given to developing typologies of families and refining concepts that describe family functioning. An example of where this has been and continues to be done is with the construct of "expressed emotion." The concept of high EE derived from investigator's attempts to understand attributes of schizophrenic families (Goldstein, 1992) and has evolved into a reliable descriptor of a characteristic associated with members of families in which a member has severe psychopathology. In fact, preliminary evidence suggests that the high

EE construct, although derived from one person, may represent a more complex relationship dynamic (Florin et al., 1992; Goldstein, 1992). Advances in refining and developing this and other constructs (and their measurement) need to be continued.

4. *Cost-effectiveness studies need to be undertaken.* Pike and Piercy (1990) explained the importance of cost-effectiveness research for family therapy. Unfortunately, little has been done to prove the cost-effectiveness of family treatment. This issue will become increasingly salient as mental health dollars become more scarce under national health care.

5. *Continued improvements need to be made in qualitative design.* The aforementioned increased acceptance of qualitative studies is encouraging. However, there is little consensus concerning standards by which to judge this research. Part of the problem is that there are still so few published examples of well-designed qualitative research. The field is also in desperate need of more studies that integrate qualitative and quantitative methodologies.

6. *Greater attention needs to be given to combining both the process and outcome perspectives.* We previously described the "new process perspective" (Gurman et al., 1986) and the importance of linking within-session behaviors to short-term as well as long-term results. This work is only being carried out by a select few individuals. The field needs to encourage clinically relevant process-outcome studies, which typically require a major investment of time, energy, and money.

7. *Programmatic research needs to be encouraged.* Some of the most meaningful findings tend to come from research efforts that are years in the making, with investigators pursuing a topic or idea through many projects that build on each other.

Unfortunately, publication pressures, financial resources, and other practical concerns discourage programmatic research and encourage moving from one unrelated study to another (Piercy & Sprenkle, 1990). As with process-outcome studies, the field needs to find ways to reward those individuals who devote time and energy to accretive research. Examples of this type of research include the work on aggressive children led by Gerald Patterson (Patterson & Chamberlain, 1988); the Relationship Enhancement (RE) research spearheaded by Bernard Guerny and associates (Hardley & Guerny, 1989), the Behavioral Marital Therapy research of Neil Jacobson (Jacobson et al., 1987), the functional family therapy research by James Alexander (Alexander & Parsons, 1982), the research on the treatment of drug abusing adolescents by Jose Szapocznik (Szapocznik et al., 1990) and those with the Center for Research on Adolescent Drug Abuse, and the Emotionally Focused Therapy research by Leslie Greenberg and Susan Johnson (Greenberg & Johnson, 1988).

8. *Large-scale, multisite studies need to be encouraged.* Many of the pressures that discourage programmatic research also discourage investigations using several different treatment facilities to study the use of family therapy in the treatment of specific problems. But, it is important that the field find ways to encourage multisite investigations. Carrying out studies using several different treatment facilities not only increases the resources (and number of subjects) that can be used in the study, but it can also increase the generalizability of results.

9. *Greater attention needs to be given to clinical significance.* Even though determining clinical significance would make research more meaningful, few family therapy researchers have attempted to report the clinical significance of their findings. Generally, results reported in terms of clinical significance have only been found in psychology journals. We feel that family therapy researchers need to begin experimenting with procedures and methods that will make their results more clinically meaningful.

For example, Jacobson and Revenstorf (1989) explain "clinically" as opposed to "statistically" significant results are achieved when a previously dysfunctional couple, family, or person receives a posttest score that is more likely to belong to a functional rather than a dysfunctional population. The researcher-clinician gap will be narrowed when researchers regularly say things like, "At posttest 67 percent of the previously dysfunctional couples scored in the normal range; 25 percent did not change; and 7 percent deteriorated," rather than the current practice of stating that "results were significant at the .05 level."

The challenge to investigators to attend more closely to clinical significance is a crucial step in building a partnership between researchers and clinicians. Researchers can offer clinicians hard data to support the effectiveness of treatment with third-party payers who are increasingly concerned with paying only for treatments that have demonstrated levels of effectiveness, specific information about how particular methods of treatment can best be delivered (e.g., how to present parent skills training), assessments of the effectiveness of new treatments and techniques, evaluations of which treatments are most effective with specific populations and problems, a technology for assessing clinical utility, and a process for gathering and weighing information that can be applied within clinical methods. Clinicians—who are ideally the major consumers of research—can help researchers focus research questions to tap real and practical clinical concerns. After all, research findings are only valuable to the extent that they are used.

CONCLUSIONS

Great advances have been made in family therapy research over the past fifteen years, despite the logistical nightmare in tracking and controlling the extraordinarily complex process of family therapy. Having carefully reviewed the literature, we believe the following conclusions are warranted:

1. Marriage and family therapy is generally effective. It is clearly superior to no treatment and produces beneficial outcomes at least as often as non-family intervention strategies.
2. Where problems have clear family relationship implications (such as marital conflict or child behavioral problems), there is a greater chance

of positive outcome when the problem is treated systemically. How-ever, there is evidence that systemic treatment doesn't always require the physical presence of all family members in the treatment room.

3. Family treatment focused on a specific problem area appears to have positive, enduring impact on the entire system and its individual mem-bers. Improvements have been reported in both individual and sys-tem-wide untreated problems when the family is engaged in family therapy.

4. Positive results can generally be achieved through brief therapy (1 to 20 sessions).

5. Family therapy is an effective adjunct in the treatment of major men-tal illnesses, such as schizophrenia, affective disorders, and eating disorders.

While evidence for the general effectiveness of family therapy is high, we are only beginning to scratch the surface of specific questions, such as "for whom is marriage and family therapy most effective?" and "what is the best approach?" For example, work in several areas (i.e., treatment of anorexia nervosa and adolescent substance abuse) has shown that family approaches are more successful with younger than older adolescents. Perhaps this is be-cause of the overwhelming centrality of family relationships in the lives of younger children. These are the kinds of specific issues that need to be ad-dressed in future research.

We have also noted throughout this chapter that there is little evidence for the superiority of one theoretical approach to treatment over another. Rather than one treatment being globally superior, it is more likely that cer-tain types of approaches will be particularly effective with certain types of clients. We urge the proponents of various models to determine with which problems their model works best.

This chapter has also attempted to depict the complex kaleidoscope that is family therapy research. We have sketched a colorful past in which research was integral to an emerging discipline. We saw how this merger faded and we have portrayed a researcher-clinician gap that we are only now beginning to bridge. We are cautiously optimistic, however, that researchers and clinicians can come together because of some of the trends we have highlighted:

1. New methods are being developed, such as task analysis, that are congruent with systems theory and that reconstruct the richness of clinical experience.

2. Qualitative methods, which frequently address questions asked by clinicians, have new-found respectability.

3. Quantitative researchers are learning to speak the language of "clini-cal significance."

4. The new process perspective is emphasizing what is happening dur-ing the course of therapy itself.

5. We are beginning to consider the clients' perspective concerning what is effective therapy.

6. Finally, and perhaps most importantly, clinicians are looking to re-searchers to document the effectiveness of treatment for managed

care organizations and other dispensers of health care dollars. The stakes are high. As this chapter is being written, government health care reform proposals are being hotly debated. Whatever the outcome, there will surely be more emphasis on accountability. It isn't a bold prediction that the future of family therapy will rest on our ability to document its efficacy.

REFERENCES

Alexander, J. F., Barton, C., Schiavo, R. S., and Parsons, B. V. 1977. Systems-behavioral intervention with families of delinquents: Therapist characteristics, family behavior and outcome. *Journal of Consulting and Clinical Psychology*. *44*:656–664.

Alexander, J. F., and Parsons, B. V. 1982. *Functional family therapy*. Monterey, CA: Brooks-Cole.

Alexander, J. F., and Parsons, B. V. 1973. Short-term behavioral intervention with delinquent families: Impact on family process and recidivism. *Journal of Abnormal Psychology*. *81*:219–225.

Anderson, C. M., Reiss, D. J., and Hogarty, G. E. 1986. *Schizophrenia and the family*. New York: Guilford Press.

Atkinson, B., Heath, A., and Chenail, R. 1991. Qualitative research and the legitimization of knowledge. *Journal of Marital and Family Therapy*. *17*:175–180.

Avis, J. M., and Sprenkle, D. H. 1990. Outcome research on family therapy training: A substantive and methodological review. *Journal of Marital and Family Therapy*. *16*:241–264.

Barton, C., Alexander, J. F., and Sanders, J. D. 1985. Research in family therapy. In *The handbook of family psychology and therapy*, L. L'Abate, ed. Homewood, IL: The Dorsey Press.

Barton, C., Alexander, J. F., Waldron, H., Turner, C. W., and Warburton, J. 1985. Generalizing treatment effects of functional family therapy: Three replications. *The American Journal of Family Therapy*. *13*(3):16–26.

Bateson, G., Jackson, D. D., Haley, J., and Weakland, J. H. 1956. Toward a theory of schizophrenia. *Behavioral Science*. *1*:251–264.

Bateson, G., Jackson, D. D., Haley, J., and Weakland, J. H. 1963. A note on the double bind—1962. *Family Process*. *2*:154–161.

Baucom, D. H., and Hoffman, J. A. 1986. The effectiveness of marital therapy: Current status and application to the clinical setting. In *Clinical handbook of marital therapy*, N. Jacobson and A. Gurman, eds. New York: Guilford Press.

Beach, S. R. H., and O'Leary, K. D. 1986. The treatment of depression occurring in the context of marital discord. *Behavior Therapy*. *17*:43–49.

Beavers, W. R., Hampton, T. B., and Hulgus, Y. F. 1985. Commentary: The Beavers System approach to family assessment. *Family Process*. *24*:398–405.

Bednar, R. L., Burlingame, G. M., and Masters, K. S. 1988. Systems of family treatment: Substance or semantics. *Annual Review of Psychology*. *39*:401–413.

Beer, J. 1993. *If you could look in a mirror through another person's eyes: An ethnography of marital therapy*. Unpublished dissertation. West Lafayette, IN: Purdue University.

Bischoff, R. J. 1993. *The development of a model of self-consultations*. Unpublished dissertation. West Lafayette, IN: Purdue University.

Bischoff, R. J., and Sprenkle, D. H. 1993. Dropping out of marriage and family therapy: A critical review of research. *Family Process*. *32*:353–375.

Boughner, H. B., Baldwin, L. M., Bubenzer, D. L., and West, J. D. Use of standardized assessment instruments: A survey. *Journal of Marital and Family Therapy*. *20*:69–75.

Broderick, C. B., and Schrader, S. S. 1981. The history of professional marriage and family therapy. In *Handbook of family therapy*, A. S. Gurman and D. P. Kniskern, eds. New York: Brunner/Mazel.

Brunk, M., Henggeler, S. W., and Whelan, J. P. 1987. Comparison of multisystemic therapy and parent training in the brief treatment of child abuse and neglect. *Journal of Consulting and Clinical Psychology.* 55:171–178.

Calvert, S. C., and Johnston, C. 1990. Acceptability of treatments for child behavior problems: Issues and implications for future research. *Journal of Clinical Child Psychology. 19*:61–74.

Cavell, T. A., and Snyder, D. K. 1991. Iconoclasm versus innovation: Building a science of family therapy—comments on Moon, Dillon, and Sprenkle. *Journal of Marital and Family Therapy.* 17:181–185.

Chamberlain, P., Patterson, G. R., Reid, J. B., Kavanagh, K., and Forgatch, M. S. 1984. Observation of client resistance. *Behavior Therapy. 15*:144–155.

Clarkin, J. F., Glick, I. D., Haas, G. L., Spencer, J. H., Lewis, A. B., Peyser, J., DeMane, N., Good-Ellis, M., Harris, E., and Lestelle, V. 1990. A randomized clinical trial of inpatient family intervention. V. Results for affective disorders. *Journal of Affective Disorders. 18*:17–28.

Corcoran, K, and Fischer, J. 1987. *Measures for clinical practice: A sourcebook.* New York: The Free Press.

Crits-Christoph, P., Baranackie, K., Kurcias, J. S., Beck, A. T., Carroll, K., Perry, K., Luborsky, L., McLellan, A. T., Woody, G. E., Thompson, L., Gallagher, D., and Zitrin, C. 1991. Meta-analysis of therapist effects in psychotherapy outcome studies. *Psychotherapy Research. 1*(2):81–91.

Crits-Christoph, P., and Mintz, J. 1991. The implications of therapist effects for the design and analysis of comparative studies of psychotherapies. *Journal of Consulting and Clinical Psychology.* 59:20–26.

Dare, C., Eisler, I., Russell, G. F. M., and Szmukler, G. I. 1990. The clinical and theoretical impact of a controlled trial of family therapy in anorexia nervosa. *Journal of Marital and Family Therapy. 16*:39–57.

Dickey, M. 1993a. A methodological review of family therapy process research. Unpublished manuscript.

Dickey, M. 1993b. Family therapy process research: Substantive review and future directions. Unpublished manuscript.

Duncan, B. L., Solovey, A. D., and Rusk, G. S. 1992. *Changing the rules: A client-directed approach to therapy.* New York: Guilford Press.

Epstein, H. B., Baldwin, L. M., and Bishop, D. S. 1983. The McMaster Family Assessment Device. *Journal of Marital and Family Therapy.* 9:171–180.

Falloon, R. H., Boyd, J. L., McGill, C. W., Williamson, M., Razani, J., Moss, H. B., Gilderman, A. M., and Simpson, G. M. 1985. Family management in the prevention of morbidity of schizophrenia: Clinical outcome of a two-year longitudinal study. *Archives of General Psychiatry.* 42:887–896.

Fisher, L., Kokes, R. F., Ransom, D. C., Phillips, S. L., and Rudd, P. 1985. Alternative strategies for creating "relational" family data. *Family Process. 24*:213–224.

Fleishmann, M. J. 1981. A replication of Patterson's 'Interventions for boys with conduct problems.' *Journal of Consulting and Clinical Psychology.* 49:343–351.

Fleishmann, M. J., and Szykula, S. A. 1981. A community setting replication of a social learning treatment for aggressive children. *Behavior Therapy. 12*:115–122.

Florin, I., Nostadt, A., Reck, C., Franzen, U., and Jenkins, M. 1992. Expressed emotion in depressed patients and their partners. *Family Process. 31*:163–172.

Gale, J., and Newfield, N. 1992. A conversation analysis of a solution-focused marital therapy session. *Journal of Marital and Family Therapy. 18*:153–165.

Giblin, P., Sprenkle, D. H., and Sheehan, R. 1985. Enrichment outcome research: A meta-analysis of premarital, marital, and family interventions. *Journal of Marital and Family Therapy. 11*:257–271.

Goldstein, M. J. 1992. Commentary on "expressed emotion in depressed patients and their partners. *Family Process.* 31:172–174.

Goldstein, M. J., Rodnick, E. H., Evans, J. R., May, P. R., and Steinberg, M. 1978. Drug and family therapy in the aftercare treatment of acute schizophrenia. *Archives of General Psychiatry.* 35:1169–1177.

Goldstein, M. J., and Strachan, A. 1987. The family and schizophrenia. In *Family interaction and psychopathology,* T. Jacob, ed. New York: Plenum Press.

Gottman, J. M. 1987. The sequential analysis of family interaction. In *Family interaction and psychopathology,* T. Jacob, ed. New York: Plenum Press.

Greenberg, L. S., Ford, C. L., Alden, L. S., and Johnson, S. M. 1993. In-session change in emotionally focused therapy. *Journal of Consulting and Clinical Psychology.* 61:78–84.

Greenberg, L. S., James, P. S., and Conry, R. F. 1988. Perceived change processes in emotionally focused couples therapy. *Journal of Family Psychology.* 2:5–23.

Greenberg, L. S., and Johnson, S. M. 1988. *Emotionally focused therapy for couples.* New York: Guilford Press.

Greenberg, L. S., and Pinsof, W. M. 1986. Process research: Current trends and future perspectives. In *The psychotherapy process: research handbook,* L. S. Greenberg and W. M. Pinsof, eds. New York: Guilford Press.

Griffith, M., and Griffith, J. 1990. Can family therapy research have a human face? *Dulwich Centre Newsletter.* 2:11–20.

Grotevant, H. D., and Carlson, C. I. 1989. *Family assessment: A guide to methods and measures.* New York: Guilford Press.

Gurman, A. S. 1983. Family therapy research and the "new epistemology." *Journal of Marital and Family Therapy.* 9:227–234.

Gurman, A. S., and Kniskern, D. P. 1978. Research on marital and family therapy: Progress, perspective, and prospect. In *Handbook of psychotherapy and behavior change: An empirical analysis,* 2nd ed., S. L. Garfield and A. E. Bergin, eds. New York: Wiley.

Gurman, A. S., and Kniskern, D. P. 1981. Family therapy outcome research: Knowns and unknowns. In *Handbook of family therapy,* A. S. Gurman and D. P. Kniskern, eds. New York: Brunner/Mazel.

Gurman, A. S., Kniskern, D. P., and Pinsof, W. M. 1986. Research on the process and outcome of marital and family therapy. In *Handbook of Psychotherapy and behavior change,* 3rd ed., S. L. Garfield and A. E. Bergin, eds. New York: Wiley.

Haas, G. L., and Clarkin, J. F. 1988. Affective disorders and the family context. In *Affective disorders and the family: Assessment and treatment,* J. F. Clarkin, G. L. Haas, and I. D. Glick, eds. New York: Guilford Press.

Haley, J. 1978. Ideas which handicap therapists. In *Beyond the double bind: Communication and family systems, theories, and techniques with schizophrenics,* M. M. Berger, ed. New York: Brunner/Mazel.

Hazelrigg, M. D., Cooper, H. M., and Borduin, C. M. 1987. Evaluating the effectiveness of family therapies: An integrative review and analysis. *Psychological Bulletin.* 101:428–442.

Henggeler, S. W., Borduin, C. M., and Mann, B. J. 1992. Advances in family therapy: Empirical foundations. In *Advances in clinical child psychology,* vol. 15, T. H. Ollendick, and R. J. Prinz, eds. New York: Plenum.

Hogarty, G. E., Anderson, C. M., Reiss, D. J., Kornblith, S. J., Greenwald, D. P., Javna, C. D., Madonia, M. J., and the EPICS Schizophrenia Research Group. 1986. Family psychoeducation, social skills training, and maintenance chemotherapy in the aftercare treatment of schizophrenia: I. One year effects of a controlled study on relapse and expressed emotion. *Archives of General Psychiatry.* 43:633–642.

Hoshmand, L. L. S. T. 1989. Alternate research paradigms: A review and teaching proposal. *The Counseling Psychologist.* 17:1–79.

Jacob, T., and Leonard, K. 1992. Sequential analysis of marital interactions involving alcoholic, depressed, and nondistressed men. *Journal of Abnormal Psychology.* *101:*647–656.

Jacobson, N. S. 1985a. Family therapy outcome research: Potential pitfalls and prospects. *Journal of Marital and Family Therapy.* *11:*149–158.

Jacobson, N. S. 1985b. Toward a nonsectarian blueprint for the empirical study of family therapies. *Journal of Marital and Family Therapy.* *11:*163–165.

Jacobson, N. S. 1991a. To be or not to be behavioral when working with couples: What does it mean? *Journal of Family Psychology.* *4:*436–445.

Jacobson, N. S. 1991b. Toward enhancing the efficacy of marital therapy and marital therapy research. *Journal of Family Psychology.* *4:*373–393.

Jacobson, N. S., Follette, W. C., and Elwood, R. W. 1984. Outcome research on behavioral marital therapy: A methodological and conceptual reappraisal. In *Marital interaction: Analysis and modification,* K. Hahlweg and N. Jacobson, eds. New York: Guilford Press.

Jacobson, N. S., Follette, W. C., and Revenstorf, D. 1984. Psychotherapy outcome research: Methods for reporting variability and evaluating clinical significance. *Behavior Therapy.* *15:*336–352.

Jacobson, N. S., and Revenstorf, D. 1989. Statistics for assessing the clinical significance of psychotherapy techniques: Issues, problems, and new developments. *Behavioral Assessment.* *10:*133-145.

Jacobson, N. S., Schmaling, K. B., and Holtzworth-Munroe, A. 1987. Component analysis of behavioral marital therapy: Two-year follow-up and prediction of relapse. *Journal of Marital and Family Therapy.* *13:*187–195.

Joanning, H., Newfield, N., and Quinn, W. H. 1987. Multiple perspectives for research using family therapy to treat adolescent drug abuse. *Journal of Strategic and Systemic Therapies.* *6:*18–24.

Joanning, H., Quinn, W., Thomas, F., and Mullen, R. 1992. Treating adolescent drug abuse: A comparison of family systems therapy, group therapy, and family drug education. *Journal of Marital and Family Therapy.* *18:*345–356.

Johnson, S. M., and Greenberg, L. S. 1988. Relating process to outcome in marital therapy. *Journal of Marital and Family Therapy.* *14:*175–183.

Kaye, J. 1990. Toward meaningful research in psychotherapy. *Dulwich Centre Newsletter.* *2:*27–38.

Kazdin, A. E. 1987. Treatment of antisocial behavior in children: Current status and future directions. *Psychological Bulletin.* *102:*187–203.

Kazdin, A. E. 1991. Effectiveness of psychotherapy with children and adolescents. *Journal of Consulting and Clinical Psychology.* *59:*785–798.

Kaslow, F. 1993. Relational diagnosis: An idea whose time has come. *Family Process.* *32:*255–259.

Keeney, B. P., and Sprenkle, D. H. 1983. Ecosystemic epistemology: Critical implications for the aesthetics and pragmatics of family therapy. *Family Process.* *21:*1–19.

Klein, N. C., Alexander, J. F., and Parsons, B. V. 1977. Impact of family systems intervention on recidivism and sibling delinquency: Preliminary findings. *Journal of Consulting and Clinical Psychology.* *45:*469–474.

Kuehl, B. P., Newfield, N. A., and Joanning, H. 1990. A client-based description of family therapy. *Journal of Family Psychology.* *3:*310–321.

Lambert, M. 1986. Implications of psychotherapy outcome research for eclectic psychotherapy. In *Handbook of eclectic psychotherapy,* J. C. Norcross, ed. New York: Brunner/Mazel.

Langsley, D., Flomenhaft, K., and Machotka, P. 1969. Follow-up evaluation of family crisis therapy. *American Journal of Orthopsychiatry.* *39:*753–759.

Langsley, D., Pittman, F., Machotka, P., and Flomenhaft, K. 1968. Family crisis therapy—Results and implications. *Family Process.* 7:145–158.

Leff, J. P., Kuipers, L., Berkowitz, R., Eberlein-Vries, R., and Sturgeon, D. 1982. A controlled trial of social intervention in the families of schizophrenic patients. *British Journal of Psychiatry.* 141:121–134.

Leff, J. P., Kuipers, L., Berkowitz, R., and Sturgeon, D. 1985. A controlled trial of social intervention in the families of schizophrenic patients: Two year follow-up. *British Journal of Psychiatry.* 146:594–600.

Lewis, R. A., Piercy, F. P., Sprenkle, D. H., and Trepper, T. S. 1990. Family-based interventions for helping drug-abusing adolescents. *Journal of Adolescent Research.* 13:35–44.

Liddle, H. A. 1991. Empirical values and the culture of family therapy. *Journal of Marital and Family Therapy.* 17:327–348.

Lipchik, E. 1991. Spouse abuse: Challenging the party line. *Family Therapy Networker.* May/June:59–63.

Luborsky, L., Crits-Christoph, P., McLellan, A. T., Woody, G., Piper, W., Liberman, B., Imber, S., and Pilkonis, P. 1986. Do therapists vary much in their success? Findings from four outcome studies. *American Journal of Orthopsychiatry.* 56:501–512.

Luborsky, L., McLellan, A. T., Woody, G. E., O'Brien, C. P., and Auerbach, A. 1985. Therapist success and its determinants. *Archives of General Psychiatry.* 42:602–611.

Mahrer, A. R. 1988. Discovery-oriented psychotherapy research: Rationale, aims and methods. *American Psychologist.* 43:694–702.

Markus, E., Lange, A., and Pettigrew, T. F. 1990. Effectiveness of family therapy: A meta-analysis. *British Journal of Family Therapy.* 12:205–221.

Martindale, C. 1978. The therapist-as-fixed-effect fallacy in psychotherapy research. *Journal of Consulting and Clinical Psychology.* 46:1526–1530.

McDaniel, S. H., Hepworth, J., and Doherty, W. J. 1992. *Medical family therapy: A biopsychosocial approach to families with health problems.* New York: Basic Books.

McGrady, B. S, and Epstein, E. E. Marital therapy in the treatment of alcohol problems. In *Clinical handbook of marital therapy,* vol. 2, N. Jacobson and A. Gurman, eds. New York: Guilford Press. (in press)

Miklowitz, D. J., and Goldstein, M. J. 1990. Behavioral family treatment for patients with bipolar affective disorder. *Behavior Modification.* 14:457–489.

Miklowitz, D. J., Goldstein, M. J., Huechterlein, K. H., Snyder, K. S., and Mintz, J. 1988. Family factors and the course of bipolar affective disorder. *Archives of General Psychiatry.* 45:225–231.

Minuchin, S., Baker, L., Rosman, B. Liebman, R., Milman, L., and Todd, T. 1975. A conceptual model of psychosomatic illness in children. *Archives of General Psychiatry.* 32:1031–1038.

Minuchin, S., Rosman, B., and Baker, L. 1978. *Psychosomatic families.* Cambridge, MA: Harvard University Press.

Moon, S. M., Dillon, D. R., and Sprenkle, D. H. 1990. Family therapy and qualitative research. *Journal of Marital and Family Therapy.* 16:357–373.

Moon, S. M., and Sprenkle, D. H. 1992. Multi-methodological family therapy research. *AFTA Newsletter.* 47(spring):29–30.

Newfield, N. A., Kuehl, B. P., Joanning, H. P., and Quinn, W. H. 1991. We can tell you about "Psychos" and "Shrinks": An ethnography of the family therapy of adolescent drug abuse. In *Family therapy approaches with adolescent substance abusers,* T. C. Todd and M. D. Selekman, eds. Boston: Allyn and Bacon.

Nichols, M. P., and Schwartz, R. C. 1991. *Family therapy: Concepts and methods,* 2nd ed. Boston: Allyn and Bacon.

O'Farrell, T. J., Cutter, H. S. G., and Floyd, F. J. 1985. Evaluation behavioral marital therapy for male alcoholics: Effects on marital adjustment and communication from before to after treatment. *Behavior Therapy. 16*:147–167.

Olson, D. H. 1976. Bridging research, theory, and application: The triple threat in science. In *Treating relationships*, D. H. Olson, ed. Lake Mills, IA: Graphic Publishing.

Olson, D. H., Bell, R., and Portner, J. 1985. *FACES III manual.* Department of Family Social Science, University of Minnesota.

Parsons, B. V., and Alexander, J. F. 1973. Short-term family intervention: A therapy outcome study. *Journal of Consulting and Clinical Psychology. 41*:195–201.

Patterson, C. H. 1984. Empathy, warmth, and genuineness in psychotherapy: A review of reviews. *Psychotherapy. 21*:431–438.

Patterson, G. R. 1974. Interventions for boys with conduct problems: Multiple settings, treatment and criteria. *Journal of Consulting and Clinical Psychology. 42*:471–481.

Patterson, G. R., and Chamberlain, P. 1992. A functional analysis of resistance: A neobehavioral perspective. In *Why don't people change? New perspectives on resistance and noncompliance*, H. Arkowitz, ed. New York: Guilford Press.

Patterson, G. R., and Chamberlain, P. 1988. Treatment process: A problem at three levels. In *The state of the art in family therapy research: Controversies and recommendations*, L. C. Wynne, ed. New York: Family Process Press.

Patterson, G. R., Chamberlain, P., and Reid, J. B. 1982. A comparative evaluation of a parent-training program. *Behavior Therapy. 13*:638–650.

Patterson, G. R., and Forgatch, M. S. 1985. Therapist behavior as a determinant for client noncompliance: A paradox for the behavior modifier. *Journal of Consulting and Clinical Psychology. 53*:846–851.

Paul, G. L. 1967. Strategy of outcome research in psychotherapy. *Journal of Consulting Psychology. 31*:109–118.

Piercy, F. P., and Sprenkle, D. H. 1990. Marriage and family therapy: A decade review. *Journal of Marriage and the Family. 52*:1116–1126.

Pike, C. L., and Piercy, F. P. 1990. Cost effectiveness research in family therapy. *Journal of Marital and Family Therapy. 16*:375–388.

Pinsof, W. M. 1981. Family therapy process research. In *Handbook of family therapy*, A. S. Gurman and D. P. Kniskern, eds. New York: Brunner/Mazel.

Rice, L. M., and Saperia, E. P. 1984. Task analysis of the resolution of problematic reactions. In *Patterns of change*, L. N. Rice and L. S. Greenberg, eds. New York: Guilford Press.

Robinson, L. A., Berman, J. S., and Neimeyer, R. A. 1990. Psychotherapy for the treatment of depression: A comprehensive review of controlled outcome research. *Psychological Bulletin. 108*:30–49.

Russell, G. F. M., Szmukler, G. I., Dare, C., and Eisler, I. 1987. An evaluation of family therapy in anorexia nervosa and bulimia nervosa. *Archives of General Psychiatry. 44*:1047–1056.

Safran, J. D., Greenberg, L. S., and Rice, L. M. 1988. Integrating psychotherapy research and practice: Modeling the change process. *Psychotherapy. 25*:1–17.

Schwartz, R. C., Barrett, M. J., and Saba, G. 1985. Family therapy for bulimia. In *Handbook for the psychotherapy of anorexia nervosa and bulimia*, D. Garner and P. Garfinkel, eds. New York: Guilford Press.

Schwartz, R. C., and Breunlin, D. 1983. Research: Why clinicians should bother with it. *Family Therapy Networker.* July–August:23–27, 57–59.

Sells, S. P., Smith, T. E., Coe, M. J., Yoshioka, M., and Robbins, J. An ethnography of couple and therapist experiences in reflecting team practice. *Journal of Marital and Family Therapy.* (in press)

Shields, C. G. 1986a. Critiquing the new epistemologies: Toward minimum requirements for a scientific theory of family therapy. *Journal of Marital and Family Therapy. 12*:359–372.

Shields, C. G. 1986b. Family therapy research and practice: Constructs, measurement, and testing. *Journal of Marital and Family Therapy.* 12:379–382.

Shields, C. G., Wynne, L. C., McDaniel, S. H., and Gawinski, B. 1994. The marginalization of family therapy: A historical and continuing problem. *Journal of Marital and Family Therapy.* 20:117–138

Shoham-Salomon, V., and Rosenthal, R. 1987. Paradoxical interventions: A meta-analysis. *Journal of Consulting and Clinical Psychology.* 55:22–28.

Smith, M., Glass, G., and Miller, T. 1980. *Benefits of psychotherapy.* Baltimore: Johns Hopkins Press.

Smith, T. E., Sells, S. P., and Clevenger, T. Ethnographic content analysis of couple and therapist perceptions in a reflecting team setting. *Journal of Marital and Family Therapy.* (in press)

Snyder, D. K., and Wills, R. M. 1989. Behavioral versus insight-oriented marital therapy: Effects on individual and interspousal functioning. *Journal of Consulting and Clinical Psychology.* 57:39–46.

Snyder, D. K., and Wills, R. M. 1991. Facilitating change in marital therapy and research. *Journal of Family Psychology.* 4:426–435.

Spanier, G. B. 1976. Measuring marital adjustment: New scales for assessing the quality of marriage and similar dyads. *Journal of Marriage and the Family.* 38:15–28.

Sprenkle, D. H., and Storm, C. L. 1983. Divorce therapy outcome research: A substantive and methodological review. *Journal of Marital and Family Therapy.* 9:239–258.

Stanton, M. D., Steier, F., and Todd, T. C. 1982. Paying families for attending sessions: Counteracting the dropout problem. *Journal of Marital and Family Therapy.* 8:371–373.

Stanton, M. D., Todd, T. C., and Associates. 1982. *Family therapy of drug abuse and addiction.* New York: Guilford Press.

Stanton, M. D., Todd, T. C., Steier, R., Van Duesen, J. M., Marder, L., Rosoff, R. J., Seaman, S. F., and Skibinski, E. 1979. *Family characteristics and family therapy of heroin addicts: Final Report 1974–1978.* Submitted to the National Institute on Drug Abuse, Grant No. R01DA 00119.

Steinglass, P., Bennett, L. A., Wolin, S. J., and Reiss, D. 1987. *The alcoholic family.* New York: Basic Books.

Stith, S. M., Rosen, K. H., Barasch, S. G., and Wilson, S. M. 1991. Clinical research as a training opportunity: Bridging the gap between theory and practice. *Journal of Marital and Family Therapy.* 17:349–353.

Szapocznik, J., and Kurtines, W. M. 1989. *Breakthroughs in family treatment.* New York: Springer.

Szapocznik, J., Kurtines, W. M., Foote, F. H., Perez-Vidal, A., and Hervis, O. 1983. Conjoint versus one-person family therapy: Some evidence for the effectiveness of conducting family therapy through one person. *Journal of Consulting and Clinical Psychology.* 51:889–899.

Szapocznik, J., Kurtines, W. M., Foote, F. H., Perez-Vidal, A., and Hervis, O. 1986. Conjoint versus one-person family therapy: Further evidence for the effectiveness of conducting family therapy through one person with drug abusing adolescents. *Journal of Consulting and Clinical Psychology.* 54:385–387.

Szapocznik, J., Kurtines, W., Santisteban, D. A., Rio, A. T. 1990. Interplay of advances between theory, research, and application in treatment interventions aimed at behavior problem children and adolescents. *Journal of Consulting and Clinical Psychology.* 58:696–703.

Szapocznik, J., Perez-Vidal, A., Brickman, A. L., Foote, F. H., Santisteban, D., Hervis, O., and Kurtines, W. M. 1988. Engaging adolescent drug abusers and their families in treatment: A strategic/structural systems approach. *Journal of Consulting and Clinical Psychology.* 56:552–557.

Szapocznik, J., Rio, A., Murray, E., Cohen, R., Scopetta, M., Rivas-Vazquez, A., Hervis, O., Posada, V., and Kurtines, W. 1989. Structural family versus psychodynamic child therapy for problematic Hispanic boys. *Journal of Consulting and Clinical Psychology. 57:*571–578.

Szmukler, G. I., Eisler, I., Russell, G. F. M., and Dare, C. 1985. Anorexia nervosa, parental 'expressed emotion' and dropping out of treatment. *British Journal of Psychiatry. 147:*265–271.

Thomas, V., and Olson, D. 1993. Problem families and the Circumplex Model: Observational assessment using the Clinical Rating Scale (CRS). *Journal of Marital and Family Therapy. 19:*159–176.

Todd, T. C., and Selekman, M. D., eds. 1991. *Family therapy approaches with adolescent substance abusers.* Boston: Allyn and Bacon.

Todd, T. C., and Stanton, M. D. 1983. Research on marital and family therapy: Answers, issues, and recommendations for the future. In *Handbook of family and marital therapy,* B. B. Wolman and G. Stricker, eds. New York: Plenum.

Tolan, P. H., Cromwell, R. E., and Brasswell, M. 1986. Family therapy with delinquents: A critical review of the literature. *Family Process. 25:*619–649.

Tomm, K. 1990. A critique of the DSM. *Dulwich Center Newsletter. 3:*5–8.

Tomm, K. 1983. The old hat doesn't fit. *Family Therapy Networker.* July–August:39–41.

Tomm, K. 1986. On incorporating the therapist in a scientific theory of family therapy. *Journal of Marital and Family Therapy. 12:*373–378.

Touliatos, J., Perlmutter, B. F., and Straus, M. A. 1990. *Handbook of family measurement techniques.* Newbury Park: Sage.

Trepper, T. S., and Barrett, M. J. 1989. *Systemic treatment of incest: A therapeutic handbook.* New York: Brunner/Mazel.

Walter, H. I., and Gilmore, S. K. 1973. Placebo versus social learning effects in parent training procedures designed to alter the behavior of aggressive boys. *Behavior Research and Therapy. 4:*361–377.

Wampler, K. S. 1982. The effectiveness of the Minnesota Couple Communication Program: a review of research. *Journal of Marital and Family Therapy. 8:*345–356.

Watzlawick, P., Beavin, J. H., and Jackson, D. D. 1967. *Pragmatics of human communication.* New York: Norton.

Wetzel, J. W. 1984. *Clinical handbook of depression.* New York: Gardner.

Wiltz, N. A., and Patterson, G. R. 1974. An evaluation of parent training procedures designed to alter inappropriate aggressive behavior in boys. *Behavior Therapy. 5:*215–221.

Wynne, L. C. 1983. Family research and family therapy: A reunion? *Journal of Marital and Family Therapy. 9:*113–117.

Wynne, L. C., ed. 1988. *The state of the art in family therapy research: Controversies and recommendations.* New York: Family Process Press.

Appendix A:
RECOMMENDED READINGS

Note: Recommended readings are categorized first by chapters of this book; then there is a second list of our overall recommendations.

Chapter 1. The Historical Context of Family Therapy

Ackerman, N. W. 1958. *The psychodynamics of family life.* New York: Basic Books.

Boszormenyi-Nagy, I. 1962. The concept of schizophrenia from the point of view of family treatment. *Family Process. 1:*103–113.

Bowen, M. 1960. A family concept of schizophrenia. In *The etiology of schizophrenia,* D. D. Jackson, ed. New York: Basic Books.

Greenberg, G. S. 1977. The family interactional perspective: A study and examination of the work of Don D. Jackson. *Family Process. 16:*385–412.

Haley, J. 1959. The family of the schizophrenic. *American Journal of Nervous and Mental Diseases. 129:*357–374.

Haley, J., and Hoffman, L., eds. 1968. *Techniques of family therapy.* New York: Basic Books.

Jackson, D. D. 1957. The question of family homeostasis. *The Psychiatric Quarterly Supplement. 31:*79–90.

Jackson, D. D. 1965. Family rules: Marital quid pro quo. *Archives of General Psychiatry. 12:*589–594.

Lidz, T., Cornelison, A., Fleck, S., and Terry, D. 1957. Intrafamilial environment of schizophrenic patients. II: Marital schism and marital skew. *American Journal of Psychiatry. 20:*241–248.

Weakland, J. H. 1960. The "double-bind" hypothesis of schizophrenia and three-party interaction. In *The etiology of schizophrenia,* D. D. Jackson, ed. New York: Basic Books.

Whitaker, C. A. 1958. Psychotherapy with couples. *American Journal of Psychotherapy. 12:*18–23.

Wynne, L. C., Ryckoff, I., Day, J., and Hirsch, S. I. 1958. Pseudo-mutuality in the family relationships of schizophrenics. *Psychiatry. 21:*205–220.

Chapter 2. The Conceptual Context of Family Therapy

Bateson, G. 1971. *Steps to an ecology of mind.* New York: Ballantine.

Bateson, G. 1979. *Mind and nature.* New York: E. P. Dutton.

von Bertalanffy, L. 1950. An outline of General System Theory. *British Journal of the Philosophy of Science. 1:*134–165.

von Bertalanffy, L. 1967. *Robots, men and minds.* New York: George Braziller.

Breunlin, D. C., and Schwartz, R. C. 1986. Sequences: Toward a common denominator of family therapy. *Family Process. 25:*67–88.

Breunlin, D. C., Schwartz, R. C., and Mac Kune-Karrer, B. M., 1992. *Metaframework for systemic therapy.* San Francisco: Jossey-Bass.

Carter, E., and McGoldrick, M., eds. 1989. *The changing family life cycle: A framework for family therapy, and* 2nd ed. Boston: Allyn and Bacon.

Davidson, M. 1983. *Uncommon sense: The life and thought of Ludwig von Bertalanffy.* Los Angeles: J. P. Tarcher.

Dell, P. F. 1982. Beyond homeostasis: Toward a concept of coherence. *Family Process. 21*:21–42.

Falicov, C. J., ed. 1988. *Family transitions.* New York: Guilford Press.

Haley, J. 1985. Conversations with Erickson. *Family Therapy Networker. 9*(2):30–43.

Hoffman, L. 1981. *Foundations of family therapy.* New York: Basic Books.

Simon, R. 1982. Reflections on family therapy: An interview with Jay Haley. *Family Therapy Networker. 6*(5):18–26.

Simon, R. 1984. Stranger in a strange land: An interview with Salvador Minuchin. *Family Therapy Networker. 8*(6):21–31, 66–68.

Sluzki, C. 1983. Interview on the state of the art. *Family Therapy Networker. 7*(1):24.

Weiner, N. 1948. *Cybernetics or control and communication in the animal and the machine.* Cambridge, MA: Technology Press.

Chapter 3. The Contemporary Context of Family Therapy

Avis, J. M. 1992. Where are all the family therapists? Abuse and violence within families and family therapy's response. *Journal of Marital and Family Therapy. 18*:225–232.

Bograd, M. 1992. Values in conflict: Challenges to family therapists' thinking. *Journal of Marital and Family Therapy. 18*:245–256.

Gergen, K. 1985. The social constructionist movement in modern psychology. *American Psychologist. 40*:266–275.

de Shazer, S. 1984. The death of resistance. *Family Process. 23*:11–16.

Goldner, V. 1985. Feminism and family therapy. *Family Process. 24*:31–47.

Goldner, V. 1988. Generation and gender: Normative and covert hierarchies. *Family Process. 27*:17–33.

Goodrich, T. J., ed. 1991. *Women and power: Perspectives for family therapy.* New York: Norton.

Gurman, A. S., Kniskern, D. P., and Pinsof, W. M. 1986. Research on marital and family therapies. In *Handbook of psychotherapy and behavior change,* 3rd ed., S. L. Garfield and A. E. Bergin, eds. New York: Wiley.

Hare-Mustin, R. T. 1994. Discourses in the mirrored room: A postmodern analysis of therapy. *Family Process.* (in press)

Hare-Mustin, R. T., and Marecek, J. 1988. The meaning of difference: Gender theory, postmodernism and psychology. *American Psychologist. 43*:455–464.

Hare-Mustin, R. T., and Marecek, J., eds. 1990. *Making a difference: Psychology and the construction of gender.* New Haven: Yale University Press.

Keeney, B. P. 1983. *The aesthetics of change.* New York: Guilford Press.

Kellner, D. 1991. *Postmodern theory.* New York: Guilford Press.

Leupnitz, D. 1988. *The family interpreted: Feminist theory in clinical practice.* New York: Basic Books.

McGoldrick, M., Anderson, C., and Walsh, F., eds. 1989. *Women in families: A framework for family therapy.* New York: Norton.

Schwartz, R. C., and Breunlin, D. C. 1983. Research: Why clinicians should bother with it. *Family Therapy Networker. 7*(4):22–27, 57–59.

Schwartz, R. C., and Perrotta, P. 1985. Let us sell no intervention before its time. *Family Therapy Networker. 9*(4):18–25.

Walsh, F., ed. 1993. *Normal family processes,* 2nd ed. New York: Guilford Press.

Chapter 4. Early Models and Basic Techniques: Group Processes and Communications Analysis

Bell, J. E. 1961. *Family group therapy*. Public Health Monograph No. 64, Washington, DC: U.S. Government Printing Office.

Bell, J. E. 1975. *Family therapy*. New York: Jason Aronson.

Bion, W. R. 1961. *Experience in groups*. London: Tavistock Publications.

Haley, J. 1963. *Strategies of psychotherapy*. New York: Grune & Stratton.

Hoffman, L. 1971. Deviation-amplifying processes in natural groups. In *Changing families,* J. Haley, ed. New York: Grune & Stratton.

Jackson, D. D. 1961. Interactional psychotherapy. In *Contemporary psychotherapies*, M. T. Stein, ed. New York: Free Press of Glencoe.

Jackson, D. D. 1967. *Therapy, communication and change*. Palo Alto, CA: Science and Behavior Books.

Lederer, W., and Jackson, D. D. 1968. *Mirages of marriage*. New York: Norton.

MacGregor, R., Richie, A. M., Serrano, A. C., Schuster, F. P., McDonald, E. C., and Goolishian, H. A. 1964. *Multiple impact therapy with families*. New York: McGraw-Hill.

Satir, V. 1964. *Conjoint family therapy*. Palo Alto, CA: Science and Behavior Books.

Sluzki, C. E. 1978. Marital therapy from a systems theory perspective. In *Marriage and marital therapy*, T. J. Paolino and B. S. McCrady, eds. New York: Brunner/Mazel.

Speck, R. V., and Attneave, C. A. 1971. Social network intervention. In *Changing families,* J. Haley, ed. New York: Grune & Stratton.

Watzlawick, P., Beavin, J. H., and Jackson, D. D. 1967. *Pragmatics of human communication*. New York: Norton.

Chapter 5. Structural Family Therapy

Colapinto J. 1991. Structural family therapy. In *Handbook of family therapy*, vol. II, A. S. Gurman and D. P. Kniskern, eds. New York: Brunner/Mazel.

Minuchin, S. 1974. *Families and family therapy*. Cambridge, MA: Harvard University Press.

Minuchin, S., Baker, L., Rosman, B., Liebman, R., Milman, L., and Todd, T. C. 1975. A conceptual model of psychosomatic illness in children. *Archives of General Psychiatry. 32:*1031–1038.

Minuchin, S., and Fishman, H. C. 1981. *Family therapy techniques*. Cambridge, MA: Harvard University Press.

Minuchin, S., Montalvo, B., Guerney, B., Rosman, B., and Schumer, F. 1967. *Families of the slums*. New York: Basic Books.

Minuchin, S., and Nichols, M. P. 1993. *Family healing: Tales of hope and renewal from family therapy*. New York: The Free Press.

Minuchin, S., Rosman, B. L., and Baker, L. 1978. *Psychosomatic families: Anorexia nervosa in context*. Cambridge, MA: Harvard University Press.

Chapter 6. Psychoanalytic Family Therapy

Ackerman, N. W. 1966. *Treating the troubled family*. New York: Basic Books.

Boszormenyi-Nagy, I. 1972. Loyalty implications of the transference model in psychotherapy. *Archives of General Psychiatry. 27:*374–380.

Boszormenyi-Nagy, I. 1987. *Foundations of contextual therapy*. New York: Brunner/Mazel.

Dicks, H. V. 1967. *Marital tensions*. New York: Basic Books.

Meissner, W. W. 1978. The conceptualization of marriage and family dynamics from a psychoanalytic perspective. In *Marriage and marital therapy*, T. J. Paolino and B. S. McCrady, eds. New York: Brunner/Mazel.

Nadelson, C. C. 1978. Marital therapy from a psychoanalytic perspective. In *Marriage and marital therapy*, T. J. Paolino and B. S. McCrady, eds. New York: Brunner/ Mazel.

Nichols, M. P. 1987. *The self in the system*. New York: Brunner/Mazel.

Sander, F. M. 1989. Marital conflict and psychoanalytic theory in the middle years. In *The middle years: New psychoanalytic perspectives*, J. Oldham and R. Liebert, eds. New Haven: Yale University Press.

Scharff, D., and Scharff, J. S. 1987. *Object relations family therapy*. New York: Jason Aronson.

Stern, D. N. 1985. *The interpersonal world of the infant*. New York: Basic Books.

Vogel, E. F., and Bell, N. W. 1960. The emotionally disturbed child as the family scapegoat. In *The family*, N. W. Bell and E. F. Vogel, eds. Glencoe, IL: Free Press.

Zinner, J., and Shapiro, R. 1976. Projective identification as a mode of perception of behavior in families of adolescents. *International Journal of Psychoanalysts*. 53:523–530.

Chapter 7. Experiential Family Therapy

Duhl, B. S., and Duhl, F. J. 1981. Integrative family therapy. In *Handbook of family therapy*, A. S. Gurman and D. P. Kniskern, eds. New York: Brunner/Mazel.

Duhl, F. J., Kantor, D., and Duhl, B. S. 1973. Learning, space and action in family therapy: A primer of sculpture. In *Techniques in family therapy*, D. A. Bloch, ed. New York: Grune & Stratton.

Greenberg, L. S., and Johnson, S. M. 1988. *Emotionally focused therapy for couples*. New York: Guilford Press.

Kaplan, M. L., and Kaplan, N. R. 1978. Individual and family growth: A Gestalt approach. *Family Process*. 17:195–205.

Keith, D. V., and Whitaker, C. A. 1977. The divorce labyrinth. In *Family therapy: Full length case studies*, P. Papp, ed. New York: Gardner Press.

Kempler, W. 1981. *Experiential psychotherapy with families*. New York: Brunner/Mazel.

Laing, R. D., and Esterson, A. 1970. *Sanity, madness and the family*. Baltimore: Penguin Books.

Napier, A. Y., and Whitaker, C. A. 1978. *The family crucible*. New York: Harper & Row.

Neill, J. R., and Kniskern, D. P., eds. 1982. *From psyche to system: The evolving therapy of Carl Whitaker*. New York: Guilford Press.

Satir, V. M. 1988. *The new peoplemaking*. Palo Alto, CA: Science and Behavior Books.

Satir, V. M., and Baldwin, M. 1983. *Satir step by step: A guide to creating change in families*. Palo Alto, CA: Science and Behavior Books.

Whitaker, C. A. and Bumberry, W. M. 1988. *Dancing with the family: A symbolic experiential approach*. New York: Brunner/Mazel.

Whitaker, C. A., and Keith, D. V. 1981. Symbolic-experiential family therapy. In *Handbook of family therapy*, A. S. Gurman and D. P. Kniskern, eds. New York: Brunner/ Mazel.

Chapter 8. Behavioral Family Therapy

Alexander, J. F., and Barton, C. 1976. Behavioral systems therapy with families. In *Treating relationships*, D. H. Olson, ed. Lake Mills, IA: Graphic Publishing.

Barton, C., and Alexander, J. F. 1981. Functional family therapy. In *Handbook of family therapy*, A. S. Gurman and D. P. Kniskern, eds. New York: Brunner/Mazel.

Birchler, G. R., and Spinks, S. H. 1980. Behavioral-systems marital therapy: Integration and clinical application. *American Journal of Family Therapy. 8*:6–29.

Bornstein, P., and Bornstein, M. 1986. *Marital therapy: A behavioral-communications approach.* New York: Pergamon.

Epstein, N., Schlesinger, S. E., and Dryden, W. 1988. *Cognitive-behavioral therapy with families.* New York: Brunner/Mazel.

Falloon, I. R. H. 1988. *Handbook of behavioral family therapy.* New York: Guilford Press.

Falloon, I. R. H. 1991. Behavioral family therapy. In *Handbook of family therapy,* vol. II, A. S. Gurman and D. P. Kniskern, eds. New York, Brunner/Mazel.

Gordon, S. B., and Davidson, N. 1981. Behavioral parent training. In *Handbook of family therapy,* A. S. Gurman and D. P. Kniskern, eds. New York: Brunner/Mazel.

Graziano, A. M. 1977. Parents as behavior therapists. In *Progress in behavior modification,* M. Hersen, R. M. Eisler, and P. M. Miller, eds. New York: Academic Press.

Holtzworth-Munroe, A., and Jacobson, N. S. 1991. Behavioral marital therapy. In *Handbook of family therapy,* vol. II, A. S. Gurman and D. P. Kniskern, eds., New York: Brunner/Mazel.

Jacobson, N. S., and Margolin, G. 1979. *Marital therapy: Strategies based on social learning and behavior exchange principles.* New York: Brunner/Mazel.

Kaplan, H. S. 1979. *The new sex therapy: Active treatment of sexual dysfunctions.* New York: Brunner/Mazel.

Masters, W. H., and Johnson, V. E. 1970. *Human sexual inadequacy.* Boston: Little, Brown.

Patterson, G. R. 1971. *Families: Application of social learning theory to family life.* Champaign, IL: Research Press.

Stuart, R. B. 1980. *Helping couples change: A social learning approach to marital therapy.* New York: Guilford Press.

Weiss, R. L. 1978. The conceptualization of marriage from a behavioral perspective. In *Marriage and marital therapy,* T. J. Paolino and B. S. McCrady, eds. Brunner/Mazel.

Wodarski, J., and Thyer, B., 1989. Behavioral perspectives on the family: An overview. In *Behavioral family therapy,* B. Thyer, ed. Springfield, IL: Charles Thomas.

Chapter 9. Bowenian Family Therapy

Anonymous. 1972. Differentiation of self in one's family. In *Family interaction,* J. Framo, ed. New York: Springer.

Bowen, M. 1978. *Family therapy in clinical practice.* New York: Jason Aronson.

Carter, E., and Orfanidis, M. M. 1976. Family therapy with one person and the family therapist's own family. In *Family therapy: Theory and practice,* P. J. Guerin, ed. New York: Gardner Press.

Fogarty, T. F. 1976. Systems concepts and the dimensions of self. In *Family therapy: Theory and practice,* P. J. Guerin, ed. New York: Gardner Press.

Fogarty, T. F. 1976. Marital crisis. In *Family therapy: Theory and practice,* P. J. Guerin, ed. New York: Gardner Press.

Guerin, P. J., Fay, L., Burden, S., and Kautto, J. 1987. *The evaluation and treatment of marital conflict: A four-stage approach.* New York: Basic Books.

Guerin, P. J., and Pendagast, E. G. 1976. Evaluation of family system and geogram. In *Family therapy: Theory and practice,* P. J. Guerin, ed. New York: Gardner Press.

Kerr, M. E., and Bowen, M. 1988. *Family evaluation.* New York: Norton.

Chapter 10.   Strategic and Systemic Family Therapies

Boscolo, L., Cecchin, G., Hoffman, L., and Penn, P. 1987. *Milan systemic therapy.* New York: Basic Books.

Cecchin, G. 1987. Hypothesizing, circularity and neutrality revisited: An invitation to curiosity. *Family Process. 26:*405–413.

Fisch, R., Weakland, J. H., and Segal, L. 1982. *The tactics of change: Doing therapy briefly.* San Francisco: Jossey-Bass.

Haley, J. 1973. *Uncommon therapy.* New York: Norton.

Haley, J. 1976. *Problem-solving therapy.* San Francisco: Jossey-Bass.

Haley, J. 1980. *Leaving home.* New York: McGraw-Hill.

Hoffman, L. 1976. Breaking the homeostatic cycle. In *Family therapy: Theory and practice,* P. J. Guerin, ed. New York: Gardner Press.

Madanes, C. 1981. *Strategic family therapy.* San Francisco: Jossey-Bass.

Madanes, C. 1984. *Behind the one-way mirror.* San Francisco: Jossey-Bass.

Madanes, C. 1990. *Sex, love and violence: Strategies for transformation.* New York: Norton.

Papp, P. 1980. The Greek chorus and other techniques of paradoxical therapy. *Family Process. 19:*45–57.

Rabkin, R. 1972. *Strategic psychotherapy.* New York: Basic Books.

Rohrbaugh, M., Tennen, H., Press, S., and White, L. 1981. Compliance, defiance, and therapeutic paradox: Guidelines for strategic use of paradoxical interventions. *American Journal of Orthopsychiatry. 51:*454–456.

Selvini Palazzoli, M., Boscolo, L., Cecchin, G., and Prata, G. 1978. *Paradox and counterparadox.* New York: Jason Aronson.

Tomm, K. 1987. Interventive interviewing: Part 1. Strategizing as a fourth guideline for the therapists. *Family Process. 26:*3–14.

Watzlawick, P., Weakland, J., and Fisch, R. 1974. *Change: Principles of problem formation and problem resolution.* New York: Norton.

Chapter 11. Emergent Models of the Nineties

Andersen, T. 1991. *The reflecting team.* New York: Norton.

Anderson, C. M., Reiss, D., and Hogarty, B. 1986. *Schizophrenia and the family.* New York: Guilford Press.

Anderson, H., and Goolishian, H. A. 1988. Human systems and linguistic systems: Preliminary and evolving ideas about the implications for clinical theory. *Family Process. 27:*371–393.

de Shazer, S. 1988. *Clues: Investigating solutions in brief therapy.* New York: Norton.

de Shazer, S. 1991. *Putting difference to work.* New York: Norton.

Gilligan, S., and Price, R. 1993. *Therapeutic conversations.* New York: Norton.

O'Hanlon, W. H., and Weiner-Davis, M. 1989. *In search of solutions: A new direction in psychotherapy.* New York: Norton.

Rolland, J. S. 1987. Chronic illness and the life cycle: A conceptual framework. *Family Process. 26:*203–221.

Schwartz, R. C. 1987. Our multiple selves. *Family Therapy Networker. 11:*25–31.

Schwartz, R. C., 1994. *The internal family systems model.* New York: Guilford Press.

White, M., and Epston, D. 1990. *Narrative means to therapeutic ends.* New York: Norton.

Wylie, M. S. 1990. Brief therapy on the couch. *Family Therapy Networker. 14:*26–34, 66.

Chapter 12. Comparative Analysis

Gurman, A. S. 1978. Contemporary marital therapies: A critique and comparative analysis of psychoanalytic, behavioral and systems theory approaches. In *Marriage and marital therapy,* T. J. Paolino and B. S. McCrady, eds. New York: Brunner/Mazel.

Madanes, C., and Haley, J. 1977. Dimensions of family therapy. *Journal of Nervous and Mental Diseases. 165:*88–98.

Sluzki, C. E. 1983. Process, structure and world views: Toward an integrated view of systemic models in family therapy. *Family Process.* *22:*469–476.

Sluzki, C. E. 1987. Family process: Mapping the journey over 25 years. *Family Process.* *26:*149–153.

Chapter 13. Research in Family Therapy: Trends, Issues, and Recommendations

Gurman, A. S., Kniskern, D. P., and Pinsof, W. 1986. Research on the process and outcome of marital and family therapy. In *Handbook of psychotherapy and behavior change,* 3rd ed., S. L., Garfield and A. E., Bergin eds. New York: Wiley.

Hazelrigg, M. D., Cooper, H. M., and Bourdin, C. M. 1987. Evaluating the effectiveness of family therapies: An integrative review and analysis. *Psychological Bulletin.* *101:*4228–4442.

Henggler, S. W., Borduin, C. M., and Mann, B. J. 1992. Advance in family therapy: Empirical foundations. In *Advances in clinical child psychology,* vol. 15, T. H. Ollindrick and R. J. Prinz, eds. New York: Plenum.

Kazdin, A. E. 1991. Effectiveness of psychotherapy with children and adolescents. *Journal of Consulting and Clinical Psychology.* *59:*785–798.

Liddle, H. A. 1991. Empirical values and the culture of family therapy. *Journal of Marital and Family Therapy.* *17:*327–348.

Moon, S. M., Dillon, D. R., and Sprenkle, D. H. 1990. Family therapy and qualitative research. *Journal of Marital and Family Therapy.* *16:*357–373.

Wynne, L. C., ed. 1988. *The state of the art in family therapy research: Controversies and recommendations.* New York: Family Process Press.

The following are among the best and most useful books about families and family therapy.

General Principles of Family Systems

Carter, B., and McGoldrick, M. 1988. *The changing family life cycle: A framework for family therapy.* 2nd ed. Boston: Allyn and Bacon.

Hoffman, L. 1981. *The foundations of family therapy.* New York: Basic Books.

Imber-Black, E., ed. 1993. *Secrets in families and family therapy.* New York: Norton.

Kerr, M. E., and Bowen, M. 1988. *Family evaluation.* New York: Norton.

Minuchin, S. 1974. *Families and family therapy.* Cambridge, MA: Harvard University Press.

Nichols, M. P. 1992. *The power of family therapy.* New York: Gardner Press.

Paolino, T. J., and McCrady, B. S., eds. 1978. *Marriage and marital therapy.* New York: Brunner/Mazel.

Watzlawick, P., Beavin, J., and Jackson, D. 1967. *Pragmatics of human communication.* New York: Norton.

Culture and Family Therapy

Boyd-Franklin, N. 1989. *Black families in therapy: A multisystems approach.* New York: Guilford Press.

Davis, L., and Proctor, E. 1989. *Race, gender, and class: Guidelines for practice with individuals, families and groups.* Englewood Cliffs, NJ: Prentice Hall.

Pedersen, P. 1987. The frequent assumptions of cultural bias in counseling. *Journal of Multicultural Counseling and Development.* *15:*16–24.

Pinderhughes, E. 1989. *Understanding race, ethnicity, power: The key to efficacy in clinical practice.* New York: The Free Press.

Sue, D. W., and Sue, D. 1990. *Counseling the culturally different: Theory and practice,* 2nd ed. New York: Wiley.

Marriage

Dicks, H. V. 1967. *Marital tensions.* New York: Basic Books.

Guerin, P. J., Fay, L., Burden, S., and Kautto, J. 1987. *The evaluation and treatment of marital conflict: A four-stage approach.* New York: Basic Books.

Lederer, W., and Jackson, D. 1968. *The mirages of marriage.* New York: Norton.

Lerner, H. G. 1985. *The dance of anger: A woman's guide to changing patterns of intimate relationships.* New York: Harper & Row.

Scarf, M. 1987. *Intimate partners: Patterns in love and marriage.* New York: Random House.

In-Laws and the Extended Family

Guerin, P. J., ed. 1976. *Family therapy: Theory and practice.* New York: Gardner Press.

Lerner, H. G. 1989. *The dance of intimacy: A woman's guide to courageous acts of change in key relationships.* New York: Harper & Row.

McGoldrick, M., and Gerson, R. 1985. *Genograms in family assessment.* New York: Norton.

Families with Babies and Small Children

Brazelton, T. B. 1983. *Infants and mothers: Differences in development.* Rev. ed. New York: Dell.

Combrinck-Graham, L. ed. 1988. *Children in family contexts: Perspectives on treatment.* New York: Guilford Press.

Faber, A., and Mazlish, E. 1974. *Liberated parents, liberated children.* New York: Grosset & Dunlap.

Ginott, H. 1969. *Between parent and child.* New York: Macmillan.

Patterson, G. 1975. *Families: Application of social learning theory to family life.* Champaign, IL: Research Press.

Families with Older Children

Bank, S., and Kahn, M. 1982. *The sibling bond.* New York: Basic Books.

Blos, P. 1979. *The adolescent passage: Developmental issues.* New York: International Universities Press.

Faber, A., and Mazlish, E. 1987. *Siblings without rivalry.* New York: Norton.

Fishel, E. 1979. *Sisters: Love and rivalry inside the family and beyond.* New York: Quill/William Morrow.

Schlaadt, R., and Shannon, P. 1986. *Drugs of choice,* 2nd ed. Englewood Cliffs, NJ: Prentice Hall.

Divorce, Remarriage, and Stepparenting

Ahrons, C., and Rodgers, R. 1987. *Divorced families: A multidisciplinary developmental view.* New York: Norton.

Isaacs, M. B., Montalvo, B., and Abelsohn, D. 1986. *The difficult divorce.* New York: Basic Books.

Vaughan, D. 1986. *Uncoupling: Turning points in intimate relationships*. New York: Oxford University Press.

Visher, E., and Visher, J. 1988. *Old loyalties, new ties: Therapeutic strategies with stepfamilies*. New York: Brunner/Mazel.

Leaving Home and the Postchildrearing Years

Levinson, D. 1978. *The seasons of a man's life*. New York: Ballantine.

Nichols, M. P. 1987. *Turning forty in the eighties*. New York: Fireside/Simon & Schuster.

Viorst, J. 1986. *Necessary losses*. New York: Simon & Schuster.

Family Therapy Technique

Anderson, C., and Stewart, S. 1983. *Mastering resistance: A practical guide to family therapy*. New York: Guilford Press.

Guerin, P. J., Fay, L., Burden, S., and Kautto, J. 1987. *The evaluation and treatment of marital conflict: A four-stage approach*. New York: Basic Books.

Isaacs, M. B., Montalvo, B., and Abelsohn, D. 1986. *The difficult divorce: Therapy for children and families*. New York: Basic Books.

Minuchin, S., and Fishman, H. C. 1981. *Family therapy techniques*. Cambridge, MA: Harvard University Press.

Minuchin, S., and Nichols, M. P. 1994. *Family healing: Tales of hope and renewal from family therapy*. New York: Touchstone/Simon & Schuster.

Pittman, F. 1988. *Turning points*. New York: Norton.

White, M., and Epston, D. 1990. *Narrative means to therapeutic ends*. New York: Norton.

Appendix B:
GLOSSARY

accommodation.   Elements of a system automatically adjust to coordinate their functioning; people may have to work at it.

anorexia nervosa.   Self-starvation leading to loss of 25 percent or more of body weight, hyperactivity, hypothermia, and amenorrhea (in females).

aversive control.   Using punishment and criticism to eliminate undesirable responses; commonly used in dysfunctional families.

basic assumption theory.   Bion's concept that group members become diverted from the group task to pursue unconscious patterns of *fight-flight, dependency,* or *pairing.*

behavior exchange theory.   Explanation of behavior in relationships as maintained by a ratio of costs to benefits.

black box metaphor.   The idea that because the mind is so complex, it's better to study people's input and output (behavior, communication) than to speculate about what goes on in their minds.

blended families.   Separate families united by marriage; stepfamilies.

boundary.   A concept used in structural family therapy to describe emotional barriers that protect and enhance the integrity of individuals, subsystems, and families.

bulimia.   An eating disorder characterized by bouts of excessive eating followed by self-induced vomiting, purging with laxatives, strenuous exercise, or fasting.

circular causality.   The idea that events are related through a series of interacting loops or repeating cycles.

circular questioning.   A method of interviewing developed by the Milan Associates in which questions are asked that highlight differences among family members.

classical conditioning.   A form of respondent learning in which an unconditioned stimulus (UCS), such as food, which leads to an unconditioned response (UCR), such as salivation, is paired with a conditioned stimulus (CS), such as bell, the result of which is that the CS begins to evoke the same response; used in the behavioral treatment of anxiety disorders.

communications theory.   The study of relationships in terms of the exchange of verbal and nonverbal messages.

complementary.   Relationships based on differences which fit together, where qualities of one make up for lacks in the other; one is one-up while the other is one-down.

concurrent therapy.   Treatment of two or more persons, seen separately, usually by different therapists.

conjoint therapy.   Treatment of two or more persons in sessions together.

constructivism.   A relativistic point of view that emphasizes the subjective construction of reality. Implies that what we see in families may be based as much on our preconditions as on what's actually going on.

contingency contracting.   A behavior therapy technique whereby agreements are made between family members to exchange rewards for desired behavior.

countertransference.   Emotional reaction, usually unconscious and often distorted, on the part of the therapist to a patient or member of a family in treatment.

cross-generational coalition.   An inappropriate alliance between a parent and child, who side together against a third member of the family.

cybernetics.   The study of control processes in systems, especially analysis of the flow of information in closed systems.

deconstruction.   A postmodern approach to exploring meaning by taking apart and examining taken-for-granted categories and assumptions, making possible newer and sounder constructions of meaning.

differentiation.   Psychological separation of intellect and emotions, and independence of self from others; opposite of fusion.

disengagement.   Minuchin's term for psychological isolation that results from overly rigid boundaries around individuals and subsystems in a family.

double bind.   A conflict created when a person receives contradictory messages on different levels of abstraction in an important relationship, and cannot leave or comment.

dyadic model.   Explanations based on the interactions between two persons or objects: Johnny shoplifts to get his mother's attention.

emotional cutoff.   Bowen's term for flight from an unresolved emotional attachment.

enactment.   An interaction stimulated in structural family therapy in order to observe and then change transactions which make up family structure.

enmeshment.   Minuchin's term for loss of autonomy due to a blurring of psychological boundaries.

epistemology.   The branch of philosophy concerned with the study of knowledge. Used by Bateson to mean worldview or belief system.

expressive role.   Serving social and emotional functions; in traditional families, the wife's role.

extended family.   All the descendants of a set of grandparents.

externalization.   Michael White's technique of getting families to fight to control their problem, as if problems were external to persons.

extinction.   Eliminating behavior by not reinforcing it.

family drawing.   An experiential therapy technique where family members are asked to draw their ideas about how the family is organized.

family group therapy.   Family treatment based on the group therapy model.

family homeostasis.   Tendency of families to resist change in order to maintain a steady state.

family life cycle.   Stages of family life from separation from one's parents to marriage, having children, growing older, retirement, and finally death.

family structure.   The functional organization of families that determines how family members interact.

family myths.   A set of beliefs based on a distortion of historical reality and shared by all family members that help shape the rules governing family functioning.

family of origin.   A person's parents and siblings; usually refers to the original nuclear family of an adult.

family projection process.   In Bowenian theory, the mechanism by which parental conflicts are projected onto the children or a spouse.

family ritual.   Technique used by Selvini Palazzoli and her Milan Associates that prescribes a specific act for family members to perform, which is designed to change the family system's rules.

family rules.   A descriptive term for redundant behavioral patterns.

family sculpting.   A nonverbal experiential technique in which family members position themselves in a tableau that reveals significant aspects of their perceptions and feelings.

feedback.   The return of a portion of the output of a system, especially when used to maintain the output within predetermined limits (negative feedback), or to signal a need to modify the system (positive feedback).

first-order change.   Superficial change in a system which itself stays invariant.

functional analysis of behavior.   In operant behavior therapy, a study of a particular behavior, what elicits it, and what reinforces it.

function of the system.   The idea that symptoms are often ways to distract or otherwise protect family members from threatening conflicts.

fusion.   A blurring of psychological boundaries between self and others, and a contamination of emotional and intellectual functioning; opposite of differentiation.

general systems theory.   A biological model of living systems as whole entities which maintain themselves through continuous input and output from the environment; developed by Ludwig von Bertalanffy.

genogram.   A schematic diagram of the family system, using squares to represent men, circles to indicate women, horizontal lines for marriages, and vertical lines to indicate children.

group dynamics.   Interactions among group members that emerge as a result of properties of the group rather than merely their individual personalities.

hierarchical structure.   Family functioning based on clear generational boundaries, where the parents maintain control and authority.

homeostasis.   A balanced steady state of equilibrium.

identified patient.   The symptom bearer or official patient as identified by the family.

instrumental role.   Decision-making and task functions; in traditional families, the husband's role.

intensity.   Minuchin's term for changing maladaptive transactions by using strong affect, repeated intervention, or prolonged pressure.

internal family systems.   A model of the mind that uses systemic principles and techniques to understand and change intrapsychic processes.

introjection.   A primitive form of identification; taking in aspects of other people, which then become part of the self-image.

invariant prescription.   A technique developed by Mara Selvini Palazzoli in which parents are directed to mysteriously sneak away together.

invisible loyalties.   Boszormenyi-Nagy's term for unconscious commitments that children take on to help their families.

joining.   A structural family therapy term for accepting and accommodating to families in order to win their confidence and circumvent resistance.

linear causality.   The idea that one event is the cause and another is the effect; in behavior, the idea that one behavior is a stimulus, the other a response.

live supervision.   Technique of teaching therapy whereby the supervisor observes sessions in progress and contacts the therapist to suggest different strategies and techniques.

marital schism.   Lidz's term for pathological overt marital conflict.

marital skew.   Lidz's term for a pathological marriage in which one spouse dominates the other.

metacommunication.   Every message has two levels, report and command; metacommunication is the implied command or qualifying message.

mirroring.   Expression of understanding and acceptance of another's feelings.

modeling.   Observational learning.

monadic model.   Explanations based on properties of a single person or object: Johnny shoplifts because he is rebellious.

multigenerational transmission process.   Murray Bowen's concept for the projection of varying degrees of immaturity to different children in the same family; the child who is most involved in the family emotional process emerges with the lowest level of differentiation, and passes problems on to succeeding generations.

multiple family therapy.   Treatment of several families at once in a group therapy format; pioneered by Peter Laqueur and Murray Bowen.

multiple impact therapy.   An intensive, crisis-oriented form of family therapy developed by Robert MacGregor; family members are treated in various subgroups by a team of therapists.

mystification.   Laing's concept that many families distort their children's experience by denying or relabeling it.

network therapy.   A treatment devised by Ross Speck in which a large number of family and friends are assembled to help resolve a patient's problems.

neutrality.   Selvini Palazzoli's term for balanced acceptance of family members.

nuclear family.   Parents and their children.

object relations.   Internalized images of self and others based on early parent-child interactions that determine a person's mode of relationship to other people.

object relations theory.   Psychoanalytic theory derived from Melanie Klein and developed by the British School (Bion, Fairbairn, Guntrip, Winnicott) that emphasizes relationships and attachment, rather than libidinal and aggressive drives, as the key issues of human concern.

open system.   A system that exchanges information or material with its environment, as opposed to a closed system that does not. Living systems are, by definition, open systems.

operant conditioning.   A form of learning whereby a person or animal is rewarded for performing certain behaviors; the major approach in most forms of behavior therapy.

ordeals.   A type of paradoxical intervention in which the client is directed to do something that is more of a hardship than the symptom.

paradox.   A self-contradictory statement based on a valid deduction from acceptable premises.

paradoxical directive.   A technique used in strategic therapy whereby the therapist directs family members to continue their symptomatic behavior. If they conform, they admit control and expose secondary gain; if they rebel, they give up their symptoms.

parental child.   A child who has been allocated power to take care of younger siblings; adaptive when done deliberately in large or single-parent families, maladaptive when it results from unplanned abdication of parental responsibility.

positive connotation.   Selvini Palazzoli's technique of ascribing positive motives to family behavior in order to promote family cohesion and avoid resistance to therapy.

postmodern.   Contemporary antipositivism, viewing knowledge as relative and context-dependent; questions assumptions of objectivity that characterize modern science. In family therapy, challenging the idea of scientific certainty, and linked to the method of deconstruction.

Premack principle.   Using high-probability behavior (preferred activities) to reinforce low-probability behavior (nonpreferred activities).

prescribing the symptom.   A paradoxical technique which forces a patient to either give up a symptom or admit that it is under voluntary control.

pretend techniques.   Madanes's playful paradoxical intervention in which family members are asked to pretend to engage in symptomatic behavior. The paradox is if they are pretending to have a symptom, the symptom cannot be real.

process/content.   Distinction between how members of a family or group relate and what they talk about.

projective identification.   A defense mechanism that operates unconsciously, whereby unwanted aspects of the self are attributed to another person and that person is induced to behave in accordance with these projected attitudes and feelings.

pseudohostility.   Wynne's term for superficial bickering that masks pathological alignments in schizophrenic families.

pseudomutuality.   Wynne's term for the facade of family harmony that characterizes many schizophrenic families.

psychoeducation.   A type of therapy developed in work with schizophrenics, which emphasizes educating family members to help them understand and cope with a seriously disturbed family member.

quid pro quo.   Literally, "something for something," an equal exchange or substitution.

reframing.   Relabeling a family's description of behavior to make it more amenable to therapeutic change; for example, describing someone as "lazy" rather than "depressed."

regression.   Return to a less mature level of functioning in the face of stress.

reinforcement.   An event, behavior, or object that increases the rate of a particular response. A positive reinforcer is an event whose contingent presentation increases the rate of responding; a negative reinforcer is an event whose contingent withdrawal increases the rate of responding.

reinforcement reciprocity.   Exchanging rewarding behaviors between family members.

resistance.   Anything that patients or families do to oppose or retard the progress of therapy.

restraining.   A strategic technique for overcoming resistance by suggesting that a family not change.

role-playing.   Acting out the parts of important characters to dramatize feelings and practice new ways of relating.

rubber fence.   Wynne's term for the rigid boundary surrounding many schizophrenic families, which allows only minimal contact with the surrounding community.

scapegoat.   A member of the family, usually the identified patient, who is the object of displaced conflict or criticism.

schizophrenogenic mother.   Fromm-Reichmann's term for aggressive, domineering mothers thought to precipitate schizophrenia in their offspring.

second-order change.   Basic change in the structure and functioning of a system.

selfobject.   Kohut's term for a person related to not as a separate individual, but as an extension of the self.

separation-individuation.   Process whereby the infant begins, at about two months, to draw apart from the symbiotic bond with mother and develop his or her autonomous functioning.

shaping.   Reinforcing change in small steps.

social learning theory.   Understanding and treating behavior using principles from social and developmental psychology as well as from learning theory.

solution-focused.   Steve de Shazer's term for a style of therapy that emphasizes the solutions that families have already developed for their problems.

structure.   Recurrent patterns of interaction that define and stabilize the shape of relationships.

structured family interview.   An assessment procedure, introduced by Watzlawick, in which families are given a series of tasks for discussion, and their interactions are observed and coded.

subsystem.   Smaller units in families, determined by generation, sex, or function.

symmetrical.   In relationships, equality or parallel form.

system, closed.   A functionally related group of elements regarded as forming a collective entity that does not interact with the surrounding environment.

system, open.   A set of interrelated elements that exchange information, energy, and material with the surrounding environment.

systems theory.   A generic term for studying a group of related elements that interact as a whole entity; encompasses general systems theory and cybernetics.

theory of logical types.   Bertrand Russell's theory of hierarchical levels of abstraction; a class is a different logical type than a member of the class.

three-generational hypothesis of schizophrenia.   Bowen's concept that schizophrenia is the end result of low levels of differentiation passed on and amplified across three succeeding generations.

token economy.   A system of rewards using points, which can be accumulated and exchanged for reinforcing items or behaviors.

transference.   Psychoanalytic term for distorted emotional reactions to present relationships based on unresolved, early family relations.

triadic model.   Explanations based on the interactions among three people or objects; Johnny shoplifts because his father covertly encourages him to defy his mother.

triangle.   A three-person system; according to Bowen, the smallest stable unit of human relations.

triangulation.   Detouring conflict between two people by involving a third person, stabilizing the relationship between the original pair.

unconscious.   Psychoanalytic term for memories, feelings, and impulses of which a person is unaware. Often used as a noun, but more appropriately limited to use as an adjective.

undifferentiated family ego mass.   Bowen's early term for emotional "stuck-togetherness" or fusion in the family, especially prominent in schizophrenic families.

Author Index

Subject Index